NINETEENTH-CENTURY BRITISH WOMEN WRITERS

NINETEENTH-CENTURY BRITISH WOMEN WRITERS

A Bio-Bibliographical Critical Sourcebook

Edited by
Abigail Burnham Bloom
Emmanuel S. Nelson, Advisory Editor

GREENWOOD PRESS
Westport, Connecticut

Library of Congress Cataloging-in-Publication Data

Nineteenth-century British women writers : a bio-bibliographical critical sourcebook /
edited by Abigail Burnham Bloom.
     p. cm.
  Includes bibliographical references and index.
  ISBN 0–313–30439–4 (alk. paper)
  1. English literature—Women authors—Bio-bibliography—Dictionaries. 2. Women and
literature—Great Britain—History—19th century—Dictionaries. 3. Authors, English—19th
century—Biography—Dictionaries. 4. Women authors, English—Biography—Dictionaries.
5. English literature—Women authors—Dictionaries. 6. English literature—19th
century—Dictionaries. I. Bloom, Abigail Burnham.
PR115.N55   2000
820.9'9287'09034—dc21   99–043163
  [B]

British Library Cataloguing in Publication Data is available.

Library of Congress Catalog Card Number: 99–043163
ISBN: 0–313–30439–4

First published in 2000

Greenwood Press, 88 Post Road West, Westport, CT 06881
An imprint of Greenwood Publishing Group, Inc.
www.greenwood.com

Printed in the United States of America

The paper used in this book complies with the
Permanent Paper Standard issued by the National
Information Standards Organization (Z39.48–1984).

10 9 8 7 6 5 4 3 2 1

Copyright Acknowledgments

The editor and publisher gratefully acknowledge permission for use of the following material:

From Anne Brontë, *The Poems of Anne Brontë: A New Text and Commentary*, edited by Edward
Chitham. © 1979 Macmillan Press Ltd. Reprinted by permission of Macmillan Ltd.

Contents

Acknowledgments

My gratitude extends to all the contributors to this volume; I have enjoyed working with all of them. I am especially grateful to those who suggested including women writers I might otherwise have overlooked. I particularly want to thank June Foley, Carol Hanbery MacKay, and Sally Mitchell for their kind help on several fronts. Although they did not write entries, Carolyn Dever and John Maynard contributed a small part of their expertise. This has been a delightful, yet time-consuming project, and I am deeply indebted to my husband, Roger F. Bloom, and our children, Alison and Zachary.

Introduction

Abigail Burnham Bloom

Nineteenth-Century British Women Writers is a reference work that can be used in several different ways. Many of those teaching Victorian literature or broader gender-oriented courses would like to expand their classes to include women writers other than those known to the canon but have not been exposed sufficiently to these writers to teach them. I conceive this bio-bibliographical study primarily as a place where professors can go to find writers and works to include in their curriculum when teaching Victorian literature and where students can discover new writers and works to explore. Thus the volume includes many women authors outside of the usual genres of novels and poetry (such as travel writers, letter writers, journal writers, and journalists) and emphasizes some of the less well-known but accessible works of the better-known writers.

Each entry is divided into four major sections. The first, Biography, contains vital information about the life of the author. The second, Major Works and Themes, includes discussion of the author's major works and the themes running through these works, as well as an orienting synopsis of how this author relates to the larger issues of Victorian literature and feminist studies. An attempt has been made to include information on how the author saw herself and what she may have intended to accomplish with her work. The third section, Critical Reception, summarizes both the contemporary and later reception accorded the author and her works. It provides an overview of how her works have been perceived from the time of their publication until the present. Bibliography, the final section, is a two-part bibliography of Works by the Author and Studies of the Author. This section begins with a short statement telling which of the works by the author are currently in print. Due to the literary productivity of many of these women, some of the works by the authors have become Selected Bibliographies, with only the major works by the author being included.

Included at the end of this volume is also a Selected Bibliography with information on recent anthologies containing writings by these women, general works of criticism on the authors themselves, and some valuable information on electronic resources available.

It should be noted that many of these authors knew one another and were influenced by one another. Their interconnections provide a fascinating web of friendships, relationships, and literary indebtedness. Thus, an asterisk at the end of a woman's name in any entry indicates that there is an entry for that woman as well.

The selection of authors was not easy. This is an era during which there was a wealth of worthy writers. I would have liked to have included everyone whose name I came across, but I did not, for example, include women who were primarily short story writers (except George Egerton) or editors. Eventually, the choices seemed arbitrary, and I think that is always the way with the selection process leading to a reference work or even an anthology unless one has the temperament and resources of Leslie Stephen.

The beginnings and ends of a century are difficult to determine. I chose to work with the time period between the writings of Dorothy Wordsworth and Charlotte Mew, while not including either of them. Dorothy Wordsworth is primarily connected to the previous century, although her Grassmere Journals were written between 1800 and 1803. However, it seems more likely that she would be taught alongside her brother (as part of the Romantics at the end of the eighteenth century) than in a course beginning with the nineteenth century. This volume rather neatly begins with Jane Austen, the first writer alphabetically and one of the earliest born. Yet her novels are frequently taught in nineteenth-century novel courses. It was difficult to determine which women to include at the end of the nineteenth and beginning of the twentieth century as well. Many were influenced by Victorian society but lived well into the twentieth century and in turn influenced the modern world.

Another difficulty has been the matter of what to call some of these women with the profusion of birth names, married names, publication names, and pseudonyms. I was delighted to refer to Elizabeth Gaskell rather than Mrs. Gaskell, but other choices were more difficult and less universally accepted. Mary Ward and Ellen Wood appear under their own first names rather than under their husband's names. After the age of eighteen, women are referred to by their last or married names wherever possible, although difficulties arose when their husbands were also writers. Common alternatives are given in the index.

Ultimately, these women should not be considered by themselves; rather, they need to be examined alongside other women writers and male writers. In order to facilitate exploring these women in different ways, I attempted to divide them into categories. I looked at them by nationality, by religion, by years when they wrote, by social class, by marital status, by political views. The task became too difficult: They spill over and don't want to be contained in any categories. I was, however, able to divide them by the genre in which they wrote despite the fact that many women wrote in several genres. I have tried to determine where their main contribution lies and then parenthetically list the other major categories in which they wrote. Writers like Lady Florence Dixie and Harriet Martineau worked in so many genres that deciding on where they should be placed seemed impossible, so I listed them as primarily novelists. The listing is not a final categorization but an attempt to provide a springboard for further exploration.

Novelists

Jane Austen

Clementina Black

Countess of Blessington (journalist, travel writer)

Mary Elizabeth Braddon

Anne Brontë (poet)

Charlotte Brontë (poet)

Emily Jane Brontë (poet)

Rhoda Broughton

Frances Hodgson Burnett

Alice Mona Caird (journalist)

Mary Cholmondeley

Marie Corelli

Dinah Maria Mulock Craik (poet, journalist, travel writer)

Lady Florence Caroline Douglas Dixie (poet, travel writer)

Emily Eden (letter writer, travel writer)

Maria Edgeworth (journalist)

George Egerton

George Eliot (journalist)

Susan Edmonstone Ferrier

Elizabeth Gaskell

Sarah Grand

Geraldine Jewsbury (journalist)

Vernon Lee (journalist)

Eliza Lynn Linton (journalist)

Lucas Malet

Harriet Martineau (journalist, travel writer)

Edith Nesbit (poet)

Margaret Oliphant Wilson Oliphant

Ouida

Charlotte Eliza Lawson Riddell

Anne Isabella Thackeray Ritchie (journalist)

Olive Schreiner

Anna Sewell

Mary Wollstonecraft Shelley

Frances Trollope (travel writer)

Mary Augusta Arnold Ward

Ellen Price Wood

Charlotte Mary Yonge

Poets

Louisa Sarah Bevington (journalist)

Mathilde Blind

Elizabeth Barrett Browning

Mary Elizabeth Coleridge (novelist, journalist)

Sara Coleridge Coleridge

Eliza Cook (journalist)

Michael Field

Dora Greenwell (journalist)

Felicia Dorothea Hemans

Mary Howitt (journalist)

Jean Ingelow (novelist)

Maria Jane Jewsbury (journalist)

Ellen Johnston

Letitia Elizabeth Landon

Amy Levy (novelist)

Alice Meynell (journalist)

Constance Naden (scientist)

May Probyn

Adelaide Anne Procter

Dollie Radford

A. Mary F. Robinson

Christina Georgina Rossetti

Elizabeth Eleanor Siddal

Katharine Tynan

Augusta Webster

Lady Jane Francesca Wilde (journalist)

Journalists

Annie Wood Besant

Barbara Leigh Smith Bodichon

Josephine Butler

Frances Power Cobbe

Emily Davies

Anna Brownell Murphy Jameson (travel writer)

Harriet Taylor Mill

Mary Russell Mitford

Florence Nightingale

Caroline Norton (novelist)

Bessie Rayner Parkes

Edith J. Simcox

Mary Fairfax Greig Somerville

Helen Taylor

Charlotte Elizabeth Tonna

Beatrice Webb

Letter Writers and Journal Keepers

Jane Welsh Carlyle

Claire Clairmont

Hannah Cullwick

Fanny Kemble (poet)

Victoria, Queen of Britain

Travel Writers

Isabella Lucy Bird

Lady Isabel Arundell Burton

Lady Elizabeth Eastlake (journalist)

Lady Lucy Duff Gordon

Mary Henrietta Kingsley

Self-Help Writers

Isabella Mary Beeton (journalist)

Sarah Stickney Ellis (novelist, poet)

Biographers/Historians

Agnes Strickland

Looking at this listing, one is struck by the number of writers working during the nineteenth century, their prolific oeuvres, and the range of their accomplishments. All of these women were aware of the lack of time available to women for serious ventures. Their lives were easily eaten up by endless household tasks and social duties. Anne Thackeray Ritchie wrote when she was eighteen, "I should like a profession so much—not to spend my life crochetting mending my clothes & reading novels—wh. seems the employment of English ladies unless they teach dirty little children to read wh. is well enough in its way—but no work to the mind" (*Anne Thackeray Ritchie: Journals and Letters*, ed. Lillian Shankman [Ohio State University Press, 1995], 43). The early letters of Jane Welsh Carlyle are filled with her frustration at her lack of time during the day to read and to write. Florence Nightingale wrote in "Cassandra," "Women never have half an hour in all their lives (excepting before or after anybody is up in the house) that they can call their own, without fear of offending or of hurting some one" (Damrosh, *Longman Anthology of British Literature* [Longman, 1999], 2:1588). Dinah Craik felt that "[t]he chief canker at the root of women's lives is the want of something to do" (Rossetti, *Maude*, ed. Elaine Showalter [New York University Press, 1993], 64). Sarah Grand wrote in *The Human Quest*, "Idleness is at the bottom of that form of heart-ache which is peculiarly the lot of women; the heart-ache which comes of an empty, purposeless existence. I don't think any part of the misery that need not be is more acute than that which comes from the want of a settled purpose in life" (Jump, *Women's Writing of the Victorian Period* [St. Martin's Press, 1999], 323). These women all found the time and the ability to write, thereby giving themselves a "purpose in life."

In addition to their writing, many of these women were deeply involved with related scholarly activities. Isabella Mary Beeton edited *The Englishwoman's Domestic Magazine* and *The Young Englishwoman*; George Eliot edited the *Westminster Review* before beginning her career in fiction writing; Charlotte Elizabeth Tonna edited the *Christian Lady's Magazine* for many years, along with several other journals as well. Charlotte Mary Yonge edited *The Monthly Packet*, a magazine for young adults, for almost forty years. Political activist Clementina Black edited *Common Cause*, while Josephine Butler edited several different journals. Eliza Cook started her own magazine, *Eliza Cook's Journal*, a journal that inspired the feminists Bessie Rayner Parkes and Matilda Hays. The Langham Place Circle, which included such women as Parkes, Barbara Leigh Smith Bodichon, and Emily Davies, took its name from the address of the *English Woman's Journal* (later the *Englishwoman's Review*). Involvement in journalism gave these writers a voice at the forefront of their culture and promoted and enhanced their varied interrelationships with other writers. Many nineteenth-century women edited the works of others, a task that involved less public prominence. For example, Sara Coleridge edited the works of her famous father, Samuel Taylor Coleridge. Jane Carlyle, Sara Coleridge, Eliot, George Egerton, and Lady Duff Gordon, among others, did literary translations. Through editing and translating these women worked within a scholarly tradition and helped to evolve a literary profession in addition to their independent creative productivity.

For many nineteenth-century women, having a voice and a forum, led—often directly—to social and political involvement. Some women, such as Frances Trollope and Elizabeth Gaskell, fought for social reform through their fiction; others sought alternative or additional means of advocating social change. Constance Naden became president of the Ladies Debating Society, a forum for the airing of developing concepts for the shaping of societal change. Mary Elizabeth Coleridge taught working-class women at her home and at the Working Woman's College. Edith Simcox was tireless in her work to improve the plight of women workers. Her involvement in union rights led her to establish and run a shirt-making factory. Augusta Webster, like Helen Taylor and Davies, fought for increased education for women. Many women, such as Besant and Sarah Grand, advocated positions that were highly controversial and often unpopular with the general public such as birth control. In the case of Besant, the advocacy of her position led to the devastating loss of custody of her two children. Florence Nightingale advocated health care reform, but in the opinion of many did not go far enough in asserting the generalized need for broader rights for women. While Eliza Lynn Linton sought reform in some areas, she was an ardent antifeminist. Many women, like Mary Ward, advocated education reform, but drew the line at suffrage for women. Lady Florence Dixie sought Home Rule for Ireland and other colonies, and Lady Wilde was also involved in the struggle for Irish independence. Toward the end of the century many women, such as Edith Nesbit, Dollie Radford, and Beatrice Webb, espoused socialism. Throughout the nineteenth century much beneficial social change became possible because of the willingness of these and other women writers to assert their opinions and to act on their beliefs.

Each of these women found a means of communicating her goals and ideals to others in society. Some received the support of their families: Anne Thackeray Ritchie's famous father encouraged her first publications and Harriet Martineau's brother told her to leave off housework and to write. To have the support or example of a literary parent or mentor opened a path for many women writers. Sara Coleridge, the daughter of Samuel Taylor Coleridge, was brought up in close contact with Robert Southey. Mary Elizabeth Coleridge followed in her family's tradition as Sara Coleridge was her great aunt. Lucas Malet was the daughter of Charles Kingsley, Adelaide Anne Procter's father was a well-known poet, and Ward was the niece of Matthew Arnold and the granddaughter of Dr. Arnold of Rugby. Even the Brontë sisters, often pictured in the isolation of the moors, had the example before them of a father who wrote and published poetry and other works. Mary Shelley had a writing father, as well as a famous poet for a husband, and the tradition of her mother, Mary Wollstonecraft, who had died just after her daughter's birth. Indeed, the work of the early feminist Wollstonecraft provided inspiration for many of the women in this volume. Taylor and her mother, Harriet Taylor Mill, worked so closely with John Stuart Mill that Mill attributed his work not to "one intellect and conscience, but [to] three" (*Autobiography of John Stuart Mill*, ed. John Jacob [Coss Columbia University Press, 1924], 185). Anna Sewell and Duff Gordon also had mothers who were published authors. Family relationships were important in the careers of the Jewsbury sisters, Maria Jane and Geraldine, as well as Claire Clairmont and Shelley who were stepsisters. In addition, Bodichon and Nightingale were cousins, as were Duff Gordon and Martineau, and Malet and Mary Kingsley. Many of these nineteenth-century women were an influence on the next generation. Trollope was the mother of three novelists, including the renowned Anthony Trollope. Oscar Wilde was the child of Lady Wilde while Hilair Belloc and Marie Belloc-Lowndes were the children of Parkes. Ritchie is sometimes seen as a bridge between the Victorian generation of her father and the modern generation of Virginia Woolf, her "adopted niece," Ritchie's sister having been married to Woolf's father.

Many of these women were greatly influenced through their readings of other's works. Emily Eden's novels were inspired by the works of Jane Austen. Indeed, Austen often served as an ideal for aspiring women writers during the nineteenth century, and critics frequently compared new novels to hers. But other women followed different models: Ouida began to write following the success of Ellen Wood's sensation novel *East Lynne*. Rhoda Broughton began to write after reading the first novel of Ritchie, *The Story of Elizabeth*. Many women poets adopted Letitia Elizabeth Landon and Felicia Dorothea Hemans as their models, even writing poems addressed to them—both Elizabeth Barrett Browning and Christina Rossetti addressed poems to Landon. Dora Greenwell dedicated sonnets to Rossetti and to Barrett Browning. Gaskell wrote a biography of Charlotte Brontë, a stunning literary accomplishment as well as a tribute to a friend. A. Mary F. Robinson wrote a biography of Emily Brontë, and Mathilde Blind wrote a biography of Eliot. Simcox was so inspired by Eliot that she wished to consecrate her entire life as a monument to Eliot. And through their conduct books, Beeton and Sarah Stickney Ellis influenced many women. Beeton, indeed, came to write after finding herself in the position of being a wife without any knowledge of how to cook, run a household, or treat servants, and wanted to help other women in need of such information. Even the fictional creation of a famous writer could become important: many women were influenced by Barrett Browning's heroine, Aurora Leigh, a model of a successful female poet who overcomes innumerable obstacles in her life.

Many nineteenth-century women were encouraged in their work by the often-interlocking friendships they established with one another. Some women, such as Anna Jameson, had wide circles of friends. Jameson had friendships with the actress Fanny Kemble (who helped her with her book on Shakespeare's heroines), the Brownings, Gaskell, and members of the Langham Place Circle. Another group of women, including Michael Field, Vernon Lee, Robinson, and to some extent Rossetti and Elizabeth Siddal, revolved around the Aesthetic Movement. The Portfolio Club, whose members included Jean Ingelow, Rossetti, Barbara Leigh Smith Bodichon, Parkes, and Procter, met for the purpose of sharing their artistic endeavors with one another. Alice Mona Caird, Dinah Craik, Webster, Olive Schreiner, and Besant all became friends. At times these friendships led to artistic collaborations. Lady Elizabeth Eastlake completed Jameson's last book after Jameson died from a cold, said to be contracted while doing research at the British Museum. Simcox worked with Mary Somerville on Somerville's autobiography. The most complete collaboration was between the poets (also aunt and niece) Katherine Harris Bradley and Edith Emma Cooper, who published their work together under the name Michael Field. They announced their relationship as poets and lovers in their remarkable poem, "It Was Deep April."

Many women wrote out of economic necessity. Margaret Oliphant nearly became destitute when her husband became ill, necessitating their relocation, and she then undertook supporting the children of her brother. Unfortunately none of the children ever became financially independent, and Oliphant constantly felt compelled to write as many books as she could as quickly as possible to support her family and the lavish lifestyle they enjoyed. Oliphant asserted in a 1879 review for *Blackwood's Edinburgh Magazine*, "Whenever it has been necessary, women have toiled, have earned money, have got their living and livings of those dependent upon them, in total indifference to all theory" ("Two Ladies," vol. 125 [1879]: 206). Mary Elizabeth Braddon supported her mother, her significant other, their five illegitimate children, and the children of his legal marriage. Marie Corelli and Craik both wrote to keep their families from poverty. Landon's writings supported her brother through college and maintained her own and her mother's households. Alice Meynell supported her family of seven children, plus the poet Francis Thompson. Trollope began writing at the age of fifty-three when she left her husband and came to the United States, ultimately producing over forty books in all. Shelley felt compelled to write after the death of her husband in order to support their son; her only apparent alternative was to surrender their child to his paternal grandfather.

Developing and maintaining a career in literature was by no means easy for women during the nineteenth century. Martineau embraced her family's impoverished situation since she no longer had to put on middle-class airs of refinement—leaving her more time for writing and the ability to write openly. Even established and respected writers such as Austen and Barrett Browning put away their writing equipment whenever company entered. The work produced by these women is a powerful witness to their determination; these were by no means the silly authors of silly novels whose works, according to Eliot, "are less the result of labour than of busy idleness" (*Selected Critical Writings*, ed. Rosemary Ashton [Oxford University Press, 1992], 320). Many became famous during their lifetimes; others have achieved posthumous esteem. Oliphant is admired today for her autobiography lamenting her inability to write as well as she hoped, because of her personal difficulties, rather than for her novels. Carlyle's friends and husband repeatedly urged her to write fiction, but her achievement rests on her letters to them. Hannah Cullwick, who worked as a housemaid all her life, has now become known because of a journal that her husband, who never acknowledged their relationship openly, encouraged her to keep. Through their writings and other literary endeavors, these women were all able to find a highly effective means of communicating their thoughts, their values, and their social and societal goals and objectives. Their lives and writings continue to surprise, delight, and fascinate us today in whatever context we choose to examine them.

Jane Austen
(1775–1817)

Emily Auerbach

BIOGRAPHY

Jane Austen is considered one of the greatest novelists of all time and is the earliest woman included in the canon of English literature. Although she spent most of her forty-one years in relative obscurity among the minor landed gentry of rural England, she transformed her limited domestic environs into a microcosm for humanity.

Jane Austen was born in Steventon, a small Hampshire village in southern England, on 16 December 1775, the seventh of eight children of a country clergyman. She spent her first twenty-five years at Steventon enjoying the lively, literate family life both her parents created. Austen's closest companion was her sister Cassandra, who later destroyed Austen's most personal letters in order to protect her privacy, leaving biographers ever after to conjecture about episodes in Austen's life.

Austen's nephew called her life "singularly barren . . . of events" because she spent most of her days engaged in needlework, piano study, visits, and balls (Austen-Leigh 8). Yet Austen was not as sheltered from the outside as many think, nor was her world a stable one. England was at war for two of Austen's four decades, two of her brothers were admirals in the navy, and her cousin's husband was guillotined in the French Revolution. England was beginning to industrialize, money was allowing people to purchase "class," and social and political tracts were challenging everything from the upbringing of girls to the British slave trade.

Perhaps this revolutionary era fostered Austen's independent spirit, which emerged in the satirical sketches and saucy burlesques she wrote as a teenager for the amusement of her family. She presents heroines who get drunk, lie, steal, and raise armies, defying every notion of proper feminine behavior. As she later wrote in a letter, "[P]ictures of perfection . . . make me sick & wicked" (*Letters*,

23 Mar. 1817). Her adolescent interest in satirizing the improbable plots, sentimental diction, and exaggerated characters of contemporary romances continued in her six completed novels.

Although Austen's fiction centers on marriage making, she remained single: She rejected a wealthy suitor the morning after accepting him. She and Cassandra donned "old maid" caps earlier than custom required, thus withdrawing themselves from the marriage market. To a niece contemplating marriage, Austen warned, "Anything is to be preferred or endured rather than marrying without Affection" (*Letters*, 18 Nov. 1814). Even a happy wife's "conjugal & maternal affections" threatened to extinguish her "delicious play of Mind" (*Letters*, 20 Feb. 1817).

Jane Austen preserved the freedom to write. As she noted about a married acquaintance in a letter to her sister, "Composition seems to me Impossible, with a head full of Joints of Mutton & doses of rhubarb" (*Letters*, 8 Sept. 1816). She worked hard at polishing her novels and referred to them as children: "I am never too busy to think of S&S [*Sense and Sensibility*]. I can no more forget it, than a mother can forget her sucking child" (*Letters*, 25 Apr. 1811). She welcomed the help her father and brothers gave her in finding publishers for her novels, recognizing that the income might bring her independence: "Tho' I like praise as well as anybody, I like . . . *Pewter* too" (*Letters*, 30 Nov. 1814).

Yet Austen shunned the spotlight and posed as one who thought little of her writing. In response to her nephew's suggestion that they combine their work, Austen wrote that his "strong, manly spirited Sketches" would not blend with her own miniature painting: "[T]he little bit (two Inches wide) of Ivory on which I work with so fine a Brush, as produces little effect after much labour" (*Letters*, 16 Dec. 1816). She chose not to repair a creaky hinge on the study door so that she could hide her manuscripts when visitors approached. Even after a boastful brother made her identity known to many, including England's Prince Regent, Austen avoided public meetings and kept her name off her title pages.

Her self-deprecatory remarks mask an underlying boldness and firmness of purpose. When the Prince Regent's librarian suggested that Austen write something more serious, such as a portrait of someone like himself, Austen replied with simultaneous humility and self-assertion: "I think I may boast myself to be, with all possible vanity, the most unlearned and uninformed female who ever dared to be an authoress" (*Letters*, 11 Dec. 1815). She declined to write historical fiction, noting she could not write seriously even to save her life: "[I]f it were indispensable for me to keep it up and never relax into laughing at myself or at other people, I am sure I should be hung before I had finished the first chapter. No, I must keep to my own style and go on in my own way" (*Letters*, 1 Apr. 1816). Austen's "own way" involved keenly observing her acquaintances and transforming daily events into six seriously comic novels of manners and morals.

Publication did not come without frustration and delay. Austen had composed three novels in the 1790s before her family moved from Steventon to Bath:

Sense and Sensibility (then "Elinor and Marianne"), *Pride and Prejudice* ("First Impressions"), and *Northanger Abbey* ("Susan"). A London publisher rejected *Pride and Prejudice*; another bought *Northanger Abbey* for £10 but never printed it. After the Austens settled at Chawton in 1809, Austen returned to these early manuscripts, revising them for publication. When *Sense and Sensibility* "By a Lady" finally appeared in 1811, critics hailed its wit and wisdom. The same publisher brought out *Pride and Prejudice* two years later, establishing Austen's reputation and smoothing the way for publication of *Mansfield Park* (1814) and *Emma* (1816). Austen did not live to see the publication of her earliest novel, *Northanger Abbey*, or of her last complete novel, *Persuasion*: Both appeared posthumously in 1818.

Despite declining health, probably due to Addison's disease, Austen continued to write in the last months of her life. She died on 18 July 1817 and was buried in Winchester Cathedral. In keeping with Austen's private life, the first inscription on her gravestone made no mention of her writing or her growing fame.

MAJOR WORKS AND THEMES

Many writers produce only one or two novels acknowledged as masterpieces, along with some embarrassingly minor novels destined for neglect. In contrast, all six of Jane Austen's completed novels have been hailed as major works.

Although not published until after her death, *Northanger Abbey* is often regarded as Austen's earliest novel. Reminiscent of Austen's adolescent burlesques, *Northanger Abbey* satirizes the unrealistic gothic romances of her day. Heroine Catherine Morland undergoes a series of misadventures because she has read Ann Radcliffe's *Mysteries of Udolpho*. Her heart beating wildly, Catherine assumes a document she has found hidden in a black cabinet will reveal hideous secrets about the Tilney family, only to discover the next morning that she has unearthed just "an inventory of linen" (172). Rather than encountering a swashbuckling villain or bloodthirsty tyrant, she meets the banal John Thorpe and the mercenary General Tilney. Like all Austen novels, *Northanger Abbey* ends with marriage for the heroine, but only after a series of mishaps forces her to see the world through wiser eyes.

Two much-quoted passages from *Northanger Abbey* concern the heroine's unconventionality and the value of novels. Austen opens the novel by highlighting her heroine's imperfections: "No one who had ever seen Catherine Morland in her infancy, would have supposed her born to be an heroine" (13). Catherine lacks romantic parentage (her father is "not in the least addicted to locking up his daughters"), beauty ("she had a thin awkward figure, a sallow skin without colour, dark lank hair, and strong features"), and delicacy (she avoids "confinement and cleanliness" by noisily "rolling down the green slope at the back of the house") (13–14). Although Austen satirizes gothic romances, she defends her own genre from those who would dismiss "*only* a novel": "or, in short, only some work in which the greatest powers of the mind are displayed, in which the most thorough knowledge of human nature, the happiest delineation of its varieties, the liveliest effusions of wit and humour are conveyed to the world in the best-chosen language" (38).

Six years after publishers acquired but failed to print *Northanger Abbey*, Austen was at work revising *Sense and Sensibility*. The first edition of the novel (1811) brought her £140, a sizable amount for the time.

Sense and Sensibility describes the courtship of two temperamentally different sisters. Practical, rational Elinor Dashwood serves as counselor to her more emotional sister Marianne and their recently widowed mother. The fate of the Dashwood women depends on whether or not the cold-hearted John and Fanny Dashwood will share their just-inherited wealth. "People always live forever when there is any annuity to be paid them," Fanny warns John, and she successfully reduces her husband's plan of a gift of £3,000 for his stepmother's family to an occasional basket of food (10).

Elinor and Marianne respond differently to disappointments in love. Steeped in sentimental novels and romantic poetry, Marianne wallows in grief when the dashing Willoughby rejects her. In contrast, Elinor suffers in stoic silence as her beloved Edward Ferrars honors a youthful engagement to the vulgar Lucy Steele. Money again shapes behavior: Willoughby rejects Marianne because of her lack of fortune, and Lucy rejects Edward once his brother garners the family inheritance. *Sense and Sensibility*'s title may refer not only to the two sisters but to the final pairing of the sober Colonel Brandon and the passionate Marianne.

After the publication of *Sense and Sensibility*, Austen turned her attention to revising *Pride and Prejudice*, which appeared in 1813. Once again, Austen focuses on a family of unmarried daughters, but her heroine is not the angelic, self-restrained Jane Bennet but her radiantly healthy, witty, and outspoken younger sister Elizabeth.

Like the Dashwood women, Elizabeth and her four sisters suffer because of unjust property inheritance laws: Their father's estate is entailed on his nearest male relative, his pompous cousin Mr. Collins. Mrs. Bennet, a "woman of mean understanding," desperately seeks husbands for her five daughters, whereas cynical Mr. Bennet retreats from his unhappy marriage by hiding in his library and ridiculing his wife (5).

Obstacles thwart Mrs. Bennet's plans: Headstrong Elizabeth refuses the tiresome clergyman Mr. Collins; Jane's suitor leaves the neighborhood; Mary becomes a tedious pedant "in consequence of being the only plain one in the family"; and the giddy Lydia and Kitty flirt with officers interested in seducing, but not marrying, them (25). Elizabeth must acknowledge the fallacy of first impressions (the novel's original title) as she concedes that Captain Wickham's charm belies his roguery, whereas Mr. Darcy's reserve masks his integrity. Although at first Mr. Darcy dismissed Elizabeth as "not handsome enough" and scorned her low birth, he admits his love for her and concedes that her aunt and uncle in trade have better breeding than his vulgar, haughty aunt, the powerful Lady Catherine de Bourgh (12).

Austen's focus takes a sharp turn as she moves from the self-confident, outspoken Elizabeth to Fanny Price, the self-deprecatory, quiet heroine of *Mansfield Park* (1814). Fanny Price is only ten years old, the daughter of an alcoholic father and slatternly mother, when she is uprooted from her home to live among the snobbish Bertram family. Like Frankenstein's creation in Mary Shelley's* novel, who becomes a monster because others treat him as monstrous, Fanny Price becomes dependent and lowly in demeanor because others deny her independence and worth, insisting from the start that she "remember that she is not a *Miss Bertram*" (10).

The Miss Bertrams may be elegant and "accomplished" (they make artificial flowers, speak French, and recite the roster of the kings of England), but they lack Fanny's loyalty and goodness. Lady Bertram offers no model, spending her days lounging on sofas, patting her pug dog, and doing needlework "of little use and no beauty" (20). Sir Thomas Bertram is away in Antigua, tending to sugar plantations dependent on slave labor. In his absence, Fanny receives only abuse ("Remember, wherever you are, you must be the lowest and last") from Aunt Norris, a mean-spirited tightwad who praises her own generosity (221).

Austen contrasts the withdrawn Fanny Price with the lively Mary Crawford, showing that Mary may sparkle, though she lacks Fanny's "affectionate heart and strong desire of doing right" (17). Although Mary's showiness initially distracts Edmund Bertram from the merits of his "timid, anxious, doubting" cousin Fanny, he comes to recognize Fanny's superiority (471). Fanny discovers "the sternness of her purpose," finding a voice to speak up to her cousins, her suitors, and even her guardian (327). Austen suggests in *Mansfield Park* that even a "gentle and retiring" young woman can come of age through a quiet kind of courage and steadfast integrity (366).

Austen turns to a radically different heroine in *Emma*: No Fanny Price, Emma thinks too well, not too little, of herself. Although Austen had labeled Elizabeth Bennet of *Pride and Prejudice* "as delightful a creature as ever appeared in print" (*Letters*, 29 Jan. 1813), she called Emma "a heroine whom no one but myself will much like" (Austen-Leigh 157). Unlike the financially vulnerable Dashwoods and Bennets, Emma Woodhouse is "handsome, clever, and rich, with a comfortable home and a happy disposition," a headstrong woman who "had lived nearly twenty-one years in the world with very little to distress or vex her" (5). Emma has "none of the usual inducements of women to marry" since she enjoys being mistress of her father's estate (84). Rather than offering his daughter guidance, Mr. Woodhouse indulges in hypochondria, continuously complaining about his health, the food, and the weather.

Emma's faults stem from "the power of having rather too much her own way, and a disposition to think a little too well of herself" (5). She plays at matchmaking, viewing others as mere puppets to manipulate. Snobbery prompts

Emma to dissuade a romance between her protégée, the orphan Harriet Smith, and the sturdy, honest farmer, Mr. Martin: "The yeomanry are precisely the order of people with whom I feel I can have nothing to do," Emma haughtily warns Harriet (29). Emma instead champions the suit of the foppish, hypocritical "gentleman" Mr. Elton, only to discover to her annoyance that his affections have settled on her (and her money) rather than on Harriet. Once rejected, Mr. Elton wastes no time in producing a Mrs. Elton, an unforgettably shallow woman who boasts of her wealthy relatives' extensive grounds and handsome carriages.

Emma's husband-to-be, Mr. Knightley, serves first as her moral preceptor, scolding her for her sporadic reading, meddling behavior, and rudeness toward the "great talker upon little matters," Miss Bates (21). Emma must learn that being "handsome, clever, and rich" does not make her a lady unless she adds kindness, tolerance, and morality. The marriage between Emma Woodhouse and Mr. Knightley again unites a spirited young woman with a more restrained and rational older man. The indomitable Emma is the only Austen heroine whose name serves as a novel's title.

The heroine of Austen's final novel has matured through painful experience. Unlike Fanny Price, who resists the persuasion of others, Anne Elliot of *Persuasion* has yielded as a motherless teenager to a family friend's warning against marrying an unpropertied man. *Persuasion* dwells not on this youthful mistake but on its later consequences as twenty-seven-year-old Anne (whose "bloom had vanished early") becomes awkwardly reacquainted with Captain Wentworth (6). Many critics have praised the mature heroine and autumnal mood of Austen's final completed novel. Rather than nursing despair, like Marianne Dashwood, Anne makes a life for herself through her "elegance of mind and sweetness of character" (5).

Unlike her sister Anne, the married Mary Musgrove has "no resources for solitude" and turns to manipulative hypochondria, boasting that her sore throats are worse than anybody else's and using her "nerves" as an excuse not to stay at her sick son's bedside when a party is in progress (37). Heroine Anne Elliot finds guidance from neither her selfish sisters nor her absurdly vain father, Sir Walter Elliot, who gazes admiringly at himself in mirrors and at his name in the Baronetage. Anne does have a model of a happily married couple, however: The vibrant Sophy Croft joins Admiral Croft at sea and is his equal partner on land, avoiding a carriage accident "by coolly giving the reins a better direction herself" (97).

In all six novels, Austen focuses on a heroine at a critical point between the state of daughter and wife. Because their parents are dead, absent, detached, or foolish, the heroines make mistakes and grow from their independent struggles. Recurring themes include the discrepancy between appearance and reality, the horror of loveless or inequitable marriages, the need to balance reason and emotion, the devastating effects of materialism and snobbery, and the inadequacy of female education, as in the description in *Emma* of Mrs. Goddard's "real,

honest, old-fashioned Boarding-school . . . where girls might be sent to be out
of the way and scramble themselves into a little education, without any danger
of coming back prodigies" (21–22). Irony laces Austen's descriptions of guardians without wisdom, clergymen without mercy, and aristocrats without good
breeding. The much-quoted opening of *Pride and Prejudice* ("It is a truth universally acknowledged, that a single man in possession of a large fortune, must
be in want of a wife") epitomizes Austen's supremely ironic voice (3).

Although all six novels concentrate on the daily lives of a few country families, readers can discover bold passages if they read between the lines, as children engaged in a "hidden pictures" activity can find subtly drawn silhouettes
of a boot or knife concealed in what looks like only a charming country scene.
One such passage occurs in *Persuasion* when Anne Elliot rejects Captain Har-
ville's assertion that women are fickle because books say so: "I will not allow
books to prove anything," Anne retorts, for "[m]en have had every advantage
. . . in telling their own story. Education has been theirs in so much higher
degree; the pen has been in their hands" (234). By taking pen in hand and
turning her rapierlike wit on society, Austen quietly but firmly challenged nearly
every assumption of her age.

CRITICAL RECEPTION

Jane Austen's novels have always provoked widely different responses and
earned her both an academic and popular following. Austen heard considerable
praise of her four published novels and knew that the Prince Regent had re-
quested her to dedicate a novel to him. Sir Walter Scott wrote favorably of her
novels as early as 1815 (*Quarterly Review*) and lauded them extensively in a
journal entry a decade after Austen's death:

That young lady had a talent for describing the involvements and feelings and characters
of ordinary life, which is to me the most wonderful I ever met with. The Big Bow-wow
strain I can do myself like any now going; but the exquisite touch, which renders ordinary
commonplace things and characters interesting, from the truth of the description and the
sentiment, is denied to me. What a pity such a gifted creature died so early. (*Journal*,
ed. J. G. Tait [1939], 14 Mar. 1826)

Not all Victorian critics agreed with Scott, however. William Wordsworth complained of Austen's "pervading lack of imagination," and Thomas Carlyle dismissed her novels as mere "dishwashings!" (Watt 3, 4). Charlotte Brontë*
bemoaned Austen's lack of emotion, observing in a letter to W. S. Williams on
12 April 1850, "She does her business of delineating the surface of the lives of
genteel English people curiously well . . . [but] the Passions are perfectly unknown to her; she rejects even a speaking acquaintance with that stormy Sisterhood" (*The Brontës: Their Friendship, Lives, and Correspondence*, ed. T. J.
Wise and J. A. Symington [Oxford, 1932], 3: 99). While George Lewes, Ben-

jamin Disraeli, and Thomas Macaulay weighed in with praise for Austen, seeing her as the first woman writer to earn comparison with Shakespeare, others continued to find Austen's world "pinched and narrow," obsessed with "marriage-ableness" (Ralph Waldo Emerson, *Journals*, ed. Edward Waldo Emerson and Waldo Emerson [Houghton Mifflin, 1913], 9: 337, 1861). Mark Twain defined a good library as one with no Jane Austen in it and wrote fellow author William Dean Howells that "it seems a great pity that they allowed her to die a natural death" (*Mark Twain–Howells Letters*, ed. Henry Nash Smith and William M. Gibson [Belknap/Harvard University Press, 1960], 2: 841).

Interest in Austen heightened with the 1870 publication of James Edward Austen-Leigh's *Memoir of Jane Austen*, yet the false image he presented of a sweetly feminine maiden aunt distorted later generations of criticism and biography. Readers in the late nineteenth and early twentieth centuries turned to Austen's seemingly idyllic rural novels for escape from their increasingly industrial, complicated age. Such nostalgia intensified during World War I, when Austen's novels became prescribed reading for shell-shocked veterans.

Austen's novels failed to soothe others, however. In "Letter to Lord Byron, Part I," 1937, W. H. Auden discerned the sharp political bite of Austen's prose, calling this "English spinster of the middle-class" surprisingly shocking for revealing so frankly "the amorous effects of 'brass' " and "the economic basis of society." In "Jane Austen," *The Common Reader, Series I* (Hogarth Press, 1925), Virginia Woolf hailed Austen as "a mistress of much deeper emotion than appears upon the surface" and praised her "impeccable sense of human values" (142, 144). Yet Woolf confessed she would not want to be alone in a room with this "most perfect artist among women" because "it seems as if her creatures were born merely to give Jane Austen the supreme delight of slicing their heads off" (149, 144).

Austen's idiosyncratic characters have seemed so real that generations of readers have found pleasure in discussing their lives *after* the novels have ended. Such devoted Austen fans who found "every dam' thing . . . remarkable about Jane" were dubbed "Janeites" in a 1924 Rudyard Kipling story ("The Janeites," *Writings in Prose and Verse of Rudyard Kipling* [Scribners, 1897–1937], 31: 175).

Austen's popular following has burgeoned, sprouting Jane Austen societies in Great Britain, North America, and Australia, hundreds of Austen-related Web sites, scores of movies, and a whole business in Austen goods, from T-shirts proclaiming "I'd rather be reading Jane Austen" to Post-It notes with favorite Austen quotations. Prequels and sequels abound as novelists feel compelled to finish *The Watsons* or *Sanditon*, revisit Austen's characters decades later (when heroes and heroines have gained weight and marriages have soured), or retell her stories from the point of view of minor characters.

Simultaneously, Austen's critical reception has grown exponentially, with her place now assured as one of the greatest novelists of all time. R. W. Chapman's scholarly editions of Austen's novels, juvenilia, and letters, combined with a wide variety of late-twentieth-century biographies and scholarly studies, have rescued Austen from the "Dear Jane" image. Critics interested in feminism, imperialism, and class structure have revealed the underlying politics of Austen's novels, whereas others have delineated the linguistic complexity of novels Austen apologetically dismissed as "trifles," masking her own seriousness as an artist. Yet Austen defies critical labels, seeming out of place when taught in eighteenth-century, Romantic, or Victorian literature classes or when presented as feminist or antifeminist, revolutionary or royalist.

As the twenty-first century begins, both popular and academic interest in Jane Austen have never been higher. She remains one of the world's few writers whose entire canon is both hailed as "classic" and widely read.

BIBLIOGRAPHY

Oxford University Press has issued the standard six-volume edition of Austen's six novels, juvenilia, and incomplete fragments (ed. R. W. Chapman) as well as her letters (ed. Dierdre Le Faye); Austen citations in this entry are from these editions. All six novels also are available in many paperback editions.

Print materials on Austen are complemented by numerous film adaptations and documentaries, as well as extensive Web sites. A good beginning site is www.pemberley.com/janeinfo.

Works by Jane Austen

Sense and Sensibility: A Novel. 1811.
Pride and Prejudice: A Novel. 1813.
Mansfield Park: A Novel. 1814.
Emma: A Novel. 1816.
Northanger Abbey and Persuasion. 1818.
The Oxford Illustrated Jane Austen. 6 vols. Ed. R. W. Chapman. 1988.
Jane Austen Letters. Ed. Deirdre Le Faye. 1995.

Studies of Jane Austen

Austen-Leigh, J. E. *A Memoir of Jane Austen.* London: Richard Bentley, 1870.
Copeland, Edward, and Juliet McMaster, eds. *The Cambridge Companion to Jane Austen.* Cambridge: Harvard University Press, 1997.
Fergus, Jan. *Jane Austen: A Literary Life.* London: Macmillan, 1991.
Honan, Park. *Jane Austen: Her Life.* New York: St. Martin's Press, 1988.
Johnson, Claudia. *Jane Austen: Women, Politics, and the Novel.* Chicago: University of Chicago Press, 1988.
Kaplan, Deborah. *Jane Austen Among Women.* Baltimore: Johns Hopkins University Press, 1992.
Kirkham, Margaret. *Jane Austen, Feminism and Fiction.* Totowa, NJ: Barnes & Noble Books, 1983.
Lascelles, Mary. *Jane Austen and Her Art.* Oxford: Clarendon Press, 1939.

Litz, A. Walton. *Jane Austen: A Study of Her Artistic Development*. New York: Oxford University Press, 1965.

Rees, Joan. *Jane Austen: Woman and Writer*. New York: St. Martin's Press, 1976.

Tanner, Tony. *Jane Austen*. Cambridge: Harvard University Press, 1986.

Tomalin, Claire. *Jane Austen: A Biography*. New York: Knopf, 1997.

Watt, Ian, ed. *Jane Austen: A Collection of Critical Essays*. Englewood Cliffs, NJ: Prentice-Hall, 1963.

Isabella Mary Beeton
(1836–1865)

Sandra L. Spencer

BIOGRAPHY

Isabella Beeton, author of *Beeton's Book of Household Management*, was born on 12 March 1836, in London, to Elizabeth Jerram Mayson and Benjamin Mayson, a linen draper. Isabella was the eldest of four children, the last being born after her father's untimely death in 1841. Her mother later married Henry Dorling, a widower who also had four young children. The couple added thirteen children of their own to their blended family. As the eldest child, Isabella actively took part in rearing her siblings and performing household chores. She was educated briefly at Miss Lucy Richardson's school in Islington and later at a German boarding school in Heidelberg. In addition to academics, she mastered both French and German and became an accomplished pianist during her stay in Germany. She also took a rudimentary cooking course offered by the boarding school. Upon returning to England, she took a private pastry-making course.

In 1856 Isabella Mayson married Samuel Orchart Beeton, a young London publisher. Shortly after marrying, she assumed an active role in the planning, writing, and editing of *The Englishwoman's Domestic Magazine* (*EDM*), a popular periodical for middle-class women that her husband published. The couple incorporated many innovative features into the periodical, including French fashions illustrated by color plates. The *EDM* was one of the first periodicals to furnish patterns of their featured fashions for subscribers.

Their first child, Samuel Orchart Beeton, was born in May 1857 and died in August. The grieving Beeton immersed herself in writing an advice book for novice homemakers, something she had sought, in vain, when she, herself, was a new bride. Her husband published the first serial part in *EDM* in late September 1859, the same month their second son, also named Samuel Orchart Beeton, was born. Although homemakers welcomed the serial parts, they soon wanted

"Mrs. Beeton's" in book form. On 1 October 1861, the volume, featuring numerous engravings and illustrations, was published.

The second Beeton son died at three years of age on New Year's Eve of 1862 while the family was on holiday in Brighton. The family moved to Greenhithe, about twenty miles from London, the following spring, where their third son, Orchart, was born on 31 December 1863, exactly a year after the death of their second son.

Beeton returned to work shortly, and the couple published a new periodical, *The Young Englishwoman*, soon thereafter. Beeton, who continued overseeing the fashion and needlework pages of *EDM*, added the responsibilities of the new periodical as well. She again became pregnant, and their fourth son, Mayson, was born on 29 January 1865. The birth itself was without complications, but Beeton developed puerperal fever and died a week later in February 1865. She was twenty-nine years old.

MAJOR WORKS AND THEMES

As a young bride, Isabella Beeton lamented that she could find no practical book of advice about supervising a household. *Beeton's Book of Household Management* (1859) filled that void. Her research resulted in one of the most innovative and accessible advice books of the time. Beeton's own inexperience was her greatest asset: She knew what novice homemakers most needed. Hence, her book had an entirely new format. In the cookery section, for example, she listed all ingredients at the beginning of recipes and used exact measurements and cooking times. She also stated the cost, number of servings, and proper season for each recipe.

Although the bulk of Beeton's book deals with cookery, the first chapter focuses on the mistress of the household, delineating fifty-four different responsibilities, including wifely virtues as well as household duties. Beeton discusses the ideal wife's cleanliness, dress, charitable activities, friendships, conversation, social etiquette, and demeanor. Advice of a more tangible nature includes how to keep household accounts, engage and supervise servants, and plan a daily agenda. With great thoroughness, Beeton covers wages for butlers, cooks, maids-of-all-work, stableboys, and twenty-one other servants.

Beeton's section on "Domestic Servants" covers specific duties of each servant and general observations on the relationship between servant and members of the household. Her section "The Rearing and Management of Children, and Diseases of Infancy and Childhood" begins with her personal philosophy about the intuitive nature of motherhood and then shifts to description of infant respiration, circulation, and digestion. Several pages are devoted to milk and food preparation, dress, teething, and childhood illnesses.

In the final two sections of the book, Beeton focuses on common medical and legal issues. In "The Doctor," she lists medical supplies every family should have on hand and gives instructions for making poultices, dispensing pills, and applying lotions. She discusses insect and snake bites, fractures, burns, and other medical emergencies. "Legal Memoranda," the shortest section of the book, contains advice on leases, insurance, wills, home purchases, and the like. Beeton sought advice from experts for the two final sections of *Household Management*. Her keen perception of what her audience needed—thorough, practical advice— resulted in a straight forward style seldom found in Victorian advice books.

CRITICAL RECEPTION

Critical response to the book was positive. Over 60,000 copies were sold the first year. Contemporary reviewers found the work impressive, but the most important testament to the book's success has been its popularity with readers. Several editions and at least twenty-five derivations of the book have been published, most with little amendment. In the preface to the 1869 edition, her husband wrote, "The arrangement of the first edition was so well-conceived that it admitted scarcely any reform, and my late wife's writing was so clear, and her directions were so practical, that only the slightest alterations and corrections were needed, except such as TIME had rendered necessary." Although *Beeton's Book of Household Management* remains culturally interesting today, the book generates little critical attention.

BIBLIOGRAPHY

Beeton's book has been updated several times, and either the book itself or one of its numerous derivations has been in print continuously.

Works by Isabella Beeton

Beeton's Book of Household Management. 1859.

Studies of Isabella Beeton

Freeman, Sarah. *Isabella and Sam: The Story of Mrs. Beeton.* New York: Coward, McCann, and Geoghegan, 1978.
Spain, Nancy. *The Beeton Story.* London: Ward, Lock, 1956.

Annie Wood Besant
(1847-1933)

Carol Hanbery MacKay

BIOGRAPHY

Born in London to what she proudly claimed as three-quarters Irish heritage, Annie Wood was raised by her widowed mother and educated privately by Ellen Marryat, who instilled in her pupil a love of learning by direct experience as well as some of her resolute Evangelicalism. Religious zeal fueled Annie's rather naive choice of marriage partner, the Church of England's Reverend Frank Besant, when she was barely twenty, but doubts about a God who would allow her infant daughter's near-death from severe bronchitis soon assailed the young mother, leading her to leave both Christianity and her husband. Working for the National Secular Society, Besant became allied with Charles Bradlaugh, with whom she was put on trial for introducing and publishing Charles Knowlton's book about birth control; the resultant notoriety contributed to her losing legal custody of both her children in 1879.

During the following decade, Besant studied for an advanced degree in science, became a Socialist, coedited with W. T. Stead *The Link*, helped the matchwork girls of Bryant and May win their strike, and was elected to the London School Board. Her career path made a lifelong turn in 1889 when she met Madame Helena Blavatsky and converted to Theosophy, becoming head of the European and Indian branches two years later. Moving to India in 1893, Besant worked for Indian self-government while rising to worldwide leadership of the Theosophical Society in 1907. Elected president of India's National Congress in 1917, she continued to make annual trips to London, speaking for women's suffrage and other social reforms. In 1924 a British tribute marked her fifty years of public service. Active in human rights to the very end, Annie Wood Besant died at her home in Madras at the age of eighty-five.

MAJOR WORKS AND THEMES

Committed to the pursuit of truth, Annie Besant began her writing career by anonymously exploring the roots of Christianity, where as a Freethinker and later Fabian Socialist, she devoted herself to educating the public about such key issues as euthanasia, birth control, marriage, and the social status of women. Editing and writing for her own journal—*Our Corner*—allowed Besant to provide a forum for debating these issues as well as for promoting the work of fellow socialists such as George Bernard Shaw. Most of her early pamphlets were published by the Freethought Publishing Company and originated in lectures she delivered for the National Secular Society.

Twice Besant wrote out full-length accounts of her life story. The first version, *Autobiographical Sketches* (1885), stressed her "deconversion" to atheism and the trial for custody of her daughter; the second, *An Autobiography* (1893), appeared after she had converted to Theosophy and viewed her life newly, recasting and examining her early years in light of their projected fulfillment through a worldwide movement that sought the universal truth informing all religious traditions. Not denying either her initial Christianity or her subsequent atheism, Besant ruthlessly engaged in the kind of self-examination that demonstrates a rational mind at work trying to understand how the individual interacts with an evolving society. Envisioning world peace and human freedom, she dedicated herself to advancing Theosophy as the dynamic synthesis that could bring about such a holistic goal.

CRITICAL RECEPTION

During her lifetime, Annie Besant was alternately reviled and championed, and her reputation has continued to fluctuate to the present day. Her evolving belief systems and her outspoken endorsement of them kept her before the public eye, making her an effective spokesperson for the causes she advocated. But because Besant's embrace of one movement usually involved criticism of its predecessor, she invoked disparagement, oftentimes for an inconsistency of thought that actually displays a coherent, logical progression. One by one, previous colleagues openly denounced her, most notably after she converted to Theosophy, but the vehemence of their attacks primarily betrays the sense of loss they felt in no longer having her as an ally.

In many respects, Besant has been best served by Indian critics and biographers, who provide fairly balanced narratives of her life and accomplishments (see most notably C. P. Ramaswami Aiyar). Writing close to the events they described, such early British biographers as Geoffrey West (1929), Gertrude Marvin Williams (1931), and Theodore Besterman (1934) lacked the perspective that hindsight and distance can provide, whereas Arthur H. Nethercot's massive two-volume endeavor betrays its own semiparodic bias by the manner of its titling. Anne Taylor's more recent accounting benefits from extensive scholarship but still seems antagonistic to its subject. It is unfortunate that fellow suffragist Elizabeth Robins did not complete her biography of Besant; it only exists in typescript at the Fales Library of New York University. Feminists have begun to discover Besant, however, and some of their biographical accounts have introduced her to a new public (see especially Rosemary Dinnage and Olivia Bennett). Most recently, Joy Dixon and Catherine Wessinger have contextualized Besant's own feminism within the enlightened aspects of her complex spirituality.

BIBLIOGRAPHY

Most of Besant's major moral, psychological, and spiritual treatises have remained in print, thanks to the Theosophical Publishing House, while both *Autobiographical Sketches* and *An Autobiography* are available from scholarly reprint presses.

Selected Works by Annie Wood Besant

Law of Population. 1878.
Autobiographical Sketches. 1885.
Why I Am a Socialist. 1886.
An Autobiography. 1893.
The Ancient Wisdom: An Outline of Theosophical Teachings. 1897.
Esoteric Christianity. 1901.
Thought Forms. With C. W. Leadbeater. 1905.
The Immediate Future and Other Lectures. 1911.
How India Wrought for Freedom: The Story of the National Congress Told from Official Records. 1915.
Duties of the Theosophist. 1917.
Psychology: Science of the Soul. 1919.
Theosophical Christianity. 1922.
The Coming of the World Teacher. 1925.

Studies of Annie Wood Besant

Aiyar, C. P. Ramaswami. *Annie Besant.* Delhi: Ministry of Information and Broadcasting, 1963.
Bennett, Olivia. *Annie Besant.* London: Hamish Hamilton, 1988.
Besterman, Theodore. *Mrs. Annie Besant: A Modern Prophet.* London: Kegan Paul, Trench, Trubner, 1934.
Bevir, Mark. "Annie Besant's Quest for Truth: Christianity, Secularism and New Age Thought." *The Journal of Ecclesiastical History* 50.1: 62–93.
Chandrasekhar, S. *"A Dirty, Filthy Book": The Writings of Charles Knowlton and Annie Besant on Reproductive Physiology and Birth Control and an Account of the Bradlaugh-Besant Trial.* Berkeley: University of California Press, 1981.
Dinnage, Rosemary. *Annie Besant.* Middlesex: Penguin, 1986.

Dixon, Joy. "Sexology and the Occult: Sexuality and Subjectivity in Theosophy's New Age." *Journal of the History of Sexuality* 7.3 (1997): 409–33.

Ellwood, Robert, and Catherine Wessinger. "The Feminism of 'Universal Brotherhood': Women in the Theosophical Movement." In *Women's Leadership in Marginal Religions: Explorations Outside the Mainstream*. Ed. Catherine Wessinger. Urbana: University of Illinois Press, 1993. 68–87.

In Honour of Dr. Annie Besant: Lectures by Eminent Persons, 1952–88. Kamachha: Indian Section of the Theosophical Society, 1990.

Melton, J. Gordon, ed. and intro. *The Origins of Theosophy: Annie Besant—The Atheist Years*. New York: Garland Publishing, 1990.

Nethercot, Arthur H. *The First Five Lives of Annie Besant*. Chicago: University of Chicago Press, 1960.

———. *The Last Four Lives of Annie Besant*. Chicago: University of Chicago Press, 1963.

Taylor, Anne. *Annie Besant: A Biography*. Oxford: Oxford University Press, 1992.

Viswanathan, Gauri. *Outside the Fold: Conversion, Modernity, and Belief*. Princeton: Princeton University Press, 1998.

Wessinger, Catherine. *Annie Besant and Progressive Messianism, 1847–1933*. Lewiston, NY: Edwin Mellen Press, 1988.

———. "Democracy vs. Hierarchy: The Evolution of Authority in the Theosophical Society." In *When Prophets Die: The Postcharismatic Fate of New Religious Movements*. Ed. Timothy Miller. Intro. J. Gordon Melton. Albany: State University of New York Press, 1991. 93–106, 218–22.

West, Geoffrey. [Geoffrey Harry Wells.] *The Life of Annie Wood Besant*. London: Gerald Howe, 1929.

Williams, Gertrude Marvin. *The Passionate Pilgrim*. New York: Coward-McCann, 1931.

Louisa Sarah Bevington
(1845-1895)

Jackie Dees Domingue

BIOGRAPHY

The eldest of eight children, Louisa Sarah Bevington defied Quaker ancestry and a privileged inheritance with outspoken censure of religion and private property ownership. Her unabashed criticism of established institutions extended even to her family's insurance business (see *Common-Sense Country*). Bevington spent most of her life in London and was married only a short time to Munich artist Ignatz Guggenberger. In addition to publishing three volumes of poetry, she achieved notoriety first as a philosophical writer and later as an enthusiastic supporter of anarchist communism.

As a social revisionist, Bevington forecast a British society that would recognize its potential for perfection at a time of progressive excitement over nineteenth-century scientific advancements. In both her prose and poetry she consistently urges that the way to facilitate such perfectibility is to accept the idea of evolutionary progress. Bevington embraced life's conflicts as part of the natural progress of humankind's social development, with the belief that one day life would be free of sorrow and abuse (see *Dame Nature's Dumb Sermon*). She also championed a philosophy of evolutionary ethics, that conscience did not emerge from biblical principles, but, rather, morality is the natural result of a constant upward course of human development. In addition, Bevington used the language of evolutionary processes (fitness, adaptiveness, purgation, self-adjustment) to substantiate the aptness of anarchist theory—including its undercurrent of violent protest—as a just response to contemporary societal ills.

In the years just preceding her death, Bevington contributed essays to several anarchist presses, including *The Torch*, a publication of William Michael Rossetti's children, and *The Commonweal*, which was started by William Morris. She also coauthored a Liberty Press pamphlet with Morris ("Why I Am an Expropriatist" in *The Why I Ams*, 1894) and translated prose and poetry by her friend Louise Michel. Bevington's inside information about an anarchist's failed testing of a bomb near the Greenwich Observatory is recorded in *Letters from the Dead* (Nicoll); the incident was later fictionalized in Joseph Conrad's *The Secret Agent*. A desire for working-class liberation inspired her vehement repudiation of economic exploitation by capitalists, and she defended the use of dynamite against authorities who could not be peacefully convinced to end their persecution of the hungry and destitute.

MAJOR WORKS AND THEMES

Although Bevington's earliest sonnets appearing in a Quaker journal in 1871 indicate an orthodox upbringing, her first volume of verse (*Key-Notes*, 1879) discloses a religious skepticism that would signify her subsequent publications and secure for her Charles Darwin's praise and a biographer's designation as the "poetess of evolutionary science" (Miles 263). In his notes and in *The Origin of Species* Darwin used the image of the tree to express evolutionary organization, which could be a link to why Bevington used the pseudonym Arbor Leigh for her first private publication of *Key-Notes* in 1876, several poems from which appeared in *Popular Science Monthly* upon the special request of Bevington's friend, sociologist and scientific ethicist Herbert Spencer. In *Key-Notes* Bevington also communicates the quintessential Victorian dilemma of an old world passing into the new: "There is not the faintest echo / From the life of yesterday: / Not the vaguest stir foretelling / Of a morrow on the way" (from "Midnight"). Bevington's assimilation of evolutionary idea into poetic thought continues in *Poems, Lyrics, and Sonnets* (1882), a collection that also addresses gender issues. Her 1895 pamphlet *Liberty Lyrics* is a tribute to anarchist comrades and urges insurrection as herald to a new world order.

In many essays, Bevington relates her preoccupation with not only how evolution discloses itself in nature but also how it affects humans' intellect and moral sense. In "The Personal Aspect of Responsibility" she explains how religion had not influenced ethical behavior, but rather a natural morality had impelled dogmatic theology. Also, the supernatural enigmas of religion are based on simple, natural truths and are actually products of the very anthropological activities they seek to transcend ("Modern Atheism and Mr. Mallock"). Bevington's 1881 *Fortnightly Review* essay, "The Moral Colour of Rationalism," is a reply on behalf of Spencer who was annoyed at a critic's statement that scientific philosophy insufficiently addressed the concept of morality. One of Bevington's most impassioned essays on how theology hinders moral advancement is "The Moral Demerits of Orthodoxy" (*Progress*, 1884), wherein she accuses "a corrupt and senile superstition" of undermining secular efforts to meet the demands of the day.

Bevington's distrust of government stemmed partly from the influences of Ralph Waldo Emerson, whom she quotes in the epigraph to *Key-Notes*; Pierre-Joseph Proudhon, whose "property is theft" maxim inspired anarchists to embrace communism as a provision for the reorganization of society; and Spencer, whose writings on social evolution and individualism Bevington refers to in many essays. The most thorough exposition of her anarchist convictions was drafted into *An Anarchist Manifesto* (1895), a treatise that outlined how revolutionary changes would occur in society, a process that could not be initiated through politics because labor and other parties destroy people's "self-reliance and self-respect, and do for them that which religion does—make them expect everything from others, nothing from themselves" (13). Bevington's political essays only rarely refer to women's concerns in particular because as an anarchist she argued for every individual's right to absolute liberty.

CRITICAL RECEPTION

Bevington achieved literary recognition in England and America following the *Nineteenth Century* publication of "Modern Atheism and Mr. Mallock" (Miles). The method of confrontational analysis she initiated with the Mallock essay continued throughout her career, and she often volleyed through issue after issue of response to her critics. She particularly enjoyed rebuttals to fellow anarchists who could not fathom, for example, her abstruse insistence that individual property did not really exist; her semantics agitated comrades who contended that the anarchists' polemic should be about oppression through control of property, not about whether property abided in substance or in theory.

Bevington's inclusion in *Poets and Poetry of the Century*, published in 1892, attests to her contemporary popularity. Her verses were praised in *The Cambridge Review* and in *The Athenaeum*; Robert Browning wrote to Bevington that he discerned in her poems "much power and beauty" (Domingue, "An Unpublished Browning Letter to Louisa Sarah Bevington"). Her work was also admired by Francis Galton, explorer and scientist best known for his studies of heredity and intelligence and whom Bevington consulted about oral hallucinations.

In the past decade Bevington's poems have been anthologized and deliberated within the context of feminist studies, but her social and political essays, which seldom address gender issues, have received little attention.

BIBLIOGRAPHY

No modern editions of Bevington's poems exist, although several of her poems are included in recent anthologies. A few of her essays are available online through the Victorian Women Writer's Project: www.indiana.edu/~letrs/vwwp.

Works by Louisa Sarah Bevington

Key-Notes. 1879.
"The Personal Aspect of Responsibility." *Mind: A Quarterly Review of Psychology and Philosophy* 4.14 (Apr. 1879): 244–55.

"Modern Atheism and Mr. Mallock." *Nineteenth Century* 6.32 (Oct. 1879): 585–603;
    6.34 (Dec. 1879): 999–1020.
"Determinism and Duty." *Mind: A Quarterly Review of Psychology and Philosophy* 5.17
    (Jan. 1880): 30–45.
"The Moral Colour of Rationalism." *The Fortnightly Review*, n.s., 30.176 (1 Aug. 1881):
    179–94.
"The Image of Truth: A Dream." *The Modern Review: A Quarterly Magazine* 3 (Oct.
    1882): 838–49.
Poems, Lyrics, and Sonnets. 1882.
"The Moral Demerits of Orthodoxy." *Progress: A Monthly Magazine of Advanced
    Thought* 4 (Sept. 1884): 128–34.
Dame Nature's Dumb Sermon. 1891.
"The Moral and Religious Bearings of the Evolution Theory." In *Religious Systems of
    the World: A Contribution to the Study of Comparative Religion.* 1892. 768–86.
" 'Leaden Instincts v. Golden Conduct.' " *Freedom: A Journal of Anarchist Communism*
    6.70 (Sept. 1892): 71–72.
"Dynamitism." *The Commonweal: A Revolutionary Journal of Anarchist-Communism*,
    n.s., 1.5 (24 June 1893): n.p.
"Why I Am an Expropriationist." *Liberty: A Journal of Anarchist Communism* 1.5 (May
    1894); *The Why I Ams.* With William Morris. 1894.
An Anarchist Manifesto. 1895.
Chiefly a Dialogue: Concerning Some Difficulties of a Dunce. 1895.
Liberty Lyrics. 1895.
"The Whereabouts of Property Ethics." *Liberty: A Journal of Anarchist Communism* 2.18
    (June 1895): 141–42.
"Money Rules the World." *The Torch: A Revolutionary Journal of Anarchist—Com-
    munism* 2.3 (18 Aug. 1895): 41–42.
Anarchism and Violence. 1896.
Common-Sense Country. n.d.

Studies of Louisa Sarah Bevington

Blain, Virginia, Patricia Clements, and Isobel Grundy. *The Feminist Companion to Lit-
    erature in English: Women Writers from the Middle Ages to the Present.* New
    Haven: Yale University Press, 1990.
Domingue, Jackie Dees. "Doctrine and Dynamite: An Edition of Louisa Sarah Beving-
    ton's Social and Political Essays." Ph.D. diss., Texas A&M University, 2000.
———. "An Unpublished Browning Letter to Louisa Sarah Bevington." *ANQ: A Quar-
    terly Journal of Short Articles, Notes, and Reviews* (2000).
Hickok, Kathleen. *Representations of Women: Nineteenth-Century British Women's Po-
    etry.* Westport, CT: Greenwood Press, 1984.
Miles, Alfred H., ed. "Louisa S. Guggenberger. 1845." In *Poets and the Poetry of the
    Century.* London: Hutchinson, 1892. 8: 261–78.
Nicoll, David. *Letters from the Dead.* London: David Nicoll, 1898.
Oliver, Hermia. *The International Anarchist Movement in Late Victorian London.* New
    York: St. Martin's Press, 1983.

Quail, John. *The Slow Burning Fuse: The Lost History of the British Anarchists*. London: Granada, 1978.

Sherry, Norman. *Conrad's Western World*. Cambridge: Cambridge University Press, 1971.

Isabella Lucy Bird (Bishop) (1831–1904)

Lila M. Harper

BIOGRAPHY

Isabella Lucy Bird (later Bishop) was one of the best known and most prolific women travel writers of the nineteenth century. She obtained a high level of respect in professional geographic societies by holding a position of impeccable respectability, both domestic and religious, and through the sheer number of miles and corresponding pages she racked up in her travels. While never publicly outspoken on women's rights, she still led the initial movement of women into the Royal Geographical Society. Her writings were popular both because they were entertaining and because they provided information useful for the expanding British empire.

Born in 1831 into a strict Church of England family, Bird had a close relationship with her younger sister, Henrietta, the audience for much of her travel writing. She was educated at home in languages and natural history, later acquiring additional training in microbiology, field photography, cartography, and basic medical aid (for both humans and horses).

After an operation for a tumor at the base of her spine, Bird made her first voyage to the United States at the age of twenty-two. She wrote an anonymous account, *The Englishwoman in America*, in 1856. A second trip followed in order to edit her father's writings on religion in America, and another (still anonymous) publication, *The Aspects of Religion in the United States of America*, in 1859.

Despite continuous ill health that required the use of a neckbrace, she continued writing while at home for ladies' magazines. Bird suffered from continuing spinal problems, insomnia, and the vague ills generally associated with depression and intellectual frustration. At the age of forty-one, she made a trip to Australia and then to California. A stopover in Hawaii introduced her to women who rode without sidesaddles, a practice that she put into operation in the Rocky Mountains. Her *A Lady's Life in the Rocky Mountains* (1879) was very popular and indicated that she could make a living through travel writing. This trip established her as a popular writer, and she realized that she could escape her social limitations through travel. She continued traveling, writing letters to her sister, then working the letters into books. When traveling, she enjoyed excellent health and thrived on the physical challenges she faced.

After Henrietta's death from typhoid fever, Bird married her sister's doctor, John Bishop, and stopped traveling and writing for the five years of their marriage until his sudden death. After widowhood, Bird again took up her career and traveled to Tibet, Persia, and Kurdistan. She gave talks to geographic societies upon her return and became one of the first women admitted to the Royal Geographical Society. Her last travels were to China and further into Tibet. She died at the age of seventy after an illness in Morocco, where she was riding 500 miles at a stretch.

MAJOR WORKS AND THEMES

Bird's travel writing career falls into three parts, identified by her changing rhetorical orientation and separated by periods of nontravel. As a young woman, she wrote in an auxiliary position, helping her father's research and writing for charitable causes, activities proper for a minister's daughter. When she began to travel again in her forties, she found relief from the confines of British social life by traveling off the beaten path. These writings show a certain nervous tension as Bird attempts to present her nonconformist behavior—traveling without a European male, riding astride, and wearing a pantslike riding costume—so it would be acceptable at home.

In 1889, after the death of her sister, and then her husband, Bird became a truly professional traveler. Ostensibly traveling in order to establish medical missions, she also sought acceptance from geographical societies, writing with an eye to the needs and interests of government officials and overseas investors. Having gained a position of respect, she emphasized now the physical hardship of her journeys, challenging Victorian assumptions about women's physical capabilities.

CRITICAL RECEPTION

Her most popular travel account, *A Lady's Life in the Rocky Mountains*, went through seven editions in its first three years of publication. The *Times*' (21 Nov. 1879, 3) review of the book played up the Wild West elements and suggested Bird was unfeminine; Bird was incensed and added a sketch of herself in later editions emphasizing the femininity of her riding dress.

Because of her Persian travels, she was seen as an authority on Far East politics. Her book on China received particular attention, as it was published shortly before the 1900 Boxer Rebellion. After her death, her obituaries noted the contrast between her poor health at home and her physical stamina abroad. Although a popular writer in her time, she has received little modern critical attention.

BIBLIOGRAPHY

Selections from Bird have been anthologized recently in *Prose by Victorian Women* (ed. Andrea Broomfield and Sally Mitchell [Garland, 1996]), *Maiden Voyages: Writings of Women Travelers* (ed. Mary Morris and Larry O'Connor [Vintage Books, 1993]), *With Women's Eyes: Visitors to the New World, 1775–1918* (ed. Marion Tinling [Archon, 1993]), and *Celebrating the Land: Women's Nature Writings, 1850–1991* (ed. Karen Knowles [Northland, 1992]). While several of her books have been reprinted, only *A Lady's Life in the Rocky Mountains* is currently in print (Comstock, 1988; Konemann, 1999).

Works by Isabella Bird

The Englishwoman in America. 1856.
The Aspects of Religion in the United States of America. 1859.
The Hawaiian Archipelago: Six Months Among the Palm Groves, Coral Reefs, and Volcanoes of the Sandwich Islands. 1875.
A Lady's Life in the Rocky Mountains. 1879.
Unbeaten Tracks in Japan: An Account of Travels in the Interior, Including Visits to the Aborigines of Yezo and the Shrines of Kikko and Isé. 1880.
The Golden Chaeronese and the Way Thither. 1883.
Journeys in Persia and Kurdistan. 1891.
Among the Tibetans. 1894.
Korea and Her Neighbors. 1897.
The Yangtze Valley and Beyond: An Account of Journeys in China. Chiefly in the Province of Sze Chuan and Among the Man-Tze of the Somo Territory. 1899.

Studies of Isabella Bird

Barr, Pat. *A Curious Life for a Lady: The Life of Isabella Bird.* London: Macmillan, 1970.
Gatti, Anne. *Isabella Bird Bishop.* London: Hamilton, 1988.
Morgan, Susan. *Place Matters: Gendered Geography in Victorian Women's Travel Books About Southeast Asia.* New Brunswick: Rutgers University Press, 1996.
Stoddart, Anna M. *The Life of Isabella Bird.* London: Murray, 1906.

Clementina Black
(1853–1922)

Andrea L. Broomfield

BIOGRAPHY

Trade union activist, suffragist, and writer, Clementina Black was born in Brighton to Clara Patten and David Black, a solicitor and town coroner. She was the eldest girl of eight children, educated by her mother and her older brothers. Because Black's father suffered from locomoter ataxia and his wife's time was taken up with nursing him, Black herself was largely responsible for teaching her younger siblings and for managing the household. At age twenty-two, after her mother died, Black taught at a local girls' boarding school to contribute to the family finances. Dissatisfaction with her life in Brighton, however, led Black and her sisters to move to London in the early 1880s. Black's sister, Constance Garnett (1861–1946), went on to become one of England's most famous translators of over seventy Russian classics, ranging from the works of Tolstoy to those of Chekhov, Gorky, and Turgenev. She is credited with igniting a passion for Russian literature in the hearts of numerous Victorians who had previously been unexposed to that country's culture.

Black's interest in trade unionism was sparked by her witnessing the 8 February 1886 march on Trafalgar Square when trade unionists, Socialists, and unemployed persons converged to protest government bans on public demonstrations. Soon thereafter, Black was appointed honorary secretary of the Women's Protective and Provident League (WPPL), the official start of her long and productive career in trade union activism. Increasingly dissatisfied with the WPPL's moderation on issues that directly affected the well-being of England's poorest women workers, Black resigned her position in 1889 to help found the militant Women's Trade Union Association (WTUA). After its collapse, she helped found the Women's Industrial Council (WIC), serving as president from 1895 to 1909, as well as becoming editor of the organization's journal, the *Women's Industrial News*, in 1895.

Not surprisingly, Black's literary output deals primarily with the causes she championed. In addition to writing extensively about labor and economics, Black also wrote essays on women's suffrage, and in 1913, she edited *Common Cause*, the official publication of the National Union of Women's Suffrage Societies. Black also wrote novels, translated several works into English, and produced book-length studies on women and labor. In 1913, she was awarded a Civil List pension of seventy-five pounds a year. When she died, she possessed only thirty-nine pounds, all of which went to her niece, whom she had raised as her own child.

MAJOR WORKS AND THEMES

Clementina Black published her first story, "The Troubles of an Automaton," in the *New Quarterly Magazine* in 1876. Her first two novels appeared shortly thereafter: *A Sussex Idyl* in 1877 and *Orlando* in 1880. Fiction brought Black little financial security, however, and after *Mericas and Other Stories* was published in 1880, she turned her attention primarily to writing articles that explored women's labor. Partly because of Black's ability to employ "New Journalism" techniques as a way of attracting and sustaining readers' attention, she quickly established herself as an authority on the topic of unskilled women workers after her first essay, "Caveat Emptor," appeared in *Longman's Magazine* in 1887. The bulk of Black's journalistic output encompasses eyewitness, first-person accounts of sweatshop conditions; polemical essays that berate middle-class complacency about working-class women; graphic renderings of working women's miserable living quarters; persuasive, melodramatic essays that urge readers to join the WIC or organize consumers' leagues; theoretical articles on economics; as well as several interviews and potted biographies of working women (condensed biographies designed to elicit an emotional response from the reader). Her work appears in an impressive array of periodicals, including the era's intellectual heavyweights such as the *Fortnightly* and *New Review*, more specialized publications such as the *Economic Journal* and *Women's Industrial News*, and popular magazines such as the *Illustrated London News*.

CRITICAL RECEPTION

Certainly Black's intimate knowledge of lower-class women's lives made her an asset to the WPPL and later the WIC, but just as important, this knowledge increased her value and reliability as an author. With readers, Black's reputation was enhanced by her continuing career as a novelist, but her relationship with several prominent middle-class women suffragists and labor organizers was at times contentious. Early in her career, Black protested parliamentary legislation designed to protect exclusively working women. As with many of her cohorts, Black contended that such legislation diminished a woman's ability to compete with men for the lowest-skilled jobs, that it kept single women from earning a living wage, and that it impeded their efforts to join established trade unions. But by 1899, Black became convinced that unskilled working women's interests needed to be protected by legislation. This contention put her at odds with colleagues who continued to maintain that protective legislation would only harm women. Nonetheless, a popular author and sought-after lecturer, Black effectively elicited support for her causes and fomented ongoing debate on women's labor. Indeed, her *Sweated Industry and the Minimum Wage* (1907) and *Makers of Our Clothes, a Case for Trade Boards* (coauthored with Adèle Meyer, 1909) were likely responsible for helping to pass the 1909 Trade Boards Act.

Although Black's career is frequently mentioned by current labor historians, she remains virtually unknown to literary scholars. Some efforts have been made to bring her name to light, in particular by critics who focus on Victorian periodicals research and feminist literary history.

BIBLIOGRAPHY

"What Is a Fair Wage?" and "The Dislike to Domestic Service" are both reprinted in *Prose by Victorian Women: An Anthology* (ed. Andrea Broomfield and Sally Mitchell [Garland, 1996]).

Selected Works by Clementina Black

"The Troubles of an Automaton." *New Quarterly Magazine* 6 (1876): 463–87.
A Sussex Idyl. 1877.
Mericas and Other Stories. 1880.
Orlando. 1880.
"Caveat Emptor." *Longman's Magazine* 10 (Aug. 1887): 409–20.
"Something about Needle-Women." *Woman's World* 1 (1888): 300–304.
"The Organization of Working Women."*Fortnightly Review* 46 n.s. (Nov. 1889): 695–704.
"On Marriage: A Criticism." *Fortnightly Review* 530 s., 47 n.s. (Apr. 1890): 586–94.
"The Coercion of Trade Unions." *Contemporary Review* 62 (Oct. 1892): 547–54.
"The Dislike to Domestic Service." *Nineteenth Century* 33 (Mar. 1893): 454–56.
"What Is a Fair Wage?" *New Review* 8 (May 1893): 587–92.
Sweated Industry and the Minimum Wage. 1907.
Makers of Our Clothes, a Case for Trade Boards. With Adèle Meyer. 1909.

Studies of Clementina Black

Cameron, Mary. "Clementina Black: A Character Sketch." *The Young Woman* 1 (1892–1893): 315–16.
Glage, Liselotte. *Clementina Black: A Study in Social History and Literature*. Heidelberg: Carl Winter Universitätsverlag, 1981.

Countess of Blessington, Marguerite Power Farmer Gardiner (1789-1849)

Ann R. Hawkins

BIOGRAPHY

Harriet Martineau* called Marguerite Power Farmer Gardiner, Countess of Blessington, one of the most "substantially successful authoresses of her time"; contemporaries like Disraeli and Jerdan estimated her yearly income from writing between £2,000 and £3,000.

As a child, she attracted attention for her imagination and ability as a storyteller, leading a neighbor to begin educating her. In 1804, when she was fourteen, her impecunious father, perceiving her beauty as a financial asset, married her to Captain Maurice Farmer over her objections. After three months of physical and psychological abuse, Margaret left Farmer and returned to her reluctant family. In 1808, still separated from her husband, Margaret fled her family under the protection of Capt. Thomas Jenkins. Her ten years with Jenkins appear to have been pleasant: Though beautiful, she recognized that she lacked reputation, and she read widely. In 1818, the death of her husband freed her to marry Charles John Gardiner, First Earl of Blessington, who reimbursed Jenkins £10,000 for her upkeep—marking the second time that Margaret Power was sold for her beauty. From 1818 to 1822, Blessington, now calling herself Marguerite, hosted a popular literary salon in London, and in 1822, she began her literary career anonymously, publishing sketches, essays, and a travel journal.

Having traveled to the Continent in August 1822, the Blessingtons met George Gordon, Lord Byron, in Genoa; and for nine weeks in 1823, Lady Blessington recorded her conversations with the poet.

From 1831 to 1849 (the year of her death), Blessington hosted a popular London salon rivaled only by Lady Holland's and appealing to literary men. Richard Robert Madden, Blessington's biographer, described Blessington as "the art of pleasing personified" able to "draw wit from a fool" (52). Of notoriety during this period was Blessington's relationship with Count D'Orsay, a member of the Blessington household on the Continent, the former husband of her step-daughter, and Blessington's companion after her husband's death.

After her husband's death in May 1829, Lady Blessington's income was reduced to a jointure of £2,000, and she returned to writing. In 1832–1833, she serialized her recollections of Lord Byron for the *New Monthly Magazine and Literary Journal*—and their popularity helped establish her literary reputation. Over the next fifteen years Blessington produced over a dozen novels, several collections of short stories and poems, and a number of popular travel books. In the 1830s and 1840s, Blessington edited two popular series of annual gift books: *The Book of Beauty* and *The Keepsake*. Beginning in 1846 she also wrote a gossip column for the *Daily News*. Despite her prolific and lucrative literary career, mounting debts forced Blessington to auction the contents of Gore House in April 1849. She died in Paris of a seizure in early June 1849.

MAJOR WORKS AND THEMES

Known for their incisive observations of social life and convention, Blessington's novels chronicle life in the years at the end of the Regency and the beginning of the Victorian eras. Like Jane Austen* and many other Romantic women writers, Blessington is concerned with the marriage market. Blessington addresses how fashionable society, particularly the corrupt London aristocracy, views honor. In *Victims of Society*, for example, the appellation of honor is tied not to personal integrity but to social convention. Comtesse Hohenlinden—whose liaisons are well known but who retains the protection of her husband—continues to visit and be visited; however, Lady Augusta Vernon, who is faithful to her husband but loses his protection, is shunned. Blessington characterized the hypocrisy of society's values in her maxim: "Be prosperous and happy, never require our services, and we will remain your friends."

Blessington's works also concern themselves with the public, even the political, realms. Her novels and travel books refer frequently to contemporary political situations both at home and on the Continent. Her novel *The Repealers* examines the social problems between tenant and landlord that "agitators" for Irish Independence create. Similarly, *The Two Friends* juxtaposes the attitudes of the "restored" French aristocracy, the landed English gentry, and the rising monied classes in England in a critique of marriage and wealth.

CRITICAL RECEPTION

Although Blessington's works were often reviewed in the nineteenth century and are worthy of study, they have received little critical comment in the twentieth. Instead, Blessington's critical reception has rested largely on her relationship with Lord Byron.

The work most frequently considered by modern scholars has been Blessington's *Conversations of Lord Byron*. These *Conversations* appear in several forms between 1832 and the 1850s. First serialized in 1832–1833, then produced as a book in 1834, her recollections also make up substantive portions of her *Idler in Italy* and *Desultory Thoughts and Reflections*. Lovell's edition of Blessington's conversations collates the serialized first edition with Henry Coburn's 1834 London edition; at the same time, it provides the "annotat[ions], underlin[ings] and margina[l] mark[ings]" of Byron's Italian mistress, the Countess Teresa Guiccioli (Lovell vii).

The primary axis of critical evaluation has been the accuracy of Blessington's recollections. Close friends of Byron—like John Cam Hobhouse or Teresa Guiccioli—commented that Blessington often captured the sound of Byron's voice. But Blessington's nineteenth-century critics complained that she was able to do so only because she had seen and transcribed Byron's own *Memoirs*. Blessington's contemporary critics considered her use of Byron's memoirs evidence of a lack of skill. But to Byron scholars, these rumors, "if true, increase the value of her book rather than diminish it" (Lovell 7).

BIBLIOGRAPHY

Currently only Ernest Lovell's critical edition of *Lady Blessington's Conversations of Lord Byron* (Princeton University Press, 1969) is in print, although her works have been reprinted in a one-volume facsimile reproduction.

Selected Works by the Countess of Blessington

Journal of a Tour Through the Netherlands to Paris, in 1821. 1822.
The Repealers. 1833.
Conversations of Lord Byron. 1834.
The Two Friends. 1835.
The Confessions of an Elderly Gentleman. 1836.
The Victims of Society. 1837.
The Confessions of an Elderly Lady. 1838.
Desultory Thoughts and Reflections. 1839.
Idler in Italy. 1839.
Idler in France. 1841.
Marmaduke Herbert. 1847.
Lady Blessington's Conversations of Lord Byron. 1969.

Studies of the Countess of Blessington

Lovell, Ernest J. Introduction to *Lady Blessington's Conversations of Lord Byron*. Princeton: Princeton University Press, 1969.
Madden, Richard Robert. *The Literary Life and Correspondence of the Countess of Blessington*. London: Newby, 1855.
Sadleir, Michael. *The Strange Life of Lady Blessington*. Boston: Little, Brown, 1933.

Mathilde Blind
(1841–1896)

James Diedrick

BIOGRAPHY

Mathilde Blind was born Mathilde Cohen in Manheim, Germany, on 21 March 1841, the second of two children born to an elderly retired banker who died in her infancy. In 1847 her mother, Friederike Ettlinger, became involved in agitation for a united and democratic Germany with Karl Blind, a radical political writer and activist whom she married in 1849. By 1849 Blind and his new family had been exiled from Germany and France, and in 1851 they were expelled from Belgium. Granted asylum in England, for the next thirty years their household became both a haven for Europe's radical exiles and an influential intellectual salon. Mathilde Blind's fervently idealistic, politically engaged poetry, which germinated in the rich soil of this radical environment, was nurtured by this expatriate community.

In 1866 her brother Ferdinand undertook a failed assassination attempt on Otto von Bismarck and hanged himself while in prison. One year later, still dressed in mourning clothes, Blind brought out her first book of poetry under the pseudonym "Claude Lake." The poems were written in the years leading up to the death of her brother and reflect the influence of the pantheism and apocalyptic yearning of the British Romantic poets on her own poetic sensibility. Many of Blind's poems also embody the same revolutionary ardor that motivated her brother.

Ironically, this first volume of poetry, which self-consciously embraces a male poetic tradition, appeared just at the time when Blind was becoming preoccupied with the oppressive gender system and the status of women. Like Mary Wollstonecraft, about whom she published an important essay in 1878, Blind located the source of gender inequity in education. The women that Blind came most to admire—George Sand, George Eliot,* Christina Rossetti,* and especially Elizabeth Barrett Browning*—all defied Victorian social conventions. When

Blind died on 26 November 1896, she bequeathed the greater part of her considerable estate to Newnham College, Cambridge, to encourage and support higher education for women.

MAJOR WORKS AND THEMES

In the 1870s Blind made the first of several trips to Scotland. Visiting the island of Iona, she discovered the legend of St. Oran, which became the subject of her first major poem, "The Prophecy of St. Oran" (1881). According to the legend, Oran consented to be buried alive in order to appease certain demons of the earth who were preventing St. Columba from building a chapel. But when St. Columba ordered the body to be dug up after three days, Oran arose from the dead to proclaim that there is no God, final judgment, or future state. St. Columba silenced Oran by ordering his body to be buried once again. In Blind's version of the legend, Oran falls in love with the daughter of a native chieftain, whose paganism eloquently resists his attempts to convert her (she calls Christianity a "joy-killing creed"); it is she who releases him from the grave, not some supernatural agency. The entire poem may be read as Blind's poetic representation of what St. Oran might have said if allowed to continue speaking after rising from the earth, filtered through her own feminist, freethinking perspective.

Blind's next major poem, *The Heather on Fire: A Tale of the Highland Clearances* (1886), was published in the midst of the Highland land war of the 1880s, rooted in the Highland Land Clearances that began in the eighteenth century and accelerated in the 1830s. In heroic couplets, it tells the story of a family destroyed by the actions of English landlords, one of whose agents boasts: "of all these dirty huts the glen we'll sweep, / And clear it for the fatted lowland sheep."

Blind gave a lecture to the Shelley Society that anticipated the title poem of her next book on an epic theme, *The Ascent of Man* (1889). "Shelley's View of Nature Contrasted with Darwin's" asserts a central role for poetry in reconciling the Rousseauian vision of a "good, sinless, and beneficent" nature with the evolutionist's view of nature as a site of lust, hunger, rapine, and cruelty. "The Ascent of Man," dedicated to Elizabeth Barrett Browning, is her own poetic attempt to represent this struggle. Like *The Heather on Fire*, it is concerned with violence, but this time the violence of both creation and civilization is represented, and the relationship between the two explored. "The Ascent of Man" struggles to discover what can be redeemed from blind violence.

Blind published two important volumes of poetry in the 1890s: *Dramas in Miniature* (1891), evenly divided between narrative poems on tragic themes and shorter lyrics, and *Birds of Passage: Songs of the Orient and Occident* (1895). The section titled "Songs of the Orient" includes the important poem "The Tomb of the Kings," resembling in spirit Shelley's "Ozymandias" but set inside a pharaoh's tomb. "Songs of the Occident" contains some of Blind's best sonnets and short lyrics, including "On a Torso of Cupid," "The Agnostic," "Rest," and seven "Shakespeare Sonnets" inspired by an extended stay in Stratford in 1894.

CRITICAL RECEPTION

The radical implications of Blind's mature poetry struck many of her contemporary readers. Indeed, the publisher withdrew *The Prophecy of St. Oran and Other Poems* from circulation in September 1881, fearing that what W. M. Rossetti called its "atheistic character" would alienate readers. *The Heather on Fire* received a warmer reception, in part because British opinion in the 1880s favored Scottish land reform. Blind's major works of poetry were extensively reviewed in British literary journals, and she was widely praised by the leading artists and intellectuals of her generation for her erudition, idealism, and moral passion. Blind is currently being rediscovered by a new generation of readers and critics, as evidenced by the selections of her poetry in anthologies and by the work of critics like Isobel Armstrong, who makes a convincing case for Blind's importance to the Victorian poetic tradition.

BIBLIOGRAPHY

Most of Blind's poetry is available on-line at the Victorian Women Writers Project: www.indiana.edu/~letrs/vwwp. In addition, selected poems can be found in recent anthologies of Victorian women's poetry.

Selected Works by Mathilde Blind

Poems [published under pseudonym Claude Lake]. 1867.
"Shelley." Review-essay of *The Poetical Works of Percy Bysshe Shelley. Westminster Review* 38 (July 1870): 75–97.
"Mary Wollstonecraft." *New Quarterly Magazine* 10 (July 1878): 390–412.
The Prophecy of St. Oran and Other Poems. 1881.
George Eliot. 1883.
Tarantella, a Romance. 1885.
The Heather on Fire: A Tale of the Highland Clearances. 1886.
Madame Roland. 1886.
The Ascent of Man. 1889.
Dramas in Miniature. 1891.
"Personal Recollections of Mazzini." *Fortnightly Review* 55 (May 1891): 702–12.
Songs and Sonnets. 1893.
Birds of Passage: Songs of the Orient and Occident. 1895.
Shakespeare Sonnets. 1902.

Studies of Mathilde Blind

Armstrong, Isobel. " 'A Music of Thine Own': Women's Poetry—An Expressive Tradition?" In *Victorian Poetry: Poetry, Poetics, and Politics.* New York: Routledge, 1993. 318–77.

Garnett, Richard. "Mathilde Blind." In *The Dictionary of National Biography*. Ed. Leslie
     Stephen and Sidney Lee. London: Oxford University Press, 1917. 22: 219–20.
———. "Mathilde Blind." In *The Poets and the Poetry of the Century*. Ed. Leslie Ste-
     phen and Sidney Lee. London: Hutchinson & Company, 1892. 7: 609–12.
Leighton, Angela. *Victorian Women Poets: Writing Against the Heart*. Hemel Hemp-
     stead: Harvester, 1983.

Barbara Leigh Smith Bodichon (1827–1891)

Lori Williamson

BIOGRAPHY

Barbara Leigh Smith, cousin of Florence Nightingale,* was born in 1827, the eldest daughter of the Radical Benjamin Leigh Smith and Anne Longden, whom he had seduced when he was forty and she only seventeen. They never married. The radical company that Leigh Smith's father kept encouraged independent freethinking and in all likelihood influenced the decisions that she made for herself and the ways in which she conceived of women's rights. When she came of age her father gave her an annual allowance of £300, providing her with a degree of financial independence that would later enable her to put her ideas into action. She also proved herself to be a proficient artist, exhibiting in London in 1859 and 1861.

In 1849 Leigh Smith attended lectures at the recently opened Bedford College in London and promoted the cause of educational reform in 1852 by setting up the coeducational, nondenominational Portman Hall School. She also became interested in women's rights, turning first to women's legal disabilities and writing a pamphlet, *A Brief Summary in Plain Language of the Most Important Laws Concerning Women* (1854), which roused considerable interest. She passed her pamphlet on to a family friend, Davenport Hill, who submitted it to the Law Amendment Society. A report advocating change in married women's property holding status was written and was followed by public meetings and a petition drafted by Leigh Smith. In 1857 the petition was presented before both Houses but was eclipsed by discussion surrounding the soon-to-be-passed Divorce Act. Nonetheless, Leigh Smith had struck a chord, and for her efforts, she earned the wrath of politicians and various publications: Any suggestion that a wife be given control over her property undermined female dependence, which was the basis of marriage.

Leigh Smith's own married life was not rooted in her dependence. In 1857, after an affair with John Chapman, the editor of the *Westminster Review*, she married a forty-six-year-old Algerian doctor, Eugène Bodichon, who did not oppose his wife's need for autonomy.

From the late 1850s onwards she devoted as much time as she could to promoting women's rights in England and worked with most of the feminist luminaries of her day. She was instrumental in setting up the Langham Place Group and in 1858 cofounded with Bessie Rayner Parkes* the *Englishwoman's Review*. The mid-1860s saw her directly involved with the London National Society for Women's Suffrage and with the first women's suffrage petition that John Stuart Mill presented in Parliament. She provided financial support to Girton College, contributing first £1000 to get the scheme off the ground, then bequeathing a further £10,000 in her will. In 1877 Bodichon fell ill and remained an invalid for the rest of her life. Her husband died in Algiers in 1885. In 1888 she signed a petition demanding that women be admitted to Cambridge degrees, and in 1891, the year of her death, she signed her last suffrage petition.

MAJOR WORKS AND THEMES

The central argument in Bodichon's major women's rights publications was that women should be given unfettered access to the public sphere and that the (man-made) obstacles that obstructed their path be removed. Her first treatise, *A Brief Summary* (1854), set out the legal disadvantages suffered by married women whose identities were subsumed in their husbands. This pamphlet was followed three years later by *Women and Work* (1857), wherein she made the "outrageous" suggestion that women could and should be anything that they wanted to be. She criticized a society that decreed that women be the dependents first of their fathers and then of their husbands and argued that work, and a sense of purpose and self-worth, was vital to mental and physical health.

Like many others who supported women's rights, Bodichon equated dependency with powerlessness, and in *Reasons for the Enfranchisement of Women* (1866), she pointed out that men had appointed themselves as spokespersons for the interests of all; this was not only unfair but also ludicrous—how could a man know what was best for a woman? Only once women had the vote would their interests be addressed, would they be given the opportunity to be treated as independent, responsible creatures, and would their status in society and in relation to men be placed on a more equitable footing.

CRITICAL RECEPTION

Barbara Bodichon demanded equality for men and women, and for these radical demands, she was often castigated in the press as being "strong-minded." It was because Bodichon was strong-minded that she had the confidence in her capabilities to carve out an independent life for herself and to encourage other women to do the same.

Ray Strachey writes (in 1928) of Bodichon as the moving force behind early feminist activity. Despite Bodichon's pivotal role, Dale Spender (1982) comments that Bodichon did not receive due recognition in the plethora of feminist studies that appeared in the 1970s. She has, however, been the subject of two major biographies and is in general judged by historians as dynamic, influential, free-spirited, motivated, and dedicated, all attributes that gave her the power to speak her mind, to speak it well, and to live her life as she wanted.

BIBLIOGRAPHY

None of her works are currently in print; however, the Victorian Women Writers Project has published three of her essays electronically: www.indiana.edu/~letrs/vwwp.

Works by Barbara Bodichon

A Brief Summary in Plain Language of the Most Important Laws Concerning Women. 1854.
Women and Work. 1857.
Memoir of Madame Luce of Algiers: Reprinted from the English. 1862.
Reasons for the Enfranchisement of Women. 1866. Read at the National Association for the Promotion of Social Science.
"Authorities and Precedents for Giving the Suffrage to Qualified Women." *Englishwoman's Review* 11 (1867): 63–73.
An American Diary, 1857–8. Ed. Joseph W. Reed, Jr. 1972.

Studies of Barbara Bodichon

Banks, Olive. *The Biographical Dictionary of British Feminists*, 1830–1930. Vol. 1. London: Harvester Wheatsheaf, 1990.
Bradbrook, M. C. *Barbara Bodichon, George Eliot and the Limits of Feminism.* London: Blackwell, 1975.
Burton, Hester. *Barbara Bodichon, 1827–1891.* London: John Murray, 1949.
Herstein, Sheila R. *A Mid-Victorian Feminist: Barbara Leigh Smith Bodichon.* New Haven: Yale University Press, 1986.
Hirsch, Pam. *Barbara Leigh Smith Bodichon: Feminist, Artist and Rebel.* London: Chatto & Windus, 1998.
Lacey, Candida Ann, ed. *Barbara Bodichon and the Langham Place Circle.* London: Routledge & Kegan Paul, 1987.
Matthews, Jacquie. "Barbara Bodichon: Integrity in Diversity." In *Feminist Theorists.* Ed. Dale Spender. London: The Women's Press, 1983. 90–123.
Reed, Joseph W., Jr., ed. *An American Diary, 1857–8.* London: Routledge & Kegan Paul, 1972.
Rendall, Jane. "Friendship and Politics: Barbara Leigh Smith Bodichon (1827–91) and Bessie Rayner Parkes (1829–95)." In *Sexuality and Subordination: Interdisciplinary Studies of Gender in the Nineteenth Century.* Ed. Susan Mendus and Jane Rendall. London: Routledge, 1989. 136–70.

Spender, Dale. *Women of Ideas and What Men Have Done to Them.* London: Routledge
& Kegan Paul, 1982.
Strachey, Ray. *"The Cause": A Short History of the Women's Movement in Great Britian.* London: G. Bell and Sons, 1928.

Mary Elizabeth Braddon
(1835-1915)

Andrew Maunder

BIOGRAPHY

Mary Elizabeth Braddon was born on 4 October 1835 in the respectable atmosphere of Frith Street, Soho, in central London. Brought up by her mother after her parents separated, she went on the stage in 1857, using the name "Mary Seyton." This experience made itself felt in a number of novels such as *Rupert Godwin* (1867), *Dead Sea Fruit* (1868), and *A Strange World* (1875). By 1860 she had left the stage and was energetically producing cheap fiction for the expanding magazine market. Success came at the age of twenty-seven with the "shocker" *Lady Audley's Secret* (1862), followed swiftly by *Aurora Floyd* (1863).

For the next twenty years she had to write continually in order to earn enough to support her mother, her partner (the impecunious publisher John Maxwell), their five illegitimate children, and the children of his legal marriage (Mrs. Maxwell, in an uncanny echo of the sensation plot, was confined in a Dublin mental institution). It is difficult to be exact about the number of novels, but from *Three Times Dead* (1860) to *Mary* (1916), there are at least seventy-seven, as well as plays, poems, and children's stories. There is also a large amount of "piratical stuff" ("Letters" 11)—anonymous or pseudonymous fiction written for the cheap magazines such as the *Halfpenny Journal* and the *Welcome Guest* as well as the more up-market *Belgravia*, which Braddon herself edited for ten years from 1866.

Henry James attributed Braddon's enormous popularity to a "grim determination to succeed," a "strictly respectful" attitude toward her audience, and an ability to keep pace with "delicate fluctuations of the public taste" (109). Both her humorous portrayal of the novelist Sigismund Smith in *The Doctor's Wife* (1864) and her letters to her mentor, Sir Edward Bulwer Lytton, reveal an ironic appreciation of public demands. "I have learned to look at everything in a mercantile sense," she told Lytton, "and to write solely for the circulating library reader, whose palette [*sic*] requires strong meat and is not very particular to the quality thereof" ("Letters" 14). Cheap reissues, foreign translations, and newspaper syndication of her works helped ensure Braddon a worldwide readership.

MAJOR WORKS AND THEMES

Braddon's novels are lively and gripping novels of mystery, detection, romance, satire, and social criticism. Her reputation has traditionally rested alongside that of her contemporaries Ellen Price Wood* and Wilkie Collins on her contribution to the genre of the sensation novel in which murder, adultery, illegitimacy, bigamy, and madness erupt within the sanctity of the domestic hearth. Braddon, however, is more subversive than Wood in her encouragement of the insubordinate desires of her female characters. Although she admitted imitating Collins, she did not share his interest in multivocal narratives. Braddon's major themes are best brought to imaginative order in *Lady Audley's Secret* in which her interest in the fictionality of the feminine ideal, the sinister workings of patriarchy, and the use of set-piece scenes and dramatic tableaux are much to the fore. Braddon's tale of a golden-haired, homicidal bigamist and of Robert Audley's amateur detective work to uncover the past of his new aunt masks far wider enquiries. Most strikingly, it dramatizes the possibilities of female rebellion and the gap between appearance and reality.

Braddon described the process of writing a new sensation novel as simply rearranging a fixed set of components: "I will give the Kaleidoscope . . . another turn, and will do my best with the bits of old glass and pins and rubbish" (Yates 2: 171). To read *Lady Audley's Secret* in its subsequent incarnations in *Aurora Floyd* (1863), *John Marchmont's Legacy* (1863), and *Eleanor's Victory* (1863) is to witness a novelist building on her own momentum. However, with commercial success came a desire for aesthetic satisfaction. "I want to be artistic," she told Lytton ("Letters" 14). Periodically her imagination turned outward as she sought her inspiration not in crime reports but in French fiction. One of her most ambitious projects was *The Doctor's Wife*, an English adaptation of Flaubert's *Madame Bovary*. Isabel Sleaford, the young heroine of the novel, is used by Braddon to question extreme romanticism fed by fiction and to highlight the sexual and emotional frustrations of women who find themselves trapped by the Victorian institution of marriage. Braddon's interest in Flaubert, Balzac, and Dumas *fils*, together with her knowledge of French romances, makes her a key figure in the history of Anglo-French literary relations. *Hostages to Fortune* (1875) is a treatment of the censorship of Dumas for the English stage. *The Golden Calf* (1883) is a subdued English version of Zola's novel of alcoholism, *L'Assommoir*. Other novels are of interest in their constructions of what might be termed female heroes—characters who appropriate all the characteristics usually ascribed to the male hero, including physical strength, intelligence, and resourcefulness.

CRITICAL RECEPTION

The impulsion to undermine Braddon's appeal pervaded the responses of the contemporary male establishment. In the account he gave of "Miss Braddon" in 1865 for the *North British Review*, W. Fraser Rae suggested that while "her achievements may not command our respect . . . they are very notable, and almost unexampled" (n.s., 4: 204) as a female sensation novelist, with the power to captivate the "unthinking crowd" (180), yet Braddon's literary status was relatively low. She was credited with "making the literature of the Kitchen the favorite reading of the Drawing room" (204), while the very qualities that readers were drawn to—her irony, her "knowing," her unladylike familiarity with the Victorian counterworld—were denounced as contaminatory. Although Braddon's immense popularity usually ensured that her sales were unaffected (or perhaps enhanced) by the moral and critical disapproval, the ephemeral quality of her work was taken for granted.

Robert Wolff's 1979 biography drew attention to both the popularity and the breadth of Braddon's influence. Elaine Showalter (1976) and Winifred Hughes (1980) were also instrumental in situating Braddon in relation to the genre of the sensation novel and the critical debates that surrounded it. In the 1990s, historicized readings of Braddon's novels, that are also informed by feminist and psychoanalytic thinking, such as those by Lyn Pykett, Ann Cvetkovich, and Pamela Gilbert, have focused on the ways in which Braddon interrogates the nature, power, and function of gender categories. Critics have also stressed the closeness of Braddon's work to forms of Victorian anxiety, particularly women's reading (Flint) and the specter of the female criminal (Helfield). Important perspectives have also been provided by writings on modern mass culture's narrative forms, including film, soap opera, and romance (Modleski). Central to all these approaches is the recognition that Braddon can no longer be viewed as literary curiosity but as a challenging writer whose range and scope invite revision.

BIBLIOGRAPHY

Only a few of Braddon's novels are currently in print, including her best-known work *Lady Audley's Secret* (Penguin, 1998) and *Aurora Floyd* (Broadview, 1998). There is a Mary Braddon Web site at: www.chriswillis.freeserve.co.uk/braddon.

Selected Works by Mary Elizabeth Braddon

Three Times Dead. 1860.
Lady Audley's Secret. 1862.
Aurora Floyd. 1863.
Eleanor's Victory. 1863.
John Marchmont's Legacy. 1863.

The Doctor's Wife. 1864.
The Lady's Mile. 1866.
Rupert Godwin. 1867.
Dead Sea Fruit. 1868.
Hostages to Fortune. 1875.
A Strange World. 1875.
The Golden Calf. 1883.
Mary. 1916.
"Devoted Disciple: The Letters of Mary Elizabeth Braddon to Sir Edward Bulwer Lytton, 1862–1873." Ed. Robert L. Wolff. *Harvard Library Bulletin* 12 (1974): 5–35, 129–61.

Studies of Mary Elizabeth Braddon

Casey, Ellen. " 'Other People's Prudery': Mary Elizabeth Braddon." *Tennessee Studies in Literature* 27 (1984): 72–82.
Cvetkovich, Ann. *Mixed Feelings: Feminism, Mass Culture and Victorian Sensationalism*. New Brunswick, NJ: Rutgers University Press, 1992.
Flint, Kate. *The Woman Reader, 1837–1914*. Oxford: Clarendon Press, 1993.
Gilbert, Pamela. *Disease, Desire, and the Body in Victorian Women's Popular Novels*. Cambridge: Cambridge University Press, 1997.
Helfield, Randa. "Poisonous Plots: Women Sensation Novelists and Murderesses of the Victorian Period." *Victorian Review* 21.2 (1995): 160–88.
Hughes, Winifred. *The Maniac in the Cellar: Sensation Novels of the 1860s*. Princeton: Princeton University Press, 1980.
James, Henry. "Miss Braddon." In *Notes and Reviews*. New York: Books for Libraries Press, 1968.
Modleski, Tania. *Loving with a Vengeance: Mass-produced Fantasies for Women*. London: Methuen, 1984.
Pykett, Lyn. *The Improper Feminine: The Women's Sensation Novel and the New Woman Writing*. London: Routledge, 1992.
Robinson, Solveig C. "Editing *Belgravia*: M. E. Braddon's Defense of 'Light Literature.' " *Victorian Periodicals Review* 28.2 (1995): 109–22.
Showalter, Elaine. "Desperate Remedies: Sensation Novels of the 1860s." *Victorian Newsletter* 49 (Spring 1976): 1–5.
Tromp, Marlene, ed. *Beyond Sensation: Mary Elizabeth Braddon in Context*. New York: SUNY Press, 2000.
Wolff, Robert. *Sensational Victorian: The Life and Fiction of Mary Elizabeth Braddon*. New York: Garland, 1979.
Yates, Edmund. *His Recollections and Experiences*. 2 vols. London: R. Bentley & Son, 1884.

Anne Brontë
(1820-1849)

Maria H. Frawley

BIOGRAPHY

The youngest member of a famous literary family, Anne Brontë has yet to achieve the recognition that many critics feel she deserves. Her distinctive status both within her family and within literary history might best be captured by beginning at the end, with her burial in 1849 in Scarborough, a seaside village roughly seventy miles from Haworth, Brontë's home. Suffering in the last stages of the tuberculosis that would kill her, Anne Brontë had traveled with her sister Charlotte* and family friend Ellen Nussey to Scarborough in the hopes that the sea air would provide some restoration and relief. Familiar with Scarborough from lengthy visits there with a family for whom she had worked as a governess, Brontë found comfort in the scenery, if not a respite from her disease. She died only a few days later and was buried, away from Haworth, where her mother and five of her siblings had been buried. The precise reasons why Charlotte Brontë chose to bury Anne in Scarborough, rather than transport her body home, are not known; scholars are sure, however, that it was Charlotte Brontë's decision. Anne Brontë's final days and burial in Scarborough are, in any case, suggestive of many issues key to understanding Brontë and her writing, perhaps most pointedly an independence and resolve not often attributed to her and a distinctive separation from her family. Finally, it is significant that Charlotte was responsible, in the end, for determining Anne's position; indeed, the control that Charlotte sought to exert over Anne's life and writing would intensify after her death, when with biographical notices and reminiscences she would influence critical commentary on Anne's achievement for generations to come.

Little more than a year and a half old when her mother, Maria Branwell Brontë died, Anne Brontë was essentially raised by her older sisters and by her Aunt Elizabeth Branwell. Aunt Branwell seems to have taken a particular interest in Anne's upbringing, and many biographers believe that her Wesleyan

Methodist heritage accounts for the specific religious inclinations that would later characterize Anne. Yet many other dimensions of Brontë's childhood and adolescence combine to account for the independence of her actions and beliefs. After the two oldest Brontë siblings, Maria and Elizabeth, died, the remaining four Brontë children—Charlotte, Branwell, Emily,* and Anne—formed a tightly knit community, entertaining each other with imaginative games and, eventually, collaboratively writing stories and poems together. Anne worked especially closely with Emily on this early writing, and some poems associated with the juvenilia, now referred to as the Gondal Saga, remain.

Because relatively little is known about Anne Brontë's life, biographers have reluctantly attempted to reconstruct her life experiences from her writing. Supplementing these limited sources are equally problematic repositories of information—Charlotte Brontë's correspondence and biographical statements as well as Elizabeth Gaskell's* famous biography, *The Life of Charlotte Brontë*, which was published in 1857. Among the most often-cited points of Anne Brontë's life that emerge from these sources are an apparent romantic interest in William Weightman, a man who served for a short time as her father's curate and who died of cholera at the age of twenty-eight in 1842; some education away from home at Roe Head and, during this time, a spiritual and emotional crisis that culminated in conversations with the Moravian minister James de la Trobe; and two stints of governess work, the first at the Ingham home of Blake Hall and the second, more long lasting, at the home of the Robinson family of Thorp Green. After returning home from Thorp Green in the summer of 1845, Brontë seems primarily to have focused on her writing, contributing first to a collection of poems put together by Charlotte Brontë, *Poems by Currer, Ellis, and Acton Bell* (1846). Continuing to use the pseudonym of Acton Bell established with this work, Brontë subsequently produced the novel *Agnes Grey*, published in 1847, and her most famous work, the novel *The Tenant of Wildfell Hall*, published in 1848.

Although biographers have precious little more to work with in reconstructing Brontë's life, interesting details continue to be found. Perhaps most intriguingly, Brontë's personal Bible has been discovered to contain notes on the flyleaves, which seem to indicate that she embarked during the years of 1841 and 1843 on a project to study the Bible on her own. The independence and initiative suggested by this endeavor—and the fact that it was evidently conducted in solitude—characterizes the poetic personas and fictional heroines of Brontë's writing as well.

MAJOR WORKS AND THEMES

Brontë's fiction and poetry reflect in many ways the tenor of her life experiences. Secrecy, solitude, and silence are hallmark themes that pervade her work, often providing her with the means to explore connections between social status and psychological experience. The seeds for these thematic interests can in fact be found in the earliest poetry, only some of which was published in *Poems by Currer, Ellis, and Acton Bell*. The Gondal figures of this early poetry are often depicted as captive or imprisoned, struggling with isolation and loneliness. Even after Brontë abandoned the Gondal Saga, these themes permeate her poetry. The personae of such poems such as "The Doubter's Prayer" embrace their privacy and yet struggle with their separation from others: "And none can hear my secret call, / Or see the silent tears I weep" (11.31–32). One of Brontë's most famous poems, "Self-Communion," struggles with the ebb and flow of her faith in private; in a characteristic moment, its speaker laments, "Such speechless raptures I have known, / But only in my dreams" (11.243–44).

Given the complexity of interests evidenced in Brontë's poetry, it is not surprising to find similar themes surfacing in her fiction. Although often read simply as a transparent account of her own experiences as a governess, *Agnes Grey* in fact uses the situation of the governess to explore the psychological ramifications of social isolation. In the novel, Brontë challenges readers to appreciate the physical and emotional difficulties endured by the governess and examines the multiple psychological strategies that her heroine develops to cope with her charges, with patronizing employers, and most significantly, with the ramifications of her isolation and marginal social position. Through her representation of Agnes's silence and solitude—sometimes chosen, sometimes forced—Brontë reveals complexities underwriting the dynamics of public and private, the concepts most crucial to Victorian domestic ideology.

In *The Tenant of Wildfell Hall*, Brontë developed a far more complex narrative technique to pursue these same issues with greater depth. Deliberately choosing a title to emphasize the theme of anonymity, Brontë examined such issues as the loss of identity in marriage; the ways that the language endorsed within patriarchy and Christianity converge to endow women with ultimately debilitating roles as angelic saviors within the home; the relationship between individuals and their surrounding communities; and the corollary difficulties of embracing secrecy, silence, and solitude. While the novel ends with a remarriage, and while the heroine Helen Huntingdon's story is enclosed within that of her second husband, a sensational story by Victorian standards resides at the core of the narrative. This story details Helen's first husband's debauchery and adultery and culminates with Helen's leaving—against his will and with their child—to live in seclusion. While clearly gripping readers with a sensational plot, Brontë used the situation not as an end in itself but rather as a means to explore with great complexity societal understandings of women's roles and responsibilities as well as the problematic nature of privacy itself.

CRITICAL RECEPTION

As is often noted, the Brontë sisters' earliest readers were intrigued by their choice of pseudonyms, which were clearly intended to thwart efforts to be read and critiqued as the work of "lady novelists." Nevertheless, both because Currer, Ellis, and Acton Bell were unidentifiable as male or female and because the works of each had obvious similarities, the novels of all three were compared and contrasted, with a surprising number of early readers arguing that they were in fact authored by one writer. The disclaimers about authorship that appeared in the prefaces to various second editions did little to move critics from discussion of this facet of the writing to other, more significant dimensions.

Poems by Currer, Ellis, and Acton Bell made little impact, despite favorable reviews in *The Athenaeum* and *Critic*. While *Agnes Grey* garnered "Acton Bell" some respect for artistic achievement, it was deemed to be inferior to *Wuthering Heights*, the novel with which it was originally published. Thus, from the very beginning of her career as a novelist, Anne struggled to be read and critiqued on her own merits, although she clearly achieved greater recognition with *The Tenant of Wildfell Hall*, particularly for the complexity and artistry of its narrative structure. Given the criminal flavor of her second novel—its exposure of debauchery, adultery, foul language, and violence in male characters, and the law-breaking action of its central heroine—it is not surprising that its earliest readers decried its author as "coarse, not to say brutal" (*Spectator*, 8 July 1848). Yet the most influential critical voice was arguably that of her sister Charlotte, who wrote (in a letter to her publisher) of *The Tenant of Wildfell Hall*, "The choice of subject in that work is a mistake: it was too little consonant with the character, tastes, and ideas of the gentle, retiring, inexperienced writer."

Despite the fact that Brontë's works were read and reviewed, it is clear that her reputation was shaped first and foremost by her sister Charlotte, views that inevitably influenced Elizabeth Gaskell in *The Life of Charlotte Brontë*. One particularly noteworthy attribute of scholarship on Anne Brontë is the extent to which views about Brontë's personality—in particular her quiet, reserved demeanor—have flavored reaction to her writing. In this century, some major Brontë scholars have attempted to pay homage to Brontë's achievements; Winifred Gerin's study *Anne Brontë* (1976) and, more recently, Edward Chitham's two works, *A Life of Anne Brontë* (1991) and *The Poems of Anne Brontë: A New Text and Commentary* (1979), are foundations on which subsequent scholars have built their own studies. More recent revival of interest in Brontë dates to the work of Elizabeth Langland, who has enabled readers to better appreciate Brontë's distinctive brand of feminism. Important work by N. M. Jacobs and Jan Gordon on Brontë's narrative technique has also contributed to a better understanding of her artistic achievements. Finally, scholars such as Elizabeth Hollis Berry, Maria Frawley, and Janet H. Freeman have begun to explore Brontë's interest in psychological processes and self-representational strategies. The variety of approaches that Anne Brontë's work generates suggest that it will continue to be read, enjoyed, and studied for years to come.

BIBLIOGRAPHY

All of the works by Anne Brontë are currently in print.

Works by Anne Brontë

Poems by Currer, Ellis, and Acton Bell. 1846.
Agnes Grey. 1847.
The Tenant of Wildfell Hall. 1848.
The Poems of Anne Brontë: A New Text and Commentary. Ed. Edward Chitham. 1979.

Studies of Anne Brontë

Allott, Miriam, ed. *The Brontës: The Critical Heritage.* London: Routledge & Kegan Paul, 1974.

Bell, Arnold Craig. *The Novels of Anne Brontë: A Study and Reappraisal.* Braunton, Devon: Merlin Books, 1992.

Berry, Laura C. "Acts of Custody and Incarceration in *Wuthering Heights* and *The Tenant of Wildfell Hall.*" *Novel; A Forum of Fiction* 30.1 (1996): 32–53.

Chitham, Edward. *A Life of Anne Brontë.* Cambridge: Basil Blackwell, 1991.

Frawley, Maria. *Anne Brontë.* New York: Twayne, 1996.

Gerin, Winifred. *Anne Brontë.* 2nd ed. London: Allen Lane, 1976.

Gordon, Jan B. "Gossip, Diary, Letter, Text: Anne Brontë's Narrative *Tenant* and the Problematic of the Gothic Sequel." *ELH* 51.4 (1984): 719–45.

Jacobs, N. M. "Gender and Layered Narrative in *Wuthering Heights* and *The Tenant of Wildfell Hall.*" *Journal of Narrative Technique* 16 (Fall 1986): 204–19.

Langland, Elizabeth. *Anne Brontë: The Other One.* Basingstoke, England: Macmillan, 1989.

———. "The Voicing of Feminine Desire in Anne Brontë's *The Tenant of Wildfell Hall.*" In *Gender and Discourse in Victorian Literature.* Ed. Antony Harrison and Beverly Taylor. De Kalb: Northern Illinois University Press, 1992. 113–23.

Liddell, Robert. *Twin Spirits: The Novels of Emily and Anne Brontë.* London: Peter Owen, 1990.

McMaster, Juliet. " 'Imbecile Laughter' and 'Desperate Earnest' in *The Tenant of Wildfell Hall.*" *Modern Language Quarterly* 43.4 (1982): 352–68.

Poole, Russell. "Cultural Reformation and Cultural Reproduction in Anne Brontë's *The Tenant of Wildfell Hall.*" *Studies in English Literature* 33 (1993): 859–73.

Scott, P. J. M. *Anne Brontë: A New Critical Assessment.* Totowa, NJ: Barnes and Noble, 1983.

Sellars, Jane. "The Art of Anne Brontë." In *The Art of the Brontës.* Ed. Christine Alexander and Jane Sellars. New York: Cambridge University Press, 1995. 134–50.

Charlotte Brontë
(1816–1855)

Maggie Berg

BIOGRAPHY

Although the famous Brontë legend of an isolated, eccentric, and frantically creative family living in a time lapse in a remote part of England is an exaggeration, the bare facts of Charlotte Brontë's life are startling enough. Born in April 1816, the third of the six children of the Reverend Patrick Brontë and his wife Maria (née Branwell), Charlotte Brontë lost her mother and her five siblings by the time she was in her early thirties. Despite these personal tragedies, Charlotte Brontë produced extensive juvenilia, an unpublished novel *The Professor, Poems by Currer, Ellis, and Acton Bell* (1846) with her sisters, and three very successful novels, *Jane Eyre* (1847), *Shirley* (1849), and *Villette* (1853).

It was the deaths of her mother (when she was only six) and her sisters that in different ways had the greatest impact on Charlotte Brontë's work. The protagonists of all her novels are orphans, and *Jane Eyre* and *Shirley* feature characters thought to be modeled on her sisters. The deaths of Maria and Elizabeth were probably caused by the terrible conditions of the school at which the four elder girls were boarding: While this experience provided Charlotte with the foundation for the depiction of Lowood School in *Jane Eyre*, Maria was the inspiration for Helen Burns. Similarly, the portraits of Shirley and Caroline, the dual protagonists of *Shirley*, are considered tributes to Emily* and Anne* who died within two months of each other while Charlotte was writing the novel.

Other aspects of Brontë's life besides the deaths of her loved ones influence her work. Her ambiguous class position—her father came from an Irish working-class family but educated himself sufficiently to attend St. John's College, Cambridge—is manifested in various ways in the novels. All of them feature, and most examine the plight of, governesses, who were the casualties of shifting Victorian demographics. Being middle class and often more highly educated than their employers, governesses nevertheless were forced by their families' financial difficulties to make their own livings, which meant that they were socially marginalized and were thought to fall short of Victorian ideals of femininity. Charlotte Brontë had two brief and unhappy periods of what she called "governessing slavery" before she finally (after a failed attempt to open her own school with Emily and Anne) began to make money from publishing. All her life, however, Brontë advocated that women be able to earn their own livings.

Charlotte Brontë's own formal education was sporadic: After ten months at Cowan Bridge School when she was eight years old, she attended and then taught at Roe Head School from 1831 to 1832 and 1835 to 1838 and did the same at the Pensionnat Heger in Brussels in 1842–43. At the latter school, when Charlotte was in her midtwenties, she fell in love with her professor, Monsieur Heger, a married man with a family. While she suffered the anguish of unrequited love after her return, Charlotte also watched her brother Branwell's decline into drug addiction and alcoholism, leading to his death in 1849. His problems were partly the result of his own illicit affair with the mother of his pupil. All of Brontë's novels, from *The Professor* and *Jane Eyre* through *Shirley* and *Villette*, describe highly charged intimate relationships between tutors and pupils.

What seems to be a life of unremitting deaths punctuated by unhappy employment and unrequited love also contained immense literary success. In 1846, Charlotte Brontë discovered a manuscript of poems in Emily's lap desk, which so impressed her that she finally persuaded both Emily and Anne to contribute to a joint publication, *Poems by Currer, Ellis, and Acton Bell* (1846). The pseudonyms were chosen, Charlotte later explained, because the sisters did not want to be either praised or blamed as *women* authors but simply as *authors*. Although the volume of poetry was virtually ignored by critics and sold only two copies, it preceded literary fame—or infamy—for all three sisters. Charlotte's first novel, *The Professor*, was still doing the rounds of the publishers in 1847 when Emily's *Wuthering Heights* and Anne's *Agnes Grey* were accepted for publication. In August, however, Charlotte received such a thoughtful refusal from Smith, Elder and Co. that she hurried to finish the novel she was then working on and six weeks later sent them *Jane Eyre*.

Jane Eyre appeared before *Wuthering Heights* and *Agnes Grey*, in October of 1847, and was an enormous success. Although it received mixed reviews and prompted speculation about the identities of the "Bells," it was a Victorian bestseller and acquired a cult status, spawning Rochester look-alikes and an "alarming revolution" in novel writing (Allott 97–98, 311–12). In July 1848, the sisters heard that Emily and Anne's publisher was selling the rights to Anne's forthcoming *The Tenant of Wildfell Hall* to an American publisher, claiming that all the Bells novels were the work of a single author. Charlotte and Anne traveled to London for the first time to introduce themselves to Charlotte's publisher, so that it became known to a few select people that they were in fact women. The meeting began a long and important friendship for Charlotte with her publisher George Smith, a relationship that sustained her after her sisters' deaths.

Charlotte Brontë's third novel *Shirley* (1849) was something of a departure from her others, being more directly concerned with the social problems of the "hungry forties" and the Chartist movement to redress working-class poverty. The novel reflects Brontë's ambivalence about her own social class in its disappointing lack of sympathy for the workers and its championing of their employers. While writing *Shirley*, Brontë experienced the hardest blow of her life. Her brother Branwell's death in September 1848 made her unwell; she had barely begun to recover when it became clear that Emily was very ill while refusing all medical aid. When Emily died of tuberculosis in December, Anne was showing signs of the same symptoms, and she, too, died the following May. Brontë's anguish is clear in the sparse description of her sisters' deaths in the "Biographical Notice" and "Preface" to the memorial edition of their novels (1850).

In 1852, while writing her last novel, *Villette*, Brontë received an unexpected marriage proposal from Arthur Bell Nicholls, the curate of Haworth. Charlotte's father was infuriated by what he considered Nicholls's presumption and made things so difficult that Nicholls resigned his post and left Haworth. Although Brontë had refused Arthur's offer of marriage, she was so impressed by his constancy that she secretly corresponded with him. Eventually Patrick Brontë relented, and Arthur not only married Brontë and returned to his position but agreed to move into the parsonage and live with his father-in-law. After Charlotte Brontë's death the two men were each other's greatest support.

Villette was partially based on Brontë's experiences at Brussels: Paul Emmanuel is likely based on her beloved teacher, Monsieur Heger. It also depicts the heroine Lucy's transfer of affection from the handsome Graham Brown, inspired perhaps by George Smith, Brontë's young publisher.

During the first months of her marriage, Brontë wrote nothing, although she read her husband a fragment of a novel, *Emma*, begun much earlier, which she said she would alter considerably. The novel was never completed. Brontë's marriage to Arthur Bell Nicholls had made her unexpectedly happy, and in the new year, just months later, she was suspected to be pregnant. She then suffered from terrible and violent nausea, from which she wasted away. Elizabeth Gaskell,* her friend and first biographer, describes Brontë's words on waking from a delirium to find her husband praying by her bedside: "I am not going to die, am I? He will not separate us, we have been so happy" (Gaskell 524). Charlotte Brontë did die, on 31 March 1855. Elizabeth Gaskell's *Life of Charlotte Brontë* was published two years later in March 1857, with a preface by Arthur Bell Nicholls. *The Professor* was posthumously published in 1857.

MAJOR WORKS AND THEMES

All of Charlotte Brontë's novels feature orphans and governesses, tutors or teachers. Three of the four also describe the protagonist's efforts to raise his or her class and economic status, thereby exemplifying the Victorian ideal of "Self-Help" (the title of a best-selling book by Samuel Smiles). The social mobility of William Crimsworth (in *The Professor*), Jane Eyre (in *Jane Eyre*), and Lucy Snowe (in *Villette*) is predicated, however, on their anomalous social status: Caught between classes, they endure loneliness and emotional deprivation until they eventually find (at least ostensibly) their appropriate places and companions. The freedom of movement experienced by Jane and Lucy is atypical of Victorian women and is largely thanks to their orphaned state. Brontë once declared that it was a pleasure to create heroines having "no father nor mother but your own imagination" (Gaskell 201), implying that her lack of literary antecedents gave her a certain license.

The anomalous social status of Brontë's heroines (her own experience) is expressed in the novels as contradictoriness. Caroline, Shirley, Jane, and Lucy all exert enormous efforts to conform socially while harboring secret rebelliousness and independence. These ambiguities are manifested textually as a juxtaposition of realism with Romanticism. Brontë's view of art seems ambivalent: While she declared that she pursued only the truths of "morality" in opposition to the jargon of "conventionality" (see "Preface" to second edition of *Jane Eyre*), she was nevertheless deeply hurt by critics' imputations that her heroines were nonconformist, irreligious, and even unfeminine. Although Brontë was politically conservative, it seems she created radical heroines.

The subversion of gender and class roles attributed to Brontë arises perhaps from her defense and celebration of individuality. The worth of each individual lies for Brontë in his or her innermost self rather than in social status (a view which Nancy Armstrong, in *Desire and Domestic Fiction* [Oxford University Press, 1987], claims inaugurated the rise of the middle classes in Britain). Jane's self-dependency, explicitly advocated in *Jane Eyre* by Helen Burns, epitomizes this individualism: "If all the world hated you, and believed you wicked, while your own conscience approved you, and absolved you from guilt, you would not be without friends" (ch. 8). Lucy Snowe and Shirley similarly rely on their own inner resources to such an extent that they threaten Victorian notions of femininity. Brontë's emphasis on emotion as the essence of self meant that she had to find a way to express something like the unconscious before Freud "discovered" it. She did so by dramatizing what Jacques Lacan in this century has called the "split subject" (*Ecrits: A Selection*, ed. Alan Sheridan [Tavistock, 1997]): Her heroines are inwardly divided and alienated from themselves.

Brontë's characters are often haunted by episodes of what William Crimsworth (in *The Professor*) calls "Hypochondria," personified as feminine. Jane and Lucy have uncanny "doubles," or manifestations of their repressed desires, in the shape of Bertha Mason (*Jane Eyre*) and the ghostly nun (*Villette*). Sandra

Gilbert and Susan Gubar regard these doubles as symptomatic of the unacknowledged tensions of Victorian women writers trapped in patriarchal literary and social values. The contradictions in Brontë's texts—stylistic as well as thematic—are the result of self-alienation, the "dis-ease" of being a woman and a writer, which, in the nineteenth century, was considered an aberration of nature.

Charlotte Brontë's exploration of the human subject is perhaps more radical than has yet been recognized. Her attempt to explain what it is that constitutes identity results in a surprising instability of gender and even of self. *Villette* and *Shirley* reveal that gender is "performative" (to use Judith Butler's term from *Bodies that Matter* [Routledge, 1993]): that it is a masquerade that iterates the norms of heterosexuality. Lucy's cross-dressing at the school fête and her experience during it of desire for another woman call attention to the "gender bending" in the novel (the nun, who is identified with Lucy, turns out to be a man in drag). Shirley (which in the nineteenth century was a man's name) is similarly confusing: Although she acts like a man, which paradoxically makes her seem more feminine, she also engages in a female homosocial, if not homosexual, relationship with Caroline. While *Shirley* most clearly describes a process whereby its heroine is heterosexualized and feminized, a similar case could be made for *Jane Eyre* and *Villette*. The slippery nature of Brontë's heroines' identities is perhaps the result of their attempts to elude the scrutinizing and controlling gazes of the male characters (notably William Crimsworth, Edward Rochester, St. John Rivers, the brothers Louis and Robert Moore, and Paul Emmanuel).

The divided selves explored in Brontë's novels (three are fictional autobiographies) result in highly ambiguous endings. The "happily ever after" plot line is troubled by entirely contrary implications. Toward the end of *The Professor*, once Crimsworth has apparently found domestic bliss with Frances and their son, he kills the boy's dog in an inexplicable fit of cruelty (to the child as well as the animal). All is not well. The ending of *Shirley* is similarly ambiguous: As the fiercely independent heroine anticipates her marriage, she is compared to a dog gnawing at its chain, and her behavior after the wedding ceremony is uncharacteristically and disturbingly passive. Jane Eyre describes her happiness at being ever more one flesh with Rochester at the end of her autobiography, but, as Bette London points out, in becoming Rochester's eyes, Jane completes her instrumentality (see London). *Villette* actually suggests two alternative endings, and Charlotte Brontë refused to satisfy those who longed to know whether or not Monsieur Paul, Lucy's fiancé, is drowned at sea.

Brontë's novels are characterized by tensions—between surface and depth, realism and romance, conformity and rebellion, and reason and passion—that have produced fruitful debates in the criticism.

CRITICAL RECEPTION

The mixed reviews of Brontë's novels only increased their commercial success. When *Jane Eyre* was published in three volumes in 1847, the 2,500 copies sold out within three months, prompting reprints in January and April of the following year. During the year of 1857 (two years after Brontë's death), for example, *Jane Eyre* sold 25,000 copies in England alone, and *Shirley* and *Villette* sold 15,000 each.

The early reviews of *Jane Eyre* were divided: While one critic declared that the obvious moral of the book was that "laws, both human and divine, . . . are not to be disobeyed when our time of trial comes" (Allott 79), Elizabeth Rigby (Lady Elizabeth Eastlake*) infamously declared Jane to be the "personification of an unregenerate and undisciplined spirit" (Allott 109). The debate over whether Brontë's work was reassuringly conservative or alarmingly subversive was exacerbated by speculation about the pseudonyms. The very qualities that were at first admired in Currer Bell's writing when it was thought to be by a man—namely, the "vigorous" (virile) style and moral frankness—were condemned as "unfeminine" when it was thought to be by a woman. Either in spite of or because of the reviews, *Jane Eyre* became something of a cult text, producing what an American reviewer called a "mental epidemic," in which men began to "swagger and swear in the presence of the gentler sex, and to allude darkly to events in their lives which excused impudence and profanity" (Allott 97–98). In recent years *Jane Eyre* has again been called "a cult text"—of feminism (see Spivak 234).

Shirley was not (and has never been) as popular as *Jane Eyre* or *Villette*. Brontë's publisher's initial silence over the first installments (while they tried to think of an appropriate response during a difficult time of her life) presaged its later reception. George Lewis in 1850 charged it with lack of unity and offensive realism in its depiction of the curates. He also triumphantly declared it quite clear that "Currer Bell is petticoated" (Allott 118). While reviewers began to agree with the latter view, Brontë's own "Biographical Notice" and "Preface" to the memorial edition of her sisters' novels made it explicit that the Bells were indeed women.

By the time *Villette* was published in 1853, Brontë's reputation was established, which perhaps contributed to its being generally well received. Some thought there were "traces . . . of the coarseness which occasionally disfigured" the earlier novels (Allott 180–81), and Matthew Arnold made the now-famous remark that Brontë's mind contained "nothing but hunger, rebellion and rage" (Allott 201). Brontë's friend Harriett Martineau,* a feminist, criticized her preoccupation with love, saying that there were other important "interests" for women (Allott 173). Brontë was so offended that she broke off the friendship (Allott 171).

The moral value of a literary work for Victorian critics depended on the author. Elizabeth Gaskell's biography, *The Life of Charlotte Brontë* (1857), aimed to exonerate Charlotte Brontë from charges of "coarseness" by presenting a lonely, timid, self-sacrificing woman who felt it her moral duty to depict "life as it really is, not as it ought to be" (Gaskell 496). The following reader's astonishment is representative: "How can so bashful a woman be so unbashful a writer?" (Allott 364). The biography effected a reversal: Rather than searching for the person behind the "naughty" books, critics began to read the novels in the light of the fact that the author was a clergyman's daughter. The edition at the end of the century of Mary (Mrs. Humphrey) Ward's* *The Life and Works of Charlotte Brontë and Her Sisters* (1899–1903) shows, by its title alone, the extent to which the Brontë story took precedence over the works themselves and also Charlotte's reputation relative to her sisters' (by the early twentieth century Emily Brontë was considered the superior writer). By the 1930s the Brontë canon was established with the publication of *The Shakespeare Head Brontë* (1931–1938), which included with the novels the juvenilia, poems, letters, and miscellaneous writings of all four Brontës.

The interest in the Brontë biography persists to this day and seems to have dominated treatment of the novels. In 1934 David Cecil influentially declared that Brontë is "her own subject" and that her work was "involuntary self-revelation" (Cecil 112). Feminist approaches of the 1960s perpetuated the bias. Margot Peters's biography *Unquiet Soul* even uses quotations from the novels to explain events in Brontë's life. Peters claims that Brontë "did not know that a writer was supposed to sublimate and objectify his [*sic*] experience" (Peters 414).

It is difficult to determine whether Brontë's assumed personal "battle between conformity and rebellion" (Peters 414) has prompted critics to find divisions or dualisms in her novels or whether it is the other way around. The psychological, feminist, Marxist, poststructuralist, and postcolonial critics of this century persist in attempting to explain contradictions. Sandra Gilbert and Susan Gubar's highly influential *The Madwoman in the Attic* (1979) takes its title from *Jane Eyre* and its theme of the "dis-ease" of Victorian women's writing from Brontë's conflict between freedom and self-repression. Terry Eagleton's *Myths of Power: A Marxist Study of the Brontës* (1975) sees the tensions in Brontë's novels as originating in her ambiguous class status. Mary Jacobus, in "The Buried Letter: Feminism and Romanticism in *Villette*," employs a deconstructionist technique to unravel the textual "doubleness" of Brontë's writing. Perhaps the most interesting and controversial of recent analyses of contradictions in Brontë's novels is Bette London's contention that although women critics and readers insist on reading *Jane Eyre* as a story of liberation, it actually describes a process of self-discipline and increasingly internalized regulation.

Attitudes toward Brontë's work illustrate the history of feminist criticism. Following Harriett Martineau's objections (above), Virginia Woolf regretted in *A Room of One's Own* (1929) that *Jane Eyre*'s unity is marred by Brontë attending to "some personal grievance" (Woolf 110). Kate Millett represents the mood of 1960s feminism when she singles out Brontë in *Sexual Politics* (the only woman writer discussed) as being "perhaps the first woman who ever admitted in print that women find men beautiful" (Millett 140). Gayatri Spivak's widely influential (beyond Brontë scholarship) 1985 essay took feminist critics to task for ignoring Bertha Mason's racial otherness. Postcolonial criticism has prompted an examination of the context of imperialism for Brontë's work. Most recently, Lori Pollock, in "(An) Other Politics of Reading *Jane Eyre*," has attempted to find a balance between indictment and defense of Brontë's politics by seeing Jane and Bertha as each other's doubles. Such balance is hard to find in Brontë criticism. However, the ambiguities in Charlotte Brontë's texts have produced excitingly partisan criticism.

BIBLIOGRAPHY

All of Charlotte Brontë's works are currently in print in numerous editions.

Works by Charlotte Brontë

Poems by Currer, Ellis, and Action Bell. 1846.
Jane Eyre, An Autobiography. 1847.
Shirley: A Tale. 1849.
Villette. 1853.
The Professor, A Tale. 1857.
"Emma: A Fragment by Currer Bell" with "The Last Sketch," by William Makepeace Thackeray. *Cornhill Magazine* 1 (1866): 485–98. Reprinted in *Brontë Society Transactions* 2 (1899): 84–101.
The Shakespeare Head Brontë. Ed. T. J. Wise and J. A. Symington. 19 vols. 1931–1938. (Includes novels, life and letters, poems, miscellaneous, and unpublished writings).
Collected Poems of Charlotte Brontë. Ed. Victor Neufeldt. 1985.

Studies of Charlotte Brontë

Allott, Miriam, ed. *The Brontës: The Critical Heritage.* London: Routledge & Kegan Paul, 1974.
Cecil, Lord David. "Charlotte Brontë." In *Early Victorian Novelists: Essays in Revaluation.* London: Constable, 1934. 109–44.
Eagleton, Terry. *Myths of Power: A Marxist Study of the Brontës.* London: Macmillan Press, 1975.
Ewbank, Inga-Stina. *Their Proper Sphere: A Study of the Brontë Sisters as Early-Victorian Female Novelists.* London: Edward Arnold, 1966.
Gaskell, Elizabeth. *The Life of Charlotte Brontë.* Ed. Alan Shelston. 1857. Harmondsworth: Penguin Books, (1975) 1981.
Gérin, Winifred. *Charlotte Brontë: The Evolution of Genius.* Oxford: Clarendon Press, 1967.
Gilbert, Sandra M., and Susan Gubar. *The Madwoman in the Attic: The Woman Writer and the Nineteenth-Century Literary Imagination.* New Haven, CT: Yale University Press, 1979.
Heilman, Robert D. "Charlotte Brontë's 'New' Gothic." In *From Jane Austen to Joseph Conrad.* Ed. Robert C. Rathburn and Martin Steinmann, Jr. Minneapolis: University of Minnesota Press, 1958. 188–32.
Jacobus, Mary. "The Buried Letter: Feminism and Romanticism in *Villette*." In *Women*

Writing and Writing About Women. Ed. Mary Jacobus. London: Croom Helm, 1979.

London, Bette. "The Pleasure of Submission: *Jane Eyre* and the Production of the Text." *ELH* 58.1 (1991): 195–213.

Maynard, John. *Charlotte Brontë and Sexuality*. Cambridge: Cambridge University Press, 1984.

Meyer, Susan L. "Colonialism and the Figurative Strategy of *Jane Eyre*." *Victorian Studies* 33.2 (1990): 247–68.

Millett, Kate. *Sexual Politics*. New York: Doubleday, 1970.

Moglen, Helen. *Charlotte Brontë: The Self Conceived*. New York: W. W. Norton, 1976.

Peters, Margot. *Unquiet Soul: A Biography of Charlotte Brontë*. New York: Doubleday, 1975.

Pollock, Lori. "(An) Other Politics of Reading *Jane Eyre*." *Journal of Narrative Technique* 26.3 (Fall 1996): 249–73.

Showalter, Elaine. *A Literature of Their Own: British Women Novelists from Brontë to Lessing*. Princeton: Princeton University Press, 1977.

Spivak, Gayatri Chakravorty. "Three Women's Texts and a Critique of Imperialism." *Critical Inquiry* 12.1 (1985): 234–61.

Tromly, Annette. *The Cover of the Mask: The Autobiographers in Charlotte Brontë's Fiction*. English Literary Studies Monograph Series No. 26. Victoria, BC: University of Victoria Press, 1982.

Woolf, Virginia. *A Room of One's Own*. London: Hogarth Press, 1929.

Emily Jane Brontë
(1818–1848)

JoAnna Stephens Mink

BIOGRAPHY

Emily Jane Brontë was born on 30 July 1818 in Thornton, Yorkshire, the fifth of six children of Patrick and Maria Branwell Brontë. She died of tuberculosis on 19 December 1848 at Haworth. Patrick Brontë was born into a humble though not impoverished family in Ireland. Remarkably for a young man of his class and time, he earned a scholarship to Cambridge University and became an ordained minister. In 1820, he was appointed perpetual curate at Haworth, an isolated and poor village in Yorkshire. Maria Branwell came from a highly respected family in Penzance, Cornwall. The (to us) early deaths of the Brontës have been the subject of many biographical studies. Maria Branwell Brontë died of cancer in 1821, when Emily was three years old. Her older, unmarried sister Elizabeth Branwell moved from Penzance to take care of the children, living in Haworth Parsonage until her death in 1842.

The two oldest girls, Maria and Elizabeth, died in 1825 within six weeks of each other, the result of harsh conditions at Cowan Bridge School, where the girls (excepting Anne*) were enrolled. Charlotte* and Emily were quickly brought home. Living quarters at the Parsonage were very cramped with four children, father Patrick, Aunt Branwell, and one or two servants. The siblings spent much time out of doors, Emily in particular finding refuge on the wild Yorkshire moors. Unlike Charlotte, Branwell, and Anne, who were away from Haworth for school and teaching positions, Emily's absences were few: to attend Roe Head School in 1835, to teach at Law Hill in 1838–1839, and to go to Brussels with Charlotte in 1842. In September 1848, Branwell died, Emily's death occurring three months later on 19 December and, finally, Anne's the following May. Charlotte, the only sibling to marry, died March 1855. Patrick Brontë died in June 1861. The entire family is buried at Haworth, except Anne, who died and was buried in Scarborough.

It is impossible to view any of the Brontë siblings independent of familial and geographic surroundings, and biography of the Brontë family has entered the realm of literary mythology. Elizabeth Gaskell's* *The Life of Charlotte Brontë* (1857), while important by providing firsthand observations of the Haworth Parsonage, did much to shape future biographical studies in her well-meaning but somewhat skewed picture of this extraordinary family. Gaskell's intent was to write a compassionate account of her friend Charlotte's remarkable life, but her reliance on Charlotte's own perception of events often caused family members, particularly father Patrick and sister Emily, to be cast in unmerited severe light. Recent biographies by Rebecca Fraser and Juliet Barker, by using new primary sources such as letters and journals, and by placing the Brontës' lives more firmly in historical perspective, have presented a more comprehensive picture of the relationships and writings of the Brontës.

Although Emily and her siblings were reared in geographically isolated Haworth, they were far from removed from events of the larger world. Their reading material was never censored. Newspapers and periodicals were part of their typical reading matter, and often echoes of political events, discussed at the dinner table, were integrated into their childhood writings. They also had access to their father's library, which included the complete works of Byron. Emily's writings, in particular, show the tortured Romantic soul, undoubtedly an influence from reading Byron and Shelley.

Emily did not make friends at school, but Charlotte's friends often visited Haworth. Such visits belie the absolute seclusion within which the Brontë children are often pictured. But, to Emily, such visits were uncomfortable, and she often withdrew to the moors. By all accounts, Emily was the most introverted of the siblings and the one most attached to the Yorkshire moors, attributes that permeate all of her writings. She was strong-willed as well. Pervasive in Brontë lore is the description of Emily, weakened by consumption (tuberculosis) and from having caught cold at Branwell's funeral, refusing medical assistance literally until hours before her death.

Emily spent more of her life at Haworth than did any of her siblings. Shortly before her seventeenth birthday, she went to Roe Head School as a pupil (and Charlotte as a teacher). Other than her six months at Cowan Bridge School, this was Emily's first time away from home. But missing the freedom of the Yorkshire landscape to such an extent that she was physically extremely ill, Emily went home after only three months. As Charlotte explained in her Biographical Notice to the 1850 edition of *Wuthering Heights*, "Liberty was the breath of Emily's nostrils; without it, she perished." Ellen Nussey, Charlotte's close friend who often visited Haworth, described Emily as pale, with "kind, kindling, liquid eyes; but she did not often look at you: she was too reserved" (qtd. in Fraser 83).

The tiny books including the stories of Angria (written by Charlotte and Branwell) and Gondal (by Emily and Anne) are often remarked upon to illustrate their precocious imaginations. And they did write when children. The first sustained writing for Emily and Anne began in 1834 with their diary papers, which includes the first extant mention of Gondal, when Emily was sixteen and Anne fourteen. Emily's accounts of her activities, though poorly spelled and punctuated, describe a carefree and cheerful household. Emily and Anne continued to write about the Gondals at least through 1845, when both were in their mid-twenties. The Gondal Saga, then, was not childhood or childish fantasy but a literary collaboration continued from adolescence through young adulthood.

In the autumn of 1837, Brontë, rather suddenly, became a teacher at Law Hill School, a rather large school near Halifax. Apparently, conditions there were harsh, and Brontë soon returned to Haworth. Her seven months' interval at Law Hill School is important, nevertheless, as many details describing Wuthering Heights are similar to High Southerland Hall, a house nearby. Top Withens, near Haworth, is another model for Wuthering Heights, so the connection to Law Hill School is not absolute. In February 1842, in order to prepare themselves to open their own school, she and Charlotte went to study foreign languages in Brussels, at the Pensionnat Heger. Emily's French essays were written at school between May and October. Emily returned to Haworth in November 1842, when Aunt Branwell died, and remained there to supervise the household, which included doing the cooking. Aunt Branwell's will provided an inheritance of £350 for Emily and each of her sisters, an inheritance they would use to help finance their volume of verse. The sisters' boarding school project, which Emily willingly supported, floundered by 1844.

In the autumn of 1845, Charlotte stumbled across a notebook of verse in Emily's handwriting. Most of Emily's poems were written during the two-year period commencing with her return from Brussels. This notebook was probably the Gondal Poems that Emily began to transcribe early in 1844 and had hidden from the rest of the family, although the family knew she wrote verse. Charlotte was surprised at the quality of the poems, however, describing them as "wild, melancholy and elevating" in her "Biographical Notice of Ellis and Acton Bell." In an 1848 letter to William S. Williams, she says "[T]hey stirred my heart like the sound of a trumpet" (qtd. in Fraser 245).

Urged (some biographers claim harassed) by Charlotte, Emily grudgingly consented to having her poems published along with those by Charlotte and Anne, but only under the condition of their being anonymous. As Charlotte describes, "[I]t took hours to reconcile her to the discovery I had made, and days to persuade her that such poems merited publication" (Biographical Notice). As was the usual practice in the 1840s, the authors were required to bear the expense of publication. They had some money, part of Aunt Branwell's legacy, which they sought to increase by speculating in shares of railway stock. Somewhat surprisingly, Emily served as business manager for the venture, avidly reading various newspaper advertisements and reports.

In May 1846, *Poems by Currer, Ellis, and Acton Bell* was published by Aylott and Jones. Emily appeared as Ellis Bell, a pseudonym that preserved both her privacy and, a plus for women who wanted to be taken seriously as writers, her gender. The authors were identified only as being from the same family, though each poem was signed by "Currer" or "Ellis" or "Acton Bell." Emily's contribution was twenty-one poems, fourteen of which were written in the two previous years. All of Emily's poems were from her manuscript notebooks and related to Gondal. She carefully edited the Gondal references, however. For example, in "Cold in the earth," she changed "Angora's shore" to "northern shore," and the published version of "The Prisoner" omits a Gondal story line and is much shorter than the manuscript version (Barker 481).

Inspired by their publishing venture, though dismayed by lack of sales, each of the sisters decided to try writing fiction. Emily's effort resulted in the phenomenal *Wuthering Heights*, published as two volumes of a triple-decker, with Anne's *Agnes Grey* comprising one volume, by Thomas Newby in December 1847. The pseudonyms were maintained; in fact, it was not until 31 July 1848 that Charlotte—over Emily's severe protestations—revealed to W. S. Williams at Smith, Elder & Co., publishers of *Jane Eyre*, the identity of "Ellis Bell." Emily seems to have been very angry, as Charlotte soon after describes to Williams: "Ellis Bell will not endure to be alluded to under any other appellation than the *nom de plume*. I committed a grand error in betraying his identity to you and Mr Smith. . . . I regret it bitterly now, for I find it is against every feeling and intention of Ellis Bell" (qtd. in Fraser 309 and Barker 563). Emily fought to preserve her privacy—and her liberty, leaving all negotiations with publishers to Charlotte.

Almost exactly a year from publication of *Wuthering Heights*, Emily Jane Brontë died on 19 December 1848 at age thirty. Charlotte describes Emily's last days: "Yet, while physically she perished, mentally, she grew stronger than we had yet known her. Day by day, when I saw with what a front she met suffering, I looked on her with an anguish of wonder and love. . . . Stronger than a man, simpler than a child, her nature stood alone. The awful point was, that, while full of ruth for others, on herself she had no pity" (Biographical Notice).

MAJOR WORKS AND THEMES

Today Emily Brontë is known primarily for *Wuthering Heights*, published in 1847 with Anne's *Agnes Grey*. Her only novel, *Wuthering Heights* has long been acknowledged as a masterpiece of poetic genius. Shy and reclusive to the extreme, during Brontë's lifetime, only 21 of her poems were published, all under the pseudonym of Ellis Bell in 1846. An additional 182 poems have since been attributed to her and published in various editions. Publication history of her poetry is described fully in Janet Gezari's Introduction, cited below. Briefly, the attribution and text of Brontë's poems were complicated by Charlotte's editing (she substantially revised most of them for the 1850 edition) and incorrect attribution. Clement Shorter's first complete edition of the poems (Hodder & Stoughton, 1910) contained 177 poems. C. W. Hatfield, who had access to more accurate transcriptions, later attributed 25 of these to Charlotte or Anne. *The Complete Poems of Emily Jane Brontë*, the first chronological arrangement, was brought out in 1923, edited by Shorter but arranged by Hatfield. The next major edition was *The Poems of Emily Jane Brontë and Anne Brontë* (the Shakespeare Head series), edited by Thomas J. Wise and John Alex Symington (Blackwell, 1934).

Gezari lauds Hatfield's edition of *The Complete Poems of Emily Jane Brontë* (Columbia University Press, 1941) as a landmark event, this edition defining the accepted canon. Until Gezari's *Emily Jane Brontë: The Complete Poems* (Penguin, 1992), the only complete edition published since 1941 was *The Complete Poems of Emily Brontë* edited by Philip Henderson (The Folio Society, 1951).

Charlotte, in her Biographical Notice to the 1850 edition of *Wuthering Heights* (published by Smith, Elder & Co.), describes her sister as having "a secret power and fire that might have informed the brain and kindled the veins of a hero." Two themes that permeate her writings are this sense of power and the freedom Brontë found walking on the moors behind Haworth. The back door of the Parsonage opened upon the moor, and among the heather and the wind Brontë found the liberty that she, to a greater extent than her siblings, craved. Rebecca Fraser describes ten-year-old Emily "roaming about the moors": "The wild landscape was already beginning to take possession of Emily's mind and became part of the imaginary land of Gondal" (53). Charlotte's close friend Ellen Nussey had many opportunities to notice Emily's withdrawal to the wind-swept heath of the Yorkshire landscape.

Brontë describes the many moods of Haworth moor in *Wuthering Heights*. The landscape could be threatening: "On an afternoon in October, or the beginning of November, a fresh watery afternoon, when the turf and paths were rustling with moist, withered leaves, and the cold blue sky was half hidden by clouds, dark grey streamers, rapidly mounting from the west, and boding abundant rain" (ch. 22). Lockwood describes its various aspects, "In winter, nothing more dreary, in summer, nothing more divine, than those glens shut in by hills, and those bluff, bold swells of heath" (ch. 32). Although most of the novel's action occurs indoors, Heathcliff and Catherine are recollected by readers of *Wuthering Heights* against the Yorkshire landscape that Emily loved. The dying Catherine entreats, "I wish I were out of doors—I wish I were a girl again, half savage, and hardy, and free" (ch. 12).

"The Prisoner," which appeared in *Poems by Currer, Ellis, and Acton Bell*, is one of Brontë's most famous, with its "powerful and intensely emotional description of the captive's vision" (Barker 481). Working through—or, sometimes, being in thrall to—contrasting emotions is a recurring theme in Brontë's poetry. Juliet Barker claims that Brontë "externalized her imagination," seeing her poems and stories "played out before her as if they were creations independent of her control" (482). This quality, however, does not mean that Brontë is a mystic, as some critics have claimed. Similarly, Brontë did not necessarily reject organized religion, even though the speaker in "No coward soul is mine" clearly does so. As Barker points out, "No coward soul is mine" is Brontë's only such comment in all of her extant writings (483).

The language of her poems and her novel conveys power; the syntax seems to convey a struggle that often focuses upon ways in which an individual is pulled by forces that can be controlled only by extreme force of will. Even when the voice is calm, we have the sense that an intense struggle has occurred. Nevertheless, the power remains as, for example, in "O God of Heaven!":

> O God of heaven! the dream of horror
> The frightful dream is over now
>
> . . . .
>
> It's over now—and I am free
> And the ocean wind is caressing me.

The speaker's struggle should not be read as Brontë's; in addition to reasons applied to any other poet, in Brontë's case, many of the poems were written as part of the Gondal Saga and as spoken by one of its turgidly romantic characters.

The individual's search for spiritual freedom is an underlying theme of *Wuthering Heights*, as might be expected from a writer who required the physical landscape to the extent that Brontë, by all accounts, did. The plethora of scholarly discussions of the novel's themes and images, most of which are readily available, point out the intricacies of this magnificent work.

CRITICAL RECEPTION

Poems by Currer, Ellis, and Acton Bell, a 170-page volume, was published in May 1846. Critical response was supportive though hardly overwhelming. However, Sydney Dobell, *The Athenaeum*'s anonymous reviewer, singled out "Ellis Bell" for particular praise: The poetry is "an inspiration, which may yet find an audience in the outer world. A fine quaint spirit has the latter [Ellis], which may have things to speak that men will be glad to hear, and an evident power of wing that may reach heights not here attempted" (qtd. in Fraser 259 and Barker 497). The reviewer in the *Dublin University Magazine* praised the "sweetness" of Currer's and Acton's poems, apparently not esteeming the power of Ellis's verses.

In spite of these positive reviews, the volume was largely ignored. Merely two copies sold during its first year, and only thirty-nine had been sold by Brontë's death in 1848. In spite of the low sales, response to the poems was encouraging enough for "the Bells" to begin to write fiction and to seek publication for their novels.

The myth that *Wuthering Heights* was not given due acclaim was begun by Charlotte, saying in her Biographical Notice, "The immature but very real powers revealed in *Wuthering Heights* were scarcely recognized"; furthermore, "its import and nature were misunderstood." But, clarifies Peterson, Charlotte may have misremembered the facts, perhaps because of her extreme suffering at the deaths of Branwell, Emily, and Anne occurring in such short succession. In fact, though unsure about the morality of Brontë's novel, literary critics "repeatedly acknowledged its originality, genius, and imaginative power" (290). Reviewers for the *Spectator, The Athenaeum*, and the *Examiner* praised Brontë's writing skill, noting its power of storytelling and description. Without exception, critics found the story compelling and extraordinary. (For detailed overview of critical history, see Peterson's essay in her edition of *Wuthering Heights*; for excerpts from primary sources, see Allott.)

Accusation of "coarseness"—profane language—may seem strange to us, but expressions such as "Go to the Deuce!" were cited as objectionable. American critics in particular accused Ellis Bell of "an ill-mannered contempt for the decencies of language" and even of "corrupt[ing] the virtues of the sturdy descendants of the Puritans" (qtd. in Peterson 290). Although the Victorian poet Algernon Charles Swinburne extolled "the passionate great genius of Emily Brontë" (qtd. in Peterson 296), most critics were unsure how to deal with the ambiguity that all of the characters in the novel portray: "In the whole story not a single trait of character is elicited which can command our admiration, not one of the fine feelings of our nature seems to have formed a part in the composition of its principal actors" is but one example (Peterson 291). In 1847, we need to remember, nineteenth-century critics and readers were used to more straightforward presentation of human strengths and flaws, which is not to say that earlier fiction overlooked the complexity of human nature. But Brontë's novel appeared to most as "morally confused" because it was difficult, even impossible, for readers to discern the villains. Even today, critics disagree as to whether *Wuthering Heights* is subversive. Charlotte attempted to defend her sister in her Editor's Preface to the 1850 edition: Emily may have been influenced by local village tales, and she "did not know what she had done."

This phrase, describing Brontë as an inspired artist unaware of the complexities of her text, guided future critics to delve into the unconscious meanings of *Wuthering Heights*. The best of the nineteenth-century studies of the novel focus on its psychological truth. Sydney Dobell, for example, discussed the conflict between Catherine's "two natures" and praised Brontë's accurate description of Catherine's delirium: Brontë appreciated that "crimes and sorrows are not so much the result of intrinsic evil as of a false position in the scheme of things" (qtd. in Peterson 292). Peter Bayne's study focused on Heathcliff's conflicted nature as well as Catherine's: "[W]e watch that boyish heart, until, in the furnace of hopeless and agonizing passion, it becomes as insensible to any tender emotion, to any emotion save one, as a mass of glowing iron to trickly dew" (qtd. in Peterson 292; see also Allott).

Most nineteenth-century critics tried to find connections that were more biographical or historical rather than focusing on the text itself. A. Mary F. Robinson,* in *Emily Brontë* (1883), drew parallels between Heathcliff's behavior and Branwell's while under the influence of alcohol and opium, sights that Emily undoubtedly witnessed frequently. This connection was one way to explain how an isolated and inexperienced young woman could describe such scenes as Hindley's drunken rages. In general, nineteenth-century critics approached the novel outwardly, in trying to find parallels between the author's life experiences and the characters and scenes that she created. Thus, connections were made to the "reality" that Brontë describes in her novel set in the wildness of the Yorkshire moors. Other critics, not satisfied with psychological or biographical approaches, sought explanation in Brontë's Gondal poems. In the 1950s, Fannie E. Ratchford made the connection between Catherine and Heathcliff and the heroine and heroes whom Brontë describes as inhabiting Gondal. However, in *Gondal's Queen: A Novel in Verse* (1955), Ratchford does not distinguish between the poems and her own "narrative prose links in the reconstruction," causing later commentators to separate Brontë's Gondal narrative from Ratchford's conjectures (Gezari xxx).

Early-twentieth-century critics C. P. Sanger and Lord David Cecil paved the way for various new interpretations of the novel. Sanger showed in *The Structure of Wuthering Heights* (1926) that Brontë had carefully worked out property and inheritance laws. In *Early Victorian Novelists* (1935), Cecil maintained the cosmic principles that organize the novel in its contrast between the "storm" of Wuthering Heights and the "calm" of Thrushcross Grange. New Criticism of the 1940s through 1960s analyzed many textual elements. Brontë's use of dual narrators, for instance, not only adds credibility, they said, because Nelly Dean and Lockwood are so realistically drawn, but also presents problems of ambiguity because of this narrative structure and the conflict between Nelly's working-class common sense and Lockwood's urbane romanticism.

Critics and biographers, such as Winifred Gerin, examined connections between Brontë's reading material and her works, the Byronic influences in particular. Other critics, such as Arnold Kettle, read *Wuthering Heights* as a critique of early-nineteenth-century England; and Sandra Gilbert and Susan Gubar opined in *Madwoman in the Attic* that Brontë revises Milton's myth of the Fall. Contemporary feminist, deconstructionist, and new historicist criticism reveal further complexities of this remarkable novel, one that will surely remain firmly placed within the canon of British literature. That *Wuthering Heights* is Brontë's only novel adds to its compelling attraction, for everyone falls under its powerful spell.

The Brontë Society was founded in 1893. The Parsonage has been restored and includes the Brontë Parsonage Museum, visited by scholars from around the world. For further information, contact The Brontë Parsonage Museum, Haworth, Keighley, West Yorkshire BD22 8DR, England. http://www.virtual-pc.com/bpmweb/.

BIBLIOGRAPHY

Wuthering Heights has been in print since it was first published. New editions of her poetry are being printed constantly. Her Belgian essays are reprinted in *The Belgian Essays*, ed. and trans. Sue Lanoff (Yale University Press, 1996).

Works by Emily Jane Brontë

Poems by Currer, Ellis, and Acton Bell. 1846.
Wuthering Heights. 1847.
Essays written in Belgium (1842), first published as *Five Essays Written in French by Emily Jane Brontë.* Trans. Lorine White Nagel. 1948.
Emily Jane Brontë: The Complete Poems. Ed. Janet Gezari. 1992.
The Brontës: A Life in Letters. Ed. Juliet Barker. 1997.

Studies of Emily Jane Brontë

Allott, Miriam F., ed. *The Brontës, the Critical Heritage.* London: Routledge, 1974.
Barker, Juliet. *The Brontës.* London: Weidenfeld, 1994.
Cecil, David. *Early Victorian Novelists: Essays in Revaluation.* Indianapolis: Bobbs-Merrill, 1935.
Chitham, Edward. *A Life of Emily Brontë.* Oxford: Blackwell, 1987.
Frank, Katherine. *A Chainless Soul: A Life of Emily Brontë.* Boston: Houghton, 1990.
Fraser, Rebecca. *The Brontës: Charlotte Brontë and Her Family.* New York: Crown, 1988.
Gerin, Winifred. *Emily Brontë: A Biography.* London: Oxford, 1971.
Ghnassia, Virginia Jill Dix. *Metaphysical Rebellion in the Works of Emily Brontë: A Reinterpretation.* New York: St. Martin's Press, 1994.
Gilbert, Sandra M., and Susan Gubar. *The Madwoman in the Attic: The Woman Writer and the Nineteenth-Century Literary Imagination.* New Haven, CT: Yale University Press, 1979.
Hewish, John. *Emily Brontë: A Critical and Biographical Study.* London: Macmillan, 1969.
Kettle, Arnold. *An Introduction to the English Novel: Defoe to the Present.* Rev. ed. New York: Harper, 1968.
Peterson, Linda H. Introduction. *Wuthering Heights.* Boston: Bedford of St. Martin's Press, 1992.
Ratchford, Fannie E. *Gondal's Queen: A Novel in Verse.* Austin: University of Texas Press, 1955.
Sanger, C[harles] P[ercy]. *The Structure of* Wuthering Heights. London: Hogarth, 1926.
Smith, Anne, ed. *The Art of Emily Brontë.* London: Vision Press, 1976.
Spark, Muriel, and Derek Stanford. *Emily Brontë, Her Life and Work.* London: Owen, 1953.
Winnifrith, Tom. *The Brontës and Their Background: Romance and Reality.* 2nd ed. London: Macmillan, 1988.

Rhoda Broughton
(1840-1920)

Anne M. Windholz

BIOGRAPHY

The strictly raised daughter of a Welsh clergyman, Rhoda Broughton grew up to become one of the most popular British novelists of the nineteenth century, associated with sensational, romantic plots, unconventionally passionate heroines, and witty social satire. Her education, directed by her father, included classical and modern languages as well as immersion in English literature. At the age of twenty-three, inspired by the example of Anne Thackeray (Ritchie)'s* *The Story of Elizabeth*, Broughton commenced her own literary career, drafting *Not Wisely But Too Well* in six weeks. She apparently pursued her writing ambitions no further until after her parents died, when her uncle, writer Joseph Sheridan Le Fanu, serialized her novel in *Dublin University Magazine*, which he then edited, and also actively promoted it to the London publisher Bentley & Sons.

The shocking subject of Broughton's first novel—the abandoned love of a young girl for a married scoundrel who ultimately murders her—would for many years color her reputation and ensure her popularity. Bentley's reader, Geraldine Jewsbury,* found the novel's subject indecent and ill-suited to a respectable publishing house. Although Broughton altered the ending to suit Bentley, the parties could not come to terms over price, and she ended up publishing the revised *Not Wisely* with Tinsley Brothers in 1867. When her fourth novel, *Goodbye, Sweetheart*, appeared in 1872, Broughton felt confident enough of her success to sign her works. By her death in 1920, she had produced twenty-six novels, more than half of which had been translated into other languages.

Rhoda Broughton was personally as popular as her novels, valued in intellectual society for her witty talk and trenchant observations. She overcame initial snubs by the Oxford elite to become one of the city's most valued and colorful personages. Invitations to her later residences in London and Headington Hill were coveted. She counted among her friends and admirers such eminent Victorians as Matthew Arnold, Thomas Hardy, and Henry James, who, although harshly critical of *Joan* (1876), remained a devoted friend until his death in 1916.

Biographers have suggested that some passionate, mistaken love affair must have blighted Broughton's youth to account for the consistency of this theme in her works, just as they assume that sibling rivalry among the Broughtons must explain plots where the machinations of one sister imperil the happiness of another. Such interpretations seem best answered by the protagonist of *A Beginner* (1894) who, on being asked how she could have written such passionate love scenes, protests that like Shakespeare and Fielding she used her imagination. Broughton's life more reliably informs her work in other ways. Her observations on the agony and ecstasy of writing emerge through the ambitious, albeit naive, heroines who take up the pen in *A Beginner* and *A Fool in Her Folly* (1920). A bitter comment in the former that "Thanks to our system of anonymous criticism . . . the writer can never know whether it is a male or female viper that spits its venom at him or her from behind a mask!" (178) articulates the same horror of bad reviews expressed in many of Broughton's letters to her publisher. Similarly, Broughton's assessment of personalities she actually encountered in society resulted in some of the most wickedly amusing caricatures in late-Victorian literature: Oscar Wilde ("Francis Chaloner") in *Second Thoughts* (1880) and Oxford scholar Mark Pattison ("Professor Forth") in *Belinda* (1883).

MAJOR WORKS AND THEMES

Belinda, Not Wisely But Too Well, and *Cometh Up as a Flower* have endured as representatives of Broughton's contribution to popular, circulating library literature of the nineteenth century. All three novels share themes common to early Broughton fiction: the naive but passionate heroine caught in a star-crossed love and often an ill-conceived marriage; the temptation of that heroine to abandon respectability and run away with her lover; and the cynical, frequently humorous assessment of conventional Victorian pieties and social customs. Though romance, failed or fulfilled, remains the raison d'être for most Broughton novels, the author's focus on contemporary manners necessarily meant that her heroines' horizons and capacities for independence broadened just as opportunities for women did at the end of the century. Broughton's later protagonists are, therefore, often motivated by ambitions at least as strong as their desire to be loved: to produce great literature, to work for social reform on issues such as temperance, women's suffrage, or the plight of factory workers. That Broughton presents such heroines as quixotic in their idealism suggests that her treatment of these issues was motivated more by any awareness of the comic potential of contemporary social crusades than by any reformist ideological agenda of her own. In *Dear Faustina* (1897), for instance, Althea Vane's commitment to the fin de siècle women's movement seems as much the result of romantic seduction by an unscrupulous New Woman as the outcome of a genuine conversion to the cause of women's rights. These and other Broughton novels usefully comment on debates about marriage and the Woman Question.

Amusement and income were Broughton's primary motivations for writing, and she had no illusions about the literary value of her earliest productions, which she described to Ethel Arnold in later years as "crude and vulgar and marred by that impropriety which is so often the fault of very young writers" (262). These faults notwithstanding, the unconventional outspokenness and daring of Broughton's heroines offered an alternative to the Victorian "Angel in the House" that readers found attractive. Broughton's challenge to standards of Victorian novel writing also extended to form. Throughout her career she criticized the practice of magazine serialization prior to book publication and contested the artificial extension of novels to three volumes that publishers and circulating libraries demanded. When *Alas!* proved a poor seller in 1890, she felt justified in abandoning the triple-decker forever. The result was a tighter prose style well suited to show off her mastery of witty dialogue and her ability to tell a good story.

CRITICAL RECEPTION

To general readers, Broughton was "Queen of the Circulating Libraries"; with critics, however, her reception was mixed. While Geraldine Jewsbury and Margaret Oliphant* offered scathing indictments of Broughton's writing, particularly her representation of women, Anthony Trollope expressed surprise that anyone could find her novels offensive. Eliza Lynn Linton* insisted that her worth was better measured by "the practical verdict of the reading world" than by "the literary trumpets of reviewers" (196). When Broughton's sales did diminish in the twentieth century, she was fairly philosophic. Observing that she had been equated with Emile Zola when young and was ranked with Charlotte Yonge* in age, Broughton concluded, "It's not I that have changed, it's my fellow-countrymen" (qtd. in Ernest Baker, *History of the English Novel*, 1967, 10: 211).

Broughton's critical reputation early in the twentieth century rested more on her later social satire than on her mid-Victorian sensationalism. Michael Sadleir, arguing that the works published after 1890 are her best in terms of style, plot, and substance, maintained: "These little books are cameos of changing fads, fashions and furies, and deserve a permanent place in the honourable tradition of polite social fiction written in English" (113). More recent critics have been most interested in her early works, largely for what their "sensationalism" signifies. R. C. Terry contends, "Broughton's significance lies in the uninhibited directness about women's strong feelings and, by implication, their sexual needs in a male-dominated society. Her presentation of headstrong girls, albeit in lush, melodramatic terms, was an act of rebellion at an unfair and sexually explosive state of affairs" (110). It is primarily as a member of the cadre of 1860s and 1870s female sensation novelists that Broughton has earned the attention of feminist scholars such as Elaine Showalter, Sally Mitchell, and Kate Flint. Helen Debenham argues that the quotations and allusions littering Broughton's first novel, so often deplored as naive pretension even by her champions, actually illustrate the "exuberant exploitation of polyphany" by which "the text reveals the inconsistencies of the dominant culture and disputes its authority." Such a reading suggests that Rhoda Broughton's significance today resides in the role her novels play in what Debenham calls "the work of culture" (22).

BIBLIOGRAPHY

Three Broughton novels have been reprinted recently: *Belinda* (Scholarly, 1970); *Cometh Up as a Flower* (Sutton, 1993); and *Not Wisely But Too Well* (Pocket Classic, 1967).

Selected Works by Rhoda Broughton

Cometh Up as a Flower. 1867.
Not Wisely But Too Well. 1867.
Goodbye, Sweetheart. 1872.
Joan. 1876.
Second Thoughts. 1880.
Belinda. 1883.
Alas! 1890.
A Beginner. 1894.
Dear Faustina. 1897.
A Fool in Her Folly. 1920.

Studies of Rhoda Broughton

Arnold, Ethel M. "Rhoda Broughton as I Knew Her." *Fortnightly Review* 108 (2 Aug. 1920): 262–78.
Debenham, Helen. "Rhoda Broughton's *Not Wisely But Too Well* and the Art of Sensation." In *Victorian Identities*. Ed. Ruth Robbins and Julian Wolfreys. New York: St. Martin's Press, 1996. 9–24.
Gilbert, Pamela. *Disease, Desire, and the Body in Victorian Women's Popular Novels.* New York: Cambridge University Press, 1997.
Linton, Eliza Lynn. "Miss Broughton's Novels." *Temple Bar* 80 (June 1887): 196–209.
Sadleir, Michael. "Rhoda Broughton." In *Things Past*. London: Constable, 1944. 84–116.
Terry, R. C. "Delightful Wickedness: Some Novels of Rhoda Broughton." In *Victorian Popular Fiction, 1860–1880*. Atlantic Highlands: Humanities Press, 1983. 102–32.
Watters, Tamie. "An Oxford Provocation & Caricature: Rhoda Broughton and Mark Pattison." *Encounter* (April 1971): 34–42.
Wood, Marilyn. *Rhoda Broughton: Profile of a Novelist.* Stamford: Paul Watkins, 1993.

Elizabeth Barrett Browning
(1806-1861)

Mary S. Pollock

BIOGRAPHY

Elizabeth Barrett Barrett (her father was Edward Barrett Moulton Barrett and she always liked the initials EBB) was born on 6 March 1806, near the home of her maternal grandparents in the County of Durham; she was the first child of Edward Moulton Barrett and Mary Graham-Clarke, the daughter of a Newcastle merchant. Three years later, Edward moved his family to a fanciful and isolated mansion in the Malvern Hills named Hope End (after the small valley that enclosed it), which he had built with the wealth accumulated by generations of Jamaican sugar planters. Here, Elizabeth passed an idyllic childhood, surrounded by adoring parents and nine siblings.

Early likenesses of Elizabeth taken by her mother, a talented portraitist, suggest humor, energy, intelligence, and a mischievous temperament. Almost everything in Elizabeth's early life seemed to support her creative impulses. She ran wild in the woods surrounding her home and, according to an account written thirty years later to Robert Browning, built there little altars to Minerva. Her father nicknamed her "the Poet Laureate of Hope End," rewarded her poetic efforts with a generous supply of pocket money, and when she was fourteen, paid the printing costs for *The Battle of Marathon* (1820), a precocious "epic" in the manner of Pope. The tutor employed for her brother Edward ("Bro") gave equal time to the sister's classical education, and after Bro entered Charterhouse, Elizabeth continued her studies independently. Elizabeth also benefited from her father's large library: She read poetry, discussed novels with her mother, and when her father proscribed the works of Gibbon and Fielding as inappropriate for a girl, she slyly substituted those of the philosophes and Mary Wollstonecraft.

After a healthy childhood, Elizabeth seemed devastated by puberty. Her emotional and physical health began to decline after the departure of Bro, her favorite sibling. Like her sisters Henrietta and Arabel, Elizabeth suffered a lengthy period of physical illnesses, and baffled physicians could not agree about her condition. Unlike her sisters, Elizabeth never completely recovered but withdrew into scholarship and invalidism. This withdrawal did not happen all at once, however. In 1826, she met the elderly scholar Uvedale Price, who was charmed by her first published collection of poetry, *An Essay on Mind, with Other Poems* (1826). Shortly thereafter, she began to develop a much deeper acquaintance with Hugh Boyd, the blind classical scholar, who encouraged her study of Greek. She persisted in this friendship, despite Boyd's demands and family pressures against the friendship, because of her own emotional and creative need—a situation that prefigured the enmeshed relationship between Elizabeth and her father later on. The Barrett family was shocked by the sudden death of Elizabeth's maternal grandmother in 1827, followed by the even more profound loss of Elizabeth's mother less than a year later.

Tensions continued to rise in the Barrett family as, unbeknownst to his children, Edward Moulton Barrett suffered serious financial losses. Since the beginning of the century, Cuban sugar had gradually driven down the price of the Jamaican sugar; the abolition of slavery in the British colonies in 1833 was the last in a series of reverses suffered by this industry, which had enriched the English middle class, including the Barretts, the Graham-Clarks, and the Browning family, with whom Elizabeth was to be connected years later. The sale of Hope End and the removal in 1837 to London was sudden and unexpected. But the final blow to Elizabeth was not the loss of her childhood home but Bro's drowning three years later at Torquay, where she had been sent for the sea air. Overcome by grief and guilt, she shut herself in a room with sealed windows and two thick doors; since she had vowed never again to break up the family in search of better health, this course was for her the only acceptable defense against the London weather, pollution, and noise. As Elizabeth's health and spirits continued to decline, she became more dependent on her father and entirely devoted to the life of the mind, cultivating an enormous correspondence, reading widely, and admitting only a select few into her presence. One of them was the essayist Mary Russell Mitford,* whose affection and conversation enriched her life and whose gift, the golden cocker spaniel named Flush, may well have saved it. Another was a family friend, John Kenyon, who suggested that Robert Browning and Elizabeth Barrett might have interests in common beyond their dedication to poetry.

In January 1845, Elizabeth received a letter from Robert Browning; it was his response to her generous assessment of his work in "Lady Geraldine's Courtship," a long ballad that anchored Barrett's *Poems of 1844*. He began, "I love your verses with all my heart, dear Miss Barrett." In closing, he went further: "I do, as I say, love these books with all my heart, and I love you, too." Browning was not admitted to Elizabeth's room until spring, and the ensuing courtship was tense. Her reservations were difficult to overcome: she was an invalid, and Robert was six years her junior. But in September 1845, the poets married secretly and departed for Italy, where they hoped Elizabeth's health would improve. With them were Flush and Elizabeth's maid, Elizabeth Wilson. To no one else had she disclosed that she and Robert Browning were more than friends; her father never forgave her and never opened her letters.

The years in Italy, from 1846 until Elizabeth's death in 1861, were arguably the most important for both poets. Their son "Pen" was born in Florence in 1849. Elizabeth's best known work, *Sonnets from the Portuguese* (1850), narrates her early relationship with Browning; but, to her own mind, the meditation on the Italian struggle for independence and reunification, *Casa Guidi Windows* (1851), and the novel poem *Aurora Leigh* (1856) were more significant. Robert's *Men and Women* (1855), written during the same period and dedicated to "my moon of poets," is perhaps his strongest work. In Italy, Elizabeth enjoyed better health than at any time since her childhood, but the deaths of Kenyon, her sister Henrietta, and her father took their toll, and she was heartbroken by the apparent reversal of the Risorgimento in the late 1850s. She died of respiratory failure during the night of 28 June 1861 in her husband's arms. Buried in the Protestant cemetery in Florence, Elizabeth Barrett Browning was mourned and remembered by the country whose cause she had championed.

Robert and Pen returned to England. The house on Wimpole Street has disappeared—only its front door remains, enshrined in the library at Wellesley College. But Casa Guidi has been renovated, a monument and resource for the study of the Brownings.

MAJOR WORKS AND THEMES

Like many other Victorian writers, Elizabeth Barrett Browning was a scholar as well as a creative artist. A classical education and a deep interest in the connections between history and contemporary life inform her poetry. Unlike the male poet-scholars of her time, Barrett had to struggle to attain the level of learning that was assumed theirs by right. Her early poetry thus expresses her love for books and her struggle for the right to scholarship. Her family indulged her talent and, at the same time, limited her access to education and experience.

The Battle of Marathon and *An Essay on Mind* were not the only poems written in the manner of Pope: When Barrett was sixteen, she wrote a discursive poem in heroic couplets, similar to *An Essay on Mind*, entitled "Essay on Woman" (1822). The first stanza invokes Pope, who "awoke the living lays" that legitimize male power; the rest, like Mary Wollstonecraft's *A Vindication of the Rights of Woman*, asserts the right of women to be poets and intellectuals; Barrett argues that women's power is yet untried, though this potential is suggested by the examples of exceptional female intellectuals. Significantly, this poem was one of the few Barrett Browning never completed, but it clearly belongs to the same period in her intellectual development as *An Essay on Mind*. This latter poem makes the relatively complex argument that poetry is ideally suited as the vehicle not only for romantic emotion but for philosophical inquiry as well. Finally, in *Aurora Leigh*, written thirty years after these early attempts at discursive poetry, Barrett Browning was able to synthesize these two themes, the fundamental nature and purpose of poetry and the potential of the woman poet.

Barrett Browning was one of the most prolific and versatile poets of the nineteenth century. After *An Essay on Mind and Other Poems* (1826), she began writing the pieces that would be included in *The Seraphim and Other Poems* (1838). The title poem in this collection shows the interest in religion that would continue to be one of Barrett Browning's themes throughout her life; *The Seraphim* also shows her command of Greek tragedy, the generic model for the work, and her continuing, if muted, interest in the cultural position of women. In *Poems of 1844*, the anchor poem, *A Drama of Exile*, echoes Barrett Browning's earlier themes—Christianity, Greek tragedy, and, by focusing on Eve's experience of the Fall, the experience of women within culture. Both collections are completed with miscellaneous lyrics, dramatic monologues, and numerous ballads, some of which were first published in journals or the popular gift annuals. Many of these poems explore another of Barrett Browning's preoccupations, the function of poetry. Translations, reviews, and essays about literature also contributed to her intellectual independence and the development of her craft.

When Robert Browning came into her life, Elizabeth Barrett was admired and respected as a "woman poet," and considering the declining market for poetry during the 1830s and 1840s, the sales of her work were significant. In fact, her work was more popular than her husband's would ever be during his lifetime. If she had not continued to develop as a poet after 1845, her work would perhaps be read today primarily as an episode in the transition from Romantic to Victorian literature and would no doubt be frequently anthologized—if only in collections of women's poetry. Browning did not influence her poetry in the usual sense of the word, but he did enable her to escape from the restrictions of her room and books and to experience life so that she could transform her own poetry. *Sonnets from the Portuguese* prefigures Barrett Browning's transformation from academic poet to observer of contemporary life. This sonnet sequence is thus only the beginning of her mature work. The rough versification in the sonnets is typical of her poetry and suggests her intention of building on poetic tradition, rather than working entirely within it. Like Gerard Manley Hopkins and Robert Browning, Barrett Browning favors slant rhyme and stretches out meter, often as far as possible while still retaining the pentameter line length required by the sonnet form. In its form and its system of allusions, the sequence shows Barrett Browning's profound understanding of Western literary history. At the same time, *Sonnets from the Portuguese* narrates her own experience *as a woman poet*, both inside and outside literary tradition, and her love for another poet, whose gender alone placed him more securely within literary history.

Ironically, the title was suggested by Browning's admiration for one of his wife's early dramatic monologues, "Catarina to Camoëns," the speaker of which is the dying and abandoned lover of the Portuguese Renaissance poet Camoëns. Contrary to the rumor of a private printing in 1847, *Sonnets from the Portuguese* was first published in 1850, along with a number of shorter pieces, including "The Runaway Slave at Pilgrim's Point," a remarkable dramatic monologue written in 1848 for an antislavery bazaar in Boston. This poem signals Barrett Browning's growing interest in politics and social issues.

Casa Guidi Windows, the two-part meditation that Barrett Browning wrote about the Risorgimento in 1847 and 1849, more clearly marks this turn in her poetic development. In Part I, inspired by a new level of civic freedom granted Florence by the Grand Duke, she anticipates the reunification of Italy, the revitalization of its culture, and its eventual freedom from the domination of other European powers, particularly Austria. The loosely rhyming verse form resonates with the more firmly structured Spenserian stanzas of Lord Byron's *Childe Harold's Pilgrimage* (1812–1818). Indeed, Part I deconstructs a central conceit in Byron's poem and the work of his Italian counterparts: that Italy's fate, like that of a fallen woman, is inevitably the result of her beauty. Barrett Browning also asserts the duty of the woman poet to comment on history and politics because her perspective offers new insights into old problems. Thus, her poetry returns to the discursive mode of *An Essay on Mind*, but with confidence rather than bravado, maturity rather than precocity. Unfortunately, two years after the Grand Duke's apparent support for the self-determination of Florence, he fled to Austria, and Austrian troops defeated Italian forces at Novara. Part II of *Casa Guidi Windows* chronicles the poet's disillusionment and Italy's political reversals. Instead of joy and hope, the poet describes the changes of heart and mind that will be necessary for a free Italy.

According to a letter to Browning in early 1845, Barrett Browning planned to write a major narrative poem for at least a decade before she began *Aurora Leigh* (1856); she devoted most of her creative energy to this project after completing *Casa Guidi Windows*. At nine books and almost 11,000 lines, it is, according to some literary historians, the longest poem in English. The protagonist of *Aurora Leigh*, like Elizabeth Barrett Browning herself, is a prolific and versatile woman poet; Aurora Leigh also earns money by writing and develops a strong critical sense of the difference between her popular work and the poetry she creates for the sake of art; she eventually settles in Italy, where she finds more freedom to pursue her poetry. Despite these parallels, *Aurora Leigh* is not the autobiographical work it is sometimes taken to be. The main character's emotional history accords not with the facts of Barrett Browning's life but with the genre of the *Künstlerroman*, particularly with Madame de Staël's *Corinne, or Italy* (1807); it resonates, as well, with Charlotte Brontë's* *Jane Eyre* and with the actual lives of the American essayist Margaret Fuller and George Sand, the contemporary French novelist whose life and works had fascinated Barrett Browning for more than a decade. The secondary plot, which traces the seduction and betrayal of Aurora's friend Marion Erle, resonates with the contemporary domestic novel, Elizabeth Gaskell's* political novels, George Eliot's* realistic fiction, and early works of French realism. The "novel poem," as Barrett Browning called it, revisits issues she had explored in her ballads and monologues, but into the story is also woven another thread from her earlier discursive work: the analysis of poetry itself—its ideal content, its form, its social and historical functions. Thus, in Barrett Browning's magnum opus, she created a synthesis of major themes and genres that had concerned her throughout her career.

Barrett Browning died five years after the publication of *Aurora Leigh*. Her health had begun to fail soon after it appeared, beloved friends had died, and the political situation in Italy seemed to be worsening. In 1860, she responded directly to Italy's woes once again in *Poems Before Congress*. And despite the resurgence of old illnesses and sorrows, Barrett Browning continued to write until she died in June the following year. During the early months of 1861, she completed some of her strongest poems, which Browning published after her death in *Last Poems* (1862): "A Musical Instrument," the controversial "Lord Walter's Wife," and "Mother and Poet," based on the experience of Laura Savio, an Italian poet whose life in some respects mirrored Barrett Browning's own. This poem resembles Browning's dramatic monologues and is one of her most technically refined short poems.

By the end of her life, Barrett Browning learned to write poetry that, in the words of her heroine Aurora Leigh, represents "this live throbbing age," conveys the complexity of human truth beyond the reach of philosophy, and takes up the task of righting social and political wrongs. Barrett Browning also developed a poetry that stretched out the boundaries of the poetic forms she had inherited, and from the beginning, she seemed instinctively to know what would entertain as well as teach.

CRITICAL RECEPTION

More than most literary reputations, Barrett Browning's has fluctuated with the critical and political issues of the time and place, partly because of her literary versatility and, perhaps even more, because of her relationship to Robert Browning.

Early in her career, although her ballads were admired, Elizabeth Barrett was revered as a "subjective poet," whose work expressed emotions and spirituality. Browning himself was attracted to these qualities in her work; the terms "subjective" and "objective," which he employs in an essay on Shelley to distinguish Romantic poetry from a poetry more resonant with external experience, echo the language he uses in his courtship letters to describe Barrett's poetry in contrast to his own. Among her other early admirers were Edgar Allan Poe, the English novelist Edward Bulwer-Lytton, and of course, Mary Russell Mitford.

After Wordsworth's death in 1850, Barrett Browning was considered as the new poet laureate, although the rationale for the suggestion must have amused her: It would be appropriate for a female monarch to have a female laureate!

In spite of the literary output of her last twelve years, which emphasizes contemporary life in the mode of literary realism, Barrett Browning's reputation for most of the twentieth century has continued to rest on her more personal poetry, particularly on *Sonnets from the Portuguese* (1850), and even on a sentimental misreading of this work as an outpouring of raw emotion. Since the sonnets have been published over and over again in greeting card format with illustrations of hearts and flowers, their complexity has almost been erased. Under the influence of feminist criticism, however, readers have become once again aware of their literary qualities. A recent gift-book edition by William S. Peterson and Julia Markus, in which the sonnets and corresponding passages from the correspondence and other poetry are printed on opposite pages, nicely encourages both romantic and scholarly readings.

Casa Guidi Windows (1851) was at first reviewed favorably. However, with the exception of an enthusiastic Italian public, Barrett Browning's readers later proved unwilling to follow her into the new territory of this work, which was both personal and political. Indeed, the dismay Henry James expressed about the poem in his group biography *William Wetmore Story and His Friends* (1903) typifies the Anglo-American reaction to this work until it, too, was rehabilitated by feminist scholars in the late 1970s and early 1980s. Barrett Browning's late political poetry, *Poems Before Congress* (1860) and *Last Poems* (1862), has met with much the same fate.

Aurora Leigh (1856), however, was received with general (though not universal) enthusiasm. George Eliot, John Ruskin, and Queen Victoria* praised it, as did Emily Dickinson's mentor Thomas Wentworth Higginson. It remained popular until the end of the nineteenth century: Readers as diverse as Oscar Wilde, Rudyard Kipling, and Susan B. Anthony admired it. But by the early twentieth century, *Aurora Leigh* was regarded as a literary oddity; in 1931, Virginia Woolf noted that the poem "overwhelms and bewilders" the twentieth-century reader, who prefers to contemplate the romance of the Brownings' life together without reading their work. However, the astonishing number of editions of *Aurora Leigh* in the late twentieth century attests to its renewed popularity. Parts of the poem have been anthologized since the first edition of Sandra Gilbert and Susan Gubar's *Norton Anthology of Literature by Women: The Tradition in English* in 1985. Cora Kaplin's 1978 Introduction to a facsimile reprint and Gardner B. Taplin's similar edition the following year brought the work back into view after it had been absent from bookstore shelves for decades. Margaret Reynolds's scholarly edition appeared in 1992, followed by Kerry McSweeney's paperback edition in 1993, and, in 1996, by Reynolds's Norton Critical Edition.

Ultimately, it is impossible to consider Barrett Browning's critical reception apart from Browning's, for, as Woolf suggests, when the Brownings' relationship took on mythic proportions in the public imagination, particularly after Rudolph Besier's famous play *The Barretts of Wimpole Street* (1931), their work was taken less seriously. During Barrett Browning's lifetime, her popularity was not paralleled by her husband's; Browning's poetry was routinely denounced as obscure. Although Browning's work began to develop a certain caché after the publication of his own novel poem, *The Ring and the Book* (1868–1869), it was not truly appreciated until the rise of modernism, a movement that valued indeterminacy, objectivity, and experimentation. On the other hand, modernism had no place for the obviously personal or didactic, elements that Barrett Browning's earlier readers had valued in her work. As Browning's reputation rose, hers fell, until, at midcentury, critics and biographers had begun to blame her for Browning's uneven production. In this phenomenon can be observed a familiar pattern: Since women artists usually do become known in terms of their husbands' work, Barrett Browning's critical reputation came to rest on *Sonnets from the Portuguese*, the poems most clearly associated with Browning. In reaction, perhaps, feminist critics have occasionally blamed Browning's handling of his wife's literary estate for her diminishing critical fortunes.

Such scholars as Dorothy Mermin, Mary Rose Sullivan, and Julia Markus, however, have written more even-handed treatments of the Brownings. In the current prevailing view, the two poets nourished and enriched each other's poetry and, at the same time, maintained individual methods and aesthetic perspectives.

BIBLIOGRAPHY

All of Barrett Browning's major works are in print. Among the best available editions are *Aurora Leigh* (ed. Margaret Reynolds [Ohio University Press, 1992]); *Casa Guidi Windows* (ed. Julia Markus [Brownings Institute, 1977]); *Selected Poems* (ed. Margaret Forster [Johns Hopkins University Press, 1988]); *A Variorum Edition of Elizabeth Barrett Browning's Sonnets from the Portuguese* (ed. Miroslava Wein Dow [Whitson, 1980]); and *Sonnets from the Portuguese, Illuminated by the Brownings' Love Letters* (ed. William S. Peterson and Julia Markus [Ecco, 1996]).

Works by Elizabeth Barrett Browning

An Essay on Mind, with Other Poems. 1826.
The Seraphim and Other Poems. 1838.
Poems of 1844. 1844.
Poems (includes first publication of *Sonnets from the Portuguese*). 1850.
Casa Guidi Windows. 1851.
Aurora Leigh. 1856.
Poems Before Congress. 1860.
Last Poems. 1862.
The Poetical Works of Elizabeth Barrett Browning. Ed. Ruth M. Adams. 1974.
The Browning Correspondence. Ed. William Kelley and Ronald Hudson. 1984–.

*Robert Browning and Elizabeth Barrett: The Courtship Correspondence 1845–1846. A
     Selection.* Ed. Daniel Karlin. 1989.
The Works of Elizabeth Barrett Browning (Wordsworth Collection). 1998.

Studies of Elizabeth Barrett Browning

Armstrong, Isobel. "The Brownings." In *New History of Literature.* Vol. 6, *The Victo-
     rians.* Ed. Arthur Pollard. New York: Peter Bedrick, 1987. 387–91, 411–12.
Cooper, Helen. *Elizabeth Barrett Browning, Woman and Artist.* Chapel Hill: University
     of North Carolina Press, 1988.
David, Deirdre. *Intellectual Women and Victorian Patriarchy: Harriet Martineau, Eliz-
     abeth Barrett Browning, George Eliot.* Ithaca: Cornell University Press, 1987.
Donaldson, Sandra. *Elizabeth Barrett Browning: An Annotated Bibliography of the Com-
     mentary and Criticism, 1826–1990.* New York: G. K. Hall, 1993.
Forster, Margaret. *The Life and Loves of a Poet: Elizabeth Barrett Browning.* New York:
     St. Martin's Press, 1988.
Gilbert, Sandra. "From *Patria* to *Matria*: Elizabeth Barrett Browning's Risorgimento."
     PMLA 99 (March 1984): 194–211.
Leighton, Angela. *Elizabeth Barrett Browning.* Bloomington: Indiana University Press,
     1986.
Markus, Julia. *Dared and Done: The Marriage of Elizabeth Barrett and Robert Brown-
     ing.* New York: Alfred A. Knopf, 1995.
Mermin, Dorothy. "The Domestic Economy of Art: Elizabeth Barrett and Robert Brown-
     ing." In *Mothering the Mind: Twelve Studies of Writers and Their Silent Partners.*
     Ed. Ruth Perry and Martine Watson Brownley. New York: Holmes & Meier,
     1984. 82–101.
Munich, Adrienne Auslander. *Andromeda's Chains: Gender and Interpretation in Vic-
     torian Literature and Art.* New York: Columbia University Press, 1989.
Reynolds, Margaret, ed. *Aurora Leigh: Authoritative Text, Backgrounds and Contexts,
     Criticism.* A Norton Critical Edition. New York: Norton, 1996.
Stone, Marjorie. *Elizabeth Barrett Browning.* New York: St. Martin's Press, 1995.
Sullivan, Mary Rose. " 'Some Interchange of Grace': 'Saul' and *Sonnets from the Por-
     tuguese."* *Browning Institute Studies* 15 (1987): 55–68.
Woolf, Virginia. *"Aurora Leigh."* In *Women and Writing.* Ed. Michèle Barrett. New
     York: Harcourt Brace Jovanovich, 1979. 133–44.

Frances Hodgson Burnett
(1849–1924)

Leonie Rutherford

BIOGRAPHY

Frances Hodgson was born in Manchester on 24 November 1849. Initially a prosperous middle-class family, the Hodgsons' fortunes failed after the death of Frances's father and the financial depression in Manchester following the cessation of cotton imports from the Southern plantations as a result of the American Civil War. This early experience of harsh conditions in the northern British manufacturing centers formed the context for her early writing for adults in the social-realist mode, such as her first major novel, *That Lass o' Lowrie's* (1877), set in the Lancashire pit district.

In 1856 the Hodgson family emigrated to Tennessee. In her 1893 autobiography, *The One I Knew Best of All*, Burnett represents this change in pastoral terms, a journey from urban, industrial sterility to a green world that nurtures both spirit and imaginative life. To supplement the family income, Frances began to submit romance and adventure tales to popular literary magazines.

In 1873 Frances Hodgson married Swan Burnett, by whom she had two sons, Lionel and Vivian. The family soon settled in Washington, D.C., where the Burnett home became one of the hubs of Washington literary and political society; this political milieu influenced some of Burnett's later writing for adults, such as *Through One Administration* (1883).

Persistent illnesses led Burnett to seek relief in the "new philosophies" of Spiritualism, Theosophy, "Mind Healing," and Christian Science. The influence of the "new thought" concerning the regenerative powers of the mind can be seen in later novels, including *A Little Princess* (1905), *The Secret Garden* (1911), and *The Lost Prince* (1915).

The publication of *Little Lord Fauntleroy* in 1886 made Burnett's fortune and reputation; it also pigeonholed her as a popular and romantic writer. The adaptation of her novel for the stage introduced Burnett to writing for the theater, which subsequently emerged as a significant part of her literary output.

In 1890 Burnett's son Lionel developed consumption. His mother took him on a European pilgrimage of pleasure, on which she was accompanied by Lionel's doctor, Stephen Townesend, who was to become her second husband. Burnett's grief over Lionel's death forms a motif in several stories published in two collections, *Giovanni and the Other* (1892) and *Piccino and Other Child Stories* (1894).

In later life, Burnett devoted herself to gardening and writing. She had always been attracted to the country house ideal, and in 1898, she leased Maytham Hall, in Kent, which was to be her home in England for almost ten years and the inspiration for *The Secret Garden*. Following her return to the United States in 1907, she continued her passion for gardening at her villa at Plandome, Long Island, where she died in October 1924.

MAJOR WORKS AND THEMES

Little Lord Fauntleroy brought together several of Burnett's favorite themes and narrative motifs: the picturesque child, whose charm encapsulates the sentimental attraction of childhood; the exemplary child, possessing innate honor and a universal generosity of spirit; the redemptive child, whose innocence comments on and redeems the fallen adult world; and finally, the romance or fairytale archetype of the "rags to riches" story. Cedric, Little Lord Fauntleroy, is vilified because of his American mother; yet when the child becomes the heir to the aging Earl of Dorincourt, his goodness, trust, and optimism redeem the misanthropic earl and restore a state of charity and goodwill in the noble family.

A Little Princess exemplifies the Cinderella archetype in Burnett's fiction. However, it also highlights Burnett's beliefs about the power of the imagination to transform reality. Sara Crewe is the daughter of a young officer who dies in India. Reduced to domestic servitude, she pretends she is a princess in luxurious surroundings, a fantasy that is transformed into reality as a result of Sara's intrinsic worthiness.

The Secret Garden celebrates the romantic and pastoral nature of childhood. In a secret walled garden, the orphaned Mary Lennox and Colin Craven, the sickly son of a widowed aristocrat, find physical and spiritual health through exercise, communion with nature, and the seasonal cycle of regeneration and rebirth. While both children are damaged, both become redemptive as they find their own health and happiness. The Yorkshire peasant boy, Dickon, a kind of Pan and Christ figure, is the ultimate example of the exemplary and redemptive child.

CRITICAL RECEPTION

Burnett's novels for adults were initially well received: Her social-realist novel *That Lass o' Lowrie's* was compared with the work of Charlotte Brontë,*

Elizabeth Gaskell,* and Henry James. This opinion was not generally shared by twentieth-century commentators, for whom Burnett was a second-rate "relic of Victorianism." More recently, however, the work of Phyllis Bixler has interpreted Burnett's adult romance in the light of traditional oral literature and the forms of popular culture.

Burnett's status as a writer now rests firmly on her children's novels. Nineteenth-century reviews of *Little Lord Fauntleroy* were generally admiring, stressing the appeal of the sentimental and romantic view of the child. Twentieth-century opinion has seen the novel as an icon of popular culture, less significant for its literary merit than for its representation of the sentimental Victorian view of childhood. However, *The Secret Garden* remains Burnett's most acclaimed novel, valued for its rich symbolic and mythic resonances and its dynamic and controversial portrayal of the child characters. While the book has long been accepted as a classic of children's literature, recent children's literature scholars such as Lissa Paul have debated the feminist significance of the novel's narrative closure.

BIBILOGRAPHY

Only Burnett's children's novels remain in print.

Works by Frances Hodgson Burnett

That Lass o' Lowrie's. 1877.
Through One Administration. 1883.
Little Lord Fauntleroy. 1886.
Children I Have Known and Giovanni and the Other. 1892.
The One I Knew Best of All: A Memory of the Mind of a Child. 1893.
The Captain's Youngest: Piccino and Other Child Stories. 1894.
A Little Princess: Being the Whole Story of Sara Crewe Now Told for the First Time.
    1905.
The Secret Garden. 1911.
The Lost Prince. 1915.

Studies of Frances Hodgson Burnett

Bixler, Phyllis. *Frances Hodgson Burnett.* Boston: G. K. Hall, 1984.
———. "The Oral-Formulaic Training of a Popular Fiction Writer: Frances Hodgson
    Burnett." *Journal of Popular Culture* 15 (Spring 1982): 42–52.
Gohlke, Madelon. "Rereading *The Secret Garden.*" *College English* 41 (April 1980):
    894–902.
Keyser, Elizabeth Lennox. " 'Quite Contrary': Frances Hodgson Burnett's *The Secret
    Garden.*" *Children's Literature* 11 (1983): 1–13.
Paul, Lissa. "Enigma Variations: What Feminist Theory Knows About Children's Literature." *Signal* 54 (Sept. 1987): 186–201.

Lady Isabel Arundell Burton
(1831–1896)

Samuel J. Rogal

BIOGRAPHY

Descendant of an established Roman Catholic family, Isabel Arundell received her education at the convent of the Canonesses of the Holy Sepulchre, near Chelmsford. Continuing her studies at Boulogne, she met the explorer and scholar Richard Francis Burton (1821–1890) in 1850; their romance dates from 1856, when they met again. Isabel Arundell felt destined to marry Richard Burton after a gypsy told her fortune. Religious differences and parental disapproval stalled their marriage until January 1861. Following the marriage, Burton involved herself in her husband's propensity for travel and writing, becoming his amanuensis and travel companion. Her husband encouraged her to generate her own travel narratives, and her pieces achieved their own popularity. Burton's travel pieces show the learning and vitality she brought to her life. Burton wrote, "I wish I were a man. If I were I would be Richard Burton; but, being only a woman, I would be Richard Burton's wife" (Blanch 43).

Burton's principal project focused upon her passion for advancing her husband's professional and literary career. She regarded Sir Richard as the most significant, but the least appreciated, Englishman of his day. By her influence she had him transferred from his consular appointment in West Africa to Brazil, where drink and dissipation became his principal concerns. Then she managed a transfer to the consulate in Damascus, then to Trieste. At the last post, the couple, although both ill, spent time traveling through south central and eastern Europe, Asia, Arabia, Egypt, and India—retracing steps of Sir Richard's former explorations. In the interim, Lady Burton worked on her husband's biography and prepared an edition of his works. When Richard Burton died in 1890 from bronchial and heart problems, his widow designed a tentlike mausoleum for his tomb, complete with camel bells. For the last six years of her life, Lady Isabel continued efforts to preserve his memory. In 1891, she received a government pension of £250. Returning to London, she took up residence with a widowed sister in Baker Street, where she died of ovarian cancer.

MAJOR WORKS AND THEMES

While attempting to elevate her husband to the pinnacle of personal and literary fame, Burton chose, in her two major books of travel narrative, to satisfy what she believed to be the intellectual needs and demands of her feminine audience. "I have followed my husband everywhere," she wrote in the "Preface" to *The Inner Life of Syria, Palestine, and the Holy Land*, "gleaning only woman's lore, and I hope that the daily jottings of my private journal will yield a sketch of the inner life of the Holy Land in general. . . . I wish to convey an idea of the life which an Englishwoman may make for herself in the East" (1: vii). A woman who enjoyed every opportunity for travel that life offered her, Burton escaped the ordinary: "The ladies [of Bombay] soon become listless, their eyes are sad, their lives are dull. They always look tired, and I do not wonder. They get up about nine, breakfast, and pay or receive visits; then tiffin, siesta, a drive to the Apollo Bunder to hear the band, or to meet their husbands at the Fort, dine, and bed, is the programme of the day" (*Arabia, Egypt, India* 259).

Burton presents herself as a woman writing for women, as well as a Roman Catholic writer. When, in August 1880, Sir Richard obtained ten days' sick leave from his consulate, she chose that they should travel to the Bavarian village of Oberammergau, known for its Passion Play, composed in the fourteenth century by the monks at Rothenbuch. Her prose description of this lengthy play conveys to readers the impression that she enjoyed pure theater more than she did the theme of the piece. Even upon the pages of the biography of her husband and of her own memoirs, Isabel Burton remains the travel writer and the amanuensis, relying heavily upon Richard Burton's published narratives, his journals, their conversations, and remembrances of her own experiences while traveling with him.

CRITICAL RECEPTION

Burton's contemporaries saw her as a subsidiary to her husband. She contributed greatly to his reputation by editing, introducing, and seeing his works through the press. She has been charged with vandalism in her wish to secure her husband's reputation by burning his papers and manuscripts after his death. As late as 1975, Joanna Richardson wrote of an Isabel Burton whose major functions in life allowed her only to "admire the scenery . . . or to tame her vagabond husband and see that he performed his consular duties." No doubt the unkindest cut of all came from a *New York Times* review of Lesley Blanche's 1954 collective biography, exposing unenlightened readers to "the fat, plain, dumpy neurotic wife of Ruffian Dick [Burton]." The literary reputation of Isabel

Burton has risen recently because of attention to the contribution of nineteenth-century women writers of prose nonfiction to the literary milieu.

BIBLIOGRAPHY

None of Isabel Burton's works are currently in print.

Selected Works by Isabel Burton

The Inner Life of Syria, Palestine, and the Holy Land. From My Private Journal. 1875.
Arabia, Egypt, India. A Narrative of Travel. 1879.
The Life of Captain Richard F. Burton. 1893.
The Romance of Lady Isabel Burton. The Story of Her Life. Told in Part by Herself and in part by W. H. Wilkins. 1897.
The Passion-Play at Ober-Ammergau. 1900.

Studies of Isabel Burton

Blanch, Lesley. *Wilder Shores of Love*. New York: Simon and Schuster, 1954.
Bowen, Elizabeth. "Lady Burton." In *Collected Impressions*. New York: Alfred A. Knopf, 1950. 98–100.
Burton, Jean. *Sir Richard Burton's Wife*. New York: Alfred A Knopf, 1941.
Casada, James A. *Sir Richard F. Burton: A Bibliographical Study*. Boston: G. K. Hall, 1990.
Curtis, Georgina P. "Isabel, Lady Burton." *Catholic World* 72 (1900): 93.
Gower, Amelia Aylmer. "Sir Richard Burton." *Belgravia* 84 (1894): 146.
"Isabel Burton." In *Personal Records*. Ed. Margaret Florence Bottrall. London: Rupert Hart-Davis, 1961. 113–16, 217–18.
Johnson, E. G. "Lady Isabel Burton." *The Dial* 22 (1897): 355.
Linton, Eliza Lynn. "The Partisans of the Wild Women." *Nineteenth Century* (March 1892): 455–64.
Lovell, Mary S. *A Rage to Live: A Biography of Richard and Isabel Burton*. New York: W. W. Norton, 1998.
McCarthy, Justin. "Sir Richard and Lady Burton." In *Portraits of the Sixties*. New York: Harper Brothers, 1903. 171–78.
Pfeiffer, John R. "Isabel Arundell Burton." In *British Travel Writers, 1837–1875*. Ed. Barbara Brothers and Julia Gergits. *Dictionary of Literary Biography*. Detroit: Gale Research, 1996. 166: 91–97.
Richardson, Joanna. "Sir Richard and Lady Burton." *History Today* 25 (May 1975): 323–31.

Josephine Butler
(1828-1906)

Ann Heilmann

BIOGRAPHY

Feminist social reformer, political writer, and activist Josephine Butler was born to Northumberland gentry and later lived in Oxford, Cheltenham, and Liverpool. Raised in an environment that combined radical liberalism, an ardent belief in human equality, and deep religious faith, she soon became sensitized to social problems. Religious doubts engendered a sense of divine mission, while early contact with public figures laid the political groundwork for her career as a radical social purity campaigner who mobilized the opposition to child abuse and the state regulation of prostitution.

Butler's most significant contribution to Victorian feminism was to establish sexual oppression as the root cause of women's social, legal, and economic subordination. Keenly aware of the politically divisive function of class and capable of intense emotional empathy, she preached the principle of sisterhood. Her spiritual fervor and tactical skills (the display of dignified femininity and the contesting of governmental seats in by-elections) influenced the suffragettes. Prefiguring modern radical feminism in her intuitive conceptualization of the personal as the political, Butler was a polemicist rather than a theorist.

Her egalitarian marriage (1852–1890) to an enlightened educationalist and radical Anglican priest, by whom she had four children, furnished the domestic and psychological support needed to sustain her political work. Encouraged by her friendship with prominent feminists (Jessie Boucherett, Anne Jemima Clough, Elizabeth Wolstenholme), she entered the public domain in the 1860s, promoting marital reform and female enfranchisement and acting as president of the North of England Council for Promoting the Higher Education of Women. Her daughter's death channeled her energies into moral reform.

After taking "fallen" women into her home and establishing two refuges, Butler scandalized Victorian moralists in 1869 by accepting the leadership of the Ladies' National Association for the Repeal of the Contagious Diseases (CD) Acts. Three Acts (1864–1868) passed to stem the spread of syphilis in the military gave a nonuniformed police force in eleven garrison towns summary powers to arrest, and enforce gynecological examinations on, any woman suspected of prostitution. Abuse of police power was endemic, and as Butler was quick to point out, the acts institutionalized the sexual double standard by victimizing working-class women. Vilified by supporters of the acts, Butler nevertheless gained widespread recognition. In 1874 she retired from the abolitionist leadership in order to concentrate on the international aspects of prostitution and child trafficking.

Following the repeal of the CD Acts in 1883–1886, Butler was largely responsible for the raising of girls' age of consent from twelve to sixteen. A tireless activist into her old age despite frequent illness and the loss of her husband, Butler edited three journals—*Shield* (1870–1886), *Dawn* (1888–1896), and *Storm-Bell* (1898–1900)—and continued to take a stand on sociopolitical matters until her death.

MAJOR WORKS AND THEMES

An accomplished pamphleteer, Butler produced some ninety tracts, articles, and books. "The Education and Employment of Women" and the Introduction to her collection *Woman's Work* highlighted the link between women's economic and sexual exploitation, pleading for improved educational and professional opportunities. In simple and clear language expressive of her oratorical skills, "Letter to My Countrywomen" explains the operation of the CD Acts, whereas "An Appeal to the People of England" and *The Constitution Violated* (1871) argue that they infringe the Magna Carta. *The Hour Before the Dawn* (1876) and "Social Purity" were written for the Social Purity Alliance, an organization Butler left when it adopted repressive policies. Not a prohibitionist as such, she was primarily concerned with the sexual abuse of women, not with individuals' moral lapses, and was dismayed when the National Vigilance Association endorsed measures that targeted prostitutes.

In later life Butler engaged with international politics. Although promoting Irish Home Rule (*Our Christianity*, 1887) and indicting the colonization of Indian women's bodies (*The Abolitionist Cause in Relation to British India*, 1895), she defended British military action against the Boers in *Native Races and the War* (1900). The book alienated many of her radical friends, yet its religious fervor and use of slavery as a metaphor for the condition of women provide a connection with earlier writings.

In addition, Butler produced two biographies of religious figures and wrote four autobiographical accounts, acknowledging her debt to her father (*Memoir of John Grey*, 1874), husband (*Recollections of George Butler*, 1892), and sister (*Harriet Meuricoffre*, 1901), as well as her *Personal Reminiscenes of a Great Crusade* (1896).

CRITICAL RECEPTION

As a woman who broke the sexual conspiracy of silence, Butler, disparaged by conservative contemporaries as "worse than a prostitute," became a role model for fin de siècle feminists, inspiring Sarah Grand's* *The Heavenly Twins* (1893). W. T. Stead's *Josephine Butler* (1887) set the tone for early twentieth-century accounts, with Millicent Fawcett and E. M. Turner's biography (1927) and Ray Strachey's *The Cause* (1928) celebrating her as a feminist heroine.

Unlike other Victorian feminists, Butler has received some degree of critical attention throughout this century, probably because her concern with sexuality was considered relevant even when her feminism was not. The establishment of women's studies has generated a number of appraisals, with emphasis recently shifting to Butler's colonial discourse.

SELECTED BIBLIOGRAPHY

Selected works on education and prostitution are accessible on microfiche, as are Butler's letters and periodicals (IDC, 3265 Johnson Ave., Riverdale, NY 10463). The Fawcett Library (London Guildhall University) has extensive holdings; see: http://www.lgu.ac.uk/fawcett/main.htm. For "The Crusade Against State Regulation of Vice," see: http://www.indiana.edu/~letrs/vwwp/butler/thoughts.html. Educational information can be accessed at: http://www.spartacus.schoolnet.co.uk. A multivolume anthology of Butler's works edited by Ingrid Sharp is forthcoming with Routledge Thoemmes Press (London).

Works by Josephine Butler

"The Education and Employment of Women." 1868. *The Education Papers*. Ed. Dale Spender. Routledge & Kegan Paul, 1987. 69–89.
"Introduction" to *Woman's Work and Woman's Culture*. 1869. British Library Microfiche Publications, 1987. vi–lxiv.
"An Appeal to the People of England." 1870. *The Sexuality Debates*. Ed. Sheila Jeffreys. Routledge & Kegan Paul, 1987. 111–50.
The Constitution Violated. 1871.
"Letter to My Countrywomen." (1871). *Sexuality Debates*. 151–69.
The Hour Before the Dawn. 1876.
"Social Purity." 1879. *Sexuality Debates*. 170–89.
Personal Reminiscences of a Great Crusade. 1896. British Library Microfiche Publications, 1987.
The Josephine Butler Letter Collection. IDC Publishers, 1983.

Studies of Josephine Butler

Boyd, Nancy. *Josephine Butler, Octavia Hill, Florence Nightingale*. London: Macmillan, 1982.
Burton, Antoinette. "Josephine Butler on Slavery, Citizenship, and the Boer War." *Social Politics* (1998): 338–61.

Butler, A.S.G. *Portrait of Josephine Butler*. London: Faber & Faber, 1954.

Caine, Barbara. *Victorian Feminists*. Oxford: Oxford University Press, 1992.

Forster, Margaret. *Significant Sisters*. Harmondsworth: Penguin, 1984.

Johnson, G. W., and L. A. Johnson. *Josephine Butler*. Bristol: Arrowsmith, 1909.

Petrie, Glen. *A Singular Iniquity*. London: Macmillan, 1971.

Uglow, Jennifer. "Josephine Butler." In *Feminist Theorists*. Ed. Dale Spender. London: Women's Press, 1983. 146–64.

Walkowitz, Judith R. *Prostitution and Victorian Society*. New York: Cambridge University Press, 1980.

Alice Mona Caird
(1854–1932)

Catherine J. Golden

BIOGRAPHY

Though little known today, the feminist novelist and journalist Alice Mona Alison Caird was once the best-known and most criticized feminist in Britain. Her 1888 essay entitled "Marriage" caused a sensation after it was picked up by the popular press. She was thirty-four years old and near the start of her professional writing career.

The available biographical material that exists on Caird is scant and sketchy. As Margaret Gullette notes, "There is no autobiography, no journal, no biography. . . . [E]ven a short life story is more of an archeological reconstruction than usual" (519). Born at Ryde, on the Isle of Wight, on 24 May 1854 (not in 1858 as has erroneously been noted), Alice Mona Alison was an "only daughter," as described in an account by Victor Plarr (166). Her mother, Matilde Ann Jane Hector, came from a wealthy Schleswig-Holstein family. Matilde married John Alison, a Scottish inventor and engineer twenty-two years her senior who made his living as a landed proprietor. The Alisons eventually moved to Lancaster Gate, Kensington, in London.

Caird began writing in a range of genres from a young age (Gullette 519–20). Little else is known of her childhood. Although she never received a formal university education, she read widely in a range of disciplines including sociology, economics, history, feminist thought, philosophy, and science (McKinney 625–26).

At the age of twenty-three, Alice Mona Alison married a wealthy Scottish landowner named James Alexander Caird. James came from a distinguished family: His celebrated agronomist father was knighted; his mother descended from the medieval Scottish poet Robert Henryson. A mild and liberal man, James Caird possessed 1,782 acres at Cassencary, their ancestral home near

Creetown, along the southwest Scottish coast; this setting is fictionalized in Caird's best-known novel, *The Daughters of Danaus* (1894).

At the time of her marriage, Caird was already involved in the ongoing debate regarding the Woman Question. Her husband did not prevent her from developing her feminist interests or her writing career. The 1880s public, fascinated by Caird, was eager to know if the "anti-marriage" woman was happily married (Gullette 518). As a young woman, she was seemingly not prepared for marriage—a point she generalizes in her fiction and nonfiction. Although she kept her personal life private, anecdotal evidence suggests hers was a relatively happy marriage. Caird had one son, Alister, born on 22 March 1884, leading Gullette to suspect she used the birth control practices she promoted (518).

First a novelist, then an essayist, Caird alternated between the two genres. Publishing her first two novels under a pseudonym, she produced six fictional works by the end of the nineteenth century including *The Wing of Azrael* (1889), *A Romance of the Moors* (1891, a short story collection), *The Daughters of Danaus* (1894), and *The Pathway of the Gods* (1898). In 1888, her famous indictment of "Marriage" appeared in the *Westminster Review*, a radical quarterly earlier associated with the work of John Stuart Mill. Caird, who promoted ideal marriages of equality, critiqued the sacred Victorian institutions of marriage and motherhood. She published her most celebrated polemical essays in a collection entitled *The Morality of Marriage and Other Essays on the Status and Destiny of Women* (1897).

Moving to London, Caird became part of an intellectual and artistic circle that included her close friends Elizabeth and William Sharp. Elizabeth shared Caird's interests in music and feminism, and the poet William Sharp introduced Caird to Dante Gabriel Rossetti, Walter Pater, Dr. Garnett, and J. A. Symonds. As her own reputation as a writer grew, she became acquainted with other liberal women writers including Dinah Maria Mulock Craik* and Augusta Webster* (McKinney 626). In the 1880s, she was connected to, but did not join, the Men and Women's Club, whose members included Emma Brooke, Olive Schreiner,* Karl Pearson, and Annie Wood Besant.* Caird did join the most egalitarian feminist club of London, the Pioneer. Also a fervent anti-vivisectionist, Caird became president of the Independent Anti-Vivisection League when George Bernard Shaw and Besant were also members.

Writing with less frequency and less intensity after the turn of the century, Caird gradually lost her audience. Surviving her husband by eleven years, she, nonetheless, wrote until one year prior to her own death in London on 4 February 1932.

MAJOR WORKS AND THEMES

The rights of women are foremost in Caird's novels and essays. She wrote to advance the women's movement. In her fictional work, Caird likens the institution of marriage to slavery and prison. She criticized the private home, arguing that women should be recognized and rewarded for maintaining it. At a time when motherhood was sacred, she censured it, calling it a supreme sacrifice. Moreover, Caird believed parents were often not the best equipped to raise their children; strikingly modern, she preferred child rearing be left to those "who have a natural gift for the work" (*Morality of Marriage* 154) (the "gifted," according to Caird, would also undergo training in child development). Likewise, her early novels offer unsatisfactory, if not tragic, depictions of marriage and motherhood. In *The Wing of Azrael* (1889), Caird pairs a despicable patriarch with a tormented wife; driven to murder her husband, the wife Viola is punished as well: She commits suicide. *The Daughters of Danaus* (1894) suggests the New Woman need not be martyred in her struggle to gain equality. Still, she leaves her heroine Hadria struggling against weighty burdens of family, marriage, and unsatisfactory motherhood. These two novels demonstrate Caird's anti-Emersonian conviction that for women in nineteenth-century society circumstance is more powerful than will. Caird's subsequent novels, including *The Pathway of the Gods* (1898), *The Stones of Sacrifice* (1915), and *The Great Wave* (1931), offer more hopeful, egalitarian fictional marriages.

Caird's essays, published in journals including *The Ladies Realm, Westminster Review, Fortnightly Review*, and *Nineteenth Century*, remain insightful today. For example, in "Does Marriage Hinder a Woman's Self-development" (1899; reprinted with *Daughters of Danaus*, 1989), Caird cleverly reverses the dynamics of gender to show how a stay-at-home husband in a female-dominated society cannot realize his scientific aspirations when saddled with housekeeping and child-rearing responsibilities. In this and other impassioned essays about marriage, the home, and children of the future, Caird shows her investment in the hotly debated Woman Question as well as her tireless commitment to the advancement of women's rights.

Caird also wrote on the topic of animal rights and embedded her convictions in her novels. For example, in *The Daughters of Danaus*, Professor Fortescue, the New Man figure, risks his reputation in the scientific world by arguing for anti-vivisection, and Hadria's unsatisfactory husband criticizes her for not having ample meat in the larder. Concerned for the welfare of women and animals, Caird also decried Fascism in her fiction.

CRITICAL RECEPTION

Caird's indictment of marriage roused unprecedented interest and "got the nineties going a little early" (Gullette 493). The *Daily Telegraph* picked up Caird's scathing 1888 critique entitled "Marriage" in a letters to the editor column called "Is Marriage a Failure?"; roughly 27,000 responses were received. Though relatively unknown before this publication, Caird became both celebrated and condemned overnight. A prominent challenger to the women's movement, Eliza Lynn Linton* wrote an essay against Caird's "Marriage" titled "The Wild Women" (1891); Caird retorted in an essay entitled "A Defence of the So-

Called 'Wild Women' " (1892; reprinted in Susan Hamilton's 1995 edition). Some of her contemporaries considered Caird " 'an unwearying pioneer of humanity' " (qtd. in Gullette 498). Her popularity, in part, can be attributed to the late Victorian fascination with the Woman Question.

Caird's fictional work as a whole did not receive much critical notice, which accounts in part for the limited biographical and critical material available today. Still, when it was first published, *The Daughters of Danaus*—now considered Caird's best work—earned gratitude from countless women readers and praise in *Shafts*, a feminist monthly that devoted parts of four issues to reviewing and quoting from it. While one *Shafts* reviewer deemed *The Daughters of Danaus* " 'one of the best books the century has produced' " (qtd. in Gullette 498), mainstream British, Scottish, and Irish papers lambasted it for its radical message about women's rights.

The 1970s reconfiguration of the literary canon and the growing interest in New Woman fiction have brought more attention to Caird, whose arguments for women's emancipation have received more praise than her artistry. A. R. Cunningham, Gail Cunningham, and Martha Vicinus, among others, refer to Caird in their discussions of New Woman fiction. *The Daughters of Danaus*, reprinted in 1989, offers readers of today a brutal critique of nineteenth-century marriage and motherhood and a compelling, outspoken feminist heroine, Hadria Fullerton Temperley, who has professional aspirations to be a composer. Moreover, Gullette, in the only published essay devoted exclusively to Caird, considers *Daughters of Danaus* "a bridge between the narrowly marriage-focused fictions of the nineteenth century and the more open-ended midlife novels that came thirty years after, such as D. H. Lawrence's *St. Mawr* and Virginia Woolf's *Mrs. Dalloway*" (503).

Caird is still less known in the 1990s than other rediscovered New Woman novelists including George Egerton,* Olive Schreiner, and Sarah Grand.* Her literary and journalistic contributions to feminism, however, warrant further examination.

BIBLIOGRAPHY

Of her fiction, only *The Daughters of Danaus* (Feminist Press, 1989) is in print. Her essays have recently been reprinted in *"Criminals, Idiots, Women, & Minors": Victorian Writing by Women on Women* (Broadview, 1996) and *Prose by Victorian Women: An Anthology* (Garland, 1996).

Selected Works by Alice Mona Caird

The Wing of Azrael. 1889.
A Romance of the Moors. 1891.
A Sentimental View of Vivisection. 1893.
The Daughters of Danaus. 1894.

The Morality of Marriage and Other Essays on the Status and Destiny of Women. 1897.
The Pathway of the Gods. 1898.
The Stones of Sacrifice. 1915.
The Great Wave. 1931.

Studies of Alice Mona Caird

Cunningham, A. R. "The 'New Woman Fiction' of the 1890's." *Victorian Studies* (Dec. 1973): 177–86.
Cunningham, Gail. *The New Woman in the Victorian Novel.* London: Macmillan, 1978.
Gullette, Margaret Morganroth. "Afterword." *The Daughters of Danaus.* New York: Feminist Press, 1989. 493–534.
McKinney, Lauren D. Introduction to "Mona Alison Caird." In *Prose by Victorian Women.* Ed. Andrea Broomfield and Sally Mitchell. New York: Garland, 1996. 625–28.
Plarr, Victor. *Men and Women of the Time: A Dictionary of Contemporaries.* 15th ed. London: George Routledge & Sons, 1899.
Vicinus, Martha. "Rediscovering the 'New Woman' of the 1890s: The Stories of 'George Egerton.' " In *Feminist Re-Visions: What Has Been and Might Be.* Ed. Vivian Patraka and Louise A. Tilly. Ann Arbor: University of Michigan Women's Studies Program, 1983. 12–25.

Jane Welsh Carlyle
(1801–1866)

Jean Wasko

BIOGRAPHY

Little in the scholarship related to Jane Welsh Carlyle is uncomplicated. Despite her claim to literary fame as one of the nineteenth century's foremost letter writers, her life, "in the Valley of the shadow" of Thomas Carlyle, seems always marginal (*Letters* 2: 74). Even those works focusing on "the Carlyles," one of Victorian England's most intriguing couples, continue to confront the problems posed by the "Froude Controversy," as biographers attempt to prove that Thomas Carlyle either worshipped his clever wife or sacrificed her genius so that she might shield him from life's ordinary trials.

Indeed, Jane Baillie Welsh, born in Haddington in 1801, gave early signs of great promise. Her father, Dr. John Welsh, the educated descendant of Scottish farmers, provided instruction for his adored daughter that suited her quick wits. She studied mathematics and Latin and produced a body of juvenilia that forecast a literary future. In 1821, Edward Irving, a tutor, in love with the "the belle of Haddington," introduced Jane Welsh to a fellow tutor, Thomas Carlyle, who instructed his "fair pupil" in German literature and encouraged her to pursue a life of the intellect. Although a disparity in social class, coupled with Carlyle's constitutional melancholy, made marriage untenable, an epistolary courtship, ideally suited to these two great letter writers, ended in marriage in 1826. Jane Welsh, it has been said, married Thomas Carlyle for his promise of genius, and for better or for worse, another subject for much speculation, he delivered beyond her imaginings.

Two years after their marriage, the Carlyles removed to Craigenputtock, a remote farm, where Jane Carlyle began what many view as a life of sacrifice. While Carlyle continued to speak of Jane's authorship, of her promise, the Craigenputtock years seemed to seal Jane's fate as buffer between Thomas Carlyle and a noisy, demanding world. Following the publication of *Sartor Resartus*, which made Carlyle the literary lion he was to remain for the rest of his days, the Carlyles took up permanent residence in Cheyne Row, London. There, life for Thomas Carlyle involved both the unremitting agony of literary production and a growing reputation as the leading thinker of the age, whereas Jane became absorbed in running a household, silencing the roosters, dogs, and parrots that threatened Carlyle's peace, suffering a series of illnesses including a serious depression, earning a reputation as a sparkling conversationalist, and always, until her death in 1866, writing letters.

While Jane Carlyle seemed to give up Jane Welsh's dreams of literary achievement, her authorship, part of the fabric of daily life, went largely unrecognized. Yet the Duke-Edinburgh edition of the Carlyle letters, when it is complete, will offer 3,500 of Jane Carlyle's brilliant letters, made possible, perhaps, by her rejection of a literary career and her immersion in the details of domestic life essential to her epistolary art.

MAJOR WORKS AND THEMES

Jane Carlyle's literary production is, with a few exceptions, entirely epistolary, and her letters offer a social history of nineteenth-century London, boasting interviews with luminaries ranging from Dickens to Darwin. Although Carlyle herself once noted that her only claim to literary fame lay in her talent for silencing offensive animals, Charles Richard Sanders, first editor of *The Collected Letters*, cites her ability to "pick up every diamond-spark, out of the common dust floor and keep it brightly available" (*Collected Letters* 1: x). Indeed, Carlyle's letters open a window on the life of a Victorian housewife, preoccupied with preparing porridge for a dyspeptic husband, redecorating her home, firing servants, banishing bedbugs, and maintaining domestic tranquility against overwhelming odds. In addition, they offer pen-portraits of her contemporaries, the leading writers and thinkers of the age, with echoes of their speech and analyses of their themes, including the Woman Question, the theory of evolution, and the crisis in faith. Intimately acquainted with the domestic side of genius, however, Jane Carlyle treated the great ideas of the age with skepticism.

Her penchant for irony highlights the gender issues that are central to her work. Living with a "sage" with a grandiose and tragic view of life, Jane Carlyle had need of the leveling power of humor, much of it directed toward debunking the self-important patriarchal world of Victorian England, incarnated in Thomas Carlyle. Moreover, since his genius was made manifest through writing and since her life was shaped by the agony of his work, Jane Carlyle struck out frequently against the tyranny of authorship and the masculine authority it conveys, finding in parody her most effective weapon for closing the gap between the lion and the lady.

In spite of her irony, however, Jane Carlyle maintains the decorum prescribed by the eighteenth-century aesthetic that requires that letters be frank, natural, spontaneous, and conversational in idiom. While her letters sparkle with the wit that is the special province of the Augustan letter writer, Jane Carlyle used her talent for conversational prose and for the dramatization of domestic life to construct a literary persona, allowing her to avoid speaking from her own heart. In donning a particular mask for a particular audience, focusing on fact to avoid feeling, and creating a subject "I" distinctly different from the authorial "I," Jane Carlyle demonstrates the complex narratology of the familiar letter, belied by eighteenth-century prescriptions.

CRITICAL RECEPTION

In a bibliographic essay, written in 1973, G. B. Tennyson raised questions about Jane Carlyle's stature as a writer: "If Jane is the commanding letter writer that her partisans claim her to be, there should be more serious criticism of her work than there is" (110). More than a decade later, in a review of volumes 10 through 12 of *The Collected Letters*, Fred Kaplan, noting the lack of scholarship generated by the letters, asks if they are being read (53). In fact, epistolary criticism has been hampered both by the lack of an aesthetic framework for criticism and by a more problematic tendency to dismiss the genre entirely. Thus in a forward to *The Collected Poems of Thomas and Jane Welsh Carlyle*, G. B. Tennyson notes that Jane Carlyle's poems, which have "some of the qualities of her engaging letters," lead "many to see her as a lost literary artist." However, in the final analysis, he concludes, "[I]t may be that Jane's greatest talent in literature lay in inspiring others" (xviii).

This view of letters, however, is changing as a result of efforts to expand the canon with various forms of vernacular literature. While twenty years ago, Charles Richard Sanders and Elizabeth Hardwick stood almost alone in providing the kind of criticism needed to establish Carlyle's reputation as an important writer, a number of recent essays, building on the foundation of an expanded canon, make significant contributions to Carlyle scholarship. In particular, work in the area of autobiography has provided impetus for several essays examining the letters of Jane Carlyle as female self-inscription. Jean Wasko argues that Carlyle "creates a subversive mode of autobiography . . . characterized by a fragmented and fluid idea of the self" as a corrective to the coherent autobiographical subject erected in the works of her husband. Sharon Hileman, also reading the letters as autobiography, recognizes complexities in epistolary narratology that have been obscured by eighteenth-century assumptions, calling attention to the disjunction between the authorial "I" and the "I" as subject and between the created reader and the actual reader(s). These studies create an opening for examining letters as female narratives that dissolve traditional boundaries between reader and writer. The long-awaited close reading of the letters of Jane Welsh Carlyle is sure to provide much-needed direction for scholars interested in the fertile field of the familiar letter.

BIBLIOGRAPHY

When the Duke-Edinburgh Edition is complete, all the known letters of Jane Carlyle will be available. Until that time, readers will have to rely on earlier collections.

Works by Jane Carlyle

Letters and Memorials of Jane Welsh Carlyle Prepared for Publication by Thomas Carlyle. Ed. James Anthony Froude. 2 vols. 1883.
New Letters and Memorials of Jane Welsh Carlyle: Annotated by Thomas Carlyle. Ed. Alexander Carlyle. 2 vols. 1903.
The Collected Letters of Thomas and Jane Welsh Carlyle. Duke-Edinburgh Edition. Ed. Charles Richard Sanders, Clyde deL. Ryals, and Kenneth Fielding. 27 vols. completed. 1970–1999. The Carlyle letters are now complete through 1852.
I Too Am Here: Selections from the Letters of Jane Welsh Carlyle. Ed. Alan and Mary McQueen Simpson. 1977.
The Collected Poems of Thomas and Jane Welsh Carlyle. Ed. Rodger L. Tarr and Fleming McClelland. 1986.

Studies of Jane Carlyle

Bloom, Abigail Burnham. "Jane Welsh Carlyle: Review of Recent Research (1974–1987)." *The Carlyle Annual* 10 (1989): 93–98.
Christianson, Aileen. "Jane Welsh Carlyle's Private Writing Career." In *A History of Scottish Women's Writing*. Ed. Douglas Gifford and Dorothy McMillan. Edinburgh: Edinburgh University Press, 1997. 232–45.
———. "Rewriting Herself: Jane Welsh Carlyle's Letters." *Scotlands* 2 (1994): 47–52.
Clarke, Norma. *Ambitious Heights: Writing, Friendship, Love—The Jewsbury Sisters, Felicia Hemans, and Jane Welsh Carlyle*. London: Routledge, 1990.
Hardwick, Elizabeth. *Seduction and Betrayal: Women and Literature*. New York: Random House, 1970.
Hileman, Sharon. "Autobiographical Narrative in the Letters of Jane Carlyle." *A/B: Auto/Biography* 4.2 (1988): 107–17.
Kaplan, Fred. "The Emerging Carlyle." Rev. of *The Collected Letters of Thomas and Jane Welsh Carlyle, vols. 10 and 12. The Arnoldian* 13 (1986): 53–56.
Skabernicki, Anne M. "Seeing Jane Plain: Recovering the Art of Welsh Carlyle." *Modern Language Studies* 27.3–4 (1997): 47–65.
———. "Two Faces of Eve: The Literary Personae of Harriet Martineau and Jane Welsh Carlyle." *The Carlyle Annual* 11 (1990): 15–30.
Tennyson. G. B. "Jane Welsh Carlyle." In *Victorian Prose: A Guide to Research*. Ed. David DeLaura. New York: MLA, 1973. 105–12.
Wasko, Jean. "The Angel in the Envelope: The Letters of Jane Welsh Carlyle." *Modern Language Studies* 27.3–4 (1997): 3–18.

Mary Cholmondeley
(1859-1925)

Carol Huebscher Rhoades

BIOGRAPHY

Mary Cholmondeley, most known for her 1899 best-seller *Red Pottage*, was born on 8 June 1859 at her father's vicarage in Hodnet, Shropshire. Educated at home, Cholmondeley grew up with the novels of Sir Walter Scott, Maria Edgeworth,* Jane Austen,* and George Eliot,* as well as theological works by William Paley, Frederic Farrar, and Joseph Butler. To amuse herself during frequent childhood illnesses, Cholmondeley wrote stories, later shifting her ambitions to novel writing, after realizing she would not likely become a great painter. At sixteen, Cholmondeley ran her father's large household while continuing to hone her writing skills and publishing stories anonymously in the *Graphic* in the 1880s.

Her first novel, *The Danvers Jewels* (1887) was serialized in the *Temple Bar*, before book publication by Bentley, as were her next three novels, *Sir Charles Danvers* (1889), *Diana Tempest* (1893), and *A Devotee* (1897). While these works were popular, none of her books either before or after received the sales and critical acclaim of *Red Pottage* (1899). Cholmondeley was then living in London and socializing with other writers, such as Henry James, Howard Sturgis, Rhoda Broughton,* and the Findlater sisters, who considered her intelligent, witty, and discerning. Despite persistent illness, Cholmondeley continued to publish short stories, novels, and a family history and to dramatize *Diana Tempest* and *Red Pottage*. She died on 15 July 1925 after several years of failing health.

MAJOR WORKS AND THEMES

Cholmondeley aspired to write serious moralistic novels in the manner of George Eliot and tempered by Emerson's Transcendentalism. While her main female characters tend to be strong-willed and have socially conscientious ambitions as well as the desire to be on an equal footing with men intellectually, they seek societal transformation through the moral and spiritual values of an earlier era rather than the more political and economical venues of the 1890s New Woman. The world of Cholmondeley's novels is further distanced from the period by the upper-class characters who cling to their family estates and traditional notions of honor and duty. Although the novels' conclusions confirm these more conservative values, the texts provide ample evidence, through irony and wit, of Cholmondeley's awareness of the foibles and stifling provincialism of the landed gentry. Through moments of irony, Cholmondeley strongly criticizes woman's position, Christian intolerance, and false intellectualism. However, with the exceptions of *Diana Tempest* and *Red Pottage*, the moralizing in the novels is too heavy-handed to be effective.

The Danvers Jewels, clearly influenced by sensationalist novels, has too much absurdity to completely engage the reader. Indeed, the only hair-raising scene occurs when the detective reveals Aurelia's wickedness by exposing the black hair under her blond wig. Cholmondeley's more serious concerns emerge in *Sir Charles Danvers*, in which the rakish Charles of the first novel is transformed into the sensitive and sensible inheritor of the family estate. It is clear early on that serious and dutiful Ruth will become his wife, but she does so only after a false engagement that is quite melodramatically ended by the appearance of a shrill American wife. Woman's duty versus happiness is explored in the novel but is unsatisfactorily explicated as the text veers from sensational scenes to Ruth's thinking made vague by Cholmondeley's displacement of moral and ethical questioning from the characters to the narrator. This tendency is moderated in *Diana Tempest* as the main character voices her concerns, seriously and wittily expressing her desire for marriage without illusions and with mutual respect. The sensational still looms large with murder intrigues that simultaneously underscore Cholmondeley's support for a morally conscientious aristocracy responsibly maintaining family rights and duties. Later novels, such as *Notwithstanding* (1913), affirm Cholmondeley's continued belief in that social order.

Cholmondeley's mixture of serious intent and wit is most felicitous in *Red Pottage* where the Reverend Gresley's pompous and provincial religiosity is satirized in counterpoint to the respect given to the aesthetic and critical development of his sister Hester. The desirability of women's profound intellectualism is reinforced by the contrast with Sibyll, the butterfly of *A Devotee*, whose shallow intellectualism is further ridiculed in *Red Pottage*. Likewise, Cholmondeley critiques true and false friendship and partnership. Serious women in the novel are sustained psychologically and spiritually by a sisterhood of true minds.

While Cholmondeley's concerns with social issues, particularly women's intellectual rights, are explored in later novels, she increasingly emphasized individual psychology. *Prisoners* (1906) delineates the deleterious effects of a selfish woman on individuals and society. In contrast, the playlet "Votes for

Men" (1909) pinpoints the absurdities of Britain's refusal to honor women's suffrage by reversing gender roles and examining power positions.

CRITICAL RECEPTION

Most critics agree that *Red Pottage* is Cholmondeley's best work, although *Diana Tempest* was also well received and has much to recommend it. When first published, most of Cholmondeley's novels were cited for their psychological and societal insights. Always considered a good but not top-ranking novelist, Cholmondeley's reputation was short-lived. *Red Pottage*, which sold over 26,000 copies almost immediately in 1899, has been revived twice to very little critical notice. Judged aesthetically deficient by Elaine Showalter (*A Literature of Their Own* [Princeton, 1977]) and insufficiently strong in its feminism by others, the book receives a deeper reading by Catherine Rainwater and William Scheick who investigate its "feminist system of human and aesthetic values" as "a superior alternative to certain conventionally revered notions" 102). This perspective, if examined in the larger context of her works, could secure for Cholmondeley a more prominent place among the novelists and social critics of her era.

BIBLIOGRAPHY

Red Pottage has recently been revived twice (1976 and 1985), but none of Cholmondeley's works are currently in print.

Works by Mary Cholmondeley

The Danvers Jewels. 1887.
Sir Charles Danvers. 1889.
Diana Tempest. 1893.
A Devotee: An Episode in the Life of a Butterfly. 1897.
Red Pottage. 1899.
Moth and Rust, together with "Geoffrey's Wife" and "The Pitfall." 1902.
Prisoners (*Fast Bound in Misery and Iron*). 1906.
The Lowest Rung. 1908. Published in the U.S. as *The Hand on the Latch*. 1909.
Notwithstanding. 1913. Published in the United States as *After All*. 1913.
Under One Roof: A Family Record. 1918.
The Romance of His Life and Other Romances. 1921.

Studies of Mary Cholmondeley

Colby, Vineta. "Devoted Amateur: Mary Cholmondeley and *Red Pottage.*" *Essays in Criticism* 20 (Apr. 1970): 213–28.
Crisp, Jane. *Mary Cholmondeley 1859–1925: A Bibliography*. Queensland, Australia: University of Queensland, 1981.

Lubbock, Percy. *Mary Cholmondeley: A Sketch from Memory*. London: Jonathon Cape, 1928.

Peterson, Linda. *Traditions of Victorian Women's Autobiography: The Poetics and Politics of Life Writing*. Charlottesville: University of Virginia Press, 1999.

Rainwater, Catherine, and William J. Scheick. "Aliens in the Garden: The Re-Vision of Mary Cholmondeley's *Red Pottage*." *Philological Quarterly* (Winter 1992): 101–19.

"Claire" (Clara Mary Jane) Clairmont (1798–1879)

Lisa Leslie

BIOGRAPHY

In her childhood, "Claire" Clairmont (born Clara Mary Jane Clairmont) enjoyed the literary society that centered on her stepfather, William Godwin, attending lectures and the theater. Claire Clairmont's mother married Godwin when Claire Clairmont was almost four, four years after the death of Mary Wollstonecraft, Godwin's first wife, left him with the responsibility of two small children. With the marriage in 1801, Claire Clairmont and her older brother Charles suddenly had two stepsisters: Fanny (illegitimate daughter of Wollstonecraft and Gilbert Imlay), aged seven, and Mary (later Mary Shelley,* daughter of Wollstonecraft and Godwin), just eight months older than Claire Clairmont. Although she was no blood relation to Wollstonecraft, whose theories of women's rights she embraced, Claire Clairmont was able to claim some connection with one of the foremost writers of feminism.

In 1814 when her stepsister Mary Wollstonecraft Godwin eloped with the still-married Percy Bysshe Shelley, Claire Clairmont accompanied them in order "to speak French," as she told a man they met in Switzerland. This journey through Europe inspired her first journal; in it she responds particularly to the landscapes through which they traveled.

Claire Clairmont continued to live with Shelley and Mary after their return to England. Her presence was embraced by Shelley but only tolerated by her stepsister. Shelley valued her company and wrote a tribute to her beautiful singing voice in his poem "To Constantia"; she also figures in several other Shelley poems. However, during a spell away from the Shelleys, Claire Clairmont initiated a brief love affair with Lord Byron; later, in Switzerland, she would introduce the two poets to each other at the beginning of the summer of 1816—an event that produced not only the novel *Frankenstein* but also one of the most important literary friendships. Claire Clairmont returned to England with the

Shelleys for the birth of Allegra, her child by Byron. Her many letters to Byron are interesting for their openness and their emotional power. These letters trace the disintegration of her extreme love for Byron into bitter hatred as she realized that her decision to give their child to Byron for a better upbringing than she as a single mother could provide meant that ultimately she had given her up completely. Allegra died in a convent in 1822 at the age of five, just four years after being sent to live with her father.

Claire Clairmont wandered in Italy with the Shelleys from 1818 until 1822, when Shelley's death forced her to take charge of her own life. A sense of rootlessness dominates her journals and letters from this period on into her later years. She worked as a governess in Russia for several years, and the letters she wrote to Mary Shelley and Jane Williams present an acute and often humorous account of life with the Russian upper classes at the time. She also relates details of the Decembrist uprising in that country in 1825.

Leaving Russia in 1827, Claire Clairmont settled for a time in Naples. The only piece of writing from this period, a fragment describing the beauty of the Neapolitan countryside, appears in her short story "The Pole," published in 1832 as "by the author of 'Frankenstein.' " Although the terms of Shelley's will would eventually provide her with financial support, the money could not be claimed while Shelley's father was still alive. While Mary Shelley despaired over Sir Timothy Shelley's long life (he lived to be ninety-two and recovered from several serious illnesses), Claire Clairmont, with her characteristic humor, managed to joke about it: "I do not believe that it is the real Sir Tim who does this—He died long ago, and they concealed it, and have got some man of sixty to live there and play the Sir Tim of ninety, in order that they may still keep their revenues" (*Correspondence* 2: 388). Resigned to being a governess, she continued to work in that profession in order to support herself. Her letters from this period give a dramatic picture of the difficult conditions of this occupation. In 1841, Claire Clairmont negotiated an annuity against her expected inheritance, finally achieving the independence she had coveted for so long.

Claire Clairmont continued her nomadic lifestyle, moving regularly and leaving a record of herself only through her letters. Her often-difficult relationship with Mary Shelley, traceable in their correspondence, ended with a family quarrel, and for the two years before Mary Shelley's death in 1851, the stepsisters had no contact. Claire Clairmont finally settled in Florence in 1872 at the age of seventy-four, maintaining a household with her niece, Paola, and a few boarders. She died quietly in 1879, almost the last of the Shelley community.

MAJOR WORKS AND THEMES

In her diaries, Claire Clairmont considers typical romantic issues such as nature, revolution, and poetry. She also undertook other literary efforts, including a novel and articles, that have not survived. These efforts suggest that she thought of becoming a writer. She also comments frequently on the necessity of freedom for women, ideas that she imbibed primarily from her admiration of Mary Wollstonecraft and from her friendship with Percy Bysshe Shelley. In an 1835 letter to Mary Shelley, she asserts: "I think I can with certainty affirm all the pupils I have ever had will be violent defenders of the Rights of Women. I have taken great pains to sow the seeds of that doctrine wherever I could" (*Correspondence* 2: 323).

Her short story "The Pole" includes a pair of sisters based on herself and Mary Shelley; Idalie (based on Mary Shelley) is a fairly conventional heroine, but the bold and intrepid traveling opera singer Marietta (based on herself) is an unusual model of femininity to put before the reading public. Despite the quality of this fiction, however, Claire Clairmont decided to stick to teaching for her income. As she wrote to a friend in 1833, "In our family if you cannot write an epic poem or a novel that by its originality knocks all other novels on the head, you are a despicable creature not worth acknowledging" (*Correspondence* 1: 295). Although she had previously helped Godwin with some of the descriptions of Russia in the beginning chapters of his 1830 novel *Cloudesley*, she never attempted writing for the public again. But the urge to write never left her, and her correspondence with Mary Shelley, Jane Williams, Antonia Clairmont (her brother's wife), and Edward John Trelawny offers insights not only to her shrewd observations of political events but also to her frequent illnesses, her jocular pessimism, her suggestions of medical remedies, her ever-continuing feminism, and her perpetual humor, which must have aided her in surviving the trials of a troubled life.

An important image that appears frequently in both Clairmont's diaries and letters is that of the traveler. Early in her diaries Clairmont instructed herself to "think of thyself as a stranger and a traveler on the globe" (*Journals* 180), and she retained this self-view until the end of her life. Her uses of the metaphor of traveling, and its connotation of rootlessness and disconnection, suggest that the force of her convictions rendered her uncomfortable in the position in society into which she was forced.

CRITICAL RECEPTION

Claire Clairmont's journals remained private, although she revised some of her first journal of the tour through Europe evidently with an eye to publication. This revision is in the style of many travel narratives, but its difference (and its value) lies in her ability to recreate the trio's interactions with local people and the discussions among her companions. The only study that looks at Clairmont's journals critically is Harriet Blodgett's *Centuries of Female Days*. It is in the genre of letters, however, that Claire Clairmont excels. Her letters to Mary Shelley and Jane Williams were valued and circulated among their friends. Mary Shelley wrote to her that "if your letters are ever published, all others that ever were published before, will fall into the shade, & you [*sic*] be looked on as the best letter writer that ever charmed their friends" (*The Letters of Mary Wollstonecraft Shelley*, ed. Betty T. Bennett, 1980–88, 3: 48).

Claire Clairmont's journals, published in 1968, are an important source of information of the life of the Shelley-Byron circle, but despite many vivid genre sketches, this has remained their perceived primary value. Her possession of some of Shelley's papers, and the attempts of an American Shelley fanatic to obtain them, inspired Henry James to write *The Aspern Papers*. Her letters and journals have been used in virtually all of the biographies of the Shelleys and Byron, and she figures to varying degrees of prominence in the stories of these lives. The publication of her letters in 1995 made available the last of her known writings. The critical reception of the letters has been enthusiastic.

BIBLIOGRAPHY

Claire Clairmont's only surviving work of fiction, "The Pole," has been republished most recently in *Mary Shelley: Collected Tales and Stories* (ed. Charles Robinson [Johns Hopkins University Press, 1976]) with an explanation of how it came to be included in the volume as well as the indisputable facts that identify Claire Clairmont as the author. Two journal fragments are printed in *Shelley and His Circle 1773–1822*: a revised section of her first journal in volume 3 (1970), and entries from 1818 in volume 5 (1973). There is also one journal entry included in Everyman's *Women Romantics 1785–1832: Writing in Prose* (ed. Jennifer Breen [J. M. Dent & Sons, 1996]). One of her letters is included in the *Virago Book of Love Letters* (ed. Jill Dawson, 1994).

Works by Claire Clairmont

"The Pole." *The Court Magazine and Belle Assemblee* (Aug. and Sept. 1832): 64–71, 129–36. ["The Author of 'Frankenstein' "].

The Journals of Claire Clairmont. Ed. Marion Kingston Stocking. 1968.

"The Journal of Claire Clairmont, August 14–22, 1814." Ed. Sir Gavin de Beer. *Shelley and His Circle 1773–1822* (an edition of the manuscripts of Shelley and others in The Carl H. Pforzheimer Library). 8 vols. Vols. 1–4: Ed. Kenneth Neill Cameron. 1961–1970. Vols. 5–8: Ed. Donald H. Reiman. 1973–1986. 3: 342–75. 1970.

"The Journal of Claire Clairmont, January 17–18 (In Part), April 23–June 1818." Ed. Marion Kingston Stocking. *Shelley and His Circle 1773–1822*. 5: 450–66. 1973.

The Clairmont Correspondence: Letters of Claire Clairmont, Charles Clairmont, and Fanny Imlay Godwin. 2 vols. Ed. Marion Kingston Stocking. 1995.

Studies of Claire Clairmont

Blodgett, Harriet. *Centuries of Female Days: Englishwomen's Private Diaries.* New Brunswick: Rutgers University Press, 1988.

Gittings, Robert, and Jo Manton. *Claire Clairmont and the Shelleys.* Oxford: Oxford University Press, 1992.

Grylls, R. Glynn. *Claire Clairmont: Mother of Byron's Allegra.* London: John Murray, 1939.

Frances Power Cobbe
(1822–1904)

Sally Mitchell

BIOGRAPHY

Feminist essayist and social reformer Frances Power Cobbe was born near Dublin to Anglo-Irish gentry. Religious doubts led her to intense private reading in philosophy and world faiths; by 1849, in a manuscript "Essay on True Religion," she calls herself a deist. Cobbe's life interests were also shaped by helping cottagers during the famine. When her father's death (in 1857) supplied a small inheritance, she spent a year in travel, joined Mary Carpenter in Bristol for an apprenticeship in practical social work, and then established herself as an author.

Cobbe's essays are marked by impassioned earnestness, careful research, concrete details, and a biting edge that compelled public attention. She published some thirty volumes and well over 100 essays in leading periodicals, produced at least 200 tracts for the antivivisection movement, and wrote more than 1,000 unsigned editorial columns for newspapers including the *Echo*, the *Standard*, and the *Daily News*.

After 1863 Cobbe shared her life with a beloved friend, sculptor Mary Charlotte Lloyd (1819–1896). Although many of Cobbe's essays promote social reforms, she also continued to explore religious topics, becoming the only woman to write regularly for *Theological Review*. Horror at the way animals were used in physiological experiments led her to establish an antivivisection society and to ask broad questions about health, medical care, and scientific values. In 1878 her efforts were largely responsible for a law giving abused wives immediate access to separation, protection orders, and child support. American suffragists used the lectures published as *The Duties of Women* (1881) in persuading complacent middle-class women to take an interest in public life.

In 1884 Cobbe retired to Wales, although she continued to write and lecture. She also assembled her papers and produced an autobiography. Her last public speech, at age eighty, was for a suffrage event. As her will directs, she is buried beside Mary Lloyd in Llanelltyd churchyard (just outside Dolgellau); a single headstone marks their joint grave.

MAJOR WORKS AND THEMES

Frances Power Cobbe's most effective essays explored contemporary issues. "Celibacy v. Marriage" (1862) and "What Shall We Do with Our Old Maids?" (1862) responded to the "problem" of "redundant females" by proposing that single women could be as happy as their married sisters. *The Red Flag in John Bull's Eyes* (1863) aroused support for the Union during the U.S. Civil War. " 'Criminals, Idiots, Women, and Minors' " (1868) promoted the Married Women's Property Act, and "Wife Torture in England" (1878) gave widespread exposure to physical abuse. Antivivisection essays emphasized the moral damage done to scientists and medical students who learned to ignore—or even enjoy—the pain caused by their experiments.

Cobbe's theological writing sought a new basis for ethics in an age of religious doubt and scientific advance. *Religious Duty* (1864) argues for an infinitely good Creator while proposing that every rational human mind can directly perceive eternal law, without the mediation of scripture, prophets, or formal religion.

In addition to her primary focus on women's rights, animal protection, and ethics, Cobbe wrote travel narratives and a variety of essays on general topics. Among them are several interesting pre-Freudian explorations of mental processes, including "Dreams as Illustrations of Unconscious Cerebration" (1871).

CRITICAL RECEPTION

Cobbe quickly established a reputation as a provocative writer whose essays were explicit, vigorous, witty, and memorable. Editors welcomed her work, knowing that it would arouse discussion, although even some activists thought her positions were too extreme. Individual essays (as well as books) were widely reviewed. As is often true of reformers, however, some essays began to look old-fashioned once the battles were won. Her theological writing, similarly, was appreciated by people who found comfort in her nondoctrinal theism but criticized both by traditional Christians and by late-nineteenth-century agnostics and atheists. Her 1894 autobiography was nevertheless enthusiastically reviewed on both sides of the Atlantic.

Genre as well as the timeliness may account for Cobbe's virtual disappearance from literary history. An 1897 article by admirer Frances Willard proposed that although "distinguished critical authorities have assigned her the rank of greatest among living English women," she has "taken duty, not love, for her theme, and the essay, not the novel, as her literary vehicle" (597). Nineteenth-century nonfiction continues to be studied, but the Victorian prose canon that took shape in the 1930s was composed of male "sages." Late-twentieth-century scholars of feminism and animal rights have aroused some interest in Cobbe's activist essays, though little attention has yet been given to her work in psychology and ethics or to the literary qualities of her prose.

BIBLIOGRAPHY

A few essays by Frances Power Cobbe are available in recent anthologies. *"Criminals, Idiots, Women, and Minors": Nineteenth-Century Writing by Women on Women* (ed. Susan Hamilton [Broadview, 1996]) includes "Celibacy v. Marriage," " 'Criminals, Idiots, Women and Minors,' " "What Shall We Do with Our Old Maids?" and "Wife Torture in England"; *Prose by Victorian Women: An Anthology* (ed. Andrea Broomfield and Sally Mitchell [Garland, 1996]) has "What Shall We Do with Our Old Maids?" "The Rights of Man and the Claims of Brutes," "Wife Torture in England," and "Schadenfreude." *The Red Flag in John Bull's Eyes* and *Why Women Desire the Franchise* are available on the Victorian Women Writers Project.

Selected Works by Frances Power Cobbe

"Celibacy v. Marriage." *Fraser's Magazine* 65 (1862): 228–35.
"What Shall We Do with Our Old Maids?" *Fraser's Magazine* (1862): 594–610.
The Red Flag in John Bull's Eyes. 1863.
"The Rights of Man and the Claims of Brutes." *Fraser's Magazine* 68 (1863): 586–602.
"The Nineteenth Century." *Fraser's Magazine* 69 (1864): 481–94.
"The Philosophy of the Poor-Laws." *Fraser's Magazine* 70 (1864): 373–94.
Religious Duty. 1864.
" 'Criminals, Idiots, Women, and Minors.' " *Fraser's Magazine* (1868): 777–94.
"Unconscious Cerebration: A Psychological Study." *Macmillan's Magazine* 23 (1870): 23–37.
"Dreams as Illustrations of Unconscious Cerebration." *Macmillan's Magazine* 23 (1871): 512–23.
"The Consciousness of Dogs." *Quarterly Review* 133 (1872): 419–51.
Darwinism in Morals, and Other Essays. 1872.
Why Women Desire the Franchise. 1877.
"The Little Health of Ladies." *Contemporary Review* 31 (1878): 276–96.
"Wife Torture in England." *Contemporary Review* 32 (1878): 55–87.
The Duties of Women. 1881.
"Progressive Judaism." *Contemporary Review* 42 (1882): 747–63.
Life of Frances Power Cobbe, by Herself. 1894.
"Schadenfreude." *Contemporary Review* 81 (1902): 655–66.

Studies of Frances Power Cobbe

Caine, Barbara. *Victorian Feminists.* New York: Oxford University Press, 1992.
Ferguson, Moira. *Animal Advocacy and Englishwomen, 1780–1900.* Ann Arbor: University of Michigan Press, 1997.

Raftery, Deirdre. "Frances Power Cobbe." In *Women, Power and Consciousness in 19th Century Ireland*. Ed. Mary Cullen and Maria Luddy. Dublin: Attic Press, 1995. 69–123.

Willard, Frances E. "Frances Power Cobbe." *Chautauquan* 7 (1897): 597–99.

Mary Elizabeth Coleridge
(1861–1907)

Simon Avery

BIOGRAPHY

An important late-nineteenth-century poet, novelist, essayist, and critic, Mary Coleridge was descended from an acclaimed literary family with Samuel Taylor Coleridge as her great-great uncle and Sara Coleridge* her great aunt. Born and brought up in London, she lived all her life in her parents' home, choosing to remain single. Her father, a Clerk of the Assize, also had strong artistic leanings, his house being something of a salon with frequent visits from Tennyson, Browning, Ruskin, Fanny Kemble,* and Holman Hunt. Tutored in the classics at home by poet and ex-Eton schoolmaster William Cory, Mary also taught herself a number of languages and read voraciously in literature and history, which she discussed with a small group of close female friends.

Throughout her life Coleridge was fiercely independent in thought. Although from a strong Church of England background, she struggled with doubt all her life, a position that is reflected in her poems "Every Man for His Own Hand" and "Doubt," and increasingly she subscribed to a more personal religion, which Robert Bridges termed a "wide spiritual outlook" (598). Influenced by her reading of Tolstoy, she taught literature to working-class women in her own home and then, from 1895, at the Working Women's College. This commitment to female education firmly aligned her with the New Woman of the fin de siècle and constitutes the subject of her poem "A Clever Woman."

Coleridge's first ambition was to be a painter—she was a close friend and champion of the Pre-Raphaelites, and a number of her poems deal with art—but she soon turned to literature. She wrote articles and reviews for several periodicals including Charlotte Yonge's* *Monthly Packet*, the *Monthly Review*, and the *Times Literary Supplement*, and her first novel, *The Seven Sleepers of Ephesus*, appeared in 1893 to admiration by Robert Louis Stevenson. Four further novels followed, the most successful being *The King with Two Faces*

(1897), based upon Gustav III of Sweden. Her greatest abilities, however, are revealed in her poetic oeuvre. Between 1882 and 1907 she wrote more than 260 brief lyrics but was extremely reluctant to publish until Robert Bridges encouraged her by offering to help edit them. *Fancy's Following*, a collection of forty-eight poems, appeared in 1896, followed by *Fancy's Guerdon* in 1897. Unlike her prose writings, which were published under her own name, her poetry appeared under the pseudonym "Anodos," a name that means "the Wanderer" and that was taken from George MacDonald's romance *Phantastes* (1858). Such masked publication clearly reflected the anxiety of influence that she experienced as a result of her literary ancestry.

Coleridge also published a collection of essays, *Non Sequitur* (1900), and, posthumously, *A Life of Holman Hunt* (1908). She died from appendicitis at the age of forty-five, and her literary remains appeared as *Gathered Leaves* in 1910.

MAJOR WORKS AND THEMES

Coleridge's novels, now forgotten, are mostly historical romances and draw upon many real figures including Gustav III of Sweden, Madame de Staël, Balzac, and the Duchess of Berri. Although they are full of action and strong characterization, they also demonstrate the fragmentariness and dreamlike quality that made her a stronger poet than novelist. Her essays, however, are generally well structured and argued (the *Times* obituary calls her "a generous and discerning Critic") and deal with a wide range of subjects, including Elizabeth Gaskell,* Elizabeth I, and the nature of heroism.

Coleridge's poetic oeuvre is her major achievement, beautifully crafted lyrics that are notable for their control, poise, and power. They are clearly the work of a transition period in literary history, many of them demonstrating the influence of the Pre-Raphaelites and especially Christina Rossetti,* whereas others prefigure the techniques and subject matter of modernism. In their brevity, depth, and compression, they are also comparable to the work of Coleridge's near-contemporary Emily Dickinson.

Coleridge has been frequently depicted as contented with the traditional roles for middle-class Victorian women, and yet her poetry, along with her life, has strong feminist overtones that have been mostly overlooked. Time and again she proposes sisterhood and a separatist female community as the way forward for women. In "The White Women," for example, she depicts a forest world inhabited by Amazonian-like females who speak the language of nature and who are free from all inhibitions, never having "bowed their necks beneath the yoke." "A Day-dream" and "The Witches' Wood" deal with similar female-centered communities. "Marriage" sharply critiques the institution as a stifling denial of identity and again offers sisterhood as a viable alternative, strongly suggesting the influence of Christina Rossetti's "Goblin Market." Indeed, many of Coleridge's poems seem to have an almost lesbian subtext.

Connected to this feminist agenda are a number of poems that employ gothic elements to reflect upon women's oppression. "The Witch," "Master and Guest," and perhaps her most famous poem, "The Other Side of a Mirror," center around the idea of woman as outsider, a wanderer figure at the margins of society or a divided self repressed by dominant sexual ideologies:

> I sat before my glass one day,
>   And conjured up a vision bare,
> Unlike the aspects glad and gay,
>   That erst were found reflected there—
> The vision of a woman, wild
> With more than womanly despair.
>   ("The Other Side of a Mirror")

Many other poems such as "Wilderspin," "The Wedding in the Snow," "Ghosts," and "Horror" demonstrate Coleridge's bizarre imagination and her love of the unearthly and surreal, a clear inheritance from Samuel Taylor Coleridge. Indeed, Mary was called "the tail of the comet S.T.C." (*Gathered Leaves* 11), and her poem "The Witch" is thought to have been written in response to his work "Christabel." Linked to this Romantic influence and the influence of other women poets such as Christina Rossetti are Mary Coleridge's other poetical concerns with the themes of isolation, lost love, and mystical experience. Overall, she is a poet of great skill, range, and vigor.

CRITICAL RECEPTION

During her lifetime, Coleridge's novels were more well known than her poetry, although the latter was praised by Bridges, Henry Newbolt, Edward Thomas, and the young Walter de la Mare, who asked for assistance with his own work. In his essay on Coleridge's poetry, Bridges rhapsodized on "the delicate harmony of special excellences that makes originality" (594), although when her collected poems finally appeared in 1908, they failed to have any great impact. A number were set to music in the pre–World War I years, but subsequently Mary Coleridge disappeared from literary history, despite Whistler's collected edition in 1954. It is only since feminist critical practices have begun to recover the vast body of poetry written by Victorian women that Coleridge has surfaced again. Yet while selections of the primary texts are now becoming available, criticism is sparse. Sandra Gilbert and Susan Gubar use "The Other Side of a Mirror" as the trope of the female writer's monstrous doppelgänger, and there are short discussions by Jean Halliday and Katharine McGowran, but otherwise the power and energy of Coleridge's work are still neglected.

BIBLIOGRAPHY

There is no collected edition of Coleridge's poems, and all her novels are out of print. Small selections of her poems can be found in recent anthologies of Victorian women's poetry.

Works by Mary Coleridge

The Seven Sleepers of Ephesus. 1893.
Fancy's Following. 1896.
Fancy's Guerdon. 1897.
The King with Two Faces. 1897.
Non Sequitur. 1900.
The Fiery Dawn. 1901.
The Shadow on the Wall. 1904.
The Lady on the Drawing-Room Floor. 1906.
A Life of Holman Hunt. 1908.
Poems. 1908.
Gathered Leaves from the Prose of Mary E. Coleridge. Ed. Edith Sichel. 1910.
The Collected Poems of Mary Coleridge. Ed. Theresa Whistler. 1954.

Studies of Mary Coleridge

Bridges, Robert. "The Poems of Mary Coleridge." *Cornhill Magazine* (Nov. 1907): 594–605.
Franklin, Colin. *Poets of the Daniel Press.* Cambridge: Rampant Lions, 1988.
Gilbert, Sandra M., and Susan Gubar. *The Madwoman in the Attic.* New Haven: Yale University Press, 1979.
Halliday, Jean. *Eight Victorian Poets Shaping the Artistic Sensibility of an Age.* Lampeter: Edwin Meller, 1993.
Jackson, Vanessa Furse. "Breaking the Quiet Surface: The Shorter Poems of Mary Coleridge." *English Literature in Transition* 39.1 (1996): 41–62.
McGowran, Katharine. "The Restless Wanderer at the Gates." In *Victorian Women Poets: A Critical Reader.* Ed. Angela Leighton. Oxford: Blackwell, 1996. 186–97.
"Miss M. E. Coleridge." Obituary in the *Times*, 28 Aug. 1907, 8.
Stevenson, Warren. "Mary Coleridge." In *Modern British Essayists First Series.* Ed. Robert Beum. *Dictionary of Literary Biography.* Detroit: Gale Research, 1990. 98: 73–76.

Sara Coleridge Coleridge
(1802–1852)

Michael A. Torok

BIOGRAPHY

Sara Coleridge, editor, poet, children's versifier, and fiction writer, was born at Greta Hall on 22 December 1802. She was the daughter of Samuel T. Coleridge, but this distinction should not diminish her own contributions to both the Romantic and Victorian eras. Her uncle, the poet Robert Southey, took her mother, Sara Fricker Coleridge, and the young Sara into his care early—giving them a loving, steady home while S. T. Coleridge was away, a frequent circumstance. At Southey's residence, Coleridge was exposed to and encouraged to absorb the contents of the grand library. In addition to her academic pursuits, she also spent time with hands-on botanical and zoological investigation.

By the age of twenty-three, Coleridge had published two difficult translations, one from Latin into English—mistakenly attributed to Southey at the time—and the other from medieval French. She published both texts anonymously. Coleridge received sporadic praise at best from her father, but he did take the occasion in 1832 to voice his admiration of her 1822 translation. He was not alone. Southey and Charles Lamb exchanged letters commending her efforts. By the age of twenty-five, she had "made herself acquainted with the leading Greek and Latin classics, and was well-skilled in French, Italian, German, and Spanish" (Coleridge, *Memoir* 53).

On 3 September 1829, Sara Coleridge and Henry Nelson Coleridge, a first cousin, were married. Between this time and the death of her husband in 1843, Sara Coleridge embraced authorship. Her first fully acknowledged work is *Pretty Lessons* (1834), a playful, instructional book of poems and lessons originally composed solely for her children. This was followed by the fairy tale *Phantasmion* (1837), which is a precursor to Christina Rossetti's* "Goblin Market." Since Coleridge initially composed both texts for the delight of children, she was lauded for her devotion and originality and shielded from the harsh public scrutiny imposed on women scholars and writers.

After her husband's death, Coleridge took over his task as literary executor of S. T. Coleridge. She had been facilitating and contributing to the work during their entire marriage. Sara Coleridge dedicated the remaining years of her life to annotating, releasing, and defending her father's works and his name as one of the foremost Romantic poets, literary scholars, and theologians of Britain. Like her father and her brother Hartley, Coleridge became addicted to opium. When she died on 3 May 1852 at fifty, she left behind a wealth of correspondence and an unfinished memoir, along with her own perspicacious insights on S. T. Coleridge's works.

MAJOR WORKS AND THEMES

Sara Coleridge's translation of Dobrizhoffer's *Account of the Abipones* in 1822 is an exemplary achievement. Lamb declared his ability in Latin lacking in comparison to Coleridge's mastery. Although the text is a little-known travelogue, her handling of the translation into English is expert and lucid. At this early time, she was already proving her abilities as a scholar and linguist. The text of *Phantasmion*, Coleridge's fairy-tale romance of Phantasmion and Iarine, can be read in numerous ways. It may be read at its face value as a beautiful, fanciful story of love, magic, and perseverance. It may be read as a Bildungsroman. And it may be read as a means through which Coleridge worked through her own relationships with the father figures in her life. One thing agreed upon by readers is the beauty of the prose, elevated to the level of poetry, throughout the work.

Coleridge's letters and her memoir give a fascinating insight into what it was like to "come of age" between the Romantic and Victorian eras. Especially for the psychoanalytic critic, these glances into the mind of Sara Coleridge are invaluable. Acting at times as a critic, as a friend, and as the voice of experience, these writings range from times of joy to grief, but all are clear, concise, and controlled.

As an editor, Coleridge tried to elucidate and clarify her father's theological beliefs, while cementing his reputation as an important thinker and philosopher. Her appendix to *Aids to Reflection* includes the essay "Essay on Rationalism," which is considered a significant addition to the studies of Samuel T. Coleridge. She kept many of her father's books in print, notably the *Biographia Literaria*, which never had a second edition before hers. She continued to organize and publish S. T. Coleridge's work until her death, the final work a collection of poetry (1852). The importance of her work in this area cannot be overemphasized.

CRITICAL RECEPTION

During her lifetime, reviewers embraced Sara Coleridge, if they knew whom to embrace. Difficulty arose when she published her first two translations, a total of five volumes, anonymously. The most frequently noted and most well-known review of Coleridge's work is a review of *Phantasmion*, which appeared in the September 1840 *Quarterly Review*. In this review the work is heralded as a poetic fairy tale and incorrectly stated to be probably the last fairy tale to come out of England.

Within the twentieth century, Coleridge has again become a subject of critical inquiry. Her work on S. T. Coleridge has stood as the basis from which many other editions of his work start. Virginia Woolf portrayed her as a woman unable to be fully realized—living in the shadow of her father—in her essay "Sara Coleridge." More recently, Bradford Keyes Mudge published *Sara Coleridge, a Victorian Daughter* as well as numerous articles. C. G. Martin found and published an unpublished letter in 1967. Nathan Cervo used Coleridge's *Memoir and Letters* as a lens through which to view Browning's Gigadibs figure in "Bishop Blougram's Apology." There is much more to be found in the works and life of Sara Coleridge, both in relation to the famous figures who surrounded her and as a writer in her own right.

BIBLIOGRAPHY

Sara Coleridge has been anthologized in recent editions of Victorian women's poetry. *Phantasmion* has been reprinted frequently, and AMS Press has reprinted her *Memoir and Letters*.

Works by Sara Coleridge

Pretty Lessons in Verse for Good Children, with Some Lessons in Latin, in Easy Rhyme. 1834.
Phantasmion. 1837.
Rev. of *Francis Beaumont and John Fletcher*, ed. Alexander Dyce. *Quarterly Review* 83 (1848): 371–416.
Rev. of *The Princess*, by Alfred, Lord Tennyson. *Quarterly Review* 82 (1848): 427–53.
Memoir and Letters of Sara Coleridge. Ed. Edith Coleridge. 1874.
With Henry Reed. *Sara Coleridge and Henry Reed: Reed's Memoir of Sara Coleridge, Her Letters to Reed, Including Her Comments on His Memoir of Gray, Her Marginalia in Henry Crabb Robinson's Copy of Wordworth's Memoirs*. Ed. Leslie Nathan Broughton. 1937.

Translations by Sara Coleridge

Account of the Abipones, an Equestrian People of Paraguay. From the Latin of Martin Dobrizhoffer, eighteen years a missionary in that country. 3 vols. 1822.
The Right Joyous and Pleasant History of the Facts, Tests, and Prowesses of the Chevalier Bayard. 2 vols. 1825.

Works by S. T. Coleridge Edited by Sara Coleridge

Specimens of the Table Talk of the Late Samuel Taylor Coleridge. 2 vols. 1835.
The Literary Remains of Samuel Taylor Coleridge. Ed. Sara Coleridge and Henry Nelson Coleridge. 4 vols. 1836–1839.

Appendix. Aids to Reflection in the Formation of a Manly Character. 1843.
Biographia Literaria. 1847.
Notes and Lectures upon Shakespeare. 1849.
Essays on His Own Times. 1850.
The Poems of Samuel Taylor Coleridge. Ed. Sara Coleridge and Derwent Coleridge. 1852.
Confessions of an Inquiring Spirit. 1853.

Studies of Sara Coleridge

Cervo, Nathan. "Sara Coleridge: The Gigadibs Complex." *Victorian Newsletter* 78 (1990): 3–9.

Martin, C. G. "Sara Coleridge: An Unpublished Letter." *Notes and Queries* 14 (1967): 51–52.

Mudge, Bradford K. "Burning Down the House: Sara Coleridge, Virginia Woolf, and the Politics of Literary Revision." *Tulsa Studies in Women's Literature* 5.2 (1986): 229–50.

———. "Exiled as Exiler: Sara Coleridge, Virginia Woolf, and the Politics of Literary Revision." In *Women's Writing in Exile.* Ed. Mary Lynn Broe and Angela J. C. Ingram. Chapel Hill: University of North Carolina Press, 1989. 199–223.

———. "On Tennyson's *The Princess*: Sara Coleridge in the *Quarterly Review.*" *The Wordsworth Circle* 15.2 (1984): 51–54.

———. "Sara Coleridge and 'The Business of Life.' " *The Wordsworth Circle* 19.1 (1988): 55–64.

———. *Sara Coleridge, a Victorian Daughter.* New Haven: Yale University Press, 1989.

Raymond, M. B. "A Letter from Sara Coleridge." *The Wordsworth Circle* 15.2 (1984): 55–65.

Woolf, Virginia. *The Diary of Virginia Woolf.* Ed. Anne Olivier Bell. San Diego: Harcourt Brace, 1985.

———. "Sara Coleridge." In *Collected Essays.* New York: Harcourt Brace, 1967. 3: 222–26.

Eliza Cook
(1818–1889)

Denise P. Quirk

BIOGRAPHY

The youngest of eleven children in a middle-class family, feminist poet and journalist Eliza Cook grew up in Southwark and nearby Horsham, Sussex. In these years in the country she developed her love of nature, which became a prominent theme in her poetry. Completely self-educated, Cook was encouraged by her mother and permitted to read whatever captured her interest. She developed a quick sense of humor and broad imagination, a thirst for knowledge, and a disdain for conventionality.

Cook's poetry, beginning with *Lays of a Wild Harp* (1835), displays her range of emotion and independent spirit. Her poems appeared regularly in the *Weekly Dispatch, Metropolitan Magazine, Literary Gazette, Morning Chronicle,* and *New Monthly*, at first anonymously, then as "C." or "E. C.," and finally under her own name. These poems brought her to the attention of the proprietor of the *Weekly Dispatch*, Alderman Harmer, under whose aegis she published *Melaia, and Other Poems* (1838). Invited to live at Harmer's home, Ingress Abbey, in Kent, Cook became attached to Harmer's granddaughter and, as a result, became the target of "absurd rumors" and "insidious" attacks that included parodies of her poems and slanderous broadsides. Cook's literary and personal reputation survived these unspecified rumors, though her frankness and her preference for short, "man-ish" hair and "half-Bloomerish," masculine attire continued to excite attention.

Cook's most significant relationship, with American actress Charlotte Cushman (1816–1876), began in 1845. Cook and Cushman were known as devoted to one another: They signaled their attachment through matching clothing, whereas Cook expressed her love and passion for Cushman in poems published throughout her life, such as "Our Rambles by the Dove," "To Charlotte Cushman," and "An Old Tune," which appear in Cook's *Poems* (1848). Cushman reciprocated by helping Cook secure American publishers and by writing the entry on Cook in Sarah Josepha Hale's *Women's Record* (1852).

In 1849, with Cushman's active involvement, Cook began publishing *Eliza Cook's Journal*, a weekly miscellany of essays, reviews, fiction, poetry, and news of current interest. At this time Cushman and Cook began to part ways. Cushman had become involved with feminist writer and translator Matilda Hays (1820–1897). Hays briefly acted opposite Cushman on the stage, and Cook accompanied them on their 1848 regional tour before Cushman and Hays set sail for the United States.

Shortly after Cushman's departure, Cook was struck with an "internal" disorder that was to plague her throughout her life. According to some contemporaries, the illness was triggered by her distress at the breakup with Cushman. During her illness, she maintained publication of the journal, but after six years, she gave up the work. Her ill health hindered her writing any new work except for *New Echoes and Other Poems* (1864) and occasional poems in the *Weekly Dispatch*. Instead, she edited and reissued one-volume editions of her collected poems, so as to make them more affordable to the middle and lower classes she considered her main audience. She also published collections of material from her journal, *Jottings from My Journal* (1860) and *Diamond Dust* (1865).

In recognition of her literary efforts, Cook was granted a Civil List Pension in 1864 of £100 per year. In 1880 she was declared "of unsound mind" and was granted a "lunatic's pension." She lived in her home in Wimbledon until 1889, when she died. Her estate included £5,057 and two houses, a testimony to the substantial royalties from her works. True to her feminism, Cook specified that monetary legacies to her nieces and great-nieces were "for their own and separate use, not entrusted to the care of their present or future husbands."

MAJOR WORKS AND THEMES

Eliza Cook's poetry was, by her description and the reactions of her contemporaries, sentimental, simple, and accessible. She explored themes of home and nature popular in Victorian literature, and many poems, including her most famous, "The Old Arm-Chair," express her grief at her mother's death before Cook was sixteen. As was typical of nineteenth-century social reformers, she encouraged the pursuit of knowledge and self-improvement among "the people," to whom she addressed her verses and essays.

Many of Cook's poems and especially her essays, published in *Eliza Cook's Journal* (1849–1854), stressed women's rights, scientific and technological progress, working-class rights, and a profound respect for religious and social freedom. Cook espoused new educational and occupational opportunities for women and the need for a married women's property act, while also honoring single women and defending the "fallen." Although she also stressed the importance of home and marriage, the focus in her essays was often on domestic violence and the need for temperance and thrift. Cook wrote many of the journal's essays herself, though some well-known writers also contributed articles and fiction, including Eliza Meteyard ("Silverpen"), Geraldine Jewsbury,* and Amelia Edwards.

CRITICAL RECEPTION

Eliza Cook's Journal was enormously popular, outselling Charles Dickens's *Household Words*, and at a price of one and a half pence, accessible to a wide readership. At the end of 1849, her journal garnered praise from over forty London and regional newspapers. Cook's poetry was widely acclaimed for its originality and its appeal to "the people," and she was compared by the *Literary Gazette* to Robert Burns. Her published portrait sold by the thousands and was said "to hang in every home in the land."

At the time of her death, Cook was proclaimed to be one of the "most popular women in England" and remembered as a "truth-seeking fearless soul" who was "careless alike of censure and applause" and willing to give "free, bold utterance to every sentiment and feeling" of her experience. Some contemporary critics castigated her poetry for its simple rhymes and folksy sentiment, and as literary tastes changed, later critics frequently echoed these judgments.

Among contemporary feminists and social reformers, however, Cook's poetry and prose also gained praise and recognition. In an 1847 lecture, radical Unitarian William Fox praised her angry political ballads such as "Godspeed the Ploughshare," written against the enclosure movement, and her journal inspired midcentury feminist editors Bessie Rayner Parkes* and Matilda Hays. Feminist historians and critics of the late twentieth century began to study Cook for her feminist politics and her role in the initiation of a feminist critical tradition. Her often hard-hitting directness has begun to earn her a place among radical social critics of the time.

BIBLIOGRAPHY

Selected poems by Eliza Cook are available in recent anthologies of poetry by Victorian women writers.

Works by Eliza Cook

Lays of a Wild Harp: A Collection of Metrical Pieces. 1835.
Melaia, and Other Poems. 1838.
Poems. 3 vols. 1848.
Eliza Cook's Journal. 1849–1854.
Poems. A New Edition, in One Volume. 1859.
Jottings from My Journal. 1860.
Poems. Selected and Edited by the Author. 1861.
New Echoes and Other Poems. 1864.
Diamond Dust. 1865.
The Poetical Works of Eliza Cook. The "Lansdowne Poets." n.d. [1870].

Studies of Eliza Cook

Hale, Sarah Josepha, ed. *Women's Record; or, Sketches of All Distinguished Women, from "the Beginning" till* A.D. *1850.* New York: Harper, 1853.

Ingram, John, "Eliza Cook." In *The Poets and the Poetry of the Century.* Ed. A. Miles. London: Hutchinson, n.d. [1899].

Merrill, Lisa. *When Romeo Was a Woman: Charlotte Cushman and Her Circle of Female Spectators.* Ann Arbor: University of Michigan Press, 1999.

Mitchell, Sally. *Fallen Angel: Chastity, Class and Women's Reading 1835–1880.* Bowling Green, OH: Bowling Green University Popular Press, 1981.

Notable Women of Our Time. London: Ward, Lock, 1882.

Robinson, Solveig C. "Defining the Nature of Good Literature: Victorian Women of Letters." Ph.D. diss., University of Chicago, 1994.

"Marie Corelli" (Mary Mackay) (1855–1924)

Annette R. Federico

BIOGRAPHY

The story of Marie Corelli's life is complicated by conjectures and unsubstantiated facts about her birth and education and by her own elaborate self-mythology. She was born Mary Mackay, daughter of the Scottish balladeer and journalist Charles Mackay, who married his second wife, Mary Elizabeth Mills, a widow who was formerly his mistress, in 1861. After Corelli's death, rumors circulated (and were variously contradicted) that she was born out of wedlock, and throughout her life, she referred to Mackay as her "stepfather" and called herself his "adopted daughter."

Biographers have viewed her lonely childhood and her father's sentimentality and indulgence as important factors in her romantic temperament. She was educated by governesses and at fourteen was sent to a convent school (she claimed in France, but probably in England). When Mrs. Mackay died in 1876, Bertha Vyver, a neighborhood friend who was a year older than Mary Mackay, moved in with the family and remained her close companion for forty-six years.

After Charles Mackay suffered a stroke in 1883, the group moved to London and were joined by Eric, Mackay's son from his first marriage, who was forty-eight years old and had been living a prodigal life in Italy and France. Eric urged his half sister to write poetry to keep the family from falling into poverty. In 1885, she sent the manuscript of a novel called *Lifted Up* to the publishers Richard Bentley & Son, using the pseudonym "Marie Corelli." It was published in February 1886 as *A Romance of Two Worlds* and initiated an extraordinary publication record: At the turn of the century, sales of Corelli's novels averaged 175,000 copies. The astonishing popular success of her first book (the critics were less enthusiastic, calling the novel "ridiculous" and "pure bosh") led to some personal embellishments: Corelli told Bentley that she was only nineteen years old and was the daughter of a Venetian who could trace her ancestry back to the musician Arcangelo Corelli. These romantic mystifications, however, were combined with hard-headed ambition and business acumen. In 1900, Corelli (with Bertha Vyver) moved to Stratford-upon-Avon, where she spent the rest of her life. She attracted curious fans and intrusive photographers, as well as the rich and famous, and often became entangled in local preservation projects and was a vocal antagonist of the Shakespeare Trust.

MAJOR WORKS AND THEMES

Although it is easy to dismiss Marie Corelli as simply a writer of melodramatic romances, it is both more fair and more exact to lay some emphasis upon the profuseness of her imagination and the variety of directions she offers for modern literary and cultural studies. Her more than twenty-five novels were in earnest opposition to Victorian materialism and the erosion of religious and romantic idealism. Corelli opposed women's suffrage and detested New Woman novels, deplored Darwinism and the encroachments of science on orthodox religion, and was blatantly anti-intellectual. Her mission was to rescue England from commercialism, religious indifference, and political corruption. Yet at the same time, Corelli's books champion women's intellectual equality with men, recast religious orthodoxy as occultism, and exploit literary Decadence to accommodate middle-class morality and taste. *A Romance of Two Worlds* (1886), *Ardath* (1889), and *The Soul of Lilith* (1892), for example, are curiously esoteric approaches to Victorian science and archaeology and participate in the late Victorian interest in psychic phenomena and "new age" spirituality. *Barabbas* (1893), an enormously popular but controversial retelling of the Crucifixion, demonstrates Corelli's daring self-righteousness and is an inventive appropriation of biblical history. Many of Corelli's novels blatantly attack the lasciviousness and greed of the British aristocracy and often oppose male infidelity and female purity in violently melodramatic narratives. *The Sorrows of Satan* (1895) was an immediate best-seller and is perhaps Corelli's most interesting novel for students of late Victorian popular fiction. A melodrama set in London "swagger" society, the novel is an exposé of the corrupt London publishing world and contains a romantic self-portrait of Corelli as an unassuming popular novelist whose morally uplifting books never fail to win readers. *The Sorrows of Satan* reveals Corelli's own resentment and anger at male critics and reviewers who relentlessly "slashed" her books, but it also is a fast-paced gothic story of a poor novelist's bargain with the devil in fin de siècle London. It is a fine example of the way Corelli's novels may cross genres, blending the conventions of romance, the gothic, the historical novel, the society novel, and even the New Woman novel, since discourses about sexuality and literature make up a large part of Corelli's work.

CRITICAL RECEPTION

Throughout her career, Marie Corelli was engaged in a fierce battle with literary critics and reviewers. Her fall in popularity was sudden and total after

World War I, and since then Corelli's reputation as a low-status author of best-sellers has hardly been disputed. Yet generations of readers have found her narrative energy and absolute moral confidence irresistible.

Several useful reconsiderations of Marie Corelli have appeared since 1992. R. B. Kershner has argued that Corelli's characteristic blend of the sexual and the spiritual, her use of myth and allusions within a present-day narrative, her attitude of persecuted artist, and her high moral claims for art make her a "Modernist hybrid" (79).

In *Literary Capital and the Late Victorian Novel*, N. N. Feltes applies a materialist analysis to Corelli's novels, looking at the empirical details of publishing history to account for Corelli's extraordinary popularity. Rita Felski, in *The Gender of Modernity*, reads Corelli as "the popular sublime," evoking the significance of transcendence as an impetus of modern mass culture. Her feminist treatment underscores the aesthetic binarisms of high and popular art with an analysis of gender binarisms. Although she sees Corelli as an "ideal candidate for rediscovery" who invites a counter reading of such epithets as "vulgar," "sentimental," and "melodramatic," Felski questions the "assumption that the noncanonical text must be legitimated as subversive in order to be considered worthy of study" (142).

BIBLIOGRAPHY

The Sorrows of Satan (Oxford University Press line of Popular Fiction, 1996, with an intro. by Peter Keating) is the only novel by Corelli currently in print.

Selected Works by Marie Corelli

A Romance of Two Worlds. 1886.
Ardath. 1889.
Wormwood. 1890.
The Soul of Lilith. 1892.
Barabbas. 1893.
The Sorrows of Satan. 1895.
The Murder of Delicia. 1896.
Temporal Power. 1902.
The Treasure of Heaven. 1906.

Studies of Marie Corelli

Bigland, Eileen. *Marie Corelli: The Woman and the Legend*. London: Jarrolds, 1953.
      Casey, Janet Galligani. "Marie Corelli and *Fin de Siècle* Feminism." *English Literature in Transition* 35.2 (1992): 163–78.
Federico, Annette. "Literary Celebrity and Photographic Realism: Marie Corelli and Late-Victorian 'Picture Popularity.'" *Nineteenth Century Studies* 11 (1997): 26–50.
Felski, Rita. *The Gender of Modernity*. Cambridge: Harvard University Press, 1995.

Feltes, N. N. *Literary Capital and the Late Victorian Novel.* Madison: University of Wisconsin Press, 1993.

Kershner, R. B. "Modernism's Mirror: The Sorrow of Marie Corelli." In *Transforming Genres: New Approaches to British Fiction of the 1890s.* Ed. Nikki Lee Manos and Meri-Jane Rochelson. New York: St. Martin's Press, 1994.

Masters, Brian. *Now Barabbas Was a Rotter: The Extraordinary Life of Marie Corelli.* London: Hamish Hamilton, 1978.

Dinah Maria Mulock Craik
(1826-1887)

Kathleen Hickok

BIOGRAPHY

Dinah Maria Mulock was born in Stoke-on-Trent, Staffordshire, in 1826. Her father, Thomas Mulock, was an Irish dissenting preacher who lost his chapel and his family by his unorthodox views and behavior. When Dinah's mother, Dinah Mellard Mulock, died in 1845, Mulock refused to support his children. So Dinah set up housekeeping for her two younger brothers and began publishing fiction, poems, children's stories, and social essays to sustain their London establishment. These appeared initially in *Chambers's Edinburgh Journal, Fraser's Magazine*, and fashionable annuals, and later in *Macmillan's Magazine, Household Words, Good Words, Cornhill, Contemporary Review*, and other respected Victorian periodicals. One brother left art school, where he had been studying alongside Holman Hunt and other future Pre-Raphaelite painters, joined the merchant marine, and died in an accident in 1847. The other emigrated to Australia in 1850. Dinah Mulock then moved in with her friend Frances Martin and continued to develop her writing career. She focused particularly upon class, gender, and family issues as they affected unmarried women.

Literary friends and acquaintances Elizabeth Gaskell,* Margaret Oliphant,* Camilla Toulmin, Mrs. S. C. Hall, Jane Carlyle,* Alexander Macmillan, and Sydney Dobell encouraged this writing. Ultimately, Dinah Craik published twenty novels, the best known being *John Halifax, Gentleman* (though Craik preferred *A Life for a Life*); various social essays, including twelve collected in *A Woman's Thoughts About Women*; several lasting children's stories, including *The Adventures of a Brownie* and *The Little Lame Prince and His Travelling Cloak*; three volumes of poetry; some travel narratives; and much periodical fiction.

In 1865 at age thirty-nine she married George Lillie Craik, a twenty-eight-year-old Macmillan's editor disabled from a railway accident; they adopted an infant girl from the parish workhouse near their Bromley home in Kent in 1869. Dinah Craik died suddenly of heart failure while preparing for daughter Dorothy's wedding in 1887. Alfred, Lord Tennyson, Matthew Arnold, Robert Browning, and John Everett Millais helped plan Craik's Tewkesbury Abbey memorial.

MAJOR WORKS AND THEMES

Dinah Craik's dominant theme is the struggle of idealistic women and men against nineteenth-century gender, class, and family structures. In novel after novel, she rewards strong, religious, earnest, hardworking men and women and exposes vain, idle, frivolous, and duplicitous ones. In *A Woman's Thoughts About Women*, Craik details her political and philosophical views on women. Paramount was unmarried women's need for "something to do"—for meaningful work with adequate pay, so they could marry for love, responsible parenthood, and a moral and useful life instead of for money and rank. In all her work, Craik presents sympathetically not only genteel, middle-class women like herself but also servants, working-class women, "lost" or "fallen" women, and aging governesses.

Craik's early novel *Olive* features a heroine like Charlotte Brontë's* Jane Eyre—orphaned, small, plain, and unconnected—who supports herself (and her mixed-race, illegitimate sister) by painting. Olive finds both independence and love and marries happily; in contrast, a childhood acquaintance who marries cynically dies young and unhappy. *The Woman's Kingdom* contrasts idealized and willful brother and sister pairs: The doctor hero and schoolteacher heroine have a successful marriage, whereas the dilettante Pre-Raphaelite painter and the femme fatale experience a superficial and ultimately devastating relationship.

In her subtly didactic children's tales, Craik's fairies and brownies are similarly winsome but dangerously amoral creatures, devoted to self-indulgence and utterly lacking in morality or genuine feeling. *Alice Learmont* is an allegory of redemption from this selfish life through home and family ties; its imagery and theme evoke "Goblin Market" (1862) by Christina Rossetti.* *The Little Lame Prince* features the crippled male recurrent in Craik's works, whose gender privileges are neutralized by physical delicacy and debility. These characters both desire and critique the complementary sex roles with which Victorians tried to resolve sexual inequality.

John Halifax, Gentleman, Craik's only adult novel with a hero, not a heroine, was her greatest popular success. Strong, honest, pure, and diligent, John Halifax grows from impoverished orphanhood to financial and personal success by manifesting all the Victorian virtues. His foils are Phineas Fletcher, a cripple who adores John, and Lord Ravenel, a discontented aristocrat who, reformed, becomes an acceptable suitor for John's daughter. The book contains many topical references, including the steam engine, the first Reform Bill, and smallpox vaccination—all desirable reforms endorsed by Halifax.

Craik's novels generally address specific English customs or laws regarding women's position and family life, revealing their effect on both the interiority and the materiality of women's lives, for example, marital rights, divorce and separation, inheritance, and adoption. *King Arthur* explores the psychology of adoption for parents and children, conveying the anguish caused by England's having no adoption provision. Other novels address even broader issues: *A Life for a Life* considers rehabilitation of criminals versus capital punishment, exploring the psychology of guilt and the practical and religious redemption of murderers, fallen women, and faithless lovers. The innovative narrative technique—the hero and heroine keep journals, which are interwoven to tell the story—highlights the striking differences Craik observed in men's and women's emotions and experiences.

Dinah Craik's feminism was conservative but genuine. In her life and literary works, she regarded ordinary women as independent and even heroic. She deplored the double standard of education, sexuality, work, and money. And she protested the attribution of inferiority to women's differences: She considered most women morally and emotionally superior and more steadfast than most men.

CRITICAL RECEPTION

In her lifetime, Dinah Craik was compared with Charles Dickens, Elizabeth Gaskell, Charlotte Brontë, and George Eliot.* Although Eliot objected strongly, the comparison continues; Eliot's *Middlemarch* (1871–1872) particularly evokes *John Halifax, Gentleman*. As Victorian values, concerns, and aesthetics receded in the early twentieth century, Craik's reputation faltered. Nevertheless, critics have noticed the influence of *John Halifax, Gentleman* upon the young Ernest Hemingway. In the second half of the twentieth century, feminist scholars renewed interest in Craik's fiction and essays, if not her poetry. Sally Mitchell places Craik in the feminine tradition, tending "toward the conservative edge of radical thought" (115); Elaine Showalter praises the "combination of didacticism and subversive feminism" whereby Craik resembles Eliot and Brontë (6). Shirley Foster concludes, "Craik's novels are essentially explorations, not statements" (67); as such, they are very convincing and highly readable.

BIBLIOGRAPHY

Books in print include *Olive, and The Half-Caste* (Oxford University Press, 1996); *A Woman's Thoughts About Women*, with Craik's essay "On Sisterhoods" and Christina Rossetti's *Maude*, ed. Elaine Showalter (New York University Press, 1993); and *The Unkind Word and Other Stories* (Short Story Index Reprint Series). *John Halifax, Gentleman* (Dent, 1983) has seldom been out of print. There are plans to reprint *The Little Lame Prince and The Adventures of a Brownie* and *A Life for a Life*.

Works by Dinah Maria Mulock Craik

The Ogilvies. 1849.
Olive. 1850.
The Half-Caste: An Old Governess's Tale. 1851.
Alice Learmont. 1852.
Agatha's Husband. 1853.
John Halifax, Gentleman (illus. John Everett Millais). 1856.
A Woman's Thoughts About Women. 1858.
A Life for a Life. 1859, 1860.
Studies from Life. 1861.
Christian's Mistake. 1865.
The Woman's Kingdom. 1869.
A Brave Lady. 1870.
The Unkind Word and Other Stories. 1870.
The Adventures of a Brownie. 1872.
The Little Lame Prince and His Travelling Cloak. 1875.
Sermons Out of Church. 1875.
Thirty Years: Poems Old and New. 1880.
Plain Speaking. 1882.
King Arthur: Not a Love Story. 1886.
Concerning Men and Other Papers. 1888.

Studies of Dinah Maria Mulock Craik

Colby, Robert. "Miss Evans, Miss Mulock, and Hetty Sorrel." *English Language Notes* 2 (1965): 206–11.

Foster, Shirley. *Victorian Women's Fiction: Marriage, Freedom and the Individual.* London: Croom Helm, 1985. 40–70.

Mitchell, Sally. *Dinah Mulock Craik.* Boston: Twayne Publishers, 1983.

Nagel, James. "*John Halifax, Gentleman* and the Literary Courtship of Clarence and Grace." In *Ernest Hemingway: The Oak Park Legacy.* Ed. James Nagel. Tuscaloosa: Alabama University Press, 1996. 59–69.

O'Toole, Tess. "Adoption and the 'Improvement of the Estate' in Trollope and Craik." *Nineteenth-Century Literature* 52 (June 1997): 58–79.

Perkin, J. Russell. "Narrative Voice and the 'Feminine' Novelist: Dinah Mulock and George Eliot." *Victorian Review* 18.1 (Summer 1992): 24–42.

Richardson, Alan. "Reluctant Lords and Lame Princes: Engendering the Male Child in Nineteenth-Century Juvenile Fiction." *Children's Literature* 21 (1993): 3–19.

Showalter, Elaine. "Dinah Mulock Craik and the Tactics of Sentiment: A Case Study in Victorian Female Authorship." *Feminist Studies* 2 (1975): 5–23.

Spilka, Mark. "Victorian Keys to the Early Hemingway." *Journal of Modern Literature* 10.1 (Mar. 1983): 125–50.

Hannah Cullwick
(1833–1909)

Brian McCuskey

BIOGRAPHY

Hannah Cullwick, who labored anonymously as a domestic servant during her lifetime, is now famous for her secret marriage to the upper-class poet and writer Arthur J. Munby. The daughter of a saddler and a housemaid, Cullwick was born in Shropshire, where she attended a charity school for two years until entering domestic service at the age of eight. In 1854, she met Munby on the street in London; long fascinated with the lives and bodies of working women, he approached the strikingly tall maid-of-all-work and struck up a conversation. For the next two decades, while Cullwick moved from place to place as a servant and Munby remained a gentleman in London, they sustained a clandestine relationship that was as emotionally complex as it was socially transgressive. They finally married in 1873, but Cullwick preferred to live and work in Munby's chambers as his servant rather than as his wife, assuming that role in public only occasionally and always reluctantly. Munby coaxed her out to musical performances, plays, and trips to the country, but Cullwick resented having to play the lady when she felt so much freer and prouder as a servant. During the four years that they lived together, the conflict between their private and public lives gradually took its toll on their marriage; Cullwick returned to Shropshire in 1877, where she lived, visited periodically by Munby, until her death.

MAJOR WORKS AND THEMES

In 1854, at Munby's request, Cullwick began writing a diary; she ultimately wrote seventeen diaries for him, finishing the last one in 1873. Because circumstances necessarily kept them apart much of the time, Munby wished to keep in closer touch with Cullwick's daily activities and, more particularly, her daily work as a general servant. Cullwick was barely literate when she began this project, but her writing improved dramatically with practice and help from Munby. The diaries, therefore, thoroughly document the social and psychological experience of working-class Victorians whom the mainstream novels largely ignore. Munby insisted that Cullwick provide detailed descriptions of her mind-numbing chores, but the diaries also reveal a keen intelligence that grapples with sophisticated questions of class and gender identity. Cullwick wonders what constitutes the difference between herself and ladies of the upper classes; she analyzes the fine distinctions that create a hierarchy within the servant class; and she negotiates the competing demands of her deeply felt duty to employers, on the one hand, and her fierce desire for independence, on the other.

Cullwick's intelligence and self-consciousness are most evident in the games of role reversal, transgression, and exaggeration that she played with Munby and described in her diaries. Social and sexual differences between them became the source of both comic and erotic pleasure and served to strengthen their emotional bond. Cullwick frequently blackened her face, blistered her hands, and washed the feet of her "Massa," as she called him; Munby often sat in her lap and admired her superior masculine strength. In public, they played the roles of haughty master and despised servant, a performance that they laughed about in private. Munby also had Cullwick photographed in a variety of transgressive costumes and poses: as a fine mistress, a black slave, a working-class man. Taken together, these games allowed the master and the servant to parody, invert, and flout the rules of a culture that refused to recognize their illicit love.

CRITICAL RECEPTION

Munby's private papers, including Cullwick's diaries, were boxed and sealed at his request until 1950; in 1972, Derek Hudson published his biography of Munby based on those papers. Hudson cites Cullwick's writing only briefly, but Leonore Davidoff gives Munby and Cullwick equal time in her seminal 1979 analysis of their diaries in relation to Victorian ideologies of class, gender, and race. In the same year, Michael Hiley published a compilation of writings about and photographs of Victorian working women with excerpted passages from the diaries and letters of both Cullwick and Munby.

Since Liz Stanley's 1984 edition of Cullwick's diaries, literary and cultural critics have examined her life and writing from increasingly sophisticated and specific theoretical positions. Peter Stallybrass and Allon White explore the conjunction of dirt, class, and sexuality in their psychoanalytic reading of the Munby-Cullwick relation as a paradigm for identifying the psychic conflicts latent in bourgeois culture; Cora Kaplan examines the same conjunction in her feminist critique of nineteenth-century cultural representations of working-class women. Combining the psychoanalytic with the feminist perspectives, recent critics such as Heather Dawkins, Julia Swindells, and Carol Mavor have used the diaries and photographs to challenge conventional notions of autobiography and to pose questions about female self-representation, subjectivity, and sexuality.

BIBLIOGRAPHY

Cullwick's diaries are held by the Library of Trinity College, Cambridge, in the Munby collection. Stanley's edition of the diaries provides lengthy and representative selections from the manuscripts; to a lesser extent, Hiley's study also draws upon and quotes from the diaries.

Works by Hannah Cullwick

Victorian Working Women: Portraits from Life. By Michael Hiley. 1979.
The Diaries of Hannah Cullwick, Victorian Maidservant. Ed. Liz Stanley. 1984.

Studies of Hannah Cullwick

Davidoff, Leonore, "Class and Gender in Victorian England: The Diaries of Arthur J. Munby and Hannah Cullwick." *Feminist Studies* 5.1 (Spring 1979): 86–141. Reprinted in *Sex and Class in Women's History.* Ed. Judith Newton, Mary Ryan, and Judith Walkowitz. London: Routledge and Kegan Paul, 1983. 16–71.

Dawkins, Heather. "The Diaries and Photographs of Hannah Cullwick." *Art History* 10.2 (June 1987): 154–87.

Hudson, Derek. *Munby, Man of Two Worlds: The Life and Diaries of Arthur J. Munby, 1828–1910.* London: John Murray, 1972.

Kaplan, Cora. " 'Like a Housemaid's Fancies': The Representation of Working-Class Women in Nineteenth-Century Writing." In *Grafts: Feminist Cultural Criticism.* Ed. Susan Sheridan. London: Verso, 1988. 55–75.

Mavor, Carol. "Touching Netherplaces: Invisibility in the Photographs of Hannah Cullwick." In *Pleasures Taken: Performances of Sexuality and Loss in Victorian Photographs.* Durham: Duke University Press, 1995. 71–116.

Stallybrass, Peter, and Allon White. "Below Stairs: The Maid and the Family Romance." In *The Politics and Poetics of Transgression.* Ithaca: Cornell University Press, 1986. 149–70.

Swindells, Julia. "Liberating the Subject? Autobiography and 'Women's History': A Reading of *The Diaries of Hannah Cullwick.*" In *Interpreting Women's Lives: Feminist Theory and Personal Narratives.* Ed. Personal Narrative Group. Bloomington: Indiana University Press, 1989. 24–38.

Emily Davies
(1830–1921)

Anita Rose

BIOGRAPHY

Sarah Emily Davies was born to John Davies, an Evangelical minister, and Mary Hopkinson, daughter of a well-to-do businessman, in Southampton on 22 April 1830. She was the fourth of five children and the second daughter. The family settled at Gateshead when Davies was eight, where, as rector, Davies's father directed a mixed-sex school. He quickly restricted enrollment to boys only, declaring that girls would "lower the tone" of the school. Thus Davies, unlike many contemporaries in the fight for women's rights, did not have the benefit of a supportive and liberal father. Instead, her father's attitudes about girl's education and women's limited abilities prepared her to face the prejudices and biases she would later encounter as a crusader for women's professional education. In 1848, Davies met and embarked on a lifelong friendship with Jane Crow and her family. Through Crow, Davies met Elizabeth Garrett (Anderson) and Barbara Leigh Smith Bodichon,* who introduced her to the organized English women's movement.

Upon her father's death in 1862, Davies moved to London, reconnecting with Bodichon and other feminists at Bodichon's Langham Place address. Here Davies began in earnest what would be her life's work: securing equal opportunities in higher education for women. She contributed regularly to periodicals such as *Contemporary Review* and briefly edited the *English Woman's Journal* and the *Victoria Magazine*. She campaigned to allow the admission of women into the University of London and to open local examinations for Oxford and Cambridge to girls.

In 1869, Davies, working with Bodichon, opened a college for women at Hitchin. In 1872, the school moved to Cambridge and was renamed Girton. After Girton was established, Davies served, reluctantly, as the school's first Mistress. When this tenure ended in 1875, she devoted her energy to ensuring educational rigor at Girton. However, despite the best efforts of Davies and others, women were not fully admitted to University at Cambridge until 1948, twenty-seven years after Davies's death.

Davies resigned from Girton's governing committee in 1904 and became more actively involved in the suffrage movement. Davies cast her first vote in 1919. She died on 13 July 1921 at her home in Belsize Park, London.

MAJOR WORKS AND THEMES

Davies was a tireless campaigner for women's education; although she recognized suffrage as an important issue, she felt strongly that without a solid and rigorous educational background, women had no chance of convincing men that women should be granted the vote. Conversely, she saw that women could better utilize this important right when their minds were suitably developed. Her *The Higher Education of Women* (1866) lays out a forthright case for the extension of women's education to professional and university levels. Unlike many Victorian feminists, she focused on the similarity, rather than difference, of the sexes, observing in the conclusion to *Higher Education* that "[n]o one urges that girls should be denied the use of cold water, or fresh air, or light . . . lest they should grow into boys," and thus it should follow that expanded educational opportunity would not turn girls into boys but into better citizens (162).

Davies initially opposed the establishment of Girton as a college for women only because she believed that the separation of men's and women's education could only serve to keep the standards for women's colleges low. She resisted the Victorian notion that concessions should be made to femininity but agreed to the establishment of a women-only Girton when it became clear that this was the only way to secure a place of any kind for women at Cambridge. Davies was pragmatic and conservative in her political thought. Unlike her more radical colleagues in the suffragist movement, she did not advocate universal suffrage. Rather, she advocated suffrage for single women householders and married women who owned property independently of their husbands. She did, however, see clearly the connection between the vote and improved educational, social, and legal status for women. In her 1905 essay "The Women's Suffrage Movement," first published in the *Girton Review* and reprinted in the 1910 *Questions Relating to Women*, she states that suffrage would have a "deep and far-reaching effect," giving women "a new standing, a new increase of power" and the ability to win concessions for themselves. Further, she argued, the power to vote would eventually bring about the removal of the barriers to women's professional education and status (204–5).

CRITICAL RECEPTION

Davies had a wide network of friends and acquaintances, welcoming the aid of sympathetic men as well as women in her efforts. She was an energetic committee worker who preferred to stay out of the limelight, often deferring to those she deemed more well qualified to debate issues. Davies's reluctance to take the limelight, preference for collaboration and committee work, political conservatism, and focus on education rather than suffrage have made her less of a "name" in the Victorian women's movement, although her role in establishing Girton College has always suggested her importance. Her work as a theorist of Victorian feminism is just beginning to be explored, and her letters and essays, in their clarity and even-handedness, are an unexpected pleasure.

BIBLIOGRAPHY

Davies's 1866 book *The Higher Education of Women*, edited by Janet Howarth, is available from Hambledon (1988). A reprint of her writings collected in 1910 under the title *Thoughts on Some Questions Relating to Women* is available from AMS Press. Four of her essays are reprinted in *Barbara Leigh Smith Bodichon and the Langham Place Group* (Routledge & Kegan Paul, 1987), edited by Candida Ann Lacey. More information on Davies's association with Girton College, Cambridge, can be found at Girton's Internet Web site: http://www.girton.cam.ac.uk; information on Davies and other nineteenth-century advocates of women's education is available on the Spartacus Educational site: http://www.spartacus.schoolnet.co.uk/index.html. At seventy-five, Davies wrote an unpublished autobiographical *Family Chronicle* for a nephew; this and other papers are collected at Girton College, Cambridge.

Works by Emily Davies

The Higher Education of Women. 1866.
Thoughts on Some Questions Relating to Women. 1910.
Additional Davies articles not collected in *Thoughts*:
"Special Systems of Education for Women." *Victoria Magazine* 11 (1868): 356.
"The Training of the Imagination." *Contemporary Review* 12 (1871): 25.

Studies of Emily Davies

Bennett, Daphne. *Emily Davies and the Liberation of Women, 1830–1921.* London: Andre Deutsch, 1990.
Caine, Barbara. *Victorian Feminists.* Oxford: Oxford University Press, 1992.
Stephen, Barbara. *Emily Davies and Girton College.* Pioneers of the Woman's Movement. 1927. Westport: Hyperion Press, 1976.

Lady Florence Caroline Douglas Dixie (1857–1905)

Duangrudi Suksang

BIOGRAPHY

Lady Florence Caroline Douglas Dixie was a writer of travel books, fiction, poetry, and political essays and a staunch feminist, who, in an interview published in the 12 April 1890 issue of the *Women's Penny Paper*, affirmed, "[T]o alter woman's position to what I think it should be I would willingly give my life" (289). She was born in London into an old and distinguished Scottish family on 24 May 1857. Lady Florence Douglas's upbringing was unconventional, for she was permitted to do everything her brothers did. Her beliefs in independence and in equality between the sexes are central to her writings and activism.

In 1875 Florence Douglas married Sir Alexander Beaumont Churchill Dixie (1851–1924), with whom she had two sons. Soon after the birth of her younger son, Dixie traveled to Patagonia with her husband. The trip inspired her first travel book, *Across Patagonia* (1880), and two novels, *The Young Castaways; or, the Child Hunters of Patagonia* (1890) and *Aniwee; or, The Warrior Queen: A Tale of the Araucanian Indians and the Mythical Trauco People* (1890). Appointed as war correspondent for the *Morning Post* during the 1880–1881 Boer War, Dixie had an opportunity to travel widely in South Africa. While in South Africa, she became involved in the movement to restore the Zulu king Cetshwayo to his throne. Her experiences in South Africa influenced her second travel book called *In the Land of Misfortune* (1882). At home, Dixie's social and political activism was evident in her support for Home Rule for Ireland and other colonies and her passionate fight for the women's suffrage. Because she adamantly believed in absolute equality between the sexes, she advocated coeducation, the rational dress reform, the reexamination of marriage vows and laws affecting women, and a change in the succession law to favor the eldest born without regard to sex. Dixie was a tireless activist who used her pen to further the causes of the disadvantaged until her death on 7 November 1905.

MAJOR WORKS AND THEMES

Dixie's autobiographical novel, *The Story of Ijain; or, The Evolution of a Mind*, written when she was nineteen and published in 1903, details her childhood and raises issues embodied in her later works. The narrator, Ijain, reflects on her childhood in Scotland and early upbringing by her mother, a convert to Catholicism. The novel shows that her sense of equality between the sexes developed early in life and became a continuing theme of her campaign for feminist causes. In it, Dixie expresses her religious doubt and criticizes orthodox upbringing. The young heroine, Lady Ijain, insists on the existence of a "Lady God" (2). Ijain's encounter with Lord den Linden at the age of fifteen recalls Dixie's meeting with George Earle Bulwer Lytton, to whom she dedicated *The Songs of a Child and Other Poems* (1902), composed under the pseudonym "Darling" between the ages of ten and seventeen. At the end of the novel, Dixie announces that she is "an antivivisectionist" (199), despite her love of hunting and shooting. Another autobiographical work is *Waifs and Strays; or, The Pilgrimage of a Bohemian Abroad*, a collection of poems written between 1870 and 1873, after the death of her brother Lord Francis Douglas in 1865, and published in 1884. The poems reveal a close relationship between the two. In the preface she describes the work as "the record of a child's pilgrimage abroad, written while following in the footsteps of a brother whose tragic death had awakened within me a longing to wander amidst the scenes in which the boy genius had lingered ere he died."

The antivivisectionism Dixie advocated at the end of *The Story of Ijain* is the focus of several of her writings expressing her objection to blood sports and exploitation of animals. In "The Massacre of the Innocents" she appeals to women to stop using feathers to decorate their hats (1427). *The Horrors of Sport* (1891; 1905 revised edition) exhibits her changed attitude and her sincere commitment to animals' rights.

Dixie's advocacy of women's rights was at the forefront of her activism. Her novels and articles reflect her belief in the natural equality between the sexes. She argued for women's professional and political participation. In "Woman's Mission," Dixie asserts, "Woman must receive an equal education to that of Man. As at an early age the boy should be taught to ride, to row, to shoot, to swim, and to practice athletic exercises, so should the girl go through a similar course of training" (114). Lady Maeva Doon, the heroine in Dixie's melodramatic novel *Redeemed in Blood* (1889), receives such an education. Like Dixie, Lady Maeva can do everything athletic that a man can—riding, shooting, running, and swimming. *Isola; or, The Disinherited* (1902), a verse play written in 1877, contains Dixie's criticisms of the religious marriage ceremony, which regards a woman as inferior to a man, and of the law of primogeniture, which recognizes only the eldest legitimate male as heir. At the end of the play, after her execution, Isola's ideal is realized in the decree of her ex-husband, who vows to rule by justice, fair play, and love. His citizens will enjoy religious freedom, and religion will play no role in marriage. Everyone will be equal, and the sexes will be brought up to respect each other. In her utopian novel *Gloriana; Or, The Revolution of 1900* (1890), she argues that to compete fairly with their male counterparts, women have to receive the same education and training as men. Dixie visualizes women gaining suffrage and finally, through the legislative process, full recognition as the physical and intellectual equals of men and subsequent access to equal opportunities in education and the professions. Dixie's final work, *Izra; or A Child of Solitude* (1906), serialized in the *Agnostic Journal* from 1902 to 1905, reiterates *Isola*'s themes of justice, fair play, and love and her concern for women's welfare. W. Stewart Ross describes it as "a work by itself. It is not a novel, it is not a book of travel—it defies classification. As a simple, sincere, high-souled knight errant of Benevolence, 'Izra' has no peer in literature, and, alas, far too few parallels in life" (*Agnostic Journal*, 30 Dec. 1905, 423).

CRITICAL RECEPTION

Lady Florence Dixie was well known to her contemporaries as a social and political activist as well as a writer. Her novels and travel books were reviewed favorably and widely, both at home and in the United States. Contemporary critics praised the revolutionary spirit in her works and recognized her as a champion of women's rights. Unfortunately, because her works are not currently in print and because there is very little scholarship on her, she remains obscure to most of today's students of Victorian literature. Among her works, *Gloriana* is most often studied by a few scholars of utopian literature. Dixie's other works, which represent her contributions to the women's movement and other reformist causes during the Victorian era, also merit renewed attention and revival.

BIBLIOGRAPHY

No works by Lady Florence Dixie are currently in print.

Selected Works by Lady Florence Dixie

Abel Avenged: A Dramatic Tragedy. 1877.
Across Patagonia. 1880.
A Defence of Zululand and Its King. Echoes from the Blue-Books. 1882.
In the Land of Misfortune. 1882.
Waifs and Strays; or, The Pilgrimage of a Bohemian Abroad. 1884.
Redeemed in Blood. 1889.

Aniwee; or, The Warrior Queen: A Tale of the Araucanian Indians and the Mythical Trauco People. 1890.
Gloriana; Or, The Revolution of 1900. 1890.
The Young Castaways; or, The Child Hunters of Patagonia. 1890.
The Horrors of Sport. 1891.
Woman's Position, and the Objects of the Women's Franchise League. 1891.
Isola; or, The Disinherited. A Revolt for Woman and All the Disinherited. 1902.
The Songs of a Child and Other Poems: Parts I & II. 1902.
The Story of Ijain; or, The Evolution of a Mind. 1903.
Izra; or A Child of Solitude. 1906.

Studies of Lady Florence Dixie

Albinski, Nan Bowman. *Women's Utopias in British and American Fiction.* London: Routledge, 1988.
Ardis, Ann. " 'The Journey from Fantasy to Politics': The Representation of Socialism and Feminism in *Gloriana* and *The Image-Breakers.*" In *Rediscovering Forgotten Radicals: British Women Writers, 1889–1939.* Ed. Angela Ingram and Daphne Patai. Chapel Hill: University of North Carolina Press, 1993. 43–56.
Frawley, Maria H. *A Wider Range: Travel Writing by Women in Victorian England.* Rutherford: Fairleigh Dickinson University Press, 1994.
Roberts, Brian. *Ladies in the Veld.* London: J. Murray, 1965.
———. *The Mad Bad Line: The Family of Lord Alfred Douglas.* London: H. Hamilton, 1981.
Stevenson, Catherine Barnes. *Victorian Women Travel Writers in Africa.* Boston: Twayne, 1982.

Lady Elizabeth Eastlake
(1809–1893)

Carol Huebscher Rhoades

BIOGRAPHY

Lady Eastlake (née Elizabeth Rigby) was born in Norwich on 17 November 1809, the fifth of Dr. Edward Rigby and Anne Palgrave's twelve children. Educated at home by governesses, she began drawing at age eight and studied French, Italian, and music. After residing in Germany from 1827 to 1829, she returned to London with her family and commenced serious studies of art and literature. She recorded her 1838–1839 journey to Russia and Estonia in *Letters from the Shores of the Baltic* (1841), her most popular and enduring work. Following a period in Edinburgh, Eastlake settled in London, marrying the painter and later president of the Royal Academy and director of the National Gallery, Charles Eastlake, in 1849. Until his death in 1865, the Eastlakes traveled extensively, researching and purchasing paintings for the National Gallery and collaborating on critiques of Italian religious art and the English edition of Kugler's history of Italian painting. Lady Eastlake continued publishing art history and criticism in the *Quarterly* and *Edinburgh Reviews* until shortly before her death on 2 October 1893.

MAJOR WORKS AND THEMES

The first woman to write regularly, although anonymously, in the conservative *Quarterly Review*, she produced essay reviews on children's books, literature, art, photography, travel, education, dress, and music. Eastlake's diverse subjects are united by her belief in English superiority and women's unique discernment of human nature and domestic detail. Assurance and knowledge permeate her oeuvre, and those writings are made lively by Eastlake's ability to describe with a delightful turn of phrase. Even Eastlake's early essays display the attributes that she deems essential in the lady writer: "all ease, animation, vivacity, . . .

leaving many a clear picture traced on the memory, and many a solid truth impressed on the mind" ("Lady Travellers" 99).

Eastlake's attention to social and domestic details in *Letters from the Shores of the Baltic* enlightens and engages readers with the extravagances of the Russian court and constricted lives of Estonian peasants. The book quickly shifts from the perils of the journey to description and critique, portraying Estonian society from the domestic arrangements to history and religious and social customs. Eastlake travels and studies the region extensively, even taking lessons in Russian and Estonian. Her intense interest makes the book authoritative and readable. Her belief in the rights and responsibilities of the aristocracy underlies criticisms of the Baltic landholding class in the *Letters* and in her only fictional writing *Livonian Tales* (1846). The longest, most developed of the three *Livonian Tales*, "The Disponent," inserts social criticism into a cliched plot of long-suffering peasants who weather their travails and are duly rewarded with high position and worldly goods. The story concludes romantically with a benevolent and newly responsible baron returning home to undo his bailiff's misdeeds, while elucidating the destructive effects of the heartless Russian bureaucracy upon peasant morale and self-respect and refuting Baltic folk "wisdom" about the silliness and contrariness of women. "The Jewess" further emphasizes women's good sense and competence.

Numerous review articles reveal Eastlake's erudition and strong opinions. "Lady Travellers" recommends several books for their enjoyable and informative female perspective but clearly favors English over German and Russian travelers. In her most notorious review, then and now, she is forgiving of the foibles of Thackeray's Becky Sharp but castigates Charlotte Brontë's* Jane Eyre as "vulgar-minded." Nevertheless, she respects Jane for her determination and firmness, qualities espoused with the intellectual equality of males and females in "The Englishwoman at School" (*Quarterly Review*, July 1878). Her "sisterhood" is clearest in *Fellowship: Letters Addressed to My Sister Mourners* (much appreciated by Queen Victoria*), which offers kind and practical solace supported by a positive religious faith. Decidedly preferring the "Quattro-Centisti" (the great painters of the Italian Renaissance), much of Eastlake's writing focused on art history and criticism with translations of Passavant, Waagen, and Kugler; lengthy essays on Michelangelo, Titian, Raphael, and da Vince; and a carefully researched completion of Anna Jameson's* *The History of Our Lord as Exemplified in Works of Art*. Insisting on having her name on the title page for these works, Eastlake was still identified as "the Author of the Baltic Letters" in reminiscences published in her last year of life.

CRITICAL RECEPTION

Lady Eastlake's works have received very little critical attention, other than the continuing dismay expressed over her review of *Jane Eyre*. Marion Lochhead's biography examines Eastlake within the Edinburgh and London literary

and artistic circles of Victorian England. While offering little analysis of Eastlake's writings, Lochhead emphasizes Eastlake's strengths from a feminist perspective: "She was not always gentle. Her strong prejudices, her outspoken
opinions, her uninhibited pungency of expression made her a formidable ad-
versary. . . . If she does not lead the procession of eminent Victorian women,
she still holds her place" (158). Joseph Garver analyzes the sensibility, romantic
pastoralism, and realism of the *Livonian Tales* with comparisons to Scott, Elizabeth Gaskell,* and George Eliot* and argues for reading the tales in light of
the "condition-of-England" debate.

Although Eastlake's work was well received during the nineteenth century,
she has been dismissed as "without any except historical interest" (Stanley J.
Kunitz, *British Authors of the Nineteenth Century* [H. W. Wilson, 1936], 206).
However, Adele Ernstrom's assessment of Eastlake's questioning of Ruskin's
dichotomy of thought and language through an analogy implicitly critical of the
realities of marriage suggests that her writings demand more serious, in-depth
analyses.

BIBLIOGRAPHY

Letters from the Shores of the Baltic was reprinted in 1970 (Arno Press, "Russia
Observed" series), and the *Journals and Correspondence* of Lady Eastlake, 2 vols., is
currently in print (AMS Press, 1995). Two selections by Eastlake are included in *Prose
by Victorian Women: An Anthology* (ed. Andrea Broomfield and Sally Mitchell [Garland,
1996]).

Selected Works by Lady Eastlake

A Residence on the Shores of the Baltic. 1841. Later editions titled: *Letters from the
        Shores of the Baltic.*
"Lady Travellers." *Quarterly Review* 76 (June 1845): 98–137.
Livonian Tales: The Disponent, The Wolves, The Jewess. 1846.
"*Vanity Fair* and *Jane Eyre.*" *Quarterly Review* 84 (Dec. 1848): 153–85.
"Modern Painters." *Quarterly Review* 98 (Mar. 1856): 384–433.
The History of Our Lord as Exemplified in Works of Art: With That of His Types; St.
        John the Baptist; and Other Persons of the Old and New Testament. Commenced
        by Anna Jameson; continued and completed by Lady Eastlake. 1864.
Fellowship: Letters Addressed to My Sister Mourners. 1868.
Handbook of Painting. The Italian Schools. Based on the Handbook of Kugler. 4th ed.
        revised and remodelled by Lady Eastlake. 1874.
Five Great Painters: Essays Reprinted from the Edinburgh and Quarterly Reviews. 1883.
Journals and Correspondence of Lady Eastlake. 2 vols. Ed. Charles Eastlake Smith.
        1895.

Studies of Lady Eastlake

Ernstrom, Adele M. " 'Equally Lenders and Borrowers in Turn': The Working and Married Lives of the Eastlakes." *Art History* 15.4 (Dec. 1992): 470–85.

Garver, Joseph. "Lady Eastlake's 'Livonian' Fiction." *Studia Neophilologica* 51.1 (1979): 17–29.

Lochhead, Marion. *Elizabeth Rigby, Lady Eastlake*. London: Murray, 1961.

Emily Eden
(1797–1869)

Eric Sterling

BIOGRAPHY

The Honourable Emily Eden (novelist, letter writer, and artist) was the seventh daughter and twelfth child (out of fourteen) of diplomat William Eden, the first Baron Auckland, and of Eleanor Elliot, the first Earl of Minto's sister. The Edens frequented aristocratic circles (primarily Whig) and were related to prominent figures such as Eleanor Eden and Vita Sackville-West. Consequently, Emily Eden enjoyed an excellent education through the teaching of governesses. Emily, along with her sister Fanny, accompanied her brother George to India and functioned as his hostess while he served as the governor-general from 1835 to 1842. She enjoyed entertaining guests and was an excellent conversationalist who spoke eloquently about politics. She did not, however, enjoy her stay in Calcutta, for the heat and loneliness afflicted her. Because George's political affairs often rendered him too busy to spend time with her, she entertained herself by writing accounts of her life in India (*Up the Country*, 1866). Furthermore, Eden's paintings appeared in a volume entitled *Portraits of the Princes and People of India* (1844). She also published two novels, *The Semi-Detached House* (1859) and *The Semi-Attached Couple* (1860 but written in 1830). Her great-niece Violet Dickinson published her letters in 1919, forty-seven years after the publication of *Letters from India*. After her return from India, she wrote and spent the rest of her life as hostess to various celebrities who visited her house, Eden Lodge, in Kensington.

Eden never married, although men, such as Lord Melbourne, expressed interest in her. She chose never to marry, partly because she saw her siblings devote so much of their time to caring for their children and partly because of her strong devotion to her brother George. In fact, her attachment to George was so strong that she did not want any man to come between them. Marian Fowler says that Eden "in personality and tastes was more 'masculine' than 'feminine,' according to her society's understanding of those terms. When Emily was growing up, women were expected to be physically delicate, shy and retiring, submissive to male authority, passive and intuitive. Their powers of reasoning were held to be inferior to men's" (16). Ignoring these stereotypes, Eden freely spoke with men about politics and other issues.

MAJOR WORKS AND THEMES

The two novels of Emily Eden are comedies of manners, the first of which focuses on city and country life. Jane Austen* was Eden's primary influence and source of inspiration; most critics mention similarities between the two writers in terms of their themes and writing styles. Eden's novels deal with aristocratic life, primarily because most of the people the author interacted with derived from the upper class. Like Austen, Eden possessed a gift for witty dialogue and biting social satire. In *The Semi-Detached House*, the pregnant heroine, Blanche, who is accustomed to city life, receives an education about people from the country and discovers, to her surprise, that the stereotypes she has accepted are baseless; the novel also focuses on the threat of the business world and the evils of anti-Semitism. *The Semi-Attached Couple* concerns a newly married couple, the Teviots, who discover how challenging a new marriage can be. The Teviots are wealthy, yet they learn that they are still somewhat unhappy and lonely. Eden's novels illuminate the author's apprehensions concerning marriage. The novels contain marriages that are acceptable but not happy or loving unions, reminiscent of the Bennet marriage in Austen's *Pride and Prejudice*.

CRITICAL RECEPTION

Emily Eden's novels were very successful; in fact, the success of *The Semi-Detached House* (published anonymously) encouraged her the following year to publish her second novel, *The Semi-Attached Couple*, which she had penned thirty years earlier. Upon learning of the popularity of *The Semi-Detached House*, she acknowledged that she had written it. B. E. Schneller remarks that Eden earned £300 for *The Semi-Detached House* from her publisher, Bentley, and was grateful to receive letters from friends who admired the humorous manner in which she characterized city and country customs (203). Her second novel also proved successful. John Gore, in a March 1924 article entitled "A Rival to Jane Austen" (published in *The London Mercury* 9.53), claims that although Eden's *Semi-Attached Couple* is not as good as *Pride and Prejudice*, it is superior to *Sense and Sensibility*. He adds that Austen compensated for her lack of worldly experience with her natural talent and common sense; Eden's works are as good as Austen's because Eden possessed the worldly experience that the other lacked, compensating for not possessing Austen's genius. Eden's collection of letters, entitled *Up the Country*, was highly received by reviewers.

Janet Courtney considers Eden a peerless writer whose works impress the reader with their wit and astuteness. Furthermore, Eden's sketches and watercolors were highly regarded.

BIBLIOGRAPHY

Up the Country has been reprinted several times. *The Semi-Attached Couple* and *The Semi-Detached House* are currently available as audiotapes.

Works by Emily Eden

Portraits of the Princes and People of India. 1844.
The Semi-Detached House. 1859.
The Semi-Attached Couple. 1860.
Up the Country: Letters Written to Her Sister from the Upper Province of India. 1866.
Letters from India. 1872.
Miss Eden's Letters. Ed. Violet Dickinson. 1919.

Studies of Emily Eden

Courtney, Janet E. *The Adventurous Thirties: A Chapter in the Women's Movement*. 1933. Freeport: Books for Libraries Press, 1967.
Dunbar, Janet. *Golden Interlude: The Edens of India 1836–1842*. London: John Murray, 1955.
Fowler, Marian. *Below the Peacock Fan: First Ladies of the Raj*. Ontario: Penguin, 1987. 13–91.
Hannay, Prudence. "Emily Eden as a Letter-Writer." *History Today* 21 (July 1971): 491–501.
Harris, Laurie Lanzen, and Emily B. Tennyson, eds. *Nineteenth-Century Literature Criticism*. 53 vols. Detroit: Gale, 1985. 10: 102–11.
Myer, Valerie Grosvenor. Introduction. *The Semi-Attached Couple & The Semi-Detached House*. New York: Dial Press, 1982. 11–16.
Schneller, B. E. "Emily Eden." In *British Women Writers: A Critical Reference Guide*. Ed. Janet Todd. New York: Continuum, 1989.
Stephen, Sir Leslie, and Sir Sidney Lee. *The Dictionary of National Biography*. 22 vols. 1921–1922. London: Oxford University Press, 1949–1950. 6: 356.
Sutherland, John. *The Stanford Companion to Victorian Fiction*. Stanford: Stanford University Press, 1989. 205.

Maria Edgeworth
(1768-1849)

Heidi Thomson

BIOGRAPHY

Marie Edgeworth was born in Oxfordshire, the third child of Richard Lovell Edgeworth and his first wife Anna Maria Elers, who died when Maria was only five years old. From the age of fourteen, she lived on her family's estate in the Irish Midlands. Her father remarried three more times and fathered twenty-two children in all, many of whom were educated by Maria, who never married. The family's Anglo-Irish status, their relative isolation, the makeup of the family, and R. L. Edgeworth's various interests contributed to Maria's understanding of herself as a writer. As child minder, assistant to her father, companion to her stepmothers (the last of whom was a year younger than Maria herself), and after the death of her father, manager of the estate, Maria gained firsthand experience in matters that inform her work.

Edgeworth's output stretches over three decades. Her early work deals largely with educational matters: In *Letters for Literary Ladies* (1795) she argues for women's education, and in *Practical Education* (1798, with her father) she argues for a rationalist, secular, and empirically oriented approach to education. The educational dimension of her stories is also obvious in Edgeworth's awareness of audience: The stories in *The Parent's Assistant* (1795) and the "Harry and Lucy" tales (*Early Lessons*, 1801) are addressed to children; the *Moral Tales* (1801) are aimed toward adolescents; and the *Popular Tales* (1804) were written for unsophisticated readers in general. Edgeworth's first novel, *Castle Rackrent, an Hibernian Tale* (1800), tells the story of the ruin of the Rackrent family as told by Thady, an Irish Catholic servant. Three more so-called Irish novels follow: *Ennui* (first published in *Tales of Fashionable Life*, 1809), *The Absentee* (first published in *Tales of Fashionable Life*, 1812), and *Ormond* (published together with *Harrington*, 1817). Edgeworth also wrote novels about contemporary English society: *Belinda* (1801), *Leonora* (1806), *Patronage* (1814), and

Helen (1834). She traveled twice to France; she visited London, where she was feted as a famous author; and she considered a visit to Walter Scott at Abbotsford in 1823 the highlight of her later years. By the 1840s she was no longer a literary lion and devoted her considerable energies to the financial management of the estate. She died peacefully at the age of eighty-one.

MAJOR WORKS AND THEMES

Edgeworth's last novel appeared three years before the accession of Queen Victoria,* but her work clearly informs the social novel of the nineteenth century. Her novels emphasize in particular how mothers are responsible for the shaping of young characters and the moral management of the larger household and the estate. Her satirical portrayal of irresponsible motherhood and the astute description of children's burdens in the family prefigure the concerns of the Brontës,* Elizabeth Gaskell,* Dickens, and others. As a writer for and about children, she is a pioneer in a genre that does not get developed until the middle of Victoria's reign. *Practical Education* is probably the most important text on education of the period and anticipates major educational legislation that did not get into effect until 1870. Edgeworth's commitment to education extended across class and gender, but unlike the more radical Harriet Martineau,* she did not challenge the social order. In contrast to the more evangelically inspired educationalists, however, Edgeworth never resorted to threats of religious damnation to admonish children.

Like the Victorians after her, Edgeworth is interested in historical and scientific origins, as her frequent references to the works of Erasmus Darwin, author of *The Botanic Garden* (1791), indicate. Her exploration of suspected breast cancer in *Belinda* (1801) illustrates her critical awareness of the medical world and problems between patients and doctors.

Edgeworth's vision of the family as the stabilizing force for society also reveals her conservatism. Convinced of the moral superiority of the Anglo-Irish landowning class, to which she herself belonged, Edgeworth usually condemns individual instances of abuse, such as the misrule of particular absentee landlords, rather than the social order that condones these abuses. Her idea of the model family extends to the idea of the model estate characterized by a benevolent hierarchical authority, and her condemnation of the abuses of colonial rule and slavery are best read in that context. Her pleas for modest reform as opposed to full-scale revolution anticipate Victorian conservatism in its desire to build up, maintain, and justify a global empire.

CRITICAL RECEPTION

As a genre the novel remained highly suspect well into the nineteenth century, and Edgeworth took care not to be associated with any flightiness. Francis Jeffrey of the *Edinburgh Review* shaped Edgeworth's formidable social and moral status as a writer who introduced large numbers of readers to "homely virtues." Edgeworth is praised by her contemporaries for her moral status and her "realistic" portrayal of the Irish, and late-twentieth-century critics continue to read *Castle Rackrent* as the "first significant English novel to speak in the voice of the colonized" (Perera 15). Jane Austen,* Scott, Macaulay, and Thackeray loved her work, and so did Ruskin, who praised her work as "the most re-readable books in existence." Edgeworth's hugely popular *Tales and Novels* (1832–1833) stayed in print throughout the nineteenth century. Her overt didacticism put off twentieth-century readers, but a renewed interest in women writers, colonial discourse, and children's writing have led to a rediscovery of Edgeworth's work from the 1980s on, leading to the recent replication of her works.

BIBLIOGRAPHY

Many of Edgeworth's novels are currently in print, and we now have the first collected edition since the nineteenth century in the twelve-volume Pickering and Chatto edition: *The Novels and Selected Works of Maria Edgeworth*, edited by Marilyn Butler et al. (1999).

Selected Works by Maria Edgeworth

Letters for Literary Ladies to which is added an *Essay on the Noble Science of Self-Justification*. 1795.
The Parent's Assistant. 1795.
Practical Education. With R. L. Edgeworth. 1798.
Castle Rackrent, an Hibennian Tale. 1800.
Early Lessons. 1801.
Moral Tales. 1801.
Popular Tales. 1801.
Leonora. 1806.
Tales of Fashionable Life. 1809.
The Absentee. 1812.
Patronage. 1814.
Ormond and Harrington. 1817.
Tales and Novels. 1832–1833.
Helen. 1834.
Maria Edgeworth: Letters from England 1813–1844. Ed. Christina Colvin. 1971.
Maria Edgeworth in France and Switzerland. Ed. Christina Colvin. 1979.

Studies of Maria Edgeworth

Butler, Marilyn. *Jane Austen and the War of Ideas*. Oxford: Oxford University Press, 1975.
———. *Maria Edgeworth: A Literary Biography*. Oxford: Clarendon, 1972.
Harden, Elizabeth. *Maria Edgeworth*. Boston: Twayne, 1984.

Kowaleski-Wallace, Elizabeth. *Their Fathers' Daughters: Hannah More, Maria Edge-worth, and Patriarchal Complicity*. New York: Oxford University Press, 1991.

McCormack, W. J. *Ascendancy and Tradition in Anglo-Irish Literary History from 1789 to 1939*. Oxford: Clarendon, 1985.

Perera, Suvendrini. *Reaches of Empire: The English Novel from Edgeworth to Dickens*. New York: Columbia University Press, 1991.

Vance, Norman. *Irish Literature: A Social History*. Oxford: Basil Blackwell, 1990.

"George Egerton" (Mary Chavelita Dunne Bright) (1859-1945)

Kimberly VanHoosier-Carey

BIOGRAPHY

Mary Chavelita Dunne Bright, as "George Egerton," published several short story collections in the 1890s that broadly fall into the classification "New Woman fiction." Egerton was born in Melbourne, Australia, to a Welsh mother who died when Egerton was fourteen and an impoverished Irish military father. At the age of twenty-eight, Egerton ran off to Norway with her father's friend, bigamist Henry Higginson. This move, combined with the blunt subject matter of Egerton's stories, marked her as a scandalous figure. While in Norway, several things happened that would influence her later work. She was subjected to Higginson's violent drunken outbursts, reproduced in stories such as "Under Northern Sky." She also became fascinated with the works of Henrik Ibsen and Scandinavian realists like Knut Hamsun, whose novel *Hunger* Egerton translated and to whom *Keynotes* is dedicated. After her return to England, Egerton married and moved to Ireland with George Egerton Clairmonte, whose name she borrowed for her pseudonym; shortly thereafter, she began writing to support herself, her husband, and in 1895, a son. After divorcing Clairmonte, she married Golding Bright, a much younger drama critic. As Egerton's early prominence faded, she returned to translating and tried playwriting, though none of her plays were popular or critical successes.

MAJOR WORKS AND THEMES

Egerton's first collection, *Keynotes* (1893), was published by John Lane as the first title in his "Keynotes" series of contemporary, woman-centered fiction. Like other New Woman fiction, the stories in *Keynotes* and the subsequent *Discords* (1894) examine women's traditional social roles. Although Egerton valorized motherhood, she stressed the dangers of women's confinement within domesticity and girls' enforced sexual ignorance. Egerton (and others) drew an analogy between marriage and prostitution; in "Virgin Soil," for instance, a daughter angrily berates her mother, "You sold me for a home, for clothes, for food" (*Discords* 157).

Throughout her stories, Egerton broadens traditional definitions of femininity, presenting a variety of female characters, including "fallen," divorced, and working women, to break away from the limited range of acceptable roles. Most characters remain unnamed in her stories, making each almost an "everywoman" and encouraging a recognition of the similarities among them, despite differences in class or status. In "A Cross Line," the main character fantasizes about performing outside the "virtuous monotony" of women's daily lives and decides that conventional standards ignore "the untamed primitive savage temperament that lurks in the mildest, best woman," which is, in fact, "the keynote of woman's witchcraft and woman's strength" (*Keynotes* 19, 22). In the utopian story that concludes *Discords*, "The Regeneration of Two," Egerton presents an alternative to such misunderstandings of women: a cooperative of women working together to create "a new standard of woman's worth" (242).

Egerton also attempts to broaden "man-made" notions of morality: In "A Psychological Moment in Three Periods" she explains, "There is no half way for a woman"—either she is completely chaste or she is marked as shameful and unnatural (*Discords* 27). Egerton's stories advocate a more flexible view and encourage sympathy with women typically seen as immoral. In "A Psychological Moment," the woman is blackmailed into moving to Paris with a married man yet retains her honor. "Gone Under" explains a woman's descent into alcoholism and prostitution after her illegitimate baby is smothered on her lover's orders.

Egerton's rewriting of conventional views is underscored by the innovative formal elements of her texts. She disrupts the stories' realistic surface by incorporating almost Modernist elements: She interweaves various narrative voices (usually female), incorporates dramatic elements as well as stream-of-consciousness passages, uses sentence-level and narrative ellipses to omit elements traditionally considered "significant," and relies on the present tense throughout to emphasize the immediacy, as well as the universality, of each (woman's) story. Most of the stories are impressionistic and episodic, presenting a single "psychological" moment or pivotal conversation that changes the main character's perspective on her role in society.

CRITICAL RECEPTION

When *Keynotes* first appeared, reviewers praised Egerton for capturing women's "souls" and accurately presenting women's varied experiences. Yet critical outrage at the shocking subject matter seems to have been the louder, more vehement response; Egerton was often cited in the 1890s debates about "erotomania" and "candour" in fiction. Because of the texts' sexual explicitness and unconventional portrayals of women, reviewers proclaimed the stories indecent. A quintessential review charges Egerton with aggressiveness and poor manners, calling *Keynotes* "questionable stories written in dubious English" that "make Mrs. Grundy's flesh creep" (*Athenaeum* 3 Feb. 1894). The popularity of the stories, however, prompted *Punch* to publish a parody of "A Cross Line" called "She-Notes" by "Borgia Smudgiton" (1894).

Recent critics tend to discuss either Egerton's gender politics or her stylistic methods. Although Egerton is positioned primarily within the context of the 1890s New Woman writers, her work has recently been discussed in terms of *écriture féminine* (Pykett), proto-Modernist techniques (Pykett, Ardis), fin de siècle redefinitions of realism (Ardis), and imperialist discourses (Chrisman). Most current critics are uncomfortable, however, with Egerton's essentialism, evident in her invocation of an "eternal feminine." McCullough reexamines this essentialism in the context of other identity politics and forms of difference.

BIBLIOGRAPHY

Only three of Egerton's texts are currently in print: *Keynotes* and *Discords* have been reprinted in a single volume by Virago (intro. Martha Vicinus, 1995), and AMS plans to reprint *The Wheel of God*.

Works by George Egerton

Keynotes. 1893.
Discords. 1894.
Symphonies. 1897.
Fantasias. 1898.
The Wheel of God. 1898.
A Leaf from the Yellow Book: The Correspondence of George Egerton. Ed. Terence de Vere White. 1958.

Studies of George Egerton

Ardis, Ann L. *New Women, New Novels: Feminism and Early Modernism*. New Brunswick: Rutgers University Press, 1990.

Chrisman, Laura. "Empire, 'Race' and Feminism at the *Fin de Siècle*: The Work of George Egerton and Olive Schreiner." In *Cultural Politics at the* Fin de Siècle. Ed. Sally Ledger and Scott McCracken. Cambridge: Cambridge University Press. 1995. 45–65.

McCullough, Kate. "Mapping the 'Terra Incognita' of Woman: George Egerton's *Keynotes* (1893) and New Woman Fiction." In *The New Nineteenth Century: Feminist Readings of Underread Victorian Fiction*. Ed. Barbara Leah Harman and Susan Meyer. New York: Garland, 1996. 205–23.

Miles, Rosie. "George Egerton, Bitextuality and Cultural (Re)Production in the 1890s." *Women's Writing* 3.3 (1996): 243–59.

Nelson, Carolyn Christensen. *British Women Fiction Writers of the 1890s*. Twayne's
    English Authors Series. New York: Twayne, 1996.
Pykett, Lyn. *The "Improper" Feminine: The Women's Sensation Novel and the New
    Woman Writing*. New York: Routledge, 1992.

"George Eliot" (Mary Anne Evans) (1819–1880)

Joan M. Lescinski

BIOGRAPHY

"George Eliot's" stance as a novelist, a moralist, and a commentator on the nineteenth century cannot be overestimated. Perhaps the greatest English woman novelist, she holds her place among the men of the nineteenth century as a writer and sage, discussing the crucial social and political issues of the age. Eliot was a moralist who led an unconventional life. She was born on 22 November 1819 in Arbury, England, to Robert and his second wife, Christiana Evans. His first wife had died some years before he married Christiana in 1813. Christened Mary Anne (but later using Mary Ann or Marian), Eliot was the youngest of Robert Evan's six children. Mary Anne was closer to her sister Christiana (b. 1814) and her brother Isaac (b. 1816) than to her older half brother Robert and half sister Frances. Her father was manager of a large estate of Sir Francis Parker-Newdigate. Elements of Eliot's life have been compared to those in her fiction. Various critics have compared Eliot's father to Caleb Garth or Adam Bede in his steady respectability.

Her father favored the quiet, bookish Mary Anne and encouraged her reading. At her death, the first book she ever received, *The Linnet's Life*, a gift from her father, was found among her effects. Because of Mrs. Evans's poor health, the children were all sent early to boarding schools. For Eliot, this meant a painful separation from her favorite brother, Isaac, but she did have the comfort of her sister Chrissey at Miss Lathom's school in Attleborough. A voracious reader, Eliot reminds us of Maggie Tulliver in *The Mill on the Floss*. With too great a truth, Maggie's father compares the intellectual strengths of his two children, "It's a pity but what she'd been the lad" (Bk. 1, ch. 3). Chrissey and Eliot remained at Attleborough until 1828, when they transferred to a school in Nuneaton. During her time there, Eliot was befriended by the head governess, Marie Lewis, who deeply influenced her and under whose encouragement Eliot moved from the traditional Anglican faith of her parents to a more Evangelical approach to religious belief.

By thirteen, Eliot had outpaced her fellow pupils and was sent to yet another school, in Coventry, run by the Misses Franklin. Although the Calvinist schoolmasters encouraged severity, Eliot thrived intellectually under the greater academic challenge. She became proficient in French and music. During this time also, her pronunciation and diction were highly trained, erasing any linguistic sign of her provincial upbringing.

Eliot left Coventry to return home in late 1835, and her mother died a few months later in February. When Chrissey married the following year, Eliot remained at home, in charge of the house for her father, continuing her studies, including Greek, Latin, German, and Italian.

During this time the interest in religion grew, and as with all important matters in George Eliot's life, it became the focus of deep reading and reflection. At this time also, her father retired and moved with Eliot to a house just outside of Coventry where she met Charles and Caroline Bray and Caroline's brother and sister, Sara and Charles Hennell. Charles Hennell's treatise *An Inquiry Concerning the Origin of Christianity*, written in 1838, deeply affected Eliot with its thesis that the New Testament was not a historically provable document but rather a compilation of myths. Eliot began to doubt her Evangelical faith and abandoned it shortly thereafter. By January 1842 she enraged her family by refusing to go to church. A compromise was reached in which she agreed to attend church as long as she had freedom to think what she liked during the services.

After her father died in May 1849, she set out with the Brays for Europe to take the Grand Tour. After a prolonged stay in Geneva, she returned in early 1850 to England, where she took up residence with the Brays. In 1851 she moved to London to live in the house of the publisher John Chapman, his wife and two children, and their governess, Elizabeth Tilley, who was also Chapman's mistress. Despite her unattractive physical appearance (Henry James called her "magnificently ugly"), Eliot found men attracted to her manner and intellect. Tilley made life uncomfortable for Eliot when Chapman began to show interest in her; so Eliot returned to the Brays for more than a year until Chapman convinced his wife and mistress that he needed her for the publishing business.

From January 1852 until July 1854, Eliot edited the *Westminster Review*. Although John Chapman was listed as chief editor, Eliot was the actual editor of this influential, intellectual journal. In addition, she wrote numerous reviews and essays for the *Westminster Review*, including "Silly Novels by Lady Novelists" in which she wrote, " 'In all labour there is profit'; but ladies' silly novels, we imagine, are less the result of labour than of busy idleness" (*Selected Critical Writings*, ed. Rosemary Ashton [Oxford University Press, 1992], 320). During this period, she became acquainted with many of the important intellectuals of her day including Herbert Spencer and his friend George Henry Lewes. To the former she proposed marriage unsuccessfully; with the latter she formed a deep, abiding relationship that lasted until his death in November 1878. She moved from Chapman's house in October 1853, from which her intimacy with Lewes may be dated. Lewes had been separated from his wife because of her infidelity, but since divorce was nearly impossible at this time in England, Lewes considered himself free of his marital obligations.

By summer of 1854, Eliot and Lewes were living together, and they departed for the continent in July of that year, Eliot representing herself as his wife. Until Lewes's death, Eliot kept her position carefully, visiting only when asked, always afraid of a scandal. Lewes was a primary influence on Eliot in encouraging her to try her hand at fiction. Previously, she had done translations and some essay writing; by 1857, she had completed the first of her fictional works, a series of three short novellas entitled *Scenes of Clerical Life*. Its success led her to the sustained efforts that produced, over the next twenty years, such masterpieces as *Adam Bede, The Mill on the Floss*, and *Middlemarch*. Although she and Lewes never married, causing a nearly lifelong estrangement from her brother Isaac, they lived happily together until his death in November 1878. Eliot wrote to her friend Barbara Bodichon,* "He is the prime blessing that has made all the rest possible to me—giving me a response to everything I have written" (Haight 280). A friend of both hers and Lewes, John Walter Cross, a man twenty years younger than Eliot, comforted her in her grief after Lewes's death and proposed three times over the next year. They married in 1880, in the final year of her life, and she died on 22 December 1880 in London. Her remains are in Highgate Cemetery in London, next to Lewes's.

MAJOR WORKS AND THEMES

Prior to her move into fiction writing, Eliot had spent a fair amount of her energy, in addition to reviewing for magazines and writing nonfiction essays, grappling with the major mystical traditions of the Christian faith, as part of her own struggle with religious belief, and translating, for example, a German *Life of Jesus* (Strauss, 1846) and Ludwig Feuerbach's *Essence of Christianity* in 1854. Between 1858 and 1872 she published works of fiction steadily. Short pieces such as the novella *The Lifted Veil*, a strange tale of clairvoyance, are just now becoming frequently discussed; whereas *Middlemarch* has been widely read and admired since publication. In addition, Eliot wrote and published poetry, "essentially the work of a novelist on leave" (*Victorian Women Poets: An Anthology*, ed. Angela Leighton and Margaret Reynold [Blackwell, 1995], 221).

Eliot's first foray into fiction came in *Scenes of Clerical Life*, published in 1858 after having been serialized in *Blackwood's Magazine*. In the first of these novellas Eliot states her desire to increase the sympathy of her readers: "Depend upon it, you would gain unspeakably if you would learn with me to see some of the poetry and the pathos, the tragedy and the comedy, lying in the experience of a human soul that looks out through dull grey eyes, that speaks in a voice of quite ordinary tones" ("Amos Barton," ch. 5, *Scenes of Clerical Life*). Eliot's ability to portray all of her characters with sympathy caused Jane Carlyle* to declare, when she had finished *Adam Bede*, that she was in charity with the whole human race.

Adam Bede, Eliot's first full-length novel, portrays an upright carpenter, a man of integrity, whose love for the flighty, pretty Hetty Sorrel brings him into conflict with his employer, the dashing but morally shallow Squire Arthur Donnithorne. When Donnithorne impregnates Hetty, she flees, commits infanticide, and is condemned to the gallows but ultimately finds comfort and salvation at the hands of both Adam and the Methodist lay preacher Dinah Morris. Adam and Dinah eventually marry, but there is a somber cast at the end of the novel to their happiness, an acceptance of a diminished reality.

Threading its way through all of her fiction is a devotion to what she calls the "truth of feeling," which she believed was "the only universal bond of union." One expression of this joining of "heart" and "mind" is attributed to Adam in *Adam Bede*:

For it seems to me it's the same with love and happiness as with sorrow—the more we know of it the better we can feel what other people's lives are or might be, and so we shall only be more tender to 'em and wishful to help 'em. The more knowledge a man has, the better he'll do's work; and feeling's a sort of knowledge. (Bk. 6, ch. 52)

Another theme that may be found in Eliot's fictional worlds is that of "internal exile," a situation in which the characters often find themselves trapped inside constraints of others or of society. Examples abound, including Janet Dempster in "Janet's Repentance" in *Scenes of Clerical Life*, Adam Bede in *Adam Bede*, Maggie Tulliver in *The Mill on the Floss*, Silas Marner in *Silas Marner*, Dorothea Brooke and Dr. Tertius Lydgate in *Middlemarch*, and Daniel Deronda in *Daniel Deronda*. Such characters almost always survive, but they suffer ostracism from those around them and rarely, if ever, find a true "soul mate" who can ease the sufferings of their sensitive souls. At best, they find a measure of internal peace, but Eliot consistently denies them the kind of happy ending so beloved of the Victorian audience.

In her fiction, Eliot shows her female characters less as victims of their situations and more as individuals capable of decision making and of "seeing" the moral ramifications of their choices in the complex Jamesian sense of that word. None of her female characters is a stereotypical female character of the nineteenth century. In many ways, her women foreshadow the greater independence, at least of thought if not of action, of modern women, something Eliot did in her own life, as well.

Her next full-length novel, *The Mill on the Floss*, traces the protagonist Maggie Tulliver from her childhood through her untimely death by drowning in the River Floss. The novel draws a marvelously detailed picture of rural England at the turn of the century. It contains a sensitive portrayal of Maggie's struggles to be loved and accepted in a rigid society that accorded girls and women little freedom and less intellectual respect. Eliot traces the downward fortunes of the Tulliver family and again reveals her concern with insightful characters who are never able fully to use the gifts they possess, particularly the intellectual ones. Maggie becomes a virtual outcast from family, friends, and society, partly through her nonconformity to stereotypical female roles and partly through an accident in which she spends a night, innocently, with a young man. The inflexible sexual mores of the small town brand her a "loose woman," completing the isolation that had been growing for her throughout her life. Many readers have found the ending of *The Mill of the Floss* unsatisfying, as Maggie dies trying to save her brother from the flood. However, this novel does portray the closeness of Eliot's early relationship with her brother Isaac and the pain caused by his separation from her. This same theme is explored in her sonnet "Brother and Sister," which concludes:

> But were another childhood-world my share,
> I would be born a little sister there.

Silas Marner, a short novel published in 1861, chronicles the life of a reclusive weaver whose painful past has caused him, like many of Eliot's characters, to be alienated from society. Somber in tone, the novel brilliantly describes the lot of a man unjustly accused of theft and ostracized from his home and the redemptive power of love.

With *Romola* (1863), Eliot widens her fictional horizons. This ambitious novel is set in late-fifteenth-century Florence at a time of religious upheaval. Eliot focuses on Tito Melema, a handsome young man who squanders money meant to ransom his foster father, the elderly Baldasare Calvo, from slavery. Eliot had gone to Florence in May 1861, where she researched the novel and began writing it by the end of the year. A story that explores fidelity and its absence, *Romola* depicts various faces of love: the ambitious and lustful side in Tito; the simple devotion of a young, lower-class woman, Tessa; and Romola's quiet, elegant faithfulness and magnanimity. A theme of rebirth and the saving power of duty and love find their climax in the end of the story where Romola, betrayed by Tito, rises above her own feelings of loss and cares for both Tessa and the children Tito had by her.

With this departure from the agrarian folk of rural England of her earlier novels, Eliot moves into a set of novels that reflect more of the complexity of nineteenth-century England. *Felix Holt, the Radical* follows, completed in 1866. The title character is an educated young man caught up in the political unrest following the Reform Bill controversies of the 1830s. The major focus, however, is on Esther Lyon, Holt's beloved, and her moral development. She finds herself caught between the love of Holt and the attentions of Harold Transome, apparent heir to Transome Court. When Harold runs for election, Holt finds himself siding with the proletariat and subsequently arrested and jailed for attempting to quell an election riot in which a constable is killed. Ultimately, Esther chooses Holt and poverty over the life of the gentry at Transome Court that she comes to see as "silken bondage." Once again, a sensitive female figure opts not for security of marriage into the gentry but for a more socially unstable life with a dynamic man in tune with the changing mores of the century.

With *Middlemarch* (1872) Eliot produces what many consider her masterpiece and one of the outstanding masterpieces of British fiction. Its subtitle—*A Study of Provincial Life*—hints at its depth and complexity as a study of human strivings. Dorothea Brooke, a young, idealistic woman, seeks a spiritual guide but has poor judgment. She marries the elderly Edward Casaubon on the mistaken idea that she can assist him in a great project of intellectual depth. She discovers, instead, a pompous and emotionally barren husband bent on denying her any intellectual or emotional freedom. Interwoven with this story is the tale of Dr. Tertius Lydgate, a progressive young doctor who hopes to establish a hospital and pursue research. Like Dorothea Brooke, he marries unwisely, choosing the shallow, selfish Rosamond Vincy whose ambitions cause them to live beyond their means and to become entangled with an unscrupulous banker, Nicholas Bulstrode. The omniscient narrator can view the interconnected lives of all the characters, but each character has a limited vision:

Your pier-glass or extensive surface of polished steel made to be rubbed by a housemaid, will be minutely and multitudinously scratched in all directions; but place now against it a lighted candle as a centre of illumination, and lo! The scratches will seem to arrange themselves in a fine series of concentric circles around that little sun. It is demonstrable that the scratches are going everywhere impartially, and it is only your candle which produces the flattering illusion of a concentric arrangement, its light falling with an exclusive optical selection. (Bk. 3, ch. 27)

Virginia Woolf called *Middlemarch* "one of the few English novels written for grown-up people," and it does indeed deny conventional solutions to the problems of complex people like Dorothea Brooke and Lydgate. Each deserves a better, more intellectually satisfying spouse, but each settles for something less. The brilliance of the character development and the richness of the world depicted help to account for the high repute in which critics have held the novel.

Daniel Deronda, written in 1876, is "the most experimental of all George Eliot's novels—experimental in the technical sense that she tried out new narrative organisation" (Beer 214). In this novel Eliot follows the fortunes of Gwendolyn Harleth and Daniel Deronda. The former is a cold, egotistical young woman who marries not for love but to save her family from bankruptcy. The title character, Deronda, dominates the second part of the story. The two sections are connected when he becomes the confidant of Gwendolyn and assumes the role of spiritual guide for her. Discovering his heritage as a Jew, Deronda accepts himself and becomes a prototype of a modern man who seeks to resolve within himself pluralistic values, in this case, his upbringing as a Christian and his birth as a Jew. In *Daniel Deronda*, Eliot explores the role not only of religion but also of community. Eliot wrote essays following the publication of *Daniel Deronda* but did not attempt another major work.

CRITICAL RECEPTION

Since Eliot was writing under a pen name, the first reception of her writing referred to her as a man, no doubt to her pleasure, since she shared the concern of many female writers of the time that her work, if known to be by a woman, would have been stereotyped as intellectually shallow, fit only for light entertainment or modest instruction. *Adam Bede* was well received, especially in its portrayal of rural England and in its excellent character development of both major and minor figures. When her identity as a woman eventually came out, readers and critics alike felt a kind of betrayal that colored subsequent commentary during her lifetime. Praise for her work was not unanimous. Some writers thought her ponderous and dull, some were envious of her achievement, and others resented her remove from what Karl calls "the fray." Eliot was also an inspiration for many women; for example, Edith Simcox* wrote her *Autobiography of a Shirtmaker* as a tribute to her. Critics, whether Victorian or modern, whether Marxist or Structuralist, have, however, consistently praised the intellectual depth of the novels. She has also been credited with being the first writer of psychological realism, writing with respect of the experiences of the ordinary man.

Henry James, in reviewing John Cross's *Life* in the *Atlantic Monthly*, praises her as having "one of the noblest, most beautiful minds of our time. . . . [Her novels have] a kind of fragrance of moral elevation; a love of justice, truth, and light; a large, generous way of looking at things; and a constant effort to hold high the torch in the dusky spaces of man's conscience" (May 1885). However, many people felt that the publication of Cross's life resulted in a downward trend in her popularity, as it detracted from the complexity of this astonishing figure. Key interpreters of her work in the early part of the twentieth century include F. R. Leavis and Virginia Woolf, both of whom rank her among the very best novelists of the nineteenth century and part of a tradition of great, moral writing.

The last forty years have produced an enormous outpouring of comment on her work, partly because of access to such materials as Gordon Haight's biographical work and edition of her letters. Thorough commentary has explored her relationship to scientific thought, social theory, feminism, Marxism, and Positivism. Feminism, in particular, has caused critics to reexamine all literature in the context of sexual politics and, in particular, to revisit and reinterpret texts by women. From F. R. Leavis in *The Great Tradition* to modern literary historians like Elaine Showalter, Eliot's novels continue to be examined in light of questions of the day. In our own time, for instance, questions about women's rights, the nature of patriarchy, and the social and political impact of sexuality are entry points to the novels. Although there had been some devaluing of Eliot by critics who wish she were more overtly antipatriarchal, the critical estimate of her work continues to be very high, an acknowledgement of the depth and complexity of the works of this most intellectual of English novelists. Recently, Frederick Karl has credited Eliot with being the "voice of a century," in that she "seems most representative, most emblematic of the ambiguities, the anguish, and divisiveness of the Victorian era" (xi).

BIBLIOGRAPHY

All of George Eliot's primary works, including fiction, letters, and criticism, are widely available. The poetry is contained in the twenty-five-volume edition of her writing (English Literature Series, 1992), and a selection may also be found in recent anthologies of poetry by Victorian women. The letters have been edited by John Cross (1885) and Gordon Haight (1954–79).

Works by George Eliot

Scenes of Clerical Life. 1858.
Adam Bede. 1859.
The Lifted Veil. 1859.
The Mill on the Floss. 1860.
Silas Marner: The Weaver Raveloe. 1861.
Romola. 1863.
Brother Jacob. 1864.
Felix Holt, the Radical. 1866.
The Spanish Gypsy. 1868.
Middlemarch: A Study of Provincial Life. 1871–1872.
The Legend of Jubal and Other Poems. 1874.
Daniel Deronda. 1876.
Impressions of Theophrastus Such. 1879.
Essays of George Eliot. Ed. Thomas Pinney. 1963.
A Writer's Notebook 1854–79 and Uncollected Writings. Ed. Joseph Wiesenfarth. 1981.
George Eliot: Selected Essays, Poems, and Other Writings. Ed. A. S. Byatt and Nicholas Warren. 1990.
George Eliot: Selected Critical Writings. Ed. Rosemary Ashton. 1992.

Studies of George Eliot

Ashton, Rosemary. *George Eliot: A Life*. London: Hamish Hamilton, 1996.
Austen, Zelda. "Why Feminist Critics Are Angry with George Eliot." *College English* 37 (1967): 549–61.
Beer, Gillian. *George Eliot*. Key Women Writers Series. Bloomington: Indiana University Press, 1986.
Bodenheimer, Rosemarie. *The Real Life of Mary Ann Evans: George Eliot, Her Letters and Fiction*. Ithaca: Cornell University Press, 1994.
Carpenter, Mary Wilson. *George Eliot and the Landscape of Time: Narrative Form and*

Protestant Apocalyptic History. Chapel Hill: University of North Carolina Press, 1986.

Carroll, David ed. *George Eliot: The Critical Heritage*. New York: Barnes & Noble, 1971.

Dodd, Valerie. *George Eliot: An Intellectual Life*. New York: St. Martin's Press, 1990.

Haight, Gordon. *George Eliot: A Biography*. New York: Oxford University Press, 1968.

Hardy, Barbara. *Particularities: Readings in George Eliot*. Athens: Ohio University Press, 1982.

Karl, Frederick R. *George Eliot: Voice of a Century: A Biography*. New York: W. W. Norton, 1995.

Leavis, F. R. *The Great Tradition: George Eliot, Henry James, Joseph Conrad*. Harmondsworth: Penguin, 1962.

Paxton, Nancy. *George Eliot and Herbert Spencer: Feminism, Evolutionism, and the Reconstruction of Gender*. Princeton: Princeton University Press, 1991.

Perkin, J. Russell. *A Reception-History of George Eliot's Fiction*. Ann Arbor: UMI Research Press, 1990.

Showalter, Elaine. "The Greening of Sister George." *Nineteenth-Century Fiction* 35 (1980): 292–311.

Witemeyer, Hugh. *George Eliot and the Visual Arts*. New Haven, CT: Yale University Press, 1979.

Woolf, Virginia. "George Eliot." In *Collected Essays*. New York: Harcourt Brace & World, 1925. 1: 196–204.

———. *Women and Writing*. Ed. Michele Barrett. Dunvegan, Ontario: Quadrant, 1984.

Sarah Stickney Ellis
(1799–1872)

Richard A. Currie

BIOGRAPHY

Sarah Stickney, writer of conduct books and fiction, was born in Hull in 1799 (sometimes recorded as 1812) and died in Hodderson, Hertfordshire, in 1872. Her father, William, was a farmer. Her mother, a Quaker, taught Sarah to read. Sarah was then educated privately when her mother died. She published several books of poetry and domestic fiction. In 1837 she became a Congregationalist and married William Ellis, who gained fame as a Christian missionary. They were married for thirty-five years and had no children. Together they were active in Christian missions, but they also attempted to aid individuals to overcome drunkenness by taking them in and patiently exhorting them "to turn from their evil ways" (Stephen and Lee 715). She also ran a school for working-class girls, Rawdon House, designed to advance her views about women. Ellis thought women should subordinate their lives to men, yet she believed they should be trained in the ability to manage their households.

MAJOR WORKS AND THEMES

Her most widely reprinted conduct book, *The Women of England: Their Social Duties and Domestic Habits*, first published in 1839, appeared in more than twenty editions. Her conduct books, including *The Daughters of England* (1842) and *The Wives of England* (1843), were widely known and influential during the nineteenth century. Besides submission to male authority, Ellis advised women to concentrate upon motherhood and the business of the home. While men engaged themselves with external matters both political and social, ladies tended their homes. Though inferior in mental and physical strength to men, Ellis maintained that a woman's strength "is in her influence" for which she is "by nature endowed with peculiar faculties . . . a quickness of perception, facility of adaptation, and acuteness of feeling" (*The Daughters of England* 9).

In addition to conduct books, Ellis sought to advance her views about women and temperance by writing fiction. Her works of fiction include *Pictures of Private Life* (1833), *Home, or The Iron Rule* (1836), and *Pique* (1850). *Fireside Stories* (1850) contains an account of how a clergyman's family deals with drunkenness at home in "The Minister's Family." Her goal was application of the principles illustrated in her conduct books "to the moral training, the formation of character, and in some degree the domestic duties of young ladies" (Stephen and Lee 715).

Ellis is vigilant in advocating that all women, no matter their station in life, maintain agreeableness, attend carefully to their dress, speak tenderly, suppress angry feelings, and master the art of conversation designed to please those, especially men, with whom they find themselves in company. She argued that women should organize their day around helping others, not themselves. Ellis advised English women that "a willing temper . . . is the great thing to be attained, a temper that does not object, that does not resist, that does not hold itself excused" (*The Daughters of England* 148).

CRITICAL RECEPTION

Ellis first used the phrase "relative creatures" to describe women's inability to envision a "just estimate of the relative importance of things in general"; thus women were "from their own constitution, and from the station they occupy in the world, strictly speaking, relative creatures" (*The Women of England* 351). The domestic ideology upheld by Ellis was challenged by writers such as Emily Davies,* Millicent Fawcett, Josephine Butler,* Francis Power Cobbe,* and others who argued for women's autonomy (Caine). Some contemporary feminist critics find Ellis negligent in developing a subordinate, rather than an autonomous, status for women. Elaine Showalter in *A Literature of Their Own* (Princeton University Press, 1977) notes of Ellis's fiction that the female protagonist must give up her life for marriage (22). Sandra Gilbert and Susan Gubar in *The Madwoman in the Attic* (Yale University Press, 1979) suggest that the dutiful Helen Burns and Miss Temple in Charlotte Brontë's *Jane Eyre* are modeled on the conduct book heroines of Ellis.

Yet recently critics have argued that Ellis advocated solidarity with women but that this solidarity was not a call for liberating them from male authority but, rather, a way of existing in a system that "could not be changed" (Shattock 152). The authors of *The Feminist Companion to Literature in English* assert that Ellis's "writing reveals a strong fellow-feeling for women's domestic trials" (Blain, Clements, and Grundy 340). Barbara Caine in *Victorian Feminists* agrees, pointing out that Ellis in *The Wives of England* was dubious about what happiness a woman could expect from marriage. Elizabeth Langland finds Ellis's work reveals "tensions in this representation of women and work that stem from conflicts between patriarchal and bourgeois ideologies" (72). While some readers have seen Ellis as "advocating a kind of subversive management of men by women," Henrietta Twycross-Martin believes that "[b]oth her conduct-books and her fiction focus on the gap between the ideology of patriarchal authority and the lived experience of women coping with men as they actually are" (9). For Ellis, women have both superior moral power to men and the subversive ability to manipulate men. Ellis remains fascinating to read as a recorder of the manners and morals of the Victorian age and controversial as to how she understood the power and position of women in society.

BIBLIOGRAPHY

No works by Sarah Stickney Ellis are currently in print.

Selected Works by Sarah Stickney Ellis

Pictures of Private Life. 1833.
The Poetry of Life. 1835.
Home; or The Iron Rule. 1836.
The Women of England: Their Social Duties and Domestic Habits. 1839.
Family Secrets; or Hints to Those Who Would Make Home Happy. 1841.
The Daughters of England. 1842.
The Mothers of England. 1843.
Mrs. Ellis' Housekeeping Made Easy. 1843.
The Wives of England. 1843.
Temper and Temperament. 1844.
The Young Ladies' Reader. 1845.
Fireside Stories. 1850.
Pique. 1850.
The Mothers of Great Men. 1859.
Share and Share Alike; or The Grand Principle. 1865.
Rainy Days and How to Meet Them. 1867.
Education of the Heart: Woman's Best Work. 1872.

Studies of Sarah Stickney Ellis

Blain, Virginia, Patricia Clements, and Isobel Grundy. *The Feminist Companion to Literature in English: Women Writers from the Middle Ages to the Present.* New Haven: Yale University Press, 1990. 340.
Caine, Barbara. *Victorian Feminists.* Oxford: Oxford University Press, 1992.
Davenport, Randi L. "*The Mother's Mistake*: Sarah Stickney Ellis and Dreams of Empire." *Victorian Literature and Culture* 22 (1994): 173–85.
The Home Life and Letters of Mrs. Ellis. Compiled by her nieces. 1893.
Langland, Elizabeth. *Nobody's Angels: Middle-Class Women and Domestic Ideology in Victorian Culture.* Ithaca: Cornell University Press, 1995.
Shattock, Joanne. *The Oxford Guide to British Women Writers.* Oxford: Oxford University Press, 1993.

Shaw, Margaret. "Reading the Social Text: The Disciplinary Rhetorics of Sarah Ellis and Samuel Beeton." *Victorian Literature and Culture* 24 (1996): 175–92.

Stephen, Sir Leslie, and Sir Simon Lee, eds. *Dictionary of National Biography.* Oxford: Oxford University Press, 1921–1922. 6: 714–15.

Twycross-Martin, Henrietta. "Women Supportive or Women Manipulative? The 'Mrs. Ellis' Woman." In *Wollstonecraft's Daughters: Womanhood in England and France, 1780–1920.* Ed. Clarissa C. Orr. Manchester: Manchester University Press, 1996. 109–20.

Susan Edmonstone Ferrier
(1782-1854)

Miles A. Kimball

BIOGRAPHY

Susan Ferrier created novels displaying marvelous satires of Scottish manners and careful meldings of Romantic sensibilities, conservative morality, and a relatively progressive feminism. Ferrier was born in Edinburgh and lived as the spinster daughter of a Scottish lawyer. As her witty letters record, she spent nearly all of her creative life as the underappreciated woman at the foot of her father's table: "My father I never see, save at meals, but then my company is just as indispensable as the tablecloth or chairs" (*Memoir* 59; 1809?). Nevertheless, Ferrier dedicated herself to her father's care, remarking that "never even for a single day could I reconcile it either to my duty or inclination to leave him" (*Memoir* 59–60; 1809?).

The blandness of this life was enlivened by Edinburgh society, connections with other Scottish novelists, and one intense friendship. Ferrier's novels show her careful observation of the breadth and eccentricity of Scottish manners. Her region and her father's connections allowed her contact with all levels of society, from rustic to urban, from humble to grand. Through her father, she came to know the families of Henry Mackenzie, author of *The Man of Feeling*, and of Sir Walter Scott, whose homes at Abbotsford and Ashestiel she visited and whose encouragement she enjoyed. Through her own reputation, she also became familiar with Joanna Baillie.

Ferrier's father served as solicitor to the Duke of Argyll, and her one great friendship, with Charlotte Clavering, the Duke's niece, arises from that connection. With Miss Clavering, Ferrier undertook to produce the novel eventually published as *Marriage* in 1818. Although initially conceived as a partnership, the novel was written almost entirely by Ferrier. After *Marriage* garnered considerable profits, Ferrier undertook to write a second novel, *The Inheritance* (1824), and a third, *Destiny, or The Chief's Daughter* (1830).

Due to her ill health and a lack of satisfaction with her writing, Ferrier completed no fiction between the publication of *Destiny* and her death in 1854.

MAJOR WORKS AND THEMES

Ferrier was no great plotter; her three novels are most conventional in this regard. In *Marriage*, she begins with a foolish union and chronicles the contrasting educations and marriages of the twin girls born as a result of it. In *The Inheritance*, Ferrier complicates the marital plans of a young heiress by eventually revealing that she is of humble birth. And in *Destiny*, she relates the progress of a Highland chief's daughter who, after being raised to a high station, falls into poverty and eventually marries a supposed dead but miraculously reappearing cousin.

On these familiar frameworks, however, Ferrier creates a humorous world peopled with wonderful portraits of Scottish types. In this regard, Ferrier shares more with Charles Dickens than Jane Austen* or Maria Edgeworth,* to whom she is usually compared; Ferrier salts her stories with caricatures that enliven the action and counteract the generally formulaic characters at the center of the plot. She succeeds equally in satirizing men and women; she paints with bravura crusty Scottish lairds and eccentric Scottish ladies, venal clergymen and timid maiden aunts.

More interesting, however, is Ferrier's use of marriage as the stage on which to work out her ideology—a mixture of Romanticism, Christianity, and feminism. Ferrier's heroines receive an education valuing natural sensibilities and common sense rather than decorative attainments like singing, dancing, and embroidery. In *Marriage* and *Destiny*, Ferrier explicitly counters the frivolous high-society education of one young woman with the humble and useful education of another; in *Destiny*, the women are stepsisters, and in *Marriage*, twins. In Ferrier's novels, women with high-society educations risk superficiality and illustrious but loveless marriages; women educated with common sense can look forward to fulfilling marriages, love, and a contented growth of faith. In this sense Ferrier's novels provide an interesting response to the difficulties of nineteenth-century womanhood, one that balances between a conservative Christianity and a desire that women should lead meaningful lives.

It is perhaps ironic that Ferrier's own education, although following the common-sense model, instead of making her a fulfilled wife and mother, left her as a spinster aunt—a caricature she clearly applied to herself in many of her letters. But Ferrier's use of a metaphorical pregnancy to describe her writing—"I begin to expect I'm with Book"—suggests that as a novelist Ferrier found a fulfillment of her own through the pen. And in her creations, her value as a humorist and a commentator on women's lives makes her well worth reading.

CRITICAL RECEPTION

Many nineteenth-century readers admired Ferrier's novels, valuing their piquant characters and moral tone. During her day, Ferrier was favorably compared to Baillie and Maria Edgeworth, and she was clearly considered a feminine counterpoint to Scott.

Most twentieth-century readers, however, while they appreciate Ferrier's characters, find her conservative morality too extreme for their tastes. The general tendency is to consider Ferrier's moralizing a flaw that reins in her exuberant satire, making it a constrained version of what it might have been. But the morality of her novels is tied too closely to their fabrics to consider it a detraction; more compelling, perhaps is to think of Ferrier's morality and satire as living in dynamic counterpoise.

A more recent line of thought has been to consider Ferrier's novels through a feminist lens, reading them as an opportunity to see the interaction of diverging impulses: a conservative desire for married love, on the one hand, and on the other, an equally fervent demand for meaningful education for women.

BIBLIOGRAPHY

None of Ferrier's works are currently in print.

Works by Susan Ferrier

Marriage. 1818.
The Inheritance. 1824.
Destiny; or The Chief's Daughter. 1830.
Memoir and Correspondence of Susan Ferrier, 1782–1854. Ed. John A. Doyle. Intro. John Ferrier. 1898.

Studies of Susan Ferrier

Craik, Wendy. " 'Man, Vain Man' in Susan Ferrier, Margaret Oliphant and Elizabeth Gaskell." *Gaskell Society Journal* 9 (1995): 55–65.
———. "Susan Ferrier." In *Scott Bicentenary Essays.* Ed. Alan Bell: Edinburgh: Scottish Academic Press, 1973. 322–31.
Cullinan, Mary. *Susan Ferrier.* Boston: Twayne, 1984.
Grant, Aline. *Susan Ferrier of Edinburgh.* Denver: Swallow, 1957.
Hart, Francis Russell. *The Scottish Novel from Smollett to Spark.* Cambridge: Harvard University Press, 1978.
Parker, W. M. *Susan Ferrier and John Galt.* London: Longmans, Green & Co., 1965.
Paxton, Nancy L. "Subversive Feminism: A Reassessment of Susan Ferrier's *Marriage.*" *Women and Literature* 4 (1976): 18–29.
Saintsbury, George. "Miss Ferrier." In *Collected Essays and Papers.* 4 vols. London: Dent, 1923. 1: 302–29.

"Michael Field" (Katherine Harris Bradley and Edith Emma Cooper) (1846-1914) and (1862-1913)

Ed Madden

BIOGRAPHY

Using the pen name "Michael Field," Katherine Harris Bradley and her niece Edith Emma Cooper wrote twenty-eight plays, eight books of poetry, and a thirty-volume private journal that documents their years together. The pen name incorporated two nicknames—Katherine known among friends as "Michael," and Edith as "Henry" or "Field." Joining the Cooper household in youth, Bradley became devoted to her niece, especially after Cooper's mother became ill, and the two remained devoted lifelong companions. After brief studies at Newnham College, Cambridge, and the College de France in Paris, Bradley published her first collection of poetry, *The New Minnesinger* (1875), as Arran Leigh; Bradley and Cooper published a second book, *Bellerophôn* (1881), as Arran and Isla Leigh—alluding surely to *Aurora Leigh*. At University College, Bristol, the two studied classical literature, which informs the first works of Michael Field, *Callirrhoë* (1884), a play about the Dionysian worship, and *Long Ago* (1889), poems based on Sappho.

In "It was deep April and the morn" (1893), a poem critics describe as an *ars poetica* or a marriage vow, Bradley and Cooper declared themselves "Poets and lovers ever more." Although Lillian Faderman maintains that Bradley and Cooper formed a nonsexual "romantic friendship," others insist that theirs was a lesbian relationship. Bradley and Cooper themselves represented the relationship as artistic, romantic, and matrimonial. Comparing themselves to the famous poet couple of the Brownings, Bradley wrote in their diaries, "*we are closer married.*" Because they not only loved one another but worked together (they described their collaboration to Robert Browning as "mosaic-work"), Bradley insists that their love is stronger, an intimacy of both romance and verse.

In 1906 Bradley and Cooper suffered the loss of their beloved dog Whym Chow, commemorated in a series of elegies, privately published as *Whym Chow,*

Flame of Love (1914). To many of their friends, their grief over a pet seemed excessive. The death occasioned a crisis of belief, and in 1907, they converted to Roman Catholicism. Both poets were diagnosed with cancer, Cooper in 1911 and Bradley in 1913, only months before Cooper's death. During this period they published two books of religious poetry, *Poems of Adoration* (1912) and *Mystic Trees* (1913). Bradley suffered a hemorrhage the day of Cooper's funeral and died less than a year later.

MAJOR WORKS AND THEMES

Women's experiences and the nature of passion—artistic, emotional, sexual, religious—are the primary themes of Field's work, and a recurrent theme of ecstasy as artistic and physical pleasure suffuses the writings. Many of the plays of Michael Field focus on historical or mythical women, especially those whose loves resist convention, and much of the poetry explores the nature of female romantic passion. Even when the writers later turned from classical to religious themes in both drama and verse, legendary loves and women's passions were still central. In the religious poetry, their unorthodox Jesus is refigured as Hermes, Bacchus, and Venus, and they figure Christian faith through their own and Mary's emotional crises. Ironically, perhaps, they chose to document female experience through a male persona. As Bradley wrote to Browning, when pleading with him to keep their identity a secret from reviewers, both their collaboration and their gender would keep their work from receiving an accurate hearing. They refused to be stifled by "drawing-room conventionalities," she told Browning, adding, "We have many things to say that the world will not tolerate from a woman's lips" (*Works and Days* 6).

When their identity became known, Bradley and Cooper maintained the literary persona of Field, as if to suggest the importance of their collaborative project and their examinations of gendered spheres, of women's sexual and social desires through daily, intimate, poetic, and practical collaborations. The name represented their work and lives together. Much of their poetry seems to have autobiographical resonance, as if through various figures and voices they might document the power and passion of their own lives together. As a number of literary critics and historians have noted, classical literature provided for many writers, including Bradley and Cooper, a realm within which to explore same-sex eroticism; *Long Ago* in its examination of Sappho's many passions (artistic, heterosexual, lesbian) seems to offer just such a realm.

Although classical themes played an important role in Field's work, their exploration of female desires was inflected by aesthetic sensualism in *Sight and Song* (1892) and by nature and the pastoral in *Underneath the Bough* (1893). *Dedicated* (1914) ends with one of Field's last and most compelling poems, "Fellowship," in which Bradley extols a return to songs of "pagan might," a final evocation of their love and art in classical terms.

CRITICAL RECEPTION

Although most of their work was dramatic, the plays of Bradley and Cooper have received very little critical attention, most considered unstageable and awkwardly ornate. Only *A Question of Memory* (1893) was staged, to negative reviews. Critics then and now insist that Field's best literary work is the poetry. Much of Field's work is notoriously hard to obtain, and the writers have failed to gain much public attention. Only a very small portion of the journals was published in T. Sturge Moore's edited volume *Works and Days* (1933), and only *Sight and Song* and *Underneath the Bough* have been republished in recent years. Like the drama, the *Whym Chow* and religious volumes remain dismissed or ignored. Selected poems have appeared in anthologies of 1890s, Victorian, or lesbian verse, but much remains unread. Critical studies have suffered as a result, and many errors, textual and biographical, persist in critical work.

Despite some favorable reviews of the early work, Victorian reviewers ignored Field after it was discovered that Michael Field was neither singular nor male but two women collaborating. Although there was an attempt to renew interest in Field's work at the beginning of the twentieth century, it remained for recent feminist and lesbian critics to begin a serious reclamation of Field. The very aspects that earlier critics would have found dismissable—their gender, their collaboration, perhaps their sexuality—are the very issues that now animate critical attention. In particular, *Long Ago*, perhaps their best work, has benefited from recent feminist studies.

BIBLIOGRAPHY

Two books of poetry by Michael Field have been reprinted in a single facsimile edition, *Sight and Song, 1892; Underneath the Bough, 1893* (Woodstock Books, 1993), and their work is included in recent Victorian women poets anthologies.

Selected Works by Michael Field

Callirrhoë, and Fair Rosamund. 1884.
Long Ago. 1889.
The Tragic Mary. 1890.
Sight and Song. 1892.
A Question of Memory. 1893.
Underneath the Bough. 1893; revised and decreased edition, 1893; revised edition, 1898.
Wild Honey from Various Thyme. 1908.
Poems of Adoration. 1912.
Mystic Trees. 1913.
Dedicated: An Early Work of Michael Field. 1914.
Whym Chow, Flame of Love. 1914.
A Selection from the Poems of Michael Field. Ed. T. Sturge Moore. 1923.

The Wattlefold, Unpublished Poems by Michael Field. Collected by Emily C. Fortey. 1930.

Works and Days: From the Journal of Michael Field. Ed. T. and D. C. Sturge Moore. 1933.

Studies of Michael Field

Faderman, Lillian. *Surpassing the Love of Men: Romantic Friendship and Love Between Women from the Renaissance to the Present.* New York: William Morrow, 1981; London: Women's Press, 1985.

Laird, Holly. "Contradictory Legacies: Michael Field and Feminist Restoration." *Victorian Poetry* 33.1 (Spring 1995): 111–28.

Moriarty, David J. " 'Michael Field' (Edith Cooper and Katherine Bradley) and Their Male Critics." In *Nineteenth-Century Women Writers of the English-Speaking World.* Ed. Rhoda B. Nathan. Westport, CT: Greenwood, 1986. 121–42.

Prins, Yopie. "A Metaphorical Field: Katherine Bradley and Edith Cooper." *Victorian Poetry* 33.1 (Spring 1995): 129–48.

———. "Sappho Doubled: Michael Field." *Yale Journal of Criticism* 8.1 (Spring 1995): 165–86.

———. *Victorian Sappho.* Princeton: Princeton University Press, 1999.

Sturgeon, Mary, *Michael Field.* London: George G. Harrap, 1922.

White, Chris. " 'Poets and Lovers Evermore': The Poetry and Journals of Michael Field." In *Sexual Sameness: Textual Differences in Lesbian and Gay Writing.* Ed. Joseph Bristow. London: Routledge, 1992. 26–43.

Elizabeth Gaskell
(1810–1865)

June Foley

BIOGRAPHY

Elizabeth Gaskell was born Elizabeth Cleghorn Stevenson in Chelsea, London, on 29 September 1810. Her parents, William and Elizabeth Stevenson, were Unitarians, and this most tolerant of nonconformist sects, which emphasizes freedom of thought and the importance of reason, would become a major force in Gaskell's life. Her father, William Stevenson, trained for the Unitarian ministry, attempted careers in "scientific" farming and magazine editing, and then held the London post of keeper of the records of the Treasury for twenty-three years, while writing pamphlets, articles, and books on subjects including agriculture and naval history.

Elizabeth, who would be nicknamed Lily, was the eighth and last child of her family and the only one except the first to survive infancy. Thirteen months after she was born, her mother died. Her father gave her over to her mother's elder sister, Mrs. Hannah Lumb, whose twenty-year-old crippled daughter, Marianne, asked to act as mother to the baby. Gaskell's childhood in the country town of Knutsford has often been considered close to idyllic. Gaskell and "my darling Aunt Lumb" had a close and loving relationship, and Gaskell's maternal grandparents, as well as numerous uncles, aunts, and cousins lived nearby. However, about a year after Elizabeth's arrival, Marianne Lumb was suddenly taken ill and died. Elizabeth not only lost her mother for the second time in her young life, but her primary caretaker became a middle-aged woman who herself was mourning the death of her only child. The deaths of mothers and children fill Gaskell's works, as do surrogate parents.

Gaskell's works also feature many men who emotionally abandon their families. William Stevenson remarried three years after his wife's death, when Elizabeth was four. He and his new wife soon had two children, but Elizabeth was evidently not asked to join this family, nor did they visit her, and during her annual visits to them in London, she suffered from her stepmother's dislike: "[V]ery very unhappy I used to be," Gaskell wrote (*Letters* 797–98). Elizabeth's brother John, twelve years her senior, did visit her in Knutsford and wrote to her. Before his initial voyage to India in 1822 as a mariner licensed by the East India Company, twelve-year-old Elizabeth visited him in Chelsea; he then wrote to her often and saw her whenever he returned to England. But John disappeared in 1828–1829 after a voyage to India. Whether he drowned, or disappeared after the ship landed, was never ascertained. Not long after John's vanishing, Elizabeth's stepmother called her to Chelsea to nurse the anxious and ill William Stevenson, who died of stroke a few months later.

From age eleven to fifteen, Elizabeth attended a girls' boarding school; after her father's death, she stayed with various relatives until, at twenty-one, she married William Gaskell. A minister at the major Unitarian chapel in Manchester, William also combined scholarship with social activism. If Elizabeth's memories of the old-fashioned country life of Knutsford would clearly influence many of her works, from *Cranford* to *Cousin Phillis*, up through her last novel, *Wives and Daughters*, her life as a minister's wife in rapidly expanding industrial Manchester would inspire other works, including *Mary Barton* and *North and South*. Throughout her married life, Elizabeth devoted much of her time and energy to domestic duties. Yet even in the early years she managed to write and to lay the foundation for a career as a writer. A few months after marriage, she became pregnant, but the child was stillborn; in 1836, Gaskell wrote a sonnet about visiting the child's grave. Meanwhile Gaskell had given birth to a second daughter, Marianne, in 1834, and wrote about the child's development from March 1835 to October 1838 in *My Diary*, intended as a gift for Marianne. Elizabeth and William jointly wrote a poem "Sketches Among the Poor," which was published in *Blackwood's Magazine* in January 1837. Also in 1837, Gaskell bore another daughter, Margaret Emily, called Meta. She then gave birth to a first son sometime between Meta's birth and that of the third daughter, Florence, in 1842, but the boy presumably died as an infant. During this time Elizabeth sent her descriptions of rural customs and an historic house to William Howitt, who printed parts verbatim in the second edition of *Rural Life of England* (1839) and in *Visits to Remarkable Places* (1840). After the birth of Florence, called Flossy, Gaskell bore another son, in 1844. Named for his father and called Willie, he died of scarlet fever at ten months. Gaskell gave birth to a fourth daughter, Julia, in 1846.

Every biography of Gaskell connects the genesis of her first novel, *Mary Barton*, with the death of Willie, and she herself alludes to it in that novel's preface. Gaskell's grief was so great, she asserted, that her husband urged her to battle it with a lengthy writing project. Her depression can hardly be doubted, but Gaskell clearly had been working toward publication. Even while she was writing *Mary Barton*, three short stories and an essay, probably written earlier, were published. Her professional career fully launched with *Mary Barton*'s publication on 25 October 1848, Gaskell's life then became divided into the "two parallel currents"—the life of the writer and the life of the woman—she would identify in her later biography of Charlotte Brontë.* Gaskell spent the next twenty-two years apparently leading the life of a conventional Victorian minister's wife and the mother of four, while also writing and attending to the publication of six novels—after *Mary Barton, Ruth* (1853), *Cranford* (1853), *North and South* (1855), *Sylvia's Lovers* (1863), and *Wives and Daughters* (1866)—more than thirty shorter works, mainly fiction, most of them published either in Dickens's journals *Household Words* and *All the Year Round* or George Smith's *Cornhill*; and the biography *The Life of Charlotte Brontë* (1857). Although Dickens praised Gaskell's work and paid her well, she resisted his editorial intervention, and their relationship was rather contentious; but she formed warm friendships with Smith, Brontë, John Forster, Florence Nightingale,* and the young American art historian Charles Eliot Norton, among other eminent Victorians. Hundreds of Gaskell's letters to family and friends, quickly written in an animated, unaffected style, attest to what the letters' collectors call her "tremendous vitality of passion" and what some of her friends describe as her "total immersion in the experience of the moment." At Knutsford, "Baby is at the very tip-top of bliss . . . oh! you would laugh to see her going about, with a great big nosegay in each hand, and wanting to be *bathed* in the golden bushes of wallflowers" (*Letters* 6). When a friend guessed that she was the anonymous author of *Mary Barton*, Gaskell wrote, "I am almost frightened at my own action in writing it" (*Letters* 67). She identified her many "me's" and their conflicts: "How am I to reconcile all these warring members?" (*Letters* 108). And in another letter she wrote, "Nature intended me for a gypsy-bachelor; that *I* am sure of" (*Letters* 310). On the difficulty of writing *North and South* in serial form: "I've been as nearly dazed and crazed with this c—, d— be h— to it, story as can be. I'm sick of writing, and everything connected with literature or improvement of the mind; to say nothing of deep hatred to my species about whom I was obliged to write as if I loved 'em" (*Letters* 325). On the controversy engendered by *Ruth*: "I think I must be an improper woman without knowing it, I do so manage to shock people" (*Letters* 223). But earlier, having shocked a member of her husband's congregation, she concluded, "So there I am in a scrape—well! it can't be helped, I am myself and nobody else, and can't be bound by another's rules" (*Letters* 63–64).

Gaskell increasingly spent time traveling outside Manchester, often abroad. She enjoyed Heidelberg, loved staying with her friend the *saloniste* Madame Mohl in Paris, and of her first trip to Rome in 1857 wrote, "I shall never be so happy again; I don't think I was ever so happy before" (*Letters* 476–77).

On 12 November 1865, the fifty-five-year-old Gaskell died suddenly, of heart failure, at the country house she had just purchased with the earnings from her writing. She died both a popular and a critically respected writer.

MAJOR WORKS AND THEMES

Gaskell's first novel, *Mary Barton* (1848), is an "industrial novel" that employs the discourse of the working class and women, giving voice to groups

traditionally silent and to such extraliterary culture as oral storytelling and workers' ballads. The narrator, a middle-class woman who insists on her lack of
authority, provides a model of compassionate empathy. Midway through the
book, Mary Barton replaces her father John as protagonist, becoming a heroine
through a courageous quest.

Ruth (1853), one of many mid- to late-nineteenth-century novels about a
"scarlet woman," portrays the seamstress heroine, Ruth Hilton, as coming to
ruin through culturally sanctioned docility and achieving rehabilitation first
through adoption by an unconventional family and then through work as a governess. Ruth successfully raises her child and dies not a pariah but a local
heroine, saint—even a Christ figure.

Cranford (1853), first published serially in Dickens's *Household Words* and
often considered Gaskell's most "beloved" and "charming" work, can also be
read as a radical experiment with narrative. Gaskell employs a group of middle-
aged spinsters, rather than one young heroine; a plot that eschews strict causality
for an episodic, repetitive, circular structure, replete with gaps; the "language
of sisterhood," including silence, gesture, and euphemism; "women's values,"
such as the avoidance of hierarchies, community over competition, forgiveness
over revenge.

North and South (1855), like *Mary Barton*, is an "industrial novel" that re-
writes a conventional romantic plot as a political one and portrays relationships
among classes as well as among sexes. However, Gaskell replaces her first
novel's earnest intervening narrator with the development of the consciousness
of the heroine, Margaret Hale, a complex character who demonstrates authority,
will, and sexual energy, along with tolerance and compassion. The book ends
with Margaret's marriage to the millowner John Thornton and their partnership
in business.

The Life of Charlotte Brontë (1857) is a rarity: the biography of a major
woman writer by a friend who is also a major woman writer. After Gaskell and
Brontë met in August 1850, they corresponded and exchanged visits. *The Life*
employs Gaskell's intense, poetic descriptive powers and parts of Brontë's letters
to portray Brontë not only as a gifted writer but also as a domestic angel who
suffered and endured as a dutiful friend, daughter, sister, and wife.

Sylvia's Lovers (1860) has a passionate heroine, Sylvia Robson, yet takes its
title from the shopkeeper Philip Hepburn and the sailor Charley Kinraid. This
historical novel, set in a Yorkshire whaling village during the events of the
French Revolution and the European wars of conquest that followed, contrasts
"history" as "his story"—men's lives, of action, adventure, and revolution—
with the ahistorical lives of women, which are the stuff of ballad and legend,
rather than literature.

Wives and Daughters (1866) is Gaskell's most ironic and relativistic work.
The "everyday" heroine, Molly Gibson, has an equally appealing stepsister, Cynthia, who identifies herself as a "moral kangaroo" and whose natural mother
proves more damaging to her than motherlessness is to Molly. Another of Gas-

kell's works that combines and comments on different sorts of discourse for men and women—here, science is the domain of men, whereas women are involved in gossip, secrets, and blackmail—this work also parodies and revises many kinds of storytelling.

Gaskell's shorter works, which include many supernatural or "gothic" stories, recently have been read as feminist in their concern with women's lives, specifically questions of power, marriage, work, and sexuality. In the poetic novella *The Moorland Cottage* (1850), the unselfish and courageous heroine wins love despite her spoiled brother and her beloved's proud father. In the novella *Cousin Phillis* (1864), often considered Gaskell's masterpiece of shorter fiction, the heroine's father teaches her to read classical and foreign literature, yet Phillis, with no opportunity to employ her learning, lives for love and, when rejected, suffers "brain fever." "Lizzie Leigh" (1850), the lead story of Dickens's first number for *Household Words*, revises the parable of the lost son to center on the mother, who offers forgiveness. "The Old Nurse's Story" (1852), first published in a special Christmas issue of *Household Words*, and now Gaskell's most anthologized supernatural tale, suggests that salvation requires sisterhood. Repeatedly, in stories like "The Poor Clare" (1856), "The Doom of the Griffiths" (1858), "Lois the Witch" (1859), "The Grey Woman" (1861), and "A Dark Night's Work" (1863), Gaskell portrays male power and women's power turned to destructiveness against themselves or other women. Gaskell's frequent use of the supernatural or gothic motif, it has been suggested, links women, as silent "other," with the otherworldly; expresses the anxieties of Victorian women; enables her to explore female sexuality within a repressive culture; and disguises her protofeminist themes.

CRITICAL RECEPTION

Although Gaskell's works enjoyed both popularity and critical esteem during her lifetime, the earlier books often provoked controversy. *Mary Barton*, an immediate success, brought praise from Thomas Carlyle and Dickens, but others objected to its mixture of documentary realism with romance or saw it as simplistically didactic, for depicting the working class sympathetically and the middle class harshly. The critics included some of Gaskell's neighbors and members of her husband's church in Manchester. *Ruth*, too, became something of a cause célèbre, for its compassionate treatment of the heroine's unmarried motherhood. Again, some Mancunians objected, and Gaskell knew of at least two men who burned a volume. Most professional reviewers responded positively, however; and Charlotte Brontë and Elizabeth Barrett Browning* were moved to maintain that, at the end, Gaskell's compassion should have extended to allowing the heroine to live. *North and South* seemed to some critics to surpass *Mary Barton* in its sympathetic treatment of both the working class and the middle class. Because it was first published serially in Dickens's *Household Words*, however, it suffered from the severe constraints of weekly serialization, and Gaskell prefaced the book publication with a complaint against the journal. *The Life of Charlotte Brontë* initially met with considerable critical acclaim but soon brought threats of lawsuits for libel, most notably from the woman the book accused of Branwell Brontë's ruin and the owners of the school identified as the model for Lowood in *Jane Eyre*. George Smith withdrew the first and second printings, and Gaskell wrote a third edition, published as "Revised and Corrected." Gaskell's *Life of Charlotte Brontë* also has recently been criticized in some revisionist biographies of the Brontës, most notably Juliet Barker's 1995 work on the entire family, for the harsh depiction of Branwell and Rev. Patrick Brontë and the softening of Charlotte's character, including the expurgation of her unrequited love for Constantin Heger. Still, many critics, while acknowledging flaws in Gaskell's work, continue to place the *Life* among the greatest English biographies.

Most significantly, however, Gaskell, as the only arguably canonical Victorian woman novelist who was a wife and mother during her writing career, has often been patronized by critics as an amateur—an earnest "authoress" for the social problem novels *Mary Barton* and *North and South*; a charming one for her most "beloved" work, *Cranford*, read as gentle, nostalgic humor; a devoted friend for *The Life of Charlotte Brontë*. Much recent scholarship has argued against this perception. Patsy Stoneman's 1987 volume on Gaskell for the Key Women Writers series of Indiana University Press details the process by which reviewers praised the anonymous *Mary Barton* for force and truth, but once "Mrs. Gaskell" was identified as the author, she received commendation for such "feminine" virtues as modesty. Most notoriously, perhaps, Lord David Cecil, in 1934, termed Charlotte Brontë and George Eliot* "eagles," but "Mrs. Gaskell, soft-eyed, beneath her charming veil . . . was a dove." Cecil maintained that Gaskell was the "typical Victorian woman," whose main quality was her "femininity"; that is, she was "gentle, domestic, tactful, unintellectual, prone to tears, easily shocked." Gaskell not only "accepted" the limitations of her gender, Cecil claimed; she did so "with serene satisfaction" (Stoneman 2).

A feminist study of Gaskell—albeit a Scandinavian one, Aina Rubenius's *The Woman Question in Mrs. Gaskell's Life and Works*—appeared in 1950; an excellent biography by A. B. Hopkins was published around the same time; and during the latter 1950s such critics as Kathleen Tillotson, Raymond Williams, and Arnold Kettle focused attention on *Mary Barton* and *North and South* as "industrial novels." Gaskell's centenary in 1965 then brought a variety of important studies, beginning with Edgar Wright's "reassessment" and J.A.V. Chappel and Arthur Pollard's first collection of Gaskell's letters.

From the mid-1970s, much of Gaskell's oeuvre received fresh examination from feminist and other perspectives, although as late as 1979 Sandra Gilbert and Susan Gubar's *The Madwoman in the Attic* dismissed Gaskell as "domestic," and as late as 1983, *The Cambridge Guide to English Literature* described Gaskell as a domestic angel "who lived in perfect harmony with her William, was happy in her four daughters, and was devotedly served by her household staff" (336).

Elizabeth Gaskell: An Annotated Bibliography of English-Language Sources, 1976–1991, by Nancy Weyant, identifies 35 new editions of Gaskell's works and 345 secondary works in fifteen years. Major studies include Angus Easson's *Elizabeth Gaskell* (1979); Stoneman's volume, which posits an interaction of gender and class in Gaskell's works; Coral Lansbury's 1984 Twayne volume; the 1991 Critical Heritage volume, edited by Easson; and Hilary M. Schor's landmark study, *Scheherezade in the Marketplace* (1992), which reads in Gaskell's novels both the story of the progress of Gaskell's heroines and the parallel story of the development of the Victorian woman novelist. The comprehensive critical biography *Elizabeth Gaskell: A Habit of Stories*, by Jenny Uglow (1993), supersedes Winifred Gerin's 1976 work; J.A.V. Chappel's *Elizabeth Gaskell: The Early Years* (1997) offers new speculation about Gaskell's childhood and adolescence; and Chappel's second edition of Gaskell's letters also has been published (1997). The Gaskell Society, founded in 1985, publishes a newsletter and a journal. It is important to note, however, that most studies of Gaskell continue to be found not in books about her alone but in journals, doctoral dissertations, and books that deal with more than one author.

Many recent studies argue that Gaskell is a radical writer in both her stories and her discourse. Such studies emphasize that Gaskell creates unconventional heroines—working-class women, fallen women, servants, and unmarried women; she shows men and unmarried women as the most effective nurturers; and she valorizes such unorthodox households as brother and sister, and groups of women. In addition, Gaskell constructs plots that bring women into public life, accept change and conflict, replace the father's story with the daughter's, depict women living in cities and working outside of marriage as positive experiences, and portray androgyny as an ideal—women learning to be active, while men learn empathy.

Many relatively recent studies, moreover, highlight Gaskell's experiments with narrative technique: her employment of the languages and perspectives of numerous "others," including her use of both "high" and "low" allusions, of parodies and revisions, interpolated stories, the digressions of speech and the incorporation of a listener's response; and a range of unconventional narrators, among them females who protect their power by concealing it. Such innovations might be interpreted as implicitly critical of traditional narrative while valorizing ways of knowing, speaking, and writing of the "other," most notably women and the working class.

BIBLIOGRAPHY

As of 2000 there is no complete edition of Gaskell's works. The World's Classics series published by Oxford University Press claims to have the most extensive collection of Gaskell's works currently in print—all six novels, the Brontë biography, and four volumes of short stories. Gaskell's novels, novellas, short stories, and *The Life of Charlotte Brontë* are available in paperback.

Works by Elizabeth Gaskell

Mary Barton. 1848.
The Moorland Cottage. 1850.
Cranford. 1853.
Ruth. 1853.
North and South. 1855.
The Life of Charlotte Brontë. 1857.
Sylvia's Lovers. 1863.
Cousin Phillis. 1864.
Wives and Daughters. 1866.
Cousin Phillis and Other Tales. Ed. Angus Easson. 1981.
My Lady Ludlow and Other Tales. Ed. Edgar Wright. 1989.
A Dark Night's Work and Other Stories. Ed. Suzanne Lewis. 1992.
The Moorland Cottage and Other Stories. Ed. Suzanne Lewis. 1995.
Private Voices. The Diaries of Elizabeth Gaskell and Sophia Holland. Ed. J.A.V. Chappel and Anita Wilson. 1996.
The Letters of Mrs. Gaskell. Ed. J.A.V. Chappel and Arthur Pollard. 2nd ed. 1997.

Studies of Elizabeth Gaskell

Boone, Joseph Allen. *Tradition Counter Tradition: Love and the Form of Fiction*. Chicago: University of Chicago Press, 1987.
Chappel, J.A.V. *Elizabeth Gaskell: The Early Years*. New York: St. Martin's Press, 1997.
D'Albertis, Deirdre. *Dissembling Fictions: Elizabeth Gaskell and the Victorian Social Text*. New York: St. Martin's Press, 1997.
Dickerson, Vanessa D. *Victorian Ghosts in the Noontide: Elizabeth Gaskell's Supernatural Stories*. Columbia: University of Missouri Press, 1996.
Easson, Angus. *Elizabeth Gaskell*. London: Routledge & Kegan Paul, 1979.
———. *Elizabeth Gaskell: The Critical Heritage*. London: Routledge, 1991.
Gallagher, Catherine. *The Industrial Reformation of Victorian Fiction: Social Discourse and Narrative Form, 1832–1867*. Chicago: University of Chicago Press, 1985.
Gillooly, Eileen. *Smiles of Discontent: Humor, Gender, and Nineteenth-Century British Fiction*. Chicago: University of Chicago Press, 1999.
Krueger, Christine. *The Reader's Repentance: Women Preachers, Women Writers, and Nineteenth-Century Social Discourse*. Chicago: University of Chicago Press, 1992.
Lansbury, Coral. *Elizabeth Gaskell*. New York: Twayne Publishers, 1984.
Rubenius, Aina. *The Woman Question in Mrs. Gaskell's Life and Works*. Cambridge: Harvard University Press, 1950.
Schor, Hilary M. *Scheherezade in the Marketplace: Elizabeth Gaskell and the Victorian Novel*. New York: Oxford University Press, 1992.
Stoneman, Patsy. *Elizabeth Gaskell*. Bloomington: Indiana University Press, 1987.

Uglow, Jenny. *Elizabeth Gaskell: A Habit of Stories*. London: Faber & Faber, 1993.

Weyant, Nancy S. *Elizabeth Gaskell: An Annual Bibliography of English-Language Sources 1976–1991*. Metuchen, NJ: Scarecrow Press, 1994.

Wright, Edgar. *Mrs. Gaskell*. Oxford: Oxford University Press, 1965.

Lady Lucie Duff Gordon
(1821–1869)

K. L. Thomas

BIOGRAPHY

Lucie Duff Gordon's published writings span only eight years of her life, but prior to this she was a respected lady of letters: a scholar and critically acclaimed translator. Lucie grew up surrounded and admired by some of the most important thinkers and artists of the Victorian era; as a child she was "doated" upon by John Stuart Mill and Jeremy Bentham, and later as the hostess of a salon studded with literati, she became the inspiration for Tennyson's *Princess* and several of Meredith's fictional characters. After her marriage in 1840, Duff Gordon published meticulously researched translations of German and French literature.

In 1861 she was forced to leave England, and her husband and three children, to seek relief from tuberculosis. She traveled first to the Cape of Good Hope and then to Egypt in 1862, where she lived until her death in 1869. Her *Letters from the Cape* was published in 1864, and *Letters from Egypt* appeared a year later. Passionately protective of her adopted home, she was critical of both European colonial forces and Ismail Pasha's repressive regime. Her letters are pertinent, agile testaments to a Victorian who was not afraid to challenge what it meant to be a traveler, English, and a woman.

MAJOR WORKS AND THEMES

Duff Gordon wrote, like her mother before her, to support her family financially. The desire to correct prejudice and misconception dominates *Letters from Egypt* (*LE*). Her book joined a glut of accounts of the Middle East published in the midcentury, but hers attracted attention as the most sympathetic, tolerant, and consequently insightful study. She herself felt that "indignant sympathy" (*LE* 229) was important. Of her cousin Harriet Martineau's* *Eastern Life, Present and Past* (1848), she writes that the "descriptions are excellent, but she evidently knew and cared nothing about the people, and had the feeling of most English people here, that the difference in manners is a sort of impassable gulf" (*LE* 3). She found Emily Lott's virulently racist *The English Governess in Egypt* (1866) "extraordinary" and was particularly incensed by the misrepresentation of harems as quasi brothels (*LE* 120–21). Indeed, she was impressed by Islam's equality for women, arguing that the faith gave women important rights and freedoms (*LE* 138).

Her letters are commentaries upon cultural translation. She mocks Western "readings" of the East; she does not, however, disturb the assumption that Egypt is a place that can be read. She offers her letters, written in what one reviewer termed an "easy, familiar, chatty style of fireside talk," as a personal guide to deciphering the country she called "a palimpsest." Although she was a fierce critic of the behavior of the dominant European culture, she did not question the "naturalness" of its dominance.

Letters from the Cape (*LC*) is also preoccupied with recovering lost layers of culture: the unearthing of what Duff Gordon saw as the land's "lost" racial history. The climax of the sixteen letters occurs when she meets the "last real Hottentot," before whom she feels like a "tyrant and oppressor . . . a murderer" (*LC* 87–88), lamenting that colonialism has reduced his race to a tragic, "mongrel" lot who work the land they once owned. Engrossed by outlining racial typologies, Duff Gordon blames the "debased" character of the Negro on the dehumanizing effects of slavery but nonetheless repeatedly deems their physiology "hideous" and "beastly." In *Letters from Egypt*, racial beauty functions as a measure and consequence of cultural authenticity; Duff Gordon aestheticizes the Egyptian physiognomy, just as she does architecture or landscape, as ancient and noble.

CRITICAL RECEPTION

Duff Gordon's letters were very popular with British and American nineteenth-century audiences. Despite a recent upsurge of interest in women's travel writing, her work is now largely neglected, but this seems to be due to her complexities rather than to her failings.

In the profoundly contradictory introduction to the first edition of *Letters*, Sarah Austen demonstrates anxiety regarding Duff Gordon's critique of Western colonizers. She emphasizes Duff Gordon's capacities for humanity and sympathy, reassuring those readers to whom "her admiration of her Arab friends will appear groundless or exaggerated" that "her object was not to blame, but to understand" (viii). Many nineteenth-century critics praised *Letters* as "quaint" and "charming" and portrayed Duff Gordon as an eccentric whose goodness had made her beloved of the oppressed natives of Egypt.

Today's critics theorizing the relationship of women travelers to colonial discourse rearticulate the same issues. In *Discourses of Difference* (1991), Sara Mills highlights Duff Gordon's use of temporal adjectives and her objectification of Egyptian bodies to demonstrate that Duff Gordon "relegates contemporary Egypt to a European past" and "Others" Egyptians (89). This judgment is rejected by Katherine Frank, who sees Duff Gordon as acculturated, rather than culturally colonialist, and by Billie Melman in *Women's Orients* (1992), who regards Duff Gordon's travel writing as "anti- or counter-orientalist." Mervat Hatem points out that Duff Gordon's antiorientalism was sincere but relative and "did not lead her to repudiate . . . key Orientalist assumption[s]" (48).

The preface to *Letters* expresses the hope that the book will awaken sentiment against the "resistless force" and "haughty indifference" of Western domination. Following the British Occupation of Egypt in 1882, the British Colonial Administration made *Letters from Egypt* required reading in all Egyptian public schools. It was read and taught as a text that legitimated the British Occupation. Duff Gordon's sympathy for the Egyptian leant itself to colonialist ends, supporting imperialist assault upon the country and people she had dearly loved.

BIBLIOGRAPHY

Duff Gordon's works have been reprinted. The most complete edition is Gordon Waterfield's Enlarged Centenary Edition (Praeger, 1969).

Works by Lucie Duff Gordon

Letters from the Cape. 1864.
Letters from Egypt. 1865.
Last Letters from Egypt with a Memoir by Her Daughter Mrs. Ross. 1875.

Studies of Lucie Duff Gordon

Frank, Katherine. *Lucie Duff Gordon: A Passage to Egypt.* London: Penguin, 1994.
Frawley, Maria H. *A Wider Range: Travel Writing by Women in Victorian England.* London: Associated University Presses, 1994.
Gendron, Charisse. "Lucie Duff Gordon's 'Letters from Egypt.' " *Ariel* 17.2 (Apr. 1986): 49–61.
Hatem, Mervat. "Through Each Other's Eyes: The Impact of the Colonial Encounter of the Images of Egyptian, Levantine-Egyptian, and European Women, 1862–1920." In *Western Women and Imperialism: Complicity and Resistance.* Ed. Nupur Chaudhuri and Margaret Strobel. Bloomington: Indiana University Press, 1992. 35–58.
Melman, Billie. *Women's Orients: English Women and the Middle East, 1718–1918.* London: Macmillan, 1992.
Mills, Sara. *Discourses of Difference: An Analysis of Women's Travel Writing and Colonialism.* New York: Routledge, 1991.

Norton, Caroline. "Lady Duff-Gordon and Her Works." *Macmillan's Magazine* 20 (Sept. 1869): 457–62.

Ross, Janet. *Three Generations of English Women*. London: J. Murray, 1888.

Waterfield, Gordon. *Lucie Duff Gordon in England, South Africa and Egypt*. London: J. Murray, 1937.

"Sarah Grand" (Frances Elizabeth Clarke McFall) (1854-1943)

JoAnna Stephens Mink

BIOGRAPHY

Frances Elizabeth Clarke, better known by her pseudonym "Sarah Grand," was born in June 1854 in Northern Ireland, the fourth child of Edward John Bellenden Clarke and Margaret Bell Sherwood Clarke, both English. Her autobiographical novel *The Beth Book* provides details of Grand's unhappy childhood. Although her parents were uninterested in her development, she was attached to her father, who died when Grand was seven. Her older brothers were educated, but Grand was not because her mother did not believe that girls needed education. After Clarke's death in 1861, the family moved near her mother's family in Yorkshire, England.

Grand's first rejection from a publisher occurred at age eleven, when she submitted songs she had composed. Her mother's reprimand, that ladies should never expect payment for work, was a rankling memory and "an important influence on her earliest feminist feelings" (Kersley 23). Deemed unmanageable, at age fourteen, Grand was sent to boarding school, which she hated. Her dissatisfaction was partly due to insufficient preparation, for which she blamed her mother; consequently, adequate education for girls became a recurring theme in Grand's writings. At sixteen, in 1871 she escaped school by marrying David Chambers McFall, an army surgeon and widower twenty-three years older than she, with two sons. During the first year of marriage, her son Archie was born. Grand was relatively contented in the marriage, but soon McFall's insensitivity and cruelty made her cold to him. Her increasing unhappiness is detailed in *The Beth Book*.

From 1873 until McFall's retirement in 1881, the family traveled extensively in the Far East. She continued to write short stories, but none was published until 1878. In 1890, encouraged by the success of *Ideala*, Grand abandoned her husband and son, from whom she remained estranged for some years. Ironically,

Grand maintained congenial relations with her stepsons. After living some years in London and Tunbridge Wells (becoming active in the women's suffrage movement there) and lecturing widely in Britain and America, Grand moved to Bath, serving six years as mayoress between 1922 and 1929. She died in obscurity in May 1943 in Calne.

MAJOR WORKS AND THEMES

Grand is credited with first using the term "new woman" in her 1894 essay "The New Aspect of the Woman Question." Her earliest publication *Two Dear Little Feet*, a 125-page monograph about the crippling effects of tight boots, reflected Grand's lifelong interest in women's fashions. She advocated sensible clothing for women and became a proponent of the Rational Dress Movement. Unlike some other feminists, Grand promoted a cultivated appearance: In "The Morals of Manner and Appearance" (1893), Grand writes, "By being inelegant, an earnest woman frustrates her own ends" (qtd. in Kucich 259).

Grand supported women's franchise by participating in several suffrage organizations, by lecturing on issues relating to women's place in society, and by exhorting in her writings better education for women, especially about intellectual issues and health concerns (particularly venereal diseases contracted from profligate husbands)—topics that also thematically connect her trilogy of *Ideala, The Heavenly Twins,* and *The Beth Book.*

The Heavenly Twins developed from the short story "The Tenor and the Boy," which forms the fourth (and, some critics claim, intrusive) section of the novel. The novel entwines the stories of Angelica and Diavolo, the female and male twins of the title; Evadne, a woman, stronger and more resolute than Ideala, who is also married to a brutish husband; and Edith, who succumbs to dementia and death as the result of contracting syphilis from her husband. The novel's major themes reflect Grand's continuing push for women's intellectual education and enlightenment about the nature of men in order to improve society as a whole.

Grand's views on marriage were more conservative than those of other New Woman writers. Her novels show an interesting juxtaposition between Victorian ethics and modern questioning of their strictures. For example, both Angelica and Beth, as well as several other female characters, audaciously confront accepted views of women's roles. Emphasis on honesty and middle-class sincerity underlies *The Beth Book,* an often painful account of Grand's own childhood and marital experiences. Other social problems that Grand tackles include land reform (*Adnam's Orchard* and *The Winged Victory*) and women sweatshop workers (*Variety*).

CRITICAL RECEPTION

Publication of *Ideala* (1888) and *The Heavenly Twins* (1893) put Grand among the first of the New Woman novelists. Contemporary critics often compared her to George Egerton,* Alice Mona Caird,* Thomas Hardy, George Gissing, and Olive Schreiner* in her development of the concept of the New Woman. Hailed as "the chief women's rights novel of the period" (Kersley 73), *The Heavenly Twins* was wildly popular on both sides of the Atlantic and made Grand a "name." Today, Sarah Grand's contributions "to the battle for aesthetic hegemony . . . [are] acknowledged" (Bonnell, "Critical Establishment" 143), as both *The Heavenly Twins* and *The Beth Book* have gained a new readership among feminist critics.

BIBLIOGRAPHY

Recently reprinted are *The Beth Book* (Thommes, 1994), *The Heavenly Twins* (Ann Arbor, 1992), and *Our Manifold Nature* (Ayer, 1994). "The New Aspect of the Woman Question" (1894) and "The New Woman and the Old" (1898) are in *Prose by Victorian Women: An Anthology* (Garland, 1996).

Selected Works by Sarah Grand

For a complete list, see Kersley's *Darling Madame* (1983).

Two Dear Little Feet (by Frances Elizabeth McFall). 1873.
Ideala: A Study from Life. 1888.
The Heavenly Twins. 1893.
Our Manifold Nature (short stories). 1894.
The Beth Book. 1897.
The Modern Man and Maid (essays). 1898.
The Human Quest. 1900.
Babs the Impossible. 1901.
Adnam's Orchard. 1912.
The Winged Victory. 1916.
Variety. 1922.

Studies of Sarah Grand

Bonnell, Marilyn. "Sarah Grand." In *British Short Fiction Writers, 1880–1914: The Realist Tradition*. Ed. William B. Thesing. *Dictionary of Literary Biography*. Detroit: Gale Research, 1994. 135: 151–64.
————. "Sarah Grand and the Critical Establishment: Art for [Wo]man's Sake." *Tulsa Studies in Women's Literature* 14.1 (Spring 1995): 123–48.
Dowling, Linda. "The Decadent and the New Woman in the 1890's." *Nineteenth-Century Fiction* 33 (1979): 434–53.
Huddleston, Joan, ed. *Sarah Grand: A Bibliography*. St. Lucia, Australia: University of Queensland Press, 1979.
Kersley, Gillian. *Darling Madame: Sarah Grand and Devoted Friend*. London: Virago, 1983.

Kucich, John. *The Power of Lies: Transgression in Victorian Fiction.* Ithaca and London: Cornell University Press, 1994.

Mangum, Teresa. *Married, Middlebrow, and Militant: Sarah Grand and the New Woman Novel.* Ann Arbor: University of Michigan Press, 1998.

―――. "Sex, Siblings, and the Fin de Siècle." In *The Significance of Sibling Relationships in Literature.* Ed. JoAnna Stephens Mink and Janet Doubler Ward. Bowling Green, OH: Popular Press, 1993. 70–82.

Senf, Carol. Introduction. *The Heavenly Twins.* By Sarah Grand. Ann Arbor: University of Michigan Press, 1992.

Dora Greenwell
(1821–1882)

Kelly Stephens

BIOGRAPHY

Dora Greenwell was a poet, essayist, and theological writer. The daughter of Dorothy Smales and William Thomas Greenwell, squire, magistrate, and deputy lieutenant of County Durham, Greenwell was well educated by a governess and through private reading. Fluent in French and Italian, she could read German, Spanish, and Latin as well as being versed in philosophy and political economics. The breadth of her knowledge is evident in her essays, and reflected in the contemporary assumption that her work "On the Education of the Imbecile" must have been written by an eminent medical man

Financial mismanagement on the part of Greenwell's father resulted in the loss of the family home, after which Dora moved to Northumberland and Lancashire, before spending her most productive years in Durham with her domineering mother. Despite this isolation, Greenwell led a significant intellectual life, forming a close friendship with the feminist activist Josephine Butler.* She knew Christina Rossetti* well; their substantial correspondence has been destroyed, but it was probably Greenwell who encouraged Rossetti's interest in antivivisection. Their friendship was memorialized in their work by the dedication of poems to each other, while Greenwell acknowledged the influence of Elizabeth Barrett Browning* by addressing two sonnets to her. Living in the north, Greenwell also participated in the intellectual life of Edinburgh. Her long friendship with the publisher Thomas Constable and his family was emotionally sustaining, as were her theological discussions with the Reverend William Knight, professor of Moral Philosophy at the University of St. Andrews.

Greenwell's most important works were published after 1860 and include both the more secular volumes entitled *Poems* (1861; 1867) and the religious verse of *Carmina Crucis* and *Camera Obscura*; the latter two use the innovative form of the prose poem to explore the difficulties of the soul's journey from doubt to faith. Her contributions to the *North British Review* were collected in *Essays*, whereas *Liber Humanitatis* contains lesser-known pieces. Her biography of the Dominican friar Lacordaire and memoir of Quaker John Woolman demonstrate an ecumenical willingness to accept the best of all religions, whereas the dialogic structure of her religious prose (described as "a conversation with myself") suggests an awareness of the competing claims of different points of view.

Greenwell's belief in the importance of human community, for which she valued both the Catholic religion and the strongly social Methodist sect, was also realized in her community work. Greenwell worked in Durham gaol and penitentiary, an experience she analyzes in "Hardened in Good" (*Essays*). Her essay "On the Education of the Imbecile" was edited and sold for the benefit of the Royal Albert Asylum at Lancaster, for which Greenwell also edited a series of works by authors such as Caroline Bowles Southey and George Macdonald. Fundamentally, however, Greenwell was an author, and when her "jail-work" seemed to interfere with her writing, she took refuge in her status as "a *professed* invalid [which] has many social immunities" and allowed the "sense of leisure and freedom" necessary for intellectual pursuits (Dorling 77).

MAJOR WORKS AND THEMES

Greenwell's oeuvre ranges widely. Many of her essays engaged with contemporary debates, revealing strong opinions and an incisive wit. In "Our Single Women" Greenwell criticizes the stereotype of "the gentle, dovelike Old Maid, . . . supposed to have some tender secret buried in her heart," arguing instead for increased opportunities for single women (Feb. 1862; *Essays* 2). "The East African Slave Trade" (1873) forcibly condemns the practice on the grounds of "the two-fold degeneracy it entails" (144), whereas "On the Education of the Imbecile" argues that there are "many incomplete and partially endowed natures . . . among us, which only *needed to have been better understood* to have been lifted to a larger, more liberal, more intellectual . . . life!" (87).

Some of Greenwell's poetry specifically canvasses social issues—"Fidelity Rewarded" is a protest against vivisection—but all her work displays a strong belief in "social interdependency" (Dorling 94) and the importance of maintaining "sympathy with man" (*John Woolman* 24). Written in 1851, "Christina" is one of the first Victorian poems to extend this sympathy to the fallen woman, although it also suggests the complex psychological dynamics that exist between the sufferer and her female saviour. Similarly, "Demeter and Cora" reveals an acute understanding of the tensions as well as the love between a mother and her daughter. It is this insight into the darker dimensions of the human psyche that distinguishes Greenwell's best poetry from the merely sentimental and that renders *Lacordaire* so readable.

Much of Greenwell's writing, poetry and prose, takes religion as its subject, her aim being to replace convention with sincerity. Her insistence on personal truth led to a recognition of Christianity as "the greatest of difficulties" (Dorling

106). Her position as a poet emphasized this difficulty, which manifested itself not only in a fraught allegiance of logic with faith but also in tensions between the celebration and suspicion of nature and a prolonged conflict between worldly satisfaction and the claims of a relationship with Christ. Greenwell discusses this in *Liber Humanitatis*, concluding that the Christian's "taste of song's sweet, intoxicating wild honey" will be "but 'sparingly, and on the tip of his spear' " (144).

CRITICAL RECEPTION

As is the case for many Victorian women writers, Greenwell was widely read in her own day, both in England and America, but is virtually unknown in ours. Well respected during her lifetime, Jean Ingelow* described Greenwell as "the most remarkable woman I have known" (Dorling 136). Sometimes, however, her intellect was seen to exceed her powers of expression. Reviewers often characterized her poetry and devotional prose as "mystical," thereby signifying a diffusion of structure or meaning. Greenwell's work was frequently compared to Rossetti's and Ingelow's, usually to her disadvantage. This tendency to hierarchical comparison survives today, although, as Janet Gray cogently argues, it serves its biographical subject ill and problematizes the feminist critical project of text and author recovery.

Greenwell has not yet proved a main beneficiary of the resurgent interest in nineteenth-century women's poetry, although Isobel Armstrong draws upon the essay "Our Single Women" in formulating her theory about the expressive poetics of Victorian women poets. Helen Groth comments on Greenwell's unification of scientific interest with a compassionate view of humanity, contextualizing Greenwell's work within both contemporary scientific debate and the work of her female peers. In general, Greenwell's religion has proved a deterrent to feminist critics who find her poetry lacking in the "essential scepticism" that she herself associated with "the poet nature" (*Liber Humanitatis* 137). However, Constance Maynard described Greenwell as "the one woman theologian of the last hundred years" (11) and found her particularly relevant to the prevailing mood of doubt after World War I. This aspect of Greenwell's work demands further attention.

BIBLIOGRAPHY

There is no recent edition of Greenwell's work, although selections of her poetry are available in recent anthologies of Victorian women's poetry. Her poetry is also included on the Chadwyck-Healey *English Poetry Full-Text Database*.

Works by Dora Greenwell

Poems. 1848.
Stories That Might Be True, with Other Poems. 1850.

A Present Heaven: Letters to a Friend. 1855. Later reprinted as *The Covenant of Life
     and Peace.* 1867.
The Patience of Hope. 1860.
Poems. 1861.
Two Friends. 1862.
Home Thoughts and Home Scenes. With Jean Ingelow et al. 1865.
Essays. 1866.
Lacordaire. 1867.
Poems. 1867.
"On the Education of the Imbecile." *North British Review*, o.s., 49, n.s., 10 (Sept. 1868):
     73–100. Reprinted and edited for the Royal Albert Idiot Asylum, Lancaster, 1869.
Carmina Crucis. 1869. Reprinted, with an introduction by Constance L. Maynard, 1906.
Colloquia Crucis: A Sequel to "Two Friends." 1871.
John Woolman. 1871.
"The East African Slave Trade." *The Contemporary Review* 22 (1873): 138–64.
Songs of Salvation. 1873.
The Soul's Legend. 1873.
Liber Humanitatis: A Series of Essays on Various Aspects of Spiritual and Social Life.
     1875.
Camera Obscura. 1876.
*A Basket of Summer Fruits: Dedicated to the American Evangelists Who Lately Visited
     England.* 1877.
Poems by Dora Greenwell. Selected, with a biographical introduction by William Dor-
     ling. 1889.
Japp, A. H., ed. "Selections from Dora Greenwell's Poetry." In *Joanna Baillie to Ma-
     thilde Blind. The Poets and the Poetry of the Century.* Ed. Alfred H. Miles. 1892.
Selected Poems. With an introduction by Constance L. Maynard. 1906.
Selections from the Prose of Dora Greenwell. Compiled, with a biographical introduction,
     by W. G. Hanson. 1950.

Studies of Dora Greenwell

Armstrong, Isobel. *Victorian Poetry: Poetry, Poetics and Politics.* London: Routledge,
     1993.
Bett, Henry. *Dora Greenwell.* London: Epworth Press, 1950.
Dorling, William. *Memoirs of Dora Greenwell.* London: James Clarke, 1885.
Gray, Janet. "Dora Greenwell." In *Victorian Women Poets.* Ed. William B. Thesing.
     Dictionary of Literary Biography. Detroit: Gale Research, 1999. 199: 140–48.
———. "Dora Greenwell's Commonplace Book." *Princeton University Library Chron-
     icle* 57.1 (1995): 47–74.
———. "The Sewing Contest: Christina Rossetti and the Other Women." *A/B: Auto/
     Biography Studies* 8.2 (1993): 233–57.
Groth, Helen. "Victorian Women Poets and Scientific Narratives." In *Women's Poetry,
     Late Romantic to Late Victorian: Gender and Genre, 1830–1900.* Ed. Isobel
     Armstrong and Virginia Blain. Basingstoke, Hamps: Macmillan Press; New York:
     St. Martin's Press, 1999. 325–51.
Kaplan, Cora. "Language and Gender." In *Sea Changes: Culture and Feminism.* Ed.
     Cora Kaplan. 1986. London: Verso, 1990. 69–94.

Leighton, Angela. "Because Men Made the Laws: Fallen Woman and Woman Poet." In *New Feminist Discourses: Critical Essays on Theories and Texts*. Ed. Isobel Armstrong. London: Routledge, 1992. 342–60.

Maynard, Constance L. *Dora Greenwell: A Prophet for Our Own Times on the Battle-ground of Our Faith*. London: H. R. Allenson, 1926.

Felicia Dorothea Hemans (1793–1835)

Kevin Eubanks

BIOGRAPHY

Felicia Browne was born in Liverpool in 1793, the daughter of George Browne, a merchant, and Felicity Wagner Browne, daughter of the Austrian Tuscany Consul. After his business failed, her father departed in 1800 for Quebec, where he later died. A precocious child, Felicia Browne studied French, Italian, Spanish, Portuguese, and German under her mother and published her first two volumes of poetry at age fourteen. Four years later, she married Captain Alfred Hemans. Hemans published regularly during these years. Ostensibly for health reasons, Captain Hemans left England permanently for Italy in 1819; Hemans and her five sons remained with her mother. Through the 1820s, Hemans's fame so grew in England and America that she could support her children through writing. In 1827 Hemans's mother died. Thereafter, Hemans, who rarely traveled before, went twice to Scotland (where she visited Walter Scott) and summered at Windermere near the Wordsworths. In 1831, her health failing, Hemans moved to Dublin, where she continued publishing until her death in 1835. Hemans's works were reprinted in England and America throughout the nineteenth century.

MAJOR WORKS AND THEMES

Hemans wrote mostly poetry: long narratives as well as hundreds of brief lyrics, many originally published in annuals and periodicals. She published two dramas; one, *The Vespers of Palermo*, was staged in London and Edinburgh. Hemans also translated numerous authors, including Camoens, Goethe, and Alfieri.

Hemans's poems are often topical: for example, *Modern Greece*, inspired by Elgin's removal to England of the Parthenon friezes. Many other poems have historical subjects, drawn from Hemans's extensive reading.

The Domestic Affections, the title of Hemans's 1812 volume, indicates one important theme in her poetry. But despite being considered the quintessential poet of hearth and home, Hemans is rarely facile in depicting domesticity. Even when claimed as the only source of true joy, home in Hemans is often nostalgically depicted as irrecoverable. In "Song of Emigration" (*Songs*), while the husband looks hopefully toward a new life, the wife mourns the loss of "Home, home and friends."

The title of her second published volume, *England and Spain; or, Valour and Patriotism*, indicates a fondness in Hemans for martial subjects. Throughout her career, Hemans celebrated those who fought for liberty from foreign tyranny, Spaniards fighting Napoleon, Scots fighting the English, or Greeks fighting Romans. A poem such as "The Homes of England," which celebrates English domesticity and the warriors who have defended it, shows Hemans at her most jingoistic. But she is also deeply aware of war's costs, especially to the domestic sphere. The title character of "The Wife of Asdrubal" (*Tales*) kills her own children after her husband surrenders to the invading Romans. Conversely, the mother in *The Siege of Valencia*, desperate to free her captured sons, betrays the city to the Moors. Often, a single poem will both celebrate bravery in and mourn the devastation of war; "Casabianca," a favorite Victorian parlor poem, is a perfect example.

Not surprisingly, Hemans's poetry frequently addresses fame and womanhood. Hemans early sought literary glory, claiming as her models the ancient "tuneful bards" ("Genius," *Poems*). However, as her reputation grew, Hemans's attitude toward fame grew more ambivalent. In her later verse, she contrasts fame with domestic happiness. The speaker in "Woman and Fame" desires not fame but "home-borne love." In "Properzia Rossi," the woman sculptor, finding no comfort in her renown, dies of unrequited love.

Another trait of Hemans's poetry, one much admired by nineteenth-century audiences, is its strain of sentimental piety. *The Sceptic* is a long, didactic poem arguing that only Christianity provides ultimate consolation in life. *The Forest Sanctuary* concerns a man who converts to Protestantism after witnessing a friend's death in the Spanish Inquisition. Religious sentiments especially predominate in Hemans's late works, such as her sonnets on "Female Characters of Scripture" and her *Hymns on the Works of Nature for the Use of Children*.

CRITICAL RECEPTION

The Restoration of the Works of Art to Italy (1816) first brought Hemans considerable favorable notice. Despite favorable reviews and poetry competition prizes, Hemans's early works sold only moderately well, rarely beyond a thousand copies. In the 1820s, however, frequent publication in annuals and periodicals increased Hemans's readership (and income) significantly, as did the 1826 American publication of her collected works. Hemans also began to receive notices in such influential periodicals as the *Quarterly Review* (1820) and the *Edinburgh Review* (1829).

Reviewers of Hemans's early works seldom saw them as distinctively "feminine." In fact, most reviewers assumed the anonymous author of *Modern Greece* to be male. But during the 1820s, critics increasingly discussed Hemans in gendered terms, praising her more "feminine" religious and domestic works over her more "masculine" military and historical ones. Jeffrey's description of Hemans's work as "a fine exemplification of Female Poetry" represents the critical consensus. Ironically, later readers often considered her poetry's supposed "femininity" a fault rather than a virtue. As tastes changed, Hemans's highly polished, sentimental verse fell out of favor.

By the twentieth century, Hemans, when not completely forgotten, was an object of satire (such as Noel Coward's parody of "The Homes of England"). But the 1980s saw a resurgence of interest in Hemans, which continues unabated. Ross sees Hemans's works as celebrating woman's concerns, offering an alternative to the predominantly masculine Romantic canon. Wolfson and Eubanks question such gendered views by exploring the creation of "Hemans" as a literary persona. Lootens considers Hemans's complex handling of British nationalism and imperialism. After almost a century of neglect, Hemans is finally regaining some of the recognition she had during her lifetime.

BIBLIOGRAPHY

A complete edition of Hemans will be out soon (ed. Paula Feldman [Johns Hopkins University Press]), and another edition is currently in print, *Felicia Hemans: Selected Texts* (ed. Gary Kelly and Susan Wolfson [Broadview, 1997]). *Records of Women* (University of Kentucky Press, 1999) is in print and a one-volume edition of her works is planned (Princeton University Press, 2000). Several of her volumes are available in facsimile editions (ed. Donald Reiman [Garland, 1978]), and selections of her works appear in most major editions of nineteenth-century British writers.

Works by Felicia Hemans

England and Spain; or, Valour and Patriotism. 1808.
Poems. 1808.
The Domestic Affections. 1812.
The Restoration of the Works of Art to Italy. 1816.
Modern Greece. 1817.
Tales, and Historic Scenes, in Verse. 1819.
Wallace's Invocation to Bruce. 1819.
The Sceptic. 1820.
Stanzas to the Memory of the Late King. 1820.
Dartmoor. 1821.
A Selection of Welsh Melodies. 1821.
The Siege of Valencia. 1823.

The Vespers of Palermo. 1823.
The Forest Sanctuary. 1825.
Hymns on the Works of Nature for the Use of Children. 1827.
Records of Woman. 1828.
Songs of the Affections. 1830.
National Lyrics, and Songs for Music. 1834.
Scenes and Hymns of Life. 1834.

Studies of Felicia Hemans

Eubanks, Kevin. "Minerva's Veil: Hemans, Critics, and the Construction of Gender."
       European Romantic Review 8 (Fall 1997): 341–59.
Jeffrey, Francis. "Felicia Hemans." *The Edinburgh Review* 99 (Oct. 1929).
Lootens, Tricia. "Hemans and Home: Victorianism, Feminine 'Internal Enemies,' and
       the Domestication of National Identity." *PMLA* 109 (Mar. 1994): 238–53.
Mellor, Anne. *Romanticism & Gender.* New York: Routledge, 1993.
Ross, Marlon. *The Contours of Masculine Desire: Romanticism and the Rise of Women's
       Poetry.* New York: Oxford University Press, 1989.
Trinder, Peter. *Mrs Hemans.* [Cardiff]: University of Wales, 1984.
Wolfson, Susan. " 'Domestic Affections' and 'The Spear of Minerva': Felicia Hemans
       and the Dilemma of Gender." In *Re-Visioning Romanticism: British Women Writ-
       ers, 1776–1837.* Ed. C. S. Wilson and J. Haefner. Philadelphia: University of
       Pennsylvania, 1994.

Mary Howitt
(1799-1888)

Margaret A. Loose

BIOGRAPHY

Inaugurating her literary career during the Janus-faced years between British Romanticism and Victorianism, Mary Botham Howitt embodies many of the literary and sociopolitical fascinations of nineteenth-century England. As a youth in Staffordshire she chafed against her Quaker family's austere tendencies to silence, plainness, and gloom, instead surreptitiously cultivating individual expression, artistic beauty, and companions of superior intellect or imagination. She acknowledged benefiting, however, from the Friends' tradition of educating women and granting them teaching and preaching positions, noting that her parents engaged the boys' school master to tutor their teenaged daughter in Latin, mathematics, and geography. In William Howitt, Mary Botham discovered a Quaker youth who delighted in conversation and intellectual pursuits and whose admiration for nature and the poetry of Byron resonated with her own, she married him in 1821 and thus began a long career of literary collaboration that complemented the efforts of each individually.

Never sectarian in her religious outlook, Howitt resigned her membership in the Society of Friends in 1847 and remained unattached to any organized religion for most of the remainder of her long life. When in midcentury spiritualism and mesmerism captured the imaginations of many respectable contemporaries, the always-inquisitive Howitts experimented in these practices as well. But it was finally, and surprisingly, to Catholicism that Mary Howitt converted in the last years of her life.

Eclectic in more than her spiritual tastes, Howitt ventured into numerous regions of Britain and Europe, frequently on walking tours, acquiring information and languages she would later use in her literary endeavors. With letters of introduction from their friend Anna Jameson,* she and her husband moved their family to Heidelberg, Germany, from 1840 to 1843, and it was during this time that she began translating books (she was the first to make Hans Christian Andersen's stories available in English). She returned to England, usually living near London to facilitate her many transactions with publishers.

In addition to her translations, Howitt herself wrote a multitude of stories and poems for children, including "The Spider and the Fly," and it is probably for these that she is most remembered. Nevertheless, she also wielded her pen in an impressive variety of genres: didactic fiction and poetry for adults, journalistic polemics addressing social issues, a verse drama, histories of Scandinavian literature and British architecture, and finally, her two-volume autobiography published posthumously in 1889. Lively, eminently readable, and socially instructive, *Mary Howitt an Autobiography* is her only remaining work in print. She lived primarily in Italy from 1771 until she died in 1888, and she was buried next to her husband in the Protestant cemetery in Rome.

MAJOR WORKS AND THEMES

Although many of William and Mary Howitt's joint projects such as *The Book of the Seasons* (1828)—Romantic in its nostalgic evocation of England's natural landscape under pressure from industrialization—met with approval from both reviewers and the public sufficient to warrant at least seventeen hefty editions, perhaps their most dazzlingly interesting collaboration was *Howitt's Journal of Literature and Popular Progress* (1847–1848), a decidedly Victorian periodical in its more or less Chartist and Co-operative approach to social problems. What makes reading the inexpensive weekly a dense sociopolitical education and a sheer pleasure is the astonishing variety of social issues at which its progressive editors took aim (as they believed) on behalf of the working classes. Perusing the fiction, poetry, engravings, reviews, letters, essays, and polemics (much of it by women) in each issue affords a view of nearly every defining debate of these revolutionary years of the nineteenth century: truly universal suffrage; prison, Poor Law, and parliamentary reform; humanity to animals; the peace and early closing movements; anti-Corn Law, antienclosure, and anti–capital punishment agitation; public health measures; temperance; Co-operative endeavors; women's economic rights; Catholic emancipation; free national education; copyright laws; communal living and child-care arrangements; Irish relief; and the abolition of slavery. While Howitt abjured any particular class loyalty as unhealthily divisive, her dedication to abolishing many injustices suffered by women and the poor remains abundantly clear.

Ballads and Other Poems (1847) achieved a "vogue" (Patson 363) and contains some of Howitt's most interesting poems (see "The Old Man's Story," for example). As a barometer of liberal sentiment toward women's economic independence and working-class agitation, her *Little Coin, Much Care* (1842) deserves attention for its equivocal portrayals of Nottingham workers and philanthropists around the time of the riots and burning of Nottingham Castle in

1831. Because of their examination of links between economics and morality, these tales are among her most noteworthy work.

Howitt remained a prolific writer after midcentury, continuing to produce volumes of poetry, prose tales, works of history and natural history, children's literature, and translations of works by Swedish, German, and Danish authors.

CRITICAL RECEPTION

Mary Howitt is now regarded as a shaper and mirror of contemporary public tastes and concerns rather than as an outright reformer or literary heavyweight. Yet situated as she was on the cusp of Romantic and Victorian ideologies, the evolution of her politics and their literary expression warrants scrutiny.

Howitt's contemporaries noticed her in a mostly favorable way, as is evident from the invitations she received to contribute to many annuals and keepsakes, to write the first of Bradshaw's Railway novels, and to contribute to Dickens's *Household Words*. In her *Autobiography*, Howitt quotes Dickens's letter to her: "Frankly, I want to say to you, that if you would ever write for [*Household words*], you would delight me, and I should consider myself very fortunate indeed in enlisting your assistance" (2: 58). She also frequently elicited praise from such reviewers as Christopher North of *Blackwood's*. Never enriched by her earnings from literary endeavors—in part because of her outright sale of copyrights and in part because of later violations of her copyrights—she did earn a sufficient living with her pen during a career spanning nearly six decades. For her literary merits, she was granted a Civil List pension beginning in 1879. Only a few biographical and/or critical studies of Howitt have appeared in the twentieth century.

BIBLIOGRAPHY

Howitt's *Autobiography* has been reprinted, and her poems appear in anthologies of Victorian women's poetry.

Works by Mary Howitt

The Book of the Seasons; or, The Calendar of Nature. With William Howitt. 1828.
Birds and Flowers, and Other Country Things. 1838.
Little Coin, Much Care: or, How Poor Men Live. A Tale. 1842.
Work and Wages: or, Life in Service. 1842.
My Own Story; or, The Autobiography of a Child. 1845.
Ballads and Other Poems. 1847.
Howitt's Journal of Literature and Popular Progress. 1847–1848.
The Poetical Works of Mary Howitt, Eliza Cook, and L.E.L. 1852.
The Cost of Caergwyn. 1864.
Mary Howitt an Autobiography. Ed. Margaret Howitt. 2 vols. 1889.

Studies of Mary Howitt

Jones, Nicholas R. "William Howitt and Mary Howitt." In *British Romantic Prose Writers, 1789–1932, Second Series*. Ed. John R. Greenfield. *Dictionary of Literary Biography*. Detroit: Gale Research, 1991. 110: 139–51.

Lee, Amice Macdonell. *Laurels and Rosemary: The Life of William and Mary Howitt*. London: Oxford University Press, 1955.

Paston, George. "William and Mary Howitt." In *Little Memoirs of the Nineteenth Century*. London: Grant Richards, 1902.

Woodring, Carl Ray. *Victorian Samplers: William and Mary Howitt*. Lawrence: University of Kansas Press, 1952.

Jean Ingelow
(1820-1897)

Heidi Johnson

BIOGRAPHY

Born in Boston, Lincolnshire, Jean Ingelow was the oldest in a family of ten children. Financial difficulties led the Ingelows first to Ipswich and finally to London in 1850. Ingelow never married and, with the success of her writing, supported her widowed mother and several charitable endeavors.

Ingelow began writing poetry for an audience of family and friends, and her initial collection, *A Rhyming Chronicle of Incidents and Feelings*, was published anonymously in 1850. This was quickly followed by a novel, *Allerton and Dreux* (1851), a story of love complicated by conflicting religious principles. An interest in writing for children was whetted by contributions to and brief editorship of *Youth Magazine*. Several volumes of her didactic children's tales appeared throughout Ingelow's lifetime, whereas six additional novels for adult audiences were moderately successful.

Fame arrived with the publication of *Poems* in 1863, which sustained its popularity through the course of thirty British editions. Volumes of new poems appearing in 1867, 1874, and 1885 achieved wide readership in Britain and also in the United States, where an estimated 200,000 copies of Ingelow's books were sold. Indeed, a petition from America unsuccessfully urged Ingelow's appointment to the post of poet laureate after Tennyson's death in 1892. Ingelow largely ceased writing in the final years of her life, perhaps due to the trauma of a beloved brother's death in 1886 but also as her poetry failed to adapt to a changing readership.

MAJOR WORKS AND THEMES

Ingelow's early years near the sea are the dominant influence reverberating throughout her adult work. This setting and an exploration of its effects on her characters inform her partly autobiographical novel *Off the Skelligs* (1872) and its sequel *Fated to Be Free* (1875), while seafaring sailors, and the women and children who remain at home, are featured prominently in her ballads, lyrics, and narrative poems, often characterized by skilled use of dialect. Ingelow's biographer, Maureen Peters, provides a highly speculative explanation for this preoccupation, as well as for Ingelow's frequent themes of lost love, failed expectations, and mourning: an early romance with a sailor who died.

Although Ingelow experimented with a number of poetic forms, her most noteworthy achievements were in lyrics, often harking back to the medieval in language and style but especially to a Wordsworthian Romanticism in their accent upon nature and childhood; Ingelow's credo was: "Imagination is such a high faculty that it should repose on things most simple and universal" (*Some Recollections of Jean Ingelow* 148). A religious emphasis also pervades her work, with characters and speakers repeatedly achieving a union with the Divine through the process of sleep and dreaming. Her subject matter and form often prompted comparison to Tennyson and Christina Rossetti,* both acquaintances of Ingelow and admirers of her poetry.

Religious and moral themes dominate most of Ingelow's children's fiction, although the fantasy that led to her most resilient success in juvenile literature, *Mopsa the Fairy* (1869), rarely surfaced in her poetry. Her adult fiction is marked by attention to the childhoods of her heroes and heroines, as well as by melodramatic and even sensational plot twists.

CRITICAL RECEPTION

Ingelow has often been dubbed a particularly "feminine" writer, and whether this characterization is used to praise or problematize her work has depended upon historical context and changing critical fashions. In her own time, Ingelow's writing garnered acclaim for its orthodox religious stance, domestic values, sentimentality, and vestiges of Romanticism. Her tentative and self-disparaging persona especially emerged when she grappled with a masculine poetic tradition, which can be discerned from the subtitle to her "Song for the Night of Christ's Resurrection: A Humble Imitation" (1867), written in response to Milton's "On the Morning of Christ's Nativity." When, however, she took on this tradition more boldly, as in *A Story of Doom* (1867), a biblical epic poem that explores women's spirituality in relation to patriarchal Christianity, her efforts were dismissed as overambitious and artistically flawed.

With the advent of feminist criticism, Ingelow's work has posed difficulties to scholars precisely because of the "femininity" and conventional outlook praised a century earlier. Ingelow's most frequently anthologized poems are "Divided" and "High Tide on the Coast of Lincolnshire (1571)," both from the 1863 *Poems*, with the latter commended for its vivid imagery, linguistic dexterity, and emotional verisimilitude by Lafcadio Hearn, who claimed that Ingelow "really wrote only one great poem" (334).

This judgment aside, one of Ingelow's chapter epigraphs in *Mopsa*, a sonnet titled "Failure," has been praised by John Hollander as not only "one of the major lost poems of the nineteenth century" (214) but "one of the finest short poems of its time" (213). Ingelow's explorations of female experience and of artistic identity have also attracted recent critical attention, especially to her long narrative poems of 1867, *Gladys and Her Island: On the Advantages of the Poetical Temperament* and *A Story of Doom*.

BIBLIOGRAPHY

Among Ingelow's novels, only her children's fantasy *Mopsa the Fairy* is in print (*Forbidden Journeys: Fairy Tales and Fantasies by Victorian Women Writers*, ed. Nina Auerback and U. C. Knoepflmacher [University of Chicago Press, 1992]); selections from her poetry have been reprinted in recent anthologies of Victorian women poets.

Selected Works by Jean Ingelow

A Rhyming Chronicle of Incidents and Feelings. Anonymous. 1850.
Allerton and Dreux; or, The War of Opinion. 1851.
Poems. 1863.
Gladys and Her Island: On the Advantages of the Poetical Temperament. 1867.
A Story of Doom. 1867.
Mopsa the Fairy. 1869.
Off the Skelligs. 1872.
Fated to Be Free. 1875.
Poems. 1913.

Studies of Jean Ingelow

Attebery, Brian. "Women Coming of Age in Fantasy." *Extrapolation* 28.1 (Spring 1987): 10–22.
Hearn, Lafcadio. "A Note on Jean Ingelow." In *Appreciations of Poetry.* Ed. John Erksine. New York: Dodd, Mead, 1916. 334–48.
Hollander, John. "A Poem Lost and Found: Jean Ingelow's Successful 'Failure.' " In *The Work of Poetry.* New York: Columbia University Press, 1997. 210–14.
Johnson, Heidi. " 'Matters That a Woman Rules': Marginalized Maternity in Jean Ingelow's *A Story of Doom.*" *Victorian Poetry* 33.1 (Spring 1995): 75–88.
Peters, Maureen. *Jean Ingelow: Victorian Poetess.* Totowa, NJ: Rowman and Littlefield, 1972.
Some Recollections of Jean Ingelow and Her Early Friends. London: W. Gardner, Darton. 1901. Rpt., Port Washington: Kennikat Press, 1972.
Wagner, Jennifer A. "In Her 'Proper Place': Ingelow's Fable of the Female Poet and Her Community in *Gladys and Her Island.*" *Victorian Poetry* 31.3 (Fall 1993): 227–39.

Anna Brownell Murphy Jameson (1794–1860)

Renée V. Overholser

BIOGRAPHY

Anna Brownell Murphy, journalist, travel writer, women's biographer, art historian, literary critic, and social activist, was born in Dublin to an Irish miniaturist and portrait painter and his English wife. The family moved to England, where Denis Murphy had so modest a success that about 1810 his daughter began work as a governess, and she was to continue contributing to the support of her family throughout her life. Her 1825 marriage to barrister Robert Jameson ended in a separation agreement in 1837, after which he provided only erratic financial support and, on his death, excluded her from his will. Throughout her career Jameson wrote from financial necessity.

The success of her earliest published work, *The Diary of an Ennuyée* (1826), a fictionalized account of the young governess's European travels with her employers, was followed by an equally popular series of biographies of famous women—female sovereigns, poets' beloveds, celebrated beauties—and by analyses of Shakespeare's heroines, which were informed by her friendships with the celebrated actresses Fanny Kemble* and Sarah Siddons. An unsuccessful effort to reconcile with her husband resulted in a travel journal that includes a compelling account of Jameson's "wild expedition" (*Letters* 93) by bateau and canoe into the Canadian wilderness.

Jameson made her mark as a professional art historian through a series of increasingly knowledgeable and self-assured articles, on early Italian painters serialized in *Penny Magazine* and on Christian iconography for *The Athenaeum*, followed by popular guides to public and private art collections in and near London. Extended continental travels, during which she haunted collections, sketching and analyzing works of art, gave firsthand authority to her aesthetic judgments as well as to analyses of continental literature and culture. She continued to travel throughout her life, with long stays in Germany, where she formed lifelong friendships with Ottilie von Goethe and her circle, and in Italy, as the senior member of the expatriate colony surrounding her close friends Elizabeth Barrett* and Robert Browning. Other important friendships included those with Lady Byron and Elizabeth Gaskell.*

Jameson's experiences had sensitized her to the need for expanded work opportunities for women, as well as to the imperatives for changes in marriage and property laws, and from the 1840s on, she played a seminal role in formulating the century's debates on these issues. Late in life she became mentor to members of the Langham Place Circle, among them Barbara Leigh Smith Bodichon,* Emily Faithfull, and Adelaide Procter.* She participated actively on the Married Women's Property Committee, and she brought her journalistic experience to the establishment and development of the *English Woman's Journal*.

MAJOR WORKS AND THEMES

Anna Jameson combined acceptance of the discourse of separate spheres with subversive analyses of art, literature, and society, designed to facilitate expansion of women's active participation in the public sphere. In *Characteristics of Women* (1832) she focused on issues of women's power, challenging constricting gender representations in sympathetic readings of such Shakespearean characters as Cleopatra, Portia, and Lady Macbeth. Her interest in women's issues intensified in *Winter Studies and Summer Rambles in Canada* (1838): She writes that she has undertaken her journey "to see, with my own eyes, the condition of women in savage life" (*Letters* 93), which she then compares favorably to societal limitations imposed on Englishwomen, suggesting the "general principle" that woman's "real dignity" and "condition" is "decided by the share she takes in providing for her own subsistence and the well-being of society as a productive labourer" (519).

Jameson's major volumes of art criticism, *Sacred and Legendary Art* (1848), *Legends of the Monastic Orders* (1850), and *Legends of the Madonna* (1852), are rigorous, systematic interpretations of Christian symbolism. In *Sisters of Charity, Catholic and Protestant* (1855) and *The Communion of Labour* (1856), published versions of her seminal lectures on female employment, Jameson argues for efforts by both men and women toward this end, for example, in establishing Protestant sisterhoods to train women for social and administrative work in hospitals, female prisons, and workhouses.

CRITICAL RECEPTION

Although her scholarship was sometimes deprecated by contemporaneous critics, Anna Jameson became a recognized art authority, widely read in Europe and the United States during her lifetime, then largely forgotten until Thomas's sympathetic biography, which echoes Jameson's own emphasis on the centrality of the relationship between art and life. Similarly, Friewald traces the necessary textual transformations demanded by the marital crisis that occasioned *Winter Studies and Summer Rambles in Canada*, whereas Desmet argues for a further purpose in *Characteristics of Women*: Jameson "not only recreates Shakespeare's characters in her own image, she invites female readers to recreate themselves" (54).

Increasingly, Jameson's intellectual power and subversiveness are recognized. Holcomb finds a "rigorous standard of accuracy and completeness" in the art criticism that derives from "self-imposed" scholarly standards (103). Frawley expands the discussion of Jameson's professionalism, analyzing the effects of her emphasis on the "utility" both of art and of her own art popularizations, which "widened the boundaries of what could be considered appropriate, proper, and within a woman's sphere" (91). Johnston's wide-ranging critical biography stresses Jameson's reformulations across gender, genre, and class boundaries in tracing "the shifts and turns she took regarding her most dominant and constant subject: women" (9). "If in her practice she rarely seems disruptive, in effect the result is polemical" (18), Johnston remarks, perhaps most remarkably when Jameson questions the "social concept of class" (234). Like Ludley, Johnston also repositions Jameson in relation to better-known male contemporaries.

BIBLIOGRAPHY

Several of Jameson's works have been reprinted: *Characteristics of Women* (AMS, 1971); *Legends of the Madonna* (Gale, 1972); *Sacred and Legendary Art* (AMS, 1976); *Sisters of Charity, Catholic and Protestant* and *The Communion of Labour* (Hyperion, 1976); *Winter Studies and Summer Rambles in Canada* (McClelland & Stewart, 1990). Jameson's essay "The Milliners" is included in *"Criminals, Idiots, Women, and Minors"* (ed. Susan Hamilton [Broadview, 1996]).

Selected Works by Anna Jameson

The Diary of an Ennuyée. 1826.
Characteristics of Women, Moral, Poetical and Historical. 1832.
Winter Studies and Summer Rambles in Canada. 1838.
Sacred and Legendary Art. 1848.
Legends of the Monastic Order. 1850.
Legends of the Madonna as Represented in the Fine Arts. 1852.
Sisters of Charity, Catholic and Protestant. 1855.
The Communion of Labour. 1856.
Memoirs of the Life of Anna Jameson. By Gerardine Macpherson. 1878.
Letters of Anna Jameson to Ottilie von Goethe. Ed. G. H. Needler. 1939.

Studies of Anna Jameson

Desmet, Christy. " 'Intercepting the Dew-Drop': Female Readers and Readings in Anna
    Jameson's Shakespearean Criticism." In *Women's Re-Visions of Shakespeare: On*

the Responses of Dickinson, Woolf, Rich, H. D., George Eliot, and Others. Ed. Marianne Novy. Urbana: University of Illinois Press, 1990. 41–57.

Frawley, Maria H. *A Wider Range: Travel Writing by Women in Victorian England*. Rutherford: Fairleigh Dickinson University Press, 1994. 71–93.

Friewald, Bina. " 'Femininely Speaking': Anna Jameson's *Winter Studies and Summer Rambles in Canada*." In *A Mazing Space: Writing Canadian Women Writing*. Ed. Shirley Neuman and Smaro Kamboureli. Edmonton: Longspoon, 1986. 61–73.

Holcomb, Adele M. "Anna Jameson (1794–1860): Sacred Art and Social Vision." In *Women as Interpreters of the Visual Arts, 1820–1979*. Ed. Claire Richter Sherman with Adele M. Holcomb. Westport, CT: Greenwood, 1981. 93–121.

Johnston, Judith. *Anna Jameson: Victorian, Feminist, Woman of Letters*. Hants, Eng.: Scolar, 1997.

Ludley, David A. "Anna Jameson and D. G. Rossetti: His Use of Her Histories." *Woman's Art Journal* 12 (Fall–Winter 1991–1992): 29–33.

Thomas, Clara. *Love and Work Enough: The Life of Anna Jameson*. Toronto: University of Toronto Press, 1967.

Geraldine Jewsbury
(1812-1880)

Elisabeth Anne Leonard

BIOGRAPHY

In *A Room of One's Own* (Hogarth Press, 1929) Virginia Woolf wrote, "We think back through our mothers, if we are women." Geraldine Endsor Jewsbury, born in the early part of the nineteenth century, before the great outpouring of novels by women writers during the Victorian era, had few women to look back to as models when she began writing. She did, however, have one significant model, her older sister, Maria Jane Jewsbury.*

Maria Jane, born in 1800, took over the role of mother and housekeeper in the Jewsbury family when her mother and Geraldine's died in 1818. Geraldine, the youngest of the Jewsbury children, was six at the time and so grew up with her sister as her mother figure. By the time she was thirty, Maria Jane had published several books and struck up friendships with other literary figures of the time, most notably the poet Felicia Hemans* and Dora Wordsworth, William's daughter. Among her books was *Letters to the Young* (1828), the edited version of letters that Maria Jane had written to Geraldine. Although the letters encouraged women not to be ambitious, particularly in literary ways, they helped Maria Jane increase her reputation as a writer and did not discourage Geraldine.

In 1832, Maria Jane married the Reverend William K. Fletcher and moved with him to India, where she died the following year. Geraldine took over her sister's responsibilities for housekeeping. Around the period of her father's death in 1840, Jewsbury was ill and experienced profound doubts about her religious beliefs. She wrote to Thomas Carlyle, as her sister had once written to William Wordsworth, and entered into a lasting, if at times rocky, friendship with Jane Welsh Carlyle,* Thomas's wife. Jane Welsh Carlyle considered Jewsbury overly emotional and passionate and at times found her much easier to get along with through letters than in person. Jewsbury, however, relied on Welsh Carlyle both for emotional support—she in some ways wanted Welsh Carlyle to be the mother/wife figure that her sister was—and for help with her writing; she submitted an early draft of her first novel, *Zoe*, to Welsh Carlyle for her comments. Welsh Carlyle was also able to provide Jewsbury with access to publishers and reviewers.

Jewsbury published *Zoe: The History of Two Lives* in 1845; it was followed by *The Half Sisters* in 1848, *Marian Withers* in 1851, and several other novels, both for adults and children. *Zoe* raised eyebrows for Jewsbury's violations of propriety. According to Joanne Wilkes, "*Zoe* was considered so likely to injure the morals of young men that it was placed in a dark cupboard in Manchester library" (xii). It included, among other things, the passionate though unconsummated love of a priest for a married woman. Her early novels depict strong women and women suffering within the limits of marriage (as Jewsbury saw Welsh Carlyle doing) and also express many of her doubts about religious practices. Jewsbury wrote her last novel in 1859. This was also the year in which Walter Mantell, with whom she was in love, refused to marry her. Her relationship with Mantell had caused her friendship with Jane Welsh Carlyle to disintegrate; Welsh Carlyle appeared both to be jealous of Mantell and to think that Jewsbury was acting disgracefully in passionately throwing herself at him. (He was not the first man she had proposed to.)

Jewsbury had been working as a reviewer on *The Athenaeum*, and when she died in 1880 of cancer, she had reviewed about 2,300 books. She also helped Lady Morgan write her *Memoirs* (1858), and she spent about the last twenty years of her life as a publisher's reader for Bentley. Although she was not a politically active feminist, having refused to sign petitions for women's rights, her novels depict what happens to women who are suppressed, whereas her own life demonstrates what a woman could do when she was allowed to be self-sufficient.

MAJOR WORKS AND THEMES

Jewsbury's novels share a concern with women's positions in society, though they have externally different subjects. Of her first three novels, *Zoe* is outwardly about religion and crises of faith, *The Half Sisters* about women's careers, and *Marian Withers* about the middle-class world of manufacturing. Jewsbury, however, shares the concern that Mary Wollstonecraft expresses in *A Vindication of the Rights of Women* (1792) about the education of young women and girls; like Wollstonecraft, she points out in her novels how deficiencies of education make women seem intellectually inferior to men. When her female characters cannot restrain their passions, it is almost always because they have not been taught how.

Zoe is set in the eighteenth century (though Jewsbury is disorganized with her chronologies; structurally the novel is rather sloppy), but though historical personages flit across its pages (Zoe once entertains Fanny Burney, for instance), it is far more of a romance than a historically accurate novel. In Everhard

Burrowes, a trained Catholic priest, Jewsbury has found a mouth for her own religious doubts and uncertainties; he sees religious denominations as ways of organizing faith for the masses rather than as true expressions of belief. Zoe herself takes the argument even further than Everhard, stating, "How much better to teach people that whatever it is really right to do, would have been equally right and equally imperative upon them, even though Moses never had delivered the ten commandments" (2: 71–72). The novel contains numerous plots and subplots, and it is at times hard to reconcile Zoe's obvious intelligence and radical ideas with her desires to move about in fashionable society. But Jewsbury creates in Zoe a woman who is both well educated and an excellent mother, thus supporting Wollstonecraft's view that education makes women better wives and mothers, and questions conventional notions about religious doctrine in relation to living morally. Jewsbury's primary argument in *The Half Sisters* is that work, even work as disreputable as acting, does not lead women into vice but rather the reverse; Bianca, an illegitimate actress who devotes herself entirely to her art, remains chaste, whereas Alice, her half sister, bored and lonely, is only prevented from running away on an adulterous affair by her husband's unexpected arrival home. Although the novel ends with Bianca forsaking the stage to marry Lord Melton, which would suggest that women cannot both work and be wives, for Jewsbury to have an illegitimate half-Italian actress marry a peer is probably radical enough. Lord Melton himself is a feminist man, arguing that if women act unprincipled, it is because they have not been taught principles. While his friend Conrad, who was once engaged to Bianca but breaks it off when he falls in love with Alice, believes that Bianca's career has "unsexed her" (216), Lord Melton says, "A woman is a rational being, with reasonable soul and human flesh subsisting, and yet she is never educated for her own sake, to enable her to lead her own life better" (219). He is capable of seeing that women have been constructed upon men's desires, and if his way of expressing it makes him a flat character, it does allow Jewsbury to give strong voice to her views about women in society.

Jewsbury's third novel, *Marian Withers*, is the story of a self-made man, John Withers, who rises from begging on the streets to owning a large cotton mill, and his daughter Marian. Here Jewsbury addresses the concerns of the manufacturing class, although she does it from the point of view of a man who wants to make life better for his workers and more profitable for himself as a consequence of his improvements; the novel does not have the gritty anticapitalist feel of the work of Elizabeth Gaskell.* Jewsbury also is able to continue writing about her concerns with women's position in society; one of Marian's friends, Hilda, marries for money and is miserable, whereas another character, Lady Wollaston, verges on an affair in part because of how confined she feels by her loveless marriage. Marian herself marries an older man who has helped her father out, but she has outgrown her fancies for dress and society and made good use of her mind in assisting her father with his operation of the mill.

Jewsbury emphasizes that it is the idle and unloved woman who marries for society's sake who suffers misery and turns away from principled behavior.

Jewsbury's later works are generally considered to be inferior. *Constance Herbert* (1855), for example, contains none of the radical questioning of cultural norms found in the earlier three books. It is a sentimental melodrama about a young woman whose mother is mad and whose father gambles away the family lands. Constance renounces marriage so as not to pass on the family insanity; as George Eliot* wrote, "[W]e are sorry that a writer of Miss Jewsbury's insight and sincerity should have produced three volumes for the sake of teaching such copy-book morality" 120). Jewsbury ceased writing fiction by 1860 and continued to write as a reviewer and publisher's reader.

CRITICAL RECEPTION

Jewsbury has not received much attention as a writer from twentieth-century scholars. This is in part no doubt due to the difficulty finding her works. Her reviews have not been collected into any single volume. Monica Correa Fryckstedt's book *Geraldine Jewsbury's* Athenaeum *Reviews: A Mirror of Mid-Victorian Attitudes to Fiction* (1986) contains an appendix listing those reviews and useful biographical material. Aside from Susanne Howe's 1935 biography, there is only one other twentieth-century book treating Jewsbury's life and work in detail, Norma Clarke's *Ambitious Heights: Writing, Friendship, Love—The Jewsbury Sisters, Felicia Hemans, and Jane Welsh Carlyle* (1990). Jewsbury's first three novels have garnered an article or two apiece; her later work is not discussed. Elaine Showalter, in her seminal text *A Literature of Their Own* (1977), makes mention of Jewsbury and her work, particularly *Zoe*, several times, but focuses more on Jewsbury's letters and reviews than on her fiction.

In her own day, Jewsbury's first novel was considered powerful and shocking. *The Half Sisters* was more well received, though not without its critics, and helped to establish Jewsbury as a significant woman novelist. *Marian Withers* was considered somewhat of a disappointment. Jewsbury was still considered a novelist of note when *Constance Herbert* was published, but while the subject matter of the book was welcome to those who had been scandalized by *Zoe*, the writing was (justly) criticized. Howe claims that Jewsbury's heart was not fully in her later novels, which seems to be a sentiment shared by Jewsbury's contemporaries. Jewsbury was admired as a reader and reviewer and had a great deal of influence in those capacities, but her fiction was not held in such high regard.

BIBLIOGRAPHY

Only three of Jewsbury's works have been reprinted in book form: *Zoe: The History of Two Lives* (Garland, 1975), *The Half Sisters: A Tale* (Oxford University Press, 1994), and *Marian Withers* (University Microfilms International, 1976).

Works by Geraldine Jewsbury

Zoe: The History of Two Lives. 1845.
The Half Sisters: A Tale. 1848.
Marian Withers. 1851.
Constance Herbert. 1855.
The Sorrows of Gentility. 1856.
Right or Wrong. 1859.
Selection from the Letters of Geraldine Endsor Jewsbury to Jane Welsh Carlyle. Ed.
     Mrs. Alexander Ireland. 1892.

Studies of Geraldine Jewsbury

Cary, Meredith. "Geraldine Jewsbury and the Woman Question." *Research Studies* 42.4
     (1974): 201–14.
Clarke, Norma. *Ambitious Heights: Writing, Friendship, Love—The Jewsbury Sisters,
     Felicia Hemans, and Jane Welsh Carlyle.* London: Routledge, 1990.
Eliot, George. "Geraldine Jewsbury's *Constance Herbert.*" Rpt. in *Selected Critical Writ-
     ings.* Ed. Rosemary Ashton. Oxford: Oxford University Press, 1992. 119–22.
Fryckstedt, Monica Correa. "Geraldine Jewsbury and Douglass Jerrold's *Shilling* Mag-
     azine." *English Studies* 66.4 (1985): 326–37.
———. *Geraldine Jewsbury's* Athenaeum *Reviews: A Mirror of Mid-Victorian Attitudes
     to Fiction.* Stockholm: Uppsala, 1986.
———. "Geraldine Jewsbury's *Athenaeum* Reviews: A Mirror of Mid-Attitudes to Fic-
     tion." *Victorian Periodicals Review* 23.1 (1990): 13–25. Abridgement of her book
     of the same title.
———. "New Sources on Geraldine Jewsbury and the Woman Question." *Research
     Studies* 51.2 (1983): 51–59.
Howe, Susanne. *Geraldine Jewsbury: Her Life and Errors.* London: George Allen &
     Unwin, 1935.
Rosen, Judith. "At Home upon a Stage: Domesticity and Genius in Geraldine Jewsbury's
     The Half-Sisters (1848)." In *The New Nineteenth Century: Feminist Readings of
     Underread Victorian Fiction.* Ed. Barbara Leah Harman and Susan Meyer. New
     York: Garland, 1996. 17–32.
Showalter, Elaine. *A Literature of Their Own: British Women Novelists from Brontë to
     Lessing.* Princeton: Princeton University Press, 1977.
Werner, Mary B., and Kenneth Womack. "Forbidden Love and Victorian Restraint in
     Geraldine Jewsbury's *Zoë.*" *Cahiers Victoriens et Edouardiens* 45 (1997): 15–
     25.
Wilkes, Joanne. Intro. *The Half Sisters: A Tale.* Oxford: Oxford University Press. 1994.
     vii–xxv.
Woolf, Virginia. "Geraldine and Jane." In *Collected Essays.* New York: Harcourt, Brace
     & World: 1967. 4: 27–39.

Maria Jane Jewsbury
(1800-1833)

Melisa Summy

BIOGRAPHY

Maria Jane Jewsbury was born in Measham, England, on 25 October 1800. Her father Thomas was a successful cotton mill owner, and her mother, also named Maria, was described as a "clever, bright, and accomplished woman." Maria Jane was the oldest of seven children; her younger sister Geraldine Jewsbury* became a famous novelist and journalist. Maria Jane's father left Measham in 1818 to seek his fortune in Manchester. Her first verses to appear in print came out in the *Coventry Herald* this same year and were titled "Curiosity and Scandal." Her mother died in Manchester in 1819, shortly after giving birth to a baby boy named Frank. This left a grieving Maria Jane in charge of the household, including the care of her six younger siblings.

Despite painting a very bleak picture in her journal of her life at this time, she did manage to continue writing, even pitching the idea of a volume of biography dedicated to great British female authors. In 1821 Jewsbury began to contribute regularly to the *Manchester Gazette*. Her first book, a compilation of verse and prose called *Phantasmagoria*, was published in two volumes in 1825. She dedicated it to William Wordsworth and wrote him an enthusiastic letter to tell him about the dedication. Jewsbury met Wordsworth a few days after a review of the book appeared and began an immediate and mutually romantic friendship with his daughter Dora that lasted the rest of her life. She began a deep, lifelong friendship with Felicia Hemans* at this time as well. She would later write to Hemans saying that she regretted her early reputation and desire for premature publication. By 1825, Maria Jane Jewsbury had become well known and loved by the reading public and was mentioned frequently in celebrity gossip sections of all of the major periodicals.

Just at the height of her popularity, she became seriously ill for the next year or two and didn't publish anything. Knowing her passion for stuffed birds, Dora

Wordsworth sent a stuffed owl to her friend during her illness to cheer her up. Jewsbury kept the owl on her desk forever afterward to inspire her as she was writing.

Her recovery from illness and much anticipated return to print came in 1827. Advice given to her sister Geraldine was published in 1828 under the title *Letters to the Young*, which became wildly popular. Her volume of domestic verses, *Lays of Leisure Hours*, was published in 1829 and dedicated to Felicia Hemans. Jewsbury also began contributing remarkable amounts of verses, sketches, and stories for annuals such as *Forget-Me-Not, The Anniversary, The Literary Souvenir, The Album, Friendship's Offering*, and various publications for children.

Her last book was published in 1830. It was a response to Madame de Staël's novel *Corinne* titled *The Three Histories: Being a History of an Enthusiast, the History of a Nonchalant, and the History of a Realist. The Three Histories* was so successful it went into three editions. It was this same year she began a rather spirited friendship with the poet Letitia Landon.* They visited often and wrote mischievous and amusing letters to each other. In 1830 Wordsworth dedicated his poem "Liberty" to Jewsbury and addressed the concluding lines directly to her.

From 1830 to 1833 she contributed to *The Athenaeum*. During this time Jewsbury fell in love with a friend of the family, a clergyman named William Fletcher. After a whirlwind courtship she married Fletcher in 1832 over her father's strong objections. Rather unexpectedly, Fletcher became the chaplain of the East India Company. They moved to India a month after their marriage. They had lived in India for a year when Maria Jane Jewsbury Fletcher contracted cholera during an epidemic and died on 4 October 1833. Extracts of Jewsbury's journals of the voyage to India and her experiences while there were published in Espinasse's *Lancashire Worthies*, 2nd Series (1874–1877), and a collection of her Lancashire carols and ballads were published in *The Rural Life*, edited by Mary Howitt.*

MAJOR WORKS AND THEMES

Phantasmagoria (1825) was a combination of verse and prose on a wide variety of topics. She went from parodying different methods of reviewing literature in a section called "First Efforts in Criticism" to poetry with lines "To Love" and lines "To Death." Her next book, *Letters to the Young*, was published in 1828. These letters of advice to her sister Geraldine struck a chord with the reading public, and the book was enormously popular. Her *Lays of Leisure Hours* (1829) was full of domestic verse so mediocre that her friends remained silent about it out of kindness. Jewsbury commented on this work in a letter to her friend Dora: "[P]ray remember that I only write verse to improve my prose." Her last book, *The Three Histories* (1830), used the cost of knowledge to women, including its values and dangers, as its central theme. Despite her reputation as a "feminine poet" and "defender of home and hearth," Jewsbury's poetry often contradicts this image. Poems such as "The Glory of the Heights" and "To My Own Heart" are poems that seem to be about the dangers of her own pride and ambition and feelings of frustration about being "trapped" by her gender.

CRITICAL RECEPTION

Wordsworth was very impressed with *Phantasmagoria* and highly praised it. Meaning well, he forwarded a copy of it to Robert Southey, the Poet Laureate, so he would review it. Jewsbury had parodied Southey's digressive reviewing style in so accurate and biting manner in the piece she called "First Efforts at Criticism" that Southey was embarrassed and offended. He reviewed the book by saying, "[T]he best advice [I] could render to the misguided young person who wrote this was to leave her wholly unnoticed." Later in her career, when Jewsbury was contributing regularly to periodicals, she became well known for her insightful essays and reviews. Her thoughtful and intelligent review of Shelley's poetry in 1831 was highly regarded in literary circles of the time. Her work was often described as displaying "quickness" and "intellectual vigor." Her book *Three Histories* was not only praised for its intellectual merit but was so immensely popular it quickly went through three editions. Today her work is inexplicably neglected for someone who was so popular with readers and so highly regarded in the literary circles of her own time.

BIBLIOGRAPHY

Maria Jane Jewsbury's poetry has been included in several recent anthologies of Romantic and Victorian poetry, such as *Romantic Women Poets: 1770–1838: An Anthology* (Manchester University Press, 1995), edited by Andrew Ashfield. Reprints of some of her essays are available in *Women's Writing of the Romantic Period 1789–1836: An Anthology* (St. Martin's Press, 1999), edited by Harriet Devine Jump, and *Maria Jane Jewsbury: Occasional Papers, Selected with a Memoir* (Oxford University Press, 1932), edited by Eric Gillette. Selected letters can be found in *Ambitious Heights: Writing Friendship, Love—The Jewsbury Sisters, Felicia Hemans, and Jane Welsh Carlyle* (Routledge, 1990), edited by Norma Clarke.

Works by Maria Jane Jewsbury

Phantasmagoria, or Sketches of Life and Literature. 2 vols. 1825.
Letters to the Young. 1828.
Lays of Leisure Hours. 1829.
The Three Histories: Being the History of an Enthusiast, the History of a Nonchalant, and the History of a Realist. 1830.
Maria Jane Jewsbury: Occasional Papers, Selected with a Memoir. Ed. Eric Gillette. 1932.

Studies of Maria Jane Jewsbury

Clarke, Norma. *Ambitious Heights: Writing, Friendship, Love—The Jewsbury Sisters, Felicia Hemans, and Jane Welsh Carlyle.* London: Routledge, 1990.

Fryckstedt, Monica Correa. "The Hidden Rill, The Life of Maria Jane Jewsbury, Parts 1 & 2." *Bulletin of the John Rylands University Library of Manchester* 66.2, 67.1 (Spring–Autumn 1984): 177–203, 450–73.

Howe, Susanne. *Geraldine Jewsbury: Her Life and Errors.* London: G. Allen & Unwin, 1935.

Levin Susan M. "Romantic Prose and Female Romanticism." *Prose Studies* 10.2 (Sept. 1987): 178–95.

Wilkes, Joanne. *Armidale Conference Papers.* Australasian Victorian Studies Association, 1988.

———. " 'Without impropriety' Maria Jane Jewsbury on Jane Austen." *Persuasions: Journal of the Jane Austen Society of North America* 13 (16 Dec. 1991): 33–38.

Ellen Johnston
(ca. 1835–1873)

Florence S. Boos

BIOGRAPHY

Ellen Johnston was one of very few Victorian women factory workers who managed to publish a volume of verse. In a fifteen-page autobiographical preface to the first edition of *Autobiography, Poems and Songs* (Glasgow, 1867) and assorted poetic exchanges in the columns of the Glasgow *Penny Post*, she also gave us a rare glimpse into the views and aspirations of people who assumed they were too poor and ill connected to achieve self-expression in print and one of the more complete accounts we have of any nineteenth-century working-class woman poet's life.

In the *Autobiography* Johnston told her readers that she was born about 1835 in Muir Wynd, Hamilton, Scotland, the only child of James Johnston, a poetically inclined stonemason, and Mary Bilsland, a dyer and dressmaker. When Ellen Johnston was an infant, her father emigrated to the United States, but anxiety apparently overcame her mother at the dockside, and she returned to Glasgow with Ellen. After several years, Mary Johnston assumed that her husband had died in America and remarried. Ellen Johnston's stepfather put her to factory work when she was eleven and engaged in other actions that "haunted me like a vampire, but at least for the present must remain the mystery of my life." She fled from her "tormenter" repeatedly, considered suicide, then gave birth at seventeen to her own daughter, Mary Achenvole, in September 1852. Shortly thereafter, Ellen began to support her extended family of four.

Her formal schooling had ended at eleven, but she read Scott's novels, Wilson's *Tales of the Border*, Burns's poetry, and other works and published her first poem in the *Glasgow Examiner* when she was nineteen. James Johnston in Maine learned what had happened to the family he left behind and "drank a death-draught from a cup in his own hand." In 1861 Mary Johnston died, and

Ellen Johnston left with her daughter for Dundee, where she worked as a factory weaver and continued to submit verses to newspapers in her spare time.

In 1865, *The Penny Post*, a working-class newspaper with a circulation of about 30,000, began to publish her poems on a regular basis, either on the front page or in a "Notices to Correspondents" section inside. In January 1867, the reformist editor Alexander Campbell actively began to solicit subscriptions in the paper's columns for prospective book publication of Johnston's collected poems, and the volume was brought into print in 1867. But the proceeds were not enough to free Johnston from factory work. An 1869 second edition omitted all reference to her illegitimate daughter but added four new poems, including her moving valedictory "The Factory Girl's Last Lay."

In late 1868, Campbell retired from editorship of *The Penny Post*, and his successor scrapped the paper's poetry columns. A solitary *Penny Post* notice solicited contributions in January 1873 for the "very ill" poet, who was now in "very distressed circumstances." Ellen Johnston died in April 1873 in the Glasgow Barony Poorhouse or its infirmary, and nothing is known of Mary Achenvole's fate. Johnston's poetry and brief memoir tell us all we know of her travails and accomplishments, but her impassioned lyrics recorded the complex blend of public introspection, active support, and stubborn independence that enabled her to bring her work into print.

MAJOR WORKS AND THEMES

Before she began her extended interactions with *The Penny Post*, Johnston had published a number of isolated poems and songs, including several in Scots. Some praised, celebrated, described, or denounced specific people or venues in her life—an employer, a workingmen's club, or her workplace. Others grieved the loss of childhood innocence and betrayals of adolescence, commemorated real or prospective romantic attachments, and satirized intolerant or exploitative people and patterns of behavior. In "O Come Awa' Jamie," for example, the speaker asked a foreman or employer to "gie us mair licht" in which to weave her quota of jute. In her best-known work, "The Last Sark, Written in 1859," a weary mother, whose husband again sought work in vain, made the timeless observation, "It is the puir man's hard-won toil that fills the rich man's purse. . . . Were it no for the working men what wad the rich men be?" After she began to write for *The Penny Post*, Johnston developed further the satiric, confessional, and performative manner of her dramatic monologues in extended dialogues, most of them with other poets—women and men—who inquired in its columns about her life. In these exchanges appeared her first direct allusions to her father and stepfather and concrete descriptions of the oppressive character of her everyday work:

> It is within the massive walls of factory dust and din
> That I must woo my humble muse, her favour still to win. . . .

> It is amidst pestiferous oil that I inhale my breath,
> 'Midst pond'rous shafts revolving round the atmosphere of death.
> ("Lines to Edith with G. D. Russell's and the Factory Girl's Cartes,"
>   *Autobiography, Poems and Songs*)

She took public solace in the consolations of art—her true companion ("my heart hath ne'er known gladness save when in fancy's dream"). In other, openly triumphal poems, such as "The Maid of Dundee to Her Slumbering Muse," she exhorted herself and occasionally "boasted" in near-euphoric tones, "Go, tell thy foes that 'twas the wrongs they've done thee, / That caused thy wailings in the Penny Post."

Ellen Johnston clearly achieved the brief flare of her success with the active support of a periodical readership, a helpful editorial patron, and epistolary friends. All those readers and friends expressed in clear material terms their conviction that her work was a heroic, even emblematic accomplishment. She also viewed her "wailings" as aspirations to overcome deprivation and isolation and wrote strong Scots verse and concrete social commentary. But her assertively "self-fashioning" efforts also reflected the very frailty and urgency of working-class poetic identity she decried. Her time was short and her "honours" transitory, but Ellen Johnston's melancholy self-awareness and performative introspection—traits normally found blended in the work of middle- and upper-class "romantic individualists" such as Byron or Emily Brontë*—were strikingly distinctive in the working-class writing of her time.

CRITICAL RECEPTION

Most older studies of British working-class poetry focus primarily on the work of English artisans and Chartists, almost all of whom were men. Susan Zlotnick notes the uniqueness of Johnston's achievement in writing about her life as a mill worker, in contrast to a dominant male working-class tradition represented by dialect poets such as Edwin Waugh, which "effectively denied [women's] existence as workers." Florence Boos examines some aspects of the complex "performative" interrelationship between Johnston's autobiography and her poems and contrasts her factory-floor radicalism with the preindustrial egalitarianism of Janet Hamilton and feminism of Marion Bernstein.

BIBLIOGRAPHY

Catherine Kerrigan included "The Last Sark" in *An Anthology of Scottish Women Poets* (Edinburgh University Press, 1991), and Johnston has been included in recent editions of Victorian women's poetry.

Works by Ellen Johnston

The Penny Post. 1865–1868, passim.
Autobiography, Poems and Songs. 1867.

Studies of Ellen Johnston

Alves, Susan. "A Thousand Times I'd Rather Be a Factory Girl: The Politics of Reading American and British Female Factory Workers' Poetry 1840–1914." Ph.D. diss., Northeastern University, 1996.

Boos, Florence. "Cauld Engle-Cheek: Working-Class Women Poets in Victorian Scotland." *Victorian Poetry* 33.1 (1995): 53–73.

King, Elspeth. *The Hidden History of Glasgow's Women: The Thenew Factor.* Edinburgh: Mainstream, 1993.

Klaus, H. Gustav. *Factory Girl: Ellen Johnston and Working-Class Poetry in Victorian Scotland.* New York: Peter Lang, 1998.

Zlotnick, Susan. " 'A Thousand Times I'd Rather Be a Factory Girl': Dialect, Domesticity, and Working-Class Women's Poetry in Victorian Britain." *Victorian Studies* 35.1 (1991): 7–27.

Fanny (Frances Anne) Kemble (1809–1893)

Barbara Penny Kanner

BIOGRAPHY

Fanny Kemble's life trajectory covered both sides of the Atlantic, taking her from youthful dramatic heroine to antislavery diarist, Shakespearean reader, and mature professional author. Had she not earned early theatrical fame, her books might not have sold. Yet both careers owed their existence to her dazzling personality, which made audiences idolize the "sublime Fanny" as lovelier and larger than life. Having left no permanent record of her stage presence or voice, Kemble's personal memoirs have become her chief contribution to the twentieth century, windows through which we glimpse a living picture of the nineteenth century's events and Kemble's place within them.

Born on 27 November 1809 into England's foremost acting family, Frances Anne was the second of Charles and Marie Thérèse Kemble's five children. From humble beginnings, Charles's father Roger Kemble had risen to establish an acting dynasty whose most noted figure was his sister, Sarah Siddons "the Tragic Muse." Deemed willful enough by her parents to require the discipline of French boarding schools, at age twenty Fanny Kemble was suddenly summoned to the stage to rescue her father's theater, London's Covent Garden, from bankruptcy. The results were astounding: Audiences were so transfixed by her passion as Shakespeare's Juliet that she became an overnight sensation. Taken to America by her father on a triumphant theatrical tour in 1832, the idealistic, egalitarian Kemble was welcomed by New Englander Catharine Sedgewick and Unitarian preacher William Ellery Channing into their antislavery crusade.

Among those whom she fascinated, however, was a man with Southern roots and different values, the wealthy Philadelphian Pierce Mease Butler. After seeing her perform, he devoted himself to courting her, and in June 1834, she married him and bid farewell to the stage. Only afterward did she learn that the Butlers' wealth came from Georgia plantations manned by slave labor, causing ethical fireworks in the marriage. Settling in Philadelphia, Kemble worked to convince Pierce to end slavery on his plantations by establishing wage labor. Frustrated by his evasive responses, she would increasingly escape from Pierce's presence to the home of her antislavery friend Catharine Sedgewick in Lenox, Massachusetts.

Sedgewick enjoyed transatlantic friendships with reform figures including British economist and London *Daily News* columnist Harriet Martineau,* critic Anna Jameson,* and feminist author Frances Power Cobbe,* who, through Sedgewick's mediation, became Kemble's lifelong correspondents. Their influence made Kemble eager to witness how the Butlers treated their slaves, but not until January 1838 did Pierce permit her to accompany him to the Georgia plantations.

During this journey, Kemble recorded in her diary her observations about the slaves' living conditions, which on both Butler Island and St. Simons Island (the Butlers' two Georgia plantations) appalled her. Refusing to keep herself apart from the slaves, she treated their illnesses, sewed them garments, gave them extra food, and grimly defied Georgia law by teaching several of them to read. From 1843 to 1845 Kemble's marriage disintegrated entirely, with countersuits for divorce and social opprobrium for Kemble as a soon-to-be divorcée. She also suffered separation from her daughters, since nineteenth-century divorce law automatically awarded custody to the father. Ultimately, she accepted that her marriage was at an end, her relationship with her daughters was severed, and she must make her own way in the world.

Kemble sailed for England in October 1845, where in 1848 she took over her ailing father's series of one-man Shakespearean readings, earning extraordinary acclaim and replenishing her finances. Meanwhile, word reached her that Pierce had filed another divorce petition citing her "wilful desertion." To fight for her parental rights, Kemble sailed for America, where she contracted for an American tour of readings that earned her $2,000 weekly and empowered her suit for periodic child custody. Pierce's divorce was granted in September 1849.

For the next ten years Kemble made numerous transatlantic crossings to be with her daughters. With the outbreak of the American Civil War, she retreated to England, which in 1862 threatened to enter the war on the side of the South. Kemble had kept her Georgia journal unpublished to avoid angering her husband, but with antislavery friends urging its publication to help keep England neutral, she yielded and handed her manuscript over to Longman Publishers. At the behest of Lincoln's government, American tycoon John Murray Forbes arranged for Harper Brothers to publish Kemble's journal in America, where it boosted late wartime morale. She remained in England until the 1867 news of Pierce's death left her free to return to America for further reading tours.

In spring of 1877, Kemble—who would remain in England for the remainder of her days—established herself in London as a grande dame entertaining a stream of distinguished visitors, among them novelist Henry James whom she had befriended ten years earlier in Rome. To his dying day James praised Kemble's storytelling powers, saying that it was she who, in 1879, told him the love story that became his novel *Washington Square*.

Also in 1878–1879, Kemble's previously serialized memoirs were published as *Records of a Girlhood*, their enthusiastic public reception making her London publisher, George Bentley, eager for more of the same. Kemble continued the account with *Records of Later Life*, published in 1882. As she grew older, Kemble spent long daily hours at her desk, writing commentary on acting and coordinating a third volume of epistolary memoirs made possible by the deaths of further friends—among them Anna Jameson—whose relatives returned the correspondence to her. In her seventies the irrepressible Kemble began writing a novel, *Far Away and Long Ago*, set in the wild, pristine America of her girlhood; it was published in 1889, her eighty-first year. When she died suddenly on 15 January 1893, her friend Henry James contributed her obituary to the London periodical *Temple Bar Magazine*.

MAJOR WORKS AND THEMES

Although Kemble's body of work contains many poems and plays, they are characterized by melodramatic diction and sentiment, and Kemble herself belittled her poems as "trumpery." Her most significant works are her life series of epistolary journals. The first one, her American travelogue *Journal of F. A. Butler* (1835), was influenced by Frances Trollope's* *Domestic Manners of the Americans* (1832) and offers witty barbs about American customs, introducing Kemble's characteristic authorial pattern of reworking her own letters and diary entries into fresh, spontaneous-sounding prose.

Kemble's next work, her plantation journal, was written with an eye to later publication for the abolitionist cause. In it, Kemble shapes her diary entries as a series of letters to a friend. Never sent, these "letters" were never intended as such but employed an imaginary audience to whom Kemble could vent her indignation, tell anecdotes humanizing the individual slaves, and weep unashamedly for the atrocities she witnessed. As a result, her plantation journal evokes a sense of moral urgency that made Kemble's abolitionist friends—who read the private manuscript—avid to have it published. When finally printed in 1863, *Journal of a Residence on a Georgian Plantation, 1838–1839* countered abstract depictions of the economic "benefits" of slavery by grippingly anatomizing the sufferings of slaves in the unimpeachable voice of a slaveowner's wife.

Kemble's youthful memoirs, serialized in the *Atlantic Monthly* as "An Old Woman's Gossip" (1875) and published as *Records of a Girlhood* (1878–1879), re-create her idealistic youth, dreams, and family theatrical heritage gleaned from family records and personal correspondence. Her second memoir, *Records of Later Life* (1882), is thematically arranged to move from her betrayed marital expectations to the 1848 triumph of her first Shakespearean readings. The book's anthology of correspondents conveys forcefully the scope and intimacy of the friendships that Kemble maintained through her letter writing. *Further Records 1848–1883* (1890), her final memoir, looks at Kemble's place in the mid-nineteenth century, particularly the years surrounding the Civil War, interweaving letters to American friends, British reformers, and government figures to foreground the shifting political scenes and social transformations that she witnessed.

CRITICAL RECEPTION

Because the young Fanny Kemble electrified theatrical critics, among them Sir Walter Scott and William Thackeray in England and Henry Wadsworth Longfellow in America, her writings also aroused their interest. However, the virtue of Kemble's serious works lay not in her style but in her ability to use personality as a vehicle for the urgency of her content—almost as if she were acting in the medium of print. Her use of this power to lend force to her moral arguments also created a political divide in the way her works were assessed.

Interspersed between the appearances of her memoirs were volumes of poetry, plays, and travel that were widely read and flatteringly reviewed primarily because both public and critics were interested in their author as a celebrity. By the end of Fanny Kemble's life, her 1890s reviewers saw her much as critics do a century later—as an historical record keeper in her life as well as in her writings, two forms of creative output for Kemble that are impossible to separate.

For twentieth-century feminist critics, however, Kemble poses a conundrum. Her works are largely free of feminist speculations except on the issue of child custody, where the obdurate laws that awarded children to divorced fathers made her a personal victim. Although her plantation journal documents repeatedly the sexual victimizations that female slaves confided to her, Kemble never links these observations to reflections on the power inequities of gender but analyzes what she sees solely in terms of racial wrongs. Even in her marriage, Kemble blamed Pierce's demands to rule her on his individual defects rather than social limitations. Having been blessed with great force of will, Kemble declared belief in the power of every individual's inner potential. It was easy for her to see the powerful nineteenth-century legal barriers that made black people's lives miserable. It was more problematic for her to recognize the insidious coercion of what twentieth-century critics have labeled "patriarchy," even with access to friends such as Frances Power Cobbe who shared feminist insights with her. To Cobbe, Kemble wrote that her own desire for women was less legal than spiritual—she looked ahead to a time when women would have a birthright of inner self-worth (Wright 199).

For this reason, Fanny Kemble's "feminism" in her journals appears indirectly, between the lines and in her remarkable, fully realized life. Like many notable nineteenth-century women, she had a family—particularly a father—whose positive belief in her was crucial in overriding the more limited cultural expectations for women in general. Kemble's written life, interpreted by herself, helps to illustrate for the twentieth-century reader how imperfectly patriarchal hegemony operated and what the possibilities for a nineteenth-century woman actually could be if her own determination favored her.

BIBLIOGRAPHY

A fair number of Kemble's works are available in reprint editions, including *Journal of a Residence on a Georgian Plantation* (University of Georgia, 1984; Beehive, 1992), *Further Records* (Ayer, 1972), *Journal 1835* (Ayer, 1972), *Fanny Kemble: A Journal of a Young Actress* (ed. Monica Grough [Columbia University, 1990]), and *Notes upon Some of Shakespeare's Plays* (AMS Press). Dana Nelson has edited *Principles and Privilege: Two Women's Lives on a Georgia Plantation* (University of Michigan Press, 1995), bringing Kemble's plantation journal and her daughter Fanny Kemble Leigh's *Ten Years on a Georgia Plantation* (1883) together in a single volume.

Selected Works by Fanny Kemble

Frances the First: An Historical Drama. 1832.
Journal of F. A. Butler. 1835.
The Star of Seville, a Drama. In Five Acts. 1835.
Poems. 1844.
Journal of a Residence on a Georgian Plantation in 1838–1839. 1863.
Records of a Girlhood: An Autobiography. 1878–1879.
Notes upon Some of Shakespeare's Plays. 1882.
Records of Later Life. 1882.
Adventures of John Timothy Homespun in Switzerland: A Play from the French. 1889.
Far Away and Long Ago. 1889.
Further Records 1848–1883. 1890.

Studies of Fanny Kemble

Allmendinger, Blake. "Acting and Slavery." *Mississippi Quarterly* 41.4 (Fall 1988): 507–13.
Armstrong, Margaret. *Fanny Kemble: A Passionate Victorian.* New York: Macmillan, 1938.
Booth, Alison. "From Miranda to Prospero: The Works of Fanny Kemble." *Victorian Studies* 38.2 (Winter 1995): 227–54.
Follini, Tamara. "The Friendship of Fanny Kemble and Henry James." *Cambridge Quarterly* 19.3 (1990): 230–42.
James, Henry. *Essays in London and Elsewhere.* New York: Harper & Brothers, 1893.
Kahan, Gerald. "Fanny Kemble Reads Shakespeare: Her First American Tour." *Theatre Survey* 24.1–2 (1983): 77–98.
Lee, Col. Henry. "Fanny Kemble." *The Atlantic Monthly* 71 (1893): 662–75.
Lombard, Mildred. "Contemporary Opinions of Mrs. Kemble's *Journal of a Residence on a Georgian Plantation.*" *Georgian Historical Quarterly* (Dec. 1950).

Marshall, Dorothy. *Fanny Kemble*. New York: St. Martin's Press, 1977.

Melchiori, Barbara. "Fanny Kemble in Rome, with Some Unpublished Letters." *English Miscellany* 20 (1969): 269–89.

Wright, Constance. *Fanny Kemble & the Lovely Land*. New York: Dodd, Mead, 1972.

Mary Henrietta Kingsley (1862–1900)

Shelly Skinner

BIOGRAPHY

In the late 1890s Mary Kingsley was well known as an ichthyologist, explorer, ethnographer, popular writer, scientific lecturer, and authority on West African culture. Kingsley was born in 1862 and spent much of her childhood and early adult life in the home caring for her ill and bedridden mother while her father, George Kingsley, traveled the world on ethnological studies. Denied a formal education, Kingsley nevertheless read her father's books about the history of African exploration and taught herself Latin, chemistry, and physics. When both her parents died in 1892, Kingsley decided to take up anthropological work and to travel to West Africa on a study of "fish and fetish." After her first trip to Sierra Leone in 1893–1894, she returned to England to provide the British Museum with several fish and insect samples. On a second trip, Kingsley arrived in Gabon in May 1895 and journeyed from Libreville along the Ogowé River as far as Talagouga and Ndjolí, exploring inland as far as 140 miles from the coast. After this expedition, she continued her travels in Calabar and Cameroon and was the first European to climb the northeast face of Mt. Cameroon (at 13,500 feet).

Kingsley funded her travels by trading in cloth, tobacco, alcohol, and rubber, and although she often stayed with European missionaries and colonial administrators, she usually hired West Africans to guide her exploration. During her second expedition, she collected a new genus of fish, six new species, a previously unknown snake, and West Africa's rarest lizard, and she also studied West African cultures, laws, and religions. After Kingsley returned to England in November 1895, she published *Travels in West Africa* in 1897 and *West African Studies* in 1899, both of which were immediate best-sellers. She also published *The Story of Africa* for *The Story of the Empire Series* in 1899 and edited and wrote an introduction for a collection of pieces by George Kingsley, which appeared in 1900 as *Notes on Sport and Travel*. While in England, Kingsley gave lectures on West African culture to scientific societies, such as the Royal Geographical Society, and wrote articles for periodicals such as the *Spectator, National Review*, and *Cornhill Magazine*. In March 1900, Kingsley again left England to travel to South Africa and served during the Boer War in a military hospital. She died of enteric fever on 3 June 1900 and was buried at sea with full military honors.

MAJOR WORKS AND THEMES

Travels in West Africa, Kingsley's most popular work, is the humorous account of her second journey to Africa in which she describes her route and records her encounters with missionaries, colonial officials, and the West African Faung. In *Travels in West Africa*, Kingsley is concerned specifically with West African religions and laws, and she explains the structure of West African culture alongside her narratives about the landscape and geography. Her second book, *West African Studies*, is a more political and heterogeneous collection that includes selections from Kingsley's lectures on West African fetish, a historical chapter on European exploration and trade in West Africa, a chapter on West African property, and a proposal for a type of indirect rule.

Because Kingsley believed that colonial administration should use African social structures to organize government and trading, she disapproved of missionary and imperialist practices that attempted to change or to destroy African customs, beliefs, or languages. Although Kingsley endorsed West African practices of polygamy because they allowed for a division of labor and a social structure in which women could pursue trade and other economic activities, she was decidedly against being labeled as a "New Woman"; she publicly opposed women's suffrage and women's inclusion in scientific societies; and she always traveled in ankle-length skirts and the paraphernalia of a Victorian lady. In her writing, moreover, Kingsley occupies an ambivalent position according to conventional Victorian sexual and racial codes. As a white, female traveler who was the epitome of femininity, she nevertheless engaged the masculine and imperialist gaze of the explorer and was often called "Sir" by her West African companions and guides.

CRITICAL RECEPTION

Kingsley's books were exceedingly popular during the late 1890s and early 1900s, but her work had become neglected by the 1930s. Critical attention diminished until several biographical narratives were published in the 1950s and 1960s. Interest in women's history revitalized scholarship on the intersections of gender and imperialism in Victorian literary history, and in the late 1980s and early 1990s Kingsley became a significant figure for feminist work on the sexual economy inscribed in travel and cultural encounter. Some scholars, including Maria Frawley and Dea Birkett, suggest that women travelers in Africa could appropriate masculine subjectivity and power. Other critics, such as Sara Mills and Alison Blunt, consider the ambivalences of gendered identity and imperialist politics in Kingsley's writing. Karen Lawrence analyzes Kingsley's trading activities as they mediate gender in cultural encounter. Although many critics have focused on Kingsley's travel writing, her political writing also will be important to future scholarship that historically and geographically locates women's lives and work.

BIBLIOGRAPHY

Travels in West Africa (ed. Elspeth Huxley [Everyman, 1993]) and *West African Studies* (Barnes & Noble, 1964) have been reprinted recently.

Works by Mary Kingsley

Travels in West Africa: Congo Français, Corsico and Cameroons. 1897.
The Story of West Africa. 1899.
West African Studies. 1899.
Notes on Sport and Travel by George Kingsley: With a Memoir by His Daughter Mary H. Kingsley. 1900.

Studies of Mary Kingsley

Alexander, Caroline. *One Dry Season: In the Footsteps of Mary Kingsley.* New York: Knopf, 1989.
Birkett, Dea. *Mary Kingsley: Imperial Adventuress.* London: Macmillan, 1992.
Blunt, Alison. *Travel, Gender, and Imperialism: Mary Kingsley and West Africa.* New York: Guilford Press, 1994.
Campbell, Olwen. *Mary Kingsley: A Victorian in the Jungle.* London: Methuen, 1957.
Ciolkowski, Laura E. "Travelers' Tales: Empire, Victorian Travel, and the Spectacle of English Womanhood in Mary Kingsley's *Travels in West Africa.*" *Victorian Literature and Culture* 26.2 (1998): 337–66.
Frank, Katherine. *A Voyager Out: The Life of Mary Kingsley.* Boston: Houghton Mifflin, 1986.
Frawley, Maria H. *A Wider Range: Travel Writing by Women in Victorian England.* Rutherford, NJ: Fairleigh Dickinson University Press, 1994.
Glynn, Rosemary. *Mary Kingsley in Africa.* London: Harrap, 1956.
Gwynn, Stephen. *The Life of Mary Kingsley.* London: Macmillan, 1932.
Holmes, I. M. *In Africa's Service: The Story of Mary Kingsley.* London: Saturn Press, 1949.
Howard, Cecil. *Mary Kingsley.* London: Hutchinson, 1957.
Hughes, Jean. *Invincible Miss: The Adventures of Mary Kingsley.* London: Macmillan, 1968.
Kipling, Rudyard. *Mary Kingsley.* Garden City: Doubleday, 1932.

Lawrence, Karen R. *Penelope Voyages: Women and Travel in the British Literary Tradition*. Ithaca: Cornell University Press, 1994.

Mills, Sara. *Discourses of Difference: An Analysis of Women's Travel Writing and Colonialism*. New York: Routledge, 1991.

Myer, Valerie Grosvenor. *A Victorian Lay in Africa: The Story of Mary Kingsley*. Southampton, England: Ashford Press, 1989.

Pearce, R. D. *Mary Kingsley: Light at the Heart of Darkness*. Oxford: Kensal Press, 1990.

Wallace, Kathleen. *This Is Your Home: A Portrait of Mary Kingsley*. London: Heinemann, 1956.

Letitia Elizabeth Landon (L.E.L.) (1802–1838)

Lucy Morrison

BIOGRAPHY

The oldest child of John and Catherine Bishop Landon, Letitia Elizabeth Landon was an enthusiastic reader from an early age and, as a teenager, wrote verses to entertain her family. Landon's neighbor, William Jerdan, then editor of the *Literary Gazette*, published her first piece, "Rome," in 1820. With financial assistance from friends, in 1821 Landon published her first volume of poetry, which sold well but brought its author no financial reward. Landon subsequently wrote for the *Gazette* from 1821 to 1824, affixing her initials to her pieces, and thus "L.E.L." entered the public sphere. She published under these initials for the rest of her life, using them both to shield her identity and to promote a curiosity that assisted the sales of her works.

In 1824, a collection of these "Poetical Sketches" entitled *The Improvisatrice, and Other Poems* brought her fame and success, and L.E.L. became a conspicuous established figure in London's literary circles. Financial security was always a driving force in L.E.L.'s life and writings—after her father's death in 1824, L.E.L. supported her brother through college and maintained her own and her mother's households. Without male protection, from the middle of the 1820s until the end of her life, the critics plagued L.E.L. about her unsuitable behavior, including rumors of affairs with various men. Supported by loyal friends such as the S. C. Halls and Edward Bulwer-Lytton, L.E.L. turned toward the more profitable venture of novels in the 1830s, and *Romance and Reality* was well received, while critics noted her growing strength as a prose writer in subsequent works. During the latter half of the 1820s and all of the 1830s, L.E.L. contributed extensively to the *New Monthly Magazine* and to many of the leading annuals of the period. She wrote both poetry and critical pieces and served as editor for Fisher's *Drawing-Room Scrap-Book*.

Following a broken engagement to Dickens's biographer John Forster in

1834, L.E.L. struggled against the criticism that was heaped upon her personally as well as professionally. In 1836, she met George MacLean, who was quickly regarded as her fiancé even while the couple seemed highly incompatible to L.E.L.'s friends. Nevertheless, L.E.L. married MacLean in June 1838 and immediately sailed to his governor's post at Cape Coast in Africa. On 15 October 1838, L.E.L. was found dead with a bottle of prussic acid in her hand, and it is unclear whether her death was an accident, suicide, or murder.

MAJOR WORKS AND THEMES

L.E.L.'s volumes of poetry in the 1820s maintained a similar pattern of one longer poem followed by shorter pieces, and her most successful volume was *The Improvisatrice*, which went through six editions in its first year of publication. L.E.L.'s focus rests consistently on the woman deserted or betrayed by an unfaithful lover, and she effusively and fluently explores the psychological results of such pain. L.E.L. adheres to the conventional expectation of woman speaking from the heart but locates power in her creations of woman as poet, singer, or prophet, with a sentimental wealth of emotional experience beyond the confines of domesticity. L.E.L. is a key figure in the transition from Romanticism to Victorian literature, responding astutely to the sinking popularity of poetry by turning her pen to novels and successfully reviving her reputation with *Romance and Reality* in 1831. Her subsequent novels, especially *Ethel Churchill*, demonstrate her increasing powers as a prose writer capable of sympathetic social commentary.

CRITICAL RECEPTION

L.E.L.'s vivid imagination ensured that her earliest works were applauded for their sentimentality and spontaneity. Critics noted her evident poetic ability even while they deplored the monotonous effusiveness of much of her work, and essentially, L.E.L.'s personal situation compelled the negative critical reception of her later volumes of poetry. Her favorably received novels reignited interest in her works in the 1830s, and her mysterious premature death promoted curiosity in the melancholy work that became, retrospectively, prophetic. Both Elizabeth Barrett Browning* and Christina Rossetti* acknowledge their debt to L.E.L. in poems addressed to her. But by the close of the nineteenth century, L.E.L.'s work had sunk into obscurity. While L.E.L.'s fascinating life received scant attention, L.E.L. has only emerged as a poet worthy of consideration in the last decade. Much of her work is still dismissed as sentimentally lighthearted, but astute critics like Glennis Stephenson have acknowledged L.E.L.'s leading position in literature of the period.

BIBLIOGRAPHY

L.E.L.'s poetry appears in most recent Romantic and Victorian anthologies; *Letitia Elizabeth Landon: Selected Writings* (ed. Jerome McGann and Daniel Riess), was published in 1997 by Broadview's Literary Texts Series. None of her novels are in print. Romantic Circles has published an electronic edition: *L.E.L.'s "Verses" and the Keepsake for 1829*, edited by Terence Hoagwood, Kathryn Ledbetterand, and Martin M. Jacobsen, available at: http://www.rc.umd.edu/.

Selected Works by Letitia Elizabeth Landon

The Fate of Adelaide; A Swiss Romantic Tale, and Other Poems. 1821.
The Improvisatrice, and Other Poems. 1824.
The Troubadour; Catalogue of Pictures, and Historical Sketches. 1825.
The Golden Violet, with Its Tales of Romance and Chivalry; and Other Poems. 1826.
The Venetian Bracelet, The Lost Pleiad, A History of the Lyre, and Other Poems. 1829.
Romance and Reality. 1831.
The Easter Gift: A Religious Offering. 1832.
Fisher's Drawing-Room Scrap-Book. 1832–1838.
Heath's Book of Beauty. 1833.
Francesca Carrara. 1834.
The Vow of the Peacock, and Other Poems. 1835.
"On the Character of Mrs. Hemans's Writings." *New Monthly Magazine* 44.176 (Aug. 1835): 425–33.
Traits and Trials of Early Life. 1836.
"The Criticism of Chateaubriand." *New Monthly Magazine* 48.189 (Sept. 1836): 62–68.
Ethel Churchill; or, The Two Brides. 1837.
Flowers of Loveliness: Twelve Groups of Female Figures Emblematic of Flowers. 1838.
The Zenana and Minor Poems of Letitia Elizabeth Landon. 1839.
The Poetical Works of Letitia Elizabeth Landon. 1844.
Poetical Works of Letitia Elizabeth Landon "L.E.L." 1873 facsimile ed. Ed. F. J. Sypher. 1990.
Letitia Landon: Selected Writings. Ed. Jerome McGann and Daniel Riess. 1997.

Studies of Letitia Elizabeth Landon

Ashton, Helen. *Letty Landon.* London: Collins, 1951.
Blanchard, L. *Life and Literary Remains of L.E.L.* 2 vols. London: Colburn, 1841.
Curran, Stuart. "Romantic Poetry: The 'I' Altered." In *Romanticism and Feminism*. Ed. Anne K. Mellor. Bloomington: Indiana University Press, 1988. 185–207.
Enfield, D. E. *L.E.L.: Mystery of the Thirties.* London: Hogarth Press, 1928.
Greer, Germaine. "The Tulsa Center for the Study of Women's Literature: What We Are Doing and Why We Are Doing It." *Tulsa Studies in Women's Literature* 1.1 (1982): 5–26.
Prins, Yopie. *Victorian Sappho.* Princeton: Princeton University Press, 1999.

Stephenson, Glennis. "Letitia Landon and the Victorian Improvisatrice: The Construction of L.E.L." *Victorian Poetry* 30.1 (1992): 1–17.

———. *Letitia Landon: The Woman Behind L.E.L.* Manchester: Manchester University Press, 1995.

Stevenson, Lionel. "Miss Landon: 'The Milk-and-Watery Moon of Our Darkness,' 1824–30." *Modern Language Quarterly* 8.3 (1947): 355–63.

"Vernon Lee" (Violet Paget) (1856–1935)

Dennis Denisoff

BIOGRAPHY

Born near Boulogne, France, Violet Paget spent much of her youth traveling in Europe and most of her life in Italy. She was educated by her mother, half brother, and governesses, but her interest in aesthetics and philosophy, which increased as she grew older, demanded a large degree of self-education as well. When she began publishing in *Frazer's Magazine* (1878–1879), she decided to adopt the pseudonym "Vernon Lee" because she believed that an assumedly male author would garner greater attention and respect. The disguise was probably unnecessary, since "everybody" soon knew who she was.

Lee's interest in aesthetics brought her into contact with Walter Pater, as well as other prominent members of the Aesthetic Movement, including Edward Burne-Jones, William Morris, Dante Gabriel Rossetti, and Oscar Wilde. Nevertheless, Lee spent most of her adult life in close, private relationships with other women, the first being her friendship with Annie Meyers in the 1870s. From 1881 to 1887, her main companion was A. Mary F. Robinson* (whose father's guests included Robert Browning, Thomas Hardy, Henry James, and George Moore), followed by what Lee called her "new love and new life" with Clementina (Kit) Anstruther-Thomson for the next ten years. Described by Lee as a "Venus de Milo," Anstruther-Thomson was a major inspiration and influence on the author's work. Lee continued to write fiction and essays throughout her life, although her reputation peaked at the end of the nineteenth century.

MAJOR WORKS AND THEMES

Lee published some forty-five works, writing in English, French, German, and Italian. Both her fiction and theoretical writings reflect her unique aestheticist views and her efforts to infuse her ideal of beauty with both a sense of social responsibility and a respect for the different ways in which people self-identify. Lee felt an especially keen discomfort with the heteronormative conventions of her time, a concern that positioned her within the current of "New Woman" writers. Many of Lee's stories and novels problematize gender issues by questioning the notion of essential identity traits and pointing to the interrelation of diverse systems of social oppression. For example, in the lengthy novel *Miss Brown* (1884), the struggle of the eponymous heroine against the objectifying misogyny of her male admirers reverberates in the character's efforts to get the aesthete community to recognize the abject poverty of many members of society. Similarly, in the story collection *Hauntings* (1890) and elsewhere, Lee uses the visual portrait as a nexus for analyzing various oppressive cultural assumptions, including heterosexuality.

One of Lee's most innovative contributions to literature regards the genre of the "genius loci" or "spirit of places." Her seven works in this genre, published from 1897 to 1925, consist of impressionistic description of various regions that she encountered during her travels. The intention was to use the text to transfer to readers the aesthetic empathy arising from one's experience of a beautiful landscape. "Empathy" was a central concept in Lee's writings on aesthetics as well.

CRITICAL RECEPTION

Lee's first major success as a writer was a series of literary portraits of musicians and singers, entitled *Studies of the Eighteenth Century in Italy* (1880). Comparable praise followed for *Belcaro* (1881), a collection of essays on art, and *Euphorion* (1884), another collection on the Renaissance. *Miss Brown*, however, was met with a negative reception because of its scathing and often clichéd attack on the dominant strain of aestheticism and the men who took part in it. Lee dedicated the novel to Henry James, who admired the author's intelligence and energy but responded to *Miss Brown* by calling the text "a deplorable mistake." Notably, almost all the critics focused on Lee's parody of the main version of aestheticism, while none addressed her more complex representation of relations between women. In later works, Lee's social analyses continued to receive lukewarm critical response. *Miss Brown* faded under the still cresting wave of the Aesthetic Movement and has only begun to resurface recently, along with her other fiction.

Many eminent Modernists admired Lee's work. Bernard Shaw praised her pacifist novel *Satan the Waster* (1920). Roger Fry wrote to tell her how much he admired her writing on aesthetics, and Virginia and Leonard Woolf's Hogarth Press published Lee's *The Poet's Eye* (1926). Despite the lack of Lee scholarship during much of the past hundred years, a recent increase in conference papers as well as a number of scholarly studies expected out in the next five years suggest that the respect for Lee's work from the likes of Shaw, Fry, and Woolf may be matched at the end of the century.

BIBLIOGRAPHY

Selections from Vernon Lee's prose have appeared in several recent anthologies: *Critical Essays on Charlotte Perkins Gilman* (ed. Joanne B. Karpinski [G. K. Hall, 1992]); *Daughters of Decadence* (ed. Elaine Showalter [Virago, 1993]); and *Prose by Victorian Women* (ed. Andrea Broomfield and Sally Mitchell [Garland, 1996]). *Miss Brown* was reprinted by Garland in 1978 but is no longer in print.

Selected Works by Vernon Lee

Studies of the Eighteenth Century in Italy. 1880
Belcaro. 1881.
Euphorion. 1884.
Miss Brown. 1884.
"Lady Tal." 1896.
Hauntings: Fantastic Stories. 1890.
Genius Loci: Notes on Places. 1899.
"The Economic Dependence of Women." 1903.
Hortus Vitae: Essays on the Gardening of Life. 1904.
Beauty and Ugliness and Other Studies in Psychological Aesthetics. 1912.
The Beautiful: An Introduction to Psychological Aesthetics. 1913.
Satan the Waster: A Philosophical War Trilogy. 1920.
The Handling of Words: And Other Studies in Literary Psychology. 1923.
The Poet's Eye. 1926.
A Vernon Lee Anthology: Selections from the Earlier Works. Ed. Irene Cooper Willis. 1929.

Studies of Vernon Lee

Cary, Richard. "Vernon Lee's Vignettes of Literary Acquaintances." *Colby Library Quarterly* 9 (Sept. 1970): 179–99.

Gardner, Burdett. *Lesbian Imagination (Victorian Style): A Psychological and Critical Study of "Vernon Lee."* New York: Garland, 1987.

Gunn, Peter. *Vernon Lee/Violet Paget, 1856–1935*. London: Oxford University Press, 1964.

Hotchkiss, Jane. "(P)revising Freud: Vernon Lee's Castration Phantasy." In *Seeing Double: Revisioning Edwardian and Modernist Literature*. Ed. Carola Kaplan and Anne B. Simpson. New York: St. Martin's Press, 1996.

Mannochi, Phyllis A. "Vernon Lee and Kit Anstruther-Thomson: A Study of Love and Collaboration Between Romantic Friends." *Women's Studies* 12.2 (1986): 129–48.

Ormand, Richard. "John Singer Sargent and Vernon Lee." *Colby Library Quarterly* 9 (Sept. 1970): 154–78.

Robbins, Ruth. "Vernon Lee: Decadent Woman?" In *Fin de Siècle/Fin du Globe: Fears and Fantasies of the Late Nineteenth Century*. Ed. John Stokes. New York: St. Martin's Press, 1992. 139–61.

Amy Levy
(1861–1889)

Audrey Horton Shifflett

BIOGRAPHY

The second daughter of Isabelle Levin and Lewis Levy, Amy Levy was born in Clapham, South London, on 10 November 1861. In 1876 the family moved to Brighton, where Levy began school. She was the first Jew to attend Newnham College, Cambridge, where she studied from 1879 until 1881. In addition to her thorough knowledge of English literature, she was fluent in French and German and read Latin and Greek.

The details of Levy's brief life are scant beyond her publication history. She revealed both her ambition to write and her feminist awareness early in life, publishing a poem, "Ida Grey," at age fourteen in a suffrage magazine, *The Pelican*. She began publishing stories in popular magazines while at Cambridge. Her first volume of poetry, *Xantippe and Other Verse*, was published in Cambridge in 1881. In this collection, she demonstrated an exceptional ability to infuse the spirit of a growing feminism with classic poetic forms and images. Her second volume of poetry, *A Minor Poet and Other Verse*, appeared in 1884, combining new poems with a few of the stronger works from her earlier volume. In 1888, she published *The Romance of a Shop*, her first novel. Her second novel, *Reuben Sachs: A Sketch*, followed at the end of that year. Set in an Anglo-Jewish community resembling Levy's own, *Reuben Sachs* caused an uproar for a depiction of materialism and ambition that some felt betrayed her own people. Her third novel, *Miss Meredith*, a lighthearted story of a governess, was serialized in the *British Weekly* from April to June 1889, then published. Over the years Levy published a variety of short stories for magazines such as *London Society, Temple Bar*, and the *Gentleman's Magazine*.

Apparently, other than occasional visits to the coast and trips to Europe, Levy lived in London. Her friends included writers Vernon Lee (Violet Paget)* and

Clementina Black.* She was a member of the socially progressive Men and Women's Club along with Olive Schreiner,* Beatrice Webb,* and Eleanor Marx, the daughter of Karl Marx who translated *Reuben Sachs* into German. Using charcoal fumes, Levy committed suicide by asphyxiation on 10 September 1889 at her parent's home at Seven Ensleigh Gardens, London. About a week prior to her death, she corrected the proof of her final volume of poetry, *A London Plane-Tree and Other Verse*; it was published posthumously.

MAJOR WORKS AND THEMES

Levy's works reveal a vast knowledge of both classical and contemporary literatures and her confident ability to experiment, imitate other writers, and use colloquial language in traditional poetic forms. In the stories "Sokratics in the Strand" and "Cohen of Trinity," for instance, she appropriates a male voice to debate questions of philosophy and existence. Such stories stand in contrast to the light romances she wrote for the popular press. "Xantippe" is outstanding among her poems. This dramatic monologue of over 275 lines gives voice to the embittered wife of Socrates. Here Levy projects a feminist image that she continued to examine in her writing—that of an intelligent woman limited within a society that fails her. Developing in an age of loquacious prose, Levy's poetic style moved from an elegiac lyricism toward a spartan forerunner of the modern. What Oscar Wilde called a "power of condensation" in her writing is especially noticeable in *A London Plane-Tree and Other Verse*. Here Levy takes London as her landscape and infuses it with her deepening resignation to despair. Between the opening image of the green tree among the city's brown and the closing image of "on me a cloud descends," the poems range from rhapsodies on aspects of city life to heart-wrenching threnodies. Her indeterminate love lyrics have fueled critical speculation about her life, of which much too little is known. A growing pessimism is revealed in her works, especially the poems and stories featuring death imagery and suicide. Levy's works are more than fatal self-fulfilling prophesies, however; they evince a compelling, often brutal, honesty and reveal an intense self-awareness and critical sensitivity.

Levy's novels critically examine the rapidly changing late-nineteenth-century society. *The Romance of a Shop* is a New Woman novel revealing both the excitement and difficulties four sisters face as they establish a photography studio to support themselves after their father's death. In *Reuben Sachs*, Levy attempted a more realistic portrayal of assimilated Anglo-Jews than George Eliot* had depicted in *Daniel Deronda*. An ill-fated love story, the novel's focus shifts from the male title character, who dies, to the lover he rejected. In a style reminiscent of Jane Austen,* Levy exposed materialism, hypocrisy, and shifting social circumstances in a direct and at times terse manner that sent shock waves through the Anglo-Jewish community in London.

CRITICAL RECEPTION

From the beginning, Levy was noticed in the press as a young writer of great promise. Although she had not surpassed "minor" status by the time of her death, she had weathered the cultural storm surrounding *Reuben Sachs* and become a rather well-known member of the London literary scene. Her greatest fame, however, came with her suicide. Other writers eulogized her, as did Oscar Wilde in *Woman's World*, calling her a "girl of genius." Her death inspired poets Eugene Lee-Hamilton and Thomas Bailey Aldrich. Posthumous reviews of her last novel and volume of poems mention the untimely death of the artist, so young and of such promise.

Levy remains a tragic figure of the instability of the 1880s. Her writings demonstrate the frustrations of a young woman writer at the dawn of the modern age, when despite progress they had made, women were still inhibited socially and economically. By the end of the century, Levy was forgotten except by a few. In 1926 before the Jewish Historical Society of England, Beth Zion Lask lamented that knowledge of the country's best Jewish writer had been suppressed through a "wilful neglect." But thankfully, after almost a century of obscurity, Amy Levy now receives increasing critical attention. Melvyn New's collection, published in 1993, makes her works available to a new audience.

BIBLIOGRAPHY

Much of Levy's work is reprinted by New. She has been published in recent anthologies of Victorian women poets and on the Victorian Women Writers Project.

Works by Amy Levy

Xantippe and Other Poems. 1881.
A Minor Poet and Other Verse. 1884.
Reuben Sachs: A Sketch. 1888.
The Romance of a Shop. 1888.
A London Plane-Tree and Other Verse. 1889.
Miss Meredith. 1889.
The Complete Novels and Selected Writings of Amy Levy, 1861–1889. Ed. Melvyn New. 1993.

Studies of Amy Levy

Beckman, Linda Hunt. "Leaving 'The Tribal Duckpond': Amy Levy, Jewish Self-Hatred, and Jewish Identity." *Victorian Literature and Culture* 27.1 (1999): 185–201.
Hunt, Linda. "Amy Levy and 'The Jewish Novel': Representing Jewish Life in the Victorian Period." *Studies in the Novel* 26.3 (1994): 235–53.
Nord, Deborah Epstein. *Walking the Victorian Streets: Women, Representation, and the City.* Ithaca: Cornell University Press, 1995.

Rochelson, Meri-Jane. "Jews, Gender, and Genre in Late-Victorian England: Amy Levy's *Reuben Sachs*." *Women's Studies* 25.4 (1996): 311–28.

Scheinberg, Cynthia. "Canonizing the Jew: Amy Levy's Challenge to Victorian Poetic Identity." *Victorian Studies* 39.2 (1996): 173–200.

Wagenknecht, Edward. *Daughters of the Covenant: Portraits of Six Jewish Women.* Amherst: University of Massachusetts Press, 1993.

Zatlin, Linda Gertner. *The Anglo-Jewish Novel in the Nineteenth Century.* Boston: Twayne, 1981.

Eliza Lynn Linton
(1822-1898)

Laurel Meredith Erickson

BIOGRAPHY

Eliza Lynn Linton's life was a contradiction. A masculine, independent woman herself, Linton built a career upon vituperative attacks of Victorian feminism as the propagator of masculine, independent, "unwomanly" women whose very existence destroyed the harmony of natural order. The daughter of a conservative clergyman, Eliza was the twelfth and final baby born into the Lynn household (her mother died a few months later). Linton described her early life at Gad's Hill (the home she herself eventually would sell to Charles Dickens) as particularly unhappy. Not as femininely charming as the idolized sister born directly before her, Linton would later account for her difference by explaining that the family had been due a boy when she was born, "and it was only the top-coating that had miscarried" (Layard 21). One sister described Eliza as more like as bear than a girl. Neglected by her father and abused by many of her siblings, Eliza Lynn retreated to the library, where she became a voracious reader. A result of her self-education was that she increasingly was unable to stomach her father's conservative views. Eliza Lynn became an early rebel. When she was twenty-three she openly defied her father's wishes and moved to London to pursue her career as a writer.

By the end of her first year in London, Eliza Lynn had written her first novel, *Azeth, the Egyptian*, and two years later she published her second, *Amymone: A Romance in the Days of Pericles*. Both are historical novels heavily influenced by her assiduous reading in the British Library. *Amymone* also is an early women's rights novel that reflected the author's association with the avant-garde of 1840s London, a world where she had refashioned herself as a Freethinker and Socialist. In 1849 Eliza Lynn was hired by the *Morning Chronicle* and gained the honor of becoming the first woman newspaper writer to draw a fixed salary, earning roughly £250 a year (Layard 60). In 1851 she quarreled with her boss, was packed off to Paris as a foreign correspondent, and soon after that was fired. That same year she threatened legal action against John Chapman, who was to publish her third novel, *Realities*. A departure from her earlier historical novels, *Realities* describes the seduction of a young actress by her stage manager. Chapman refused to accept the novel on account of the sensual nature of Eliza Lynn's writing, and the author was forced to publish it at her own expense.

In 1853 Eliza Lynn was hired as a contributor to Dickens's *Household Words*. Although Linton remained a prolific writer of fiction throughout her life, it was her polemical writing in the popular press that firmly established her career. When she began writing for the *Saturday Review* in the 1860s, her writing took a decidedly antifeminist turn. There is no easy explanation for her reversal concerning the Woman Question. She had by this time made a disastrous marriage to the engraver William James Linton. They married in 1858, but by 1867 William had moved to America without her. Linton herself explained her antifeminist position as a reaction to the tragedy of her independent life (although her genuineness is questionable). She asserted that her own life was an example of the "gigantic mistake" of feminism, a movement that "makes women hard and men hysterical, which gives to each sex the vices of the other while destroying its own hitherto distinctive virtues" (qtd. in Layard 140). Her critics suggested that her antifeminist writing paid better than feminist writing. Regardless, Linton became one of the most vocal and animated nineteenth-century opponents of women's rights, coining such popular catchphrases as the "Girl of the Period," the "Shrieking Sisterhood," and the "Wild Women" in her pungent descriptions of feminism's vices.

Linton's fiction also took a decidedly antifeminist turn, although the black-and-white position on gender Linton assumed in her essays became increasingly muddled. The masculine antiheroine in *The One Too Many* (1894), for example, does not fare that badly (marriage to a policeman) compared to the sweet heroine (death by drowning). Perhaps most surprising from an author who advocated strict gender division along the lines of biological difference is Linton's *The Autobiography of Christopher Kirkland*. A fictionalized account of her own life, Linton decided to rewrite herself as the male "Christopher" (a switch that also involved changing her husband into a wife, "Esther," who eventually moves to America to fight for women's rights). Although some overlooked it, most critics found the sex reversal odd and troublesome. Linton wrote another fictional autobiography, *The Second Youth of Theodora Desanges* (this time from a female point of view), and a memoir, *My Literary Life*. Both were published posthumously.

MAJOR WORKS AND THEMES

The depravity of masculine, educated women who clamor for equal rights remains a persistent theme throughout Linton's work and was the subject of three collections of essays. The issue pops up in almost all of Linton's novels but most notably in *The Rebel of the Family*, which addresses the dangers of female same-sex desire within the women's movement, *The One Too Many*, which caricatures the vicissitudes of the Girton girl, and *In Haste and Leisure*, which attacks the frivolous activity within feminist women's societies.

Linton's career appears to be defined by her antifeminist writing, but her novels address a variety of issues pertinent to her day, including religious doubt, science, socialism, and free thought. She also harbored an interest in spiritualism and occultism. Linton writes about her own spiritual rebellion in *Christopher Kirkland*, tracing her evolution through asceticism, atheism, agnosticism, and finally "altruism." The most successful of all her novels was *The True History of Joshua Davidson, Christian and Communist*, which attacks religious orthodoxy by recasting the trials of Jesus's life within the hypocrisies of modern religion.

CRITICAL RECEPTION

Although Linton's tendency toward polemics and caricature might make her fiction easy to ridicule by twentieth-century standards, in the nineteenth century she was a respected writer. Her novels addressed the serious issues of her time—from the Woman Question and social problems to politics and religion. Linton considered George Eliot* her personal rival, although she grudgingly admitted Eliot's superiority as a writer. Her writing leans toward the sensational; murder and madness are frequently the catalysts for plot. Editors expressed concern over the sensuality of Linton's writing and a certain discomfort with the often drawn-out descriptions of her female characters' limbs and complexions. As is to be expected of any polemical writer, reviews of Linton's novels tended to be mixed. Over the course of her career, the artistic merit of Linton's novels often was conflated with their political content.

SELECTED BIBLIOGRAPHY

None of Linton's books currently are in print, but several essays have been reprinted in recent anthologies of prose by Victorian women.

Works by Eliza Lynn Linton

Azeth, the Egyptian. [1846.]
Amymone: A Romance in the Days of Pericles. 1848.
Realities: A Tale. 1851.
Witch Stories. 1861.
Grasp Your Nettle. 1865.
Lizzie Lorton of Greyrigg. 1866.
Sowing the Wind. 1867.

Ourselves: Essays on Women. 1869.
The True History of Joshua Davidson, Christian and Communist. 1872.
The Mad Willoughbys and Other Tales. 1875.
Patricia Kemball. 1875.
The Atonement of Leam Dundas. 1876.
The World Well Lost. 1877.
Under Which Lord? 1879.
The Rebel of the Family. 1880.
With a Silken Thread, and Other Stories. 1880.
"My Love!" 1881.
The Girl of the Period, and Other Essays from the Saturday Review. 1883.
Ione. 1883.
The Autobiography of Christopher Kirkland. 1885.
Paston Carew, Millionaire and Miser. 1886.
The One Too Many. 1894.
In Haste and Leisure. 1895.
Dulcie Everton. 1896.
'Twixt Cup and Lip. Etc. 1896.
My Literary Life. 1899.
The Second Youth of Theodora Desanges. 1990.

Studies of Eliza Lynn Linton

Anderson, Nancy Fix. *Woman Against Women in Victorian England: A Life of Eliza Lynn Linton.* Bloomington: Indiana University Press, 1987.
Layard, George Somes. *Mrs. Lynn Linton: Her Life, Letters & Opinions.* London: Methuen, 1901.
Van Thal, Herbert, *Eliza Lynn Linton: The Girl of the Period.* London: George Allen & Unwin, 1979.

"Lucas Malet" (Mary St. Leger Kingsley Harrison) (1852–1931)

Patricia Lorimer Lundberg

BIOGRAPHY

"Lucas Malet" was a daughter of Charles Kingsley, Anglican Canon and novelist, and cousin to Mary Henrietta Kingsley,* intrepid traveler. A lonely child educated at home, she married William Harrison, her father's curate, in 1876. Although she studied art with Edward Poynter at the Slade School, both father and husband discouraged any career. Forbidden to read novels until age twenty, she wrote them to release pent-up frustrations as a clergyman's wife. She crafted a pseudonym from her father's mother's aunt Malet and her grandmother Mary Lucas Kingsley. After three novels of renunciation, she explored asceticism in two essays. Her best work followed 1887, when she began *The History of Sir Richard Calmady* (1901). This date marks the birth of Lucas Malet as an acclaimed writer of realistic fiction. Reading Darwin, Whitman, Fielding, Sterne, Scott, and Plato at the time, she counted George Eliot,* Flaubert, DeMaupassant, Zola, Balzac, and Dostoevski among her influences (Dolman 149). Her first major success—and scandal—was *The Wages of Sin* (1891), which fractured her marriage to the Rector of Clovelly but assured entry into London literary circles.

Malet once told an interviewer, "Nature jumbled things up altogether in the construction of her whole family and distributed male and female characteristics at random" (Dickens 522). Her novels hint at lesbian tendencies, but correspondence suggests she had a male lover. Childless, she adopted her cousin Gabrielle Vallings and encouraged dual careers as operatic soprano and novelist while discouraging marriage. They moved to Switzerland in 1923 but eventually fled in poverty, dependent on Civil List and Royal Literary Fund grants and the largess of novelist Robert Hitchens. After Malet died of cancer at Tenby, Wales, Vallings was forced to auction the Kingsley literary estate.

MAJOR WORKS AND THEMES

Malet dared to explore subjects that shocked husband and audiences alike but won her critical acclaim, social fame, and sporadic fortune. Her best work includes searching analyses of the consequences of seduction in *Wages of Sin* and portrayal of the bitterness of disability—and a powerfully drawn seductress—in *Sir Richard Calmady*. *Mrs. Lorimer* (1882), *Colonel Enderby's Wife* (1885), and *A Counsel of Perfection* (1888) feature gender-bending explorations of self-sacrifice, written while she struggled futilely to fashion herself as a model of renunciation, a country parson's wife. *Little Peter* (1888) looks compassionately at the deformed and intrudes her anguished self-portrait as one of the "little writers of little books . . . diligently trying to persuade themselves and others that they are great writers of great books, and discoverers of a universal panacea for the healing of nations" (85). *The Gateless Barrier* (1900) creates a gothic love story between the ghost of a Romantic maiden and her reincarnated lover, a tale of suppressed sexuality and female empowerment in the realm of the supernatural (Lorimer Lundberg, "Dialogic Fiction"). *The Far Horizon* (1906) and *Adrian Savage* (1911) also earned critical acclaim. Elegantly written and deeply psychological, the novels problematize language, genre, gender, and class to disrupt social and cultural icons.

CRITICAL RECEPTION

Lucas Malet enjoyed a major literary reputation, her books were published in multiple editions in London and New York and widely reviewed. *Wages of Sin* became book of the year. *Sir Richard Calmady* drew critical applause—and vilification for an "unpleasant" theme "running counter . . . to the healthy instincts of the higher types of humanity" (J. Courtney, "Lucas Malet's Novels," 540). Malet's reputation also suffered from contemporary devaluing of women writers' work and her bold marital separation and conversion to Catholicism. Poverty and health breakdowns eventually forced her to compromise her high standards. Once compared favorably with friends George Meredith and Henry James, she was forgotten. Yet James and Hardy both wrote novels that appropriated Malet in theme and plot; *Jude the Obscure* especially echoes her *The Wages of Sin* (Schaffer). Recent scholars have rediscovered the remarkable fiction of Lucas Malet.

BIBLIOGRAPHY

No novel is in print, but the Indiana University Victorian Women Writers Project has published *The History of Sir Richard Calmady* electronically: http://www.indiana.edu/~letrs/vwwp/.

Selected Works by Lucas Malet

Mrs. Lorimer: A Sketch in Black and White. 1882.
Colonel Enderby's Wife: A Novel. 1885.
"Youngest of the Saints [General Gordon]." *Fortnightly Review* 44 (1885): 395–412.
"The Other Side of the Moon [H. F. Amiel]." *Fortnightly Review* 45 (1886): 615–32.
A Counsel of Perfection. 1888.
Little Peter: A Christmas Morality, for Children of Any Age. 1888.
"The Progress of Women in Literature." *Universal Review* 2 (1888): 295–301.
The Wages of Sin. 1891.
The Carissima: A Modern Grotesque. 1896.
The Gateless Barrier. 1900.
The History of Sir Richard Calmady: A Romance. 1901.
"The Feminine Note in Fiction." *Bookman* 27.159 (1904): 116–18.
"The Threatened Resubjection of Women." *Fortnightly Review* 83 (1905): 806–19.
The Far Horizon. 1906.
The Score. 1909.
The Wreck of the Golden Galleon. 1910.
Adrian Savage. 1911.
The Tutor's Story. An Unpublished Novel by the Late Charles Kingsley Revised and Completed by His Daughter Lucas Malet (Mrs. Mary St. Leger Harrison). 1916.
Deadham Hard: A Romance. 1919.
The Tall Villa. 1920.
Da Silva's Widow and Other Stories. 1922.
"A Conversion." *World Fiction* (1922): 64–76.
The Survivors. 1923.
The Dogs of Want: A Modern Comedy of Errors. 1924.
The Private Life of Mr. Justice Syme (completed by Gabrielle Vallings). 1932.

Studies of Lucas Malet

Archer, William. "Lucas Malet." In *Real Conversations*. London: Heinemann, 1904. 216–34.
[Courtney, Janet]. "Lucas Malet's Novels." *Fortnightly Review* 71 (1902): 532–40.
———. "Novelists of the Nineties. . . ." *Fortnightly Review* 137 (1932): 230–41.
Courtney, William. "Lucas Malet." In *Feminine Note in Fiction*. London: Chapman, 1904. 87–114.
Dickens, Mary Angela. "A Talk with 'Lucas Malet.' " *Windsor Magazine* (Oct. 1899): 522–24.
Dolman, Frederick. " 'Lucas Malet' at Home. . . ." *The Young Woman* 4.41 (1896): 145–49.
Lorimer Lundberg, Patricia. "Dialogic Fiction of the Supernatural: 'Lucas Malet.' " *English Literature in Transition 1880–1920* 41.4 (Sept. 1998): 389–407.
———. "Lucas Malet." In *British Women Writers: A Critical Reference Guide*. Ed. Janet Todd. New York: Continuum, 1989. 435–36.
Schaffer, Talia. "Malet the Obscure. Thomas Hardy, 'Lucas Malet,' and the Literary Politics of Early Modernism." *Women's Writing* 3.3 (1996): 261–85.

————. "Some Chapter of Some Other Story: Henry James, Lucas Malet, and the Real Past of *The Sense of the Past." Henry James Review* 17 (1996): 109–28.

Srebrnik, Patricia. " 'Lucas Malet.' " In *Late Victorian and Edwardian British Novelists, First Series*. Ed. George M. Johnson. *Dictionary of Literary Biography*. Detroit: Gale Research, 1995. 153: 177–85.

————. "The Re-Subjection of 'Lucas Malet': Charles Kingsley's Daughter and the Response to Muscular Christianity." In *Muscular Christianity: Embodying the Victorian Age*. Ed. Donald E. Hall. Cambridge: University of Cambridge Press, 1994. 194–214.

Harriet Martineau
(1802–1876)

Pamela Corpron Parker

BIOGRAPHY

As a professional writer, outspoken intellectual, popular educator, and reformer, Harriet Martineau was a major figure in Victorian Britain. She supported herself with her writing for over forty-five years, publishing well over a hundred separately printed titles, numerous periodical articles, and almost 2,000 newspaper articles. Furthermore, her numerous essays addressing what was then called the "Woman Question" and her social activism for causes such as improved education for women, divorce reform, universal suffrage, and repealing the Contagious Diseases Acts establish her as an important forerunner to contemporary feminism.

Martineau was born on 12 June 1802 in industrial Norwich to Elizabeth (Rankin) and Thomas Martineau, Unitarian textile manufacturers and wine merchants. Her *Autobiography* (written in 1855; published posthumously in 1877) describes her unhappy upbringing as the sixth of eight children, particularly her resentment toward her overbearing mother. By her own account, Martineau turned adversity to advantage. As a solitary, sensitive child, she found solace in religion and a rigorous course of studies. With her older siblings as her teachers, she studied French, Latin, composition, and arithmetic at home; at eleven years of age, she received two additional years of formal education at a local Unitarian school and later continued her studies with professional tutors at home. By sixteen, her growing deafness increased her isolation and depression, prompting her parents to send her to live with an aunt in Bristol. There she was influenced by the Unitarian minister Lant Carpenter, who encouraged her intellectual growth and prompted her interest in the utilitarian and necessarian philosophies of Locke, Hartley, and Priestly.

Martineau credits her deafness for helping her escape from the usual female occupations of governess or teacher and enabling her to consider writing as an occupation. Her younger brother James, her closest and most supportive sibling, encouraged her to submit her first article ("Female Writers on Practical Divinity") to *The Monthly Repository*, a Unitarian periodical, in 1822. In her *Autobiography*, Martineau recounts the "evening [that] made me an authoress" with pleasure. After reading her essay, her brother James said, "Now, dear, leave it to other women to make shirts and darn stockings; and you devote yourself to this" (1: 97). She took his advice and wrote early in the morning and late in the evening when her household duties were complete. A series of personal and financial setbacks thrust Martineau into writing as a full-time occupation: Her oldest brother Thomas died, the family's business failed, and her father's depression and poor health eventually led to his death. In addition, her engagement to John Hugh Worthington dissolved as a result of his increasing mental illness and subsequent suicide. In the years following, Martineau's writing provided a focus for her energies, and her family's sudden poverty provided her with a socially acceptable reason to throw herself into her work. As she explains in her *Autobiography*: "I began to feel the blessing of a wholly new freedom. I, who had been obliged to write before breakfast, or in some private way, had henceforth liberty to do my own work in my own way; for we had lost our gentility (1: 114). All of these events forced Martineau from the conventional script of many Victorian women's lives: marriage, maternity, and emotional and economic dependence. From this point on, Martineau became a regular contributor to *The Monthly Repository* on topics such as theology, philosophy, and female education. A prolific if sometimes uncritical writer, she gained immediate financial and literary success in 1832 with the publication of *Illustrations of Political Economy*, a series of twenty-five didactic narratives explaining the principles of classical economics. The phenomenal popularity of the tales enabled her to move to London, the center of literary and political activity.

Society in America (1837) went beyond a simple travel narrative to analyze American culture's deviance from its democratic principles. Martineau's first novel, *Deerbrook* (1839), a domestic novel set in provincial England, met with only moderate success, even though Martineau considered it her best work. Martineau, seriously ill, took up lodgings at Tynemouth and remained confined to her couch for the next five years. Her illness did not interrupt her writing considerably; she published *The Hour and the Man* (1841), a fictional biography of Toussaint L'Ouverture, a series of children's stories entitled *The Playfellow* (1841), and the popular *Life in the Sick-Room* (1844), her ruminations on the life of an invalid.

After a controversial "cure" through mesmerism (see her *Letters on Mesmerism* [1845]), she moved to the Lake District in 1845, where she designed her own home (now a museum), ran a small farm, and revelled in her domestic independence and proficiency. There she became friends with Dorothy and William Wordsworth, Matthew Arnold, Charlotte Brontë,* and George Eliot,* and she reviewed many of their works for the *London Daily News*. Martineau also wrote several social histories of England during this period, particularly *The*

History of England During the Thirty Years' Peace, 1816–1846 (1849–1850), which incorporated social and economic analysis into its narrative. She translated and abridged Comte's *Positive Philosophy* (1853), the groundwork for Martineau's commitment to positivism and a clear departure from her earlier religious orthodoxy. In 1855 doctors diagnosed her with heart disease, and she wrote her autobiography with all the urgency of one convinced she was terminally ill. To her own surprise and satisfaction, she lived twenty more years in fairly robust health and continued her prodigious literary output.

Martineau's astounding popularity gave her access to most of the important people of the Victorian era and gave her greater opportunity to espouse her ideas of radical reform, particularly public education, laissez-faire economics, and female equality. Throughout her career, she maintained her commitment to correcting injustice and viewed her writing as primarily pedagogical in orientation. Likewise, she maintained her confidence in the human capacity for reason, enlightened education, and informed social change. Her independent nature might be exemplified best by her repeated refusal of Civil List pensions and by her desire to be buried without religious rites.

MAJOR WORKS AND THEMES

The wide range of genres Martineau pursued during her forty-five-year literary career defy her neat categorization as an author and testify to her intellectual breadth and prolific output. A novelist, autobiographer, historian, economist, sociologist, philosopher, translator, popular educator, and career journalist, Martineau published numerous books and contributed to a variety of prominent nineteenth-century periodicals. As one of the leading writers for the *London Daily News* from 1852 to 1866, she wrote obituaries of many of the famous personalities of nineteenth-century England, later compiled and published as *Biographical Sketches* (1869). Though most of her books are now out of print, her place as an important Victorian intellectual and social commentator has been increasingly noted in numerous anthologies of British literature and critical studies of the nineteenth century, particularly those focusing on prose and women writers. The *Autobiography, Illustrations of Political Economy, Society in America*, and *Deerbrook* have received most recent critical attention.

Although the last twenty years of Martineau's life are not included in her *Autobiography*, it provides fascinating insights into her life and works, as well as the complex culture from which she emerged. Of particular interest are her account of the coronation of Queen Victoria,* her observations of Victorian London, and her many references to famous literary personalities. In her *Autobiography*, the major concerns of her life and career are consistently revealed: disdain for abusive authority, confidence in the benefits of education and self-reliance, and a desire for greater justice for all. Her capacity for honest self-reflection is somewhat compromised by her construction of herself as a model of feminine self-sufficiency, yet the *Autobiography* is remarkable for its unapologetic explanation of Martineau's life as a professional writer. She is more defensive about her movement away from religious orthodoxy and suppresses painful private details, such as her troubled engagement with John Hugh Worthington and her later estrangement from her brother James.

Despite Martineau's initial difficulty finding a publisher for *Illustrations of Political Economy*, it was an immediate success, selling 10,000 copies in twenty-five monthly installments from 1832 to 1834. Martineau's economic tales were hotly anticipated by readers such as Queen Victoria, Samuel Taylor Coleridge, and Sir Robert Peel, and politicians supplied her with bluebooks and suggestions for new tales that supported future legislation. Martineau used narrative exposition, representative characters, and exemplary dialogue to explain the economic theories of Adam Smith, David Ricardo, and T. R. Malthus. Her narrative innovations provided models for later industrial fiction such as Elizabeth Gaskell's* *North and South* and Charles Dickens's *Hard Times*. Throughout *Illustrations* and her other economic tales, such as *Poor Laws and Paupers* (1841–1843), Martineau struggles to reconcile her confidence in individual autonomy with a more deterministic view of human existence.

Society in America (1837) and *A Retrospect of Western Travel* (1838) are innovators in travel writing and sociological study. They provide Martineau's impressions of her 1834–1836 trip to America as well as her condemnation of slavery and gender inequality. In a controversial chapter of *Society in America* entitled the "Political Nonexistence of Women," she argues for women's greater access to the political process:

Governments in the United States have power to tax women who hold property; to divorce them from their husbands; to fine, imprison, and execute them for certain offenses. Whence do these governments derive their powers? They are not "just," as they are not derived from the consent of the women thus governed. (*Society in America* 1: 148)

Martineau forcefully criticizes the hypocrisy of a democratic government that gives women and slaves no legal representation and few educational and vocational opportunities.

Deerbrook, published in 1839 in three volumes, examines the lives of two middle-class sisters who move to a provincial town. Their story follows the Austenian model of the romantic plot complicated by good-natured busybodies and malcontent relations. Of particular interest is the portrayal of Maria Young, a physically disabled governess, whose singleness and bodily afflictions echo Martineau's own life and provide her with an opportunity to comment on the vocational and emotional difficulties of single working women.

From her earliest writings, Martineau concerned herself with the subordination of women. "Female Writers on Practical Divinity" and "On Female Education" (1822 and 1823), both published in *The Monthly Repository*, promote women's qualifications as writers on divine and moral subjects and reveal her belief in superior female morality. While she argued that male and female differences were largely a result of educational differences, she maintained the sanctity of women's domestic duties and positions as "relative creatures." In *How to Observe Manners and Morals* (1838), she argued that "the degree of degradation of women is as good a test as the moralist can adapt for ascertaining the state of domestic morals in any country" (151). Throughout her life, Martineau embraced Enlightenment views of women as rational beings and believed women could gain equality through education and self-improvement. For Martineau, work was the salvation of the poor and the idle, particularly women.

CRITICAL RECEPTION

Harriet Martineau acknowledged her place as a popularizer rather than originator of great ideas. As a regular obituary writer for the *Daily News*, and convinced she would die an early death, Martineau wrote an obituary for herself. She modestly assessed her contributions: "With small imaginative and suggestive powers, and therefore nothing approaching to genius, she could see clearly what she did see, and give clear expression to what she had to say. In short, she could popularize, while she could neither discover nor invent" (29 June 1876). Yet Martineau experimented with new narrative methods and ideas, articulated clearly the positions of radical reform, and exemplified a life of purposeful productivity. She was a thoroughgoing professional by any era's standards, and the breadth of her contributions makes her an important figure in Western intellectual history.

Martineau's outspoken opinions on everything from "the Woman Question" to the abolition of slavery, economics to philosophy, and mesmerism to colonial rule in India earned her many epithets both positive and negative from her contemporaries. The 1833 *Quarterly Review* labeled Martineau an "unfeminine . . . female Malthusian" (49: 97). Thomas Carlyle described her as "one of the strangest phenomena" (*The Correspondence of Thomas, Carlyle and Ralph Waldo Emerson, 1834–1872*, 2 vols. [Osgood, 1883], 1: 126), and John Stuart Mill called her a "mere tyro" and accused her of reducing the system of laissez-faire economics to "an absurdity" (*Collected Works*, ed. Francis E. Mineka [University of Toronto, 1963], 14: 53). Fellow invalid Elizabeth Barrett Browning* gave her qualified praise as "the most logical intellect of the age, for a woman" (*Letters of the Brownings to George Barrett*, ed. Paul Landis, [University of Illinois, 1958]). In his 14 March 1846 assessment in the *People's Journal*, William Howitt praised her "beautiful spirit" and intellectual breadth: "Everywhere she seems at home, and everywhere she teaches us some invaluable lesson of life." George Eliot called Martineau a "trump—the only English women that possesses thoroughly the art of writing" (*Letters*, ed. Gordon Haight, 9 vols. [Yale], 2: 4).

Critical interest in Harriet Martineau and her writings has surged in recent years as a result of feminist revisionary efforts and the greater critical acceptance of "nonliterary" works as the legitimate foci of scholarly inquiry. More specifically, a growing emphasis on the emerging discourses of economics, philosophy, and sociology is exemplified by recent historical retrospects in these fields in which Martineau is frequently credited with the title of "first woman" economist, philosopher, or sociologist. Furthermore, Martineau is of particular interest to those studying the genre of women's autobiography (see Peterson), travel writing, and the emerging field of disability studies. Valerie Sanders (1990) and Elisabeth Arbuckle (1983) have both published collections of Martineau's letters; Valerie Kossew Pichanick (1980), Susan Hoecker-Drysdale (1992), and Shelagh Hunter (1995) provide the best and most recent critical biographies.

In earlier assessments of her work, such as R. K. Webb's 1960 biography, Martineau is notable mostly for defying the conventional expectations of her sex as a professional writer and social critic. Pichanick's well-regarded biography is more balanced: "She seized upon the vital issues of the day, and with that dispatch and fluency which made her a considerable journalist, she informed her public" (243). Hunter's assessment is more laudatory: "The interest of the phenomenon she became lies less in the quality of her prolific writings than in their combination of the personal and the representative" (195). In his introduction to Martineau in *Prose by Victorian Women*, Herbert Northcote particularly praises *Society in America*, calling it one of "the most important sociological documents of nineteenth-century American culture and history. Although sorely neglected today, it equaled Alexis de Toqueville's *Democracy in America* (1835; 1840) in popularity and influence" (35). In *Intellectual Women and Victorian Patriarchy*, Deirdre David argues that Martineau's career "is defined by her auxiliary usefulness to a male-dominated culture" (31), but she goes on to praise her as a "splendid Victorian, certainly as intelligent as any of her male contemporaries, and, I daresay, twice as energetic and tough minded" (93).

Gayle Graham Yates's collection of Martineau's writing on women is of particular interest to feminist scholars. She calls her "a giant among early feminists" (18) and argues that her "faith in individual women's accomplishments was a central point of Martineau's feminism from the beginning" (20). Martineau faithfully recorded the contributions of other prominent Victorian women, including Charlotte Brontë, Margaret Fuller, and Florence Nightingale,* and gave women prominent roles in her fiction. Martineau's writings demonstrate well her support for the education of women, her agitation for better pay and working conditions for women, and her interest in the conditions of their domestic lives. She not only influenced a generation of women writers, both minor and major; she contributed to the growing body of work that focused on middle- and working-class subjects.

In addition to her collection of Martineau's letters, Sanders has written the only book-length study of Martineau's fiction. In *Reason over Passion*, Sanders makes a convincing case for Martineau's place as an innovator in the social problem novel genre, foreshadowing later works by Charlotte Brontë, Gaskell, Eliot, Trollope, Dickens, and Thackeray. Likewise, Catherine Gallagher includes an astute though brief analysis of Martineau's contributions to what she calls industrial fiction, arguing that Martineau's interpretation of political economy makes her fiction more mechanistic. Critics often question whether Martineau's didacticism compromised her art, but few fail to acknowledge that her writing contributed to the emergence of the middle and working class as legitimate literary subjects. As Pichanick argues, *Deerbrook*'s "chief importance was in breaking with the silver-spoon tradition and in giving the middle-class hero a place in English literature" (120).

Martineau herself saw her role as primarily pedagogical and moral. She believed fictional narrative provided the best agent for communicating morals and philosophy (Sanders 10). In a letter to her brother James, Martineau denied having any "uncommon talents" or "an atom of genius." She admitted only that "various circumstances have led me to think more accurately than some women, [and] I believe I may write on subjects of universal concern as to inform some minds and stir up others" (*Autobiography* 1: 141–43).

BIBLIOGRAPHY

While the majority of Martineau's works are out of print, several have been reprinted recently, including the *Autobiography* (Virago, 1983), *Deerbrook* (Virago, 1983), *How to Observe Manners and Morals* (Transaction, 1989), *Martyr Age of the United States* (Ayer, 1978), *A Retrospect of Western Travel* (Greenwood, 1970; Reprint Services, 1991), and *Society in America* (Transaction, 1981).

Selected Works by Harriet Martineau

Illustrations of Political Economy. 9 vols. 1832–1834.
Society in America. 3 vols. 1837.
How to Observe Manners and Morals. 1838.
A Retrospect of Western Travel. 2 vols. 1838.
Deerbrook. 3 vols. 1839.
Martyr Age of the United States. 1839.
The Hour and the Man. 3 vols. 1841.
The Playfellow. 1841.
Poor Laws and Paupers. 4 vols. 1841–1843.
Life in the Sick-Room: Essays by an Invalid. 1844.
Letters on Mesmerism. 1845.
The History of England During the Thirty Years' Peace, 1816–1846. 2 vols. 1849–1850.
The Positive Philosophy of Auguste Comte. Translated by Harriet Martineau. 3 vols. 1853.
Biographical Sketches. 1869.
Autobiography with Memorials by Maria Weston Chapman. 3 vols. 1877.
Harriet Martineau's Letters to Fanny Wedgwood. Ed. Elisabeth Arbuckle. 1983.
Harriet Martineau: Selected Letters. Ed. Valerie Sanders. 1990.

Studies of Harriet Martineau

David, Deirdre. *Intellectual Women and Victorian Patriarchy: Harriet Martineau, Elizabeth Barrett Browning, George Eliot.* Ithaca: Cornell University Press, 1987.

Frawley, Maria. "Harriet Martineau in America: Gender and the Discourse of Sociology." *Victorian Newsletter* 81 (1992): 13–20.

Freedgood, Elaine. "Banishing Panic: Harriet Martineau and the Popularization of Political Economy." *Victorian Studies* 39.1 (Autumn 1995): 33–53.

Gallagher, Catherine. *The Industrial Reformation of English Fiction, 1832–1867.* Chicago: University of Chicago Press, 1980.

Hobart, Ann. "Harriet Martineau's Political Economy of Everyday Life." *Victorian Studies* 37.2 (Winter 1994): 223–52.

Hoecker-Drysdale, Susan. *Harriet Martineau: First Woman Sociologist.* New York: Berg, 1992.

Hunter, Shelagh. *Harriet Martineau: The Poetics of Moralism.* Brookfield, VT: Scolar Press, 1995.

Peterson, Linda H. "Harriet Martineau: Masculine Discourse, Female Sage." In *Victorian Sages and Cultural Discourse.* Ed. Thais Morgan. New Brunswick: Rutgers University Press, 1990. 171–86.

Pichanick, Valerie Kossew. *Harriet Martineau: The Woman and Her Work.* Ann Arbor: University of Michigan Press, 1980.

Sanders, Valerie. *Reason over Passion: Harriet Martineau and the Victorian Novel.* New York: St. Martin's Press, 1986.

Thomas, Gillian. *Harriet Martineau.* Boston: Twayne, 1985.

Webb, R. K. *Harriet Martineau: A Radical Victorian.* New York: Columbia University Press, 1960.

Yates, Gayle Graham. *Harriet Martineau on Women.* New Brunswick: Rutgers University Press, 1985.

Alice Meynell
(1847–1922)

Janna Knittel

BIOGRAPHY

Poet, journalist, Socialist, feminist, Catholic convert, and mother, Alice Thompson (later Meynell) was born to artistic and wealthy parents in Barnes, west of London. She was raised in Italy and returned to England with the family when she was eighteen. Seemingly suffering from depression, the young Alice Thompson took a rest cure. During this retreat, she followed her mother in converting to the Roman Catholic Church.

She married journalist Wilfred Meynell in 1876, a year after her first volume of poetry was published. Together they edited several periodicals. Meynell also was a regular contributor to the *National Observer*, the *Pall Mall Gazette*, and American publications. Immersed in journalistic writing, she apparently wrote no poems in ensuing years.

Her journalistic endeavors were financially necessary. Wilfred Meynell did not have the means to which the young Alice Thompson was accustomed. The Meynells raised seven children and also cared for the poet Francis Thompson during his recovery from drug addiction.

These demands exacerbated Meynell's ill health. But in 1900, she and her husband took their first vacation together in twenty-three years. This trip to Italy initiated a long-awaited period of travel and adventure, including a six-month-long lecture tour of the United States.

She died in London at age seventy-five after several weeks of illness but not before creating a "List of Poems to be published in book form (if occasion occurs posthumously)" (qtd. in Viola Meynell 345).

MAJOR WORKS AND THEMES

Although her early poetry incorporates the conventions of contemporary women's poetry, Meynell later avoided such melancholy and sentimentalism in favor of a political and intellectual stance. Motherhood is a frequent theme. In contrast to the idealized Victorian mother, Meynell was busy with work, distant, and often distracted. This distance drives her to speak differently about the mother-child relationship than readers typically expect. As Angela Leighton claims, "Meynell writes with a new restraint and sceptical distance about a subject which has conventionally lain outside the sphere of serious literature" (259). This can be seen especially in poems like "The Modern Mother" and "The Girl on the Land," in which "the giver of life is [also] the giver of difference, separation, danger" (Leighton 263).

As president of the Society of Women Journalists beginning in 1897, Meynell joined the forefront of the women's movement. Her suffragist work later led her to write poems in protest of World War I. "Parentage," contradicting Augustus Caesar's declaration that unmarried citizens are "slayers of the people," proclaims that, "she who slays is she who bears, who bears." Though the poem also asserts, "Those who slay / Are fathers," Meynell stresses that women—who bear the children and bear the pain of their loss—are complicit in wartime killing.

Many of Meynell's essays have been collected into volumes. These include personal essays, art criticism, and literary criticism. She also edited the works of other women poets, including Elizabeth Barrett Browning* and Christina Rossetti.*

CRITICAL RECEPTION

Much of the contemporary criticism of Meynell's poetry reasserts that she is a woman writer. A 1914 review claims, apparently with some astonishment, "In her essays you realize that a woman may have ideas as well as feelings, reasons as well as intuitions" (qtd. in Tuell 137). Such naïveté notwithstanding, Meynell consistently received positive criticism. Her first volume of poems, *Preludes* (1875), garnered praise from John Ruskin, William Michael Rossetti, Lord Tennyson, and George Eliot.* In 1895, Meynell was nominated for Poet Laureate. All seven volumes of poetry published between 1893 and 1903 received positive reviews. In sum, "By the time of her death in 1922, . . . Meynell was still considered one of the foremost women poets of the day" (Leighton 255).

In the latter half of the twentieth century, Meynell's reputation dwindled. Until recently, her work has seldom been included in either anthologies or curricula. The poems traditionally anthologized, such as "The Shepherdess," are not considered the best by feminist critics and have encouraged judgments of her work based only on a small selection of poems.

Since the advent of the Modernist movement, Meynell has been labeled a stereotypical Victorian poetess. Readers in an age of free verse have considered her passionless for adhering to precise prosody. Though such reserve may be daunting to modern readers used to radical poetic statements, Meynell's intellectualism redefines the Victorian poetess in significant ways. The stereotype depicts women who write primarily about internal struggles, playing out and sentimentalizing the few acceptable roles available to them. By writing about politics and casting a critical eye on the institution of motherhood, Meynell carved out a new niche for women's poetry.

BIBLIOGRAPHY

The following works by Meynell have been reprinted recently: *Ceres' Runaway and Other Essays* (Ayer, 1977); *Rhythm of Life and Other Essays.* (Ayer, 1986); *Second Person Singular and Other Essays* (Ayer, 1977); *Prose and Poetry* (Ayer, 1977); *The Colour of Life: and Other Essays on Things Seen and Heard* (Ayer, 1977); and *Essays* (Greenwood, 1970). Meynell's poetry is also included in modern anthologies of poetry by women.

Works by Alice Meynell

Poetry

Preludes. 1875.
Poems. 1893.
Collected Poems of Alice Meynell. 1893.
Other Poems. 1896.
Later Poems. 1901.
The Shepherdess and Other Verses. 1902.
A Father of Women and Other Poems. 1917.
Poems. 1921.
The Last Poems of Alice Meynell. 1923.
The Poems of Alice Meynell: A Centenary Edition. 1947.
Prose and Poetry. 1947.
The Poems of Alice Meynell. 1990.

Prose

The Colour of Life: and Other Essays on Things Seen and Heard. 1896.
The Rhythm of Life and Other Essays. 1896.
London Impressions. 1898.
The Spirit of Place and Other Essays. 1899.
Ceres' Runaway and Other Essays. 1909.
Mary, the Mother of Jesus: An Essay. 1912.
Childhood. 1913.
Essays by Alice Meynell. 1914.
Essays. 1916.
Hearts of Controversy. 1917.
The Second Person Singular, and Other Essays. 1921.

Studies of Alice Meynell

Badeni, June. *The Slender Tree: A Life of Alice Meynell.* Padstow, Cornwall: Tabb House, 1981.

Leighton, Angela. *Victorian Women Poets: Writing Against the Heart*. London: Harvester Wheatsheaf, 1992.

Meynell, Viola. *Alice Meynell: A Memoir*. London, Jonathan Cape, 1929.

Tuell, Anne Kimball. *Mrs. Meynell and Her Literary Generation*. New York: Dutton, 1925.

Harriet Taylor Mill
(1807-1858)

Jo Ellen Jacobs

BIOGRAPHY

Mention Harriet Taylor Mill (HTM) and listeners inevitably respond, "Oh, she's the one John Stuart Mill (JSM) had the intimate friendship with and eventually married, right?" This reaction is not what either HTM or JSM would have wanted, nor what HTM deserves. She wrote over 300 pages of published and unpublished writing, including her famous "Enfranchisement of Women" (1851). A passionate writer committed to fundamental women's issues such as the deplorable state of women's education, the unfairness of marriage and divorce laws, and the ubiquity of domestic violence, HTM's voice reflected her anger and determination to make a practical difference in the world. Whether encouraging her daughter to read Mary Wollstonecraft when she was fourteen or trying to influence a domestic violence trial while it was in progress, HTM committed her life to changing the world into a more equitable and more just one. She criticized women like George Sand who discarded the opportunity to participate in the political arena and praised French laborers and Cornish miners for experimenting in socialism. HTM was much more than an overpraised, silent partner to JSM.

HTM began life in 1807 as the eldest daughter of a Unitarian man midwife. Growing up with a testy father and a bitter mother, Harriet escaped into marriage to John Taylor when she was eighteen. She wrote a piece for the Society for the Diffusion of Useful Knowledge and published poems, reviews, and articles for *The Monthly Repository* in the early 1830s. During this period of writing and simultaneously her third pregnancy in five years, Harriet Taylor met JSM. She soon arranged her life so that she would remain legally wed but could spend much of her life with JSM.

During the twenty years of their unmarried relationship, HTM continued to write both her own essays and coauthored newspaper articles, essays, and books with JSM. After nursing John Taylor twenty-four hours a day for six weeks, he died in 1849. HTM and JSM married in 1851. Despite evidence to the contrary, historians of philosophy have generally refused to acknowledge any important or positive contribution of HTM to those works published in JSM's name. Yet careful examination of all of the newly published writings of HTM reveal that during the brief years before Harriet Taylor Mill's death in 1858, JSM and HTM wrote *On Liberty* and the *Autobiography*, neither of which was published until after her death. HTM's daughter, Helen Taylor,* a woman who would become a feminist activist and writer, continued a form of intellectual partnership with JSM after HTM's death.

MAJOR WORKS AND THEMES

HTM's writing can be grouped under two headings, those concerned directly with women and those not inherently related to women's issues. One theme woven throughout the first category is a refusal to privilege public over private. For example, HTM argued that the restrictions on public education for women were damaging, but so were the constraints of Victorian social life, including access to sexual knowledge, that result in a lack of self-knowledge as well as entrance into a marriage contract without the knowledge needed to consent properly.

Like other Victorian writers, HTM compared the status of women to slavery. She pealed away the layers of the analogy suggesting that both slavery and marriage were based on the threat of physical force, so that until domestic violence laws were improved, raw physical brutality operated in marriage, just as it did in slavery. Language and law reinforced the cultural assumption obvious in the phrase spoken incredulously by men about interference with "*their* wives or children." (Frances Power Cobbe* would, years later, use almost precisely the same language with even the same word italicized.) Lack of economic freedom and fear of physical force were the sources of both slavery and the plight of Victorian women.

The most obvious connections to HTM's work are to the Radical Utilitarians and Radical Unitarians in whose traditions HTM was nurtured. However, the parallels to the Owenite views of women, property, sexuality, and religion are also instructive. HTM's promotion of a companionate view of marriage, coupled with her argument for liberal divorce laws and, in an ideal world, a complete lack of governmental oversight of marriage, added to the discussion of marriage during this period. She was openly critical of both Sarah Stickney Ellis's* and Anna Jameson's* views of women's role in marriage.

In addition to her discussion of women's issues, HTM wrote about ethics, religion, arts, socialism, and the role government should have in citizen's lives. The damage of conformity, the value of eccentricity, and the need to limit both governmental and societal interference in an individual's actions and speech were recorded in HTM's essays twenty years before these topics appear in *On*

Liberty. Her poetry was mediocre, but her passion for the arts was a lifelong joy, and her reviews were astute. HTM's arguments for experiments in socialism have been criticized by many Mill scholars. She was clearly much less committed to the benefits of capitalism in the everyday lives of the working classes than was JSM. Her atheism, although only expressed privately or behind the cover of anonymous essays, was still sufficient to be the cause of consternation among many of her critics in the history of philosophy.

CRITICAL RECEPTION

To date there has been no biography or book-length study of HTM's life or ideas. Critiques of her have typically been buried in works on JSM. Until the 1950s HTM was vilified either as an intellectual vamp whose bad ideas influenced whatever claims of JSM's the critic rejected or as an emotional solace but intellectual lightweight. None of these evaluations were based on a study of any of HTM's actual writing. F. A. Hayek published *John Stuart Mill and Harriet Taylor: The Friendship and Subsequent Marriage*, the first publication of some of HTM's letters and a couple of her unpublished essays in 1951. Yet, between 1950 and 1970, the critics of HTM continued to fall into the same patterns identified before 1950.

In 1970, Alice Rossi recognized some of the causes of the disdain for HTM in her introduction to *Essays on Sex Equality*. Eugene August's biography of JSM published the same year began to explore the possibility of a true collaboration between HTM and JSM, but by the middle of the 1970s, the familiar vitriolic reception of HTM was back in vogue. In the 1990s HTM's ideas have begun to receive more detailed study.

BIBLIOGRAPHY

The Complete Works of Harriet Taylor Mill, edited by Jo Ellen Jacobs (Indiana University Press, 1998), includes all of HTM's published and unpublished essays, as well as all of her extant letters.

Works by Harriet Taylor Mill

Book reviews, poems, and "The Seasons." *The Monthly Repository*. 1831–1832.
"Life of William Caxton." In *Lives of Eminent Persons*. 1833. 1–32.
Newspaper articles. *Morning Chronicle, Daily News*, and *Sunday Times*. 1846–51.
"On the Probable Futurity of the Labouring Classes." In *Principles of Political Economy*. 1848.
"Enfranchisement of Women." *Westminster Review* (July 1851): 289–311.
"Remarks on Mr. Fitzroy's Bill for the More Effectual Prevention of Assaults on Women and Children." 1853.
Essays on Sex Equality. With John Stuart Mill. Ed. Alice S. Rossi. 1970.
The Complete Works of Harriet Taylor Mill. Ed. Jo Ellen Jacobs. 1998.

Studies of Harriet Taylor Mill

Allen, Virginia. " 'On Liberty' and Logic: The Collaboration of Harriet Taylor and John Stuart Mill." In *Listening to Their Voices: The Rhetorical Activities of Historical Women*. Ed. Molly Meijer Wertheimer. Columbia: University of South Carolina Press, 1997. 42–68.

August, Eugene. *John Stuart Mill: A Mind at Large*. New York: Charles Scribner's Sons, 1975.

Hackleman, Leah. "Suppressed Speech: The Language of Emotion in Harriet Taylor's The Enfranchisement of Women." *Women's Studies: An Interdisciplinary Journal* 20.3–4 (1992): 273–86.

Hayek, F. A. *John Stuart Mill and Harriet Taylor: Their Friendship and Subsequent Marriage*. New York: Augustus M. Kelley, 1951.

Jacobs, Jo Ellen. *Harriet Taylor Mill: Portrait of a Victorian Radical*. Bloomington: Indiana University Press, forthcoming.

———. "Harriet Taylor Mill's Collaboration with John Stuart Mill." In *Interruptions: The Voices of Women Philosophers*. Ed. Cecile Tougas and Sara Ebenreck. Philadelphia: Temple University Press, 2000. 155–66.

———. " 'The Lot of Gifted Ladies Is Hard': A Study of Harriet Taylor Mill Criticism." *Hypatia* 9.3 (1994): 132–62; rpt. in *Hypatia's Daughters: Fifteen Hundred Years of Women Philosophers*. Ed. Linda Lopez McAlister. Bloomington: Indiana University Press, 1995.

Mendus, Susan. "John Stuart Mill and Harriet Taylor on Women and Marriage." *Utilitas* 6.2 (1994): 287–99.

Zerilli, Linda. "Constructing 'Harriet Taylor': Another Look at J. S. Mill's Autobiography." In *Constructions of the Self*. Ed. George Levine. New Brunswick: Rutgers University Press, 1992. 191–212.

Mary Russell Mitford
(1787–1855)

Lauren McKinney

BIOGRAPHY

Mary Russell Mitford is best known for the informal essays or "sketches" she wrote describing the local inhabitants and environment of her village, Three Mile Cross. Compiled into a series of volumes entitled *Our Village: Sketches of Rural Life, Character, and Scenery* (1824–1832), these essays were immediately and widely admired. Later writers and critics credited Mitford with inventing a new literary genre, the geographically descriptive essay. Her sketches are valuable for both their local descriptions and her idiosyncratic technique. Most of her most vivid work was written between 1819 and 1830, before the railroads and the First Reform Bill; for this reason, later Victorians saw Mitford's writing as offering a final view of preindustrial England.

Mitford was born in Alresford, Hampshire, to George Mitford, a nonpracticing physician with a propensity for gambling, and Mary Russell Mitford, heiress of a moderate fortune. Mary was their only child and was considered something of a prodigy; allegedly, she could read before age three. Her parents sent her to Mrs. St. Quintin's school in London when she was ten, which was where Caroline Lamb and Laetitia Landon (L.E.L.)* were also educated. Mitford assiduously continued her education on her own after four years at Mrs. St. Quintin's. The record of the circulating library in Reading, where the family lived at the time, indicates that in one month Mitford checked out fifty-five books.

She started publishing her poetry in 1810, with her small volume *Poems*. Shortly before 1820, she also began keeping a detailed journal, writing plays, and submitting essays to periodicals. By this time, Mitford's father had gambled away or spent all of the £20,000 in Irish lottery money that Mitford had won at age ten; thus, she began to look toward writing as a profession. Economic straits forced the Mitfords to move to a simple cottage in Three Mile Cross, the location that proved so rich a source of material for *Our Village*. In addition to writing sketches until near the end of her life, she also corresponded prolifically with other literary figures, including Elizabeth Barrett Browning* and John Ruskin.

MAJOR WORKS AND THEMES

Although Mitford's father was a vociferous Whig, she herself never sided overtly with any political party, and indeed she ridicules one-sided politicians in the *Our Village* sketch "The Election." Nevertheless, she developed a strong affinity toward the laboring classes; she commented once that Balzac's settings were too frequently the boudoir and the opera and that he had no love for the people. This affinity resulted in a sensitive, if perhaps idealized, interpretation of the lives of country laborers, instead of through political activism. At the same time, Mitford abhorred sentimentality and sometimes mimicked pastoral ideas of "the country" in her writing.

Compared with later Victorian thinkers, Mitford does not on the surface appear intellectual, simply because she rarely discusses ideas in the abstract. She focused her thoughts on the specifics of her local world, allowing her wide literary background to subtlely inform that view. Although Mitford wrote some poetry in the 1810s and some tragedies in the 1820s, her most innovative work is the descriptive sketch, as found in the *Our Village* compilations, which were published in five volumes as they were written: in 1824, 1826, 1828, 1830, and 1832. Many of the sketches were initially published in *Lady's Magazine*. Later sketches followed the same vein but are generally considered stilted: *Belford Regis* in 1834 and *Country Stories* in 1837. The uniqueness of Mitford's *Our Village* sketches lies in their spontaneous style (written "on the spot and at the moment," as she writes in the preface to the first volume) and in an extraordinary detail that by no means diminishes the fresh, unlabored style. Thus, Mitford paints a thorough and multidimensional picture of her locale.

CRITICAL RECEPTION

Although Mitford's goal was to exclude what she called sentimentality and pathos, it is not always clear to her readers whether she achieved it. H. F. Chorley, a close friend of Mitford's, admitted that she "enamels too brightly." By all accounts, though, her work was received well by contemporary casual readers; the circulation of *Lady's Magazine* increased from 250 to 2,000 upon publication of her essays. By midcentury, Mitford had also come to the attention of critics. Elizabeth Barrett Browning* called Mitford a "sort of Crabbe prose in the sun." Tennyson was so enchanted by her sketch "Dora Creswell" that he adapted it for his poem "Dora." Anne Thackeray Ritchie* greatly admired Mitford's work and wrote the introduction to the first collected works in 1906. Many minor writers in midcentury claimed their indebtedness to her prose style, including S. C. Hall, who wrote popular sketches on Ireland, and Susanna Moodie, who recorded the trials of frontier life in Canada.

Mitford's *Our Village* deserves attention for several reasons: its innovative style, its popularity among Mitford's contemporaries, the critical consideration it received, and its direct influence on other writers. Mitford's domestic subject matter and her informal, rambling style have probably prevented her work from being considered "serious." It is clear, however, that the sketches resonated deeply with later Victorians due to the wholeness and clarity of her interpretations of village life. In other words, what later Victorians nostalgically perceived as the innocence of lost village life was preserved for them in Mitford's prose.

BIBLIOGRAPHY

Several of Mitford's works have been reprinted: *Belford Regis, or Sketches of a Country Town* (Ayer, 1977), *Country Stories* (Ayer, 1977), and *Our Village* (Woodstock, 1996). Three of her essays are included in *Prose by Victorian Women* (ed. Andrea Broomfield and Sally Mitchell, Garland, 1996).

Works by Mary Russell Mitford

Poems. 1810.
Our Village: Sketches of Rural Life, Characters, and Scenery. 1824–1832.
Belford Regis, Or Sketches of a Country Town. 1834.
Country Stories. 1837.
Recollections of a Literary Life, or Books, Places, and People. 1852.
The Life of Mary Russell Mitford, Told in Her Letters. Ed. A. G. L'Estrange. 1882.
Our Village: Sketches of Rural Life, Characters, and Scenery. Introd. Anne Thackeray Ritchie. 1906.
The Letters of Mary Russell Mitford. Introd. R. Brimley Johnson. 1924. Norwood Editions, 1978.
Raymond, Meredith, and Mary Rose Sullivan, eds. *Women of Letters: Selected Letters of Elizabeth Barrett Browning and Mary Russell Mitford.* 1987.

Studies of Mary Russell Mitford

Edwards, Peter David. *Idyllic Realism from Mary Russell Mitford to Hardy.* New York: St. Martin's Press, 1988.
Hunter, Shelagh. *Victorian Idyllic Fiction: Pastoral Strategies.* Atlantic Highlands: Humanities Press, 1984.

Constance Naden
(1858-1889)

Emily R. Anderson

BIOGRAPHY

Constance Caroline Woodhill Naden was a poet, philosopher, and scientist. Born in Birmingham, on 24 January 1858, she was the only child of Thomas and Caroline Anne (Woodhill) Naden. Her mother died shortly after childbirth, and Naden was raised by her maternal grandparents. Her childhood was somewhat lonely, but Naden found refuge in her grandparents' library. Although she attended school, Naden primarily educated herself. At the age of eighteen, she met Dr. Robert Lewins (1817–1895), who would become a lifelong friend and mentor.

Naden resumed her formal education in 1881, at Mason College, where she had been attending lectures informally for two years. Though never applying for a degree, she was one of the school's most successful students and won several awards. She learned French, Latin, Greek, and German, and she studied chemistry, botany, physiology, geology, biology, zoology, and physics. *Songs and Sonnets of Springtime*, her first volume of poetry, appeared in 1881. While at school, Naden continued to write poetry, but she focused on her scientific and philosophical work. She published regularly, during the next several years, in the college magazine and several scientific journals, using various pseudonyms. A commanding speaker, she gave lectures at the scientific societies to which she belonged, championed and organized for women's rights, and was president of the Ladies' Debating Society.

Naden continued to publish essays, give lectures, and write poetry until she left Mason College in 1887. She published a new volume of poetry, *A Modern Apostle; The Elixir of Life; The Story of Clarice; and Other Poems*, in this same year, then forswore poetry to focus on her philosophical and scientific work. In June, her grandmother died, and Naden, deeply affected, left England to travel with a friend, Madeline Daniell. When she returned in the following year, she had contracted a fever. She continued to write and speak, however, until she began suffering serious abdominal pains. In November 1889, Naden consulted a surgeon, who suggested an operation to remove ovarian cysts. While the operation was necessary and skillfully managed, it proved fatal. Her father and Daniell were present when Naden died, on December 23, at the age of thirty-one.

MAJOR WORKS AND THEMES

Among Naden's recurring themes were the sciences and philosophy and particularly Hylo-Idealism, the philosophical belief system to which Lewins converted Naden in 1881. One attraction of this system of beliefs, which emphasized the unity between the material world and subjective perception, was its compatibility with evolution and its emphasis on education. Naden's many essays, published in various journals and proceedings, explain and defend Hylo-Idealism, the principles behind evolution, atheism, and other scientific and philosophical positions she supported.

Naden's devotion to science and education is evident in her poetry. Many of her early poems are about nature, including one of the best-received, "Six Years Old" (1881), and about science, such as "Lament of the Cork-Cell" (1881), a poem remarkable for raising the death of a cell to tragic proportions. Among her later poems are "The New Orthodoxy" (1887), in which a woman chastises her lover for scoffing at Herbert Spencer and Darwin, and the delightful "Solomon Redivivus" (1887), in which King Solomon describes evolution: "We were a soft Amoeba / In ages past and gone, / Ere you were Queen of Sheba, / And I King Solomon" (lines 21–24).

Much of Naden's poetry is overtly feminist. "Love *versus* Learning" (1881) describes the sorrow of a woman whose beloved scoffs at her intelligence and education, and "The Two Artists" (1881) mocks a painter and his devastation at learning that his subject is wearing makeup. In her lectures and poetry, Naden staunchly defended the rights of women and women's suffrage, and many of her poems are devoted to the relationships between men and, particularly, educated women. While Naden chastised women who too readily conformed to society's expectations, her poetry reveals that she was sympathetic toward women's plight.

CRITICAL RECEPTION

Naden encountered difficulty in publishing her second volume of poetry, perhaps because of its radical content. Several prominent readers, however, applauded her work. W. E. Gladstone cited her, along with Elizabeth Barrett Browning,* Christina Rossetti,* and Emily Brontë,* as among the best female Victorian poets. Oscar Wilde publicly praised her poems and named his first short story "The Canterville Ghost, A Hylo-Idealistic Romance," after her philosophical work. Despite this praise, Naden's poems and essays were not universally read, and her fame did not long survive her.

Her philosophical tracts were much less admired, outside of the organizations for which she wrote them. Thomas Carlyle was a vehement critic of Lewins and his beliefs, which Naden never ceased defending. Herbert Spencer himself, though, compared Naden to George Eliot* (as did a phrenologist, who examined Naden's skull), while expressing reservations about the intellectual development of women in general and predicting a physical price for such mental exercise. Even her defenders were quick to point out that despite her intellect she acted as feminine as a Victorian woman should. Most in the intellectual community, though, and certainly those who knew her recognized a rare genius.

After a small flurry of publications and collections following her death, critical attention to Naden disappeared. Her poetry is, perhaps, less interesting formally than that of other Victorian women, but its feminism, its humor, and the novelty of its subjects demand attention.

BIBLIOGRAPHY

Various of Naden's poems have appeared in several recent anthologies of Victorian women's poetry and in several anthologies produced around the time of her death. All of her poetry can be found on the Victorian Women Writers Project (http://www.indiana.edu/~letrs/vwwp/). The prose collections below contain original work as well as some of the essays originally published in *Journal of Science*, from 1881 to 1884, in *Knowledge*, in 1885, in *Agnostic Annual*, from 1885 to 1890, in *Mason College Magazine*, from 1881 to 1887, and in the proceedings of the societies to which she belonged.

Works by Constance Naden

Songs and Sonnets of Springtime. 1881.
What Is Religion? A Vindication of Neo-Materialism. 1883.
A Modern Apostle; The Elixir of Life; The Story of Clarice; and Other Poems. 1887.
Induction and Deduction: A Historical and Critical Sketch of Successive Philosophical Conceptions Respecting the Relations of Inductive and Deductive Thought, and Other Essays. Ed. Robert Lewins. 1890.
"On Mental Physiology and Its Place in Philosophy." *Proceedings of the Aristotelian Society* 1.3 (1890): 81–82.
"On Rationalist and Empiricist Ethics." *Proceedings of the Aristotelian Society* 1.3 (1890): 79.
Further Reliques of Constance Naden: Being Essays and Tracts for Our Time. Ed. George M. McCrie. 1891.
Selections from the Philosophical and Poetical Works of Constance C. W. Naden. Ed. Emily Hughes and Edith Hughes. 1893.
The Complete Poetical Works of Constance Naden with an Explanatory Fore-word by Robert Lewins. 1894.

Studies of Constance Naden

Hughes, William R. *Constance Naden: A Memoir*. London: Bickers and Son; Birmingham: Cornish Brothers, 1890.

Moore, James R. "The Erotics of Evolution: Constance Naden and Hylo-Idealism." In *One Culture: Essays in Science and Literature*. Ed. George Levine and Alan Rauch. Madison: University of Wisconsin Press, 1987. 225–57.

Smith, Philip E., II. "Robert Lewins, Constance Naden, and Hylo-Idealism." *Notes and Queries* 25 (1978): 303–9.

Smith, Philip E., II, and Susan Harris Smith. "Constance Naden: Late Victorian Feminist Poet and Philosopher." *Victorian Poetry* 15 (1977): 367–70.

Edith Nesbit
(1858–1924)

Margaret Elizabeth Strickland

BIOGRAPHY

Renowned children's author and prominent Fabian Socialist Edith Nesbit, or "Daisy" as she was known to her friends, was born in London, the youngest of six children. Her father single-handedly directed an agricultural college before his death in 1862. Nesbit's mother administered the college herself for five years before moving the family to the Continent to improve the health of her eldest daughter. Sent off to "deplorable" boarding schools, Nesbit became unhappy and repeatedly ran away until the family returned to England and settled in Kent in 1871. The instability of her childhood is reflected in her concern with stability of place, security, and serenity in her children's books.

Inspired by the poetical works of Christina Rossetti,* Nesbit was already writing poems and submitting them to magazines by the age of fifteen. In 1880, already seven months pregnant with their first child, she married Hubert Bland. Nesbit financially supported her family after Bland contracted smallpox and his business partner deserted him, taking their funds. She handpainted greeting cards engraved with her own verses and wrote short stories, the first of which was published in *Sylvia's Home Journal*.

In 1886, close friend and literary companion Alice Hoatson moved in with Nesbit and Bland, later giving birth to two children by Bland. Hoatson became house manager and children's nurse as Nesbit's literary career became more demanding. Nesbit's unconventionality was also apparent in other areas of her life. Along with her husband, George Bernard Shaw, H. G. Wells, and others, Nesbit founded the Fabian Society and wrote a few socialist tracts. She wore her hair short, smoked in public, dressed in billowing dresses, and had extramarital affairs—perhaps to counter those of her philandering husband.

Nesbit did not discover her talent for children's literature until the success of *The Story of the Treasure-Seekers* (1899), the story of the Bastable children's strange adventures told from a child's viewpoint in a realistic manner. She continued writing novels for children until her death, alternating between realism and fantasy. When Hoatson's carelessness and parental neglect caused the death of Nesbit's youngest son, relations between Nesbit and Hoatson became strained. Bland's death in 1814 and Nesbit's second marriage to Thomas Tucker three years later compelled Hoatson to move out. Nesbit, in her will, disinherited Hoatson's two children. Nesbit died in 1924 due to heart disease and lung cancer; she is buried in Jesson St. Mary's Kent.

MAJOR WORKS AND THEMES

Early in her career, Nesbit and Bland published collaborative short stories and novels for *The Weekly Dispatch*, including *The Social Cobweb* (1884) and *Something Wrong* (1886). In 1885, they published a joint novel, *The Prophet's Mantle*, under the pseudonym "Fabian Bland," that dealt with socialist themes. It was also during this time that Nesbit began publishing her many books of poetry; her most notable collections include *Lays and Legends* (1886), *Songs of Love and Empire* (1898), and *Ballads and Lyrics of Socialism* (1908).

Nesbit's most popular works were those written for children, often stemming from her own childhood experiences. She penned a series of twelve stories, "My School-Days," for *The Girl's Own Paper* in 1896–1897 based on her adventures with her brothers and her unhappy school experiences. These reminiscences were collected and published under the title *Long Ago When I Was Young* in 1966. The absence of her father was a loss that affected Nesbit deeply, and absent or dead fathers are a recurring theme in many of her books. In *The Railway Children* (1906) the heroine is reunited with her father at the end of the story in an emotional meeting. The Bastable stories, beginning with *The Story of the Treasure-Seekers* (1899) and continued in *The Wouldbegoods* (1901) and *The New Treasure-Seekers* (1904), all contained happy memories from Nesbit's childhood when her family was living at Halstead Hall in Kent.

Her novels about middle-class children emphasized compassion, fairness, loyalty, self-sacrifice, and conformist gender roles. However, in her short stories, gender roles are less confined and more ambivalent. In "The Last of the Dragons" (1899) the Princess of Cornwall is a better fencer than all of the princes and is the one who conquers the dragon—with affection.

In contrast to the Bastable series, which are grounded in real childhood memories, the magic series shows Nesbit at her most creative. *The Phoenix and the Carpet* (1904) and *The Story of the Amulet* (1906) intermingle real-life situations with magical and dangerous elements to fascinate and delight Nesbit's young readers.

CRITICAL RECEPTION

In spite of Nesbit's ambitions to be a poet, it was her children's literature in which her strongest talents of invention and expression as an author came together. Nesbit is often referred to as the "grande dame" of children's fantasy because she was the first author to write novels about magic entering into the ordinary lives of children. These magical and fantastical stories have influenced several twentieth-century authors, such as C. S. Lewis and Edward Eager.

Not completely satisfied with her success as a children's author, Edith Nesbit continued writing short stories, novels, and poems for adults throughout her life. "Man-Size Marble," from *Grim Tales* (1893), is thought to be her most skilled piece in the gothic genre. Much of her adult fantasies, however, tend to lack intensity and real horror, Nesbit is at her best when using her personal fears as a source for her stories.

In her heart, Nesbit longed to be a poet most of all. Her first collection of poems, *Lays and Legends* (1886), received high praise and encouraged Nesbit to write more poetry. Although Nesbit has claimed, "Only my socialist poems are *real* me, and not drama," she published some highly personal poems. Angela Leighton has commented that Nesbit's most successful poems are those that reveal her inner self (*Victorian Women Poets: Writing Against the Heart* [Harvester Wheatsheaf, 1992]). Despite recent attempts to uncover forgotten works of Nesbit, the popularity of Nesbit's children's fantasies during the late Victorian period still overshadow what she considered to be her more serious literary attempts.

BIBLIOGRAPHY

Nesbit's most popular children's works have been continuously in print. Recent collections of Edith Nesbit's children's stories include *Beautiful Stories from Shakespeare for Children* (Smithmark, 1997), and *Whereyouwantogoto and Other Unlikely Tales* (Shambhala, 1993), and *English Fairy Tales* (Wordsworth Editions, 1999). A selection of her poetry is available in recent anthologies of Victorian women writers. Fairy tales by Nesbit appear in *Forbidden Journeys: Fairy Tales and Fantasies by Victorian Women Writers* (University of Chicago, 1992), *Victorian Fairy Tales: The Revolt of Fairies and Elves* (Routledge, Kegan & Paul, 1989), and *The Victorian Fairy Tale Book* (Pantheon, 1990). *Ballads and Lyrics of Socialism, The Rainbow and the Rose*, and *Songs of Love and Empire* are available on the Victorian Women Writers Project Web site: http://www.indiana.edu/~letrs/vwwp/.

Works by Edith Nesbit

The Prophet's Mantle. [Fabian Bland.] With Hubert Bland. 1885.
Lays and Legends. 1886.
Grim Tales. 1893.
A Pomander of Verse. 1895.
Songs of Love and Empire. 1898.
The Book of Dragons. 1899.
The Story of the Treasure-Seekers. 1899.
The Wouldbegoods. 1901.

Five Children and It. 1902.
The Red House. 1902.
The New Treasure-Seekers. 1904.
The Phoenix and the Carpet. 1904.
The Rainbow and the Rose. 1905.
The Railway Children. 1906.
The Story of the Amulet. 1906.
The Enchanted Castle. 1907.
Ballads and Lyrics of Socialism. 1908.
The House of Arden. 1908
Harding's Luck. 1909.
The Magic City. 1910.
The Magic World. 1912.
Wet Magic. 1913.
Long Ago When I Was Young. 1966.

Studies of Edith Nesbit

Briggs, Julia. *A Woman of Passion: The Life of E. Nesbit, 1858–1924.* New York: New
      Amsterdam Books, 1987.
Carpenter, Humphrey. *Secret Gardens: The Golden Age of Children's Literature.* Boston:
      Houghton Mifflin, 1985.
Foster, Shirley, and Judy Simons. *What Katy Read: Feminist Re-Readings of "Classic"
      Stories for Girls.* Iowa City: University of Iowa Press, 1995.
Moore, Doris Langley. *E. Nesbit: A Biography.* New York: Chilton, 1966.
Streatfield, Noel. *Magic and the Magician: E. Nesbit and Her Children's Books.* London:
      Benn, 1958.

Florence Nightingale
(1820–1910)

Sandra J. Peacock

BIOGRAPHY

Florence Nightingale, the second child of William Edward Nightingale and Frances Smith, was born in 1820 in the Italian city after which she was named. Her family was wealthy, and she never lacked material comforts. As a young girl she was educated at home, and in accordance with her father's liberal views on education, she studied philosophy, history, and languages, including classical Greek.

Nightingale's life may be divided into three distinct stages. Until age thirty-one, she was tormented by feelings of alienation from family and close friends; her desire for an independent, useful life clashed with her family's insistence that she lead the idle life of a bourgeois daughter. In her private notes and diary entries, Nightingale recorded her anguish, including the fear that she was a "monster" (Woodham-Smith 6). Early in life she began to escape into daydreams that at times consumed her waking hours and threatened her sanity. In 1837, she claimed that God spoke to her, calling her to a life of service.

She turned to religion to determine God's plan for her, and in 1844 she concluded that she had been called to nursing. Her parents rejected this ambition as entirely unsuitable, and for nearly a decade Nightingale's life was marked by surreptitious study of medicine and public health issues, punctuated with bouts of psychological and physical breakdown. When she visited Egypt and Greece in 1849–1850, her private diaries record religious visions, irrepressible daydreams, and periods of utter despair. While in Greece in June 1850, she wrote in her diary of her desire to "go up to the Eumenides Cave & ask God there to explain to me what were these Eumenides which pursued me. I would not ask to be released from them . . . but to be delivered from doing further wrong" (Calabria 66).

Later in 1850, Nightingale won parental permission to pursue a career in nursing, and she soon visited a German Protestant nursing order. In 1853, she took a position at a struggling London hospital for impoverished gentlewomen. The same year, the Crimean War broke out, and reports of terrible conditions in army hospitals reached England and provoked public outrage. Nightingale's friend Sidney Herbert, then the secretary of war, asked her to lead a group of nurses to the Crimea and supervise the reorganization of the army's medical facilities.

Nightingale's well-publicized activity in the Crimean War ushered in the next stage of her life. During this second, public phase, she achieved an extraordinary level of celebrity for a Victorian woman. Upon her return to England, Nightingale was hailed as a heroine by both the army and the general public, and she was acknowledged as an expert on both military living conditions and public health generally. Through constant correspondence and personal contact with important politicians, she worked for the improvement of army hospitals and sanitary conditions around the Empire. She avoided unwanted visitors on the grounds of ill health but worked furiously in private. Using funds subscribed by a grateful public after her Crimean achievements were publicized, she opened a training school for nurses in London in 1860.

In 1872 Nightingale entered the final stage of her life by gradually relinquishing her public duties and turning her attention instead to religious thought. The ultimate public recognition of her contributions came when she received the Order of Merit in 1907, three years before her death.

MAJOR WORKS AND THEMES

Until relatively recently, Nightingale was known primarily for her publications on sanitary conditions in the British army and on the training of nurses. Her massive study of army medical care appeared in 1858, and her *Notes on Nursing* followed in 1860. Both offer Nightingale's views on sanitation, disease, preventive medicine, and nursing. Her personal letters, diaries, and writings on religion, however, illuminate a wider array of interests. The most compelling and revealing is a polemical essay, "Cassandra," a brief but fierce attack on the Victorian bourgeois family. She describes in bitter words the futility of female existence in such families, day after day circumscribed by trivial duties, with a daughter's actions decided by the whims of parents or the demands of frivolous social obligations. Nightingale lamented that "women never have half an hour in all their lives . . . that they can call their own" (Stark 34). In the end, she invoked the image of a female Christ, "a woman, who will resume, in her own soul, all the sufferings of her race," and become the "Saviour of her race" (Stark 50).

"Cassandra" is but a small segment of a larger work, *Suggestions for Thought*, of which only six copies were privately printed during Nightingale's lifetime. The original work was over 800 pages long, but excerpted versions with commentary are available. Nightingale envisioned these *Suggestions* as a blueprint for a new religion, an eclectic blend of Unitarianism, mysticism, and reconstructed Christianity that would allow humans to realize the divine within them and understand God's purpose for them. Though she dedicated it to "Searchers After Truth among the Artizans of England," the bulk of *Suggestions* is both a critique of bourgeois treatment of women and a serious contribution to Victorian theological debate. Nightingale's letters and diaries are also valuable sources for readers interested in Victorian religion, travel, and women's experience generally.

CRITICAL RECEPTION

It is difficult to separate the critical reception of Nightingale's written work from the critical reception of her person and career. During her lifetime, Nightingale was hailed as a selfless heroine, the "Lady with the Lamp" who devoted her energy to improving the medical care of British soldiers and the British public. Her well-publicized life provided an exemplar of the contributions that energetic, dedicated women could make to society. The inner Nightingale has only gradually emerged.

Nightingale's complex, often contradictory, personality provoked polarized reactions among her biographers. In *Eminent Victorians* (1918), Lytton Strachey savaged her as a ruthless manipulator who relied on male stooges to work her will for relentless improvement—of the state, the War Office, the British soldier, and the worker. More recently, F. B. Smith portrayed her as a calculating schemer motivated only by a desire to enhance her reputation and power. He referred to the "narcissistic quality of her personality" and described her as forever veering "between self-admiration and self-contempt" (Smith 22). Other biographers have been more balanced, and some have enriched our understanding of Nightingale's complex nature through sympathetic consideration of the psychological torment she expressed in the autobiographical fragments.

Nightingale's writings have also met with contradictory reactions. Scholars of Victorian women and feminism have eagerly embraced "Cassandra" and *Suggestions for Thought*, rediscovering Nightingale as a critic of the bourgeois family and as a serious participant in the debates over religion that convulsed the later Victorian period. Myra Stark asserted that " 'Cassandra' should rightly take its place among the classics of Victorian feminism" (Stark 14). By contrast, F. B. Smith agreed with Thomas Carlyle, who "dismissed it as the bleating of a sheep lost in the wilderness" (Smith 188).

Scholars generally agree that while an expert on aspects of public health and hospital administration, Nightingale was a driven woman who expected her friends to share her level of fierce commitment to the cause of improving conditions for soldiers. They also agree, for the most part, that while her ideas on religion are not entirely original, her *Suggestions* does bear scrutiny as a powerful critique of bourgeois society and an attempt to reconcile science with faith. Even the most enthusiastic scholars concede that Nightingale, who saw clearly a source of Victorian oppression of women, was no more than an ambivalent supporter of women's rights and feminism. As one recent biographer says, the study of Nightingale's broad array of writings has fleshed out the "imposing, monolithic Victorian heroine" and revealed instead a "contradictory and thoroughly entertaining nineteenth-century woman" (Hobbs 4).

BIBLIOGRAPHY

In recent years "Cassandra" has been published in several different formats, as have her letters and nursing works, and many of her other works are appearing for the first time. For courses in Victorian literature, the works edited by Stark, Calabria, and Calabria and Macrae are recommended and easily available.

Selected Works by Florence Nightingale

Notes on Matters Affecting the Health, Efficiency, and Hospital Administration of the British Army. 1858.
Notes on Nursing: What It Is and What It Is Not. 1860.
Cassandra: An Essay. Ed. Myra Stark, with an epilogue by Cynthia MacDonald. 1979.
Florence Nightingale in Rome: Letters Written by Florence Nightingale in Rome in the Winter of 1847–1848. Ed. Mary Keele. Memoirs of The American Philosophical Society 143. 1981.
The History of Nursing: An Index to the Microfiche Collection. Vol. 1, *The Adelaide Nutting Historical Nursing Collection.* 1983. (Contains the complete report on army hospitals and *Suggestions for Thought*.)
Letters from Egypt. A Journey on the Nile, 1849–1850. Selected and Introduced by Anthony Sattin. 1987.
Ever Yours, Florence Nightingale. Selected Letters. Ed. Martha Vicinus and Bea Nergaard. 1990.
As Miss Nightingale Said . . . Florence Nightingale Through Her Sayings—A Victorian Perspective. Ed. Monica Baly. 1991.
Cassandra and Other Selections from Suggestions for Thought. Ed. Mary Poovey. 1992.
Suggestions for Thought. Selections and Commentaries. Ed. Michael D. Calabria and Janet A. Macrae. 1994.
Calabria, Michael. *Florence Nightingale in Egypt and Greece. Her Diary and "Visions."* 1997.

Studies of Florence Nightingale

Bishop, W. J., and Sue Goldie, comps. *A Bio-Bibliography of Florence Nightingale.* London: Dawsons of Pall Mall, 1962.
Boyd, Nancy. *Three Victorian Women Who Changed Their World: Josephine Butler, Octavia Hill, Florence Nightingale.* Oxford: Oxford University Press, 1982.
Bullough, Vern, Bonnie Bullough, and Marietta P. Stanton, eds. *Florence Nightingale and Her Era: A Collection of New Scholarship.* New York: Garland, 1990.
Cook, Sir Edward. *The Life of Florence Nightingale.* 2 vols. London: Macmillan, 1913.

Hobbs, Colleen. *Florence Nightingale*. New York: Twayne, 1997.

Landow, George P. "Aggressive (Re)interpretations of the Female Sage: Florence Nightingale's 'Cassandra.' " In *Victorian Sages and Cultural Discourse: Renegotiating Gender and Power*. Ed. Thais Morgan. New Brunswick: Rutgers University Press, 1990. 32–45.

Poovey, Mary. "A Housewifely Woman: The Social Construction of Florence Nightingale." In *Uneven Developments. The Ideological Work of Gender in Mid-Victorian England*. Chicago: University of Chicago Press, 1988. 164–98.

Showalter, Elaine. "Florence Nightingale's Feminist Complaint: Women, Religion, and *Suggestions for Thought*." *Signs* 6.31 (1981): 395–412.

Smith, F. B. *Florence Nightingale. Reputation and Power*. New York: St. Martin's Press, 1982.

Snyder, Katherine V. "From Novel to Essay: Gender and Revision in Florence Nightingale's 'Cassandra.' " In *The Politics of the Essay: Feminist Perspectives*. Ed. Ruth-Ellen Boetcher Joeres and Elizabeth Mittman. Bloomington: Indiana University Press, 1993. 23–40.

———. "Nofriani Unbound: The First Version of Florence Nightingale's 'Cassandra.' " *Victorian Literature and Culture* 24 (1996): 251–88.

Strachey, Lytton. *Eminent Victorians*. London: Chatto & Windus, 1918.

Woodham-Smith, Cecil. *Florence Nightingale*. New York: McGraw-Hill, 1951.

Caroline Norton
(1808–1877)

Nikki Lee Manos

BIOGRAPHY

The Honorable Caroline Elizabeth Sarah Norton was an Irish beauty born in 1808. At the age of seventeen, she entered London's marriage market, expecting to find a husband who would bring her wealth and social prominence. The notoriety that dogged her throughout her life barred her from such a conventional fate, for Norton played a dominant role in not one but two scandals of national consequence in nineteenth-century Britain.

Although a presentable match, George Norton quickly proved to be below his wife in more than social standing. In 1836, having survived a physically abusive marriage for eight years and given birth to three sons, Norton found herself locked out of her home and denied access to her personal belongings and family. George Norton next sued for divorce on the grounds of adultery. He lost his suit, but Norton, a married woman, had no legal means either to defend her name in a court of law or to extricate herself from an embittered marriage.

The rumors of adultery resurfaced with a vengeance ten years later. News that the Cabinet had voted to repeal the Corn Laws was published prematurely in the press. Rumor quickly targeted Norton as responsible for the leak due to her romantic ties to the politician Sidney Herbert. Norton lost her coveted position as a political confidant.

Norton never questioned, at least publicly, the notion of separate spheres, yet she was the great-granddaughter of the Irish dramatist and Whig politician Richard Brinsley Sheridan. Her family encouraged her to view herself as gifted with high intelligence and artistic talents. Writing brought her solace from her disastrous marriage as well as the means to keep her family solvent. She published books of poetry, had a play performed, and contributed miscellaneous works to magazines and annuals.

At Caroline Norton's death in 1877, the British legislative and court system had granted married women a legal existence. Besides the right to fight for the custody of their children, they were entitled, as single women were, to their earnings, their inheritance, and the right to enter into contracts. The legal victory came too late for Norton. She remained legally and emotionally tied to her husband. Two years after his death at the age of sixty-seven, an ailing Caroline Norton married her lifelong friend Sir William Stirling-Maxwell. She died three months later.

MAJOR WORKS AND THEMES

Norton's writing developed in response to her unending marital troubles. She published *A Voice from the Factories* (1836) to earn money, but her focus— abusive child labor practices—reflected her distress over the loss of her children. She honed her journalistic skills to battle eloquently for the right to live her life. When her pamphlet *The Separation of Mother and Child by the Law of Custody of Infants Considered* (1837) failed to reform child custody laws, she published *A Plain Letter to the Lord Chancellor on the Infant Custody Bill* (1839) and intensified her lobbying campaign. Parliament passed the Infant Custody Bill in 1839, granting married women limited rights to their infant children, and Norton began visiting her remaining two children.

When Norton's husband won his suit in 1853, her property was transferred to him, including copyrights. Norton responded by renewing her lobbying efforts, this time for divorce law and property reform. Her series of inspired pamphlets—*English Laws for Women in the Nineteenth Century* (1854), *A Letter to the Queen on Lord Cranworth's Marriage and Divorce Bill* (1855), *A Review of the Divorce Bill of 1856*—were instrumental in passing the Marital Causes Bill in 1857 and the Married Women's Property Acts in 1870, 1882, and 1893.

Norton wrote successfully in a number of formats. She earned enough to support herself and her sons by publishing over a hundred works of fiction and lyrics of popular songs. Her three-volume romances are remarkable for their unusual plot twists and intriguing heroines. *Stuart of Dunleath* (1851), *Lost and Saved* (1863), and *Old Sir Douglas* (1867), in particular, underscore her talent for comic relief, artful dialogue, and psychological insights. The recent publication of Norton's lengthy correspondence to Lord Melbourne is indispensable for establishing Norton's significance. She was a charismatic figure of the nineteenth century who pioneered expanding the conventional boundaries of women's writing.

CRITICAL RECEPTION

Writers such as Dickens, Disraeli, and Thackeray used Norton's propensity for scandal as the basis for their plots and characterizations. George Meredith solidified Norton's reputation for coming generations in the best-selling roman à clef *Diana of the Crossways* (1885). Meredith seemed to adhere to the facts of Norton's life in his roman à clef, yet he ignored unsettling details and presented rumor as fact. In the guise of his heroine's action, he depicted Norton as responsible for the Corn Law scandal, selling the secret to the press, and motivated by unrestrained physical passion. Meredith surmised correctly that scandal would fashion future opinion of Norton, which it has until the last few decades.

Norton has been viewed traditionally as a minor Victorian poet and witty conversationalist who entertained the most prominent men of her day. A more complex assessment is emerging. Norton is now recognized as one of the most successful literary women of the nineteenth century and a forerunner of the women's movement of the fin de siècle era.

Norton used her intellectual and artistic gifts to unmask the legal inequities that had barred her from her property, notably, her children. Her lifelong reform goals appeared limited, ostensibly to protect women when their husbands proved unworthy. Nevertheless, her essays, novels, and correspondence—offering a sustained written record of private anguish—document an emerging woman's voice in public arenas outside the courts. Her writings, moreover, mark changing notions of family and women's sexuality.

BIBLIOGRAPHY

Several of Caroline Norton's works have been reprinted, including *English Laws for Women in the Nineteenth Century* (intro. Joan Huddleston [Academy Chicago, 1982]), *Lost and Saved* (intro. Sylvia Bailey Shurbutt [Scholars' Facsimiles & Reprints, 1988]), and *A Voice from the Factories* (intro. Jonathan Wordsworth [Woodstock Books, 1994]).

Works by Caroline Norton

A Voice from the Factories. 1836.
The Separation of Mother and Child by the Law of Custody of Infants Considered. 1837.
Stuart of Dunleath. 1851.
English Laws for Women in the Nineteenth Century. 1854.
Lost and Saved. 1863.
Old Sir Douglas. 1867.
The Letters of Caroline Norton to Lord Melbourne. Ed. James O. Hoge and Clarke Olney. 1974.
Selected Writings of Caroline Norton. Introd. James O. Hoge and Jane Marcus. 1978.

Studies of Caroline Norton

Acland, Alice. *Caroline Norton.* London: Constable, 1948.
Chedzoy, Alan. *A Scandalous Woman: The Story of Caroline Norton.* London: Allison & Busby, 1992.

Clarke, Michael. "William Thackeray's Fiction and Caroline Norton's Biography: Narrative Matrix of Feminist Legal Reform." *Dickens Studies Annual* 18 (1989): 337–51.

Forster, Margaret. *Significant Sisters: The Grassroots of Active Feminism, 1839–1939.* London: Secker & Warburg, 1984.

Meredith, George. 1897. *Diana of the Crossways.* Intro. Lois Josephs Fowler. New York: Norton, 1973.

Perkins, Jane Gray. *The Life of Mrs. Norton.* London: John Murray, 1910.

Poovey, Mary. *Uneven Developments: The Ideological Work of Gender in Mid-Victorian England.* Chicago: University of Chicago Press, 1988.

Margaret Oliphant Wilson Oliphant (1828–1897)

Deirdre d'Albertis

BIOGRAPHY

Margaret Oliphant, one of nineteenth-century Britain's most prolific novelists and, arguably, its most accomplished professional woman of letters, began her long life as a writer with the publication in 1849 of *Passages in the Life of Mrs. Margaret Maitland*. Although well known to her contemporaries as a reviewer, essayist, travel writer, literary critic, biographer, historian, and editor (Henry James remarked that "few authors of our time have been so organised for liberal, for—one may almost put it—heroic production" [James 358]), Oliphant is best remembered as a novelist and short story writer with prodigious powers of invention. Unusual stamina enabled Oliphant to withstand a series of disasters in her personal life while maintaining a high standard of professional productivity: "From the time she was twenty to her death in her seventieth year she wrote on an average at least six volumes a year—one every two months" (Gwyn 26). Yet Oliphant was destined to fail when it came to earning the respect of her literary peers. Compared unfavorably then as now with such women novelists as George Eliot* and Charlotte Brontë,* Oliphant herself attributed the less-than-satisfactory fate of her literary reputation to pressing material circumstances—widowed early in life, she assumed sole financial responsibility for her family from that time forward—that forced her to become more prolific than she might otherwise have been. Oliphant's posthumously published *Autobiography* reveals the self-doubts and ongoing struggles of an intelligent, self-critical woman writer who resented the myth of domestic womanhood enshrined by her culture. "[W]henever it has been necessary," Oliphant asserted in an 1879 review for *Blackwood's Edinburgh Magazine*, "women *have* toiled, have earned money, have got their living and livings of those dependent upon them, in total indifference to all theory" ("Two Ladies" 206). Equally hostile to domestic ideologues who would keep women out of the marketplace and to nineteenth-century feminists who agitated for economic and social reform of that same marketplace, Oliphant managed to create a relationship with publishers and the reading public based on values of industry, reliable service, and good workmanship that inevitably carried the taint of commerce into what was meant to be the realm of art.

Born at Wallyford, Musselburgh, in Midlothian, Scotland, Oliphant was raised by her intelligent, fiercely loving mother, Margaret Oliphant Wilson, to relish storytelling. Her somewhat distant and unremarkable father, Francis Wilson, a customs official, played a less crucial role in the formation of his daughter's literary and intellectual ambitions. As adherents to the newly formed Free Church of Scotland, the Oliphant family entered eagerly into debates over religious doctrine, a passion reflected in the novelist's later writings about dissent and clerical life. Her mother encouraged her to begin writing in her teens, and the fledgling author published her first novel at the age of twenty-one. In 1852 Margaret Wilson married her cousin, the stained-glass artist Francis Wilson Oliphant, and the young couple settled in London. This brief, happy apprenticeship period for Margaret Oliphant as a writer was soon interrupted by financial worries, the death of two children in infancy, and her husband's rapidly deteriorating health. Diagnosed with tuberculosis, Frank Oliphant and his family were advised to relocate to a milder climate; he died in 1859 in Rome. As a consequence, Oliphant found herself stranded in Italy with three young children to support (all of whom would eventually predecease her).

Recently formed ties to the publishing house of Blackwood's sustained the young writer through this and succeeding financial crises. In her history of the accomplishments of William Blackwood and his sons, *Annals of a Publishing House*, Oliphant describes herself as "a sort of general utility woman," always on call to provide a last-minute review or essay to fill out the latest edition of *Blackwood's Edinburgh Magazine* (known colloquially as "Maga") (*Annals* 2: 475). Despite the genuine personal ties that formed between the widow and her various publishers over the years, even Blackwood's reserved the right to reject manuscripts deemed for whatever reason to be unprofitable. In 1861, Oliphant reached a daunting impasse with Blackwood's; unable to sell her copiously, if unevenly produced fiction, she was nearly overwhelmed by the prospect of being unable any longer to support her dependents. In her *Autobiography* and elsewhere, Oliphant recollects that it was only under such extreme pressure that she was able to change tack and begin work on those stories and novels reckoned to be her greatest critical and financial success, the "Chronicles of Carlingford" series.

Although Oliphant managed to overcome early personal and professional hardships, the burden of providing for her own children was increased by the addition of three of her widower brother's children to the household (her two sons and a nephew Frank were all educated at Eton at Oliphant's expense). Despite the many demands placed upon her erratic income from writing, Oliphant characteristically rejected the imperative to economize in favor of entertaining, travel, and cultivation of the good life. Her convivial instincts, coupled with a desire to manage and provide for others rather than be perceived as dependent herself, led the author to overextend the limits of her own hospitality to an often astonishing degree. One of her son Cyril Oliphant's friends, reminisced, "The little house in Clarence Crescent overflowed with her courtiers. The words which she wrote of Mrs. Duncan Stewart would have as aptly described her own case. 'In the middle of the flutter of general company, she had always (as indeed every one has) a constant circle of intimates, always the same, and sometimes not quite worthy of the idol they surrounded.' A witty friend once said of her that she was always surrounded by people who called each other 'Parasites' " (Sturgis 237). As a result, one contemporary reviewer succinctly noted that for most of Oliphant's adult life "the actual had her by the throat" (Gwyn 34). She maintained a voluminous correspondence with her publishers, most of which was devoted to forestalling or renegotiating payment of debts with the promise of manuscripts and essays to come. Sustained by almost superhuman industry—commonly drafting a three-volume novel while undertaking piecework for Blackwood's—Oliphant attained a level of productivity impressive even in the era of Dickens and Trollope. As Anne Thackeray Ritchie* remarked of the older woman's literary career, "[T]he very bountifulness of her gift was her temptation" (Ritchie 26). Lonely and dispirited, Oliphant died in 1897 at the age of sixty-nine in Wimbledon, still hard at work on several projects at once, having lost her last remaining children, Cyril ("Tiddy") and Francis Romano ("Cecco") in 1890 and 1894, respectively.

MAJOR WORKS AND THEMES

Oliphant's early work, unsurprisingly, features Scottish scenes: For instance, the historical novel *Caleb Field* (1851), *Merkland* (1851), and *Katie Stewart* (1853) are most often discussed in terms of larger developments in Scottish regional fiction, whereas later works such as *The Minister's Wife* (1869), *Effie Ogilvie* (1886), and *Kirsteen* (1890) may also be linked to that tradition. Yet Oliphant soon looked beyond her native Scotland to write about English characters and themes. The young novelist tried her hand at nearly every prominent genre of the period, from domestic romance with *The Athelings* (1857) to sensation novels with *Salem Chapel* (1863). The latter volume formed part of the aforementioned "Chronicles of Carlingford" (1862–1876), which also include *The Rector and the Doctor's Family* (1863), a collection of two stories published in a single volume, *The Perpetual Curate* (1864), *Miss Marjoribanks* (1866), and *Phoebe Junior: A Last Chronicle of Carlingford* (1876). The "Chronicles" were first serialized in Blackwood's and then separately published; contemporaries were quick to note Oliphant's obvious indebtedness to Trollope's popular Barsetshire Chronicles. Critics also tended to compare Oliphant's treatment of domestic subjects with George Eliot's handling of similar themes—a comparison not entirely welcome to the less frenetically productive author.

In the "Chronicles," Oliphant renders minutiae of social relations in provincial England with attention both to gentry and clergy, professional families, and tradesmen in Carlingford, affording readers an especially valuable glimpse into the everyday lives of the English middle classes in the middle years of the century. Church politics figure prominently in the novels, as do concerns with vocation generally. Most strikingly, doubtless because of hardships associated with domesticity in her own case, Oliphant reveals herself in these novels to be one of the great, clear-eyed historians of the Victorian family. Her plots generally feature a tart deflation of masculine pretensions. There is no wise, omnipotent patriarch to be found in the fiction; rather, unsentimental portraits abound of weak-willed husbands, fathers, and brothers supported by independently minded, eminently capable women. Henrietta Corkran, describing a meeting with the "popular authoress" at Eton, immediately sensed a distinct mingling of impatience and irreverence in Oliphant's outlook on the opposite sex: "Mrs. Oliphant struck me as being rather antagonistically inclined towards the lords of the creation, for I recollect that she made me laugh by remarking that men would be much improved if a good sound whipping was administered to them about once a month" (Corkran 337).

Indeed, Oliphant could never quite forgive Charlotte Brontë for being a great writer who was obsessed with romantic love between men and women: "There is but one strain of intense sentiment in these books—the desire of a lonely creature longing for its mate, an all-engrossing thought . . . that yearning of the woman toward the man which . . . has produced the greater part of all distinctively feminine distresses" ("The Old Saloon" 757). In contrast to Brontë's "strain of intense sentiment," Oliphant portrayed relations between the sexes in a manner that is both comical and critical. Her heroines prefer to rely on their own—often hilariously inadequate—resources rather than look to men for guidance or support: Lucilla Marjoribanks's imperious management of her father's household in *Miss Marjoribanks* and Nettie Underwood's determined reign over a family of helpless incompetents in *The Doctor's Family* both bespeak an exasperated dismissal of male authority, as well as a certain wistfulness at the failure of most men to challenge their dominion.

Oliphant did not confine herself to the subgenre of domestic fiction, and as she grew older, she became increasingly interested in writing about mysticism and the afterlife. Her remarkable tales of the supernatural are collected in *Stories of the Seen and the Unseen* (1902). Oliphant's vivid treatment of the occult has captured the attention of modern readers, leading to the fairly reliable reissue from time to time of these titles.

Oliphant spent at least as much time penning nonfiction as she did novels and short stories. As "general utility woman," she was commissioned, for instance, to edit the prestigious Blackwood's Foreign Classics series. Other nonfiction projects included biographies of Edward Irving, Scottish founder of the "Catholic Apostolic Church," and the travel writer and journalist Laurence Oliphant, a distant cousin, as well as of Thomas Chalmers and of her friend John

Tulloch. Oliphant's travel writing remains valuable for those interested in the history and architecture of Italian cities; her well-regarded *Literary History of England* (1882) displays characteristic tastes of the age. Yet Oliphant probably wielded her greatest literary influence in her role as a reviewer for Maga. Lamenting her role as a veritable one-woman critical institution, Henry James objected that when it came to criticism, "no one . . . practiced it more in the hit-or-miss fashion and on happy-go-lucky lines than Mrs. Oliphant herself. She practiced it, as she practiced everything, on such an inordinate scale that her biographer, if there is to be one, will have no small task in the mere drafting of lists of her contributions . . . no woman had ever, for half a century, had her personal 'say' so publicly and irresponsibly" (James 358).

Ironically, Oliphant's last work—the apologia she composed for publication after her death, has been judged by many to be her most powerful. As Virginia Woolf noted, Oliphant's autobiography is one of the most moving and in many ways characteristic life stories of the Victorian period (Woolf 91). Published posthumously in 1899, the *Autobiography* has been edited and reprinted by Q. D. Leavis and, more recently, by Elisabeth Jay, who has significantly altered the formal organization of the volume as it was originally prepared by Oliphant's first editor, Mrs. A. L. Coghill. Unlike the more controlled life writings of such Victorian sages as Mill and Darwin, or even Ruskin and Wilde, Oliphant's autobiography is best read in conjunction with Trollope's account of a life spent writing to order. In contrast, however, to Trollope's carefully cultivated equipoise, the maternal sufferings of Oliphant suffuse the memoir with barely suppressed emotion. As a monument to the loss of her children, as well as a lament for the art she failed to realize in her novels, Oliphant's autobiography stands as one of the great self-reflective documents of the age.

CRITICAL RECEPTION

Was Margaret Oliphant nothing more than a hack writer—heroic in terms of industry, perhaps—but a hack, nevertheless? Toward the end of her life and immediately after her death, Oliphant's reputation suffered its greatest decline. Popular throughout much of the century (Queen Victoria,* for instance, was an avid reader of Oliphant's fiction), the novelist was ultimately judged harshly for those habits of regularity and reliability that first secured her a place in the profession of letters. Even her most sympathetic supporters acknowledged the unevenness of her oeuvre. Fellow Scots writer J. M. Barrie speculated after Oliphant's death that her spontaneous and even, at times, slipshod method of composition was essential to the unique character of her novels: "[W]hether they would have been greater books had she revised one instead of beginning another is probably to be doubted. . . . Condensation, a more careful choice of words, we all learn these arts in the schools nowadays, they are natural to the spirit of the age; but Mrs. Oliphant never learned them, they were contrary to her genius (as to some other novelists greater than she), and they would probably have trammelled her so much that the books would have lost more than they gained" (Barrie vii).

Central to the harsh judgment of nineteenth-century critics (and to some extent, the disdain of many twentieth-century readers as well) has been a perception that Oliphant chose to devote the greater part of her creative energies not to her literary vocation but to ever-expanding domestic obligations. Shortly after her death, Stephen Gwyn asserts: "Mrs. Oliphant was a woman and a mother, and the innermost preoccupation of her mind—the point to which her fluctuating thoughts would always swing back—was her children. It may have been an accident—but more likely it is not—that the women who have been great artists have been childless women" (Gwyn 37). Only now have readers begun to explore the fruitful tension between Oliphant's role as mother and her role as writer; along with a reappraisal of definitions of artistic genius and critical questioning of any easy assumption that "the women who have been great artists have been childless women," Oliphant's career has emerged as an important example of a writer whose ambivalence about the restrictions of both roles produced a uniquely critical body of writing. Certainly, late-twentieth-century feminist readers have found much to appreciate in Oliphant's acerbic commentary on Victorian domestic ideology. Although not herself an active participant in the mid-Victorian feminist movement, Oliphant persistently interrogated habits of thought that excluded women from commerce and the professions. Oliphant's "practical feminism," as scholar Elizabeth Langland suggests, may not conform to modern-day notions about the politics of gender, but if we can come to appreciate her extraordinary position in relationship to her own culture, we have much to learn about the ways in which such anomalous women have both accommodated themselves to and undermined systems of oppression.

BIBLIOGRAPHY

Oliphant published over a hundred volumes of fiction and nonfiction. Although many of her novels have been reprinted, only her *Autobiography* has remained consistently in print.

Selected Works by Margaret Oliphant

Passages in the Life of Mrs. Margaret Maitland. 1849.
Caleb Field. 1851.
Merkland. 1851.
Katie Stewart. 1853.
The Athelings. 1857.
The Rector and The Doctor's Family. 1863.
Salem Chapel. 1863.
The Perpetual Curate. 1864.
Miss Marjoribanks. 1866.
The Minister's Wife. 1869.
Phoebe, Junior: A Last Chronicle of Carlingford. 1876.

"Two Ladies." *Blackwood's Edinburgh Magazine* 125 (Feb. 1879): 206–24.
A Beleaguered City. 1880.
Hester. 1883.
Effie Ogilvie. 1886.
"The Old Saloon: The Literature of the Last Fifty Years." *Blackwood's Edinburgh Magazine* 141 (June 1887): 737–61.
Kirsteen. 1890.
Annals of a Publishing House: William Blackwood and His Sons. 1897.
Stories of the Seen and the Unseen. 1902.
Autobiography and Letters of Mrs. Margaret Oliphant. Ed. Mrs. Harry Coghill. 1899. Rpt., 1974. Intro. Q. D. Leavis.
The Autobiography of Margaret Oliphant: The Complete Text. Ed. Elisabeth Jay. 1990.

Studies of Margaret Oliphant

Barrie, J. M. "Introductory Note." *A Widow's Tale and Other Stories by Mrs. Oliphant.* Edinburgh: William Blackwood and Sons, 1898.
Clarke, John Stock. *Margaret Oliphant: A Bibliography.* Victorian Fiction Research Guides 11. St. Lucia, Qld.: University of Queensland, 1986.
Colby, Vineta, and Robert Colby. *The Equivocal Virtue: Mrs. Oliphant and the Victorian Literary Market Place.* New York: Archon Books, 1966.
Corbett, Mary Jean. *Representing Femininity: Middle-Class Subjectivity in Victorian and Edwardian Women's Autobiographies.* New York: Oxford University Press, 1992.
Corkran, Henrietta. *Celebrities and I.* London: Hutchinson, 1902.
Gwyn, Stephen. "The Life and Writings of Mrs. Oliphant." *Blackwood's Edinburgh Magazine* 190 (July 1899): 26–47.
James, Henry. *Notes on Novelists and Some Other Notes.* London: J. M. Dent & Sons, 1914.
Jay, Elisabeth. *Mrs. Oliphant: "A Fiction to Herself," a Literary Life.* Oxford: Clarendon Press, 1995.
Langland, Elizabeth. *Nobody's Angels: Middle-Class Women and Domestic Ideology in Victorian Culture.* Ithaca: Cornell University Press, 1995.
Peterson, Linda H. "Audience and the Autobiographer's Art: An Approach to the Autobiography of Mrs. M.O.W. Oliphant." In *Approaches to Victorian Autobiography.* Ed. George P. Landow. Athens: Ohio University Press, 1979.
Ritchie, Anne Thackeray. *From the Porch.* London: Smith, Elder, 1913.
Sturgis, Howard Overing. "A Sketch from Memory." *Temple Bar* 118 (Oct. 1899): 233–48.
Trela, D. J. *Margaret Oliphant: Critical Essays on a Gentle Subversive.* Selinsgrove: Susquehanna University Press, 1995.
Williams, Merryn. *Margaret Oliphant: A Critical Biography.* London: Macmillan, 1986.
Woolf, Virginia. *Three Guineas.* New York: Harcourt, Brace, 1938.

"Ouida" (Marie Louise de la Ramée) (1839–1908)

Sandra Hannaford

BIOGRAPHY

"Ouida," whose assumed name is a childhood mispronunciation of "Louise," was born Marie Louise Rame on New Year's Day in 1839 in Bury St. Edmunds, a provincial English town she never revisited and rarely spoke of after her departure in 1857. Ouida idolized her father, Louis Rame, an exotic character to the Bury townspeople, some of whom suspected him to be a Bonapartist agent because of his French origin and frequent absences from his wife and child. He taught his native language by profession. His most important influence on his daughter was to instill in her a love for nature and reading literature. While her mother lived with her until Mrs. Rame's death in 1893, her father had the most impact on the young Ouida. Although he was unattractive and middle-aged when her parents married, Ouida identified strongly with her father's French heritage. Despite his virtual absence in her life, Ouida romanticized her childhood memories of her father in the mysterious heroes of her early novels. Ouida never married, though she preferred the company of men to any woman other than her mother.

In 1871 Ouida permanently settled in Italy, the scene of many of her later novels. There she surrounded herself with luxury and dogs until she saw her popularity wane and her financial problems increase. Ouida gave her critics ammunition by leading a life as colorful as that of her amoral characters. She died of pneumonia in 1908. Bury St. Edmunds, recognizing her love for animals, erected a fountain for dogs and horses in her memory. The inscription reads: "Here may God's creatures whom she loved assuage her tender soul as they drink."

MAJOR WORKS AND THEMES

Ouida was inspired to write by the success of Ellen Wood's* *East Lynne*. Like the plots of many of the sensation novels, Ouida's plots revolve around hidden identities, romantic heroes, melodramatic action, and opulent settings.

She wrote in "Romance and Realism," "I do not object to realism in fiction; what I object to is the limitation of realism in fiction to what is commonplace, tedious, and bald" (Stirling 15). Unhampered by the necessity of earning a living or domestic duties, Ouida's upper-class characters ruthlessly pursue their every desire, be it love or power. For biographer Elizabeth Lee, "Love and intrigue are her sole themes. Her characters exist only to make love and be made love to" (243).

Recently scholars have commented on Ouida's female characters. Natalie Schroeder points out that her female characters are defeated "by a patriarchal society in which a woman's beauty and strength fade with her youth, while males reach the fullest vigor of manhood with age" (99–100). Pamela K. Gilbert suggests that "she grants these women a remarkable power and energy in manipulating and controlling their environment, and a capacity for doing damage that may have been a potent attractant for female readers who felt that their own control of their lives was at best tenuous" (144). Both in her own personal life and in the lives of many of her heroines, Ouida clearly refused to bow to the dictates of conventional Victorian feminine behavior. But Ouida did not become locked into the pattern of her early, best-selling novels. She was inspired by her reading; for example, she patterned *Folle-Farine* (1871) on Goethe's *Faust*. In her later novels, Ouida's heroes and heroines are frequently from the peasant class or they are animals.

CRITICAL RECEPTION

Ouida wrote a total of forty-six novels, as well as collections of short stories and essays; among these are philosophical and critical treatises, dramas, and several children's books. Although not popular with the critics, Ouida's books found a wide audience for most of her life.

The success of *Under Two Flags* (1867), which has been dramatized several times, led to the popularity of the French Foreign Legion in novels and films. As Pamela Gilbert points out, this novel combines the high-society romance with the adventure novel. While styling her prose as excessive and flamboyant, Monica Stirling calls *Under Two Flags* a "rapidly moving, highly coloured, frequently preposterous, and frequently touching novel" (65). Unlike her contemporaries, recent critics focus on the social implications of Ouida's writing. Many critics see her as rebelling against conventional Victorian ideals. Even as Ouida herself decried female suffrage and the "New Woman" (Ouida singled out the phrase from an essay by Sarah Grand*), her most memorable fictional heroines are, as she herself was, decidedly determined women. Natalie Schroeder believes that Ouida, like Mary Braddon,* "depict[s] women who are attempting to escape from their limited social spheres . . . [Her female characters] emerge as far more interesting than and superior to their male adversaries" (100–101). Praising the readability of her fiction, John Sutherland suggests that "Ouida deserves rather more of a literary reputation than posterity has allowed her" (xiii).

BIBLIOGRAPHY

A Dog of Flanders (Dover, 1992) and *Under Two Flags* (ed. John Sutherland [Oxford, 1995]) have been issued recently in paperback; *Under Two Flags* and *The Massarenes* have been reprinted by AMS Press.

Selected Works by Ouida

Held in Bondage. 1863.
Strathmore. 1865.
Chandos. 1866.
Cecil Castlemaine's Gage, and Other Novelettes. 1867.
Idalia. 1867.
Under Two Flags. 1867.
Folle-Farine. 1871.
A Dog of Flanders, and Other Stories. 1872.
Signa. 1875.
Moths. 1880.
In Maremma. 1882.
The Massarenes. 1897.
La Strega, and Other Stories. 1899.

Studies of Ouida

Bigland, Eileen. *Ouida: The Passionate Victorian*. London: Jarrolds, 1950.
Dobrée, Bonamy. *Milton to Ouida: A Collection of Essays*. London: Frank Cass, 1970.
Ffrench, Yvonne. *Ouida: A Study in Ostentation*. London: Cobden-Sanderson, 1938.
Gilbert, Pamela K. *Disease, Desire, and the Body in Victorian Women's Popular Novels*. Cambridge: Cambridge University Press, 1997.
Lee, Elizabeth. *Ouida: A Memoir*. London: T. Fisher Unwin, 1914.
Schroeder, Natalie. "Feminine Sensationalism, Eroticism, and Self-Assertion: M. E. Braddon and Ouida." *Tulsa Studies in Women's Literature* 7.1 (Spring 1988): 87–103.
Stirling, Monica. *The Fine and the Wicked: The Life and Times of Ouida*. New York: Coward-McCann, 1958.
Sutherland, John. Introduction. *Under Two Flags*. Oxford: Oxford University Press, 1995.

Bessie Rayner Parkes (Belloc) (1829-1925)

Christine Swiridoff

BIOGRAPHY

Although most remembered for her central role in the mid-Victorian women's rights movement, Bessie Rayner Parkes also edited journals and wrote essays, poems, and travel sketches. Born on 16 June 1829 in Birmingham and educated in Warwickshire, Parkes grew up primarily in London. Her father, Joseph Parkes, was a radical lawyer, a historian of the Chancery Bar, and founder of the Reform Club, and her mother, Elizabeth Priestly, belonged to a prominent Unitarian family.

After completing school, Parkes published three volumes of poetry in the 1850s. During that time, conversations with like-minded young women about the Woman Question prompted her to write *Remarks on the Education of Girls* (1854). With Barbara Leigh Smith (later Bodichon*), Parkes helped organize the Married Women's Property campaign late in 1855. By 1857, the Campaign had proved a failure, but the experience showed Parkes the need for a public forum to discuss women's concerns. Parkes had edited the *Waverley Journal*, a Scottish periodical, for a brief time in 1856 and 1857 and believed that a periodical devoted to the issues affecting women would provide a useful platform. With this aim, Parkes cofounded, with Barbara Leigh Smith, and coedited, with Matilda Hays, *The English Woman's Journal* (1858–1864). Promoting employment for women was a primary endeavor, and at the *Journal*, Parkes started a register of unemployed women, which Jessie Boucherett took over and used to establish the Society for the Promotion of the Employment of Women in July 1859. Led by Bessie Parkes, Barbara Leigh Smith, and Emily Davies and named after the *Journal*'s address, the Langham Place Circle became the center of the middle-class women's rights movement in Britain during the 1850s and 1860s and promoted women's employment, educational reform, women's suffrage, and women's legal condition.

Her conversion to Roman Catholicism in 1864 and a severe illness in 1865 restricted Parkes's active participation in the women's rights movement. Her marriage to French barrister Louis Belloc in 1867 prompted her further withdrawal from the public, although she did participate in the early women's suffrage campaign in 1866–1867. Her husband's death in 1872 shook Parkes deeply, and she lived with her children, Hilaire and Marie (Belloc-Lowndes), between France, her primary home during their marriage, and England. In 1925, Parkes died at age ninety-five in Sussex.

MAJOR WORKS AND THEMES

Given Parkes's involvement in the women's movement, it is not surprising that much of her work revolves around the theme of women's rights. Perhaps her most important works, *Essays on Woman's Work* (1865) and *Remarks on the Education of Girls* (1854), address the need for improving women's access to both profitable employment and education. In addition, her poetry often reflects her views on the Woman Question. The narrative poem *Summer Sketches* resists conservative notions of woman's natural sphere and argues for women's development. "To an Author Who Loved Truth More than Fame" is a fascinating view of the challenges faced by the woman writer who refuses to buckle under the "torture of the critic's pen." Parkes worked to draw attention to the stories of successful, meritorious women. She paid tribute to Adelaide Procter* and Elizabeth Barrett Browning,* dedicating poems to them, collected biographies of women in *Vignettes* (1866), and wrote numerous essays both on notable women and on important issues affecting the condition of women.

Religious faith is also a central theme in Parkes's work, becoming increasingly dominant following her conversion to Catholicism, most notably in her assembly of biographies in *Historic Nuns* (1898) and record of nineteenth-century religious revival in *The Flowing Tide* (1900). Later in her life, Parkes's works also became increasingly reflective. *A Passing World* (1897) and *In a Walled Garden* (1895) are collections of sketches covering a range of subjects from the Franco-German War to Catholicism to recollections of her many literary friends.

CRITICAL RECEPTION

Bessie Parkes's work in periodicals is significant, though her aim, as she explained, was not to create literary or monetary success but to provide a forum for "serious and sensible discussion." Never a radical, Parkes advocated moderate reform in her writings and editorial policies.

Contemporary reviews of Parkes's books were consistently favorable, although her later works received the most critical attention. Her aspirations to be a poet were subsumed by other interests; she published only a few poems after her three volumes of poetry in the 1850s, which were collected in *Fifty Years* (1904).

Because of her pioneering work and involvement in the mid-Victorian debates over the legal, economic, and social condition and rights of women, Parkes continues to be a significant figure for feminist historians, but she has been largely forgotten except for her editorship of *The English Woman's Journal* and her contributions to the mid-Victorian women's rights movement. Now that some of her poems with feminist themes are accessible in the recent anthologies of poetry by Victorian women, Bessie Parkes may begin to receive wider recognition and should prove an interesting addition to Victorian literature classes.

BIBLIOGRAPHY

The Bessie Rayner Parkes Collection is held at Girton College, Cambridge. *In a Walled Garden* (1895) and *Poems* (1852) are available on the Victorian Women Writers Project: http://www.indiana.edu/~letrs/vwwp/.

Works by Bessie Rayner Parkes (Belloc)

Poems. 1852.
Remarks on the Education of Girls. 1854.
Summer Sketches and Other Poems. 1854.
Gabriel. [A Poem]. 1856.
Ballads and Songs. 1863.
Essays on Woman's Work. 1865.
Vignettes: Twelve Biographical Sketches. 1866.
La Belle France. 1868.
Peoples of the World . . . With . . . Illustrations. 1870.
In a Walled Garden [Miscellaneous Essays]. 1895.
A Passing World. [Miscellaneous Essays]. 1897.
Historic Nuns. 1898.
The Flowing Tide (A Record of the Religious Revival on the Nineteenth Century). 1900.
Fifty Years. [Poems]. 1904.

Studies of Bessie Rayner Parkes (Belloc)

Herstein, Sheila R. "*The English Woman's Journal* and the Langham Place Circle: A Feminist Forum and Its Women Editors." In *Innovators and Preachers: The Role of the Editor in Victorian England.* Ed. Joel Wiener. Westport, CT: Greenwood Press, 1985.
———. "The Langham Place Circle and Feminist Periodicals of the 1860s." *Victorian Periodical Review* 26 (1993): 24–27.
Lowndes, Marie Belloc. *I, Too, Have Lived in Arcadia: A Record of Love and Childhood.* London: Macmillan, 1941.
Strachey, Ray. *The Cause: A Short History of the Women's Movement in Great Britain.* London: G. Bell & Sons, 1928.

May Probyn
(ca. 1856?–1909?)

Christine Swiridoff

BIOGRAPHY

Little is known of novelist and poet May Probyn beyond a few hints from her published works. Marion Thain has recently witten that she lived from 1856 or 1857 until 29 March 1909. She resided in Weybridge and London and was publishing from 1878 to 1895. Hers is a life yet to be unearthed, and based on the quality of her work, such excavation promises to be rewarding.

While poetry soon became her primary craft, Probyn's first published pieces were prose works. Her first work, *Once! Twice! Thrice! and Away! A Novel* (1878), an adventure novel, was followed by *Who Killed Cock Robin?*, "Robert Tresilian," a short story, and two volumes of poetry in the early 1880s. Although these earlier works went out of print, Probyn continued to be published in periodicals, including *Macmillan's Magazine, Month, and Littell's Living Age*, and in anthologies such as A. H. Mile's *The Poets and the Poetry of the Century* (1891). Probyn had contact with several other poets, including Vernon Lee,* A. Mary F. Robinson,* and Katharine Tynan.* She converted to Roman Catholicism in 1883, and her deepening religious beliefs are reflected in her subsequent, and final, volume of poetry, *Pansies* (1895).

MAJOR WORKS AND THEMES

In addition to her focus on religion in her later poetry, Probyn also addressed political and feminist issues and often reworked the themes other women poets of the age. Several of her more interesting poems deal with feminist themes. An interesting view of relationships between men and women is presented in "Ballade of Lovers," a biting commentary on the double sexual standard of the century and the differences between the sexes. In "The Model," the male artist produces his idea of woman as he poses and refashions his model to portray

Mary or Herodias, seeing only the image he creates, not the woman. "The Model" is similar to Christina Rossetti's* "In an Artist's Studio" in its critique of the male artist's gaze; however, unlike Rossetti's silent model, Probyn gives her artist's model a voice in this dramatic monologue. In its theme of the temporality of beauty and of love, "The Model" also resembles Elizabeth Siddal's* "The Lust of the Eyes," for Probyn's artist's model realizes the fleeting, ephemeral nature of her lover's affection now that her looks have altered.

Like many other Victorian women poets, May Probyn also addressed social and political issues. "The End of the Journey" tells the story of a fallen woman, a Native American, killed by the father of their child. Like the loyal yet readily discarded woman in "Ballade of Lovers," the woman in "The End of the Journey" clings at her lover's knee though he has seduced and abandoned her, and her love is rewarded with cruel death. Although "The End of the Journey" lacks the sharp political punch and social indictment of Elizabeth Barrett Browning's* "The Cry of the Children" and "The Runaway Slave at Pilgrim's Point," like these political poems, "The End of the Journey" provokes both the reader's anger at injustice and sympathy for the dispossessed and outcast.

As is common with Victorian poetry, love is a frequent subject of Probyn's poems. Rather than the romantic sentiment we find in works such as Elizabeth Barrett Browning's *Sonnets from the Portuguese*, most often love in Probyn's poems is decidedly unromantic: The speaker of "More Than They That Watch for the Morning" declares never to have loved; "Uncertainties" tells a tale of missed opportunities and a lost chance for love; the look of a lover fades as quickly as a bloom, according to "Blossom."

Many of the poems on love are excellent examples of Probyn's wit, and this humor is evident in the series of playful poems "Triolets." The pursuit of love turns humorously disastrous in "Masquerading," for the lover finds that he has unknowingly declared his love to the wrong woman. With the simple image of a foot on the hem of a dress, Probyn pokes fun at the disillusioned lovers in "I. Before" and "II. After," paired poems comparing the fantasies of new romance and the changes in a relationship after these initial passions fade. "Love in Mayfair" is even more satirical, for its speaker is a woman whose love is inspired only by a man's "twenty thousand a year."

CRITICAL RECEPTION

If we can judge by her publication in periodicals and anthologies and the song made of her poem "Come What Will, You Are Mine" after the turn of the century, Probyn's work did achieve a certain degree of popularity. However, she received little critical attention. Only one work—her last, entitled *Pansies*—was reviewed in major periodicals. This volume of ballads and religious poetry was received well by the critics, declared by a *Bookman* reviewer to be the "richest in colour" of "all the English Catholic poetry of the day" (1895). An *Athenaeum* reviewer found Probyn's ballads to be somewhat difficult to read but "distinctively interesting and impressive," considering her religious poems to "come nearer to achievement" (1895). "The Beloved" is compared to work by Christina Rossetti, though Probyn lacks her "culminating effect of emotion" according to this reviewer. In a time when Victorian women writers are being reconsidered and rediscovered, scholars may well turn to look again at Probyn.

BIBLIOGRAPHY

Probyn is included in *The Oxford Book of English Verse*, edited by Sir Arthur Quiller-Couch (Oxford University Press, 1939, 1961) but disappears, along with most other women poets, from *The New Oxford Book of English Verse* (Oxford University Press, 1972), edited by Helen Gardner. Currently, the best and most thorough coverage of Probyn's poetry is in *Victorian Women Poets: An Anthology*, edited by Angela Leighton and Margaret Reynolds (Blackwell, 1995).

Works by May Probyn

Once! Twice! Thrice! and Away! A Novel. 1878.
"Robert Tresilian. A Story." In *The Sea-Side Annual for 1880*. 1880.
Who Killed Cock Robin? [a tale]. 1880.
Poems. 1881.
A Ballad of the Road, and Other Poems. 1883.
Pansies; A Book of Poems. 1895.

Studies of May Probyn

Review of *Pansies; A Book of Poems*. *The Athenaeum* 105 (1895): 831.
Review of *Pansies; A Book of Poems*. *Bookman* 8 (1895): 90.
Thain, Marion. "May Probyn." In *Victorian Women Poets*. Ed. William B. Thesing. *Dictionary of Literary Biography*. Detroit: Gale Research, 1999. 199: 243–51.

Adelaide Anne Procter
(1825-1864)

Cheri Lin Larsen Hoeckley

BIOGRAPHY

Adelaide Anne Procter was born into the London literary scene on 30 October 1825. Her parents, Bryan Waller Procter and Anne Skepper Procter, lived at 25 Bedford Square with her mother's mother and stepfather, the influential judicial figure and friend of the Lake Poets, Basil Montagu. Her father also wrote poetry under the pseudonym Barry Cornwall. Family friends included many prominent Victorian writers—Charles Dickens, Thomas Carlyle, and Leigh Hunt, among others. Adelaide and her five younger siblings were a regular part of the lively household's circle of visitors and entertaining.

Adelaide fostered an early interest in poetry and intellectual pursuits. Her mother transcribed Adelaide's favorite lines of poetry so the child could carry them with her. She studied languages, piano, and Euclidean geometry. With two of her sisters, Procter converted to Catholicism in 1851. After her conversion, she supported Catholic charities, especially those for women. Her philanthropic interests also included many secular activities to advance women's rights. Procter's only journey out of England was an 1853 visit to her Catholic aunt in Turin. The journey prompted some lively letters home, which Dickens quoted at length in a posthumous introductory biography to her collected works. Her witty and vivacious letter writing voice permeates Procter's unpublished letters, as well.

In 1856 Procter and several friends—including Bessie Rayner Parkes,* Barbara Leigh Smith (Bodichon),* Matilda Hays, and Emily Faithfull—established offices in Langham Place to promote activities that fostered women's professional and educational opportunities. Befitting her talents and reputation as a poet, Procter contributed both verse and prose to the Langham Place publication *The English Woman's Journal*. She also edited *Victoria Regia*, a richly bound volume of poetry designed to demonstrate the capabilities of the Victoria Press,

Emily Faithfull's all-female printing house run from the offices. Her enthusiasm for Langham Place endeavors extended her involvement there well beyond literary activities. For instance, when the newcomer Jessie Boucherett proposed the organization that would become the Society for the Promotion of the Employment of Women, Procter offered her services as general secretary, devoting herself to clerical duties with an energy that prompted Boucherett to remember the poet as the Society's "animating spirit."

A battle with tuberculosis that began in her twenties finally diminished Procter's activity. In 1862 she visited Malvern hoping the famous waters would provide a cure. She returned to London and resumed writing and activism until the following year, when her illness demanded bed rest. Procter died at home attended by her mother and her sister on 2 February 1864.

MAJOR WORKS AND THEMES

Domestic themes, sentimental piety, and an interest in feminine duty most notably mark Procter's poetry. However, her artful combination of these traditional female concerns with an interest in women's rights often lends her verse a surprising complexity and ironic texture. Perhaps the strongest testimony to her adroitness at juxtaposing disparate themes lies in the difference between the periodicals that most sought her for publication. The educated and politically interested female readers of *The English Woman's Journal* regularly delighted in her poetry. Without any perceptible shift in style or content, she also wrote verse that Dickens sought out for his more traditional family-oriented periodicals *Household Words* and *All the Year Round*.

Procter's published collections reveal her ingenuity in combining her domestic, religious, political, and economic interests in verse. Her largest works are two separately published volumes, both titled *Legends and Lyrics*, and each compiling poems that appeared originally in periodicals. Procter also collected previously unpublished poems in *A Chaplet of Verses* to benefit the Catholic Women's Night Refuge, a London shelter for homeless women and children.

CRITICAL RECEPTION

In the decade following her death, Procter's popularity rivaled that of Tennyson. Dickens's introductory biography to *Legends and Lyrics* largely determined the critical vantage point on Procter for the next century; in fact, with the exception of the memoirs left by members of the Langham Place Circle, most essays on Procter until the 1970s are clearly derivative of Dickens's text, often quoting him verbatim. Dickens stresses Procter's filial loyalty and her personal piety and commitment to duty; although he was her periodical editor for nearly ten years, he offers no critical discussion of her work. This focus on Procter's appropriate femininity gained support through the early twentieth century when her poetry was largely preserved as hymns. Her most notable lyric is "The Lost Chord"—which Sir Arthur Sullivan set to music—but others survive in current hymnals.

Obituaries and reviews written by her Langham Place friends emphasize a trait that Dickens downplays: Procter's characteristic wit. That quality emerges unexpectedly in her poetry, often producing ironic complexity that allows her to critique the gendered status quo in verses extolling female submission. This wit, and its resultant archness in much of her poetry, has gained Procter recent critical attention. While not denying the prevalence of domestic and pietistic themes in her poetry, criticism of Procter at the end of the twentieth century is revealing the simultaneous sexual, political, and economic depths that frequently complicate her work.

BIBLIOGRAPHY

After lapsing out of print for most of the twentieth century, Procter's poetry is resurfacing as a staple figure in anthologies of nineteenth-century women poets such as *Nineteenth-Century Women Poets* (ed. Isobel Armstrong and Joseph Bristow [Clarendon Press, 1996]) and *Victorian Poetry and Poetic Theory* (ed. Thomas J. Collins and Vivienne Rendle [Broadview, 1999]).

Works by Adelaide Anne Procter

Legends and Lyrics. A Book of Verses. 1858.
Legends and Lyrics: A Book of Verses. 1861.
Victoria Regia: A Volume of Original Contributions in Poetry and Prose. Ed. Adelaide
        Anne Procter. 1861.
A Chaplet of Verses. 1862.

Studies of Adelaide Anne Procter

Armstrong, Isobel. "A Music of Thine Own: Women's Poetry—an Expressive Tradition?" In *Victorian Women Poets: A Critical Reader.* Ed. Angela Leighton. Oxford: Blackwell, 1996. 245–76.
Belloc, Bessie Rayner. *In a Walled Garden.* London: Ward and Downey, 1895.
Boucherett, Jessie. "Adelaide Anne Procter." *The English Woman's Journal* 13 (Mar. 1864): 17–21.
Dickens, Charles. "Introduction." *Legends and Lyrics: A Book of Verses.* London: George Bell and Sons, 1892. xiii–xxiv.
Gregory, Gill. "Adelaide Procter's 'A Legend of Provence': The Struggle for a Place." In *Victorian Women Poets: A Critical Reader.* Ed. Angela Leighton. Oxford: Blackwell, 1996. 88–96.
———. *The Life and Works of Adelaide Procter.* Brookfield, VT: Ashgate, 1998.
Lohrli, Anne. Household Words. *A Weekly Journal 1850–1859. Conducted by Charles Dickens.* Toronto: University of Toronto Press, 1973.

"Dollie" Radford
(1858-1920)

Christine Pullen

BIOGRAPHY

Caroline Maitland—or "Dollie" as she was always known—was born in Worcester in 1858. Her father, a master tailor, was a well-educated man, but he possessed an unconventional personality, and his maverick lifestyle created problems for his family. Her mother was just eighteen when Dollie was born. She subsequently gave birth to five more children, four of whom died in infancy or early childhood. She herself died when Dollie was nine years old. In her early teens Dollie attended a local boarding school but following her grandmother's death (and probable legacy) went to London to complete her education at Queen's College, Harley Street.

Radford's poetic ability was evident from an early age. At eighteen she won a local poetry prize for women. Her literary achievement attracted the attention of the eminent literary scholar Dr. F. J. Furnivall, who befriended her during her final year at Queen's College. Probably through her acquaintance with Furnivall, she was introduced to Eleanor Marx and rapidly became a favorite with the Marx family. It was while reading at the British Museum with Eleanor that she first encountered Ernest Radford. Dollie and Ernest Radford were married in 1883.

Like Eleanor Marx, Ernest Radford had become a member of H. M. Hyndman's Social-Democratic Federation. When the Federation split, Radford followed William Morris into the Socialist League. Dollie Radford, who also joined the League, was particularly drawn to Morris's utopian vision of socialism. Despite their initial happiness, ideological differences caused tension in the Radford's relationship, and financial worries compounded their difficulties, as Ernest Radford, having abandoned his career as a barrister, was attempting to earn a living by freelance lecturing and writing—mainly poetry. Dollie Radford also regularly contributed stories and poems to contemporary journals, and in 1891, her first volume of verse, *A Light Load*, was published. In 1892 Ernest Radford suffered a cataclysmic mental collapse from which he never fully recovered. From this time onward, Dollie Radford, who by now had three children, had to carry the additional burden of her husband's illness. In 1898 she suffered a further blow when Eleanor Marx committed suicide—as their mutual friend, the Jewish poet Amy Levy,* had done nine years earlier. Radford's only novel, *One Way of Love*, on the theme of the woman betrayed, appeared some months after Eleanor's death at the end of 1898.

From 1900 onward the Radfords lived in Hampstead, an area of London renowned for its artistic and literary associations. Despite their problems, they enjoyed a lively social life, and their wide circle of literary acquaintance included George Bernard Shaw, H. G. Wells, W. B. Yeats, and D. H. Lawrence. Dollie Radford provided the model for the character of Hattie Redburn in Lawrence's *Kangaroo*.

In 1900 Radford published *The Poet's Larder*, a collection of short stories on the theme of men and women. In 1907 *A Ballad of Victory and Other Poems* appeared. In 1910 her collected *Poems* were published. By this time her health was poor, and in 1911 she underwent major surgery. Ernest Radford died in September 1919, and his widow survived him by only five months, succumbing to cancer in February 1920.

MAJOR WORKS AND THEMES

A significant theme in Radford's poetic oeuvre is that of pain and loss. Even in her earliest and "lightest" collection, *A Light Load*, a somber note can be heard. However, as in her life, in her poetry, angst is always tempered by hope. Although not religious in the conventional sense, Radford possessed a deeply spiritual side to her character. She lived in an age when the simultaneous advance of socialism and feminism appeared to offer the prospect of a new dawn of freedom and equality. A utopian vision of the future is a consistent feature of the poetry written by women of the era, but all too frequently, utopianism stripped their verse of any degree of psychological veracity. In Radford's case, below the superficial surface, a more sophisticated analysis of the human psyche can be discerned.

Some of her most joyful and witty poems were those inspired by domestic life, for example, the poems dedicated "To My Children" and her tribute to the pleasures of a cigarette—"A Novice." It is in her later poems, such as "To the Caryatid" and "I Could Not Through the Burning Day," included in *A Ballad of Victory and Other Poems* and her final volume of *Collected Poems*, that the "darker" and more serious side of Radford's poetic vision emerges with greater clarity.

CRITICAL RECEPTION

On the whole, Radford's poetry was well received by her contemporaries, although she suffered somewhat from comparison with her husband. Notices that reviewed their work in conjunction, such as that in *The Athenaeum* of 21 September 1896, reflect the endemic sexual bias of the period. Among her literary admirers were Arthur Symons, William Archer, and Richard Le Gallienne. In 1902 Archer included a review of Radford's verse alongside that of many of her more distinguished compeers in his *Poets of the Younger Generation*. Like other critics, he readily acknowledged her abilities as a lyricist, describing the verse as "exquisite." However, unlike others, he also acknowledged her serious underlying message, paying tribute to her eloquent expression of the "resolute religion of her heart."

Unfortunately, as in the case of so many female poets of her era, Radford's poetry gradually fell out of favor and, consequentially, out of print. The limited selection of her poems included in present-day anthologies—generally samples of her more frivolous verse—represent her as little more than a lightweight sentimental lyricist. This contemporary view is summed up by Angela Leighton in her study *Victorian Women Poetry: Writing Against the Heart* (Harvester Wheatsheaf, 1992), in which she dismisses Radford's verse as a "sentimentalist model" of Victorian women's poetry. A comprehensive reevaluation of the entire spectrum of Radford's work is long overdue.

BIBLIOGRAPHY

A very small number of Radford's poems are included in present-day anthologies. Her "Soliloquy of a Maiden Aunt" is included in *The New Oxford Book of Victorian Verse* (ed. Christopher Ricks [Oxford University Press, 1987]) and three of her verses are featured in *Winged Words: An Anthology of Victorian Women's Poetry and Verse* (comp. Catherine Reilly [Enitharomon, 1994]). However, a number of her complete volumes, including *A Light Load* and *A Ballad of Victory and Other Poems*, are available on the Victorian Women Writers Project.

Works by Dollie Radford

A Light Load. 1891.
Songs for Somebody. 1893.
Goodnight. 1895.
Songs and Other Verses. 1895.
One Way of Love: An Idyll. 1898.
The Poet's Larder and Other Stories. 1900.
The Young Gardeners' Kalendar [sic]. 1904.
A Ballad of Victory and Other Poems. 1907.
Collected Poems. 1910.
"The Ransom: A Poetic Play." *Poetry Review* 6.2 (Mar.–Apr. 1915): 118–53.

The Goose Girl at the Well: A Fairy Play: By Louis Davis. Songs by Dollie Radford. n.d.

Studies of Dolly Radford

Reviews of *Songs and Other Verses. The Athenaeum* (21 Sept. 1895): 378; (25 Dec. 1897): 881; *Bookman* (Aug. 1895): 146.

Symons, Arthur. *Poets and Poetry of the Nineteenth Century: Christina G. Rossetti to Katherine Tynan*. Ed. Alfred H. Miles. London: George Routledge & Sons, 1907. 9: 409–12.

Charlotte Eliza Lawson Riddell
(1832–1906)

Andrew Maunder

BIOGRAPHY

Charlotte Eliza Lawson Riddell was born Charlotte Cowan on 30 September 1832 in Carrickfergus, Ireland, where her father was High Sheriff of County Antrim. After her father's early death, she and her invalid mother moved to Dundonald, County Down, the setting for her novel *Berna Boyle* (1884). In 1855, Cowan set off for London, hoping to make a living by writing. Her subsequent experience of the London publishing scene makes itself felt in such novels as *The Moors and the Fens* (1858) and *A Struggle for Fame* (1883). By 1857, she had married Joseph Hadley Riddell, variously described as a civil engineer and "inventor," and was energetically supplying the circulating libraries with a steady stream of works including *The Ruling Passion* (1857) and *The Rich Husband* (1858). Popular success came at the age of thirty-two with the best-seller *George Geith of Fen Court* (1864), followed by *The Race for Wealth* (1866).

For the next forty years Riddell had to write continually in order to earn enough to support her impecunious husband, who went bankrupt several times in the 1860s and left massive debts when he died in 1880. It is difficult to be exact about the number of novels and collected volumes of short stories. Like other women writers, Riddell used pseudonyms—"R. V. Sparling," "Rainey Hawthorne," "F. G. Trafford"—to disguise her identity. Nonetheless, from *Zuriel's Grandchild* (1855) to *Poor Fellow* (1902), there are at least thirty full-length works in addition to a considerable amount of writing for popular journals including *Once a Week, Temple Bar, London Society*, and also the *St. James Magazine* and *Home* (both of which Riddell herself edited in the 1860s). A power in the literary marketplace in the late 1860s and 1870s, her influence with publishers nonetheless began to wane in the 1880s. By the end of the century she was living a frugal and reclusive existence in Upper Halliford, Middlesex. In May 1901, Riddell was the first author to receive a yearly pension (£60) from the Society of Authors. She died at Hounslow on 24 September 1906.

Helen Black, who interviewed Riddell in 1893, attributed her success to her "noble self-reliant spirit" in the face of "continuous misfortune" (25). Riddell's own feelings about her career are perhaps best articulated in her portrayal of the aspiring author Glenarva Westley in *A Struggle for Fame*, an autobiographical novel that reveals a grim appreciation of the difficulties women faced in the literary world. Glenarva's career as a novelist is ill-fated because she cannot overcome the obstacles placed in her way by the male literary establishment: lack of encouragement, the humiliation of being publicly ridiculed and chastised, overexposed to the spotlight of female publicity, guilt at abandoning traditional female roles. As well as suggesting a general inability on the part of Victorian women to deal with literary celebrity, the novel also offers (through a series of thinly disguised pen portraits) a revealing insight into the workings of the mid-Victorian publishing industry.

MAJOR WORKS AND THEMES

Riddell's range as a writer was extremely wide, and her works encompass several categories: mystery, crime, the supernatural, domestic realism, romance, satire, and social criticism. However, her initial popular success rested alongside that of her contemporaries Mary Elizabeth Braddon* and Ellen Wood* on her contribution to the genre of the sensation novel in which respectability concealed shocking depths of unknown crime. As unsettling as Braddon in her suggestion that social and moral chaos infected the institutions of marriage and the home, Riddell echoes Wood in her use of a high-handed, moralizing narrator. Riddell's most successful novel was *George Geith of Fen Court* in which her interest in dark family secrets, in sin and suffering, in the fictionality of the feminine ideal and the corruption of commercial life are much in evidence. This fashionable "bigamy novel," which tells the story of a vicar turned city accountant plagued by financial disaster, bereavement, and a blackmailing wife who returns from the dead was also made into a successful play (1877). Almost as popular with readers was *Phemie Keller* (1866), a controversial story of the illicit love felt by a sixteen-year-old wife for her elderly husband's nephew. Endowed with considerable ability to invent good plots and dramatic situations, the passion and power of Riddell's stories appealed to Victorian readers looking for an escape from the boredom of their daily lives.

Although Riddell published several other sensation novels including *Above Suspicion* (1876), she was also known for her "city" novels, set in London's financial district. *City and Suburb* (1861) was followed by *The Race for Wealth* (1866), a moralistic story of the different approaches taken by two fortune-seeking brothers and *Far Above Rubies* (1867) in which a husband loses his family's estate by investing in a fraudulent limited liability company. *Mortmontly Estate* (1874) is a wish-fulfillment novel about a wife who saves her husband's paint manufacturing company from bankruptcy. The male heroes of these city novels are the "urban gentry": accountants, engineers, architects, chemists. The much admired insider's view of city life (the details were gleaned from Riddell's husband and from her own experiences of working as a clerk in the early years of their marriage) is embellished with many topographical details—a characteristic that prompted comparisons with Balzac. In their condemnation of material greed and unscrupulous financiers, the novels have something in common with Charles Dickens's *Little Dorrit* (1855–1857) and Anthony Trollope's *The Way We Live Now* (1874–1875); but works like *Too Much Alone* (1860) also place great stress on the thoughts and feelings of unhappy wives who are neglected, abused, or impoverished by their husbands or lovers. Other novels such as *Austin Friars* (1870) are of interest in their constructions of what might be termed women heroes: characters who appropriate all the characteristics usually ascribed to the male hero, including financial intelligence and resourcefulness.

CRITICAL RECEPTION

Riddell received a mixed reception from contemporary critics. In the account he gave of Riddell on 5 October 1861, the writer for the *Saturday Review* ranked her alongside George Eliot* as the leading exponent of literary realism. Riddell's *City and Suburb* "struck into a new vein of social life, and proved how full of interest modes of existence might be that had hitherto been held as too homely and prosaic for fiction." Comparisons with Charlotte Brontë* and Elizabeth Gaskell* followed. Among other reviewers, however, Riddell's critical stock stood less high. In an article appearing in the *Fortnightly Review*, in 1865, George Henry Lewes condemned her "extravagant sentimentality" and her lack of "truthfulness, insight and good sense." As a female sensation novelist or "passion novelist," as an 1866 reviewer for the *Spectator* termed her, Riddell was judged unladylike and contaminatory. Other contemporaries, such as Anne Thackeray Ritchie,* while agreeing that Riddell was "morbid" and "introspective," nonetheless recognized the appeal that her tales of neglect and unrequited passion held for a large number of women readers.

After her death in 1906 Riddell's reputation went into an eclipse. Her works went out of print and remain so. Helen Black's interview with Riddell in *Notable Women Authors of the Day* (1893) contains the fullest portrait of her. It is only recently that critics have begun to draw attention to both the popularity and the breadth of Riddell's achievements. Monica Correa Fryckstedt (1986) has situated Riddell in relation to the popular fiction market of the 1860s. John R. Reed has highlighted the closeness of Riddell's city novels to Victorian anxieties about business practices. An important perspective has also been provided by Patricia

Srebrnik (1994) in an analysis of Riddell's popular appeal to both male and female readers. As a writer, Riddell is far more influential than is generally acknowledged, but unlike the writers she can be seen to have influenced— Thomas Hardy, George Gissing, George Egerton,* Sarah Grand*—her achievements remain for the most part unacknowledged.

BIBLIOGRAPHY

None of Riddell's novels are currently in print.

Selected Works by Charlotte Eliza Lawson Riddell

Zuriel's Grandchild. 1855.
The Ruling Passions. 1857.
The Moors and the Fens. 1858.
The Rich Husband. 1858.
Too Much Alone. 1860.
City and Suburb. 1861.
George Geith of Fen Court. 1864.
Phemie Keller. 1866.
The Race for Wealth. 1866.
Far Above Rubies. 1867.
Austin Friars. 1870.
Mortmontly Estate. 1874.
Above Suspicion. 1876.
A Struggle for Fame. 1883.
Berna Boyle. 1884.
Poor Fellow. 1902.

Studies of Charlotte Eliza Lawson Riddell

Black, Helen C. *Notable Women Authors of the Day.* Glasgow: David Bryce and Son, 1893.
"City and Suburb." *Saturday Review* (5 Oct. 1861): 356–57.
Cross, Nigel. *The Common Writer: Life in Nineteenth Century Grub Street.* Cambridge: Cambridge University Press, 1985.
Ellis, Stewart M. *Wilkie Collins, Le Fanu and Others.* London: Constable, 1934.
Fryckstedt, Monica Correa. *On the Brink: Novels of 1866.* Uppsala: Studia Anglistica Upsaliensia, 1986.
Lewes, George Henry. "Criticism in Relation to Novels." *Fortnightly Review* 3 (1865): 352–61.
"Phemie Keller." *Spectator* (31 Mar. 1866): 361.
Reed, John R. "Friend to Mammon: Speculation in Victorian Literature." *Victorian Studies* 27 (1983–1984): 179–202.
Showalter, Elaine. *A Literature of Their Own: British Women Novelists from Brontë to Lessing.* Princeton: Princeton University Press, 1977.

Srebrnik, Patricia Thomas. "Mrs Riddell and the Reviewers: A Case Study in Victorian Popular Fiction." *Women's Studies* 23 (1994): 69–84.

Thackeray, Anne. "Heroines and Their Grandmothers." *Cornhill Magazine* 11 (1865): 630–40.

Anne Isabella Thackeray Ritchie (1837–1919)

Carol Hanbery MacKay

BIOGRAPHY

In her life and art, Anne Thackeray Ritchie's experience seems to parallel that of the Victorian woman, whose complexity was not always realized. Yet Ritchie negotiates the circumstance of apparently taking a secondary position to her novelist father William Makepeace Thackeray, turning it into a creative mode of actively connecting lives and retelling a woman's story. In this respect, her literary career consists of a female meditation on the perfunctory observation proffered by Thackeray in his *History of Pendennis* that we are all isolated universes walking around under our separate hats. Ritchie's writing evinces a subtly covert quality that reconciles sadness with conviction and renewal. Today's critic may begin with her father because both her age and our own have often reached her through him—and admittedly she seemed to place him paramount in her life—but Ritchie's extraordinary growth through transcending her father's accomplishments helps us to understand her style, her subject matter, and her outlook.

Raised by her grandmother and her father, shuttling between homes in Paris and London, Ritchie formed a very strong tie with her younger sister Harriet, known as "Minny." Their mother, Isabella Shawe Thackeray, suffered a severe case of postpartum depression shortly after Minny's birth, living out the rest of her years until her death in 1893 under private care. Those early years in Paris, restive under the care of her Calvinist grandmother, contributed to Anny's cosmopolitan, boundary-crossing perspective, which was augmented by frequent travel on the Continent with her father. She also grew up surrounded by Thackeray's literary friends, most especially the Brownings and the Carlyles and the Tennysons. Neither literature nor literary figures were foreign to Ritchie; their familiarity and her intimacy with them provided a privileged entrée into the world of letters. Often her father's first reader by virtue of serving as his amanuensis, Ritchie was accorded his respect and confidence as partner to his writing process.

Ritchie published her first essay, entitled "Little Scholars" (1860), under Thackeray's editorship in the *Cornhill Magazine*, but it had already been accepted as an anonymous submission by publisher George Smith. Along with publication of several more essays and sketches, she was soon a proud first novelist with serialization of *The Story of Elizabeth* (1862–1863). During these years, Thackeray even referred to her as likely to surpass him; recognizing her genius, he alternately guarded her possessively and wished her independent happiness. Needless to say, Ritchie was grief-stricken at his death in 1863, seeking solace with her sister in a cottage provided for them by family friend and photographer Julia Margaret Cameron on the Isle of Wight. But Ritchie never really stopped writing, first recording her feelings in her journal and letters, then returning to fiction (most notably *The Village on the Cliff* in 1867) and the articles that filled the pages of the *Cornhill*, the *Pall Mall Gazette*, and *Macmillan's Magazine* for decades to come.

Minny Thackeray's marriage to Leslie Stephen in 1867 hardly disrupted the sisters' household, as they simply moved him into their home, but Minny Stephen's untimely death in 1875 caused a second great void in Ritchie's life. (Stephen's second marriage, to the widowed Julia Duckworth, would produce another great writer, namely, Virginia Woolf.) Anne Thackeray surprised everyone two years later, however, by marrying her second cousin, Richmond Ritchie, some seventeen years her junior. Anne Thackeray Ritchie continued to write throughout marriage and motherhood (Hester was born in 1878, William in 1880), eventually leaving fiction behind for increased returns to the past through personal memoir writing—ostensibly about others but always figuring in her own subjective responses and intuitive explorations.

Ritchie's major undertaking in the 1890s was the series of biographical introductions to her father's works, which allowed her to abide by his proscription that she never write a sustained biography of him yet permitted her own opportunity to set the record straight about him and his creative sources. The early twentieth century saw her reissuing and expanding those introductions in a centenary edition (1910–1911), continuing to contribute reminiscences to a variety of periodicals, and receiving increased recognition for her endeavors. She was elected to the presidency of the English Association in 1912 (her inaugural address was entitled "A Discourse on Modern Sibyls"), although that year also marked the death of her husband. Ironically, the *Dictionary of National Biography*, founded by brother-in-law Leslie Stephen, only accorded Anne Thackeray Ritchie an entry as a footnote to Richmond and his career as a civil servant in the India Office. During World War I, Ritchie worked closely with one of Dickens's daughters to raise money for the war effort, but after a bomb blew out the windows of her London home, she retreated to Freshwater, to the cottage called "The Porch" on the Isle of Wight, where she died in the company of her daughter in 1919.

MAJOR WORKS AND THEMES

Perhaps Anne Thackeray Ritchie's chief contribution to literature inheres in her creative mode—her ability to recast or reconceive previous forms, turning them into something uniquely her own, notably demonstrated in her "domestic" fairy tales and biography operating equally powerfully as autobiography. In the fictional realm, her primary characters are women who have been passed by in some manner and yet make peace with themselves—much as Ritchie might have been eclipsed by Thackeray's reputation and yet made her own way. Intent on telling women's stories—in fiction and nonfiction, as part of a necessary corrective to literary history—Ritchie recognizes the significance of place as a critical tool, evidenced especially in her introductions to the works of Maria Edgeworth,* Mary Russell Mitford,* and Elizabeth Gaskell,* as well as in her biographical introductions to her father's canon. Her essays typically develop a theme and then embellish it through concentric layers, revealing implications and intricate relationships previously unnoticed or unacknowledged.

Ritchie's literary career commenced through an interplay between serialized fiction and shorter, more occasional sketches published in *Cornhill Magazine*. *The Story of Elizabeth* (1863) and *The Village on the Cliff* (1867) are rather remarkable early novels. The young Miss Thackeray's immediate contribution to novel writing seems to lie in dispersed focus, establishing either dual heroines or multiple subjectivities. Her style is quite impressionistic even in these initial "Victorian" works. Moreover, she takes conventional plotlines or romance outlines and twists them to create a sense of enlightened resignation in their resolutions. Next in succession is *Old Kensington* (1873), which convincingly invokes its neighborhood ambience as well as approaches stream of consciousness in presenting the thoughts of its female protagonist Dolly Vanborough. *Miss Angel* (1875) constitutes Ritchie's sole foray into historical fiction; based on the life of the eighteenth-century painter Angelica Kauffmann, this tale with its ready-made plot frees the author even more to explore narrative consciousness, in this case expertly handling both free indirect discourse and interior monologue.

By midcareer, Ritchie's short fiction and essays were being variously collected and reprinted in single volumes, such that eventually the firm of Smith, Elder could publish a set of ten volumes of "The Works of Miss Thackeray" (1875–1890). Most intriguing of this middle period's short fiction is Ritchie's rewriting of fairy tales in a contemporary, "domesticated" fashion. Tales like "Cinderella" and "Beauty and the Beast," collected in volumes like *Five Old Friends and a Young Prince* and *Bluebeard's Keys and Other Stories*, are rendered in the style of domestic realism, which is highly appropriate to Ritchie's muted conclusions. Her "happy endings" reveal themselves as tragicomedy, itself indicative of the author's covert feminism. Cinderella, for instance, achieves her marriage goal through the traditional virtues of passivity and obedience, but her unconscious reimaging of the self points up her growing dissatisfaction. In addition, character-narrator Miss Williamson stands both inside and outside the domestic circle, commenting on and self-consciously critiquing that boundary line. Ritchie thus subtly suggests that on their own terms, within a liberated confinement, women can begin to postulate mental and physical independence from the patriarchal order.

Ritchie's covert feminism can be seen in her choice of subject matter, in her fascination with the telling of women's lives. Her book-length study *Madame de Sévigné* (1881) for Margaret Oliphant's* series of "Foreign Classics for English Readers" testifies to a particularly happy conjunction. Here we recognize one expert letter writer evoking a seventeenth-century predecessor; observing that "[t]here is something almost of a great composer's art in the endless variations and modulations of this lady's fancy," Ritchie might as well be sketching a self-portrait. A similar project is at work in *A Book of Sibyls* (1883), which invokes the lives and accomplishments of four eighteenth-century foremothers— Anna Letitia Barbauld, Maria Edgeworth,* Amelia Opie, and Jane Austen.* Utilizing her novelist's ability to build empathetic layers on a specific reality, especially through setting, Ritchie dealt with each of these progenitors individually in four articles published over a twelve-year period before she perceived that the true form of her self-reflective tribute constituted a single volume.

Drawing on her fiction-writing and research skills, Ritchie increasingly turned to memoir writing, but her memoirs are particularly powerful because they so vividly recreate "living" conversations with the literary figures she had known since childhood. Her almost eidetic memory made it possible for her to reproduce actual dialogues, to reconstitute them in their precise milieu. Ritchie accomplishes this "life-writing" especially efficaciously in *Records of Tennyson, Ruskin, and Robert and Elizabeth Browning* (1892) and *Chapters from Some Memoirs* (1894). All of this memoir writing would seem to be a prelude to the writing of her biographical introductions to her father's works. Published first in 1898–1899, each of these thirteen extended introductions is mimetic of the work in question to some degree as well as rehearsing the creative impulses that generated it—thus providing Ritchie a review of some of her own key source points.

The empathetic whimsy that was so apparent in the life relations of Anne Thackeray Ritchie can just as readily be recognized today in the style and scope of her written words. As her subjective voice recounts these periods of fecundity, she reflects back on her own story and resources, which she had begun to playfully recall in the series of autobiographical essays that are perhaps more aptly titled in their American incarnation, *Chapters from Some Unwritten Memoirs*. This 1894 volume shows Ritchie gradually reexamining her literary roots in the context of her early experiences with such figures as Frederick Chopin, Charlotte Brontë,* and Fanny Kemble.* After having more completely laid her father's memory to rest in the revised and expanded centenary biographical introductions, Ritchie was then ready to dwell more openly on the subject of female friendship. In a sense she had already started this undertaking for some of her literary foremothers, but now, in her last decade, she does the same for contemporary female friends—colleagues such as Gaskell, Cameron, and Emily Tennyson—claiming them much more on her own terms of female configuration than through the memory-evoking patterns that her father's influence directed. In each of these accountings, Ritchie's immediate impressionism conveys her own personality to her readers as much as it does her subject matter, pulling her readership into her world just as she is reaching out to them.

CRITICAL RECEPTION

During her lifetime, Ritchie's work was extremely well received. She was regularly published in the *Cornhill* and other periodical outlets, sometimes anonymously, most frequently as Anne Isabella Thackeray or "Miss Thackeray." In this respect, her reputation was very much self-earned, only faintly tinged with nostalgic affection for her father's fiction. Her contemporary readership both appreciated and celebrated her unique voice. One budding young novelist, Rhoda Broughton,* cited with anticipatory delight her own growth into authorship, given that Miss Thackeray had published her first work when "a girl hardly older than myself." At the other end of the spectrum of fame and accomplishment, George Eliot* confided that the only fiction she took time to read was that of Anthony Trollope and Anne Thackeray, whose stories "I cannot resist when they come near me."

Ritchie's male critics were perhaps even more adulatory. Robert Louis Stevenson, for example, wrote a poem upon reading *A Book of Sibyls*. Another close acquaintance and admirer, Henry James, responded with near awe to her gift for discernment. In his 1884 essay on the art of fiction, he referred to her anonymously as "a woman of genius," citing especially her manner of invoking momentary mental images to germinate the seeds of her fiction—in this case, using a girlhood memory of growing up in Paris to infuse life into the early scenes of her first novel. Some of their correspondence at Harvard's Houghton Library has been reproduced by Winifred Gérin in the appendix to her biography of Ritchie.

At her death, Ritchie was acknowledged by an obituary article in the *Cornhill* for the wide range of her accomplishments and *literary connectiveness*, but despite the appreciations of fellow novelists like George Meredith and Thomas Hardy, the memory of her work was beginning to go into decline. Virginia Woolf astutely noted this trend in her *Times Literary Supplement* obituary, admitting in ironic eulogy that Ritchie will nonetheless be "the unacknowledged source of much that remains in men's minds about the Victorian age." Entitled "The Enchanted Organ," Woolf's more thorough tribute to her aunt-by-marriage occurred on the occasion of the publication of Ritchie's journals and diaries by her daughter Hester. The same spirit of loving respect for eccentric acumen had caused Woolf to cast her Aunt Anny in the character of Mrs. Hilbery in her novel *Night and Day* (1919).

After the publication of Woolf's review essay in 1924, over half a century elapsed before Ritchie began again to move toward center stage. By then most of her works were out of print, with only a few scholarly reprints making their way to libraries. But the 1980s saw a resurgence of interest in Ritchie, starting with Gérin's full-length biography and continuing with a series of articles by Carol Hanbery MacKay highlighting new ways of reading Ritchie's style and subject matter for their protofeminism.

Meanwhile, additional primary material has continued to surface, and the body of Ritchie's correspondence and manuscript holdings now resides at the University of London Library and at Eton College Library. Katherine Hill-Miller has recently focused on Ritchie's relationship to Thackeray as engendering "a blurred self-image"—a "dual sense of self as daughter and son"—while Manuela Mourão has been closely examining the nonfictional prose for its subtle subversion, uncovering the "guarded feminist interventions of a successful woman intellectual." Equally important are the introductions to reprints supplied by editors whose efforts make it possible for students of Ritchie to study and write about her work within a more informed scholarly community. As evidence of this trend, Ritchie's work is more frequently under discussion at academic conferences; see, for example, Robin Sheet's forthcoming analysis of "Bluebeard's Keys" as rejecting Thackeray's "brooding and sardonic pessimism at the same time that it refutes the misogyny of Victorian children's literature." Given Anne Thackeray Ritchie's profound significance as both a stylist and an early feminist, we can only hope that this recent revival of interest portends an increased and enthusiastic following.

SELECTED BIBLIOGRAPHY

Two early novels, *The Story of Elizabeth* and *Old Kensington*, have been reprinted and introduced by Esther Schwartz-McKinzie (Thoemmes Press, 1995), whereas three of her fairy tales—"Cinderella," "The Sleeping Beauty in the Wood," and "Beauty and the Beast"—have been reproduced, the first by Jack Zipes in *Victorian Fairy Tales: The Revolt of the Fairies and Elves* (Methuen, 1987), the last two by Nina Auerbach and U. C. Knoepflmacher in *Forbidden Journeys: Fairy Tales and Fantasies by Victorian Women Writers* (University of Chicago Press, 1992). The protofeminist essay "Heroines and Their Grandmothers" has been reissued by Andrea Broomfield and Sally Mitchell in their volume *Prose by Victorian Women: An Anthology* (Garland, 1996), while Ritchie's 1893 "Reminiscences" (introducing a volume of Julia Margaret Cameron's photographs entitled *Alfred, Lord Tennyson and His Friends*) has been abridged by Harriet Devine Jump in her collection *Women's Writing of the Victorian Period 1837–1901: An Anthology* (St. Martin's Press, 1999). And both *Madame de Sévigné* (1973) and *From the Porch* (1971) have existed in scholarly reprints for some time.

Works by Anne Thackeray Ritchie

The Story of Elizabeth. 1863.
The Village on the Cliff. 1867.

Five Old Friends and a Young Prince. 1868.

To Esther and Other Sketches. 1869.

Old Kensington. 1873.

Bluebeard's Keys and Other Stories. 1874.

Toilers and Spinsters and Other Essays. 1874.

Miss Angel [based on the life of artist Angelica Kauffmann]. 1875.

Madame de Sévigné. 1881.

Miss Williamson's Divagations. 1881.

A Book of Sibyls: Mrs Barbauld, Miss Edgeworth, Mrs Opie, and Miss Austen. 1883.

Mrs Dymond. 1885.

Records of Tennyson, Ruskin, and Robert and Elizabeth Browning. 1892.

Chapters from Some Memoirs. [Harper's: *Chapters from Some Unwritten Memoirs*.] 1894.

Introduction to the Biographical Edition of the *Works of William Makepeace Thackeray*. 13 vols. 1898–1899.

Blackstick Papers. 1908.

Biographical Introductions to the *Centenary Edition of the Works of William Makepeace Thackeray*. 26 vols. 1910–1911.

From the Porch. 1913.

From Friend to Friend. Ed. Emily Ritchie. 1919.

Thackeray and His Daughter: The Letters and Journals of Anne Thackeray Ritchie, with Many Letters of William Makepeace Thackeray. Ed. Hester Thackeray Ritchie. 1924.

The Two Thackerays: Anne Thackeray Ritchie's Biographical Introductions to the Centenary Edition of the Works of William Makepeace Thackeray. Introduction by Carol Hanbery MacKay and bibliographical apparatus by Peter Shillingsburg and Julia Maxey. 2 vols. 1988.

Anne Thackeray Ritchie: Journals and Letters. Ed. Abigail Burnham Bloom and John Maynard. Commentary and notes by Lillian F. Shankman. 1994.

Studies of Anne Thackeray Ritchie

Fuller, Hester Thackeray, and Violet Hammersley, comp. *Thackeray's Daughter: Some Recollections of Anne Thackeray Ritchie*. Dublin: Euphorion, 1951.

Gérin, Winifred. *Anne Thackeray Ritchie: A Biography*. Oxford: Oxford University Press, 1981.

Hill-Miller, Katherine C. " 'The Skies and Trees of the Past': Anne Thackeray Ritchie and William Makepeace Thackeray." In *Daughters and Fathers*. Ed. Lynda E. Boose and Betty S. Flowers. Baltimore: Johns Hopkins University Press, 1989. 361–83.

MacKay, Carol Hanbery. "Biography as Reflected Autobiography: The Self-Creation of Anne Thackeray Ritchie." In *Revealing Lives: Gender in Autobiography and Biography*. Ed. Marilyn Yalom and Susan Groag Bell. Albany: SUNY Press, 1990. 65–80, 217–20.

———. "Hate and Humor as Empathetic Whimsy in Anne Thackeray Ritchie." *Women's Studies: An Interdisciplinary Journal* 15.1–3 (1988): 117–33; rpt. in *Last Laughs: Perspectives on Women and Comedy*. Ed. Regina Barreca.

———. " 'Only Connect': The Multiple Roles of Anne Thackeray Ritchie." *Library Chronicle of the University of Texas*, n.s., 30 (1985): 83–112.

———. "The Thackeray Connection: Virginia Woolf's Aunt Anny." In *Virginia Woolf and Bloomsbury: A Centennial Celebration*. Ed. Jane Marcus. Bloomington: Indiana University Press and London: Macmillan, 1987. 66–95.

Mourão, Manuela. "Delicate Balance: Gender and Power in Anne Thackeray Ritchie's Non-Fiction." *Women's Writing* 4.1 (1997): 73–89.

Woolf, Virginia. "The Enchanted Organ." 1924. In *Collected Essays*. Ed. Leonard Woolf. New York: Harcourt, Brace, 1967. 4: 73–75.

Zuckerman, Joanne. "Anne Thackeray Ritchie as a Model for Mrs Hilbery in Virginia Woolf's *Night and Day*." *Virginia Woolf Quarterly* 13 (1973): 32–46.

A. Mary F. Robinson
(Darmesteter Duclaux)
(1857–1944)

A. I. Parejo Vadillo

BIOGRAPHY

Robinson was one of the most highly admired poets of her day. Her drawing room in London, and later in Paris, attracted the most important personalities of London's literary life, including Oscar Wilde, George Moore, Vernon Lee,* Walter Pater, Louisa S. Bevington,* and Augusta Webster.* Robinson's only sister and lifelong companion, Mabel, distinguished herself as a fiction writer, but it was Mary Robinson who soon became a leading figure in London's poetic circles. Her first volume of verse, *A Handful of Honeysuckle* (1878), quickly established her fame as the new Letitia Elizabeth Landon.*

Robinson's aesthetic ideas placed her within the Aesthetic Movement initiated by the Pre-Raphaelites and theorized by Pater. Her precise and melodious compositions gained the admiration of critics and poets alike. A deep lover of the Renaissance, a student of aesthetics and of the classics, she studied classical and literary studies at University College, London. In 1881, she published *The Crowned Hippolytus*, a very fine translation of Euripides that she dedicated to her friend A. J. Symonds. It was, however, her lesbian relationship with the aesthetic critic and writer Vernon Lee that involved her with the most important women writers of their time, including Emily Pfeiffer, Mathilde Blind,* and Amy Levy.* They traveled together to Oxford to stay with Mary Ward,* and every summer they rented a house in the countryside where they worked (Marandon 36).

In 1888, Robinson met James Darmesteter, and very quickly, to the astonishment of the literary world, they got engaged. Lee reacted very badly to the news and broke up their relationship. In 1889, Robinson married James, and they moved to Paris. Under her new name, Mary Darmesteter, she published another volume of verse, *Retrospect* (1893), and established herself as a literary critic. Between 1889 and 1894 (when James Darmester died suddenly), she published numerous volumes of literary criticism, both in French and English, and contributed poems and essays to periodicals such as *The Athenaeum, The Revue de Paris, Cosmopolis* and *The Fortnightly Review*. In 1901 she married Emile Duclaux (director of the Pasteur Institute) and became Mary Duclaux, a prose writer.

When Emile Duclaux died in 1904, Mary Duclaux continued her wide-ranging literary career. She stayed in France during World War I, and she published *Images and Meditations* (1923), a collection about the horrors of war. After the German occupation of Paris in World War II, the poet and her sister moved to Aurillac, where she died in 1944.

MAJOR WORKS AND THEMES

Robinson's most influential work lies within her poetry. Placed within the aesthetic circles of London, her writings responded to the theory of "art for art's sake." Influenced by Pater, Baudelaire, Gautier, and Vernon Lee, Robinson understood the world aesthetically, and poetry allowed her to transcend reality, as poems such as "The Idea," "Song," or "Art and Life" clearly and beautifully show. However the publication of *The New Arcadia* (1884) marked a change within her aesthetics, as she incorporated in her poems a study of the social tensions that affected fin de siècle England. Perhaps due to its highly polemical reception, Robinson returned to her earlier concerns in *An Italian Garden, a Book of Songs* (1886) and *Songs, Ballads and a Garden Play* (1888).

Both in her poetry and in her literary criticism Robinson questioned and challenged the sexual politics of England. Especially interesting are her critical biographies of women writers such as Emily Brontë (1883) and Margaret of Angoulême (1886), both for the "Eminent Women Series." She also supported young women writers such as Marie Lenéru or Colette in the twentieth century.

In addition to her primary focus on aesthetics, her interest in the past—in Greek studies, the Renaissance, and the Medieval (George Moore met her dressed in medieval costumes)—appears continuously in both her lyrical and narrative poetry and in her literary criticism.

CRITICAL RECEPTION

Robinson quickly established a reputation as a very crafted poet. Her poetry was widely reviewed in the major magazines and periodicals, and both critics and the public passionately read her work. The publication of *The New Arcadia*, however, changed this view completely. She was then described as an "aesthetic pessimist," and her description of rural England as a dystopia, the result of "her morbid fancy." By contrast, J. A. Symonds thought that this was one of the biggest achievements in contemporary poetry and suggested that Robinson send the volume to Walt Whitman, whom he greatly admired. Critics preferred Robinson's "dainty exquisiteness," as a critic of the *Spectator* put it, to her more social work. Her biographies were highly appreciated, and her work on contemporary French and English writing gained her a reputation as a distinguished critic.

In the preface to her *Collected Poems* (1902) Robinson wrote, "Mary Darmesteter has no longer a right to exist. As regards the English public Madame Duclaux has given no proof of her existence; she has, she hopes, before her a modest future of French prose, and leaves her English verses to Mary Robinson" (vii). It was this multiplicity of names, her displacement in Paris, and her change to prose that may account for Robinson's marginality. Today, her work has started to receive some interest, but very little attention has yet been given to her prose work.

BIBLIOGRAPHY

A few poems by A. Mary F. Robinson are available in recent anthologies of Victorian women's poetry such as *Victorian Poetry and Poetic Theory* (ed. Thomas J. Collins and Vivienne Rundle [Broadview, 1999]) and *British Women Poets of the 19th Century* (ed. Margaret Randolph Higonnet [Meridian/Penguin, 1996]).

Works by A. Mary F. Robinson

Poetry

A Handful of Honeysuckle. 1878.
The Crowned Hippolytus. Translated from Euripides, with new Poems. 1881.
The New Arcadia and Other Poems. 1884.
An Italian Garden, A Book of Songs. 1886; 1897.
Songs, Ballads and a Garden Play. 1888.
Retrospect and Other Poems. 1893.
The Collected Poems, Lyrical and Narrative. 1902.
The Return to Nature. Songs and Symbols. 1904.
Images and Meditations. A Book of Poems. 1923.

Fiction

Arden. 1883.

Criticism

Emily Brontë. Eminent Women Series. 1883.
Margaret of Angoulême, Queen of Navarre. Eminent Women Series. 1886.
The End of the Middle Ages. Essays and Questions in History. 1889.
Froissart. 1894. Translated from the French by E. F. Poynter. 1895.
The Life of Ernest Renan. 1898.
Grands Ecrivains d'Outre-Manche: Les Brontë, Thackeray, les Browning. 1901.
"Introduction." *Casa Guidi Windows*, by Elizabeth Barrett Browning. 1901.
The Fields of France. Little Essays in Descriptive Sociology. 1903.
The French Ideal: Pascal, Fénelon and other Essays. 1911.
Mme de Sévigné. Textes Choisis et Commentés. 1914.

A Short History of France, From Caesar's Invasion to the Battle of Waterloo. 1918.
Twentieth Century French Writers. Reviews and Reminiscences. 1919.
Victor Hugo. 1921.
Poèmes de Robert Browning. Précedés d'une Étude sur sa Pensée et sa Vie. 1922.
The Life of Racine. 1925.

Studies of A. Mary F. Robinson

Blain, Virginia. "Sexual Politics of the (Victorian) Closet; or, No Sex Please—We're Poets." In *Women's Poetry, Late Romantic to Late Victorian.* Ed. Isobel Armstrong and Virginia Blain. London: Macmillan, 1998. 135–63.

Marandon, Sylvaine. *L'Oeuvre Poétique de Mary Robinson 1857–1944.* Bordeaux: Pechade, 1967.

Parejo Vadillo, A. "New Woman Poets and the Culture of the *salon* at the *Fin de Siècle.*" *Women: A Cultural Review* 10.1 (1999): 22–34.

Reynolds, Margaret. " 'I Lived for Art, I Lived for Love': The Woman Poet Sings Sappho's Last Song." In *Victorian Women Poets. A Critical Reader.* Ed. Angela Leighton. London: Blackwell, 1996. 277–306.

Robertson, E. S. *English Poetesses.* London: Cassell & Co., 1883. 376–81.

Symons, Arthur "A. Mary F. Robinson-Darmesteter." *Poets and Poetry of the Century.* Ed. A. H. Miles. London: Hutchinson, 1891–1897. 8: 521.

Van Zuyle Holmes, Ruth. "Mary Duclaux: Primary and Secondary Checklists." *English Literature in Transition* 10.1 (1967): 27–46.

Christina Georgina Rossetti (1830–1894)

Alan S. Weber

BIOGRAPHY

Christina Georgina Rossetti was born in London on 5 December 1830 into an artistic and literary family of Italian émigrés. Much of what we know about Rossetti's life comes from two posthumous biographies by people who knew her well—Mackenzie Bell's 1898 study and her brother William Michael Rossetti's "Memoir" in the 1904 edition of her poems. A scattering of her letters, edited by William Michael, Janet Camp Troxell, and Lona Mosk Packer, has also survived. Widely acknowledged as one of the foremost Victorian poets, Rossetti, in addition to her several volumes of verse, also wrote nursery rhymes (*Sing-Song*), two collections of short stories (*Commonplace and Other Short Stories* and *Speaking Likenesses*, for children), a short story for girls (*Maude*), and six prose devotional works, including a commentary on the Apocalypse.

Rossetti's father Gabriele was a Neapolitan political exile who fled to London in 1824, where he married Frances Polidori, the daughter of the poet and translator Gaetano Polidori. Gaetano Polidori later printed Rossetti's first poems on his private press in 1847. Gabriele taught Italian at King's College School, where his sons Dante Gabriel and William Michael were educated. As was common in middle-class Victorian households, Rossetti and her sister Maria were educated at home by their mother, and both sisters worked briefly as governesses. As revealed in her early letters, a playful, competitive atmosphere tinged with ambition reigned among the Rossetti siblings, who were all encouraged in their artistic pursuits. In the 1850s, Rossetti assisted her mother in running an unsuccessful day school. Rossetti's brothers, along with James Collinson, Thomas Woolner, John Everett Millais, Holman Hunt, and Frederick Stephens, founded the Pre-Raphaelite Brotherhood (PRB) in 1848, a loosely defined association of painters, writers, and sculptors. Rossetti was instrumental in the early years of the PRB, although she was never fully admitted as a member of the circle. She contributed several poems, however, to the short-lived PRB journal *The Germ*. Her contributions were either unsigned or appeared under the pseudonym "Ellen Alleyn." Her artistic activities on the fringe of the PRB, as well as her own occasionally self-deprecatory remarks, reveal the straitened roles accorded to many female artists of the period.

Although she traveled abroad twice in the 1860s to northern France and Italy, most of her life was spent quietly in London. She was very close to her mother Frances, from whom she assumed a strict Anglican sense of propriety. She rejected two suitors during her lifetime, the painter James Collinson and the philologist and Dante translator Charles Bagot Cayley. Both men were probably declined as the result of religious scruples on Rossetti's part. Rossetti was troubled by poor health from her adolescence onward, and in 1871 she was diagnosed with Graves' disease (a type of hyperthyroidism). William Michael reports that she was an almost constant and "sadly-smitten invalid" from the ages of thirty to thirty-nine, yet she maintained "courage, patience, and even cheerfulness" during these years ("Memoir," *Poetical Works* 1).

Rossetti spent her later years caring for her maternal aunts and her mother Frances, who died in 1886. Her later work after *A Pageant and Other Poems* (1881) consisted primarily of works of devotional prose and biblical commentary, published by the Society for Promoting Christian Knowledge.

MAJOR WORKS AND THEMES

Literary critics writing after Rossetti's death have insisted on reading her poems biographically. Although this has led to many insights into her poetry, William Michael warns us that the full details of Rossetti's inner life were not shared even with her family. Her first recorded lines of juvenilia clearly reveal the impulsive and innovative nature of her early poetry:

> Cecilia never went to school
> Without her gladiator
>   ("Memoir," *Poetical Works* xlix)

This sort of playful bizarrerie, however, was increasingly to be replaced by an aesthetic of resignation, despondency, and suffering as she grew into adolescence. William Michael observed that "in innate character she was vivacious, and open to pleasurable impressions; and, during her girlhood, one might readily have supposed that she would develop into a woman of expansive heart, fond of society and diversions. . . . What came to pass was of course quite the contrary" ("Memoir," *Poetical Works* lxvi). The change from vivacious child to despondent young adult is perhaps mirrored in one of Rossetti's earliest compositions, *Maude* (written 1850), a story for girls that was not published until 1897. The story describes the accidental death of a young poet Maude, who epitomizes the guilt, doubt, and awkwardness of adolescence in addition to the elation and self-confidence of a precocious female artist assured of her gifts. Maude constantly fears, however, that she is placing her desire for fame and recognition before her love for God. In her recent edition of *Maude* (New York University Press, 1993), Elaine Showalter has wisely paired the piece with Dinah M. Craik's* *A Woman's Thoughts About Women* (1857). Craik believes that "the chief canker at the root of women's lives is the want of something to do" (64). This was both Maude's and Rossetti's concern: Victorian middle-class society, which prevented women from entering the traditional professions, had not made proper social, intellectual, or spiritual provisions for unmarried women. Much of the despondency and doubt of Rossetti's poems is perhaps rooted in her anxiety over her social role, since in rejecting her suitors she was also rejecting the standard Victorian position of women as wives. Poetry gave Rossetti something to do, but something that perhaps should not have been placed before marrying or even devoting oneself entirely to God, as her sister Maria was eventually to do by entering an Anglican sisterhood.

Another primary concern of Rossetti's poetry is of course religion, and specifically a dualistic conception of Christianity in which heaven and earth are very separate and very different worlds. In an 1870 letter to her brother Dante Gabriel, Rossetti writes, "It is not in me, and therefore it will never come out of me, to turn to politics or philanthropy with Mrs. Browning: such many-sidedness I leave to a greater than I, and, having said my say, may well sit silent" (Rossetti, *Family Letters* 31). Rossetti is commenting on her limited range of subjects (although this should not be seen as a fault); but "many-sidedness" also implies "multiplicity" for her—the pleasures and desires of the created world that distract and lead the soul away from God. This religious univocality sometimes exacerbated an overscrupulosity that did not escape her family, as when she pasted strips of white paper over offensive lines in her copy of Swinburne's poems.

Rossetti published two poems in *The Athenaeum* (14 and 28 Oct. 1848) and seven pieces in *The Germ* (1850), but her first major public recognition came in 1862 with the appearance of *Goblin Market and Other Poems*. The title poem "Goblin Market" has been frequently reprinted and anthologized and was well received by a workingman's society when first read in public by Rossetti's publisher Alexander Macmillan prior to its publication. It has been successful not only for its mastery of rhythmic techniques but also because it defies easy categorization. Part children's fairy story, part moral fable, and part allegory, the poem tells of two sisters, Laura and Lizzie, who are tempted to buy fruits from furry, ratlike Goblin men in the marketplace. With their chant "Come buy, come buy," the goblins tempt Laura to eat, after which she falls rapidly into decline. Lizzie then proceeds to the marketplace and defies the seductive goblins who smear the juices of their fruits on her unyielding face. Laura is restored by sucking the juices from Lizzie's face. The precise meaning of the goblins—whether temptation, the devil, or the world—as well as the function of the juices (which serve as a *pharmakon*, both a poison and antidote) has troubled critics.

Some of the overtly sexual imagery ("We must not buy their fruits: / Who knows upon what soil they fed / Their hungry thirsty roots?" [*Complete Poems* 1: 12, ll. 43–45]) disturbed Victorian critics but has fascinated modern ones. While "Goblin Market" warns against succumbing to the world and its temptations, at the same time it celebrates that world through its meter and tantalizing descriptions of the luscious goblin fruits. The poem therefore never slips into unnecessary preachiness or simple moral proscription.

The Prince's Progress and Other Poems (1866), her second volume of verse, is similar in design and scope to *Goblin Market*, but the characters are less engaging. The opening long narrative poem, also like "Goblin Market," consists of a moral fable concerning a Prince who obtains an Elixir of Life from an old Alchemist in order to make himself and his bride immortal. But after dallying on the way, he arrives to witness his bride's funeral and realizes that he has "loitered on the road too long, / [and] trifled at the gate" (*Complete Poems* 1: 108, ll. 483–84). The poem reveals the vague mysticism and conscious medievalism of other Pre-Raphaelite art.

The title piece of Rossetti's collection of short stories *Commonplace and Other Stories* (1870) tells of three unmarried women—Lucy, Catherine, and Jane Charlmont—and their financial and personal struggles after their father's death. In the story, Lucy Charlmont falls for Alan Hartley's shallow flattery, but after her obsession is past, she finds happiness in a worthier man, Arthur Tresham. Her sister Jane, on the other hand, marries for money. Stretching to 140 pages, the story certainly could have been developed into a full-length novel. One regrets that Rossetti never tried her hand in this genre, but her talent obviously lay more in the line of the sonnet and narrative poem. The story "Nick" in the collection is worthy of mention for its humorous use of the Midas tale: A jealous and stingy man becomes whatever he wishes for one hour. He only ends up tormenting himself, however, by wishing for mean and petty things. *Commonplace* demonstrates that Rossetti's work is not without humor, irony, or satire, as might appear from a cursory reading of her religious poetry.

Sing-Song: A Nursery Rhyme Book appeared in 1872, beautifully illustrated by Arthur Hughes, who also provided drawings for *Speaking Likenesses*. To judge their success as children's poems, one must of course consult younger readers shortly before bedtime. Her other work for children, the short story collection *Speaking Likenesses* (1874), opens with the story of Flora, who holds a disagreeable and selfish birthday party. Dismayed by the fights and turmoil, Flora falls asleep and in a dream joins an Alice-in-Wonderland party with a nasty birthday Queen and unpleasant guests who mirror her own disastrous party. After being starved and abused at the Queen's party (the boys and girls play "Hunt the Pincushion," with Flora as the pincushion), she awakes a much more enlightened child.

A Pageant and Other Poems (1881) begins with a brief verse pageant presenting the twelve months. The collection also contains the two sonnet sequences "Monna Innominata" and "Later Life," which is described as a "Double Sonnet of Sonnets." These two cycles demonstrate her mastery over the sonnet form. "Monna Innominata" artfully extends the already overelaborated Petrarchan tradition; the poems are written in the voice of the heroine, not the famed and immortal Beatrice and Laura, but unnamed ladies, "donne innominate."

Rossetti continued to write poetry throughout her life—new items were added to reprintings of her collected poems (*Poems: New and Enlarged Edition*, 1890) or reprinted from her prose works (*Verses*, 1893)—but after 1881 she turned her attention primarily to devotional prose. This shift may have been occasioned by the deaths of her brother Dante Gabriel in 1882 and her mother Frances Polidori in 1886, who was her religious model and guiding light. Also, Dante Gabriel had turned increasingly toward the sensual in his art, and Rossetti had directly witnessed the destructive effects of this turn. Her later emphasis on the afterlife and moral rectitude may have been an attempt to psychically rebalance the Rossetti family after Dante Gabriel's excesses and depressions. Victorian women were commonly expected to maintain the moral center of the family.

Rossetti commented on the Christian feasts in *Called to Be Saints: The Minor Festivals Devotionally Studied* (1881), although she claimed no originality for her exegesis. In 1883, she composed a similar work of commentary and exegesis on the decalogue entitled *Letter and Spirit: Notes on the Commandments*. In 1885, she compiled *Time Flies: A Reading Diary*, which provides a short religious meditation or poem for each day of the year as well as for the movable feasts. The work is similar in conception to her 1874 piece, *Annus Domini: A Prayer for Each Day of the Year, Founded on a Text of Holy Scripture*, a similar sort of spiritual diary. Her final work, *The Face of the Deep: A Devotional Commentary on the Apocalypse* (1892), was a lengthy verse-by-verse exposition of the last book of the New Testament.

CRITICAL RECEPTION

Rossetti has never fallen out of critical favor and is still the subject of book-length studies today. During her lifetime, her poetry was in general favorably reviewed in the leading literary journals. Algernon Charles Swinburne, Edmund Gosse, and Edmund Stedman all wrote laudatory estimations of her work. Her first volume of verse, *Goblin Market*, was anonymously reviewed in *The Athenaeum, British Quarterly Review*, and the *Saturday Review* and did receive some negative responses. While most critics praised the volume for its freshness, originality, and use of the fantastic, the reviewer of the *Saturday Review*, for example, complained that the story of the title poem was "flimsy and unsubstantial" (13 [24 May 1862]: 595–96).

Rossetti was frequently compared not only to Dante and Petrarch, whose influence she felt through her family's devoted scholarly interest in these poets, but also to the seventeenth-century English metaphysical poets Herbert, Crashaw, and Donne. The demanding tone and paradoxical self-effacing self-centeredness of Herbert is clearly echoed in such poems as Rossetti's "A Better Resurrection" (*Complete Poems* 1: 68):

> Cast in the fire the perished thing,
>   Melt and remould it, till it be
> A royal cup for Him my King:
>   O Jesus, drink of me. (ll. 21–24)

Although her subsequent volume of poetry, *The Prince's Progress* (1866), was not as well received as *Goblin Market*, she was gaining widespread recognition as a serious poet. *A Pageant and Other Poems* (1881), especially the "Monna Innominata" cycle of sonnets contained therein, secured her fame as an eminent national poet on par with Elizabeth Barrett Browning.* The anonymous reviewer of the *Literary World* (12 [5 Nov. 1881]: 395–96) believed that Rossetti's "Monna Innominata" sonnets surpassed Elizabeth Barrett Browning's *Sonnets from the Portuguese* in beauty of form and "self-forgetfullness of spirit." The comparison between Rossetti and Elizabeth Barrett Browning was to become commonplace in literary handbooks in the early part of the twentieth century.

With her death in 1894 came an outpouring of eulogies and retrospective evaluations of her poetic achievement, as well as an entry by Richard Garnett in *The Dictionary of National Biography* (1897). After the appearance of Mackenzie Bell's 1898 biography (the first major critical study of her life and poetry) and the "Memoir" of William Michael Rossetti (1904), much of the Rossetti criticism became biographical in nature in the early years of the twentieth century. At the centenary of her birth in 1930, a wealth of major studies and biographies appeared including works by Mary Frances Sanders, Edith Birkhead, Dorothy Margaret Stuart, and Eleanor Walter Thomas. From then onward, criticism of Rossetti followed general trends in literary criticism with a marked increase in Freudian and psychoanalytical critiques of her work in the 1940s and 1950s. Rossetti has been the focus of recent feminist criticism, with biographies, editions, and critical interpretations by Elaine Showalter, Angela Leighton, Kathleen Jones, and Jan Marsh. Antony Harrison's *Christina Rossetti in Context* emphasizes the need to read Rossetti in historical context, a critical methodology that he feels has been hindered by the New Critical bias in past Rossetti scholarship. *The Achievement of Christina Rossetti*, edited by David A. Kent, is a valuable collection of essays reassessing all aspects of Rossetti's life and work, and Edna Kotin Charles's *Christina Rossetti: Critical Perspectives, 1862–1982* surveys the major criticism of Rossetti.

BIBLIOGRAPHY

The standard modern edition of Rossetti's poetry, still in print, is *The Complete Poems of Christina Rossetti: A Variorum Edition*, edited by R. W. Crump in 3 volumes (Louisiana State University Press, 1979–1990).

Works by Christina Rossetti

Poetry

Verses. 1847 [private printing].
Goblin Market and Other Poems. 1862.
Poems. 1866.
The Prince's Progress and Other Poems. 1866.
Sing-Song: A Nursery Rhyme Book. 1872.
Goblin Market, The Prince's Progress, and Other Poems. 1875.
A Pageant and Other Poems. 1881.
Poems. New and Enlarged Edition. 1890.
Verses. Reprinted from *Called to Be Saints, Time Flies*, and *The Face of the Deep.* 1893.
New Poems, Hitherto Unpublished or Uncollected. Ed. William Michael Rossetti. 1896.
The Poetical Works of Christina Georgina Rossetti. Ed. William Michael Rossetti. 1904.
The Complete Poems of Christina Rossetti: A Variorum Edition. 3 vols. Ed. R. W. Crump. 1979–1990.

Prose

Commonplace and Other Short Stories. 1870.
Annus Domini: A Prayer for Each Day of the Year, Founded on a Text of Holy Scripture. 1874.
Speaking Likenesses. With Pictures Thereof by Arthur Hughes. 1874.
Seek and Find. A Double Series of Short Studies of the Benedicite. 1879.
Called to Be Saints: The Minor Festivals Devotionally Studied. 1881.
Letter and Spirit. Notes on the Commandments. 1883.
Time Flies: A Reading Diary. 1885.
The Face of the Deep: A Devotional Commentary on the Apocalypse. 1892.
Maude: A Story for Girls. Intro. William Michael Rossetti. 1897.
Maude. With Dinah Mulock Craik, "On Sisterhoods" and *A Woman's Thoughts About Women.* Ed. Elaine Showalter. 1993.
Selected Prose of Christina Rossetti. Ed. David A. Kent and P. G. Stanwood. 1998.

Letters

Harrison, Antony H., ed. *The Letters of Christina Rossetti.* 2 vols. 1999.
Rossetti, William Michael, ed. *Rossetti Papers 1862 to 1870.* 1903.
Rossetti, William Michael, ed. *The Family Letters of Christina Rossetti.* 1908.
Troxell, Janet Camp, ed. *Three Rossettis: Unpublished Letters to and from Dante Gabriel, Christina, William.* 1937.
Packer, Lona Mosk, ed. *The Rossetti-Macmillan Letters.* 1963.

Studies of Christina Rossetti

Bell, Mackenzie. *Christina Rossetti.* London: Burleigh, 1898.
Battiscombe, Georgina. *Christina Rossetti: A Divided Life.* London: Constable, 1981.
Charles, Edna Kotin. *Christina Rossetti: Critical Perspectives, 1862–1982.* Selinsgrove: Susquehanna University Press, 1985.

Crump, R. W. *Christina Rossetti: A Reference Guide*. Boston: G. K. Hall, 1976.

Harrison, Antony. *Christina Rossetti in Context*. Chapel Hill: University of North Carolina Press, 1988.

Jones, Kathleen. *Learning Not to Be First: The Life of Christina Rossetti*. New York: St. Martin's Press, 1991.

Kent, David A. *The Achievement of Christina Rossetti*. Ithaca: Cornell University Press, 1987.

Leighton, Angela. "Christina Rossetti." In *Victorian Women Poets: Writing Against the Heart*. London: Harvester Wheatsheaf, 1992. 118–63.

Marsh, Jan. *Christina Rossetti: A Writer's Life*. New York: Viking Penguin, 1995.

Mayberry, Katherine J. *Christina Rossetti and the Poetry of Discovery*. Baton Rouge: Louisiana State University Press, 1989.

Packer, Lona Mosk. *Christina Rossetti*. Berkeley: University of California Press, 1963.

Rosenblum, Dolores. *Christina Rossetti: The Poetry of Endurance*. Carbondale: Southern Illinois University Press, 1986.

Shove, Fredegond. *Christina Rossetti: A Study*. Cambridge: Cambridge University Press, 1931.

Stuart, Dorothy Margaret. *Christina Rossetti*. London: Macmillan, 1930.

Thomas, Eleanor Walter. *Christina Georgina Rossetti*. New York: Columbia University Press, 1931.

Waller, R. D. *The Rossetti Family 1824–1854*. Manchester: Manchester University Press, 1932.

Olive Schreiner
(1855–1920)

Elizabeth J. Deis

BIOGRAPHY

Olive Emilie Albertina Schreiner was born in Wittebergen, South Africa, the ninth child of missionary parents, Rebecca and Gottlob Schreiner. The Schreiners, Evangelical Lutherans, had been recruited for missionary service by the London Missionary Society, but because of disagreements with others in that society, Gottlob Schreiner was in service with the Wesleyans at the time of Olive Schreiner's birth. In 1865 her father was forced to leave the ministry; unable to establish a business, he went bankrupt, and the family scattered. Schreiner went to live with an older brother, and though she received formal education there for the first time, her free thinking was a source of conflict. From the early 1870s to 1881, Schreiner either stayed with siblings or worked as a governess; she also read many of the major philosophical, scientific, and literary works by nineteenth-century writers. She kept a journal throughout this period, composed numerous stories, and began writing (sometimes simultaneously) the three novels she produced in her lifetime—*Undine, The Story of an African Farm*, and *From Man to Man*. This period was the first of many difficult ones in Schreiner's life: In addition to her struggles with religion, she dealt with at least one unhappy romantic encounter, the onset of the asthma attacks that plagued her throughout her life, and the death of her father in 1876.

When Schreiner left South Africa for Great Britain at age twenty-six, her character was essentially formed. Highly emotional, she was plagued with a sense of loss, of loneliness and isolation, and of life's uncertainty, but she was also determinedly rational, a religious freethinker who was fascinated with modern science (her life's dream was to become a doctor). In addition to the loss of five siblings to early deaths, another formative element in Schreiner's youth was her difficult relationship with her mother, contrasting with a warmer relationship with her father. From her earliest years Schreiner was known for her overabundance of physical and intellectual energy (people often complained about her habit of pacing the floor and talking to herself for hours at a time, day or night) and her independence. These features combined to make her both fascinating and irritating to others. She was a strong-minded individualist who was at the same time insecure and desperate for the supportive love of others and for a clear sense of identity.

Schreiner spent her first years in Britain attempting to stay healthy long enough to begin medical training. However, her career as a writer was established when she brought her manuscript of *The Story of an African Farm* to Chapman and Hall in April 1882. George Meredith, then serving as a reader for the firm, liked the novel, and Chapman and Hall published *The Story of an African Farm* in 1883 (the author's name given as "Ralph Iron"). Schreiner immediately became a significant figure in London's intellectual and political circles, befriending in particular Eleanor Marx and Havelock Ellis. Schreiner and Ellis had a close relationship that may or may not have been sexual, as well, but the independent spirits and insecurities of both kept them from formalizing the relationship. In 1885, Schreiner became one of the original members of the Men and Women's Club. This club was supposed to provide a setting in which men and women could discuss sexuality openly, and its members did focus for some time on questions relating to the morality, economics, and causes of prostitution, but the ideas of Karl Pearson, later known for his studies of eugenics, dominated most of their discussions. Schreiner was attracted to Pearson, but when it became clear that her affection was not returned, and also that she was not able to stay healthy or to make real progress on her novel *From Man to Man*, Schreiner decided to return home, sailing at the time of the Dock Strike in 1889.

In South Africa, Schreiner struggled to find relief from her chronic asthma and to stay safe in a time of political turmoil. On 24 February 1894, following a brief return visit to England, Schreiner married Samuel Cron Cronwright, an ostrich farmer who shared her liberal political and religious views. Schreiner was attracted to Cronwright and also longed to have children. The only pregnancy Schreiner carried to term produced a baby girl who lived one day (30 Apr.–1 May 1895). Schreiner's personal life darkened from this point until her death. In 1898, her good friend Eleanor Marx committed suicide, and Schreiner's relationship with Cronwright became increasingly tense. They separated informally when Schreiner traveled to England in 1913. She returned to Cape Town alone in August 1920 and died at Wynberg, a suburb of Cape Town, in December.

The work that Schreiner did after the death of her baby was almost entirely political, and her impact, growing out of her writings and personal influence, was substantial. Schreiner had met Cecil Rhodes in 1890, and through much of the subsequent decade, she argued with and ultimately campaigned against him and the combination of capitalism and racism he promoted. Schreiner was also an active supporter of women's causes during this period, attempting through the work of the Women's Enfranchisement League to win votes for women in the Cape Colony. She published her most influential nonfiction work, *Woman & Labour*, in 1911. After Schreiner's death, acting as her sole heir and the executor of her estate, Cronwright published both *From Man to Man*, which Schreiner felt that she had never completed, and *Undine*, which she had not wished to publish. He did, however, inter her remains as she had wished: in a sarcophagus with her baby and her pet dog at Buffels Kop, overlooking the South African Karoo.

MAJOR WORKS AND THEMES

The Story of an African Farm, Schreiner's best-known and most successful work, portrays the anguish of religious doubt as well as the difficulties for women created by institutionalized sexism. Set almost exclusively on an ordinary Boer farm, the novel treats a particular community in a particular national context and thus conveys political themes, as well. The lives of the characters in this work are stunted by oppression: Children are treated ruthlessly by their elders; farmworkers are persecuted by property owners; black house servants and travelers are ignored, teased, or assaulted by whites; women of all ages and races are restricted physically, intellectually, and emotionally by men.

In this difficult context, two cousins, Emily and Lyndall, grow into adulthood. The girls share a close and loving relationship, although Emily is a conventional young woman who looks forward to getting married and settling down on the farm that she will inherit, whereas Lyndall is restless, strong-minded, and independent. Lyndall is passionately devoted to books and ideas but eventually comes to realize the difference between high ideals and reality, particularly in the lives of women. Through Lyndall's discussions of sociopolitical issues as well as religion and spirituality, and the narration (by means of allegory) of the young farmworker Waldo's spiritual growth, the novel argues that suffering and isolation are basic to human experience, though exacerbated by sociopolitical conditions. Only by radically modifying one's expectations of success or gratification can one manage to live anything like a happy life. Beyond this simple fact, there is much that mortals will never understand.

The themes in this novel, like those developed in Schreiner's other works, reflect the author's own experiences but also parallel ideas central to middle and late Victorian culture, although Schreiner was much more direct and outspoken about issues that concerned her than were her English contemporaries. Schreiner's religious doubts—doubts compounded by her commitment to rational thought and her understanding of modern science—parallel those of Alfred Tennyson or Matthew Arnold, but she resolved those doubts to some degree by adopting Herbert Spencer's ideas about limitations inherent in the human condition. Schreiner's novels reflect her unhappy relationships with men, due at least in part to the oppression of Victorian sexism, issues also treated by English writers such as Elizabeth Barrett Browning,* George Eliot,* and George Meredith, although Schreiner's direct attacks on marriage in *African Farm* made women worldwide feel that Schreiner alone had articulated the complicated resentments and needs that haunted them. Finally, like Mary Wollstonecraft and John Stuart Mill, Schreiner pointed out the links between social problems and women's limited opportunities—links connecting gender, economics, and politics—particularly in *From Man to Man* (which treats these issues as they relate to marriage and prostitution) and *Woman & Labour.*

CRITICAL RECEPTION

The combination of acclaim and denunciation that characterized the critical reception given Schreiner's *African Farm* in the 1880s was typical of the reception of all of her works in her lifetime; given the intellectually radical temper of the fin de siècle, positive responses outweighed negative ones. Admirers of this novel usually responded to its frank questioning of the bases for religious belief, the strong feminist ideas voiced by Lyndall, the examination of the effects of British colonialism, or the evocative descriptions of South Africa. Conservative reviewers expressed horror because of their negative views of those same issues.

Schreiner's reputation has benefited both from the recent efforts of feminist critics to rediscover a tradition of women's writing and from recent studies of colonial literature; since the mid-1970s, Schreiner and her works have been treated in numerous books and articles. Fortunately for researchers, the biography by Ruth First and Ann Scott is extraordinarily thorough and well written. Finally, *African Farm* and other works by Schreiner are interesting to new formalist critics because of their inventive form: Schreiner's extensive descriptions of setting and her dreamy allegorical passages interrupt but parallel the plot, whereas characters designated as "strangers" appear in the works, play key roles, and then disappear. Olive Schreiner's independent personality, her clearheaded and pragmatic feminism, and the special perspective her South African roots gave her combine to make her a unique, fascinating, and important figure in literary history.

BIBLIOGRAPHY

Only three of Schreiner's works—*The Story of an African Farm, Dream Life and Real Life*, and *Woman & Labour*—have been reprinted, and only *The Story of an African Farm* (Peter Smith, 1975; Penguin, 1985; Dover, 1998; Oxford, 1999) is generally available.

Works by Olive Schreiner

The Story of an African Farm. 1883.
Dreams. 1890.

Dream Life and Real Life. 1893.
Trooper Peter Halket of Mashonaland. 1897.
An English South African's View of the Situation. Words in Season. 1899.
Woman & Labour. 1911.
Stories. Dreams and Allegories. 1923.
Thoughts on South Africa. 1923.
The Letters of Olive Schreiner. 1924.
From Man to Man Or, Perhaps Only. . . . 1926.
Undine. 1929.
A Track to the Water's Edge: The Olive Schreiner Reader. Ed. Howard Thurber. 1973.
An Olive Schreiner Reader: Writings on Women and South Africa. Ed. Carol Barash. 1987.
Letters: Vol. I. 1871–99. Ed. Richard Rive. 1988.
My Other Self: The Letters of Olive Schreiner and Havelock Ellis, 1884–1920. Ed. Yaffa C. Draznin. 1993.

Studies of Olive Schreiner

Beeton, Ridley. *Olive Schreiner: A Short Guide to Her Writings.* The Human Sciences Research Council Publication No. 51. Cape Town: Howard Timmins, 1974.

Berkman, Joyce Avrech. *The Healing Imagination of Olive Schreiner: Beyond South African Colonialism.* Amherst: University of Massachusetts, 1989.

———. *Olive Schreiner: Feminism on the Frontier.* St. Alban's: Eden Press Women's Publications, 1979.

Brandon, Ruth. *The New Women & the Old Men: Love, Sex, and the Woman Question.* London: HarperCollins, 1991.

Cronwright-Schreiner, S[amuel] C[ron]. *The Life of Olive Schreiner.* London: Unwin, 1924.

First, Ruth, and Ann Scott. *Olive Schreiner: A Biography.* New Brunswick: Rutgers University Press, 1980.

Horton, Susan R. *Difficult Women, Artful Lives: Olive Schreiner and Isak Dinesen, in and out of Africa.* Baltimore: Johns Hopkins University Press, 1995.

Monsman, Gerald. *Olive Schreiner's Fiction: Landscape and Power.* New Brunswick: Rutgers University Press, 1991.

Parkin-Gounelas, Ruth. *Fictions of the Female Self: Charlotte Brontë, Olive Schreiner, Katherine Mansfield.* New York: St. Martin's Press, 1991.

Van Wyk Smith, Malvern, and Don Maclennan, eds. *Olive Schreiner and After: Essays on Southern African Literature, in Honour of Guy Butler.* Cape Town: David Philip, Publisher, 1983.

Walkowitz, Judith R. "Science, Feminism and Romance: The Men and Women's Club 1885–1889." *History Workshop: A Journal of Socialist and Feminist Histories* 21 (1986): 37–59.

Anna Sewell
(1820–1878)

Robert Dingley

BIOGRAPHY

Anna Sewell was born in 1820 into a Quaker family living at Great Yarmouth in Norfolk. Her father pursued a somewhat unstable business career. The principal influence on Anna's personal and intellectual development was her mother, Mary, who began, at the age of sixty, a career as the author of ballads and tracts for the laboring classes. When Sewell was fourteen, she sustained a serious fall that left her permanently lamed; she became thereafter a semi-invalid, unable to limp more than a few yards, subject to periods of mental prostration, and reliant on a pony and trap for transport. Much of her early adult life was passed at various English and European spas, but these quests for health were unsuccessful, and after the late 1850s, Sewell was more or less confined to her parents' successive houses. In 1871 her health declined further, and she began writing what she described in her diary as "the history of a horse." *Black Beauty*, her only book, was finally completed in 1877, and Sewell died the following year.

MAJOR WORKS AND THEMES

In writing *Black Beauty*, Sewell was consciously working within the conventions of the tract fiction in which her mother specialized, a fiction designed to further the moral education of children and working-class readers by presenting simple narratives in which virtues like thrift, temperance, and knowing one's place receive their just reward. Thus, just as Mary Sewell chronicled in *Patience Hart's First Experiences in Service* (1862) the exemplary career of an industrious housemaid, so her daughter wrote the autobiography of a horse who earns honorable retirement after a life of hard work and dutiful obedience. But if Beauty embodies most of the qualities of an ideal subordinate, many of his owners fail to honor their reciprocal responsibilities toward him, and Sewell's book is designed to promote a more compassionate treatment of working horses (which were liable, in the nineteenth century, to be treated as dispensable extensions of industrial machinery). Within this general reformist program, moreover, Sewell foregrounds for condemnation the widespread use of the bearing-rein, a form of harness designed to give carriage horses a "showy" appearance but that caused great suffering. Because it seeks to target a specific abuse, *Black Beauty* can thus be illuminatingly aligned not only with tract literature but also with much mainstream fiction of the 1860s and 1870s—with the novels of Charles Reade or Wilkie Collins, for example, who often constructed narratives around social and moral problems that they felt required remedial legislative action.

Sewell's moral concern was not, however, confined to the brutal treatment of horses. Although there had been earlier animal autobiographies written specifically for children, *Black Beauty* also draws on a sophisticated adult tradition of ironic narrative in which a nonhuman observer provides ingenuous commentary on human society. Beauty observes his various possessors with an innocent outsider's eye, and his naive perceptions intermittently offer a challenging critique of the "superior" species. The old horse Captain, for example, has taken part in the Charge of the Light Brigade; when Beauty asks what the fighting was about, Captain replies: "[T]hat is more than a horse can understand, but the enemy must have been awfully wicked people, if it was right to go all that way over the sea on purpose to kill them." The indictment of war is the more forceful for Captain's trusting assumption that human beings must know best. Again, the cruelty with which her grooms and masters treat the spirited mare Ginger lends itself to feminist reading as a veiled transposition of the violence inherent in gendered sexual relationships between humans (a point developed by Coral Lansbury, who draws analogies between Ginger's maltreatment and the sadistic practices depicted in Victorian pornography). Moreover, Beauty's status as the exploited servant, or slave, of a "higher" order can be seen to reflect other power relationships in nineteenth-century culture—between employers and workforce in industrial capitalism, for example, and between imperial colonists and subject populations. Beauty's color is no accident (Sewell's book is clearly modeled on Harriet Beecher Stowe's *Uncle Tom's Cabin*, 1852), and the most poignant moments in the narrative occur when Beauty, while recognizing the inevitability of servitude, nevertheless longs wistfully for freedom.

CRITICAL RECEPTION

Black Beauty became a best-seller almost immediately, and early reviews testified to its instructive value both for children and for adults professionally concerned with the care of horses. The book enjoyed still wider currency when it was distributed, both in Britain and America, by associations concerned with the prevention of cruelty to animals. But while Sewell's book has generated countless sequels and imitations (not to mention several film treatments), it has attracted little critical attention. Specialists in children's literature like Margaret Blount and Peter Hollindale have situated it within the generic conventions of juvenile fiction, and the feminist critics Ruth Padel and Coral Lansbury have explored the book's displaced treatment of sexuality and gender issues. Robert Dingley has examined the book's intertextual relationship with *Uncle Tom's Cabin*, and Susan Chitty remains Sewell's only serious biographer.

BIBLIOGRAPHY

The best edition of *Black Beauty* is the World's Classics text with notes and a perceptive introduction by Peter Hollindale (Oxford University Press, 1992), but *The Annotated Black Beauty*, edited by Ellen B. Wells and Anne Grimshaw (J. A. Allen, 1989), should also be consulted for its wealth of information on horses and their treatment in the nineteenth century.

Work by Anna Sewell

Black Beauty: His Grooms and Companions: The Autobiography of a Horse. 1877.

Studies of Anna Sewell

Blount, Margaret. *Animal Land: The Creatures of Children's Fiction.* London: Hutchinson, 1974.
Chitty, Susan. *The Woman Who Wrote Black Beauty: A Life of Anna Sewell.* London: Hodder and Stoughton, 1971.
Dingley, Robert. "A Horse of a Different Color: *Black Beauty* and the Pressures of Indebtedness." *Victorian Literature and Culture* 25 (1997): 241–51.
Lansbury, Coral. *The Old Brown Dog: Women, Workers and Vivisection in Edwardian England.* Madison: University of Wisconsin Press, 1985.
Padel, Ruth. "Saddled with Ginger: Women, Men and Horses." *Encounter* 55.5 (Nov. 1980): 47–54.
Stibbs, Andrew. "*Black Beauty*: Tales My Mother Told Me." *Children's Literature in Education* 22 (1976): 128–34.

Mary Wollstonecraft Shelley
(1797–1851)

Elizabeth C. Denlinger

BIOGRAPHY

What did it mean to be Mary Shelley? Historically it has meant that, even more than many other women writers, she has been identified by her relationships: daughter to Mary Wollstonecraft, author of *A Vindication of the Rights of Woman*, and to William Godwin, best known for his novel *Caleb Williams*; and lover and wife of Percy Bysshe Shelley, the Romantic poet with whom, at sixteen, she eloped. Until recently, her name was associated almost exclusively with her first novel, *Frankenstein, or the Modern Prometheus* (1818). The reality of her life, of course, was more complex.

Mary Wollstonecraft Godwin was born on 30 August 1797 in London. Her parents, opposed on principle to marriage, and yet both well aware of the prejudice that attached to unmarried mothers and their children, had undergone the ceremony the previous March. Mary Wollstonecraft survived her second daughter's birth by only ten days, and the infant Mary, as well as her half sister Fanny, the offspring of another connection, were left to William Godwin to raise. For four years he managed alone; however, in 1801 he remarried, to a widow named Mary Jane Clairmont who had two children of her own.

In the writings of Mary Shelley, what emerges most clearly from this early experience is the fierce and nearly solitary dyad of father and daughter, a literary pairing that may be taken as half autobiography and half fantasy. A stepmother was neither a comfort nor a welcome interruption to the four-year-old Mary Wollstonecraft Godwin. Shelley's second novel *Matilda*, written in 1819, takes the figure to an emotional extreme in dealing with a father's incestuous desire for his daughter. The motif of the father and daughter pair alone in the world reappears in Shelley's novel *Lodore* (1835) as well as in short stories, for example "The Mourner" (1829), in which a young woman blames herself for her father's drowning.

Mary Godwin was never sent to school; her first lessons were received from her father, and later a governess was hired. William and Mary Jane Godwin ran a business publishing and selling children's books for which the young Mary, aged ten, wrote an extension of a comic ballad by Charles Dibdin, "Mounseer Nongtonpaw." It was her first published work, and popular enough to be pirated.

When she was sixteen, Mary Godwin met Percy Bysshe Shelley for the second time, and the two fell in love. Shelley was a follower of Godwin's political philosophy, which emphasized rationality, benevolence, and the capacity for moral improvement; he was also becoming a primary source of financial support for the impecunious philosopher. Although married at this point, rather unhappily, to the former Harriet Westbrook, Shelley was never one to pass up what he wanted. Within weeks he and the philosopher's daughter had eloped—taking with them Claire Clairmont,* the stepsister with whom Mary Godwin would have an ambivalent relationship for the whole of their lives. They went to Europe, where the Napoleonic Wars had recently ended; this honeymoon without a wedding resulted in Mary Godwin's first book, *History of a Six Weeks' Tour through a part of France, Switzerland, Germany, and Holland* (1817). A fairly conventional travel narrative, this work reveals little of the emotion of the adventure, but reading it along with the journal that the pair kept together provides both a romantic and a Romantic picture of the trip.

The years of her connection with Percy Shelley, 1814 to 1822, were the crucial ones in Mary Shelley's life. Composed of travels between Europe and Britain, they were punctuated by babies and books, of which many more of the latter than the former reached full growth; for while Percy Florence Shelley, born in 1819, lived to be the comfort of Mary Shelley's later life, none of the three other children to whom she gave birth lived to be four.

Yet it would be a misrepresentation to write of this period as defined solely by grief, however much this came to be the dominant note of after-years. More quotidian anxieties beset Mary Godwin and Percy Shelley as well, the most important of these being lack of money, brought on partly by the easygoing spending habits of a young man brought up to wealth but also by Shelley's continued financial support of William Godwin and other friends.

During this period, the summer of 1816 must be noticed, as it has become one of the most famous seasons in literary history. Bringing with them their child William, as well as Claire Clairmont, Shelley and Mary Godwin returned to Europe, this time spending the summer in Switzerland, near the shores of Lake Geneva. Claire Clairmont was the reason for the choice of venue and for the trip itself: While still in London she had introduced herself to George Gordon, Lord Byron, became, briefly, his mistress, and was already pregnant with their child. The scene of Byron, his physician Polidori, Percy Shelley, Claire Clairmont, and Mary Godwin trying their hands at ghost stories has become an emblem of talents gathered: two poets, one famous and one still obscure; the youngest of the group still a girl, finding unlooked-for powers in her disturbing dream.

The trio of Percy Shelley, Mary Godwin, and Claire Clairmont returned to England but did not settle in London, since all were determined to conceal Claire Clairmont's pregnancy and, later, her child. Relations with the Godwins were strained and at times broke off altogether; both William and Mary Jane Godwin had condemned the elopement, whereas William Godwin continued to accept, and even demand, money from Percy Shelley. Fanny Imlay Godwin, Mary's half sister, was placed in the uncomfortable position of being Godwin's messenger. The reasons for her suicide in October 1817 are obscure, although the sense of being unwanted seems to have been one of them. Mary Godwin's and Percy Shelley's grief was compounded by Harriet Westbrook Shelley's suicide by drowning in December of that year, and both the Shelleys—as they became very shortly afterward—were stricken with grief and guilt.

In the spring of 1818 the Shelleys traveled to Italy with Claire Clairmont, her child Allegra, and their children William and Clara Everina. They would spend the rest of their married life there, writing, studying languages, keeping abreast of the Italian and Greek struggles for national independence, visiting galleries and ruins, and creating their own circle of English, Italian, and Greek friends.

The series of deaths that had begun in England continued here. Their relentlessness would have been a horror for anyone and later made its way, on a larger scale, into *The Last Man* (1826). William and Clara died months apart in 1819, and Claire Clairmont's daughter Allegra in 1822. William Shelley's death was especially agonizing for the couple, and their differing reactions caused a breach in their marriage; the birth of Percy Florence in November 1819 did not heal it. The fault was widened by Mary Shelley's emotional withdrawal and Percy Shelley's flirtations with other women. In time relations might have been mended, but in July 1822, Percy Shelley, his friend Edward Williams, and a cabin boy, sailing a small boat Byron had named the *Don Juan*, were caught in a squall. Percy Shelley had never learned to swim; it may not have been of any use anyway, since all aboard were drowned.

Mary Shelley was now, at the age of twenty-four, a widow with a small child, Percy Florence. Paralyzed with grief, she did not leave Italy for nearly a year. When she returned to England, she was pressed by financial trouble. Sir Timothy Shelley, Percy Florence's grandfather, refused her any support for the boy unless she relinquished custody, an impossibility for her. The situation changed later, but Sir Timothy kept them on such a short supply of money that Mary Shelley could not afford not to write. She turned out book reviews, short stories for the popular annuals, volumes of brief biographies, and novels. Determined to make a safe life for Percy Florence, she sent him to Harrow, one of the oldest and most established of the public schools.

Gradually she remade a social world: She repaired her relationship with Godwin, remaining close to him until his death in 1836, and formed deep friendships with a number of women. Shelley was romantically linked with several men— never in such a way as to injure her reputation (among them John Howard Payne and Washington Irving)—but did not remarry. When Percy Florence, who had become an amiable and conventional young man, did marry, he chose a young woman who was entirely congenial to his mother; they remained a close family until Mary Shelley's death, at the age of fifty-three, from a brain tumor.

MAJOR WORKS AND THEMES

Mary Shelley's first novel, *Frankenstein* (1818), remains her best known. The number and variety of interpretations critical, theatrical, and cinematic to which it has been subject are the best illustration of its continuing power over readers and viewers. The idea of a man creating another life carries with it all the tension and imaginative possibility immanent in a powerful trope: Victor Frankenstein's work is both like and unlike childbirth, conjures up visions of a science both omnipotent and monstrous, looks forward to cloning and backward to alchemy.

It is worth noting that *Frankenstein* starts from a "what-if" clause, as does Shelley's third published novel *The Last Man*. (*Valperga*, a novel of the Guelphs and the Ghibellines, intervened.) This is now perhaps, after *Frankenstein*, the most frequently read of Shelley's novels. Written after Byron's death in 1824, *The Last Man* takes as its subject a plague that kills off the human race. The melancholia pervading the book, and the care given to its characters, among which are portraits of both Byron and Percy Shelley, allowed Mary Shelley a vehicle of expression for her grief that is equally engaging to the reader. Today, of course, incurable plagues are even more compelling, and the novel has gained a resonance that it could not have had in 1826.

Lodore and *Falkner*, the two novels that Shelley produced during or just before the reign of Queen Victoria,* are not of as much critical interest as *The Last Man, Frankenstein*, or *Matilda*. This is partly because they do not appeal so immediately to late-twentieth-century critical preoccupations as subjects such as eschatology, incest, and artificial life forms do; however, as Victorian works they are interesting in that they engage with subjects that were the material of many rather sensational late-eighteenth-century novels: sensibility, duelling, abduction. Indeed, while Mary Shelley's life is one of the emblematic ones of British Romanticism, her novels—except for *Frankenstein* and *The Last Man*—are often more easily explained in the cultural terms of the periods preceding and following. Thus, while Elizabeth Raby in *Falkner* braves social condemnation by going to visit her father in prison (he has confessed to having abducted and inadvertently caused the death, many years before, of the mother of the man with whom she is in love), her filial piety is one of the hallmarks of Victorian social belief, as is the happy ending in which all parties are reconciled.

Students of the period would be well advised to read Shelley's final travel work, *Rambles in Germany and Italy in 1840, 1842, and 1843* (1844). This work, recounting Shelley's travels with Percy Florence and friends of his from Cambridge, gives a strong sense of the transformation that was wrought in her between her first tragic sojourn in Italy and her return there. If one of the characteristics of the Victorian era in Britain is an emphasis on prolonged mourning, Shelley is certainly a sterling example, sensing herself deservedly to be "the companion of the dead" who, "while yet very young" had "reached the position of an aged person, driven back on memory for companionship with the beloved," for whom "the shades that gathered round the scene were the realities" (*Rambles* 1: 140).

All of her books after the death of Percy Bysshe can be interpreted as partaking of grief work, in some degree, and the *Rambles* is notable because that grief has become a specifically Victorian one: long, gentle, clung to for its own sake, and this time unclothed in fiction. If others have defined Mary Shelley by her relations, she defined herself largely by their loss.

CRITICAL RECEPTION

A moderately successful novel in Shelley's lifetime, *Frankenstein* was then, as now, her most popular work. Its first adaptation for the stage took place soon after she returned from Italy, and there have been so many since then (the monster has truly a life of its own) that Steven Earl Forry has devoted a whole book, *Hideous Progenies*, to them.

However, as had been her mother's fate, Mary Shelley's works sank into obscurity soon after her death. There was no shortage of biographies, but interest in her life with Percy Shelley was far greater than that given to her novels. Since the late 1970s, however, Shelley's work has gained ever-greater numbers of readers and critics. With most of her novels are available in paperback, Mary Shelley has taken her place next to her husband in the canon. For this she has academic feminism to thank. Shelley was not an outspoken feminist herself; the vilification her mother underwent posthumously, the quiescence of any organized women's movement during her lifetime, and her own reluctance to put herself into the public gaze for any cause may all be adduced as reasons for this. However, as she wrote in 1838, "If I have never written to vindicate the Rights of women, I have ever befriended women when oppressed" (*Journals* 557). The longing for the comfort of the bourgeois family and the politically liberal tenor of her novels have made them attractive choices for critics like Anne Mellor and Betty T. Bennett. *Frankenstein* and *The Last Man*, both presenting the most powerful appeals to readers' imaginations, will remain the most accessible of her novels, but Victorianists will find interest in her later works, both fiction and nonfiction, that have yet to be the focus of extended critical work.

BIBLIOGRAPHY

All of Mary Shelley's major works are in print. A great deal of information is available at Resources for the Study of Mary Shelley's *Frankenstein*: http://www.georgetown.edu/ irvinemj/english016/franken/franken.html.

Selected Works by Mary Shelley

History of a Six Weeks' Tour through a part of France, Switzerland, Germany, and Holland. 1817.
Frankenstein, or the Modern Prometheus. 1818.
Valperga. 1823.
The Last Man. 1826.
The Fortunes of Perkin Warbeck, a Romance. 1830.
Lodore. 1835.
Falkner. A Novel. 1840.
Rambles in Italy and Germany in 1840, 1842, and 1843. 1844.
Matilda, a.k.a. *Mathilda* (written 1819–1820). 1959.
Shelley and His Circle. Ed. Kenneth N. Cameron, Donald H. Reiman, and Doucet Devin Fischer. 8 vols. 1961–.
Collected Tales and Stories. Ed. Charles E. Robinson. 1976.
The Letters of Mary Wollstonecraft Shelley. Ed. Betty T. Bennett. 3 vols. 1980–1988.
The Mary Shelley Reader: Containing Frankenstein, Mathilda, Tales and Stories, Essays and Reviews. Ed. Betty T. Bennett. 1991.
The Journals of Mary Shelley, 1814–1844. Ed. Paula Feldman and Diana Scott Kilvert. 1995.
Maurice, or, The Fisher's Cot. Ed. Claire Tomalin. 1998.

Studies of Mary Shelley

Bennett, Betty T. "Finding Mary Shelley in Her Letters." In *Romantic Revisions.* Ed. Robert Brinkley and Keith Hanley. Cambridge: Cambridge University Press, 1992. 291–306.
———. *Mary Wollstonecraft Shelley: An Introduction.* Baltimore: Johns Hopkins University Press, 1998.
Botting, Fred. "Reflections of Excess: *Frankenstein,* the French Revolution and Monstrosity." In *Reflections of Revolution: Images of Romanticism.* Ed. Allison Yarrington and Kelvin Everest. London: Routledge, 1993. 26–38.
Conger, Syndy M., Frederick S. Frank, and Gregory O'Dea, eds. *Iconoclastic Departures: Mary Shelley After Frankenstein: Essays in Honor of the Bicentenary of Mary Shelley's Birth.* Madison, NJ: Fairleigh Dickinson University Press, 1997.
Fisch, Audrey A., Anne K. Mellor, and Naomi Schor, eds. *The Other Mary Shelley: Beyond Frankenstein.* New York: Oxford University Press, 1993.
Forry, Steven Earl. *Hideous Progenies: Dramatizations of Frankenstein from Mary Shelley to the Present.* Philadelphia: University of Pennsylvania Press, 1990.
Garrett, Margaret Davenport. "Writing and Re-Writing Incest in Mary Shelley's *Mathilda.*" *Keats-Shelley Journal* 45 (1996): 44–60.
Gilbert, Sandra, and Susan Gubar. *The Madwoman in the Attic: The Woman Writer and the Nineteenth-Century Literary Imagination.* New Haven: Yale University Press, 1979.
Hill-Miller, Katherine. *My Hideous Progeny: Mary Shelley, William Godwin, and the Father-Daughter Relationship.* London: Associated University Presses, 1995.
Levine, George, and U. C. Knoepflmacher, eds. *The Endurance of Frankenstein: Essays on Mary Shelley's Novel.* Berkeley: University of California Press, 1979.

McWhir, Anne. "Teaching the Monster to Read: Mary Shelley, Education, and *Frankenstein*." In *The Educational Legacy of Romanticism*. Ed. John Willinsky. Waterloo, Ontario: Wilfrid Laurier Press, 1990. 73–92.

Mellor, Anne K. *Mary Shelley: Her Life, Her Fiction, Her Monsters*. New York: Methuen, 1988.

Palacio, Jean de. *Mary Shelley dans son oeuvre: Contribution aux études Shelleyennes*. Paris: Klincksieck, 1969.

Poovey, Mary. *The Proper Lady and the Woman Writer: Ideology as Style in the Works of Mary Wollstonecraft, Mary Shelley, and Jane Austen*. Chicago: University of Chicago Press, 1984.

St. Clair, William. *The Godwins and the Shelleys*. New York: Norton, 1989.

Sunstein, Emily W. *Mary Shelley: Romance and Reality*. Boston: Little, Brown, 1989.

Elizabeth Eleanor Siddal (1829–1862)

Rhonda Brock-Servais

BIOGRAPHY

William Michael Rossetti, chronicler of the Pre-Raphaelite Brotherhood (PRB) wrote the earliest biography of Elizabeth Siddal. However, Rossetti was ambivalent about his sister-in-law and subtly devalues her life in an effort to add to the Dante Rossetti legend. Elizabeth Siddal was born on 25 July 1829 to working class parents. An apocryphal story tells of her youthful discovery of poetry; the paper used to wrap butter contained verses by Tennyson and became a prized possession. She was "discovered" by the PRB in 1850—a milliner's assistant. Traditionally, Siddal has been portrayed as innocent and passive. In the most famous story of her career, Siddal modeled Ophelia, floating in a bathtub warmed by candles, which went out; she remained there uncomplaining. She may have become secretly engaged to Rossetti in 1851, but little supports such an early date. By 1852, she posed only for Rossetti, shortly thereafter becoming his "student." Impressed by her work, John Ruskin offered to buy each completed piece. Although Siddal favored this arrangement, Rossetti negotiated an annual income in exchange for whatever she might produce. During the late 1850s she was frequently sick and alone. Most biographers assert that illness and addiction to laudanum made her distant, difficult, and dependent. Early in 1860, Rossetti was called to what was believed to be her deathbed, where he promised to marry her immediately upon recovery. The wedding took place on 23 May 1860. A stillborn daughter followed a year later. On 11 February 1862, she died of a laudanum overdose. The inquest ruled her death "accidental," despite rumors of suicide. Stories of her bleak final years only add to the Dante Rossetti myth. Swinburne, a dissenting voice and a good friend, protested that she was never the tragic figure found in her portrayals. Strangely, her biography does not end with death; in an extravagant show of grief, Rossetti placed the sole copy of his poems in her casket. In 1869 he had her body exhumed to retrieve them.

MAJOR WORKS AND THEMES

Siddal's entire poetic corpus consists of fifteen poems and a few fragments. Her subject matter (both poetic and artistic) came from old ballads and medieval tales; dominant themes are alienation, guilt, early death, and the impossibility of earthly love. "Early Death," "He and She and Angels Three" (reminiscent of Rossetti's "Blessed Damozel"), and "Lord May I Come?" all feature death and the meeting of lovers in an afterlife. Although her themes are common to the entire Pre-Raphaelite movement, they become unique because of the strength of the female voice. The speakers of "Love and Hate" and "The Passing of Love" display anger and rebellion—emotions practically unheard of in the Victorian woman. Two poems, "Gone" and "The Lust of the Eyes," have male speakers— challenging standard gender assumptions. Both speakers relate to women only through exteriors. The speaker of "Gone" can only recall his lost "tender dove" through associations with material objects. "The Lust of the Eyes" is a harsh look at masculine attitudes and begins, "I care not for my lady's soul." Given Siddal's supposed innocence, these are startling observations concerning gender relations in society and the PRB.

"At Last," "Lord May I Come?," and "A Year and a Day" all express a deep pain with life. "A Year and a Day" is accepted as a retelling of the Ophelia story. Oscar Wilde encountered it while in prison and declared it "A-I." In these lines Ophelia voices her thoughts—something unusual in standard Victorian representations. The poem opens with an ironic treatment of spring. Despite the renewal surrounding her, the speaker desires only escape from this world. Because of her lover's desertion, life has become a burden. In the first stanza, she expresses the excruciating slowness with which her life proceeds—every hour is painful to her. In the second stanza, she lies still in the grass and feels it fold over her body as if she were already in her grave. The third stanza finds her trying to articulate, more precisely, her mental condition. It is linked to the fourth through the water imagery of tears, rain, and a river. The rushing river and the birds, reminders of the fullness of life, serve only to intensify her unhappiness. In the final stanza, a "silence falls upon [her] heart." She envisions herself lying in the grass "Like beaten corn of grain." A husk of her former self, her kernel, her ability to give love, has been beaten out of her. The violence of this final image is somewhat shocking, given the peaceful death usually associated with Ophelia.

CRITICAL RECEPTION

William Rossetti published Siddal's complete works between 1895 and 1906. They were omitted from the Pre-Raphaelite canon and treated as curiosities—

confessional and derivative. In 1965 Oswald Doughty called Siddal's poems, "plaintive little lock-sick verses, all pathos and self-pity" (*A Victorian Romantic: Dante Gabriel Rossetti* [Frederick Muller, 1949]). Despite the admiration of several important cultural contemporaries (Ruskin, Browning, Tennyson, Swinburne, and Wilde), she was dismissed. However, like the work of other women poets, Siddal's poetry is being reevaluated. In 1980 Berg wrote, "Her poetry is certainly superior to other peripheral Pre-Raphaelites who have received far greater attention." Until recently, studies on the PRB and Rossetti regarded her primarily as burden or inspiration, but several new biographies dispute the characterization of her as a passive and self-abnegating person. Further, contemporary critics assert her poetry is more meaningful than a ploy to win back Rossetti's love. For many people, Elizabeth Siddal symbolized Pre-Raphaelitism, but that is true only of her exterior. The PRB, despite its worship of women, had few women artists and poets. The interior life of women, they imply, does not matter, but Elizabeth Siddal, in her poetry, demonstrates quite clearly that it does.

BIBLIOGRAPHY

All of Siddal's works have now been published, and current Victorian women's and Pre-Raphaelite anthologies usually contain selections: *Nineteenth-Century Women Poets* (ed. Isobel Armstrong and Joseph Bristow [Clarendon Press, 1996]), *An Anthology of Pre-Raphaelite Writing* (ed. Carolyn Hares-Stryker [New York University Press, 1997]), and *The Pre-Raphaelites* (ed. Jerome Buckley [Academy Chicago, 1986]).

Works by Elizabeth Siddal

Poems and Drawings of Elizabeth Siddal. Ed. Roger Lewis and Mark Samuel Lasner. 1978. (This book also contains original publication information on each of her poems.)

Studies of Elizabeth Siddal

Berg, Maggie. "A Neglected Voice: Elizabeth Siddal." *Dalhousie Review* (1980): 151–56.
Cherry, Deborah, and Griselda Pollock. "Woman as Sign in Pre-Raphaelite Literature: A Study of the Representation of Elizabeth Siddal." *Art History* 7.2 (1984): 206–27.
Donaldson, Sandra. " 'Ophelia' in Elizabeth Siddal Rossetti's Poem 'A Year and a Day.' " *Pre-Raphaelite Review* (Nov. 1981): 127–33.
Fredeman, William. *Pre-Raphaelitism: A Biblio-critical Guide*. Cambridge: Harvard University Press, 1965.
Hunt, Violet. *The Wife of Rossetti: Her Life and Death*. London: Bodley Head, 1932.
Marsh, Jan. *The Legend of Elizabeth Siddal*. London: Quartet, 1989.
———. *Pre-Raphaelite Sisterhood*. New York: St. Martin's Press, 1985.

Rossetti, William Michael. "Dante Rossetti and Elizabeth Siddal." *Burlington Magazine* 3 (1903): 273–95.

———. *Dante Gabriel Rossetti: His Family Letters with a Memoir*. London: Ellis and Elvey, 1895.

Edith J. Simcox
(1844-1901)

Constance M. Fulmer

BIOGRAPHY

Edith Jemima Simcox was a remarkable scholar, social reformer, and writer who was born on 21 August 1844 and died on 15 September 1901. She was totally devoted to improving the circumstances of women's lives. With her friend Mary Hamilton she started a shirtmaking cooperative, Hamilton and Company, in the Soho District of London, in order to employ women and to offer them decent working conditions. She was actively involved in the establishment of trade unions, served as a representative to the International Trade Union Congress on at least eight occasions, worked to promote women's suffrage, and was elected to the London School Board. She was well acquainted with the leaders of these movements and with many other outstanding intellectual, political, and literary figures.

Simcox was an ardent admirer of the novelist George Eliot* and wanted everything that she accomplished to serve as a tribute to Eliot. She was frequently one of the callers at Eliot's Sunday afternoon gatherings of the literary elite and recorded in her *Autobiography of a Shirtmaker* detailed accounts of the conversations that took place on these occasions.

From age twenty-five Simcox was a regular contributor to the major periodicals using the pseudonym "H. Lawrenny" as well as her own name and was the author of three books. She often delivered public speeches as a part of her work in establishing trade unions and supporting women's causes.

Her two older brothers, George Augustus and William Henry, were educated at Oxford University and were distinguished authors. Edith Simcox made her home with her mother, Jemima Haslope Simcox, and lovingly cared for her during her final illness. The two women are buried together.

In her personal journal, which she called *Autobiography of a Shirtmaker* and in which she made entries more or less regularly from May 1876 to January

1900, she mentions that as a child she preferred boy's games and that she and her brothers were often referred to as "the three boys." She alludes to her "young manhood," describes herself as "half a man," frequently refers to her androgyny, and makes many interesting observations on gender issues.

All of her writings attest to the depth and diversity of her knowledge; she translated German texts and considered compiling a German dictionary. At the Trade Union Congress in Paris, she made an extemporaneous speech in French; she read Latin and Italian and refers to teaching herself Greek and Dutch. She spoke with authority on topics related to ethics, science, art, and literature. She wanted all of her work to "have a social bearing" and to be useful in "setting the world to rights."

MAJOR WORKS AND THEMES

The *Autobiography of a Shirtmaker* is a repository of facts and feelings for anyone who is interested in Victorian literature and society. In her journal Simcox describes both her day-to-day activities and her private reflections including her reactions to her associates, her writing and other accomplishments, and her disappointments—all from the perspective of a woman working successfully in public roles usually reserved for men.

Her books are *Natural Law: An Essay in Ethics*, in which she formulates her own system of ethics; *Episodes in the Lives of Men, Women, and Lovers*, a series of twelve fictional vignettes; and *Primitive Civilizations, or Outline of the History of Ownership in Archaic Communities*, in which she describes the acquisition of property in ancient Assyria, Egypt, China, and Babylon.

She was a regular contributor to the *Academy, Fraser's Magazine, Fortnightly Review, Nineteenth Century, Macmillan's Magazine, North British Review, Saint Paul's*, and *Longman's*. In the final journal entry on 29 January 1900, she mentions writing a *Nineteenth Century* article that is titled "The Native Australian Family." Her periodical writings reflect her fervent attempts to ensure the social and moral well-being of men, women, and children and reveal her enthusiasm for women's issues and for economic and educational reform and her extensive knowledge of an amazingly wide variety of topics.

CRITICAL RECEPTION

Edith Simcox was well respected in her own day as a writer and as a public speaker. She expressed surprise that one reviewer of *Episodes in the Lives of Men, Women, and Lovers* commended her creativity in writing fiction. In recent years she has been known primarily because of her admiration of George Eliot and is frequently mentioned in biographies of Eliot. Her *Autobiography* was used by Keith A. McKenzie as the basis of his book *Edith Simcox and George Eliot* (Oxford, 1961; Greenwood, 1978). Gordon S. Haight used McKenzie's transcript in writing his *George Eliot: A Biography* (Oxford, 1968) and published extensive excerpts in Volume 9 of *The George Eliot Letters* (Yale, 1974).

BIBLIOGRAPHY

Articles by Simcox have been reprinted recently in *Prose by Victorian Women* (ed. Andrea Broomfield and Sally Mitchell [Garland, 1996]). Simcox's *Autobiography of a Shirtmaker* has been published as *A Monument to the Memory of George Eliot* (ed. Constance M. Fulmer and Margaret E. Barfield [Garland, 1998]).

Works by Edith J. Simcox

"Review of *Middlemarch.*" *Academy* 4 (1 Jan. 1873): 1–4; rpt. *A Century of George Eliot Criticism*, ed. Gordon S. Haight, 1965; *George Eliot and Her Readers*, ed. John Holmstrom and Laurence Lerner, 1966; *George Eliot: The Critical Heritage*, ed. David Carroll, 1971.
Natural Law: An Essay in Ethics. 1877.
"George Eliot." *Nineteenth Century* 9 (May 1881): 778–801; rpt. *Littell's Living Age* 149 (1881): 791–805.
Episodes in the Lives of Men, Women, and Lovers. 1882.
"Eight Years of Co-operative Shirtmaking." *Nineteenth Century* 15 (June 1884): 1037–54.
Primitive Civilizations, or Outline of the History of Ownership in Archaic Communities. 1894.
A Monument to the Memory of George Eliot: Edith J. Simcox's Autobiography of a Shirtmaker. Ed. Constance M. Fulmer and Margaret E. Barfield. 1998.

Studies of Edith J. Simcox

Fulmer, Constance M. "Edith Simcox: Feminist, Reformer, and Erudite Reviewer." *Victorian Periodicals Review* 31.1 (1998): 105–21.
McKenzie, Keith A. *Edith Simcox and George Eliot.* Oxford: Oxford University Press. 1961; Westport, CT: Greenwood, 1978.

Mary Fairfax Greig Somerville (1780-1872)

Kathryn A. Neeley

BIOGRAPHY

Mary Somerville was the leading woman of science in Great Britain during the nineteenth century and a highly successful scientific author in an era when scientific books and articles played an important role in general intellectual life. Somerville's greatest strength was in mathematics, but her expertise extended throughout the physical sciences.

Born in Scotland into a middle-class family, Somerville spent her youth in and around Edinburgh. After the death of her first husband, Samuel Greig, in 1807, Somerville became first a protégé and then an integral part of the intellectual circle associated with the *Edinburgh Review*. With her marriage in 1812 to William Somerville and a subsequent move to London, Somerville expanded her scientific expertise and her association with the scientific and intellectual elite of Great Britain. Her closest scientific collaborators included John Herschel, Charles Babbage, and Michael Faraday. She was also well acquainted with Walter Scott and the painters James Nasmyth and J.M.W. Turner. She served as a mentor to Ada Byron Lovelace.

Somerville was well known personally to the scientific communities of Britain and France long before she established her reputation as a scientific author with her first book, which was published in 1831 when she was nearly fifty-one years old. Her works bear little resemblance to the dominant forms of scientific writing that are produced today. They combine strong analytical and technical treatment of esoteric concepts with qualities that are often both painterly and poetic.

Somerville moved to Italy with her family in 1838 and remained there until her death in 1872. She produced four books on scientific subjects, two of which went through several editions. Near the end of her life, she drafted an autobiography, which was edited by her daughter Martha Somerville and friend Frances Power Cobbe.* Throughout her career, Somerville received extraordinary support from William Somerville, who served as a willing and effective intermediary between her and the predominantly male scientific community. She received numerous scientific honors from Britain, the United States, Italy, and elsewhere.

MAJOR WORKS AND THEMES

Mary Somerville's scientific writings contributed to one of the most important cultural projects of Victorian Britain: establishing science as a distinct, integral, and unifying element of culture. Achieving this objective required not only the dissemination and interpretation of new scientific discoveries, but also a new rhetoric of science that established its practical, spiritual, intellectual, and aesthetic value and portrayed it as progressive yet compatible with traditional values.

Her first book, *Mechanism of the Heavens* (1831), was a rendering in English of Laplace's *Mécanique Céleste*, which was considered to be the most important scientific book written since Newton's *Principia*. To contextualize Laplace's work, Somerville wrote a preliminary dissertation, or introduction, to *Mechanism of the Heavens*. The *Preliminary Dissertation* was published separately in 1832. It provided the outline for *On the Connexion of the Physical Sciences* (1834), which summarized current knowledge in all areas of the physical sciences and went throughout numerous editions as new discoveries and theories emerged. *Physical Geography* (1848) used geography as the organizing principle for presenting a comprehensive description of the physical features, natural processes, and life forms of the earth. *On Molecular and Microscopic Science* (1869) surveyed the state of knowledge and recent discoveries in the emerging sciences of chemistry and biology. In each of these books, she reached out to increasingly broad audiences.

Her last work was her autobiography, *Personal Recollections* (1873). This work reveals little of Somerville's scientific thinking but does provide insight into the challenges she faced and the success she achieved as a female intellectual.

CRITICAL RECEPTION

Responses to Somerville's work within her lifetime were almost uniformly positive. Her works, especially her first three, were praised for their perspicacity, timeliness, precision, clarity, professional tone, breadth, and aesthetic appeal. She was compared favorably to great figures in science, including Newton and Alexander von Humboldt. One key to the favorable reception of her work was the close associations she maintained with most of the leading scientists of her day, many of whom reviewed and critiqued her works before publication. Another significant factor in her success as a writer on science was her ability to manage her identity as a woman by adopting a style that focused on the subject rather than on her own voice.

By the time of her death, Somerville had achieved near-mythic status in Britain. The advancement of science since Somerville's time has meant that her works no longer enjoy state-of-the art status. They continue to hold great interest, however, because of the way they reflect both the power of science to capture imagination and the influence of cultural factors in the development of science. They provide a window into a particularly lucid and illuminated mind and into one of the most formative periods in the evolution of modern scientific culture.

BIBLIOGRAPHY

Two of Mary Somerville's major works are currently in print: *On the Connexion of the Physical Sciences* is available from Ayer Company Publishers, and *Personal Recollections* is available from AMS Press. Somerville's work does not easily lend itself to anthologizing because any single passage cannot adequately capture the network of subtle intellectual and symbolic connections that permeate her writings. For a reader interested in Somerville's scientific writing, the *Preliminary Dissertation* to *Mechanism of the Heavens* is probably her most manageable work. It is relatively brief, treats the history of astronomy and related sciences in an accessible way, and is usually available through interlibrary loan in cases where local libraries do not own a copy. Perhaps more significantly, the *Preliminary Dissertation* is a microcosm of Somerville's scientific writing, in the sense that it develops most of the key themes and exemplifies most of the important techniques that characterized her writing as a whole. For a reader interested in autobiography or various aspects of history in the nineteenth century, *Personal Recollections* is probably the most useful of Somerville's works.

Works by Mary Somerville

Mechanism of the Heavens. 1831.
Preliminary Dissertation to Mechanism of the Heavens. 1832.
On the Connexion of the Physical Sciences. 1834.
Physical Geography. 1848.
On Molecular and Microscopic Science. 1869.
Personal Recollections from Early Life to Old Age, of Mary Somerville. 1873.

Studies of Mary Somerville

Neeley, Kathryn A. *Mary Somerville: Science, Illumination, and the Female Mind.* Cambridge University Press, 2000.
Patterson, Elizabeth C. *Mary Somerville and the Cultivation of Science, 1815–1840.* The Hague: Martinus Nijoff, 1983.

Agnes Strickland
(1796-1874)

Robert C. Petersen

BIOGRAPHY

For thirty years Agnes Strickland was Victorian England's most popular female writer of history. She born in London and raised at Reydon Hall in Suffolk, where she and her five sisters were given educations that made all but one into journalists, occasional poets, and writers of memoirs and books of history. Strickland's sister Catharine Traill wrote a book entitled *The Backwoods of Canada* (1836), whereas Susanna Moodie, another sister, wrote a classic account of immigrant life in Canada entitled *Roughing It in the Bush* (1852).

Agnes and her elder sister Elizabeth, known as Eliza, however, entered the London literary world, mixing with figures like Thomas Campbell, Bulwer Lytton, and Walter Scott. They also met the literary hostess Lady Fanny Morgan and, through her, the publisher Henry Colburn and the noted poet Letitia Landon.* Like many other women writing at this time, Strickland produced poems for periodical publication, historical novels, and didactic fiction for children. Her first effort as biographer was *Queen Victoria* from her Birth to her Bridal* (1840). The twelve-volume *Lives of the Queens of England* (1840–1848) made Agnes Strickland into a literary celebrity. The significant contribution Eliza Strickland made to this project, in terms of research and the actual writing of nineteen of the thirty-three biographies of England's queens from Matilda of Flanders to Anne, was generally unknown during the sisters' lifetimes.

This project was the beginning of Strickland's career as royal biographer and historian. She became a writer of history when she gained admission, with the help of Lord Melbourne, when he was Home Secretary, to the State Papers Office. Strickland edited a collection of letters of Mary, Queen of Scots; with Eliza, she wrote a series entitled *Lives of the Queens of Scotland* (1850–1859) and a book entitled *Lives of the Tudor Princesses* (1867); and she wrote by herself a parallel study of Stuart princesses published in 1870, *Lives of the Last*

Four Princesses of the House of Stuart. To do this work, she made trips to Scotland and Wales, and she consulted archives in Edinburgh, Paris, and The Hague. In France, with the aid of Foreign Minister Guizot, himself an historian, Strickland unearthed a cache of letters written by James II's consort Mary Beatrice of Modena that had been largely untouched by earlier researchers.

Strickland settled in Southwold with her younger sister Jane in 1864 and died there a decade later. She is buried in St. Edmund's churchyard. Jane Strickland published a biographical study of her sister in 1887.

MAJOR WORKS AND THEMES

At the time Strickland began the series *The Lives of the Queens of England*, British historians were reinterpreting the reigns of the Stuart monarchs. Her accounts of the lives of the consorts of Charles I, Charles II, and James II appeared just as male historians were arguing that the seventeenth century marked the triumph of Protestantism and representative British political institutions. Strickland's lives of the royal Stuart women view the Cromwellian interregnum and the Glorious Revolution from the royalist perspective and reconstruct events through the eyes of female participants. Where Thomas Babington Macaulay's history of England through James II can be called a Whig interpretation, Strickland's is a Tory reading of the period.

Her decision, perhaps largely unconscious, to write the lives of Queens, many of them consorts with limited political power, might be read as acceptance of the marginalized status of many women in the Victorian period. It could as easily be read as an act totally subversive of Victorian norms, for Strickland's texts reveal conflicting impulses and narrative strategies. On the one hand, her biographies are chronological, story driven, and controlled by a narrator who identifies herself as an historian. At the same time, they are also discursive, atemporal, and even controlled by the materials unearthed by Strickland's research. The one pattern treats Mary Beatrice of Modena, for example, as heroine of historical romance and a figure illustrative of cultural norms—as pious Catholic queen and model daughter, wife, and mother. The other resists the control of any static paradigm and casts Mary Beatrice's life in the mode of feminist autobiography. It is hard not to read Strickland's own conflicted sense of self into such a text.

CRITICAL RECEPTION

In the best sections of the *Lives of the Queens of England* and Strickland's other biographies of England's royal women, her work is fresh and original. At the time she published it, it was also controversial. Some reviewers objected to Strickland's treatments of the Stuarts as too sympathetic. There were even rumors in the contemporary press that she was about to become a Roman Catholic. Strickland's edition of Mary, Queen of Scots's letters, and her two series on

English and Scottish queens, and other books went through multiple editions. Her original research and lively style brought Strickland a wide, popular readership. In 1865, she talked to undergraduates at Oxford about the writing of history, and she was invited to come to Edinburgh in 1871 to participate in the celebration of Walter Scott's birth a century before.

Strickland gets brief mention in current studies of nineteenth-century British historians. Part of the reason may be an assumption that her original popularity means she was a scribbler for hire, a popularizer, and not an historian at all. Certainly, Strickland lacked academic credentials and institutional support while writing in a genre dominated by her male contemporaries. Tastes have also changed, and Strickland's books are out of print. Nevertheless, examination of her writing does show something about the popularization of history and about the increasingly central role women took as literary figures in the Victorian period.

BIBLIOGRAPHY

Four of Agnes Strickland's poems are reprinted in Paula Feldman's anthology *British Women Poets of the Romantic Era* (Johns Hopkins, 1997). Richard West reprinted *Tales from English History*, a children's book, in 1978, and Telegraph Books reprinted the *Lives of the Queens of England* in 1981, although they are not now in print.

Works by Agnes Strickland

Tales from English History. 1836.
Queen Victoria from Her Birth to Her Bridal. 1840.
Lives of the Queens of England. 12 vols. 1840–1848.
Letters of Mary Stuart. 1842.
Lives of the Queens of Scotland. 8 vols. 1850–1859.
Lives of the Tudor Princesses. 1867.
Lives of the Last Four Princess of the House of Stuart. 1870.

Studies of Agnes Strickland

Ballstadt, C.P.A. "The Literary History of the Strickland Family." Ph.D. diss., University of London, 1965.
Delorme, Mary. " 'Facts, Not Opinions'—Agnes Strickland." *History Today* 38 (Feb. 1988): 45–50.
Peterman, Michael. "In Search of Agnes Strickland's Sisters." *Canadian Literature* 121 (Summer 1989): 115–24.
Pope-Hennessy, Una. *Agnes Strickland: Biographer of the Queens of England.* London: Chatto & Windus, 1940.
Strickland, Jane Margaret. *Life of Agnes Strickland.* Edinburgh: Blackwood and Son, 1887.

Helen Taylor
(1831-1907)

Juliette Berning Schaefer

BIOGRAPHY

Helen Taylor, journalist and advocate for women's rights and universal education, was born youngest of three and only girl in London to Harriet and John
Taylor, a wholesale druggist. In 1831, Helen's mother met John Stuart Mill, and
for twenty years, while Harriet remained married to John Taylor, they were
devoted companions. In 1851, a year after John Taylor died, Harriet Taylor
married John Stuart Mill. Ultimately, Helen spent most of her life with them.
When Harriet Mill* died in 1858, Helen Taylor, who was in Scotland acting
professionally, rushed to be with Mill. For the remaining fourteen years of Mill's
life, Helen Taylor, as her mother had before her, worked for the same causes,
meticulously edited his writings, and assumed his correspondence. She edited
and wrote the introduction for his posthumously published autobiography. Mill
humbly and generously attributed his work not to "one intellect and conscience,
but [to] three" (Coss 185).

   Helen Taylor's views were extremely radical, democratic, and individualist.
She was active in advocating the Contagious Diseases Acts, opposing the Irish
coercion policy of the liberal government, fighting for the English branch of the
Irish Ladies' Land League, the Land Reform Union and the League for Taxing
Land Values. She participated in the Democratic Federation, later the Social
Democratic Federation, helped to found the Metropolitan Mistresses Association
that was intended to aid women teachers, and joined the Moral Reform Union.
In 1885 she offered herself as the radical candidate for Parliament; the campaign
was tumultuous and controversial, and her nomination was ultimately refused.
Taylor lived until 1907, an additional thirty years after Mill's death, and is
buried in the cemetery at Torquay; the inscription on her tombstone reads: "She
fought for the people."

MAJOR WORKS AND THEMES

Taylor believed in individuality, universal education, representation, and suffrage and struggled against political and religious conformity. Taylor and Mill campaigned for equality before the law with no legal disabilities imposed on men or women by reason of sex. Her appeal for individuality as a means of bettering humankind is apparent in her "The Election of Representatives" (1865), which addresses the need for every individual to be represented.

Mill credited Taylor with the formation of the suffrage movement because she assisted members of the Langham Place Group and was one of the founding members of the National Society for Women's Suffrage. In "The Ladies' Petition" (1867), she demands changes in law by explaining and arguing for Mill's Petition. In 1881, in "Women's Rights as Preached by Women," she defends Mill's (and possibly her mother's) "admirable book" "The Subjection of Women" and his attempts to pass the "Ladies' Petition" fourteen years previously. However, she explains that "what would then have been acceptable as a first concession of voting-power to women, will seem, we believe, to most thoughtful persons, a compromise too inadequate and insignificant for acceptance now ("Women's" 475).

Of importance to Taylor, and Mill, was inequality, before the law and in the home. She considered the differences between men and women unnecessarily emphasized, resulting in injustice, tyranny, and slavery in family life among all classes. In "Women and Criticism" (1866), Taylor argues that "women might possibly prove equal to men if they were placed in the same circumstances" (336). She suggests "experimenting" with women's rights as the country had "experimented" with industrial laws. In " 'Nurses Wanted' " (1865) she addressed the absurd contention that women and men should be governed by separate spheres for which there is no logical reasoning, as in the profession of nursing, which claims to be "congenial to the best instincts of women" (539) but is refused "all reward and all honour" (540). Her suggestion was to "turn their ambition to a better world, where there is no distinction of sex." In 1872, Taylor, an excellent speaker because of her acting experience, addressed the Edinburgh branch of the National Society for Women's Suffrage where she accused men of giving to themselves "the right to dictate to women what they should and should not be, and do, and learn."

After Mill's death in 1873, Taylor's campaign for universal education became intense. This is revealed by her service on the London School Board for nine years, her speeches, essays, and actions. She fought for universal free education, the provision of food and shoes for students (for which she occasionally used her own money), the abolition of corporal punishment, and smaller classes. In "London School Board" (1876) and "Banquet to Miss Helen Taylor" (1877), where her speeches are quoted, Taylor states that education is necessary for both boys and girls, and women are as instrumental in this teaching as men. Her views regarding education were inextricably bound to her beliefs about the betterment of humankind, individuality, and women's rights.

Perhaps because of her extensive work with Mill, and other influential men, Taylor insisted that women include men in their crusades. In "Influence of Women on Temperance" (1877), she berates women who have "exclusively ladies' temperance societies" and suggests that because "intemperance is the same degradation to a man as to a woman, they [should] work only with men for its suppression and not as a means of separate associations" (54). In "Women's Rights as Preached by Women" (1881), Taylor asserts that "the interests of men and women in this matter [the women's rights movement] are not antagonistic or divided, but harmonious and identical" (Robson and Robson 301). It was her contention that inequality would be prevented by discouraging the idea of separate spheres.

CRITICAL RECEPTION

The reception and acceptance of Taylor's works were due in large part to Mill's influence and recommendation of her. Even after Mill's death, she is referred to as his daughter. However, Taylor had many critics; Ruth Borchard states that "enough is known of Helen to make it perfectly clear that concerning her . . . [Mill] was labouring under a complete delusion. She was a worthy, intellectual, somewhat unbalanced woman, of the highest moral sentiments, who displayed a superior, irritable attitude to all around her and was much given to reforming her inferiors" (136). After winning her seat on the London School Board in 1879 Taylor "was loathed by the official Liberal party caucus and was referred to behind her back as 'the acid maiden' " (Hollis 93). Taylor may have been criticized because she was parent and community centered but not child centered. Her arguments are tightly constructed and thoroughly argued, and her speeches were often attended because of her impassioned stage presence. Recent scholarship regards Taylor as an integral factor in Mill's life and work, as well as in her own causes.

BIBLIOGRAPHY

"Women and Criticism" is reprinted in *"Criminals, Idiots, Women and Minors"* (ed. Susan Hamilton [Broadview, 1996]; "Women and Criticism" and "The Ladies' Petition" have been published in *Prose by Victorian Women: An Anthology* (ed. Andrea Broomfield and Sally Mitchell [Garland, 1996]); and "Women and Criticism," "The Education of Women," "The Contagious Diseases Acts," "Nursing," "Election to the London School Board" 1 and 2, "Parliamentary Suffrage for Women," "The Ladies' Petition," "Women's Suffrage 3," and "Women's Rights as Preached by Women," as well as "Self-Education" and "Propagandizing for the Cause," coauthored with Mill, have been published in *Sexual Equality: Writings by John Stuart Mill, Harriet Taylor Mill, and Helen Taylor* (ed. Ann P. Robson and John M. Robson [University of Toronto Press, 1994]).

Selected Works by Helen Taylor

" 'Nurses Wanted.' " *The Reader* (13 May 1865): 539–40.
"The Election of Representatives." *The Reader* (10 June 1865): 651–52.
"Women and Criticism." *Macmillan's Magazine* (14 Sept. 1866): 335–40.
"The Ladies' Petition." *The Westminster Review* (31 Jan. 1867): 63–79.
"Address to the Third Annual Meeting of the Edinburgh Branch of the National Society for Women's Suffrage, 1872." In *Women in Public: The Women's Movement 1850–1900. Documents of the Victorian Women's Movement*. Ed. Patricia Hollis. 1979. 294–95.
"Industrial Education for Ladies." *The Westminster Review* (Jan. 1874): 1–6.
"London School Board." *Englishwoman's Review* (15 Nov. 1876): 504–5.
"Banquet to Miss Helen Taylor." *Englishwoman's Review* (15 Feb. 1877): 72–75.
"Influence of Women on Temperance." *The Westminster Review* (15 Feb. 1877): 53–57.
"Women's Rights as Preached by Women." *The Westminster Review* (1 Oct. 1881): 469–78.

Studies of Helen Taylor

Borchard, Ruth. *John Stuart Mill the Man*. London: Watts, 1957.
Broomfield, Andrea. "Forging a New Tradition: Helen Taylor, Eliza Lynn Linton, Millicent Garrett Fawcett, and the Victorian Women of Letters." Ph.D. diss., Temple University, 1994.
Broomfield, Andrea, and Sally Mitchell, eds. *Prose by Victorian Women: An Anthology*. New York: Garland, 1996. 449–51.
Coss, John Jacob, ed. *Autobiography of John Stuart Mill*. New York: Columbia University Press, 1924.
Hollis, Patricia. *Ladies Elect: Women in English Local Government 1865–1914*. Oxford: Clarendon, 1987.
———, ed. *Women in Public: The Women's Movement 1850–1900. Documents of the Victorian Women's Movement*. Boston: George Allen & Unwin, 1979.
Kamm, Josephine. *John Stuart Mill in Love*. London: Gordon & Cremonesi, 1977.
Nicholls, C. S., ed. *The Dictionary of National Biography: Missing Persons*. New York: Oxford University Press, 1993. 483–85.
Pappe, H. O. *John Stuart Mill and the Harriet Taylor Myth*. Melbourne, Australia: Melbourne University Press, 1960.
Rendall, Jane, ed. *Equal or Different: Women's Politics 1800–1914*. Oxford: Basil Blackwell, 1987.
Robson, Ann P., and John M. Robson, eds. *Sexual Equality: Writings by John Stuart Mill, Harriet Taylor Mill, and Helen Taylor*. Toronto: University of Toronto Press, 1994.

Charlotte Elizabeth Tonna
(1790–1846)

Mary Lenard

BIOGRAPHY

Charlotte Elizabeth Tonna was born in Norwich, the daughter of a clergyman. She lost her hearing at the age of ten, but this did not keep her from reading, and she became fascinated with imaginative literature, especially Shakespeare. Later in life, she came to see this fascination as sinful because it served no useful, religious purpose, but this early reading in drama, poetry, and fiction probably provided excellent preparation for her future writing career.

Tonna married an army officer, Captain Phelan, and moved to his small estate in Ireland. While in Ireland, she developed a sincere affection for the Irish people but at the same time grew increasingly severe and Evangelical in her religious convictions. She began publishing religious tracts through the Dublin Tract Society, using the name "Charlotte Elizabeth." Tonna's marriage was unhappy, and she separated from her husband, returning to England in 1824. She continued to write tracts for children and the lower classes and didactic fiction on subjects that interested her, such as the abolition of slavery, Zionism, and religious struggles in Ireland. After Phelan's death, she married Lewis Tonna, a religious writer twenty years younger than herself, who encouraged her literary efforts. She was prolific as a writer and editor, publishing continuously and editing the *Christian Lady's Magazine* from 1834 to 1846, the *Protestant Annual* in 1840, and the *Protestant Magazine* from 1841 to 1846. During the 1840s Tonna became convinced that industrialism threatened the physical and spiritual welfare of the poor, and she attacked the factory system in *Helen Fleetwood* (1841), *The Wrongs of Woman* (1843–1844), and the anonymous, nonfictional *The Perils of the Nation* (1842). Tonna died in 1846, leaving an extensive legacy of literary works and active involvement with a number of social causes.

MAJOR WORKS AND THEMES

Tonna was heavily influenced by the conservative reaction against the French Revolution. Her adored father was a Tory and a Church of England clergyman, and this family background, in addition to the paranoid political atmosphere of the Napoleonic era, probably caused Tonna's hostility to Roman Catholicism and her political conservatism. Her stay in Ireland only intensified her antipathy toward the Catholic Church, since she saw it as the means by which the Irish people were enslaved in ignorance and superstition, a view she professed in her novel *Derry* (1833). In contrast, her attitude toward Judaism was relatively enlightened. In her novel *Judah's Lion* (1843), Tonna argued that the Jews could only fulfill themselves by recognizing Jesus Christ, but she also respected them as recipients of God's covenant, and she strongly disapproved of anti-Semitism.

Since Tonna thought that literature for its own sake was sinful, all of her works were didactic in nature, and many were written in support of social and political causes. Some of these causes, like her anti-Catholicism, are distasteful to modern readers. However, Tonna was also indefatigable in her support of the poor and oppressed. She wrote poems and one novel, *The System* (1827), to expose the evils of slavery but found an even more passionate voice supporting factory reform.

Joseph Kestner has argued that the social reform novel was one genre in which Victorian women could speak with power and authority, and Tonna certainly exemplifies this insight. She constructed herself as a woman driven to political writing by a strong sense of religious mission. Tonna therefore created a role that transcended women's political disenfranchisement, and she continually justified this "talent of female influence" in her works (see "Politics," *Christian Lady's Magazine* [Mar. 1834]: 250). As Christine Krueger has pointed out, Tonna's sermonlike novels skillfully invoke God's authority in support of political goals. This formula was a powerful persuasive tool, but Tonna had yet another weapon: her potent use of pathos. Tonna's best works, *Helen Fleetwood* and *The Wrongs of Woman*, contain moving portrayals of physical and emotional suffering that are used to evoke audience sympathy. Tonna's contributions to social reform literature and her use of the *Christian Lady's Magazine* as a forum to influence politics through her female readers mark her as a key figure in both Victorian studies and women's studies.

CRITICAL RECEPTION

Tonna was well known in the Evangelical community, and her tracts and novels went through multiple editions. Her factory reform novels were recognized as significant influences on public opinion, even by Chartist leaders. Tonna also provided a model for other women writers, namely Harriet Beecher Stowe, who introduced an American edition of Tonna's works in 1845. The rise of more aesthetic and formal standards in literary criticism caused Tonna's work to fade quickly from literary history, however, and it was almost entirely ignored until the women's movement created new interest in women's literature. Since the late 1970s, the scholarly world has become increasingly familiar with her name.

BIBLIOGRAPHY

Tonna's works are not in print.

Selected Works by Charlotte Tonna

Izram: A Mexican Tale. 1826.
Osric: A Missionary Tale. 1826.
The System: A Tale. 1827.
Derry: A Tale of the Revolution. 1833.
Chapters on Flowers. 1836.
Helen Fleetwood. 1841.
Personal Recollections. 1841.
The Perils of the Nation. 1842.
Judah's Lion. 1843
The Wrongs of Woman. Serialized in *Christian Lady's Magazine*, 1843–1844.
Works of Charlotte Elizabeth. Introd. Mrs. H. B. Stowe. 1845. *Posthumous and Other Poems*. 1847.

Studies of Charlotte Tonna

Corbett, Mary Jean. "Feminine Authorship and Spiritual Authority in Victorian Women Writers' Autobiographies." *Women's Studies* 18 (1990): 13–29.
Fryckedstedt, Monica. "Charlotte Elizabeth Tonna and *The Christian Lady's Magazine*." *Victorian Periodicals Review* 14 (1981): 43–51.
———. "The Early Industrial Novel: Mary Barton and its Predecessors." *Bulletin of the John Rylands University Library* 63 (1980): 11–30.
Kanner, Barbara, and Ivanka Kovacevic. "Blue Book into Novel: The Forgotten Industrial Fiction of Charlotte Elizabeth Tonna." *Nineteenth-Century Fiction* 25 (1970): 152–73.
Kaplan, Deborah. "The Woman Worker in Charlotte Elizabeth Tonna's Fiction." *Mosaic* 18 (1985): 51–63.
Kestner, Joseph. "Charlotte Elizabeth Tonna's *The Wrongs of Woman*: Female Industrial Protest." *Tulsa Studies in Women's Literature* 2 (1983): 193–214.
———. *Protest and Reform: The British Social Narrative by Women*. Madison: University of Wisconsin Press, 1985.
Kovacevic, Ivanka. *Fact into Fiction*. Leicester: Leicester University Press, 1975.
Koweleski, Elizabeth. "The Heroine of Some Strange Romance: The Personal Recollec-

tions of Charlotte Elizabeth Tonna." *Tulsa Studies in Women's Literature* 1 (1982): 141–53.

Krueger, Christine. *The Reader's Repentance*. Chicago: University of Chicago Press, 1992.

Frances Trollope
(1779–1863)

Ann-Barbara Graff

BIOGRAPHY

Frances ("Fanny") Milton Trollope began writing at the age of fifty-three solely for reasons of financial necessity. Prolific, she published forty books from 1832 until her death in 1863; so admired as a novelist, travel writer, and social satirist, critics commonly asked, "Who will be the next Mrs Trollope?" Remarkably soon after her death, her fame was eclipsed by that of her son, Anthony Trollope, and despite her important contributions to contemporary debates about the condition of women, slavery, and child labor, her works have only recently recaptured the attention they deserve.

Born on 10 March 1779 near Bristol, Fanny was educated by her father, a widowed cleric. She befriended Hannah More, Samuel Taylor Coleridge, and Mary Mitford,* among other local notables, but never entertained literary aspirations herself. In 1803, the family moved to London, and in 1809, at the age of thirty, Fanny married Thomas Anthony Trollope, a barrister at Lincoln's Inn. The marriage, at first quite satisfactory, produced seven children; however, relations grew strained as Thomas Anthony's health failed, his practice shrunk, an anticipated inheritance fell through, and debts from renovations to their home in Harrow mounted. Fleeing the bailiff, Fanny Trollope, three of her children, and Auguste Hervieu, her supposed lover and the children's drawing master, sailed to America to reside with Frances Wright at Nashoba, a slave emancipation colony. The party did not stay at Nashoba, preferring to quickly remove themselves to Cincinnati. Trollope began writing theatricals to supplement Hervieu's wages but entertained a grand dream of building a bazaar, a European-style social club, where women and men could mingle freely. In fact, the Bazaar (referred to as Trollope's Folly) opened and closed in 1829, a victim of unscrupulous contractors and Trollope's inability to recognize the tenacity of the American separate sphere ideology. Creditors seized everything. Without enough money to return to England, and barely enough money to survive in America, Trollope began to write down her observations of American society with an eye to publication. Hervieu's savings enabled the family to return to England penniless, where Fanny Trollope's volume appeared. Buoyed by the overwhelming success of *Domestic Manners of the Americans* (1832), Trollope continued writing until her death in 1863.

MAJOR WORKS AND THEMES

From the beginning of her career, Frances Trollope wrote as a reformer and social satirist, distinguishing herself as a champion of the dispossessed, addressing such themes as political injustice, moral hypocrisy, and sexual inequality in various genres including the novel, verse satire, gothic romance, detective story, and travelogue. Having experienced financial hardship (brought on by her husband's mismanagement of their affairs and by legal prerogatives that denied her access to her own funds) and having investigated and documented the ill treatment of slaves, women, and children in her travels throughout the United States, Britain, and Europe, Trollope wrote with a passion and authority that were difficult to challenge. At a time when it was unusual for women to write about topical political issues, Trollope wrote purposively to affect the political consciousness of her readers and the legislative agenda of the House of Commons; as a consequence, her critics routinely maligned her as unfeminine, coarse, vulgar, and bitter. Undaunted, Trollope persisted in each volume subverting generic conventions and popular expectations to inscribe a feminist, egalitarian alternative.

Domestic Manners of the Americans, Trollope's first work and the first of four books about America, explored the weaknesses and benefits of the democratic republicanism. Criticized by American reviewers as revenge for the failure of her Bazaar, the English read it voraciously in light of the controversy surrounding the extension of the suffrage in the Reform Bill of 1832. The narrative has three parts: an adventure story, an account of life in Cincinnati (for Trollope, a culture wasteland), and a traditional traveler's account. Unique in form and content, Trollope uses multiple narratives, reportage, and vignettes of domestic life to compare American and English systems of government, comment on American customs, and critique the American character, which she found hypocritical especially concerning the treatment of women, slaves, and Native Americans. Most troubling to Trollope was the circumscribed role of women in America, what she called "lamentable insignificance," as women had little opportunity for education and seemed trapped in their domestic sphere, marrying too young to develop a sense of self-sufficiency and then restricted from social interaction outside the home.

Following the success of *Domestic Manners*, Trollope began experimenting with the novel as a form of social criticism and, in quick succession, wrote *Jonathan Jefferson Whitlaw* (1836), *Michael Armstrong* (1840), and *Jessie Phil-*

lips (1844). *Jonathan Jefferson Whitlaw* was one of the first novels in English to depict the evils of slavery. Based on her experiences in the South, Trollope recounts the sexual sadism and brutality of slaveholders, the trauma of separation on slave families, and the insufficiency of efforts to deal with slavery in this frank story of rape and murder on a slave plantation. Given the similarities between it and *Uncle Tom's Cabin* (1851), it is likely that Harriet Beecher Stowe read *Whitlaw*; however, Trollope's narrative is more realistic, her resolution more militant: Trollope's slave heroine murders Whitlaw and goes unpunished, problematizing the question of justice in a slave society.

Michael Armstrong exposes the conditions under which children worked in the northern textile mills. Fanny traveled to Lancashire, its mills, slums, and churches to research her subject, writing in the novel: "Let none dare to say this picture is exaggerated, till he has taken the trouble to ascertain by his own personal investigation that it is so" (186). Horrified by what she saw, Trollope wanted to awaken a sense of national guilt not only at the conditions in the mills but also at the Parliamentary Commission charged with reform. In the novel, nine-year-old Michael is adopted by a mill owner (in a questionable act of private philanthropy) and then apprenticed to a remote mill where children are worked to death. The plot is driven by Miss Brotherton, an heiress and prototypical Trollopian heroine, who searches for Michael and uncovers how the system of child labor functions over the course of her investigation. The critics were disturbed by the political content of *Michael Armstrong*, and Trollope was rebuked for being an agitator; however, in 1847, the Factory Act was passed, forbidding the employment of children in the textile mills.

Jessie Phillips is an indictment of the 1834 Poor Law reforms, especially the bastardy provisions that were revised to prevent unwed mothers from demanding support from the fathers of their children and the relief reforms that placed greater emphasis on workhouse rather than outdoor relief. In this "fallen woman" novel, a young girl, believing the promise of marriage from a squire's son, submits to his advances and gets pregnant only to be ostracized by the community and taken to the workhouse. Jessie escapes the workhouse in time to give birth to her child; however, the child's father (coincidentally nearby) kicks the baby to death. Of course, Jessie is charged with the crime. In this novel, Trollope confronts the insensitivity and obduracy of the welfare system and its prejudiced application to women. As a result of the novel's popularity, the bastardy clause was amended to return rights to unwed mothers.

Mocking her critics who insisted she write "domestic" fictions, that is, novels about submissive women, Trollope wrote *The Widow Barnaby* (1839), a comic novel about a recent widow "fair, fat and forty" who unabashedly seeks her fortune and sexual gratification, and *One Fault* (1840), one of the first novels to dramatize an unhappy marriage, in which the fault of the title lays in the jealous character of the husband. In *One Fault*, Trollope even provides a new model of female conduct; as the narrator explains, if the long-suffering heroine had been "a high-spirited violent woman . . . her liberal, gentlemanlike, and honourable husband might have been cured, after a few years of struggling, of those pampered vices of temper which now neutralized or smothered all his good qualities" (2: 153).

CRITICAL RECEPTION

Though realism was regarded as a "low" form (especially inappropriate for women) in her own lifetime and few of her works were republished after 1858, it is difficult to question Trollope's popularity and contribution to the condition of women, slavery, and child labor debates in the 1830s and 1840s. In the twentieth century, her popularity rested exclusively on her relationship with her son, Anthony Trollope, and on *Domestic Manners of the Americans*; however, recently her work has undergone reappraisal by feminist scholars like Helen Heineman and Teresa Ransom, who have made a case for her as an innovative writer who drew complex female characters; wrote sexually frank, realistic social fictions; and expanded the conventions of female authorship. Ransom has even challenged conventional wisdom about Trollope's influence on Anthony's fiction, arguing that *The Warden* (1855) and *He Knew He Was Right* (1869), for instance, can be read as reworkings of his mother's *The Vicar of Wrexhill* (1837) and *One Fault*. Important work has yet to be done on Frances Trollope, but clearly there is new scholarly interest.

BIBLIOGRAPHY

Several of Trollope's novels have been reprinted recently: *Domestic Manners of the Americans* (Penguin, 1997); *The Vicar of Wrexhill* (Sutton, 1999); and *The Three Cousins* (Sutton, 1999).

Selected Works by Frances Trollope

Domestic Manners of the Americans. 1832.
The Refugee in America. 1832.
The Abbess: A Romance. 1833.
Tremordyn Cliff. 1835.
The Life and Adventures of Jonathan Jefferson Whitlaw: or Scenes on the Mississippi. 1836.
Paris and the Parisians in 1835. 1836.
The Vicar of Wrexhill. 1837.
The Widow Barnaby. 1839.
The Life and Adventures of Michael Armstrong, the Factory Boy. 1840.
One Fault: A Novel. 1840.
The Widow Married: A Sequel to the "Widow Barnaby." 1840.
Charles Chesterfield: or the Adventures of a Youth of Genius. 1841.
The Barnabys in America: or Adventures of a Widow Wedded. 1843.
Jessie Phillips; A Tale of the Present Day. 1844.

Father Eustace. 1847.
The Three Cousins. 1847.
Mrs Mathews, or Family Mysteries. 1851.
The Life and Adventures of a Clever Woman, Illustrated with Occasional Extracts from Her Diary. 1854.
Gertrude, or, Family Pride. 1855.

Studies of Frances Trollope

Ellis, Linda Abess. *Frances Trollope's America: Four Novels.* American University Studies Series IV; English Language and Literature, Vol. 145. New York: Peter Lang, 1993.

Giltrow, Janet. "Painful Experience in a Distant Land: Mrs. Moodie in Canada and Mrs. Trollope in America." *Mosaic* 14 (Spring 1981): 131–44.

Grube, Alberta Fabris, and Jacques Portes. "An English Lady Looks at America: Frances Trollope's *Domestic Manners of the Americans.*" In *Criss-Crossing Perspectives, 1788–1848.* Ed. Jacques Portes. Paris: Centre d'Etudes Nord-Americanes, E.H.E.S.S., 1987.

Heineman, Helen. *Frances Trollope.* Boston: Twayne, 1984.

Neville-Sington, Pamela. *Fanny Trollope: The Life and Adventures of a Clever Woman.* New York: Viking, 1997.

Ransom, Teresa. *Fanny Trollope: A Remarkable Life.* New York: St. Martin's Press, 1995.

Katharine Tynan
(1859-1931)

Susan Schreibman

BIOGRAPHY

Katharine Tynan is probably best remembered today as an early contributor to the Irish Literary Renaissance and a close friend and important correspondent to the youthful W. B. Yeats. She deserves, however, to be remembered for more than this. She was a prolific and professional writer whose career spanned over fifty years, during which she engaged in a variety of mediums, including poetry, fiction, autobiography, and journalism.

In the late 1860s Tynan suffered near blindness due to a chronic ulcerated-eye condition. She was eventually cured by a Dublin specialist but left purblind for the rest of her life. Despite this handicap, Tynan was an inveterate reader and was encouraged to write by her father, Andrew Tynan. He provided her with what Virginia Woolf wrote that every women writer should have: a room of one's own and an income. In her late teens her father furnished a room for Tynan in which to write in the family home at Whitehall outside Dublin. And not only were all her expenses taken care of, but she was, after her mother's death, to become her father's intellectual and social companion. Her Sunday "at homes" at Whitehall were a literary event commented on by many writers of the time, such as Douglas Hyde, George Russell (AE), and W. B. Yeats.

Tynan had already established her reputation as a poet and writer when she, in 1893, married Henry Albert Hinkson, a writer and barrister, at the relatively late age of thirty-four. She moved with Hinkson to England where her five children were born; three survived into adulthood. The family returned to Ireland in 1911, first living in Dalkey, County Dublin, then moving to County Mayo when Hinkson was appointed resident magistrate in October 1914. In 1913, *Twenty-Five Years*, the first of Tynan's six volumes of memoirs, was published. The following spring she traveled to Rome in the company of Lady Aberdeen, the wife of the Lord-Lieutenant of Ireland, to observe the International Women's Congress.

In 1919 Hinkson died suddenly, and Tynan's life changed again. She had found life in Mayo lonely, and after several years in Dublin and London, she moved with her daughter Pamela, who also became a writer, to Cologne, where it was possible to live cheaply with a foreign income. Tynan's last published book of memoirs, *Life in the Occupied Area* (1925), is a record of this time. During her last years, Tynan continued to publish poetry, novels, and articles on love and marriage, always from a Catholic point of view.

MAJOR WORKS AND THEMES

Tynan was an eclectic writer. This was due, in part, to the necessity of having to help to financially support her family. When her family was young, her need to churn out romances to bring in a second income might help to account for her largely formulaic writing. She was a prolific writer: During her lifetime she wrote or edited (in addition to uncollected articles, sketches, and introductions to other writers' works) more than 200 books, including *Child at Prayer: A Book of Devotions for the Young* (1923), many books on Irish themes, including *Ballads and Lyrics* (1891), a collection compiled in the early years of the Celtic Renaissance, *The Cabinet of Irish Literature* and *The Wild Irish Harp*, over fifteen collections of poems, even a book of Irish history, *Katharine Tynan's Book of Irish History* (1918). She also wrote over 100 novels, the vast majority of them set in Ireland.

Not only were many of Tynan's texts firmly rooted in a Catholic ethos and a Christian morality, but several, such as *A Nun, Her Friends and Her Order: Being a Sketch of the Life of Mother Mary Xaveria Fallon, etc.* (1891), *The Rhymed Life of St. Patrick* (1907), and *Story of Our Lord for Children* (1923), were based on Christian historical themes. During the Great War, Tynan wrote several collections of poems that directly responded to the conflict. These collections, coupled with several later collections, are fascinating as they tend to reflect the war and postwar conflicts, disappointments, and guilt of a society trying to come to term with its loss.

Tynan's six collections of autobiography are a mixture of sentimental prose, a smattering of self-analyses, sketches of friends, most of them famous, and long passages devoted to the everyday happenings of a quite extraordinary life.

CRITICAL RECEPTION

Tynan was an immensely popular writer during her lifetime, and many of her books went into several printings. By the time W. B. Yeats met Tynan in 1885, she had already established herself as a poet to be reckoned with. Earlier that year Kegan Paul had brought out *Louise de la Vallière, and Other Poems*; although it was initially subsidized by her father, it quickly went into a second printing. It was favorably reviewed by Christina Rossetti.* Tynan soon came under Yeats's influence, and much of her early poetry and sketches were highly regarded in both Ireland and England for capturing the spirit of the early Celtic Revival.

As a novelist Tynan had a wide readership. Her last novel, *The Forbidden Way* (1931), for example, was reissued five times in three years. Early in her career she found a romantic formula on which she was able to embellish the colorful character sketches at which she was so adept.

Today much of Tynan's work seems dated. Her late poetry has more in common with her early poetry than with her modernist contemporaries, and her novels rarely seem to rise above the formulaic. Yet some of her fiction was enlightened in its championing the rights of women, as was much of her later journalism. Although by today's standards Tynan's pronouncements on class and race are outdated, her work provides an important record of the Victorian class values of her time, and as such there is much in her writing that is of real interest, possibly more for *what* is being said as opposed to *how* it is said.

BIBLIOGRAPHY

Poetry by Katharine Tynan has been collected in several anthologies including *Pillars of the House: An Anthology of Verse by Irish Women from 1690 to the Present* (ed. A. A. Kelly [Wolfhound, 1987]) and recent anthologies of Victorian women's poetry. There is also a Local Ireland, Katharine Tynan biographical entry: http://www.local.ie/content/697.shtml. The Special Collections Department of The John Rylands University Library, University of Manchester, has an extensive collection of books and manuscripts (primarily correspondence) relating to Katharine Tynan, Henry Hinkson, and Pamela Hinkson. The Archives Department at University College Dublin has an uncataloged collection of papers relating to Katharine Tynan's work.

Selected Works by Katharine Tynan

Poetry

Louise de la Vallière, and Other Poems. 1885.
Ballads and Lyrics. 1891.
The Wind in the Trees: A Book of Country Verse. 1898.
Experiences. 1908.
Flowers of Peace: A Collection of the Devotional Poems of Katharine Tynan. 1914.
Flowers of Youth: Poems in Wartime. 1915.
The Holy War. 1916.
Evensong. 1922.
Collected Poems. 1930.
Twenty-four Poems. 1931.

Autobiographical Writing

Twenty-five Years: Reminiscences. 1913.
The Middle Years. 1916.

The Years of the Shadow. 1919.
The Wandering Years. 1922.
Memories. 1924.
Life in the Occupied Area. 1925.

Fiction

A Cluster of Nuts: Being Sketches Among My Own People. 1894.
An Isle in the Water. 1895.
The Land of Mist and Mountain. 1895.
The Way of a Maid. 1895.
Led by a Dream, and Other Stories. 1899.
The Adventures of Carlo. 1900.
That Sweet Enemy. 1901.
A Red, Red Rose. 1903.
The Adventures of Alicia. 1906.
A Little Radiant Girl. 1914.
Countryman All: A Collection of Tales. 1915.
Lord Edward Fitzgerald: A Study in Romance. 1916.
The Second Wife Together with a July Rose. 1921.
Mad Marriage. 1922.
The Briar Bush Maid. 1926.
The Wild Adventure. 1927.
Lover of Women. 1928.
The Forbidden Way. 1931.
Irish Stories: 1893–1899. Ed. Peter van de Kamp. 1993.

Studies of Katharine Tynan

Connerton Fallon, Ann. *Katharine Tynan.* Boston: Twayne, 1979.
Gaddis Rose, Marilyn. *Katharine Tynan.* Cranbury, NJ: Associated University Press, 1974.
McHugh, Roger, ed. *W. B. Letters to Katharine Tynan.* New York: McMullen, 1953.
van de Kamp, Peter. "Some Notes on the Literary Estate of Pamela Hinkson." In *Yeats Annual No. 4.* London: Macmillan, 1986. 181–86.

Victoria, Queen of Britain (1819-1901)

Adrienne Munich

BIOGRAPHY

As the most prominent women in the long period (1837–1901) named for her, Queen Victoria has been the subject of innumerable biographical writings. Briefly then, she was born in 1819 to the fourth son of King George III, Edward, Duke of Kent, and his wife, Victoire, the former Dowager Princess of Leiningen, a widow in the Saxe-Coburg line who did not speak English when her daughter was born in Kensington Palace. Victoria's unhappy and cloistered childhood after her father's death when she was eight months old was succeeded by happy years when she ascended the throne at eighteen, married her cousin Albert of Saxe-Coburg, and produced nine live children in twenty years. Her idyllic marriage ended with Albert's death in 1861 when they were both forty-two years old. Victoria reinvented herself as a widow. Titled Empress of India in 1876, her influence continued to grow, and her image pervaded her Empire. When she died in January 1901 there were few who did not feel that her death marked not only the end of the century but the end of an era.

MAJOR WORKS AND THEMES

Victoria always wrote with her readers in mind, and none of her writing can be read without an awareness of Victoria's sovereignty, her perspective as a woman who has an available scope larger than any other Victorian woman. From the age of thirteen, she wrote a daily journal entry, including her wedding day and the blissful morning after, to two weeks before her death. The early entries—from age thirteen to eighteen—were read by her mother and her governess. Nevertheless, even the early journals reveal something of Victoria's precise intelligence and her careful evaluation of surroundings, a foundation of the

Queen's writing style. She is accurate regarding facts and meticulous regarding grammar. When Victoria became Queen, the journals assume the emphatic tone of a woman of immediate, passionately held views and feelings. Her letters, particularly to her large family, reveal her manner of organizing and understanding the world of which she was at the center. Letters to family and memos to her household and ministers display the Queen's assertive voice, her passion for particularity, her mercurial but deeply felt opinions about almost every topic dear to her subjects, from wars and the character of her ministers, and indeed all the servants of the realm, to the experience of childbirth, to the status of animals, to the errors of missionary work in the Empire. Victoria's great influence on foreign affairs was revealed upon the posthumous publication of nine volumes of letters.

Her letters, particularly the remarkable five volumes to her eldest daughter Victoria, Crown Princess Frederick of Prussia, show her intimate side and her opinions on current issues, authors (whom she met personally), the arts and artists, and details of family life as it intersects with politics. In addition, most of her letters to her ministers and to family members—and she managed to forge alliances through marriage to most European kingdoms—demonstrate her command of pertinent information. In addition, she expressed herself on most issues of interest to women.

CRITICAL RECEPTION

Although she published best-selling volumes of her journals of her family life in the Scottish Highlands, these popular publications, presenting the royal family in leisure, with no allusion to political life, were effectively dismissed, in part through their perceived triviality, signaled by the often-quoted flattery of Prime Minister Benjamin Disraeli's comment to her, "We writers, M'am." Disraeli's remark has stood as a negative evaluation of *Leaves from the Journal of Our Life in the Highlands* and *More Leaves*. In addition to the *Highland* journals, there is an immense body of Victoria's published writings—journals, letters, speeches—that rivals in sheer quantity any of the Queen's energetic professional contemporaries, much of which has been considered useful for historical or biographical reasons. After her death, the 122 volumes of journals were mercilessly edited by Beatrice, youngest of her nine children. Were these volumes intact, history would have one of the most remarkable and detailed views of an entire era, from a singular viewpoint. Despite her undisputed centrality to the age and the great quantity of the written record, her unique status as a Victorian woman writer, who is also Queen, has yet to be systematically considered.

BIBLIOGRAPHY

None of Victoria's writing is in print.

Selected Works by Queen Victoria

Leaves from the Journal of Our Life in the Highlands from 1848 to 1861. Ed. Arthur
    Helps. 1868.
More Leaves from the Journal of a Life in the Highlands from 1862 to 1882. 1882.
Letters of Queen Victoria. Ed. Arthur Christopher Benson and Viscount Esher (First
    Series) and George Earle Buckle (Second and Third Series). 9 vols. 1907–1931.
*The Girlhood of Queen Victoria: A Selection from Her Majesty's Diaries Between the
    Years 1832 and 1840.* Ed. Viscount Esher. 2 vols. 1912.
Letters of Queen Victoria, from the Archives of the House of Brandenburg-Prussia. Ed.
    Hector Bolitho. 1938.
*Queen Victoria: Leaves from a Journal, A Record of the Visit of the Emperor and
    Empress of the French to the Queen and of the Visit of the Queen and H.R.H.
    The Prince Consort to the Emperor of the French.* Ed. Raymond Mortimer. 1961.
*Regina vs. Palmerston: The Correspondence Between Queen Victoria and Her Foreign
    and Prime Minister, 1837–1865.* Ed. Brian Connell. 1961.
Private Correspondence of Queen Victoria and the German Crown Princess: 1858–1885.
    Ed. Roger Fulford. 5 vol. 1964–1976.
*Dear and Honoured Lady: The Correspondence Between Queen Victoria and Alfred
    Tennyson.* Ed. Hope Dyson and Charles Tennyson. 1971.
Advice to a Grand-daughter: Letters from Queen Victoria to Princess Victoria of Hesse.
    Ed. Richard Hough. London: Heinemann, 1975.
Queen Victoria in Her Letters and Journals: A Selection. Ed. Christopher Hibbert. 1985.

Studies of Queen Victoria

Homans, Margaret. *Queen Victoria: Power, Representation, and the Woman Monarch.*
    Chicago: University of Chicago Press, 1998.
Homans, Margaret, and Adrienne Munich, eds. *Remaking Queen Victoria.* Cambridge:
    Cambridge University Press, 1997.
Houston, Gail. *Royalties: The Queen and Victorian Writers.* Charlottesville: University
    Press of Virginia, 1999.
Munich, Adrienne. *Queen Victoria's Secrets.* New York: Columbia University Press,
    1996.
St. Aubyn, Giles. *Queen Victoria: A Portrait.* New York: Athenaeum, 1992.
Strachey, Lytton. *Queen Victoria.* New York: Harcourt Brace, 1921.
Thompson, Dorothy. *Queen Victoria: The Woman, the Monarchy, and the People.* New
    York: Pantheon, 1990.

Mary Augusta Arnold Ward (Mrs. Humphry Ward) (1851–1920)

Gisela Argyle

BIOGRAPHY

From the start of her career, Mary Augusta Ward (neé Arnold) used her marital title, Mrs. Humphry Ward. The choice is symptomatic of her negotiations of a host of typical Victorian conflicts: matriarch versus woman of letters, scholar versus best-selling novelist, promoter of higher education for women versus opponent of female suffrage, philanthropist versus propagandist for the British war effort. In contrast to her own *A Writer's Recollections* (1918), her nephew Aldous Huxley's satire "Farcical History of Richard Greenow" in *Limbo* (1920; Chatto & Windus, 1970) testifies to the next generation's incomprehension of her "schizoid" positioning. The granddaughter of Dr. Arnold of Rugby and fond niece of Matthew Arnold early and readily assumed the vocation of a woman of letters and continued to pursue it as wife and mother. Her husband, Thomas Humphry Ward, was a Fellow at Oxford and, later, political-leader writer and art critic for the *Times*. While at Oxford, Mary Ward engaged herself in two major campaigns: on behalf of the "Liberal camp" in the religious debate with a pamphlet that would grow into *Robert Elsmere* (1888) and on behalf of women's higher education, as cofounder and first secretary of Somerville Hall (1879). After the great success of *Robert Elsmere* she turned herself into a "money-generating fiction-machine" (Sutherland), in support of her extended family and a lavish upper-class lifestyle. As a novelist, she outlived her audience, and the younger generation of writers ignored or scorned "Ma Hump." On her death the *Times* primarily commemorated not the writer but her philanthropic achievements, especially the Passmore Edwards Settlement in London, since then renamed for her, and the Play Centres.

MAJOR WORKS AND THEMES

Ward's best novels are *Robert Elsmere* (1888), *The History of David Grieve* (1892), *Marcella* (1894), *Helbeck of Bannisdale* (1898), *Eleanor* (1900), and *The Marriage of William Ashe* (1905). For many of her readers and reviewers she was a successor to George Eliot,* whom she had actually met as a young girl. All these novels participate strongly in the genre of the Bildungsroman. She presents a character's principles and vocation, including women's semi-public philanthropic or political activity, on the one hand, and private affection and loyalty, on the other, as dynamically interrelated, for good or ill. And the protagonists share the author's own "intoxication" with nature (*Recollections*), which she enhances by setting each novel in new locales. However, unlike George Eliot, Ward did not backdate any of her novels. Starting with her de-cision to recast a pamphlet in defense of religious skepticism as a novel, in *Robert Elsmere*, she continued to use her "novels of propaganda" for testing topical religious and social issues in the medium of "sensuous life" (*Recollec-tions*).

Her portrayals of both religious controversy and social and industrial reform are typically gendered. Like George Eliot in an earlier generation, she denies her heroines the full privileges of education and vocation that she herself en-joyed, with the result that the ultimate message seems to resemble that of the socially and religiously conservative novel *The Clever Woman of the Family* (1865) by Charlotte Yonge.* In her finest novel, *Helbeck of Bannisdale*, the typically strong-willed heroine is fatally torn between the Jesuitical "tyranny" of the man she loves and "a strange and desolate liberty" bequeathed to her by her agnostic father. However, Ward permits her heroines to make a persuasive case for their own judgment and conduct, without either Yonge's moralism or George Eliot's authorial irony. In the context of social and industrial reform, her heroines at their best are painfully conscious, as she herself was, of the inconsistency between their socialist convictions and their elite tastes; indeed, unlike Gissing, she hardly presents the intended beneficiaries in their own agency. The heroines' "natural" lack of political nerve and skill restricts them, if they don't wish to risk more harm than good, to the role of Lady Bountiful under a husband's expert judgment: " 'A woman has enough to govern herself' " (epigraph in *Marcella*). But in both *Marcella* and its sequel, *Sir George Tressady* (1896), Marcella's "natural" social pity adds motivation to men's convictions, even converting otherwise indifferent men to political engagement.

Ward best applied her critical principles in the fine, cosmopolitan introduc-tions to the Haworth Edition of the Brontë* novels (1899–1900); she never wrote the planned critical treatment of George Eliot. However, in her program-matic preface to the sixth edition of *David Grieve*, she defended "the novel with a purpose" and its "thought-stuff" against her negative reviewers by setting it in the larger historical and European tradition of Cervantes, Rousseau, George Sand, and Goethe, citing their novels' inclusivity of discourses, in anticipation, as it were, of Bakhtin. Except for less essayistic and descriptive "surplusage" (Ward's introduction to *Shirley*), her technique did not change. Stylistically she remained an "eminent Victorian," unaffected by the new preoccupations with narrative perspective and presentment of consciousness—Henry James, a loyal friend and benevolent critic, used to "rewrite" her novels while reading them.

CRITICAL RECEPTION

Traditional in narrative technique and topical in their subject matter, her best six novels were all popular successes or even best-sellers, both in Britain and America, as well as being reviewed as serious fiction. Her "grave" fiction (Gladstone), belonging to the "new didacticism" of the 1880s and 1890s, was read by men in public life as a corollary to the periodicals and disseminated radical ideas to a large public. This topicality quickly made her fiction seem outdated and useful only as social history. Q. D. Leavis ranked her, with H. G. Wells, as one of the "sincere" novelists, who make "for more desirable (*but not finer*) feeling" (*Fiction and the Reading Public*, 1932 [Russell & Russell, 1965] 70; emphasis added), which explains why Ward could not belong to the "great tradition" as defined by F. R. Leavis in 1948 (*The Great Tradition* [Chatto & Windus, 1960]). However, besides Sutherland's definitive biography, there have now appeared new editions and reprints of her novels as well as reevaluations of her fiction, life-writing, and literary criticism. For today's scholarly interests, Ward is preeminently instructive.

BIBLIOGRAPHY

Of all Ward's writings, only three novels are in print: *Eleanor, Lady Rose's Daughter*, and *The Marriage of William Ashe* (all reprinted by Buccaneer, 1977).

Selected Works by Mary Ward

Robert Elsmere. 1888.
The History of David Grieve. 1892.
Marcella. 1894.
Sir George Tressady. 1896.
Helbeck of Bannisdale. 1898.
Intro. *Life and Works of the Sisters Brontë*. Haworth Edition. 7 vols. 1899–1900. Rpt.,
       AMS Press, 1973.
Eleanor. 1900.
Lady Rose's Daughter. 1903.
The Marriage of William Ashe. 1905.
A Writer's Recollections. 1918.

Studies of Mary Ward

Ashton, Rosemary. "Doubting Clerics: From James Anthony Froude to Robert Elsmere via George Eliot." In *The Critical Spirit and the Will to Believe*. Ed. David Jasper and T. R. Wright. New York: St. Martin's Press, 1989. 69–87.

Bellringer, Alan W. "Mrs. Humphry Ward's Autobiographical Tactics: *A Writer's Recollections*." *Prose Studies* 8.3 (Dec. 1985): 40–50.

Bindsley, Anne M. *Mrs. Humphry Ward: A Study in Late-Victorian Feminine Consciousness and Creative Expression*. Stockholm: Almqvist and Wiksell International, 1985.

Colby, Vineta. *The Singular Anomaly: Women Novelists of the Nineteenth Century*. New York: New York University Press, 1970.

Fasick, Laura. "Culture, Nature, and Gender in Mary Ward's *Robert Elsmere* and *Helbeck of Bannisdale*." *Victorian Newsletter* 83 (Spring 1993): 25–31.

Gladstone, W. E. "*Robert Elsmere*. The Battle of Belief." *Nineteenth Century* 23 (May 1888): 766–88; rpt. in *Later Gleanings*. New York: Charles Scribner's Sons, 1897. 77–117.

Peterson, William S. *Victorian Heretic: Mrs. Humphry Ward's "Robert Elsmere."* Swansea: Leicester University Press, 1976.

Sutherland, John. *Mrs. Humphry Ward: Eminent Victorian, Pre-Eminent Edwardian*. Oxford: Oxford University Press, 1987.

Sutton-Ramspeck, Beth. "The Personal Is Poetical: Feminist Criticism and Mary Ward's Readings of the Brontës." *Victorian Studies* 34.1 (Autumn 1990): 55–75.

———. "The Slayer and the Slain: Women and Sacrifice in Mary Ward's *Eleanor*." *South Atlantic Review* 52.4 (Nov. 1987): 39–60.

Wilt, Judith. " 'Transition Time': The Political Romances of Mrs. Humphry Ward's *Marcella* (1894) and *Sir George Tressady* (1896)." In *The New Nineteenth Century: Feminist Readings of Underread Victorian Fiction*. Ed. Barbara Harman and Susan Meyer. New York: Garland, 1996.

Beatrice Webb
(1858–1943)

Deborah Epstein Nord

BIOGRAPHY

Beatrice Webb is best remembered as leader of the Fabian Society and coauthor, with her husband Sidney Webb, of important tomes of social and political history, among them *The History of Trade Unionism* (1894), *Industrial Democracy* (1897), and the nine-volume *English Local Government* (1903–1929). In her own right, however, she was a brilliant diarist and autobiographer who chronicled her intellectual and political evolution and her struggles for independence as a late-century Victorian woman. Descended from north-of-England Radicals and religious nonconformists, she was born into the entrepreneurial upper middle class. Her father, Richard Potter, was a railway magnate and lumber merchant; and her mother, Laurencina Heyworth Potter, a bluestocking and would-be novelist, devoted herself to the study of languages and political economy. Raised with her eight sisters by nannies and governesses in a Gloucestershire mansion and in a London flat, Potter Webb received no formal education but read widely and voraciously. Herbert Spencer, friend of her mother's and philosopher of social evolution, guided her in her studies.

When Webb was a young, unmarried woman searching for what she called "creed" and "craft" in the 1880s, her cousin Charles Booth invited her to work on his monumental study of poverty in London. Her contributions to Booth's *Life and Labour of the People in London* (1889–1903) consisted of studies of three metropolitan groups: dock laborers, sweatshop workers, and Jewish immigrants. The most striking piece of writing to emerge from this experience was "Pages from a Work-Girl's Diary," an account of Webb's masquerade as a seamstress seeking employment in an East End tailor's shop.

Webb was drawn to Fabian Socialism by her interest in empirical research, by her nascent belief in state regulation of labor—the result of her investigations of unregulated London trades—and finally, by reading *Fabian Essays*, published in 1889 and edited by George Bernard Shaw. Sidney Webb's essay in that collection, on the "historic basis" of socialism, relied on the evolutionary social theories of Herbert Spencer and Auguste Comte. In 1891 Webb joined the Fabian Society and became secretly engaged to Sidney, the son of a milliner and hairdresser; she married him in 1892 following the death of her father. As a working partnership they produced major works of historical research, helped to establish the London School of Economics, launched the *New Statesman*, and waged an ultimately unsuccessful campaign for the reform of the Poor Law.

MAJOR WORKS AND THEMES

Beatrice Webb kept a diary from the age of fifteen until her death in 1943. *The Diary of Beatrice Webb*, published in four volumes between 1982 and 1985, documents the personal struggles of an intellectually ambitious and emotionally fragile woman who desperately wished to break out of the strictures of upper-middle-class Victorian femininity. It traces her political evolution from Spencerian individualism to Fabian collectivism and records with accurate and painful detail what she called the London "marriage market." The diary is, as well, a thorough and useful history of the rise of the Labour Party and contains vivid and occasionally ruthless descriptions of political figures in the world of British socialism.

Webb made artful use of the diary herself when, in the throes of a deep personal crisis during World War I, she decided to write the story of the first few decades of her life. She produced the autobiography *My Apprenticeship*, probably her best and most enduring book, in 1926. Shaken by the war and uncertain of the public and personal paths her life had taken, Webb looked back in search of a triumphant and coherent chronology. Following in the tradition of other important Victorian autobiographers, she structured her life's story around her conversion to socialism and the discovery of her vocation, the craft of social investigation. Complicating and transforming this structure was the story of gender, of trying to forge a life of accomplishment and purpose when marriage to a suitable man was all that was expected of her. "I saw myself as one suffering from a divided personality," she wrote in *My Apprenticeship*, "the normal woman seeking personal happiness in love given and taken within the framework of a successful marriage; whilst the other self claimed, in season and out of season, the right to the free activity of a 'clear and analytic mind'" (239). Like certain heroines of Victorian fiction, Webb sought to reconcile romantic love with independence, and she wrote her autobiography as an intellectual woman's courtship novel. *My Apprenticeship* culminates in Beatrice and Sidney Webb's marriage, a "working comradeship founded in a common faith" (354). This narrative of Webb's life illustrates, as well, the intimate connection between religious impulse and socialist politics in the last decades of the nineteenth century.

CRITICAL RECEPTION

For many decades the Webbs were criticized and caricatured as positivists and technocrats. Virginia Woolf commented in her diary on the Webbs' lack of interest in either esthetic or emotional life, and Beatrice Webb drew criticism from feminists for her supposed indifference to women's rights. The Webbs have been satirized as a manipulative, Gradgrindian pair, most notably in H. G. Wells's *The New Machiavelli* (1911), and reviled by anti-Communists for their support of the Soviet Union in the 1930s. In recent years, however, the publication of Beatrice Webb's diaries, feminist readings of her autobiographical works, and a revival of interest in her early efforts as social investigator have led to a reassessment of Webb as a writer and personality distinct from her husband. The image of a more introspective, talented, and tormented woman has emerged; and her struggles against the sexual and marital conventions of her generation and class have taken on paradigmatic significance.

BIBLIOGRAPHY

The Letters of Sidney and Beatrice Webb, ed. Norman MacKenzie (3 vols., Cambridge University Press, 1978), and *The Diary of Beatrice Webb*, ed. Norman and Jeanne MacKenzie (4 vols., Harvard University Press, 1982–1985), have recently been published, as have reprints of *My Apprenticeship* (Cambridge University Press, 1979) and *The Co-operative Movement in Great Britain* (Ashgate, 1987).

Works by Beatrice (Potter) Webb

"Pages from a Work-Girl's Diary." *Nineteenth Century* 25 (Sept. 1888): 301–14.
"The Docks," "The Jewish Community," and "The Tailoring Trade." In *East London*. Ed. Charles Booth. 1889.
The Co-operative Movement in Great Britain. 1893.
The History of Trade Unionism. Coauthor Sidney Webb. 1894.
Industrial Democracy. Coauthor Sidney Webb. 1897.
English Local Government. Coauthor Sidney Webb. 9 vols. 1903–1929.
My Apprenticeship. 1926.
Our Partnership. 1948.
The Letters of Sidney and Beatrice Webb. Ed. Norman MacKenzie. 3 vols. 1978.
The Diary of Beatrice Webb. Ed. Norman MacKenzie and Jeanne MacKenzie. 4 vols. 1982–1985.

Studies of Beatrice Webb

Adam, Ruth, and Kitty Muggeridge. *Beatrice Webb: A Life, 1858–1943*. London: Secker & Warburg, 1967.
Caine, Barbara. "Beatrice Webb and Her Diary." *Victorian Studies* 27.1 (Autumn 1983): 81–89.

———. "Beatrice Webb and the 'Woman Question.' " *History Workshop Journal* 14 (Autumn 1982): 23–43.

Cole, Margaret. *Beatrice Webb*. New York: Harcourt, Brace, 1946.

Hynes, Samuel. "The Art of Beatrice Webb." In *Edwardian Occasions*. New York: Oxford University Press, 1972. 153–73.

Lewis, Jane. *Women and Social Action in Victorian and Edwardian England*. Stanford: Stanford University Press, 1991.

MacKenzie, Jeanne. *A Victorian Courtship: The Story of Beatrice and Sidney Webb*. New York: Oxford University Press, 1979.

Nord, Deborah Epstein. *The Apprenticeship of Beatrice Webb*. Ithaca: Cornell University Press, 1989.

Sanders, Valerie. " 'Fathers' Daughters': Three Victorian Anti-Feminist Women Autobiographers." In *Mortal Pages, Literary Lives: Studies in Nineteenth-Century Autobiography*. Ed. Vincent Newey and Philip Shaw. Brookfield, VT: Ashgate Publishing, 1996. 153–71.

Augusta Webster
(1837–1894)

Christine Sutphin

BIOGRAPHY

Augusta Webster was born Julia Augusta Davies in Dorset to Julia Hume Davies and Vice-Admiral George Davies. She spent her earliest years on board her father's ship the *Griper* in several ports in southern England. The family later lived at Banff Castle, Scotland, and at Penzance in Cornwall, then moved to Cambridge. Augusta attended the Cambridge School of Art, learned French during brief stays in Geneva and Paris, and taught herself Greek, Italian, and Spanish. In 1863 she married Thomas Webster, subsequently a lecturer at Trinity College, with whom she had one child, Margaret Davies Webster. In 1870 the Websters moved to London where Augusta became involved in social and political issues. She wrote and spoke eloquently on women's suffrage and higher education, advocated state-supported education for the poor, and was twice elected to the London School Board.

Webster's first collections of poetry, *Blanche Lisle, and Other Poems* (1860) and *Lilian Gray* (1864), and her only novel, *Lesley's Guardians* (1864), were published under the pseudonym of "Cecil Home." Her translations of Aeschylus and Euripides and all her later publications appeared under her own name. Webster was acclaimed during her lifetime, both for her writing and for her philanthropic efforts. Her obituary in *The Athenaeum* described her "as a poet of remarkable intellectual strength" and as a noble humanitarian commensurate with George Eliot* and Frances Power Cobbe* (Watts).

MAJOR WORKS AND THEMES

Of all her work, Webster's poetry is the most impressive, especially the dramatic monologues in *Dramatic Studies* (1866) and *Portraits* (1870). Webster was influenced by Robert Browning, but as both Angela Leighton and Susan

Brown have pointed out, Browning concentrates on the psychological divisions within his personae, whereas Webster's characters' dilemmas stem as much or more from social constraint: "It is characteristic of Webster to give full scope to the argument from circumstance and economic conditions" (Leighton 184). Nowhere is the commentary on social constraints more powerful than in Webster's "A Castaway," in which a high-class prostitute analyzes the contradictory ideology surrounding women's sexuality, laissez-faire economics, and her ambivalence about her position in life.

Webster's monologues often give voice to women. In two of the most effective—"Circe" and "Medea in Athens"—Webster examines mythic figures to create expressions of women's desire for sex and power, as well as to comment on the politics of heterosexuality, not only in an imagined "classical" period but in her own. Significantly, Circe asserts that her cup does not change men into swine; instead it reveals their true nature:

> . . . Change? there was no change;
> Only disguise gone from them unawares:
> And had there been one true right man of them
> He would have drunk the draught as I had drunk,
> And stood unharmed and looked me in the eyes.
>   ("Circe," *Portraits* 21)

Webster's portrayal of conventional women is also telling. In "The Happiest Girl in the World," "Faded," and "By the Looking-Glass," she examines the ambivalence of women in love, the mixed messages they receive from their culture, and the high value placed on physical beauty. Webster adopts male personae to powerful effect in such poems as "A Preacher" and "A Soul in Prison." In these poems Webster tackles the problem of religious doubt, an unusual subject for a Victorian woman.

In her later career, Webster turned to verse-drama. *The Sentence* (1887), set during the reign of the Roman emperor Caligula, is generally considered her most successful work in this genre. Webster also wrote a number of lyrics; particularly noteworthy are her "English rispetti" based on an Italian form. Webster's sonnet sequence, *Mother and Daughter* (1895), though unfinished at her death, is a significant contribution to women's revision of a traditionally male genre.

In addition to her poetry, Webster should be remembered for *A Housewife's Opinions* (1879), a collection of essays written for the *Examiner*, in which she expresses trenchant opinions on subjects from women's suffrage to the necessity of recognizing the difference between poets' lives and their personae.

CRITICAL RECEPTION

Christina Rossetti* and W. M. Rosseti praised Webster's poetry. Reviews consistently noted her originality, dramatic power, and intellectual force. The

Dictionary of National Biography declared, "Some of her lyrics deserve a place in every anthology of modern English poetry" (Lee 1027). One explanation for Webster's exclusion from the canon is that she lacked the powerful literary connections that would have kept her reputation alive. No diaries and few letters survive to support biographical work. In addition, some of the genres she chose are not widely read. Another possibility is that the social and political content of much of her strongest work did not appeal to later scholars. Webster did not appear in several important anthologies of nineteenth-century writers compiled in the 1920s and 1930s, an omission that meant that even specialists in the Victorian period have been largely unfamiliar with her work.

In the 1990s Dorothy Mermin calls her "the best of the poets whose reputations died with the century" (*Godiva's Ride* 53) and adds that "despite their excellence, her poems remain almost entirely unknown" (80), whereas Angela Leighton concludes that her "omission from the list of major women poets of the nineteenth century has gone unchallenged for too long since Christina Rossetti . . . first challenged it" (201). Webster's work remained out of print for about a hundred years. Her headnote in Clarendon Press's *Nineteenth-Century Women Poets* (ed. Isobel Armstrong and Joseph Bristow, 1996) begins: "Given the impressive technical and imaginative strengths of her work, there can be no doubt that Augusta Webster ranks as one of the great Victorian poets" (590). Her recent inclusion in anthologies and a forthcoming edition of her poems will help to reestablish Webster as a major voice in Victorian literature.

BIBLIOGRAPHY

Some of Webster's poems have been published in *Victorian Women Poets* (ed. Angela Leighton and Margaret Reynolds [Blackwell, 1995]), *Nineteenth-Century Women Poets* (ed. Isobel Armstrong and Joseph Bristow [Clarendon Press, 1996]), and *The Victorians* (ed. Valentine Cunningham [Blackwell, 1997]). *Augusta Webster: Portraits and Other Poems* (ed. Christine Sutphin) was published by Broadview Press in 2000.

Selected Works by Augusta Webster

Blanche Lisle, and Other Poems. 1860.
Lesley's Guardians. 1864.
Lilian Gray, a Poem. 1864.
Dramatic Studies. 1866.
A Woman Sold and Other Poems. 1867.
Portraits. 1870 (enlarged ed. 1893).
The Auspicious Day. 1872.
Yu-Pe-Ya's Lute. A Chinese Tale in English Verse. 1874.
Disguises: A Drama. 1879.
A Housewife's Opinions. 1879.
A Book of Rhyme. 1881.
In a Day: A Drama. 1882.

Daffodil and the Croäxaxicans. 1884.
The Sentence: A Drama. 1887.
Mother and Daughter. An Uncompleted Sonnet Sequence. 1895.

Studies of Augusta Webster

Boos, Florence. "Augusta Webster." In *Victorian Poets After 1850*. Ed. William E. Fredeman and Ira B. Nadel. *Dictionary of Literary Biography*. Detroit: Gale Research,
1985. 35: 280–84.

Brown, Susan. "Determined Heroines: George Eliot, Augusta Webster, and Closet Drama
by Victorian Women." *Victorian Poetry* 33 (Spring 1995): 89–109.

———. "Economical Representations: Dante Gabriel Rossetti's 'Jenny,' Augusta Webster's 'A Castaway,' and the Campaign Against the Contagious Diseases Acts."
Victorian Review 17 (Summer 1991): 78–95.

Demoor, Marysa. "Power in Petticoats: Augusta Webster's Poetry, Political Pamphlets,
and Poetry Reviews." *Belgian Essays in Literature and Language* (1997): 133–
40.

Lee, Elizabeth. "Augusta Webster." In *Dictionary of National Biography*. 1917. Ed. Sir
Leslie Stephen and Sir Sidney Lee. London: Oxford University Press, 1937–1938.
Vol. 20.

Leighton, Angela. "Augusta Webster." In *Victorian Women Poets: Writing Against the
Heart* London: Harvester Wheatsheaf, 1992.

Sutphin, Christine. "The Representation of Women's Heterosexual Desire in Augusta
Webster's 'Circe' and 'Medea in Athens.' " *Women's Writing* 5.3 (1998).

Watts, Theodore. "Mrs. Augusta Webster." *The Athenaeum* (15 Sept. 1894): 355.

Lady Jane Francesca Wilde (1821?-1896)

Dejan Kuzmanovic

BIOGRAPHY

Jane Elgee was born in Dublin into a prosperous, Protestant, Anglo-Irish family who supported the English rule, yet in her twenties she became involved with the nationalist Young Ireland movement and began writing for their newspaper the *Nation*. Her passionate revolutionary poetry brought her swift and lasting fame, and her pen name, Speranza, became a symbol of the Irish struggle for independence. Oscar Wilde was greeted by Irish Americans in 1882 as "Speranza's Son," and in 1891, 78 percent of the readers of a Dublin magazine named her the greatest living Irishwoman. Although she wrote all her life and translated poetry and prose from several European languages, her later work never approached the popular success of her early poetry.

In 1851, Jane Elgee married William Wilde, a prominent eye and ear surgeon, medical commissioner for the Irish census, and an authority on ancient Irish history, knighted for his achievements in 1864. Their conjugal happiness was tested by Sir William's adulterous affair, which caused a public scandal and a trial, harming their finances more than their reputation. In fact, Lady Wilde was a popular social hostess, very aware of the cultural importance of that role, and her famous at-homes gathered Dublin's most distinguished (and notorious) artists, writers, scholars, wits, and Bohemians.

Sir William's death in 1876 left Lady Wilde with nothing but debts and liabilities. Her many publications brought her little money, and her application for a literary pension from the government kept being refused until 1890. In 1879, she moved to London, where her son Oscar, a rising celebrity, introduced her to the society. While in Dublin she was almost unanimously respected and loved, her London acquaintances responded to her eccentricities in mixed ways. Her uncompromising individualism and brilliant conversation were admired, but her outlandish manners and old-fashioned clothes caused amazement and gossip.

Financial difficulties and various family problems marred Lady Wilde's last years. She found some consolation in Oscar's success, although she never saw any of his celebrated plays. By the mid-1890s, she gradually ceased publishing and entertaining and rarely left her house. The final blow was Oscar's imprisonment for "gross indecency" with other men in 1895, after which her health quickly deteriorated, and she refused to see friends, choosing to spend her last months in solitude. A month before death, she asked that Oscar be brought from prison to see her but was refused. At her request, the funeral was modest and private. No payment was made for a permanent tomb, so her remains were removed after seven years (both her sons being dead by then), and today nothing marks the place of her burial.

MAJOR WORKS AND THEMES

Lady Wilde's most effective poems, such as "The Stricken Land" or "The Famine Year," chronicle the tragedy of the Irish famine, exhorting patriotism and rebellion. Militant in tone, drawing from biblical, classical, and Irish oral traditions, they overflow with revolutionary zeal. Her essays on Ireland also sizzle with rousing, romanticized, sometimes politically irresponsible nationalism. The famous *"Jacta Alea Est"* ("The Die Is Cast," 1848) calls the Irish to arms against the English rule, ignoring the fact that the decimated population hardly had strength or energy for fighting. *The American Irish* (1878), written thirty years later, contains the same inflammatory rhetoric, unresponsive to political changes that have meantime occurred. While moving as descriptions and condemnations of English misrule in Ireland, her political pamphlets occasionally uncritically glorify everything Irish and denounce everything English.

Her insightful essays on women combine enlightened feminism with a more conservative rhetoric. In "The Bondage of Woman" she argues that women can attain political and sensual equality while preserving their feminine charm and fulfilling the "womanly duties" to their husbands. In "Venus Victrix," she praises strong, independent women, yet asserts that sympathy and sacrifice are the essence of womanhood. In other essays, she emphasizes women's achievements in literature and arts, calls for a female university and governmental support of exceptional women, and praises the Married Woman's Property Act for enabling women's financial independence in marriage, but in "Genius and Marriage" she instructs the woman married to "a genius" to efface herself and be entirely dedicated to her husband's work.

Lady Wilde's two collections of Irish folklore, reviews and essays on an impressive variety of subjects, from "The Destiny of Humanity" (1877) to "The Laws of Dress" (1881), and voluminous correspondence also testify to her vast reading, intelligence, humor, and emancipated opinions.

CRITICAL RECEPTION

Since most of Lady Wilde's writings are politically charged, it is hardly surprising that their early critical reception betrays political bias. Her passionate advocacy of Irish liberty and condemnation of English tyranny seduced her Irish readers into regarding her more as a precious national symbol than a writer to be evaluated, whereas it provoked her English critics to judge her with particular severity. While the Irish press praised the beautiful imagery and peculiar, powerful rhythm of her poems, English newspapers mocked her melodramatic style and questioned her facts. Her widely read books on Irish folklore and various essays encountered similarly mixed, politically motivated reception.

Today Lady Wilde is known either as Speranza or as the "Mother of Oscar," and the interest in her is primarily biographical. Regrettably, none of her works are currently in print, and there is virtually no scholarship on it. Her work certainly deserves more attention, in particular by those interested in the literary aspects of the Irish struggle for independence, Irish folklore, or nineteenth-century feminism.

BIBLIOGRAPHY

Selections from Lady Wilde's poetry can be found in several anthologies of Victorian women's poetry such as *Victorian Women Poets: An Anthology* (ed. Angela Leighton and Margaret Reynolds [Blackwell, 1995]) and *Nineteenth-Century Women Poets* (ed. Isobel Armstrong and Joseph Bristow [Clarendon Press, 1996]).

Works by Lady Wilde

Poems. 1864.
The American Irish. 1878.
Driftwood from Scandinavia. 1884.
Ancient Legends, Mystic Charms and Superstitions of Ireland. 1887.
Ancient Cures, Charms and Usages of Ireland. 1890.
Notes on Men, Women and Books. 1891.
Social Studies. 1893.

Studies of Lady Wilde

Horan, Patrick. *The Importance of Being Paradoxical: Maternal Presence in the Works of Oscar Wilde*. Madison: Fairleigh Dickinson University Press, 1997.
Melville, Joy. *Mother of Oscar: The Life of Jane Francesca Wilde*. London: John Murray, 1994.
Wyndham, Horace. *Speranza: A Biography of Lady Wilde*. New York: Philosophical Library, 1951.

Ellen Price Wood (Mrs. Henry Wood)
(1814–1887)

Janet L. Grose

BIOGRAPHY

Ellen Price Wood, best known as the author of *East Lynne*, was born in Worcester on 17 January 1814, the eldest daughter of a successful glove manufacturer. She loved books as a child and developed her writing skills during her teens, when the early stages of a lifelong illness and a resulting spinal curvature generally kept her confined to a reclining position. In 1836 she married Henry Wood, a businessman whose banking and shipping interests often kept him in France, where the Woods lived and traveled for two decades.

By the time she wrote *East Lynne* (1861), the Woods were living in London, where the author wrote short stories and novels steadily for more than three decades and ultimately finished almost forty long novels and over 300 short stories. For the last two decades of her life, she also owned, contributed to, and edited a monthly periodical, the *Argosy*. Many of her Johnny Ludlow stories appeared in the *Argosy* before being collected and published by Richard Bentley.

Most of Wood's manuscripts and letters were destroyed, but according to the accounts we do have, Ellen Wood was a quiet, humble, and religious person. Her marriage and family life seem to have been basically traditional and quite fulfilling. She died on 10 February 1887, was buried in Highgate Cemetery, and was mourned widely in both literary and personal circles.

MAJOR WORKS AND THEMES

East Lynne, by far Wood's most successful work, was her first full-length novel and the product of many years of planning and two years of actual composition. Published serially in *Colburn's New Monthly Magazine* in twenty-one parts, from January 1860 to September 1861, and then in three volumes in 1861, *East Lynne* was one of the early hugely popular "sensation novels" that became so prominent during that decade. It is the story of Lady Isabel Vane, a young woman who leaves her husband and children for another man, has an illegitimate child, is badly scarred in a railway accident, and then, disguised, endures the humiliation and pain of being governess to her own children while watching her former husband adore his new wife.

East Lynne has many of the scandalous details of the typical sensation novel, and it may seem to be morally heavy-handed, since the adulterous Isabel is duly punished for her sins. However, the novel is thematically much more complex than such a reading indicates, particularly since the reader is encouraged to sympathize with Isabel. The very fact that the heroine rejects her traditional patriarchal home in favor of life with a notorious rake suggests a possible rejection of the "Angel in the House" stereotype. As Stevie Davies has suggested, Wood's decision to use her husband's name as her authorial persona indicates a desire to appease Victorian gender ideals while subversively challenging them in her fiction. Certainly, in *East Lynne* and her other works, there seems a likelihood of discrepancy between the narrator's opinions, which often echo those of Victorian propriety, and the author's opinions, which may be significantly more radical.

Although Wood is best known for her sensation fiction, her works also reveal that she was adept at portraying the daily life of the middle class. Her characters are colorfully developed through dialogue and action. Wood was also keenly aware of social issues, as her exploration of working-class strikes in *A Life's Secret* (1862) and temperance in *Danesbury House* (1860) reveals. Her love of Worcestershire and her fascination with boys are evident in the *Johnny Ludlow* stories.

All of Wood's fiction reflects her intense interest in people. She was not a prominent member of Victorian literary circles, nor was she a vocal advocate of women's rights. However, her works reveal that even when she did not overtly defy prescriptions of gender and morality in her fiction, she certainly did explore options far beyond those advocated in conduct books. The body of her work reveals her to be a wonderful mix of influences: She was a product of conservatism, both religious and domestic; she was also, however, an author who took risks, experimenting with scandalous plots, dark characters, and the hidden realities of Victorian life that many in her society were reluctant to acknowledge.

CRITICAL RECEPTION

Not surprisingly, Ellen Wood began to receive a great deal of critical attention following the publication of *East Lynne*, which sold over half a million copies before 1900, was pirated in America, adapted for the stage in England, and translated into numerous languages. Oddly enough, however, the novel was rejected twice by Chapman and Hall and once by Smith and Elder before Richard Bentley accepted it, thereby establishing a long and lucrative relationship with Wood as her publisher.

Like Wilkie Collins's *The Woman in White* before it and Mary Elizabeth Braddon's* *Lady Audley's Secret* after it, *East Lynne* was an obvious success with the public, was in great demand in the circulating libraries, and was particularly popular with female readers. It also received generally positive critical review. A sure mark of its importance in major literary circles was the enthusiastic and unusually long review in the *Times*. Although she did receive some criticism for her melodramatic and shocking plots, Wood nevertheless established a literary reputation that assured her a readership for future novels. The *Johnny Ludlow* stories were particularly popular and generated critical praise for her depiction of her home county of Worcestershire and of boys' nature, a talent enhanced by Wood's experiences with her brothers and their college friends.

By the end of the century, Wood's readership was diminishing, and many of her books were no longer in print. This trend continued for several decades, until both fiction by Wood and essays about her were rarities. In the last three decades, however, interest in feminist criticism and sensation fiction has revived *East Lynne* from obscurity. Modern critics are also looking at Wood's fiction from new perspectives, and the author once considered simply a conservative voice of middle-class values is being explored as a progressive voice of protest against the confinement implied by the traditional Victorian patriarchal family.

BIBLIOGRAPHY

East Lynne (intro. Sally Mitchell [Rutgers University Press, 1984]; ed. Norman Page and Kamal Al-Solaylee [Dent, 1994]) is the only work by Wood currently in print.

Selected Works by Ellen Price Wood

Danesbury House. 1860.
East Lynne. 3 vols. 1861.
A Life's Secret. 1862.
Mrs. Halliburton's Troubles. 1862.
The Castle's Heir. 1863.
The Shadow of Ashlydyat. 1863.
Verner's Pride. 1863.
Lord Oakburn's Daughters. 1864.
The Red Court Farm. 1868.
Roland Yorke. 1869.
Johnny Ludlow, six series. 1874–1889.

Studies of Ellen Price Wood

Al-Solaylee, Kamal. Introduction. *East Lynne.* Ed. Norman Page and Kamal Al-Solaylee. London: Dent, 1994. xv–xxiii.

Balee, Susan. "Correcting the Historical Context: The Real Publication Dates of *East Lynne.*" *Victorian Periodicals Review* 26.3 (1993): 143–45.

Davies, Stevie. Introduction. *East Lynne*. London: Dent, 1984. v–xii.

Langbauer, Laurie. "Women in White, Men in Feminism." *Yale Journal of Criticism* 2.2 (1989): 219–43.

Loesberg, Jonathan. "The Ideology of Form in Sensation Fiction." *Representations* 13 (1986): 115–38.

Mitchell, Sally. Introduction. *East Lynne*. New Brunswick: Rutgers University Press, 1984. vii–xviii.

Showalter, Elaine. "Desperate Remedies: Sensation Novels of the 1860s." *Victorian Newsletter* 49 (1976): 1–5.

Shuttleworth, Sally. "Demonic Mothers: Ideologies of Bourgeois Motherhood in the Mid-Victorian Era." In *Rewriting the Victorians: Theory, History, and the Politics of Gender*. Ed. Linda M. Shires. New York: Routledge, 1992. 31–51.

Sterner, Mark. "The Changing Status of Women in Late Victorian Drama." In *Within the Dramatic Spectrum*. Ed. Karelisa V. Hartigan. Lanham: University Press of America, 1986. 199–212.

Walker, Gail. "The 'Sin' of Isabel Vane: *East Lynne* and Victorian Sexuality." In *Heroines of Popular Culture*. Ed. Pat Browne. Bowling Green, OH: Popular, 1987. 23–31.

Wood, Charles W. *Memorials of Mrs. Henry Wood*. London: Bentley, 1894.

Charlotte Mary Yonge
(1823-1901)

Marylu Hill

BIOGRAPHY

By the time of her death in 1901, Charlotte Mary Yonge's career almost completely spanned the Victorian era. A near-contemporary in age to Queen Victoria,* Yonge represented through her novels many of the now-stereotypical values of the Victorian age—home, family, church, and stability. But—and perhaps of more interest to modern readers—Yonge's novels of nineteenth-century life captured the upheavals faced within the English family caused by changes in attitudes toward gender roles, education, religion, and class. While remaining a staunch conservative throughout her life, Yonge presented powerful images of Victorians—particularly Victorian women—in crisis.

Charlotte Mary Yonge was born in 1823 in the town of Otterbourne, Hampshire, to solidly middle-class parents. In contrast to her constant depictions of large families in her fiction, Yonge was the elder of only two children. Her education took place largely at home, where she was taught by her father, a retired army officer with strong clerical connections; from him she received training in ancient and modern languages, history, literature, and—most crucially for the formation of her character—a conservative High Church religious education. The arrival in 1836 of John Keble, the leading light of the Tractarian, or Oxford, movement, as vicar of nearby Hursley parish brought Yonge into the compass of Tractarian theology and provided the single-most important shaping influence on her as a writer. Yonge became a "catechumen" of Keble, and until his death in 1866, he was her most-valued reader and commentator on her literary work.

With the publication of *The Heir of Redclyffe* (1853), Yonge rocketed to literary fame. *The Heir of Redclyffe*, a tale of spiritual versus worldly desires personified by two cousins at odds with each other, was an immediate bestseller and clearly left its mark on at least one generation of Victorians. Yonge was an immensely prolific writer, often writing several works simultaneously; in total she produced over 160 titles, in addition to editing and contributing to *The Monthly Packet*, a juvenile magazine, from 1851 to 1890. She also taught daily in the village school—like many of her spinster heroines—and had advanced notions of early childhood education in that she believed learning was most effective when it stimulated a child's natural curiosity and interests. By the time she died in 1901, Yonge was recognized as something of a Victorian sage for at least two generations of readers, especially adolescent girls.

MAJOR WORKS AND THEMES

Charlotte Yonge's fiction covers an amazing variety of topics and time periods, but for the modern reader, her novels of domestic life and the impact of domesticity upon both unmarried and married women in the family are of the greatest interest. In her best novels—which include *The Heir of Redclyffe, The Daisy Chain* (1856), *Heartsease* (1854), *Hopes and Fears* (1860), *The Clever Woman of the Family* (1865), *The Pillars of the House* (1873), and *The Three Brides* (1876)—there runs a quietly subversive thread in the midst of her repeated assurances that women are subservient to men. In each of the novels listed above, as well as many of her other works, Yonge suggests that not only are women the heart of the home, but all true power, that is, spiritual, moral, and maternal power, emanates from feminine rather than masculine ideals. For example, as Barbara Dennis has recently noted, the subtext of *The Heir of Redclyffe* is that "good" women, like Mrs. Edmondstone or her daughter Amy, are the true rulers of hearts and souls and, as such, are "formidable role models" in a positive sense for young women. Likewise, seemingly passive and shy Violet Martindale of *Heartsease* turns out to possess the gentle power by which all the other characters are influenced and shaped for the better. In a time period where mother figures tend to be missing or useless, as we find in Charles Dickens, the Brontës,* and George Eliot,* Yonge creates powerful and efficient mother figures who embody Ruskin's ideal of womanly influence and guidance in "Of Queens' Gardens."

But not all mothers are good mothers in Yonge's fictional world; a refreshing aspect of her novels is her ability to offer many contrasting types to avoid the strictly sentimental. Each of her major works has an example of bad mothering—Flora May in *The Daisy Chain*, who disregards her infant's needs to pursue status as a member of Parliament's wife; Lady Martindale and her aunt Mrs. Nesbit (her surrogate mother), who both perpetuate a chain of inattention to their families; and Mrs. Curtis in *The Clever Woman of the Family*, who is simply rather weak and silly. These women fail because they do not exercise their true power through mothering and instead focus on worldly desires.

In contrast to the mother characters, Yonge also creates an engaging group of spinsters within her novels whom she alternately critiques and applauds. All her spinsters (or near-spinsters, meaning at the end they surprisingly marry after all) can be read as aspects of Yonge herself; frequently, like Theodore in *Hearts-ease* or Ethel May in *The Daisy Chain*, they are described almost exactly the way Yonge described herself in an autobiographical fragment as a young girl—darkly handsome, intellectual, occasionally shrill-voiced, and always anxious to be of use. The trials her spinster characters go through offer moving testimony to the plight of the superfluous woman, particularly one whose intelligence and talents remain largely untapped by life. The two most contrasting portraits are perhaps Ethel May—whose nearsighted awkwardness and gawky qualities combined with her quick intellect endeared her to many Victorian readers—and Rachel Curtis in *The Clever Woman of the Family*—who is opinionated, bossy, headstrong, and steeped in theories. Yonge uses very different methods to finally achieve the same purpose of helping these two women find their "true" feminine side. But Yonge is not interested in the worldly femininity of ladylike airs; instead, she depicts a growth in character that permits these young women to shift from theoretical "book" knowledge to a knowledge based on experience of real emotions. "Cleverness" in all her spinsters (and many of her men besides) must be replaced with "wisdom" gained from an intuitive compassion for others and a feminine sense of the healing nature of domestic life. The "Woman Question" for Yonge is thus misdirected because it places an emphasis on the self's own needs rather than the needs of others—a distinction upheld by the twin codes of religion and true womanhood.

It is further worth noting that in Yonge's world of compassionate mothers and busy spinsters her male figures tend to be either passive, weak, and susceptible to worldly temptation or domesticated, feminized, and often celibate. For example, Arthur Martindale in *Heartsease* almost brings his family to ruin due to his childish avoidance of all responsibility. Mr. Edmondstone in *The Heir of Redclyffe* is well meaning but vacillating and generally useless in decision making—his wife makes all the important decisions. Even the likable Dr. May in *The Daisy Chain* is impetuous and often petty and childish in his emotions—it is his foolhardy driving, for example, which causes the death of Mrs. May in the first pages of the novel.

The most admirable men in Yonge's novels are clearly feminized males—men who have embraced the domestic and spiritual hearth. John Martindale, Alick Keith, and Guy Morville are all examples of men who have learned to value domestic ideals—and, what is more, know how to create them in the best "womanly" fashion. Even superior knowledge in men is suspect unless it clearly serves the greater spiritual and domestic good; thus, Norman May, anxious for academic honors, is inferior to his less-learned, more womanly brother Richard in terms of spiritual development for much of the novel. Accordingly, for both men and women, knowledge must be tempered by experience and compassion.

Finally, the modern reader can turn to Charlotte Yonge's novels for any variety of insights into human character and Victorian social mores. Yonge consistently offers perceptive psychological insights into family politics, particularly when a new in-law joins the family dynamic. Her portraits of sibling and parental jealousy and maneuvering at the entry of a daughter- or sister-in-law are very realistic, most notably in *Heartsease* and *The Three Brides*. Parent/child relations are also generally presented with great veracity, and Yonge highlights the problematic issue of filial obedience when a parent is clearly in the wrong or at best has neglected his or her parental duties.

Students of class and empire in the Victorian novel will also find much to work with in Yonge's novels, especially with her sometimes paradoxical attitudes toward class (which can best be understood perhaps through her religious background). Her family's involvement with the army and colonial interests also give her fiction a wider range of awareness than might otherwise be supposed. Finally, as critics of Victorian children's books already know, Yonge offers an intriguing window into the world of Victorian childhood. Her portraits of children are generally very real, particularly in her ability to capture the animal spirits of large families.

CRITICAL RECEPTION

Despite her best-selling status in midcentury, by the end of her life, Yonge was already being dismissed as too "goody-goody" by younger readers. Certainly her critical reception, while fairly strong at the time of *The Heir of Redclyffe* (and including such admirers as Alfred Tennyson, Dante Gabriel Rossetti, Henry James, and William Morris), never reached the height of a Dickens, Eliot, or Hardy. Although her works have maintained a faithful core of readers into this century, critics and writers of the early twentieth century have tended to equate Yonge's novels with Victorian effusions of sentimentality and, as such, place her among other eminent Victorians against whom the modernists rebelled. In addition, there remains the criticism that Yonge simply wrote too much, and subsequently wrote herself out—a criticism that the sheer volume of her works seems to bear out.

But interest in Charlotte Yonge was deservedly revived with the growth of the women's movement of the 1970s, and her novels about headstrong and impetuous heroines have undergone interested scrutiny in the light of twentieth-century feminism. Recent critical works on Yonge by June Sturrock and Barbara Dennis emphasize the complexity of Yonge's attitudes toward the "Woman Question" and her role in the Tractarian movement, in contrast to pervading assumptions about her conservatism and her peripheral status in the Oxford movement. Her ideas on education, especially female education, are beginning to draw more attention as seen in recent rereadings by Shirley Foster and Judy Simons in *What Katy Read* and Judith Rowbotham in *Good Girls Make Good Wives*. A new edition of *The Heir of Redclyffe* has recently been published by Oxford University Press that permits readers once again to gauge its central importance for Victorian readers and also to prove again the immense readability of Yonge at her best. As one critic, Edith Sichel, stated in 1901, "We do not so much read her stories as live next door to her characters." Even at the distance of over a century, Yonge's characters in her strongest novels remain surprisingly alive with plenty to say to modern readers.

BIBLIOGRAPHY

With the exception of a limited number of her novels, including *The Heir of Redclyffe* (ed. Barbara Dennis, Oxford University Press, 1997), *Heartsease* (AMS Press), *Hopes and Fears* (AMS Press), and *The Trial* (Sutton Publishing, 1999), Yonge's works are largely out of print. In the 1980s, Virago Press reprinted *The Daisy Chain* and *The Clever Woman of the Family* (rpt. 1999).

Selected Works by Charlotte Mary Yonge

The Heir of Redclyffe. 1853.
Heartsease, or The Brother's Wife. 1854.
The Daisy Chain. 1856.
Dynevor Terrace, or The Clue of Life. 1857.
Hopes and Fears, or Scenes from the Life of a Spinster. 1860.
The Trial [a sequel to *The Daisy Chain*]. 1864.
The Clever Woman of the Family. 1865.
The Pillars of the House. 1873.
The Three Brides. 1876.

Studies of Charlotte Mary Yonge

Battiscombe, Georgina, and Marghanita Laski. *A Chaplet for Charlotte Yonge.* London: Cresset, 1965.
Coleridge, Christabel. *Charlotte Mary Yonge: Her Life and Letters.* London: Macmillan, 1903.
Dennis, Barbara. *Charlotte Yonge (1823–1901): Novelist of the Oxford Movement.* Lewiston, NY: Edwin Mellen Press, 1992.
Foster, Shirley, and Judy Simons. *What Katy Read: Feminist Re-Readings of "Classic" Stories for Girls.* Iowa City: University of Iowa Press, 1995. [Chapter on *The Daisy Chain*]
Rowbotham, Judith. *Good Girls Make Good Wives: Guidance for Girls in Victorian Fiction.* Oxford: Basil Blackwell, 1989.
Sandbach-Dahlstrom, Catherine. *Be Good Sweet Maid: Charlotte Yonge's Domestic Fiction: A Study in Dogmatic Purpose and Fictional Form.* Stockholm: Almqvist and Wiksell International, 1984.
Sturrock, June. *"Heaven and Home": Charlotte M. Yonge's Domestic Fiction and the Victorian Debate over Women.* Victoria, British Colombia, Canada: English Literary Studies, 1995.
———. "A Personal View of Women's Education, 1838–1900: Charlotte Yonge's Novels." *Victorians Institute Journal* 7 (1992): 7–18.
Wheatley, Kim. "Death and Domestication in Charlotte M. Yonge's *The Clever Woman of the Family.*" *Studies in English Literature* 36 (1996): 895–915.

Selected Bibliography

ANTHOLOGIES

Abrams, M. H., ed. *The Norton Anthology of English Literature*. 7th ed. Vol. 2. New York: W. W. Norton, 2000. Besant, E. Brontë, Browning, M. Coleridge, (Mulock) Craik, Eliot, Ellis, Field, Hemans, Landon, Martineau, Nightingale, Rossetti, Shelley.

Damrosh, David, gen. ed. *The Longman Anthology of British Literature*. Vol. 2. New York: Longman, 1999. Austen, Beeton, Bird, A. Brontë, C. Brontë, Browning, Cobbe, Eliot, Ellis, Field, Gaskell, Hemans, Kemble, Kingsley, Martineau, Nesbit, Nightingale, Norton, Rossetti, Trollope, Q. Victoria.

Gilbert, Sandra M., and Susan Gubar, eds. *The Norton Anthology of Literature by Women: The Tradition in English*. 2nd ed. New York: W. W. Norton, 1996. Austen, C. Brontë, E. Brontë, Browning, M. Coleridge, Edgeworth, Eliot, Gaskell, Meynell, Nightingale, Rossetti, Schreiner, Shelley.

Haight, Gordon S., ed. *The Portable Victorian Reader*. New York: Penguin Books, 1972. Bodichon, C. Brontë, Carlyle, Eliot, Gaskell, Martineau, Q. Victoria.

Jump, Harriet Devine, ed. *Women's Writing of the Victorian Period 1837–1901: An Anthology*. New York: St. Martin's Press, 1999. Beeton, Besant, Bevington, Bird, Black, Bodichon, C. Brontë, E. Brontë, Browning, Butler, Caird, Carlyle, Cobbe, M. Coleridge, S. Coleridge, Cook, Craik, Cullwick, Eastlake, Eliot, Ellis, Field, Gaskell, Grand, Johnston, Kemble, Landon, Linton, Martineau, Naden, Nesbit, Nightingale, Norton, Oliphant, Ouida, Probyn, Procter, Ritchie, Robinson, Rossetti, Shelley, Simcox, Q. Victoria, Wilde.

Trilling, Lionel, and Harold Bloom, eds. *The Oxford Anthology of English Literature: 1800 to Present*. Vol. 2. New York: Oxford University Press, 1973. E. Brontë, Browning, Rossetti.

Wu, Duncan, ed. *Romanticism: An Anthology*. Oxford: Blackwell, 1994. (Barrett) Browning, Edgeworth, Hemans, Landon, Norton, Shelley.

POETRY

Armstrong, Isobel, and Joseph Bristow, eds. *Nineteenth-Century Women Poets*. Oxford: Clarendon Press, 1996. Blind, Braddon, A. Brontë, C. Brontë, E. Brontë, Brown-

ing, M. Coleridge, S. Coleridge, Cook, Craik, Eliot, Ellis, Field, Greenwell, He-
mans, Howitt, Ingelow, M. Jewsbury, Johnston, Kemble, Landon, Levy, Meynell,
Mitford, Naden, Nesbit, Norton, Parkes, Procter, Rossetti, Sewell, Siddal, Tynan,
Webster, Wilde.

Ashfield, Andrew, ed. *Romantic Women Poets: 1770–1838: An Anthology*. Manchester:
Manchester University Press, 1995. Barrett (Browning), C. Brontë, E. Brontë, S.
Coleridge, Hemans, M. Jewsbury, Landon, Norton.

Collins, Thomas J., and Vivienne Rundle, eds. *Victorian Poetry and Poetic Theory*.
Ontario: Broadview, 1999. Braddon, C. Brontë, E. Brontë, Browning, M. Cole-
ridge, Cook, Eliot, Field, Greenwell, Hemans, Ingelow, Landon, Levy, Norton,
Procter, Robinson, Rossetti, Siddal, Webster, Wilde.

Cunningham, Valentine, ed. *The Victorians: An Anthology of Poetry and Poetics*. Oxford:
Blackwell, 1997. Blind, A. Brontë, C. Brontë, E. Brontë, Browning, Coleridge,
Craik, Eliot, Field, Gaskell, Howitt, Ingelow, Kemble, Landon, Levy, Meynell,
Norton, Parkes, Procter, Rossetti, Siddal, Webster.

Higonnet, Margaret Randolph, ed. *British Women Poets of the 19th Century*. New York:
Meridian/Penguin, 1996. Blind, A. Brontë, C. Brontë, E. Brontë, Browning, M.
Coleridge, Eliot, Field, Greenwell, Hemans, Ingelow, Kemble, Landon, Levy,
Meynell, Nesbit, Radford, Robinson, Rossetti, Webster.

Karlin, Daniel, ed. *The Penguin Book of Victorian Verse*. London: Penguin, 1997. Blind,
A. Brontë, C. Brontë, E. Brontë. Browning, M. Coleridge, Eliot, Field, Howitt,
Ingelow, Landon, Levy, Meynell, Probyn, Procter, Rossetti, Webster.

Leighton, Angela, and Margaret Reynolds, eds. *Victorian Women Poets: An Anthology*.
Oxford: Blackwell, 1995. Bevington, Black, Blind, A. Brontë, C. Brontë, E.
Brontë, Browning, M. Coleridge, S. Coleridge, Cook, Eliot, Field, Greenwell,
Hemans, Howitt, Ingelow, M. Jewsbury, Johnston, Kemble, Landon, Levy, Mey-
nell, Naden, Nesbit, Norton, Parkes, Probyn, Procter, Robinson, Rossetti, Siddal,
Webster, Wilde.

Norris, Pamela, ed. *Sound the Deep Waters: Women's Romantic Poetry in the Victorian
Age*. Boston: Bulfinch/Little, Brown, 1991. A. Brontë, C. Brontë, E. Brontë,
Browning, M. Coleridge, Eliot, Greenwell, Ingelow, Levy, Meynell, Nesbit, Proc-
ter, Radford, Rossetti, Siddal.

Reilly, Catherine, comp. *Winged Words: An Anthology of Victorian Women's Poetry and
Verse*. London: Enitharmon Press, 1994. Bevington, Blind, E. Brontë, Browning,
M. Coleridge, Cook, Craik, Eliot, Field, Greenwell, Howitt, Ingelow, Kemble,
Levy, Meynell, Nesbit, Norton, Probyn, Procter, Radford, Robinson, Rossetti,
Siddal, Tynan, Webster, Wilde.

Ricks, Christopher, ed. *The New Oxford Book of Victorian Verse*. Oxford: Oxford University Press, 1987. Bevington, C. Brontë, E. Brontë, Browning, M. Coleridge,
Eliot, Field, Greenwell, Ingelow, Levy, Meynell, Nesbit, Procter, Radford, Robinson, Rossetti, Siddal, Tynan.

Wain, John, ed. *The Oxford Anthology of English Poetry*. Vol. 2. Oxford: Oxford University Press, 1990. E. Brontë, Browning, Ingelow, Meynell, Rossetti.

PROSE

Broomfield, Andrea, and Sally Mitchell, eds. *Prose by Victorian Women: An Anthology*.
New York: Garland, 1996. Bird (Bishop), Black, Caird, Cobbe, Eastlake, Eliot,
Grand, Lee, Linton, Martineau, Mitford, Oliphant, Ritchie, Simcox, Taylor.

Hamilton, Susan, ed. *"Criminals, Idiots, Women and Minors": Victorian Writing by Women on Women*. Peterborough, Ontario: Broadview, 1996. Caird, Cobbe, Jameson, Linton, Martineau, Oliphant, Taylor.

Lacey, Candida Ann, ed. *Barbara Leigh Smith Bodichon and the Langham Place Group*. New York: Routledge & Kegan Paul, 1987. Bodichon, Cobbe, Parkes, Procter.

Mundhenk, Rosemary J., and LuAnn McCracken Fletcher, eds. *Victorian Prose: An Anthology*. New York: Columbia University Press, 1999. Bodichon, C. Brontë, Carlyle, Cobbe, Craik, Eastlake, Eliot, Ellis, Gordon, Kingsley, Martineau, Nightingale, Norton, Oliphant, Tonna, Q. Victoria, Ward.

GENERAL BIBLIOGRAPHY

Ardis, Ann L. *New Women, New Novels: Feminism and Early Modernism*. New Brunswick: Rutgers University Press, 1990.

Auerback, Nina. *Communities of Women: An Idea in Fiction*. Cambridge: Harvard University Press, 1978. Austen, C. Brontë, Gaskell.

———. *Woman and the Demon: The Life of a Victorian Myth*. Cambridge: Harvard University Press, 1982.

Bodenheimer, Rosemarie. *The Politics of Story in Victorian Social Fiction*. Ithaca: Cornell University Press, 1988. C. Brontë, Eliot, Gaskell, Jewsbury, Trollope.

Boone, Joseph Allen. *Tradition Counter Tradition: Love and the Form of Fiction*. Chicago: University of Chicago Press, 1987. Austen, E. Brontë, Eliot, Gaskell.

Colby, Robert A. *Fiction with a Purpose: Major and Minor Nineteenth-Century Novels*. Bloomington: Indiana University Press, 1967.

Colby, Vineta. *The Singular Anomaly: Women Novelists of the Nineteenth Century*. New York: New York University Press, 1970. Lee, Linton, Schreiner, Ward.

Cunningham, Gail. *The New Woman and the Victorian Novel*. New York: Macmillan Press, 1978. C. Brontë, Caird, Egerton, Gaskell, Malet, Wood.

Cvetkovich, Ann. *Mixed Feelings: Feminism, Mass Culture, and Victorian Sensationalism*. New Brunswick: Rutgers University Press, 1992. Braddon, Eliot, Wood.

David, Deirdre. *Intellectual Women and Victorian Patriarchy: Harriet Martineau, Elizabeth Barrett Browning, George Eliot*. Ithaca: Cornell University Press, 1987.

Foster, Shirley. *Victorian Women's Fiction: Marriage, Freedom and the Individual*. London: Croom Helm, 1985. C. Brontë, Craik, Eliot, Gaskell, Sewell.

Gates, Barbara T. *Kindred Nature: Victorian and Edwardian Women Embrace the Living World*. Chicago: University of Chicago Press, 1998.

Gilbert, Pamela K. *Disease, Desire, and the Body in Victorian Women's Popular Novels*. Cambridge: Cambridge University Press, 1997. Braddon, Broughton, Ouida.

Gilbert, Sandra M., and Susan Gubar. *The Madwoman in the Attic: The Woman Writer and the Nineteenth-Century Literary Imagination*. New Haven: Yale University Press, 1979. Austen, A. Brontë, C. Brontë, E. Brontë, Browning, M. Coleridge, Eliot, Rossetti, Shelley.

Harman, Barbara Leah, and Susan Meyer. *The New Nineteenth Century: Feminist Readings of Underread Victorian Fiction*. New York: Garland, 1996. A. Brontë, Grand, G. Jewsbury, Oliphant, Ward.

Hickok, Kathleen. *Representations of Women: Nineteenth-Century British Women's Poetry*. Westport: Greenwood Press, 1984.

Homans, Margaret. *Bearing the Word: Language and Female Experience in Nineteenth-

Century Women's Writing. Chicago: University of Chicago Press, 1986. C. Brontë, E. Brontë, Eliot, Gaskell, Shelley.

Hughes, Winifred. *The Maniac in the Cellar: Sensation Novels of the 1860s.* Princeton: Princeton University Press, 1980. Braddon, Wood.

Kestner, Joseph. *Protest and Reform: The British Social Narrative by Women, 1827–1867.* Madison: University of Wisconsin Press, 1985.

Kranidis, Rita S. *Subversive Discourse: The Cultural Production of Late Victorian Feminist Novels.* New York: St. Martin's Press, 1995. Caird, Cholmondeley, Egerton, Grand.

Krueger, Christine. *The Reader's Repentance: Women Preachers, Women Writers, and Nineteenth-Century Social Discourse.* Chicago: University of Chicago Press, 1992. Eliot, Gaskell, Tonna.

Langbauer, Laurie. *Novels of Everyday Life. The Series in English Fiction, 1850–1930.* Ithaca: Cornell University Press, 1999. Oliphant, Yonge.

Langland, Elizabeth. *Nobody's Angels: Middle-Class Women and Domestic Ideology in Victorian Culture.* Ithaca: Cornell University Press, 1995. Eliot, Gaskell, Oliphant.

Leighton, Angela. *Victorian Women Poets: Writing Against the Heart.* London: Harvester Wheatsheaf, 1992. E. Brontë, Browning, M. Coleridge, Eliot, Field, Hemans, Landon, Meynell, Procter, Rossetti, Webster.

Leighton, Angela, ed. *Victorian Women Poets: A Critical Reader.* Oxford: Blackwell, 1996.

Manos, Nikki Lee, and Meri-Jane Rochelson, eds. *Transforming Genres: New Approaches to British Fiction of the 1890s.* New York: St. Martin's Press, 1994. Corelli, Grand, Kingsley.

Mellor, Anne K. *Romanticism & Gender.* New York: Routledge, 1993. Austen, E. Brontë, Hemans, Landon.

Mermin, Dorothy. *Godiva's Ride: Women of Letters in England 1830–1880.* Bloomington: Indiana University Press, 1993.

Michie, Elsie B. *Outside the Pale: Cultural Exclusion, Gender Difference. and the Victorian Woman Writer.* Ithaca: Cornell University Press, 1993. C. Brontë, E. Brontë, Eliot, Gaskell, Shelley.

Moers, Ellen. *Literary Women.* New York: Oxford University Press, 1977.

Nelson, Carolyn Christenson. *British Women Fiction Writers of the 1890s.* Twayne's English Authors Series. New York: Twayne, 1996. Caird, Cholmondeley, Egerton, Grand, Lee.

Nestor, Pauline. *Female Friendships and Communities: Charlotte Brontë, George Eliot, Elizabeth Gaskell.* Oxford: Clarendon Press, 1985.

Newton, Judith Lowder. *Women, Power, and Subversion: Social Strategies in British Fiction, 1778–1860.* Athens: University of Georgia Press, 1981. Austen, C. Brontë, Eliot.

Poovey, Mary. *The Proper Lady and the Woman Writer: Ideology as Style in the Works of Mary Wollstonecraft, Mary Shelley, and Jane Austen.* Chicago: University of Chicago Press, 1984.

———. *Uneven Developments: The Ideological Work of Gender in Mid-Victorian England.* Chicago: University of Chicago Press, 1988. C. Brontë, Nightingale, Norton.

Pykett, Lyn. *The "Improper" Feminine: The Women's Sensation Novel and the New Woman Writing.* New York: Routledge, 1992. Braddon, Grand, Wood.

Ross, Marlon. *The Contours of Masculine Desire: Romanticism and the Rise of Women's Poetry*. New York: Oxford University Press, 1989. Hemans, Landon.

Shires, Linda M., ed. *Rewriting the Victorians: Theory, History, and the Politics of Gender*. New York: Routledge, 1992.

Showalter, Elaine. *A Literature of Their Own: British Women Novelists from Brontë to Lessing*. Princeton: Princeton University Press, 1977.

———. *Sexual Anarchy: Gender and Culture at the Fin de Siècle*. New York: Viking, 1990.

Thompson, Nicola. *Reviewing Sex: Gender and the Reception of Victorian Novels*. New York: New York University Press, 1996. E. Brontë, Yonge.

Tillotson, Kathleen. *Novels of the Eighteen-Forties*. Oxford: Oxford University Press, 1956. C. Brontë, Gaskell.

ELECTRONIC RESOURCES

Alan Liu's "Voice of the Shuttle" from the University of California at Santa Barbara: http://vos.ucsb.edu/shuttle/english.html.

CETH Directory for Electronic Texts in the Humanities: http://scc01.rutgers.edu/ceth.

Gaslight Electronic Text, 1800–1919: http://www.mtroyal.ab.ca/programs/arts/english/gaslight.

Victorian Database Online: http://www.victoriandatabase.com.

Victorian Women Writers Project: http://www.indiana.edu/~letrs/vwwp/.

VICTORIA Research Web: http://www.indiana.edu/~victoria.

Index

About the Editor and Contributors

EMILY R. ANDERSON is currently working on her Ph.D. in English at the University of California, Berkeley. Her work is on nineteenth-century literature, primarily by women, and the development of novelistic language and narrative strategies. She has recently presented papers on, among others, Constance Naden.

GISELA ARGYLE is Associate Professor in the Division of Humanities, York University (Ontario). She has recently written articles on Charlotte Brontë and George Meredith and a book on German allusions.

EMILY AUERBACH is Professor of English at the University of Wisconsin, Madison, and creator of the award-winning "Courage to Write" series of public radio programs and written guides on women writers. Her book *Searching for Jane Austen* is forthcoming.

SIMON AVERY is Lecturer in English Studies at the University of Hertfordshire. He has published work on the Brontës, Christina Rossetti, and nineteenth-century women's poetry, as well as on teaching and learning in higher education. He is currently coauthoring a critical study of Elizabeth Barrett Browning and completing a Ph.D. thesis on the representation of politics and power structures in her work.

MAGGIE BERG is Full Professor at Queen's University, Kingston, Canada. She has written books on Charlotte and Emily Brontë, most recently *Wuthering Heights: The Writing in the Margin* (1996), and articles on Luce Irigaray and is currently writing a book on Anne Brontë.

ABIGAIL BURNHAM BLOOM is Managing Editor of the journal *Victorian Literature and Culture*. She is coeditor, with John Maynard, of *Anne Thackeray Ritchie: Journals and Letters* (1994) and author of the forthcoming article

"Trancendency through Incongruity: The Background of Humor in Carlyle's *Sartor Resartus*" in *The Victorian Comic Spirit*. She teaches at New York University and the New School University and has written and lectured on the Carlyles and the Brontë sisters.

FLORENCE S. BOOS is Professor of English at the University of Iowa. Her publications have included several articles on Scottish women working-class poets, and she is at work on a two-volume edition of William Morris's poetic cycle *The Earthly Paradise* (2000).

RHONDA BROCK-SERVAIS is Visiting Assistant Professor at Converse College in Spartanburg, South Carolina. Her dissertation topic is the Victorian literary fairy tale.

ANDREA L. BROOMFIELD is Assistant Professor of English at Wheaton College in Illinois. She is coeditor, with Sally Mitchell, of *Prose by Victorian Women: An Anthology* (1996), and she is the author of several articles pertaining to women essayists and the Victorian periodical press. She is currently at work on a manuscript that explores the developing tradition of Victorian women's nonfiction prose.

RICHARD A. CURRIE received his Ph.D. in Victorian Literature from New York University and has published on Dickens in *Dickens Quarterly, Dickens Studies Annual*, and *English Studies*. His most recent article is on *The Mill on the Floss* for the *Victorian Newsletter*.

DEIRDRE D'ALBERTIS, Associate Professor of English at Bard College, is author of *Dissembling Fictions: Elizabeth Gaskell and the Victorian Social Text* (1997).

ELIZABETH J. DEIS is Elliott Associate Professor of Rhetoric and Humanities at Hampden-Sydney College. She has published an edition of George Meredith's 1895 *Collection of Three Stories* and other articles on Meredith and is writing a study of portrayals of marriage in Victorian fiction.

DENNIS DENISOFF is Assistant Professor at the University of Waterloo. He has published a study of the lesbian poet Erin Mouré, entitled "Erin Mouré: Her Life and Works" (*Canadian Writers and Their Works*, 1995), and has coedited *Perennial Decay: On the Aesthetics and Politics of Decadence* (1999).

ELIZABETH C. DENLINGER received her Ph.D. from New York University in 1996. She is a research assistant for *Shelley and His Circle* and is currently working on a volume on the representation of prostitution in eighteenth-century Britain.

JAMES DIEDRICK is Professor of English at Albion College, specializing in nineteenth- and twentieth-century British literature. He has published *Understanding Martin Amis* (1995); entries on Charles Dickens and Edith Simcox for the *Dictionary of Literary Biography* (1987, 1998); and articles on Walter Scott, Charlotte Brontë, George Eliot, John Ruskin, and Charles Dickens.

ROBERT DINGLEY is Senior Lecturer in the School of English, Communications and Theatre at the University of New England, New South Wales. He has written extensively on Victorian literature, and his edition of George Augustus Sala's account of colonial Australia, *The Land of the Golden Fleece*, was published in 1995.

JACKIE DEES DOMINGUE is an Instructor at Blinn College in Bryan, Texas. Her work on Louisa Bevington includes a Ph.D. dissertation for Texas A&M University entitled "Doctrine and Dynamite: An Edition of Louisa Sarah Bevington's Social and Political Essays" and the essay "An Unpublished Browning Letter to Louisa Sarah Bevington." She has also presented papers on Samuel Taylor Coleridge and apocalyptic eschatology.

LAUREL MEREDITH ERICKSON is a Lecturer in the Department of English at the University of Michigan. She recently completed her dissertation, "Odd Women: Late-Victorian Fiction and the Work of Female Desire," and has published an article on Wilkie Collins's *The Woman in White* and a review essay on psychoanalysis and lesbianism.

KEVIN EUBANKS teaches English at the University of Tennessee, Knoxville. His recent publications include studies of Felicia Hemans and of Bertolt Brecht.

ANNETTE R. FEDERICO, Associate Professor of English at James Madison University, is the author of *Masculine Identity in Hardy and Gissing* (1991) and several articles on Victorian fiction. She has an essay on Marie Corelli in *Victorian Women Writers and the Woman Question* (1999), and she is currently at work on a book on Marie Corelli and late-Victorian literary culture.

JUNE FOLEY earned her Ph.D. in English and American Literature at New York University. She is Adjunct Assistant Professor at NYU's Gallatin School and a Core Faculty member at The New School. She has published and spoken on Elizabeth Gaskell, Charles Dickens, George Eliot, and Jane Austen; her most recent article is "*The Life of Charlotte Brontë* and Some Letters of Elizabeth Gaskell" in *Modern Language Studies* (1997).

MARIA H. FRAWLEY is Associate Professor of English at the University of Delaware, where she teaches Victorian literature, twentieth-century British literature, and women's literature. She is the author of *A Wider Range: Travel Writing by Women in Victorian England* (1994) and of *Anne Brontë* (1996) as well as of articles on nineteenth-century women's writing. The recipient of an NEH fellowship, she is currently at work on a study of Victorian invalids and their narratives of illness.

CONSTANCE M. FULMER is Professor of English at Pepperdine University in Malibu, California. With Margaret E. Barfield she has edited Edith J. Simcox's *Autobiography of a Shirtmaker* (1997). She has read papers on Simcox at two National Women's Studies Association conferences and at four Eighteenth and Nineteenth Century British Women Writers conferences.

CATHERINE J. GOLDEN is Associate Professor of English at Skidmore College. She is editor of *The Mixed Legacy of Charlotte Perkins Gilman* (with Joanna S. Zangrando, 2000); *Unpunished*, a hitherto unpublished feminist detective novel by Charlotte Perkins Gilman (with Denise D. Knight, 1997), and *The Captive Imagination: A Casebook on "The Yellow Wallpaper"* (1992). She is also the author of many essays and reviews on Victorian literature and book illustrations published in *Victorian Poetry, Victorian Studies, Victorian Periodicals Review, Salmagundi, Woman's Art Journal, CEA Critic*, and *Profession 95*.

ANN-BARBARA GRAFF is completing her doctoral dissertation on the construction of gender, race, and national identity after Darwin at the University of Toronto.

JANET L. GROSE is Assistant Professor of English at Union University, Jackson, Tennessee. Her most recent publication is "G.W.M. Reynolds's 'The Rattlesnake's History': Social Reform Through Sensationalized Realism" in *Studies in the Literary Imagination* (1996).

SANDRA HANNAFORD is presently a Ph.D. candidate and sessional instructor at Memorial University of Newfoundland. Her doctoral thesis research is in the area of the history of the book in nineteenth-century Newfoundland. She is currently editor of *Postscript* and a contributor to *Makers of Western Culture, 1800–1914* (forthcoming).

LILA M. HARPER is currently Adjunct Instructor at Central Washington University. Her Ph.D. is from the University of Oregon, and her dissertation, "Solitary Travelers: Nineteenth-Century Women's Travel Narratives," is being revised for publication. She has also written biographical entries on Harriet Martineau and Lucie Duff Gordon.

ANN R. HAWKINS is Assistant Professor of English at Austin Peay State University where her specialization is Romanticism. She is currently working on a book on Byron's *Manfred*.

ANN HEILMANN is a Lecturer in English at the University of Wales, Swansea, where she teaches nineteenth- and twentieth-century literature and women's writing. Having edited *The Late-Victorian Marriage Question: A Collection of Key New Woman Texts* (1998) and taken on the general editorship of a new Routledge Thoemmes Press series, "Sources of Feminism," she is now working on another anthology project, *Sarah Grand: Sex, Subversion and Social Purity* (coedited with Stephanie Forward), and completing research on two studies of New Woman fiction.

KATHLEEN HICKOK is Associate Professor of English and Women's Studies at Iowa State University. Her most recent publication, " 'Burst Are the Prison Bars': Caroline Bowles Southey and the Vicissitudes of Poetic Reputation," appears in *Romanticism and Women Poets: Opening the Doors of Reception*, edited by Harriet Kramer Linkin and Stephen C. Behrendt (1999).

MARYLU HILL is Assistant Professor in the Core Humanities Program at Villanova University. Her first book, *Mothering Modernity: Feminism, Modernism, and the Maternal Muse*, a study of Victorian mothers and modernist daughters, was published in Garland's "Origins of Modernism" series in the fall of 1998. She is currently working on Victorian photography and literary depictions of the past.

CHERI LIN LARSEN HOECKLEY is Assistant Professor of English at Westmont College. She has published articles on marital property in Adelaide Procter's poetry and in Elizabeth Barrett Browning's *Aurora Leigh*. These essays relate to her larger project examining the Married Women's Property movement and Victorian women writers.

JO ELLEN JACOBS is Chair of the Philosophy Department at Millikin University. She has recently edited *The Complete Works of Harriet Taylor Mill* (1998) and has written *Harriet Taylor Mill: Portrait of a Victorian Radical* (forthcoming); "Harriet Taylor Mill's Collaboration with John Stuart Mill: The Means and Meaning of Their Collaborations" (*Interruptions: The Voices of Women Philosophers*, forthcoming); and " 'The Lot of Gifted Ladies Is Hard': A Study of Harriet Taylor Mill Criticism" (*Hypatia* [1994]; *Hypatia's Daughters: 1500 Years of Women Philosophers*, 1995).

HEIDI JOHNSON, a doctoral candidate at the University of Iowa, is completing her thesis on women sleuths and legal constructions of class and gender in Victorian literature and culture.

BARBARA PENNY KANNER, Continuing Research Scholar in the University of California, Los Angeles, History Department and the UCLA Center for the Study of Women, is the author of many book-length bibliographic guides to British women's social history, including *Women in Context: 200 Years of British Women Autobiographers* (1997); *Women in English Social History*, 3 vols. (1987–1990); and *The Women of England from Anglo-Saxon Times to the Present* (1979). Her current projects include a study of women educators in Britain's universities from the late nineteenth century to 1930, an examination of the Webling family of late-nineteenth-century child actresses and their association with John Ruskin, and a chapter in the anthology *Voices of Women Historians* (1999).

MILES A. KIMBALL is Director of the Professional Writing Program at Murray State University; he received his Ph.D. from the University of Kentucky; and he is currently writing a book about nineteenth-century attitudes toward language.

JANNA KNITTEL earned her Ph.D. in English at the University of Oregon. Her research interests include so-called minor women poets, primarily British and American poets from the latter half of the nineteenth century. Currently, she is completing postgraduate work at the University of Kansas.

DEJAN KUZMANOVIC is a Ph.D. candidate in English at Rice University working on a dissertation that explores the rhetoric of seduction and influence in late-Victorian and modernist British literature and culture. He has contributed to *The Encyclopedia of Gay Histories and Cultures* (1999).

MARY LENARD received her Ph.D. in English from the University of Texas at Austin in 1996 and is currently teaching at Alma College. She recently published *Preaching Pity: Sentimentality and Social Reform in Victorian Culture* (1998).

ELISABETH ANNE LEONARD is presently working on a Ph.D. in English Literature at Kent State University. Besides being the editor of *Into Darkness Peering: Race and Color in the Fantastic* (Greenwood, 1997), she has published an article on A. S. Byatt in *Extrapolation*, an article on composition in *CCC*, and numerous articles for reference books.

JOAN M. LESCINSKI, a member of the Sisters of St. Joseph of Carondelet, is President and Professor of English at Saint Mary-of-the-Woods College near Terre Haute, Indiana. She has written and spoken extensively on the British novel, including works by Austen, Dickens, Hardy, and Eliot.

LISA LESLIE is currently completing her Ph.D. dissertation on Claire Clairmont, Mary Shelley, and Percy Bysshe Shelley at the University of Liverpool in England. She has read papers on Claire Clairmont at conferences in Moscow, Salzburg, Groningen, and Glasgow, as well as in England and America.

MARGARET A. LOOSE is a graduate student in English Literature at the University of Iowa and a Regional Delegate to the Modern Language Association. Her most recent publication is "Katherine Anne Porter's *Ship of Fools*" in *Reference Guide to American Literature* (1994).

PATRICIA LORIMER LUNDBERG is Associate Professor of English and Women's Studies and Interim Dean of Arts and Sciences at Indiana University Northwest. Among her recent publications are articles on feminist dialogics, George Eliot, Charlotte Brontë, and Lucas Malet. She is at work on a critical biography of Lucas Malet (Mary St. Leger Kingsley Harrison).

CAROL HANBERY MacKAY is Associate Professor of English at the University of Texas at Austin. Author of *Soliloquy in Nineteenth-Century Fiction* (1987), she is currently completing a book-length study that interrelates the self-performance strategies of Julia Margaret Cameron, Anne Thackeray Ritchie, Annie Wood Besant, and Elizabeth Robins.

ED MADDEN, Assistant Professor of English at the University of South Carolina, has published essays on Radclyffe Hall, Tony Harrison, AIDS elegies, and queer theory and Victorian poetry. He is currently completing a book on images of Tiresias in modernist literature and coediting, with Marie Honan, a collection on queer theory in Irish studies.

NIKKI LEE MANOS, Professor of English at Marymount College, Tarrytown, New York, has recently published articles and papers focused on the 1890s, New Women Writers, and George Meredith's *Diana of the Crossways*. She is coeditor, with Meri-Jane Rochelson, of *Transforming Genres: New Approaches to British Fiction in the 1890s* (1994).

ANDREW MAUNDER holds a doctorate from the University of Nottingham and currently teaches in the Faculty of Humanities at the University of Hertfordshire. He has published articles on Anthony Trollope, Victorian serials, and the Victorian theater and has completed a critical edition of Ellen Price (Mrs. Henry) Wood's *East Lynne*.

BRIAN McCUSKEY is Assistant Professor of English at Utah State University, where he teaches nineteenth-century British literature and contemporary literary theory. His articles on Victorian fiction and domestic service have appeared in *Dickens Studies Annual* and *Nineteenth-Century Prose*. He is currently writing a book about the representation of servants in Victorian literature and culture.

LAUREN McKINNEY, Assistant Professor of English at Eastern Mennonite University in Harrisonburg, Virginia, is currently researching Irish women writers of the Celtic Twilight.

JOANNA STEPHENS MINK is Professor of English at Minnesota State University. Her most recent book is *Common Ground: Feminist Collaboration in the Academy*, a collection of scholarly essays coedited with Elizabeth Peck (1998).

SALLY MITCHELL, Professor of English and Women's Studies at Temple University, is currently working on a biography of Frances Power Cobbe. Her most recent books are *Daily Life in Victorian England* (Greenwood, 1996) and *The New Girl: Girls' Culture in England, 1880–1915* (1995).

LUCY MORRISON is Assistant Professor of English at Pennsylvania State, Hazelton, and is the coauthor of *A Mary Shelley Encyclopedia* (Greenwood, forthcoming).

ADRIENNE MUNICH, Professor of English and Women's Studies at Stony Brook, is the author of *Andromeda's Chains* (1989) and *Queen Victoria's Secrets* (1996) and the coeditor of *Arms and the Woman* (1989) and *Remaking Queen Victoria* (1997). She is also coeditor of the journal *Victorian Literature and Culture*.

KATHRYN A. NEELEY is Associate Professor of Technology, Culture, and Communication in the School of Engineering and Applied Science at the University of Virginia. She teaches and writes about the history of scientific and technical communication and the public understanding of science, with special emphasis on the contributions of women and the relationship of science and technology to literature and the arts. She has recently completed a biography of Mary Somerville, *Mary Somerville: Science, Illumination, and the Female Mind* (2000).

DEBORAH EPSTEIN NORD is Professor of English and Director of Women's Studies at Princeton University. She is the author, most recently, of *Walking the Victorian Streets: Women, Representation, and the City* (1995) and is currently working on a study of gypsy figures in nineteenth-century British culture.

RENÉE V. OVERHOLSER teaches at Hunter College, City University of New York, and is Assistant Editor for Pictures of the journal *Victorian Literature and Culture*. She is working on a study of Algernon Swinburne and Gerard Manley Hopkins.

A. I. PAREJO VADILLO is currently completing a Ph.D. on late-nineteenth-century women poets and the poetics of space at Birkbeck College, University of London. Her research interests include fin de siècle women's poetry, modernity, space, and technologies of mass transportation. She has recently published an article on New Woman poets in *Women: A Cultural Review* and is a contributor for Annotated Bibliography for English Studies.

PAMELA CORPRON PARKER is Assistant Professor of English and Codirector of Women's Studies at Whitworth College in Spokane, Washington. She is cofounder of the Conference on Eighteenth- and Nineteenth-Century British Women Writers and a former Lilly Fellow. Her publications include articles on Elizabeth Gaskell, nineteenth-century philanthropy, and British women's biographies. She is currently at work on a book tentatively entitled "Good Women, Good Work: Women Writers, Victorian Biography, and Philanthropy."

SANDRA J. PEACOCK is Assistant Professor of History at Georgia Southern University. She is the author of *Jane Ellen Harrison: The Mask and the Self* (1988) and is currently working on a study of Victorian women and religion.

ROBERT C. PETERSEN, Associate Professor of English at Middle Tennessee State University, teaches courses in modern and contemporary British literature, as well as a course in Japanese fiction in translation. He has just completed a research project on the novelist Banana Yoshimoto. Dr. Petersen has published work on authors as diverse as Caroline Gordon, L. P. Hartley, and Lewis Carroll.

MARY S. POLLOCK is Associate Professor at Stetson University, where she teaches in the English Department and the Women and Gender Studies Program. She has published numerous articles on women's music, literature by women writers, and Victorian literature. She has just completed a critical study of Elizabeth Barrett and Robert Browning, entitled "Eros and Argument: The Poetry of the Brownings, 1845–1861."

CHRISTINE PULLEN has a degree in the Humanities from Middlesex University and is currently nearing completion of her Ph.D. on Amy Levy at Kingston University. She has delivered various papers on women poets of the 1880s and is preparing a critical biography of Levy for publication.

DENISE P. QUIRK, a former editor of trade and textbooks, is a Ph.D. candidate in the Department of History at Rutgers University. Building on her interest in gender, imperialism, and the feminist periodical press, she is currently researching her dissertation on nineteenth-century British women's public culture.

CAROL HUEBSCHER RHOADES has taught Swedish language and British literature at the University of Texas at Austin where she earned her doctorate in Comparative Literature. She is completing a book entitled "Routes of Power: Woman's Journey in the Novels of George Eliot and Fredrika Bremer."

SAMUEL J. ROGAL chairs the Division of Humanities and Fine Arts at Illinois Valley Community College. A specialist in eighteenth-century British studies, he has authored books and articles on Methodism and the hymnody of the period. In addition, Rogal has authored two volumes on W. Somerset Maugham and works on eighteenth-century agriculture and medicine. His current project focuses on a seven-volume biographical dictionary of eighteenth-century Methodism.

ANITA ROSE is an Assistant Professor in the Department of English at Concord College, Athens, West Virginia. She has published work on Victorian feminist and utopian Elizabeth Burgoyne Corbett and Scottish philosopher William Hamilton.

LEONIE RUTHERFORD teaches literature, media, and cultural studies in the School of English, Communication, and Theatre at the University of New England. She has recently published a book on the colonial poet and suffragist Louisa Lawson and a chapter on children's film in *Writing the Australian Child: Texts and Contexts in Fiction for Children* (1997).

JULIETTE BERNING SCHAEFER is currently Adjunct Associate Professor of English at Madonna University in Livonia, Michigan. She has written a dissertation titled "*Lloyd's Penny Weekly Miscellany of Romance and General Interest*: A Study of Its Cultural and Historical Context in Relation to Its

Working-Class Readers" (1996). She is currently working on papers concerning the poetry and short stories in *Lloyd's* and their relationship to the working-class readers.

SUSAN SCHREIBMAN is Professor of Professional and Technical Communication at New Jersey Institute of Technology. She is the editor of *Collected Poems of Thomas MacGreevy: An Annotated Edition* (1991). Her current research, The Thomas MacGreevy Hypertext Chronology, is a digital archive exploring the life, work, and relationships of Thomas MacGreevy.

AUDREY HORTON SHIFFLETT has a master's degree in English from the University of South Carolina. A freelance editor, she is the production coordinator for *Marian McPartland's Piano Jazz*, a production of South Carolina Educational Radio, heard weekly on National Public Radio.

SHELLY SKINNER is a Ph.D. candidate in the English Department at Syracuse University, writing a dissertation on tourism and geography in late-nineteenth- and early-twentieth-century British fiction and travel writing.

SANDRA L. SPENCER is Lecturer in English at the University of North Texas, Denton, Texas. Spencer's favorite area of interest is Victorian women and publication. Her most recent publication, "Words, Terms, and Other 'UnChancy' Things: Rhetorical Strategies and Self-Definition in 'The Laws Concerning Women,' " appeared in 2000 in *Women's Writing Special Edition: Margaret Oliphant*.

KELLY STEPHENS is a graduate student at the University of Sydney, Australia, and has completed a thesis on the intersection between religious discourse and poetic identity in the works of nineteenth-century British women poets. She has published articles on Christina Rossetti and Emily Brontë and biographical criticism of Victorian women's poetry.

ERIC STERLING received his Ph.D. from Indiana University and is Associate Professor of English at Auburn University, Montgomery. He has published a book on Renaissance drama, *The Movement Towards Subversion: The English History Play from Skelton to Shakespeare* (1996), as well as articles and encyclopedia entries on authors of various countries and centuries.

MARGARET ELIZABETH STRICKLAND received an M.A. in English Literature with a certificate in Women Studies from Texas A&M University. She is currently pursuing a Ph.D. with an emphasis in nineteenth-century literature.

DUANGRUDI SUKSANG, Professor at Eastern Illinois University, has published papers on women's utopias and book reviews in *Utopian Studies*. She is currently working on a reissue of Elizabeth Corbett's feminist utopia *New Amazonia: A Foretaste of the Future* (1889).

MELISA SUMMY is a Ph.D. candidate in English Literature at Miami University of Ohio. She recently presented a paper on *Dracula* at the annual Interdisciplinary Nineteenth-Century Studies conference and has an essay being published on Edmund Husserl in the *Dictionary of Literary Biography* volume on Twentieth Century European Cultural Theorists. She is currently finishing her thesis on abjection in the late Victorian horror novel.

CHRISTINE SUTPHIN is Professor of English at Central Washington University. She is currently editing a collection of Augusta Webster's poetry for publication in 1999.

CHRISTINE SWIRIDOFF is currently a doctoral student in the English Department at Temple University. Her research interests focus on Victorian literature and British and American women writers.

K. L. THOMAS holds a master's from Cornell University and is completing a doctorate at Oxford University on postal reform in the nineteenth century. She has also written on lesbian identity in the Victorian era.

HEIDI THOMSON received her Ph.D. from the University of Illinois at Urbana-Champaign and is currently a Senior Lecturer in English Literature at Victoria University of Wellington, New Zealand. She is one of the editors of *The Novels and Selected Works of Maria Edgeworth* (1999).

MICHAEL A. TOROK completed his Ph.D. in Creative Writing at the University of Southwestern Louisiana. Having become interested in the Romantic and Victorian periods, Michael works to conjoin his studies with his creative work. He has recently enjoyed joint teaching a course on the Victorian women poets and has presented papers at several conferences.

KIMBERLY VaNHOOSIER-CAREY completed her doctorate at the University of Texas at Austin in 1997 and is currently a Visiting Assistant Professor at the Georgia Institute of Technology in Atlanta. She has published an article on the representation of female experience in D. H. Lawrence's *The Plumed Serpent*. She is working on a book-length study of turn-of-the-century and Modernist women writers' experimentation with gender and narrative.

JEAN WASKO is Professor of English and Chair of the Department of Literature and Language Arts at Fontbonne College. Her research interest lies in the familiar letter, and she has written and published on Jane Welsh Carlyle and Virginia Woolf.

ALAN S. WEBER is a Center for Medieval and Renaissance Studies Associate Fellow at the State University of New York, Binghamton. He has published articles on Matthew and Arthur Hugh Clough and his book *Nineteenth Century Science* appeared in 1999.

LORI WILLIAMSON received her Ph.D. in British history from the University of Toronto in 1994 and currently holds a research fellowship at the University of Wolverhampton. Her research interests lie mainly within modern British social and cultural history. Her doctoral thesis on the nineteenth-century feminist and reformer Frances Power Cobbe was published under the title *Power and Protest: Frances Power Cobbe and Victorian Society* (2000). She is currently working on the semiotics of nursing and nurses in the nineteenth and twentieth centuries, has published in the *International History of Nursing Journal*, and is compiling a five-volume set of reprints centered around Florence Nightingale and the history of nursing.

ANNE M. WINDHOLZ teaches in the Department of English and Journalism at Augustana College in Sioux Falls, South Dakota. Her publications include articles in *The 1890s: An Encyclopedia of British Literature, Art, and Culture* (1993), in *British Short Fiction Writers, 1880–1914: The Realist Tradition* (*Dictionary of Literary Biography*, Volume 135, 1994), and most recently, in *Victorian Periodicals Review* (1990, 1996). Windholz is currently writing a book entitled "British Magazines and the Re-Colonizing of America, 1880–1900."

ISBN 0-313-30439-4

HARDCOVER BAR CODE